THE
TALENT
MANAGEMENT
HANDBOOK

SECOND EDITION

CREATING A SUSTAINABLE
COMPETITIVE ADVANTAGE
BY SELECTING, DEVELOPING,
AND PROMOTING
THE BEST PEOPLE

**Edited by
Lance A. Berger
Dorothy R. Berger**

Mc
Graw
Hill

New York   Chicago   San Francisco   Lisbon   London
Madrid   Mexico City   Milan   New Delhi   San Juan
Seoul   Singapore   Sydney   Toronto

The McGraw·Hill Companies

Copyright © 2011 by The McGraw-Hill Companies, Inc. All rights reserved. Printed in the United States of America. Except as permitted under the United States Copyright Act of 1976, no part of this publication may be reproduced or distributed in any form or by any means, or stored in a database or retrieval system, without the prior written permission of the publisher.

1 2 3 4 5 6 7 8 9 10   DOC/DOC   1 9 8 7 6 5 4 3 2 1 0

ISBN   978-007-173905-4
MHID   007-173905-X

This publication is designed to provide accurate and authoritative information in regard to the subject matter covered. It is sold with the understanding that neither the author nor the publisher is engaged in rendering legal, accounting, securities trading, or other professional services. If legal advice or other expert assistance is required, the services of a competent professional person should be sought.
—*From a Declaration of Principles Jointly Adopted by a Committee of the American Bar Association and a Committee of Publishers and Associations*

Library of Congress Cataloging-in-Publication Data

The talent management handbook : creating a sustainable competitive advantage by selecting, developing, and promoting the best people / [edited] by Lance Berger, Dorothy Berger. – 2nd ed.
    p. ; cm.
  Includes index.
  ISBN 978-0-07-173905-4 (alk. paper)
  1. Career development. 2. Employee motivation. 3. Creative ability in business. I. Berger, Lance A. II. Berger, Dorothy R.

  HF5549.5.C35T35 2011
  658.3'14—dc22
                                                           2010041289

McGraw-Hill books are available at special quantity discounts to use as premiums and sales promotions or for use in corporate training programs. To contact a representative, please e-mail us at bulksales@mcgraw-hill.com.

This book is printed on acid-free paper.

Contents

Contents

Part VI   Innovative Thinking that Can Shape Your Organization's Approach to Talent Management   503

Preface

T HE TALENT MANAGEMENT HANDBOOK HELPS ORGANIZATIONS DRIVE AND SUSTAIN excellence by proactively using talent management processes to create a culture for success. Based on our research, consulting assignments, and the input of this book's preeminent contributors, we conclude that the core talent management framework required for creating a culture for success consists of three elements. These are:

- A talent management creed composed of a widely publicized set of core principles, values, and mutual expectations that mutually guides the behavior of an organization and its people. Collectively, the stated principles depict the type of culture an organization strives to create to achieve its unique portrait for success. The principles of the creed are embedded into both its talent management strategy and in its talent management system through incorporating its doctrines into selection criteria, competency definitions, performance criteria, and internal selection and development processes, and all other human resources policies and programs.
- A talent strategy makes explicit the types of people in whom the organization will invest. The highest investments are rooted in the organization's talent creed and each person's potential for contributing to organizational success now and in the future.
- A talent management system consists of a set of procedures, systems, and processes that translate an organization's talent creed and strategy into a diagnostic and implementation program for investing in the people who exemplify the culture that will achieve organization excellence.

This book is organized into six parts. The chapters are arranged to provide readers with a logical path to creating the talent management framework described above.

Part I establishes the talent management framework. It shows how the different elements of a creed, talent strategy, and the building blocks of a talent management system are integrated into a unified approach that creates and sustains organizational excellence. The building blocks represent assessment tools rooted in the organization's creed that include competencies, performance appraisal, potential forecast, and succession and career planning. The building blocks enable the organization to classify its employees based on actual and potential contribution to organizational success and to suggest the types of investment needed to enhance individual contribution.

Part II describes the types of investments an organization must make to assure that its human resources can perform at the highest competitive levels now and in the future based on the assessment of its people. This section covers the use of training, development, coaching, mentorship, and leadership within a talent management plan. Together Parts I and II provide critical input to helping an organization attract, select, retain, and engage its people.

Part III presents approaches that are used to allocate financial rewards to employees based on their actual and potential contribution to employee success.

Part IV links talent management, culture, and business excellence. It describes how organization philosophies, beliefs, and values establish the parameters that govern the selection, development, and advancement of the people who shape the culture for success that drives business excellence. They include elements such as: ethics, sustainability, diversity, engagement, innovation, and creativity.

Part V covers a diverse collection of critical topics that include defining the link between business planning and talent management, workforce analysis, and recruitment, outplacement, and information systems that complement other talent management processes.

Part VI encourages the reader to be imaginative in approaching the unique talent management requirements of their organization. It includes ways to use a "people equity framework" to rethink talent management, use novel "collaborative approaches to marshall or marshall talent," consider the "global state of talent management," "deploy a special model for talent manager excellence," and use talent management "leadership" to drive success in the government.

Contributors

Angelita Becom, Senior Consultant, Sibson Consulting, Raleigh, North Carolina (Chapter 7)

Craig M. Berger, Director of Education, Society for Environmental and Graphic Design, Washington, DC (Chapter 49)

Dorothy R. Berger, Partner, Lance A. Berger & Associates, Ltd., Bryn Mawr, Pennsylvania (Chapter 1)

Lance A. Berger, Managing Partner, Lance A. Berger & Associates, Ltd., Bryn Mawr, Pennsylvania (Chapter 1)

Nila G. Betof, Ph.D., Chief Operating Officer, The Leader's Edge, Bala Cynwyd, Pennsylvania (Chapter 41)

Richard E. Boyatzis, Ph.D., Professor in the Departments of Organizational Behavior, Psychology, and Cognitive Science, Case Western Reserve University, Cleveland, Ohio (Chapter 21)

Mark Graham Brown, President, Mark Graham Brown & Associates, Manhattan Beach, California (Chapter 6)

Reginald F. Butler, Cultural Transformation Services Managing Director, PricewaterhouseCoopers LLP, Tampa, Florida (Chapter 40)

Max Caldwell, Managing Director, Towers Watson, New York, New York (Chapter 36)

Dennis Carey, Vice Chairman, Korn/Ferry International, Scottsdale, Arizona (Chapter 17)

Kevin Cashman, Senior Partner, Korn/Ferry Leadership and Talent Consulting, Minneapolis, Minnesota (Chapter 17)

Craig Chappelow, Global Portfolio Manager, Assessments, Center for Creative Leadership, Greensboro, North Carolina (Chapter 22)

Joyce Cohen, Senior Consultant, Career Systems International, Sherman Oaks, California (Chapter 15)

Paul Conley, Consultant, Towers Watson, Minneapolis, Minnesota (Chapter 28)

Robert Conlon, Senior Vice President, Sibson Consulting, Chicago, Illinois (Chapter 44)

Elizabeth Craig, Research Fellow, Accenture, Boston, Massachusetts (Chapter 42)

Sharon L. Cresswell, Talent Management: Competencies and Curriculums, Baker Hughes Corporate, Houston, Texas (Chapter 18)

Beverly Crowell, Senior Consultant, Career Systems International, Sherman Oaks, California (Chapter 15)

Murray M. Dalziel, Ph.D., Professor of Management and Director, University of Liverpool Management School, Liverpool, England (Chapters 2 and 12)

Lisa Edwards, Senior Director for Talent Management, Corbis, Seattle, Washington (Chapter 19)

Marc Effron, President, The Talent Strategy Group, New York, New York (Chapter 54)

JP Elliott, Senior Consultant, Sibson Consulting, Los Angeles, California (Chapter 10)

Denise Fairhurst, Senior Consultant, Towers Watson, New York, New York (Chapter 36)

Marc Feigen, Founder, Feigen & Company, New York, New York (Chapter 17)

John W. Fleenor, Research Director, Center for Creative Leadership, Greensboro, North Carolina (Chapter 22)

David C. Forman, Chief Learning Officer, Human Capital Institute, Washington, DC (Chapters 30 and 53)

Ron Garonzik, Ph.D., Vice President, Hay Group, Boston, Massachusetts (Chapter 4)

Guy Gauvin, Executive Vice President of Global Services, Taleo, Dublin, California (Chapter 50)

Marshall Goldsmith, Executive Coach, Leadership Development and Behavioral Change, San Diego, California (Chapter 16)

Dick Grote, President, Grote Consulting Corporation, Frisco, Texas (Chapter 5)

Michael Haid, Senior Vice President, Global Solutions, Right Management, Philadelphia, Pennsylvania (Chapter 23)

Stephen F. Hallam, Ph.D., Professor of Management, University of Akron, Akron, Ohio (Chapter 38)

Teresa Alberte Hallam, Ph.D., Senior Lecturer, University of Akron, Akron, Ohio (Chapter 38)

Theodore A. Hartz, MBA, Executive Director of Customized Learning Solutions Drexel University Goodwin College of Professional Studies, Co-Director Drexel/Torrance Center for Creativity and Innovation, Drexel University, Philadelphia, Pennsylvania (Chapter 35)

Mayra Hernandez, CEO, Impactomb, New York, New York (Chapter 24)

David Insler, Senior Vice President, Sibson Consulting, Los Angeles, California (Chapter 7)

Deb Jacobs, Partner, Axiom Consulting Partners, New York, New York (Chapter 24)

Randy Jayne, Ph.D., Managing Partner, Heidrick & Struggles, Global Aerospace, Defense, and Aviation Practice, McLean, Virginia (Chapter 47)

Jason Jeffay, Partner and Global Talent Management Leader, Human Capital business, Mercer, Atlanta, Georgia (Chapter 45)

Dan Kadrlik, Stock Plan Consultant, Executive Pay and Benefits, Target Corporation, Minneapolis, Minnesota (Chapter 28)

Beverly Kaye, Ph.D., Founder and CEO, Career Systems International, Sherman Oaks, California (Chapter 15)

Anne Kelly, Principal, Center for Human Capital Innovation (CHCI), Washington, DC (Chapter 55)

Jim Kochanski, Senior Vice President, Sibson Consulting, Raleigh, North Carolina (Chapter 10)

Dale E. Kunneman, Vice President Human Resources Global Products, Baker Hughes Corporate, Houston, Texas (Chapter 18)

John B. Larrere, National Practice Leader, Leadership and Talent, Hay Group, Philadelphia, Pennsylvania (Chapter 4)

Rick Lash, Ph.D., Canadian Leadership and Talent Practice Leader, Hay Group, Toronto, Canada (Chapter 46)

Gerald E. Ledford, Jr., Ph.D., President, Ledford Consulting Network, LLC, Redondo Beach, California (Chapter 29)

David Lee, Principal, HumanNature@Work, Bar Mills, Maine (Chapter 33)

Tom McMullen, North American Reward Practice Leader, Hay Group, Chicago, Illinois (Chapter 46)

Haig R. Nalbantian, Senior Partner and Director of Global Research and Commercialization, Human Capital business, Mercer, New York, New York (Chapter 45)

Ed Newman, Founder, The Newman Group, and Leader, Futurestep, US, Los Angeles, California (Chapter 43)

E. Michael Norman, Senior Vice President, Sibson Consulting, Los Angeles, California (Chapter 44)

J. Evelyn Orr, Intellectual Property Development Consultant, Korn/Ferry Leadership and Talent Consulting, Minneapolis, Minnesota (Chapter 3)

Andy Pellant, Managing Partner, Emergentedge, Hertford, England (Chapter 31)

Jack J. Phillips, Ph.D., Chairman, ROI Institute, Inc., Birmingham, Alabama (Chapter 19)

James F. Reda, Founder and Managing Director, James F. Reda & Associates, LLC, New York, New York (Chapter 8)

Fredericka K. Reisman, Ph.D., Professor, Director Drexel/Torrance Center for Creativity and Innovation, Drexel University, Philadelphia, Pennsylvania (Chapter 35)

Andrew S. Rosen, Executive Vice President, ORC Worldwide, New York, New York (Chapter 26)

William J. Rothwell, Ph.D., SPHR, Professor of Workforce Education and Development, Department of Learning and Performance Systems, College of Education, The Pennsylvania State University, University Park, Pennsylvania (Chapter 11)

Mark Royal, Senior Consultant, Hay Group, Chicago, Illinois (Chapter 27)

Kim E. Ruyle, Vice President of Product Development, Korn/Ferry Leadership and Talent Consulting, Minneapolis, Minnesota (Chapter 3)

Tony Santora, Executive Vice President, Global Solutions, Right Management, Philadelphia, Pennsylvania (Chapter 48)

Deborah Schroeder-Saulnier, Director of Marketing, Senior Vice President, Global Solutions, Right Management, Philadelphia, Pennsylvania (Chapter 34)

Melvin Scales, Senior Vice President, Global Solutions, Right Management, Philadelphia, Pennsylvania (Chapter 48)

William A. Schiemann, CEO, Metrus Institute, Somerville, New Jersey (Chapter 51)

Allan Schweyer, Principal, Center for Human Capital Innovation (CHCI), Washington, DC (Chapter 55)

Jim Shanley, Partner, The Shanley Group, Hillsborough, North Carolina (Chapter 54)

Molly Dickinson Shepard, Chief Executive Officer, The Leader's Edge, Bala Cynwyd, Pennsylvania (Chapter 41)

Yaarit Silverstone, Talent & Organization Performance Managing Director, Accenture, Atlanta, Georgia (Chapter 39)

Doris Sims, SPHR, Founder and President, Succession Builders LLC, Flower Mound, Texas (Chapter 13)

Catherine M. Sleezer, Competencies and Curriculum Supply Chain, Baker Hughes Corporate, Tulsa, Oklahoma (Chapter 18)

David Smith, Talent & Organization Performance Managing Director, Accenture, Hartford, Connecticut (Chapter 42)

Melvin L. Smith, Ph.D., Professor in the Department of Organizational Behavior, Case Western Reserve University, Cleveland, Ohio (Chapter 21)

Aaron Sorensen, Ph.D., Senior Consultant, Sibson Consulting, Chicago, Illinois (Chapter 44)

Mel Stark, Vice President, Hay Group, Jersey City, New Jersey (Chapter 27)

Jodi L. Starkman, Executive Vice President, ORC Worldwide, New York, New York (Chapter 26)

Owen Sullivan, Chief Executive Officer, Right Management, Philadelphia, Pennsylvania (Chapter 32)

Sylvester Taylor, Director, Assessments, Tools, and Publications, Center for Creative Leadership, Greensboro, North Carolina (Chapter 22)

Robert J. Thomas, Institute for High Performance Executive Director, Accenture, Boston, Massachusetts (Chapter 39)

Kaye Thorne, Founder and Managing Partner, Talent Perspectives, Dorset, England (Chapter 25)

Francesco Turchetti, Director Talent Management, Baker Hughes Corporate, Houston, Texas (Chapter 18)

Dave Ulrich, Ph.D., Professor, Ross School of Business, University of Michigan, Ann Arbor, Michigan, and Partner, The RBL Group, Provo, Utah (Chapter 52)

Michael Ulrich, Research Associate, The RBL Group, Provo, Utah (Chapter 52)

Ellen Van Oosten, Department of Organizational Behavior, Weatherhead School of Management, Case Western Reserve University, Cleveland, Ohio (Chapter 21)

Karol M. Wasylyshyn, Psy.D., President, Leadership Development, Philadelphia, Pennsylvania (Chapter 20)

Kevin D. Wilde, Vice President, Organization Effectiveness and Chief Learning Officer, General Mills, Minneapolis, Minnesota (Chapter 14)

Jeana Wirtenberg, Ph.D., Director, External Relations and Services, Institute for Sustainable Enterprise, Fairleigh Dickinson University, Teaneck, New Jersey (Chapter 37)

Martin G. Wolf, Ph.D., President, Management Advisory Services, Jalisco, Mexico (Chapter 9)

Allen Zeman, Ph.D., President, Center for Human Capital Innovation (CHCI), Washington, DC (Chapter 55)

Part I

Creating a Talent Management Program for Organization Excellence

Chapter 1

Designing and Assembling the Building Blocks for Organization Excellence: The Talent Management Model

Lance A. Berger, Managing Partner
Dorothy R. Berger, Partner
Lance A. Berger & Associates, Ltd.

SUCCESSFUL ORGANIZATIONS PROACTIVELY AND SYSTEMATICALLY TAKE ACTION TO ENSURE that they have the human resource capability to meet their current and future business requirements. These organizations have made talent management a critical force in their drive for excellence. Although there are a variety of approaches to talent management, our experience and research indicates that the underlying model used by high-performing organizations consists of three linked elements: a creed, a strategy, and a system. In this chapter, we will discuss each of the elements as we construct a talent management model for organization excellence.

Talent Creed

A talent management creed is composed of a widely publicized set of core principles, values, and mutual expectations that guide the behavior of an institution and its people. Collectively, the stated principles depict the type of culture an organization strives to create to achieve its unique portrait of success. The principles of the creed are embedded into both its talent management strategy and in its talent management system by incorporating its doctrines into selection criteria, competency definitions, performance criteria, and internal selection and development processes. An excellent example of such a creed is the Johnson & Johnson Credo. Johnson & Johnson is consistently among the top group on Fortune's Most Admired Companies list. Johnson & Johnson states that "Our Credo is more than just a moral compass. We believe it's a recipe for business success." The Credo is available on the Johnson & Johnson Web site. Another highly successful company with an explicit creed is Microsoft. Microsoft believes that its values guides its employees' behaviors and must shine through in all its employees' interactions with one another and with stakeholders.

Most recently, creeds have been updated to include social responsibility, sustainability, ethical behavior, innovation, and creativity. Starbuck's creed includes reference to social and ethical responsibility. It states: "The following six Guiding Principles will help employees measure the appropriateness of their decisions: Provide a great work environment and treat each other with respect and dignity; Embrace diversity as an essential component in the way we do business; Apply the highest standards of excellence to the purchasing, roasting and fresh delivery of our coffee; Develop enthusiastically satisfied customers all of the time; Contribute positively to our communities and our environment; Recognize that profitability is essential to our future success."

Part IV, Theme 2 of this book presents a thorough treatment of these ideas and their influence on talent management.

Talent Strategy

A talent strategy makes explicit the type of investments an organization makes today in the people whom it believes will best help it achieve competitive excellence in the future. A talent management strategy views a workforce as a portfolio of human resource assets that are differentiated based on an assessment of each person's current and potential contribution to organization success. The types of people that will receive different types of investment are rooted in the organization's talent creed. We have found that, regardless of the content of an organization's creed, the talent strategies of most high performing organizations contain the following three directives:

1. Cultivate the Superkeeper.™
2. Retain key position backups.
3. Appropriately allocate training, rewards, education, assignments, and development (TREADs).

Cultivate the Superkeeper™

This directive involves the identification, selection, development, and retention of Superkeepers.™ Superkeepers™ are a very small group of individuals (about 3 percent of an organization) who have demonstrated superior accomplishments, have inspired others to attain superior accomplishments, and embody the creed, core competencies, and values of their organization. Their loss or absence severely inhibits organization growth because of their disproportionately powerful impact on current and future organization performance. Bill Gates once said, "Take our twenty best people away from us and I can tell you that Microsoft would be an unimportant company."

Retain Key Position Backups

The second directive comprises the identification and development of high-quality replacements for a small number of positions designated as key to current and future organization success. Gaps in replacement activity for incumbents in key positions are highly disruptive, costly, and distracting to an organization. To achieve organizational excellence, key positions should be staffed by, and have replacements that have, historically exceeded organization performance expectations, show a commitment to develop others, and are role models for the organization's creed. One of the most important talent management decisions the organization will make is the designation of key positions. In our experience, every organization likes to think of all its positions as key. We estimate that, when honestly rationalized, no more than 20 percent of an organization's jobs should be designated as key.

There are a number of useful criteria for determining whether a position is *key*. Following is a short list of some of them:

Immediacy: The short-term loss of the incumbent would seriously affect profit, revenue growth, operations, work processes, products, services, employee morale, stakeholder satisfaction, competitive advantage, or the prestige of the organization.

Uniqueness: The position requires a competency or set of competencies that is, or will be, unique to the organization or its industry.

Demand: The job market for incumbents holding the position is tight now or will be in the future.

Strategic Impact: The loss of a qualified incumbent for even a modest amount of time would affect the future success of the organization.

Basic: The organization could not survive without the incumbent.

Ed Newman (Chapter 43) provides an additional definition of key (critical) jobs that will be useful to readers.

Allocate TREADs Appropriately

TREADs refer to investments made by an organization today in the form of training, rewards, education, assignments, and development activities. The return on most of these investments, however, will not be realized until the future. To properly invest its TREADs, an organization must classify each of its employees based on his or her actual or potential for adding value to the organization. The employee groups, for investment purpose, can be classified on the basis of their level of performance and competencies, their leadership and development of others, and their position as role models for the organization's creed. These classifications are as follows: Superkeepers™, those employees who greatly exceed expectations now and are projected to do so in the future (3 percent); Keepers, those employees who exceed expectations now and are projected to do so in the future (20 percent); Solid Citizens, those employees who meet organization expectations (75 percent); and Misfits, those employees who are below organization expectations (2 percent). Employees are placed in this category when they are either weak performers or lack the competencies for doing their job. Poor allocation of TREADs can lead to unwanted turnover, morale, and performance problems, particularly in Superkeeper™ and Keeper groups. In the best performing organization, 5 percent of the resources are allocated to the Superkeepers™, 25 percent of the resources are allocated to the Keepers, 68 percent of the resources are allocated to the Solid Citizens, and 2 percent go to resurrecting some of the Misfits with potential for performance improvement. Part II, "Training, Coaching, and Development," describes in detail how TREADs can be used effectively in a talent management program.

Table 1-1 provides a strategic perspective on TREADs allocation by employee classification.

	Compensation	Training/Development	Career Paths	Visibility
Superkeeper™	Accelerate much faster than pay markets	Major investments	Very rapid	Very high recognition
Keeper	Accelerate faster than pay markets	Substantial investments	Rapid	High recognition
Solid Citizen	Accelerate moderately until competitive level is reached	Investments only to enhance competencies for current/future business situations	Moderate to none	Recognition
Misfit	No increase	Only to improve fit now or for next job if it has a reasonable probability of success	None	

Table 1-1 TREADs Allocation by Employee Classification

Talent Management System

Once an organization commits to excellence by embracing a creed and a strategy, the two strategic talent management drivers explained above, it will need to put into place a human resources system to ensure talent management implementation.

A talent management system is a set of procedures and processes that translate an organization's talent creed and strategy into a diagnostic and implementation program for achieving organization excellence. Most successful talent management systems consist of the following four components: (1) assessment tools, (2) multi-rater assessment, (3) diagnostic tools, and (4) monitoring processes.

Assessment Tools

Our research, conducted since the first edition of *The Talent Management Handbook*, continues to show that the infrastructure of human resources systems and processes for failed organizations is typically an incoherent mosaic of unconnected, incomplete, missing, and inconsistent assessment tools and methods. This means performance appraisals, assessments of potential, competency evaluations, career planning, and replacement planning (the core elements of talent management) are unlinked and largely irreconcilable. Additionally, the return on the cost of implementing these programs as separate and distinct is low, time expenditure high, credibility low, and employee dissatisfaction pervasive.

Successful organizations use a talent management model that contains the five assessment tools, or building blocks, listed below. The five assessment tools should be linked to ensure that each assessment is consistent with the four other evaluations. Collectively, the assessments can serve as the basis for making investment decisions consistent with the three part strategy outlined above.

Competency Assessment. Competencies are the building blocks of a talent management system. They are any behavior, skill, knowledge, or other type of stated expectation that is crucial to the success of each employee and to the success of the entire organization. Competencies used for employee assessment must always include the organization's creed. Our research has determined that most organizations use between four and nine competencies in their talent management process.

Table 1-2 illustrates a list of nine representative core competencies and their definitions. The list has undergone little change since the first edition of this book.

Core Competency	Attributes
Action Orientation	Targets and achieves results, overcomes obstacles, accepts responsibility, establishes standards and responsibilities, creates a results-oriented environment, and follows through on actions.
Citizenship	Demonstrates a commitment to the organization's stated creed, values, ethical codes, and principles of sustainability. Is honest, candid, and transparent in personal and business relationships. Exhibits integrity and builds trusting relationships with others.
Communication	Communicates well, both verbally and in writing. Effectively conveys and shares information and ideas with others. Listens carefully and understands various viewpoints. Presents ideas clearly and concisely and understands relevant detail in presented information.
Creativity/Innovation	Generates novel ideas and develops or improves existing and new systems that challenge the status quo, takes risks, and encourages innovation.
Customer Orientation	Listens to customers, builds customer confidence, increases customer satisfaction, ensures commitments are met, sets appropriate customer expectations, and responds to customer needs.
Interpersonal Skill	Effectively and productively engages with others and establishes trust, credibility, and confidence with them.
Leadership	Motivates, empowers, inspires, collaborates with, and encourages others to succeed. Develops a culture where employees feel ownership in what they do and continually improve the business. Creates a clear vision, accurately communicates the vision, and gets others to behave in a way to support the vision.

Table 1-2 Nine Representative Competencies (continued on next page)

Core Competency	Attributes
Teamwork	Knows when and how to attract, develop, reward, be part of, and utilize teams to optimize results. Acts to build trust, inspire enthusiasm, encourage others, and help resolve conflicts and develop consensus in supporting high-performance teams.
Technical/Functional Expertise	Demonstrates strong technical/functional proficiencies and knowledge in required areas of expertise. Shows knowledge of company business and proficiency in the strategic and financial processes, including profit and loss (P&L) planning processes and their implications for the company.

Table 1-2 Nine Representative Competencies (continued)

A comprehensive treatment of competencies is covered in Part I, "Building Block 1."

Performance Appraisal: A performance appraisal is a measurement of actual results achieved within those areas for which the employee is held accountable and/or the competencies deemed critical to job and organization success. There are only a relatively small number of ways organizations measure employee performance. Dick Grote, in Chapter 5, describes a cogent view of performance appraisal. His model envisions performance appraisals consisting of organization competencies, job family competencies, key job responsibilities, and goals and major projects. Martin Wolf in Chapter 9 classifies performance appraisal systems as being a combination of trait-, behavior-, knowledge/skill-, or results-based. A range of performance appraisal approaches is covered in Part I, "Building Block 2."

Potential Forecast: A potential forecast is a prediction of how many levels (organization/job) an employee can progress within an organization based on his or her past or current performance appraisals, training and development needs, career preferences, and actual and projected competency levels and positions that represent realistic future job opportunities. Like any forecast, an individual's potential is subject to periodic evaluation. It is heavily influenced by the quality of the input provided by different assessor groups and by a variety of situational factors associated with job conditions at different moments in time. Murray Dalziel (Chapters 2 and 12) feels that collectively three critical attributes can be used to assess potential no matter what assessment process or rating system is used. These attributes are as follows:

"How does the individual set his or her business agenda?"
"How does the person take others with him or her?"
"How does the person present him- or herself as a leader?"

It would be reasonable to assume that periodic multi-rater assessments based on these attributes could generate a reasonable forecast of potential. A complete review of potential forecasting can be found in Part I, "Building Block 3."

Measurement Scales for Performance and Potential: Our large-scale study of organizations involved in some type of successful talent management process showed that the vast majority use a simple five-point scale to measure performance and potential. The most common scale for performance measurement is as follows: greatly exceeds expectations (5), exceeds expectations (4), meets expectations (3), below expectations (2), greatly below expectations (1). The most common scale for potential assessment is: high potential (5), promotable (4), lateral or job enrichment (3), marginal (2), none (1). Our conclusion is that most organizations discover that simpler is better. The scales are straightforward and they achieve credible results.

Succession Planning: In the broadest sense, the process that seeks to identify replacement candidates for current incumbents, and potential future job openings, and to assess the time frames in which they can move to these positions.

Career Planning: This process identifies potential next steps in an employee's career and his or her readiness for movement to new positions. Career planning merges the organization's assessment of employee growth readiness (succession plan), employee career preferences, and the likelihood that positions in a career path will become available.

Table 1-3 illustrates, in the form of a bench strength summary, the merging of succession and career planning.

Position	Potential	Performance	Next Position	Status	Replacement(s)	Status
Bednarik, Charlene Executive VP (Female) **Keeper**	P	EE	President and CEO	Now	Logan, Bill	12–24 Mos.
Mantle, Morris Executive VP **Superkeeper™**	U	GEE	VP and CFO	Now	LeClerc, Juan	12–24 Mos.
Maris, David VP and CFO **Key position**	NP	ME			Blocking Mantle, M. Jones, G. Surplus	Now Now
Williams, Otis (Minority) VP, HR	P	EE	EVP Quality	Now	Martinez, P. Gonzalez, P. Surplus	12–24 Now Now
Hingis, Martin VP, VP-R&D **Key position**	NP	GBE (performance problem)			Void	

Potential: P (Potential–1 or more levels); U (Unlimited Potential); LR (Lateral Rotational); NP (No Potential)
Performance: GEE (Greatly Exceeds Expectations): EE (Exceeds Expectations); ME (Meets Expectations); BE (Below Expectations); GBE (Greatly Below Expectations)
The Bench Strength Summary captures the key elements for aligning people with organization needs. Five action items with recommendations are identified:
Void: Positions with no replacements. 1. Select from talent pool. 2. Add to talent pool and accelerate development. 3. Identify backups. 4. Begin external recruitment. 5. For key positions accelerate the process.
Surpluses: Positions with more than one replacement. 1. Redirect career paths. 2. Move high potentials quickly. 3 Job rotation inside unit. 4. Task force assignments.
Blocking: Non-promotable managers with promotable subordinates. 1. Move incumbent or backup within one year. 2. Job rotation outside unit. 3. Special projects.
Performance Problems: Employees not meeting expectations. 1. One more accomplishment review. 2. Focus on results and competency improvement. 3. Terminate (consult HR department).
Superkeeper™: Very accelerated career paths and compensation growth, high development investment; formal mentor and sponsor arrangement.

Table 1-3 Illustrative Bench Strength Summary

Bill Rothwell and six other experts provide an extensive treatment of succession and career planning in Part I, "Building Block 3."

Multi-Rater Assessment

The best talent management systems utilize the input on an ongoing basis of different raters. Critical assessments come from the "vertical and horizontal organization," since most decisions on succession planning, career planning, and job assignments require the approval and ownership of progressively higher levels of management as well as different functions. Performance appraisals almost always are confirmed by two levels of supervision. This multi-rater approach should be utilized in the other types of assessment and extended to more assessors. The addition of assessors and assessment tools necessitates a reconciliation process to ensure a consistent and mutually agreeable basis upon which TREADs investments can be made.

Final assessment, and decisions, regarding upward mobility or job reassignment must minimally include input from the following:

- *Employee*. The owner of the career plan that is aligned with the succession plan.
- *Boss*. The primary assessor who, in most cases, is most familiar with the employee.
- *Boss's boss*. The key link in the vertical succession and career plan.
- *Boss's peer group*. Source of potential new assignments in the same or other function.

Kevin Wilde in Chapter 14 discusses the "influencers" in the talent review and further information on multi-rater assessment can be found in Part II, "Coaching, Training, and Development."

Diagnostic Tools

Diagnostic tools are analytical devices an organization uses to convert the assessment of its people into a talent management plan. The five core diagnostic tools that are typically used by high performing organizations involve identifying the following strategic drivers:

1. *Superkeeper™ reservoir*. Superkeepers™ are employees whose performance greatly exceeds expectations, who inspire others to greatly exceed expectations, and who embody institutional competencies (including the creed). An organization must ensure that it has a cadre of these critical employees, since they will ensure its sustainability.
2. *Key position backups*. The "insurance policies" that ensure organization continuity. Every key position should have at least one backup at the "Keeper" (exceed job expectations) level.
3. *Surpluses*. Positions with more than one replacement for an incumbent. While ostensibly a positive result of the talent management process, it can be a potential source of turnover and morale problems if the replacements are blocked by a non-promotable incumbent and/or there is no realistic way most of the promotable replacements can advance.

4. *Voids*. Positions without a qualified backup. Once voids are identified, the organization should determine whether it will transfer someone from the surplus pool, develop alternative candidates, or recruit externally.
5. *Blockages*. Non-promotable incumbents standing in the path of one or more high-potential or promotable employees.
6. *Problem employees*. Those not meeting job expectations (measured achievement or competency proficiency). They should be given the opportunity to improve, receive remedial action, or be terminated. The time frame for observed improvement should be no longer than six months.
7. *TREADs allocation*. The value of investments in training, rewards, education, assignments, and development based on an employee's current and projected contribution to the organization—that is, the investment in Superkeepers™ and Keepers, key position backups, and solid citizens. See allocation of TREADs above.

Monitoring the Process

The robustness of any talent management process should be periodically measured to ensure that it continues to be effective. Monitoring enables an organization to fine-tune its talent management system on an ongoing basis in accordance with its creed and talent management strategy. The best-performing companies minimally use the following four broad measures:

Quality. Is the talent management strategy delivering results as measured by the maintenance of a sufficient reservoir of Superkeepers™ and backups for key positions with at least Keeper-level replacements? Are TREAD investments aligned with actual and forecasted employee contribution? Are the results of the talent management process seen at tactical levels, as evidenced by higher organization performance, lower turnover rates, reduction in both voids and surpluses, weeding out of the misfits, employee performance distributions aligned with overall company performance, pay decisions aligned with performance, and high levels of employee engagement and morale?

Timeliness. Does the talent management system work in a stated time frame or is it viewed as too protracted as a decision-making process?

Credibility. Are management and employees engaged by system? Do people believe the system works and is fair?

Summary

In this chapter, we have created a talent management model based on the practices of high-performing organizations. It consists of three linked elements: a creed, strategy, and system. The model requires that the principles of the organization's creed are embedded into both its talent management strategy and in its talent management system by incorporating its doctrines into selection criteria, competency definitions, performance criteria, and internal selection and development processes.

The talent management strategy contains the following three directives:

1. Cultivate the Superkeeper™.
2. Retain key position Keeper backups.
3. Appropriately allocate training, rewards, education, assignments, and development (TREADs).

The talent management system utilizes a set of procedures and processes that translate the organization's creed and strategy into a diagnostic and implementation program for achieving organization excellence based on four components: (1) assessment tools, (2) multi-rater assessment, (3) diagnostic tools, and (4) monitoring processes.

Chapter 2

Formulating Competencies

Murray M. Dalziel, Ph.D., Professor of Management and Director
University of Liverpool Management School

AN AMERICAN-BASED FAST-MOVING CONSUMER GOODS COMPANY DECIDES TO EXPAND aggressively in Europe and Asia. It hires a team of international search consultants who attract some of the best marketing talent from some of the most prominent firms in the consumer goods sector. Twenty-four months later, 70 percent of the new hires are gone.

A large financial services company embarks on an ambitious acquisition binge. In short order it acquires five medium-sized competitors. After 24 months, its share price collapses as the costs for IT integration fails.

A successful technology firm hires a new chief financial officer. With an accounting degree, an MBA from one of the best business schools, and experience in progressively different roles in finance in a number of Fortune 100 companies, he was the ideal candidate. However, 18 months later he is gone. "He never fit in here," claims the company's CEO.

How to Derail Your Company by Ignoring Competencies

The fast- moving consumer goods company, obtaining hiring recommendations from an executive search firm, assumed that people who came from some of the best "brands" companies in the world, with pedigree marketing experience, would be able to lead them to new levels of market penetration. But many of these hires were not assessed on, nor did they have the competencies needed to succeed, especially in new markets where they were expected to take independent responsibility for generating new campaigns. Often the circumstances they faced were quite different from what they had experienced elsewhere in their careers. Many of the hires came from companies with tight procedures about brand development and rollout. They had taken on increasingly important parts of that process in their previous companies. In this company, though, they were expected to take more responsibility and to dramatically increase levels of creativity and originality. However, this was now an environment that was rather free flowing and certainly not procedural. The result was that many could not adapt. They were either fired for their failure or left on their own accord.

The financial service company had assumed that combining IT platforms was a relatively straightforward technical task. Senior management failed to check whether in their company (or in any of their acquisitions) they had the project management skills to execute the plan. Worse, each of the IT departments had different skill requirements and no attempt was made to bring these together into a coherent whole. Consequently, as one of the executives put it, "We had all the skills you could possibly need, but they were thinly spread through so many people that it was unlikely that in our lifetime we could have completed a project."

The technology company had merely looked for someone with the right credentials. It did not make transparent that many of the skills needed as a CFO are not only technical but also leadership skills. "His approach to relationships was definitely a scorched earth strategy," remarked the CEO.

These three failure cases show why, from a business perspective, "competency models" are imperative. Today most large companies have one, if not several, competency models. But in many companies they are seen as the rather esoteric tool of the human resources department. This is a great pity because competency models have real business purpose and can underpin the social architecture that all successful businesses need.

Using Competency Models

There are many ways to develop and use competency models. We will describe four:

- Using commonly available models
- Generating a model for a specific role
- Job-family models
- Behavioral benchmarking

Which method should be used depends on why an organization wants to use a model. We will refer back to the cases at the beginning of this chapter to show how different methods fit different business situations.

Warning: Competencies Could Also Be Bad for Your Company

Whatever method is used there is a serious warning before proceeding. Competencies are quite ubiquitous in companies today. There is a tendency for these to look like a laundry list of desirable attributes that you would want anyone to possess. Some lists are copied from one company to another. We saw a competency model that had been developed for middle-level managers in a multinational chemical company being used wholesale in a regional retail bank for all managerial staff! As the case vignettes at the beginning of the chapter point out, an imperative is to ensure that the competency model you are using fits a particular business situation.

Competencies are also by their nature somewhat individualistic. But organizations are not mere aggregates of individuals. Organizations are formed through interaction between individuals. Relationships are at the core of an organization, and if the competency model does not take that into account, it cannot serve the organization well.

A competency model is also by definition written at a particular point in time. There has to be a consideration of the dynamic qualities of an organization. Will these attributes define what is needed in the future? Under what circumstances will any of these attributes become obsolete? Failure to ask these types of questions will ensure that your competency model will not serve your company well.

Commonly Available Models

There is now a whole industry in describing the characteristics of great leaders. One of the best of these is Daniel Goleman's Emotional Intelligence. Emotional Intelligence in its rawest form involves understanding how people control their emotions, which are deeply rooted in their brain chemistry. In his book *Working with Emotional Intelligence*, Goleman primarily uses the research of David McClelland and his colleagues at McBer and Company, pioneered in the 80s and continued to this date. He ties that with modern theories of how the brain functions, showing how these characteristics work and why they are important. More importantly, he demonstrates that people are capable of learning and developing these characteristics because these traits are tied to the brain and, far from being hard-wired from birth, are constantly rearranging themselves. The brain is one of the more pliable organs we possess.

Goleman has extended this argument to show that these elements are very much about "Social Intelligence." This is why the generic model is a useful model for organizations to use as a generic competency model. Most of organizational life is about what people do with other people. There may indeed be roles which depend on individuals isolated from each other, but these are extremely rare. How our brain functions, how we react, and how we interact with others is critical. Goleman proposes that social and emotional intelligence is shown in four areas: self-awareness, social awareness, self-management, and relationship management (see Figure 2-1).

Self Awareness	**Social Awareness**
• Emotional Self-Awareness	• Empathy
	• Organizational Awareness
Self-Management	**Relationship Management**
• Achievement Orientation	• Coach and Mentor
• Adaptability	• Influence
• Emotional Self-Control	• Inspirational Leadership
• Positive Outlook	• Teamwork

Figure 2-1 Social and Emotional Intelligence Quadrants

Within each of these are a set of competencies or characteristics that can be behaviorally observed. The technology firm hiring its new CFO would have been well served by choosing some of these to base its selection decision.

Each of these competencies has a set of behavioral descriptions. Figure 2-2 shows the descriptors for Positive Outlook (Self-Management quadrant). Notice how these are arranged at different levels. People can display competencies in different ways. Even though these are generic behaviors in any given situation, you need to determine what is more important for a particular role in your business situation. The CFO could easily have shown in his career or at the interview that he "viewed the future with hope" but perhaps "seeing possibilities rather than problems" was more important. Figure 2-3 shows the descriptors for Teamwork (Relationship Management quadrant). The CFO might have been able to "solicit input from others" when what was really required was to "encourage others" or "build bonds."

Since emotional and social intelligence is so important to success and is clearly observable, then, in the absence of any other strong driving business reason, businesses would do well to consider them in selection.

Many organizations also use these characteristics to give feedback to their employees about what is working and what is not working. Feedback given using a 360 process where data is gathered from the boss, peers, and direct reports (some organizations even go further and add customers), directed by a qualified advisor, can be immensely helpful in redirecting people to behaviors which will improve their performance. This provides a generic basis for benchmarking competencies.

The technology firm who failed with its CFO should have used these criteria as one part of the selection. But if the firm had ignored them in favor of technical skills, it could have minimized problems by providing him with early feedback about how he was relating and its effects on people around him. Management is a "contact sport," which is why "social intelligence" is critical.

Positive Outlook

Balanced optimism about life

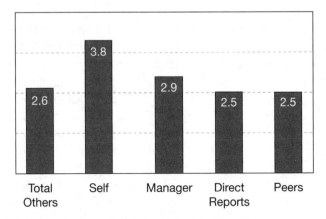

4. Sees possibilities rather than problems

3. Sees opportunities rather than threats

2. Sees more positives than negatives

1. Views future with hope

Figure 2-2 Behavioral Description: Self Management

Teamwork

Working with others towards a shared goal. Creating group synergy in pursuing collective goals.

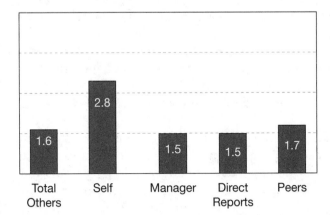

4. Builds bonds

3. Encourages others

2. Solicits input

1. Cooperates

Figure 2-3 Behavioral Description: Relationship Management

Building a Model for a Critical Role

Generic models like Goleman's emotional and social intelligence are very useful for describing behaviors and competencies across an organization or across a range of roles. Some managers will find them somewhat dissatisfying because they do not capture precisely what is required in a given role. The financial services company unable to integrate its IT platform probably needed to better define a key role or set of skills associated with the "project manager" job. They can do that two different ways—use a panel of managers to describe what they see as the defining characteristics of project managers or actually conduct research to identify the critical things that differentiate people who are good in this role from those who are typical. These are not mutually exclusive; some organizations do both.

What is really important is to look at all aspects of a person. Think of all the attributes a person can possess as contained in an iceberg. On the surface (above the water line), what is needed to be a financial services IT project manager? This might be knowledge of alternative IT platforms and certification in project management methodologies. You then want to drive deeper than this. What do outstanding project managers show or know that average performers do not show with the same degree of consistency? Perhaps outstanding project managers have a deeper appreciation for more than one part of the business as well as technical skills. Next, look below the surface from how we observe a person—first at his or her self-image. How do outstanding project managers look at themselves in comparison to average performers? Perhaps the outstanding performers see themselves as facilitators and coaches for their teams and not as drivers to obtain results. They are obtaining results in a different way.

The next level digs further below the surface and looks for the traits that the person brings to the role that will make a difference. Conceivably, outstanding project managers have an insatiable thirst to improve and make a difference, while the average ones have more needs for control. The next level should look at the fundamental motivational issues that make a difference. Perhaps project managers have a greater desire to make a difference to the organization, while average managers are more concerned about the image they have projected.

These are the types of questions that should be teased out either in a panel session with managers who know people in this role very well or addressed empirically by interviewing and observing actual project managers.

When specific roles are critical for organization outcomes, then they merit their own competency model.

These methods can be used for any critical role in an organization. Today many organizations want to look at their overall leadership and see the leadership as a key role. This is what the fast-moving consumer goods company should have been thinking about. Rather than hire great marketing people who could not perform in their culture or market situation, they might have thought about the attributes that would have made them successful in that particular company. In general, in times of great change, there are opportunities to relook at the characteristics the company wants to see in key leaders who will drive the strategy or the change. As the fast-moving consumer goods company discovered, functional skills or even success in other companies are not necessarily the best predictors in new situations.

Research could have been carried out as to what makes the difference in this company. But management teams often have strong views about leadership. Discussing these issues in a management group can be a valuable exercise. But management discussions about the characteristics of potential leaders need discipline. Too often these sessions generate lists that are too long. Therefore, any potential candidate is unlikely to meet the criteria. Other groups produce lists that are unrealistic.

There are three connected methods management groups can use to build a model of competencies that they agree should drive leadership or key roles in their company. First, managers can use a list (as in Figure 2-1) and agree which of these characteristics are most important in their company. If they had only to choose five, which of these would differentiate the best performers from average performers? Which two or three would have the most devastating impact if missing? This requires a hard discussion about what matters for this company. If there is an agreement on 8 to 12 characteristics that foster superior performance or would be killers if missing, the management team should have a discussion about how these are displayed in their company. For example, what would "Inspirational Leadership" look like in roles in this company? How would you know someone was showing this to a very high standard?

Second, the management team can decide on the key requirements for the role. For the fast-moving consumer goods company, how are these leaders assigned to expanding business in new territories supposed to add value? They might have a debate that ends up with a list of the seven (plus or minus two) accountabilities that define the role. This might include "modify brand strategies to meet key customer needs in their markets" and "build an organization capable of delivering the right product at the right time to trade distributors." Then the management team constructs a matrix where they map out the critical competencies they have decided at stage two and show how these enable people in the role to enact their accountabilities in superb ways. Alternatively, a management group could start at this step and, having agreed on the key accountabilities for the role, answer the question, "What attributes, characteristics, skills, or competencies will enable the person in the role to perform this accountability in an outstanding manner?"

Third, the management group should think concretely about whom they see as the top performers in these key roles. Keep a picture of them in mind, and then take some people who are typical but not below average performers and form a picture of them in the management team's minds. What does the management team see the top performers doing that is different from the average performers? What makes them outstanding? What motivates them? How do they think? Make sure you focus not only on results but also on what they are actually doing. Again, a management group can start here and go back through the first two steps in any order.

When going through this type of exercise, keep in mind that for some management groups, this may be the first time they have engaged in a discussion about needed capabilities. Some may find these exercises "academic" and not "action-oriented." Facilitators may need to keep them on track. The top management team having a discussion about the types of capabilities people require is probably one of the most important discussions they can have and is a prerequisite to good talent management. Facilitators also need to ensure that the discussion is grounded on what the business needs to be successful.

The range of issues dealt with by Figure 2-1 is worth returning to. Some management groups produce descriptions of competencies that are too one-sided. Different business situations will pull for different attributes and how these attributes are displayed. But avoid making them unbalanced. Unbalanced models (which, for example, have a lot of competencies about thinking and achieving but not many on influencing or energizing) often will lead organizations to select singular leaders who do not adapt.

Building Models for Job Families

To ensure that the IT function in the newly integrated financial services firm performs well over time, the team must decide what will be required for the whole function and ensure that the function is attracting the right technical skills as well as the right behavioral attributes. The primary goal is to find the right set of technical attributes for people to perform in a given function. This has to start with the leadership group coming together and agreeing on where the business is going and what the individuals in this functional area must contribute. Attributes must be embedded in business logic and not technical or HR logic. Otherwise, over time the descriptions are seen as somewhat general. If the management team can complete the statement "this is what we must get right. . .," then the technical and behavioral attributes will resonate and have real value for the organization.

Only after agreeing on what the business has to get right should the team proceed and look at the skills and other attributes. To do this, start from the entry level and answer the question, "What do people need in order to perform well at this level?" Then imagine a second level and answer the question, "What would a person have to demonstrate in order to move to this level?" Repeat this question for the next level. If the team sees more than four levels in their function, then level 5 should be the leadership grouping.

This method should produce a chart with the skills that a function needs in order to complete its mission. The chart should be usable. Managers should be able to compare their people and decide which skills they possess and whether they possess enough know-how at each level of the function.

Behavioral Benchmarking

When organizations are faced with changed or new situations (such as faced by the consumer goods company), they often sponsor more rigorous studies of their best people's actions, how these best people compare to others in the organization, or to stars in benchmark companies. "Behavioral Benchmarking" is probably the most recent evolution from the competency approaches. For example, when a telecommunications company spun off its wireless division, they benchmarked the top team against others in the industry. When a new CEO joined a fast-growth software company, he commissioned a study of how his "stars" compared to outstanding performers in other fast-growth companies. In order to obtain more focus on top-line growth, the CEO of a large consumer goods company commissioned a study of his leaders against leaders who were known to produce high growth. He used the findings on the gaps to refocus leadership teams at the top of his organization.

Behavioral Benchmarking is different from using a generic model because you will want to pinpoint comparisons with specific people in roles in other companies. This usually requires outside help, although some organizations might form a consortium to develop models across a number of organizations. In selecting an external organization, you need to understand the nature of their database. How extensive is it? Does it cover industries that you want to benchmark against? What levels are the people you are benchmarking against? Are they at levels comparable to what you are focusing on in your organization? Are the performance attributes of the comparison group known? A pragmatic approach that many organizations use to test this is to rigorously assess both outside and internal candidates for given roles. Of course, you want to select the best person, but you can take this one level further and seek to understand what differentiated the "outsiders" from the "insiders."

Competency Models Underpin HR Systems and Processes

Competency models used in any of these approaches are fundamental underpinnings of HR systems. Many organizations have had different language to describe their recruitment standards, training requirements, or promotion criteria. Using a common competency model, they can create a common language through which all of these important organizational initiatives can converge.

Large organizations, often operating across many countries, also need a common language to talk about people. Failure to do this can lead to spotty performance from one unit to the next, which is not explained merely by market forces or the inability to plan for global succession because of the inability to compare talent across borders. Competency models provide a common model for talking about people.

Conclusion

The fundamental premise on how to build a competency model should be on the driving business issues that the company faces. If the fast-moving consumer goods company had done that, it would have been able to go to market faster and have a greater impact when launching in new markets. If the financial services company had done that, its acquisitions and customer retention rates would have been much higher; and if the technology firm had hired its CFO on the basis of a competency model, its share price would have been protected.

References

Goleman, D. *Working with Emotional Intelligence*. New York: Bantam Books, October 1998.

McClelland, D. C. "Toward a Theory of Motive Acquisition," *American Psychologist* 20, no. 5, May 1965, pp. 321–333.

McClelland, D. C. "Testing for Competence Rather Than for Intelligence." *American Psychologist* 28, no. 1, January 1973, pp. 1–14.

Chapter 3

Fundamentals of Competency Modeling

Kim E. Ruyle, Vice President of Product Development
J. Evelyn Orr, Intellectual Property Development Consultant
Korn/Ferry Leadership and Talent Consulting

COMPETENCIES ARE AT THE CORE OF ALL TALENT MANAGEMENT PRACTICES. COMPETENCIES provide a clear and consistent vocabulary for talent management programs and the messages that inform and engage the key stakeholders—executive management, line management, high-potential employees, and the general employee population.

A competency is a measurable skill, attitude, or attribute that contributes to success on the job. Examples include Business Acumen,[1] Perspective, Planning, Patience, and Listening (Lombardo and Eichinger 2009). Competencies enable us to make meaningful contributions that support the organization. And because competencies shape our behavior, they, to a large extent, determine how we do our jobs and how we accomplish goals.

Numerous research studies have established the value of competencies. Competencies promote alignment of talent management practices, and research by Becker and Huselid (1998), Huselid, Becker, and Beatty (2005), and others have demonstrated the positive financial impact of alignment with talent management systems. A benchmarking study by the American Productivity and Quality Council in 2006 found that every one of the organizations identified as a "best practice organization" had developed a behavioral competency model designed to guide selection, promotion, development, and succession planning (Hollenbeck 2009). Other studies have shown that a competency-based executive assessment and selection process can generate as much as an additional $3M annual profit per candidate selected (Russell 2001), that the application of competencies is positively correlated with job satisfaction (Towler and Britt 2006), and that competencies are linked to increased profit and reduced turnover (Pluzdrak 2007).

Extensive research has been conducted on competencies over the past 20 years. We know which competencies are in relative high supply in the labor pool (e.g., Drive for Results) and which are in short supply (e.g., Dealing with Ambiguity). We know which are relatively difficult to develop (e.g., Conflict Management) and which are easiest (e.g., Action Oriented). And, very importantly, we know which competencies are most related to performance at various stages of career development.

Everyone possesses some skill level in all competencies. We're better at some than others, and our relative strengths and weaknesses in competencies give us a distinct leadership texture. Your leadership texture will determine how others perceive you. The words they select to describe you generally reflect their perception of your relative strengths, those competencies that are at the forefront of your personal leadership texture. For any individual, the most effective leadership texture is defined by the context—the person's role and position level and by certain organizational-level factors such as business strategy and organizational culture. Some competencies are more important to the performance of a financial analyst than they are for a customer service associate, some are more important to the performance of an individual contributor than they are for a manager, and some are more important to people working in an organization that focuses on operational efficiency as opposed to an organization that focuses on breakthrough innovation.

Competencies can be grouped into unique combinations that are used to define success for a particular context. These particular competency models are often referred to as competency success profiles. Common applications of success profiles include the following:

- Role-specific success profiles based on job analyses are often used to create job descriptions, guide behavioral-based interviews, generate development plans, aid in selection for assignments and promotions, and, generally inform workforce planning activities.
- Position level-specific success profiles are often used to enhance career planning and development.
- Core organization competency profiles reflect the set of critical competencies required throughout the firm to shape the organizational capabilities and culture required to achieve the strategic intent.

An accurate competency success profile represents the ideal leadership texture for a particular context. It describes those people who perform well and deliver results in that particular context, the people who are deemed competent. Those who most closely mirror the competencies in the success profile will be considered the most competent, the star performers. They will deliver the highest value to their organizations, and to the extent that they perform in a meritocracy, will receive rewards that reflect their results. Because they have the right leadership texture, they will approach their work with positive attitudes. They will make sound decisions and exhibit appropriate behaviors.

Competencies are the building blocks of performance. They can be measured and they can be learned. Learning means acquiring the ability to do something new, to do something that couldn't be done before the learning took place. Competencies are learned by degrees, and to the degree that you have learned a competency, you will have the ability to do something new, to behave in a different way, to display a new attitude, to deliver enhanced results.

Although competency success profiles are created to be unique to a specific context, the uniqueness comes primarily from the particular combination of competencies, not from the competencies that comprise the profile. There are a number of commercially available, research-based leadership competency models available on the market. Because the good ones are based on research, they have a lot in common, and they are able to describe the majority of skills and attributes that determine success for most contexts. Except for specific functional-technical skills, it rarely makes sense to develop homegrown competencies. Utilizing a research-based commercially available competency set will save time and money, and will provide normative data related to skill levels, supply in the workforce, and developmental difficulty. Several vendors have a variety of tools based on their competency set: 360 assessment instruments, interview guides, and developmental materials.

Functional-technical competencies are a special breed. They can be legitimately included in a research-based set of leadership competencies as a placeholder, of sorts, because all leaders require a level of functional-technical competences. However, the importance of functional-technical skills, in general, diminishes significantly as a person's career progresses. Even for new technical hires in engineering, finance, or IT, functional-technical skills may account for no more than 25 percent of job performance (Schmidt and Hunter 1998).

Other leadership competencies such as Conflict Management, Organizing, Interpersonal Savvy, and Organizational Agility are very important for success even for individual contributors in the most technical of positions. While people in these positions are often hired for functional-technical competence, they are far more likely to have performance problems, even derail, because of deficiency in other leadership competencies. For senior executives, functional-technical competencies typically contribute very little to leadership effectiveness.

Competency success profiles can be created by analyzing data from several sources:

- Research and empirical studies and normative data that indicate what's most important for a defined role, such as chief financial officer, or for a defined context such as a turnaround situation
- Executives or executive leadership teams who, typically with the assistance of a competency expert, have identified the competencies that most closely map to business-specific factors such as strategy, mission, vision, and values

- Subject matter experts who are exemplary performers in the targeted role led by a skilled facilitator

It's common to use a combination of these methods, and any of them will likely result in placing competencies into one of at least two classifications. Price-of-admission competencies are those important for the context but in high supply in the target population. Price-of-admission competencies add little value to and are often excluded from a success profile. They are useful to identify, however, so they can be used in résumé screening during selection processes. Competitive-edge competencies, on the other hand, are those that truly differentiate exemplary performers from the average. It's important to identify and include competitive-edge competencies in the competency success profile.

Regardless of the method or combination of methods used to create a success profile, it's a best practice to have a team of key stakeholders validate it through a group process facilitated by a skilled competency practitioner. This helps achieve buy-in and support from key leaders who are in a position to promote it in the organization.

Case Study

A venture-funded start-up business was established in response to a perceived opportunity created by the collapse of global fisheries and rising demand for fresh fish. The intention is to grow the venture into a global, vertically integrated operation to (1) commercially farm fish, (2) provide fresh fish to major wholesale markets, and (3) operate a series of upscale seafood restaurants.

The company's farming operations will initially consist of three large commercial fish farms located in oceans off three coasts. In the first year, 15 restaurants are planned to open in major global cities; more than half of the initial restaurants will be located in North America, but several restaurants will also open in the first year in Europe, Asia, South America, and Mexico. Very aggressive growth plans are in place that will add two fish farms and double the number of restaurants within five years. The executive management team has crafted mission, vision, and value statements and defined the strategic focus and unique value proposition, as shown in Figure 3-1.

Kimbo/Fish International

Mission

Serve fresh fish to the world while delivering:

- Sustainable, earth-friendly aquaculture
- Efficient global logistics operations
- Unique fine dining experiences

(continued)

Figure 3-1 Kimbo/Fish International Company Blueprint

Vision

Become the world's first truly global and vertically integrated fishery and to be recognized as a leading:

- Supplier of fresh fish to major global markets
- Provider of consistent fine seafood dining experiences in major world cities
- Pioneer and promoter of earth-friendly fish farming methods

Values

- Growth focus—Drive relentlessly to achieve and exceed growth expectations.
- Transparency—Make sure important information is freely accessible to all employees.
- Collaboration—Minimize organizational boundaries; collaborate effectively across them.
- Constructive conflict—Resolve issues head-on.
- Accountability—Everyone bears responsibility for delivering results.
- Risk taking—Embrace and reward calculated risk taking.

Strategic Focus

Operational Efficiency

Unique Value Proposition

Based on positioning as a global and vertically integrated fresh fish supplier with core capabilities in:

1. Earth-friendly aquaculture
2. Efficient global logistics and distribution
3. Delivery of fine dining experiences

Figure 3-1 Kimbo/Fish International Company Blueprint

Recognizing the value that would be provided by a core leadership success profile for the organization, the CHRO engaged a competency expert consultant to work with the senior management team. The process they followed consisted of the following:

1. Select a best-in-class, research-based library of competencies that promotes the integration of competencies throughout talent management processes.
2. Employ a competency expert to analyze and map the organization's business drivers and strategy to the competencies.
3. Through a facilitated workshop of key stakeholders, develop and validate a core leadership success profile to be used throughout the organization.
4. Identify key strategic jobs in the organization that will be targeted for role-specific competency modeling.
5. Through a facilitated workshop of subject matter experts, develop and validate competency success profiles for key strategic jobs that supplement the core success profile.

6. Design and implement a comprehensive plan to roll out the competency success profiles to the organization.

The consultant, working from a commercial research-based competency library, mapped competencies to the organization's strategy, mission, vision, and values and created the matrix shown in Figure 3-2 to guide a competency modeling workshop. The matrix has a number of columns as follows:

- The first column lists the competency title with the associated number from the library.
- The second through seventh columns indicate by virtue of a 1 or 0 whether the competency is correlated with a particular factor. All the competencies in the matrix were selected as a starting point because they map relatively strongly to the organization's strategy and unique value proposition; thus, they all receive a value of 1 in the column headed "Strategy." Those competencies receiving a value of 1 in the second column are mapped to the organization's vision statement. The values in the column headed "Executive Success" come from research available through the competency library vendor; those competencies with a value of 1 have relatively high correlations with executive success. The consultant added additional columns to reflect research correlating competencies to learning agility, a key predictor of potential, and emotional quotient, an indicator of interpersonal skills.
- The values are summed in the eighth column, and the competencies are ranked from the highest score to the lowest. For instance, Dealing with Ambiguity and Motivating Others receive a score of 7 because they are mapped to each of the seven factors examined. On the other hand, Delegation, Informing, and several others are only mapped to two factors.
- The final column indicates the level of difficulty of developing the competency on a five-point descriptive scale from Easiest to Hardest.

Competencies Initially Considered	Strategy	Vision	Mission	Values	Executive Success Research	Learning Agility	EQ	Sum	Developmental Difficulty
2 Dealing with Ambiguity	1	1	1	1	1	1	1	7	Harder
36 Motivating Others	1	1	1	1	1	1	1	7	Moderate
12 Conflict Management	1	1	1	1	0	1	1	6	Hardest
33 Listening	1	1	1	1	0	1	1	6	Easier
46 Perspective	1	1	1	1	1	1	0	6	Moderate
51 Problem Solving	1	1	1	1	1	1	0	6	Moderate

Figure 3-2 Competency Mapping Matrix (continued on next page)

Competencies Initially Considered	Strategy	Vision	Mission	Values	Executive Success Research	Learning Agility	EQ	Sum	Developmental Difficulty
52 Process Management	1	1	1	1	1	1	0	6	Moderate
14 Creativity	1	1	1	0	1	1	0	5	Moderate
15 Customer Focus	1	1	1	0	1	0	1	5	Easiest
48 Political Savvy	1	1	1	1	1	0	0	5	Hardest
50 Priority Setting	1	0	1	1	1	1	0	5	Easier
65 Managing Vision and Purpose	1	1	1	1	1	0	0	5	Moderate
5 Business Acumen	1	1	1	0	1	0	0	4	Moderate
16 Timely Decision Making	1	1	0	1	0	1	0	4	Easiest
31 Interpersonal Savvy	1	0	1	1	0	0	1	4	Harder
32 Learning on the Fly	1	0	0	1	1	1	0	4	Moderate
39 Organizing	1	0	1	0	1	1	0	4	Easier
47 Planning	1	1	1	1	0	0	0	4	Easiest
53 Drive for Results	1	0	1	1	1	0	0	4	Easier
58 Strategic Agility	1	1	1	0	1	0	0	4	Harder
59 Managing through Systems	1	1	1	1	0	0	0	4	Harder
64 Understanding Others	1	0	0	1	0	1	1	4	Hardest
17 Decision Quality	1	1	0	0	1	0	0	3	Easier
28 Innovation Management	1	1	0	0	1	0	0	3	Hardest
37 Negotiating	1	0	1	0	1	0	0	3	Harder
38 Organizational Agility	1	0	1	1	0	0	0	3	Harder
42 Peer Relationships	1	0	0	1	0	0	1	3	Easier
56 Sizing Up People	1	0	0	0	0	1	1	3	Harder
60 Building Effective Teams	1	0	0	1	0	0	1	3	Harder
18 Delegation	1	0	0	1	0	0	0	2	Easier
27 Informing	1	0	0	1	0	0	0	2	Easiest
29 Integrity and Trust	1	0	0	0	0	0	1	2	Easier
35 Managing and Measuring Work	1	0	1	0	0	0	0	2	Easier

Figure 3-2 Competency Mapping Matrix (continued)

After preparing the matrix, the consultant facilitated a competency modeling workshop with key stakeholders from senior and mid-level management to work through the matrix and identify those competencies that should be included in a core leadership success profile for the organization. Participants considered each competency in the matrix and classified them into competitive-edge, differentiating, and price-of-admission competencies. Significant discussion ensued and difficult decisions were facilitated by the consultant to determine which, if any, price-of-admission competencies would be included in the final success profile. The final result is shown in Figure 3-3.

Kimbo/Fish International Leadership Success Profile	
Competencies	**Primary Application**
Dealing with Ambiguity	Development—Aggressively develop this.
Business Acumen	Price-of-Admission—Screen for this.
Conflict Management	Development—Aggressively develop this.
Customer Focus	Price-of-Admission—Screen for this.
Informing	Development—Aggressively develop this.
Integrity and Trust	Price-of-Admission—Screen for this.
Learning on the Fly	Price-of-Admission—Screen for this.
Listening	Development—Aggressively develop this.
Motivating Others	Development—Aggressively develop this.
Negotiating	Selection Criteria—Interview for this.
Organizing	Selection Criteria—Interview for this.
Perspective	Development—Aggressively develop this.
Planning	Selection Criteria—Interview for this.
Political Savvy	Development—Aggressively develop this.
Priority Setting	Selection Criteria—Interview for this.
Problem Solving	Price-of-Admission—Screen for this.
Process Management	Selection Criteria—Interview for this.
Drive for Results	Price-of-Admission—Screen for this.
Sizing Up People	Selection Criteria—Interview for this.
Managing through Systems	Development—Aggressively develop this.
Building Effective Teams	Development—Aggressively develop this.
Understanding Others	Development—Aggressively develop this.

Figure 3-3 Leadership Success Profile

Twenty-two competencies were selected to reflect the essential leadership texture for the organization. This profile supports the organization's strategy and values, is further supported by research, and, by virtue of the participation of stakeholders, is well understood by executives and managers who are in a position to explain and champion it throughout the organization.

Another outcome of the competency modeling workshop is classification within the profile to provide guidance for employees, especially managers who are selecting and developing talent. Some competencies are price-of-admission competencies. They are important for the desired leadership texture but are in high supply in the labor pool. They are easily evaluated during the résumé-screening process to ensure that job candidates meet a minimum standard. Other competencies are identified as selection criteria; they are competitive-edge competencies that are often addressed in interviews. And finally, other competencies are identified for development. These competencies are targeted for inclusion in development initiatives, coaching and mentoring programs, and when considering the developmental power of job assignments.

The competencies composing the core leadership success profile apply to all employees in the firm, but there are other competencies not included, functional/technical competencies, for instance, that are important to specific jobs. After completing the core success profile, the consultant assisted the organization in the second phase of the project, which was to identify key strategic jobs in the firm and identify additional competencies that would complement the core success profile.

The consultant worked with a team of HR managers and selected line managers to analyze the strategic importance of jobs and identify those that would receive additional competency modeling work. The team categorized jobs to differentiate between those that are not only difficult but also are essential to the strategic success of the organization. Those are the positions addressed in job-specific competency profiling.

Once key jobs were identified, the consultant led select subject matter experts, including successful incumbents and bosses, in the creation and validation of role-specific success profiles. The consultant framed the exercise by posing the following questions:

- What are the strategic goals of the organization or function or level?
- What are the deliverables/expectations of the job?
- What differentiates high performers?
- What are the challenges incumbents will face (politics, lack of resources, etc.)?

After discussing and reaching some agreement among the group, the consultant documented the general themes related to the questions for participants to reference during the exercise. Participants began the process of individually reviewing competencies and sorting them into groups such as Mission Critical, Nice to Have, Not Important. After each participant finished the exercise, the consultant consolidated and analyzed the data. The consultant then led the group in considering the research, developmental difficulty, and alignment to role-specific expectations and challenges. The group also conducted a thematic analysis to ensure a balanced profile. The consultant was careful to frame this exercise by being clear about the outcome. The group was asked to provide their best recommendation for the success profile, and the final decision was made in consultation with the executive leadership team. The profiling exercise provided a key opportunity for subject matter experts to get involved, which enhanced the degree to which the group adopted and championed the success profile and would endorse it once in effect.

Summary

Through research, it is known what leaders do and what competencies are required to be successful. Although the names, the numbers, and the specificity of the competencies may be different for different competency libraries developed by different authors/vendors, the content, themes, and essence are about the same (Tett, Guteman, Bleier, and Murphy 2000). The degree to which leadership competencies help an organization achieve its business objectives depends in equal parts on the quality of competency model development and the quality of execution. When best practices are applied, competencies become the thread that ties an organization's business strategy to all of its talent management practices.

References

Becker, B. E., and M. A. Huselid. 1998. High performance work systems and firm performance: A synthesis of research and managerial implications. *Research in Personnel and Human Resources Journal* 16(1):53–101.

Hollenbeck, G. P. 2009. Executive selection: What's right . . . and what's wrong. *Industrial and Organizational Psychology* 2:130–143.

Huselid, M. A., B. E. Becker, and R. W. Beatty. 2005. *The workforce scorecard: Managing human capital to execute strategy.* Boston: Harvard Business School Publishing Corporation.

Lombardo, M. M., and R. W. Eichinger. 2009. *FYI for your improvement: A guide for development and coaching.* Minneapolis: Lominger Limited.

Pluzdrak, N. L. 2007. *The correlation of leadership competencies and business results: A case study on the ROI of leadership competencies.* Dissertation. Pepperdine University.

Russell, C. J. (2001). A longitudinal study of top-level executive performance. *Journal of Applied Psychology* 86(4):560–573.

Schmidt, F. L., and J. E. Hunter. 1998. The validity and utility of selection methods in personnel psychology: Practical and theoretical implications of 85 years of research findings. *Psychological Bulletin* 124:262–274.

Tett, R. P., H. A. Guterman, A. Bleier, and P. J. Murphy. 2000. Development and content validation of a "hyperdimensional" taxonomy of managerial competence. *Human Performance* 13(3):205–251.

Towler, A., and T. Britt, T. 2006. *Leadership competencies and organizational outcomes: A longitudinal study.* Paper presented at the Annual Conference of the Society for Industrial and Organizational Psychology, Dallas.

Notes

1. All competencies referenced in this chapter are from the Leadership Architect®
   Competency Library, a research-based set of 67 competencies and 19 stallers and stop-
   pers. These competencies with their associated definitions and developmental remedies
   are the copyrighted and proprietary intellectual property of Lominger International,
   A Korn/Ferry Company. All rights are reserved.

Chapter 4

Creating the Workforce of the Future: Projecting and Utilizing New Competencies

Ron Garonzik, Ph.D., Vice President
John B. Larrere, National Practice Leader, Leadership and Talent
Hay Group

Introduction

In our work with clients, we have steered away from a "one size fits all" approach to management and leadership competency modeling that pays insufficient attention to role demands and the peculiar organizational hierarchies that determine the strategic perspective required from senior management positions, in particular. Such generally applied competency models, while useful in shaping work culture and establishing new values, have fallen short when applied to career pathing and succession management needs. This has become essential in light of the increasing complexity of jobs, the flattening of organizational hierarchies, and increasingly the wide application of matrixed and interdependent roles. In our experience, there is a more nuanced view of competencies required for future workforce needs that applies to three broad transitional levels of organizations, as will be explored in this chapter:

- At entry levels of the organization, individual contributors, or first-line managers preparing to perform as high-functioning professional managers of others
- As one progresses to mid-management levels, demonstrating excellence in *something* of value to the business and/or running of the organization, and obtaining required seasoning as a manager of managers

- At the executive levels, synthesizing years of capability, knowledge, and skills required for business delivery or functional leadership in roles of strategic consequence

We briefly make note of a number of dynamics that, if unmanaged, can interfere with the acquisition of critical competencies and capabilities during these key transitions, as well as of consequences for effectiveness in role performance.

Strategy shapes talent demands. Business strategy has direct implications for organizational strategy. In turn, organizational strategy influences the size, complexity, and accountability of roles. For instance, functional organizations consolidate decision making at the top; matrixed organizations spread decision making power across units to account for geography, industry sector, and product considerations. Collectively, these contextual variables impact talent requirements and can make or break success in role performance.

The higher the organizational level, the more talent becomes a function of role demand versus the available supply of talent that can "move up." Most organizations, following the logic of having a healthy supply of high-potential individuals in the pipeline as a measure of success, have some system in place for identifying "high potential" at different levels of seniority. Organizations, however, can fall into the trap of assuming that anointed "high flyers" will be good at almost any leadership role, yet the evidence is to the contrary: *High potential is a temporary state, not necessarily an enduring trait.*

While managers progress through the organizational hierarchy, "potential" takes on different significance. At lower levels, the challenge is to develop a flexible range of capabilities that would enable managers with suitable potential to move into a variety of positions (skill and know-how permitting). At higher levels, the issue is less about long-term potential but rather increasingly more about *potential for what the specific job requires* and and how the role contributes to strategy and business results.

The more pressing the organization's need for delivery of results from a role, the more explicit the organization must be about the demands inherent in such roles as a consequence of short-term suitability. *Superstar* crashes are most often a consequence of "hi pos" stretched beyond their level of capability and experience, to the detriment of the business and these individuals' careers. It is not enough to consider whether someone is ready for a move to a bigger role. Those responsible for overseeing such moves also need to look at how individuals will fit into the specific requirements of different roles, with the ingredients for success varying considerably from one role to another.

The availability and cohesiveness of core talent management processes required to support business objectives. Organizations can unwittingly be complicit in the derailing of careers by mismanaging career progression central to the effective deployment of talent. Following are some common ways this plays out:

- *The laissez-faire mistake.* Thinking that the organization's responsibility ends when it identifies potential. By assuming that the cream will rise to the top, the organization can waste the latent potential in the workforce by failing to nurture and develop it.

- *The job rotation mistake.* Making the assumption that a job rotation or an overseas assignment is, in itself, a developmental experience, without providing either the framework to orient the person to what exactly he or she is supposed to learn from the assignment or a debriefing to ensure that the desired development did indeed take place.
- *The our-best-talent-can-manage-anything mistake.* Making promotions or lateral moves that stretch the person to the point of breaking, without providing support and a safety net; worse, subsequently blaming the person for failing to adapt quickly enough.
- *The moving too fast mistake.* Moving the high-potential individual from one role to another too quickly, eliminating the opportunity to learn from deep experience and from his or her mistakes. Worse yet, moving a high-potential person before the consequences of his or her mistakes become clear, thereby rescuing the individual, rather than allowing him or her to fail and learn from their mistakes.

All of these scenarios can impede the acquisition of capability essential to effective performance across work levels.

Organizational Transitions with Varying Implications for Talent and Competencies

Our experience in helping clients manage talent has indicated that the devil is truly in the details. Simple competency solutions oversimplify complex human resource and organizational challenges, with adverse impact that can hinder the longer-term growth potential of key talent. Take for instance, the urging of managers to leverage and build on personal strengths at the expense of broadening one's capability by focusing on relative areas of weakness. This approach may have some advantages at lower-level positions, but is likely ill-placed advice for more senior position holders. As an illustration, a manufacturing supervisor may be expected to get personally involved in driving task delivery to high standards of excellence requiring personal attention to detail and hands-on oversight. But such a behavioral orientation typically interferes with effectiveness in more senior-level management roles.

Nevertheless, there are a handful of personal characteristics predictive of longer-term success that can be assessed in lower-level positions that go beyond specific skills and know-how required to perform effectively in any job. These factors remain constant as employees rise to higher-level positions, yet eventually must take a back seat in relevance to more role-specific competencies that become more central to effective performance in specific jobs. With higher-level positions, competency requirements become more complex and differentiated as a consequence of level and role type. Hay Group research points to essential competency differences among senior executive positions, even though they may be uniformly populated by "high potential" leaders.

Entry levels and learning professional excellence. Assuming the educational requirements, a key challenge from a talent management perspective involves the identification of employees with the potential to grow beyond the entry job level into outstanding professional managers or leaders. There are a number of popular, scalable frameworks for defining long-term potential, and with overlap of constructs among them. Hay Group utilizes four research-based competencies—*Growth Factors*—consistent with research in social psychology and adult development that have shown strong predictive ability in assessing long-term potential for professional growth. These factors are designed to be recognizable early in a person's career (though they do not necessarily predict success in entry-level roles), support learning from developmental opportunities, and success in a broad range of leadership roles, to be relatively enduring and relatively difficult to learn in a classroom training setting (hence, from the organization's viewpoint, worth selecting for), and work well across diverse global populations (and do not discriminate against diverse groups).

- *Eagerness to learn.* The willingness to take a risk in exchange for the opportunity to learn something new. This factor reflects an individual's confidence in stretching beyond their comfort zone, as well as their ability to listen to, and learn, from others.
- *Breadth of perspective.* The ability to incorporate multiple perspectives and disciplines in evaluating and solving problems. It involves viewing a given job within the broader picture of the organization as a whole, and grows in importance as a manager rises to more senior levels.
- *Understanding others.* The capacity to accurately perceive others' perspectives and experiences. This factor captures an individual's motivation and ability to learn from others—particularly those with different perspectives—by listening with care and respect.
- *Personal maturity.* The ability to view criticism and difficulties as opportunities for learning and growth. Every senior manager knows the path to leadership can be challenging, even painful, with setbacks along the way. This factor captures a person's resilience to maintain emotional balance and keep learning in the face of turmoil.

Although there may be some similarity among commonly available measures of "high potential," a critical miscalculation we have seen is the confounding of immediate *performance* with the evaluation of longer-term *potential*. It is certainly not unusual to encounter mid-career "stars" who had a rocky start during the first few working years. People may fail to deliver exemplary output because of a mismatch with job requirements, lack of proper managerial oversight, or other exogenous factors. On the other hand, it's quite common to encounter the early career "star" deliverer with little real potential for long-term growth as measured by the above Growth Factors—sometimes as a consequence of interest and personal values (a dedicated engineer with little professional interest beyond an engineering career). Thus, there is the need to treat performance and potential-for-growth as independent factors.

Demonstrating excellence in a defined area. During mid-career years, managers face the challenge of combining mastery and experience with some awareness of antici-pated career aspiration and preference—that is, "Where do I see myself at the top of my game?" and "How divergent do I see myself progressing from my educational and early work experiences?" Self-awareness becomes a determining feature of success as manifest through the lens of self-image ("I may have been trained as an engineer but have come to see myself as a general manager."), exposure to opportunity ("I don't have the managing a P&L and business delivery team experiences required to become a significant general manager."), and sense of one's own capability ("Even though I'm willing to work as a general manager, I simply don't see myself as ready and able to work in that capacity."). Ideally, employees are converging between the previously independent variables of demonstrated performance and estimated potential to stretch one or two positions beyond one's current job. The key test within these organizational strata is to be seen by one's colleagues and superiors as someone who demonstrates specialization and excellence in *something* related to the business at hand: leading a sales team, strategy development, line HR expertise, and so on. These levels are char-acterized by increasing complexity in understanding the business and implications across a range of internal and external variables: the competitive landscape, business scope and scale, the life cycle of the business, and the local/global nature of the busi-ness. Positions in this section of the organization span from the entry- to management- to director-level positions, and include the technical professionals—"experts" in defined areas who are likely to remain on dedicated technology-oriented tracks.

Regardless of managerial or technical expertise, as one progresses up the organi-zational ladder, one should be increasingly cognizant of the impossibility of carrying out one's work independently. Therefore, a premium is placed on learning to manage interdependent relationships. Demonstrated competence within this mid-career period should enable employees to manage the variable of diminishing hierarchy. Fewer large organizations are purely hierarchical in nature—a movement likely to be further accentuated in the future. Working collaboratively within some kind of matrixed organizational structure has become more the norm. The hallmark of this type of structure is learning to live with and manage shared accountability, where one's freedom of action is bounded by matrix-guided approvals and decision making. The essential tension of working at this level is the challenge, which goes with the absence of clean lines of unequivocal accountability, of gaining sufficient leadership experience required for top management roles.

From a competency development perspective, one needs to manage a sort of yin/yang of demonstrating excellence, without becoming organizationally pigeonholed by that very area of expertise. This is of particular relevance in today's transformed workplace where the patriarchic ("Don't worry—we'll take care of your career.") organ-ization has become a vestige of a bygone era. Employees must be adaptive to the demands of organizations that are leaner, more nimble, and competitive in response to changing market conditions. This new orientation to the workplace is captured in Douglas T. Hall's work on the *protean career* (Hall 1976, 2002). Derived from Greek mythology, Proteus, the form-shifting god of the sea, has become a symbol for career management. Hall sees the protean career as: "A process which the person, not the organization, is managing. The protean person's personal career choices and search for self-fulfillment are the unifying or integrative elements in his or her life (Hall 1976, 201)." Personal responsibility for making the *right* career choices presupposes intentional clarity about career aspirations and a good dose of assertiveness and self-confidence to reject or shape job opportunities that may distort the arc of one's career.

Synthesis—Becoming an Executive or Senior Professional

In entering the executive ranks, managers have assumedly demonstrated "high potential,"— the convergence of strong results and potential, to take on roles with increasing levels of strategic relevance. But what of the potential to succeed when managers are stretched into unfamiliar territory? It is easy to get it wrong in determining the degree of stretch. Just because a promising manager is currently doing a great job does not mean he or she will automatically perform as well in another role—and certainly not necessarily as a *leader*. The fallout from promoting someone wrongly at more senior levels can be disastrous, both for the individual and the company. The individual can become stressed and demotivated, underperform, and induce dissatisfaction in the people working for him or her. Then how to choose the right person for more senior positions? The state of being called "high potential" does not necessarily carry over from one situation to the next. Great performance is a state, the condition of enjoying a good match between a person's capabilities and the requirements of the job—and it lasts as long as that match stays in balance, with challenges that are neither too easy nor too hard. Deciphering the demands of senior management positions represents an important breakthrough in addressing these concerns.

In many organizations, outmoded assumptions continue to be made about what is required of effective executives. There remains a strong belief that within an organization's top tiers, most roles are similar in terms of the required skills and behaviors. Certainly specific roles require specialized knowledge: The CFO needs to understand corporate finances; the head of HR should be well versed in people policies and issues. But beyond such professional knowledge, many organizations assume the same general attributes apply to all senior leaders. Thus, it should be no problem to move a talented performer from one role to another. However, Hay Group research shows that beyond some clear role similarities, executive positions differ in many ways that, if not addressed, can derail even the best managers. The vast majority of today's executive roles tend to fall into one of three *types*, depending on their proximity to business outcomes and the degree to which people and resources are directly controlled (see Table 4-1). Organizations will need to continue to address the important competency distinctions among these roles—in particular, to ensure that by the time managers reach executive ranks they have developed competencies required for success in roles that vary from one's organizational upbringing.

Leadership Type	Operational Roles	Collaborative Roles	Advisory Roles
LEVELS OF WORK — Strategic — Global Enterprise Leadership	Top leaders of large, complex international organizations, typically publicly traded, high-profile conglomerates that span diverse technologies.	N/A	N/A
Enterprise Leadership	Leads all aspects of business to generate results. Typically the highest-level leadership role in a diverse enterprise with multiple business units, lines, and markets.	N/A	N/A
Strategy Formation	Focused on the achievement of bottom-line results where global or business-critical objectives must be achieved. Typically more complex general manager or sales roles.	Develops and delivers strategically important programs critical to the organization's mission through coordination and direction of diverse resources over whom direct control is not exercised.	Focuses on the alignment and integration of strategies for a function that is a critical driver of business success. Partners in determining business strategy and provides strategic advice that supports the achievement of critical business objectives.
Strategic Alignment	Focuses on the achievement of bottom-line results where product and market developments demand significant change to current business capabilities. Typically general manager or sales roles.	Defines and delivers specific and measurable long-term programs and results through a complex network of resources and partners over whom direct control is not exercised.	Focuses on the alignment and integration of policy in a strategically important and diverse area. Provides advice and guidance that support the achievement of major business objectives. Seen as thought leader internally.
Tactical — Strategic Implementation	Integrates and balances operational or sales resources to extend current business capabilities, ensuring that market demands are met in the short and medium term. Manages a large, complex operating unit to predetermined requirements.	Delivers specific, measurable results across a broad complex area through a network of diverse resources and partners over whom direct control is not exercised.	Focuses on the translation and application of policy in diverse although usually related areas.
Tactical Implementation	Manages defined resources to ensure achievement of clearly specified objectives such as volume, cost, quality, and service to meet schedule and customer requirements.	Delivers specific, measurable results in a discrete, defined area through a network of internal and external resources and partners over whom direct control is not exercised.	Focuses on the translation and application of policy in a specific functional area.

Table 4-1 Leadership Roles Matrix

Leadership Type	Operational Roles	Collaborative Roles	Advisory Roles
Strategic			
Global Enterprise Leadership	• Symbolic leadership • Externally focused • High level of social responsibility • Focused on building top team and organizational capability • Unique competencies related to values or strategy	N/A	N/A
Enterprise Leadership	If top CEO: • High level of teamwork • Wide range of sophisticated or unique competencies based on organization Otherwise: • Same as level below plus • High levels of integrity, coaching, and customer focus	N/A	N/A
Strategy Formation	• Competencies from level below plus • Strategic focus with broader, longer-term view • Higher levels of developing others • Sophisticated influence, strategies based on in-depth understanding of others and organization's politics	• Networks and builds relationships • Takes a strong leadership role • Greater level of organization commitment; models loyalty • Encourages development and provides feedback • Integrity	[Insufficient data due to small sample size for this role and level.]
Strategic Alignment	• Competencies from level below plus • Focuses on providing strong visionary leadership • Willing to apply rules flexibly	• Seeks information to support decisions, negotiate, and influence others • More likely to seek input of others • Integrity	• Broad and strategic business perspective (understanding the organization in the market) • Complex influence skills based on deep understanding of people, organization, and business • High integrity
Strategic Implementation	• Competencies of level below plus • Demands high performance form the team • More likely to act consistently with values and beliefs	• More initiative than preceding level • More likely than other collaborative managers to set challenging goals	• Continues to focus advice and service on the larger organization • Continues to model loyalty to the organization • Coaches and develops others • More likely to take a leadership role than at preceding level
Tactical Tactical Implementation	• Focuses on business results • Focuses on own team, coaching, supporting, gaining input • More likely to take on challenges than peers in other roles	• Demonstrates responsive rather than proactive initiative • Demonstrates pattern recognition more than insight	• Focuses on service to the larger organization • Models loyalty to the organization • Manages subordinates one-on-one rather than as a team • Accepts need for flexibility

LEVELS OF WORK

Table 4-2 Leadership competencies

- *Operational roles* are the more traditional management positions. Executives in these roles are directly accountable for results through the control of significant resources. At the lower levels, operational managers may oversee a department or team. Higher up, they may be in charge of a business unit—or an entire company. Operational leaders are intensely focused on results. They're always pushing, raising the bar, and taking risks. They know their organization, the market, the challenges, threats, and opportunities. And they shape that knowledge into a vision. They need high degrees of self-confidence and flexibility. As the SVP of a technology firm observed, "I want to be flexible, but I don't want to make compromises that will put the business at risk."

- *Advisory roles* provide advice and support in a specific area. These leaders seldom have direct accountability for results. Yet their intellectual challenges can be huge. At the tactical level, they interpret and implement policies and provide expert advice. At the strategic level, they're the thought leaders who shape policy. Advisory leaders tend to be behind-the-scenes operatives who, lacking control, must use influence and organizational knowledge to make things happen. Successful advisory leaders know how to maneuver through the organizational landscape. They are great with people and often highly conceptual, using knowledge and experience to create business solutions. The advisory leaders we studied also exhibited exceptionally high levels of integrity. They were not afraid to provide organizational conscience by standing firm or challenging others. As a senior HR executive noted: "I've reached the stage in my career where I have more confidence in doing what I feel is the right thing."

- *Collaborative roles* are hybrids of sorts that are emerging as a mainstay of today's flatter, matrix-structured organization. These leaders have significant accountability for results but little direct operational control. They work through others. In larger organizations, collaborative leaders often head up such areas as brand and product management, marketing, and supply chain management. These leaders draw on the competencies of their advisory and operational peers. With their accountability comes a focus on results. With their lack of control comes a need for influence and organizational understanding. Successful collaborative leaders are highly proactive, extremely flexible, and tenacious in seeking information. As an executive responsible for a major region of a global technology firm, noted: "It's tricky. I'm responsible for a billion in revenue and 110,000 people. But I have none of the levers to throw. Everybody who works for me has another boss. I don't control their pay or rating. Yet I'm accountable for the geography's performance."

Common Executive Pitfalls

There are a number of common pitfalls for executives operating at the upper organization levels. We include a number of frequently observed scenarios that can limit one's potential for career advancement:

Lack of job diversification can result in sidetracking. There are risks in being perceived as "the expert," especially at executive levels. Many low-level executives, often for reasons beyond their control, have too narrow a set of career experiences and therefore lack a full repertoire of professional capabilities that can open doors to top-level career options. As the funneling of senior leadership positions results in fewer and fewer job options, such leaders can be thrust into a functional sidetrack to the "main show"—because they are of less value in executive positions requiring broader enterprise accountability. What does the ideal career trajectory include? Setting aside specific job titles, senior executives should have experience working across all three role types, as detailed above. By the time individuals reach senior executive roles, they need to have demonstrated success driven by the strength of their conceptual or analytical ability—resulting from positions in which their skills have been honed in making coherent arguments, assertions, and strategies that others have latched onto because of their quality of thought. Advisory positions are typically ideal training grounds for such capability. At some point in their career paths, senior executives should have demonstrated success in managing and cooperating with people who do not have direct accountability to them. They should have had opportunities to have developed and demonstrated "referent power" (French and Ravens 1959); the power that comes from admiration and mutual respect and enhances the ability to work collaboratively in teams. Referent power also enables the successful delivery of results as a consequence of people *wanting* to work with the manager. Finally, senior leaders should have had opportunity to deliver a measurable, bottom-line result and to implement a strategy to the point of completion. Leaders who have only held line positions often fail to apply a keen intellect that differentiates strategy and vision. Those without experience in matrixed situations (leading without authority) will find it difficult to run without the ball and thereby enable the team to "score more points while on the field of play." At the top executive team levels, they must hand off, or simply fail to do the job effectively. Similarly, those leaders who have not delivered bottom-line results and successful operations should not expect to deliver sustainable results without some operational savvy. In this manner, the synthesis of these three modes of work make up the full complement of executive competencies that enable effectiveness at this level: delivering intellectually through the power of one's thought, effectively by demonstrating emotional intelligence required of interdependent relationships and by focusing on a bottom-line way of operating that drives results for stakeholders.

Otherwise worthy high potentials can be left to over-ripen in a particular function or job mode. As is frequently the case, it is too late to move leaders into a line (business delivery) position after they are CFO of a global division or head of corporate strategy. The line role for which they are capable is usually two levels below the level at which they are currently engaged. Because the line role carries more influence than it deserves, moving them to a line job at the same level can cause organizational disruption (due to overreaching one's experience and capability) and wreak havoc on the business. It also mismatches compensation; a person will not want to take the reduced role for reduced pay and yet it will be higher than other people delivering similar results. Line managers need to handle a matrix role before they develop an exaggerated sense of their own efficacy. Advisory/staff role job holders need to have an early line role to be able to grasp the full scope of delivery. The role of talent management is to not let people get to top of their functions without out-of-silo successes.

Sitting in the right pew, but in the wrong church. Every organization has its own culture, a set of shared assumptions that has been learned over time, is taught to new members, and is believed to be the correct way to perceive, think, and feel (Schein 1986). As is especially the case with external hires, they may have what it takes to succeed in top-level jobs from a professional standpoint but lack the appropriate sensitivity and flexibility to adapt to a new work setting because they were raised under a different set of shared assumptions. As a case in point, a Hay Group study (McClelland 1998) illustrates the power of cultural fit. Forty-nine percent of high-potential talent hired to a global fast-moving consumer goods company failed within two years of hire. The external hires did not lack industry experience, skill, or even a string of successes, but they failed to navigate the new organization's operating model successfully. A targeted competency-based assessment, including selection for idiosyncratic cultural competencies, reduced that failure rate to 6 percent within the same period of time.

The unique talent management benefits/deficits of smaller organizations. Smaller organizations typically lack the variety of roles that are formative in preparing for senior-level accountability—a potential downside for those executives in search of a job in a larger organizational setting. Yet if the top management team functions in a strategic decision-making (vs. information sharing) manner, these executives often have the opportunity for broad exposure to running the business that they might not otherwise receive—even in comparison to larger organizations. If the CEO maintains all the control, visioning, and strategizing, executives will suffer from lack of hands-on decision making, and other market-making opportunities. This kind of dependency makes it unlikely that an internal candidate will emerge. The CEO then must turn to more expensive outside candidates as an exit strategy. They will often have to turn to venture capital firms and untested outsiders to fund and manage continued operations and reap the rewards of their life's work.

The role for boards in ensuring that talent management for top positions is producing results. As the recent banking crisis indicated, it can be very difficult to find CEOs who will fit the time and circumstances. Many boards went begging for talent with little to show for it. As a consequence of this meager supply of top talent, boards are taking a more active role in ensuring the efficacy of talent management strategies. Boards can be on the lookout for the pitfall of endorsing the development of "generic" top leaders, at the expense of talent in alignment with the explicit needs of the business and organization. We have seen boards become mesmerized by high-potential leaders with whom they happen to be familiar, but who may lack the experiences necessary to succeed. Yet boards should be wary about promoting CEO candidates who have not had the benefit of endeavoring to create sustained revenue growth. Success in managing costs is only half the equation. Boards should meet a variety of senior executives as part of their interaction with management. They can be apprised of the results these executives have delivered to date, their various experiences, an assessment of their competence, and the likely roles they can be expected to fill. Having dinner or a chat with these potential successors is helpful but certainly not a substitute for due diligence.

Summary and Implications

There is little mystery about the competencies of relevance to future workforce needs. The real challenge rests in implementation of talent strategy that accounts for a wide range of business and organizational variables.

A summary of to-dos in ensuring that employees are developing the competencies they will need to have in place as they progress through their careers:

- Insist that strategy is decoded into specific implications for future roles and people.
- Insist that high-potential individuals show success at all three modes of leadership/jobs.
- Define the "future-focused" behaviors, assigned to particular roles, that will predict leadership success based on your strategy.
- Embed those behaviors in your performance and talent management activities.
- Ensure that HR creates robust platforms and that line managers execute and own them.
- Reclaim talent as a corporate asset—reject "tick the box" succession planning. There are tasks to learn and experience in each role, and incumbents need to have sufficient time to learn them and demonstrate results.
- Review talent objectively against current and future roles.

In this way organizations can avoid the pitfall of creating simplistic development initiatives that are unconnected to complex business needs at particular levels and for particular roles.

References

French, J. R. P., B. Raven. 1959. The bases of social power. In D. Cartwright (ed.) *Studies in social power*. Ann Arbor, MI: University of Michigan Press.

Hall, D. T. (1976). *Careers in organizations*. Glenview, IL: Scott, Foresman, p201.

Hall, D. T. (2002). *Careers in and out of organizations*. Thousand Oaks, CA: Sage Publications.

McClelland, D. C. (1998). Identifying competencies with behavioral-event interviews. *Psychological Science* 9(5):331—339.

Schein, E. H. What you need to know about organizational culture. *Training and Development Journal* 40(1):30–33.

Chapter 5

Designing a Performance Appraisal for Driving Organization Success

Dick Grote, President
Grote Consulting

"**W**HAT IS A PERFORMANCE APPRAISAL?" THROUGHOUT THIS CHAPTER, I WILL RELY ON an answer that, while universally accepted in most organizations, is rarely verbalized: "A performance appraisal is a formal record of a supervisor's opinion of the quality of an employee's performance." The operant word in this definition is *opinion*. In most organizations, every individual with supervisory responsibilities is asked on an annual basis to complete the company's performance appraisal form, assessing just how well a direct report did his or her assigned job.

The performance appraisal forms in some companies are complex and all-encompassing. Alcon Laboratories, the 15,000-employee company that specializes in eye-care pharmaceutical products, uses a 13-page performance appraisal form—unless you work in one of Alcon's matrix-type organizations, in which case the form is 19 pages. It is easy to imagine the howls of supervisory protest that would arise if a company created a new performance appraisal form that was even half that size. Interestingly, not only does Alcon have the longest performance appraisal form I have encountered, the company also achieves 100 percent uncomplaining compliance.

At the other extreme is Hunt Oil, a successful American petroleum company. Their form is the result of a 15-minute brainstorm between CEO Ray Hunt and his VP-HR. The appraisal form is a list of 13 open-ended questions that they want every supervisor to annually discuss with each direct report. The questions they came up with are straightforward: "What did you do in the last year that you're most proud of?" "Where do you see yourself in two or three years?" "What does the company need to do to help you be more successful?" Anyone could generate an equally useful set of questions that we would like our supervisors to discuss on a regular basis with each of their team members. That is the extent of Hunt Oil's performance appraisal system. There is no paperwork to be completed, save for the requirement that each supervisor write a memo to Hunt each year providing a brief assessment of each direct report's performance over the year and a statement either that he or she had conducted his or her conversations with each employee, or that he or she hadn't conducted all of them and why. Ray Hunt calls each of his managers who reported that he hadn't conducted all of his conversations. He asks them one question: "Why didn't you do what I asked you to do?" Like Alcon Laboratories, Hunt Oil has no problem achieving 100 percent compliance with its performance appraisal requirements.

The approaches to performance appraisal taken by Alcon Laboratories and Hunt Oil are very different. But they do have two things in common: Both have firm and dedicated top-management support and both meet the definition of a performance appraisal.

Behavior and Results

For the great majority of companies, the Alcon process would be excessively burdensome, while the Hunt Oil process would be too casual. But consider another commonality these two strikingly different appraisal systems possess: They both focus on behavior and results, the two components of human performance.

Human performance is a function of how well the individual contributes to the organization in two loosely correlated areas: achieving the results—the goals, objectives, key job responsibilities, and so on—that the company expects, and demonstrating the behaviors—the competencies, conduct, demeanor—that the organization requires of all its employees.

A summary of the elements of each component follows:

Element	Focus
Results	**WHAT** the individual achieved
	Actual job outputs
	Business results
	Measurable outcomes and accomplishments
	Objectives achieved
	Adherence to schedules / deadlines / budgets
	QQCT—Quality/Quantity/Cost/Timeliness

Element	Focus
Behaviors	**How** the individual performed
	Adherence to organizational values
	Competencies/Performance Factors
	Traits/Attributes/Characteristics/Proficiencies
	Personal style, manner, and approach
	Teamwork/team player
	KASH—Knowledge/Attitudes/Skills/Habits

Every effective performance appraisal system provides for the assessment of the individual's performance in each dimension.

The Behavioral Dimension

Currently, it is common for organizations to create a set of competencies that they expect all members of the organization to demonstrate. Frequently, these competencies are linked back to the organization's mission and vision and values, and displaying these behaviors, the thought goes, will make it more likely that the organization's values will be manifested in the way each team member does his or her job. The person may not accomplish much—that falls into the *Results* area—but by holding people accountable for demonstrating a set of important behaviors or competencies in their performance appraisal will help focus their attention on those behavioral components of the job that the company considers vital.

Competencies tend to be of two types. The first, usually called *core* or *cultural* or *organizational* competencies, are those that apply to every member of the organization. It matters not whether you're a senior vice president or a newly hired intern. Therefore, there cannot be too many core or organizational competencies, since there aren't all that many behaviors that apply equally well to every person in the organization. A few years ago I worked with Lucasfilm to help the company create a performance management system that would apply to all six of George Lucas's separate companies that he was bringing together when he created his new corporate headquarters. I worked with the CEO, key executives, and the presidents of Skywalker Sound, Industrial Light and Magic, and the other four operating companies to develop a set of core competencies that would apply to all of these formerly highly independent businesses. We settled on three: *Accountability*, *Achievement Orientation*, and *Teamwork*. No matter which of George Lucas's companies you work for, or what your job, you are expected to demonstrate those three competencies.

Three is probably the smallest number of core or cultural competencies a company would determine. The largest number in my experience resulted from my work with JCPenney when Allen Questrom, CEO at that time, was charged with engineering the turnaround of the then-teetering retail giant. Eleven competencies were listed on the company's performance appraisal form, and the turnaround (assisted by a great many other factors) was a remarkable success.

For most organizations, somewhere between three and seven organizational competencies is recommended. It is a small enough number for people to remember, and it can encompass a sufficiently important range of behaviors that will make a significant difference if displayed by everyone.

Job Family Competencies

Obviously there are many competencies that don't apply to everyone in the organization. Developing and retaining talent, for example, might be a vitally important competency for someone in a leadership position, but one that would be irrelevant for a pipefitter. Likewise, safety is a crucial competency for the pipefitter, but of limited relevance to someone in a systems analyst position.

Too many organizations make the mistake of trying to identify the vital competencies required for success in every job in the organization. Identifying competencies for every position is a huge undertaking, and the enormous administrative burden imposed by a project of this magnitude will never generate the corresponding payoff. It is easier, and more effective, to think not in terms of individual *jobs*, but instead of *job families*. While there may be hundreds of different job titles within a single organization, there are never more than half dozen or so job families. For example, the job families typically present in an organization are *Professional/Technical, Operations, Administrative, Sales*, and *Supervisory/Managerial*. Some organizations will have a large cadre of employees in the *Customer Service* job family. Hospitals frequently create a *Clinical* job family. Many organizations identify a separate set of job family competencies for those in *Executive* jobs.

While there may be hundreds of different jobs, there usually is a small number of job families, and organizations are better off determining the competencies that are critical to success in each job family than in trying to isolate the specific competencies required for every job.

Even jobs that on the surface seem entirely different (for example, financial analyst, petroleum engineer, training course developer, and research chemist) are all members of the *Professional/Technical* job family. Each one, with no overlap in their job responsibilities, is a college-educated, professionally trained, exempt individual contributor who may supervise at most an administrative assistant. The competencies—the behavioral factors that are prerequisites for success—that apply to every member of this cohort are remarkably similar. Among them might be *Adaptability/Flexibility, Conceptual Thinking, Decision Making, Initiative/Action Orientation*, and *Judgment and Problem Solving*. It is far easier to determine the competencies required by members of a job family (and allow individual managers of job incumbents in these positions to add or subtract or place particular emphasis on particular ones) than it is to do a factor analysis of the success components in each individual position.

Organizational competencies and job family competencies together make up the two components of the behavioral aspect of the job. The missing factor is the *Results* dimension.

Results

"So what have you done for me lately?" That, in its bluntest form, is the question we ask when we assess the *Results* dimension of job performance. And just as there were two different competencies that made up the behavioral aspect of human performance, there are likewise two key components that compose the *Results* area.

The first, *Key Job Responsibilities*, can be lifted verbatim from the individual's job description. This assumes that the individual has a well-written and accurate job description. Therefore, as part of effective performance management procedures, the manager needs, on about an annual basis, to work with each direct report to identify the key job responsibilities of the incumbent and the measures of success for performing each aspect of the job.

The easiest way is to identify key job responsibilities is to think in terms of the job's "big rocks." While all of us do dozens of tasks and duties and chores every day, we do all these activities in the service of accomplishing a small number of key job responsibilities or major job components—the "big rocks" of our jobs.

Big Rocks

"Big rocks" should be stated in the simplest verb/noun form, with no reference to quality of performance, or frequency, or measures of success. For a nurse, for example, the big rocks might include such items as: provide patient care; assess patients; educate patients and their families; coordinate services; ensure patient and physician satisfaction. These cover at least 90 percent of what a typical hospital nurse's job description might include. Notice four key characteristics of the items on the list, however: First, each big rock in the nurse's job is a simple and straightforward verb/noun statement of exactly what the key job responsibility is. There is no reference to how often it's done, or how important it is, or how success will be measured. Keeping it simple is a key determinant of success in designing a performance appraisal. Second, it is simply stated. Third, there's no overlap. Finally, there should be few big rocks. Although the nurse does many different things a day, they are all done to further the accomplishment of a small number of key job responsibilities. No job has more than a half dozen big rocks.

It is only when we identify the big rocks of a job in this simple way can we understand and assess how well the job is being performed. So the next step for each big rock is to develop a set of measures or examples of fully successful performance for each of the big rocks. For the nurse's big rock "Assess patients," the measures and examples of successful performance might include "assessment for signs and symptoms of abuse or neglect are performed and documented" and "reporting procedures are followed." Notice that many of the measures have no quantitative or countable elements.

Are These Valid Performance Measures?

The answer to whether these are valid performance measures is "absolutely." A common error is to fall victim to the *myth of quantifiability*, the bogus notion that in order for a measure to be objective, it must be amenable to quantitative, independently verifiable proof. Objectivity has nothing to do with quantifiability. It has to do with being fair and assessing what you have observed without bias interference. If our concern is with the quantity of work produced or cost or timeliness, there will be available, quantifiable measures. Instead of using quantitative measures, we instead use descriptive ones and describe through the use of examples just how well the job was done.

Projects and Goals

Few of us spend all of our time doing only what is spelled out in our job descriptions. We get tugged away by special projects and task forces that may be highly worthwhile tasks but that lie outside the boundaries set by a job description. A well-designed performance appraisal provides as much attention (and allows for as much credit) to our successes in goals and special projects as to the completion of our job description duties.

The Missing Piece

An effective performance appraisal form, one that communicates through the dimensions it assesses just what the organization considers to be important, concentrates on both the person's performance in the *behaviors* arena and the *results* domain. But there is still one piece missing: a focus on the person's specific accomplishments or achievements, regardless of the domain he or she falls into. Rarely does the appraisal form ask the supervisor to specifically identify the three, for example, most important contributions the person made over the course of the year.

Furthermore, virtually every organization has a mission statement or a statement of its vision and values. Everyone needs to be accountable for supporting the mission, vision, and values and for demonstrating them in their day-to-day job performance. Therefore, an optimum performance appraisal form, one that truly drives organizational success, has a final section that asks the question, "What did this individual do in the past 12 months that. . . ." And in that space appear the words of the mission or values statement. The form should allow appraisers to not only consider how a direct report met day-to-day operational and behavioral responsibilities but identify what he or she did that most helped the organization achieve its mission. The inclusion of that question will communicate to all that this company takes its mission and vision and values seriously. Figure 5-1 lists, items and components of an ideal performance appraisal form.

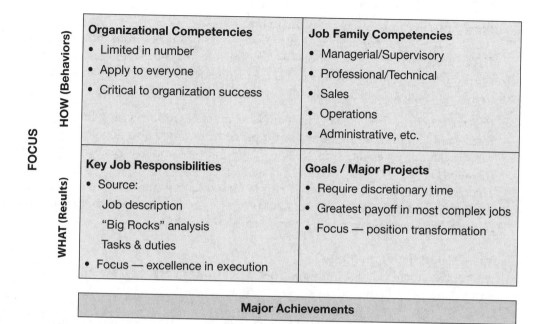

Figure 5-1 An Ideal Performance Appraisal Form

How to Create the Ideal Performance Management System

From my experience, I have developed ten tips that, if wisely applied, will result in the creation of a performance management system that accomplishes its goals:

One—Get Top Management Actively Involved

Without top management's commitment and visible support, no program can succeed. Top management must establish strategic plans, identify values and core competencies, appoint an appropriate Implementation Team, demonstrate the importance of performance management by being active participants in the process, and use appraisal results in management decisions.

Two—Establish the Criteria for an Ideal System

Consider the needs of the four stakeholder groups of any appraisal system: Appraisers who must evaluate performance; Appraisees whose performance is being assessed; Human Resources professionals who must administer the system; and the Senior Management group that must lead the organization into the future. Identifying their expectations at the start helps ensure their support once the system is designed. Ask each group: "What will it take for you to consider this system a smashing success?"

Three—Appoint an Implementation Team

This task force—a diagonal slice of appraisers and appraisees from different levels and functions in the organization—is responsible for (1) developing appraisal forms, policies, and procedures, and (2) ensuring successful deployment. Effective implementation teams usually divide themselves into two subgroups:

- *Policies, Practices, Procedures.* This team is responsible for designing the appraisal forms and recommending policies and procedures. They also develop measurement systems to ensure the system is operating properly once it has been installed.
- *Understanding, Support, Acceptance.* This team works as a mini advertising agency, arranging communication plans and programs to ensure understanding and support by everyone who will be affected by the system.

Four—Design the Form First

The appraisal form is a lightning rod that will attract everyone's attention. Design the form and get lots of feedback and revise accordingly.

Five—Build Your Mission, Vision, Values, and Core Competencies into the Form

The real objective of any performance management system is to ensure that the company's strategic plan and vision and values are communicated and achieved. Core competencies expected of all organization members should be included, described, and assessed. To avoid cynicism include your mission statement clearly and visibly in the performance appraisal system. Values become real only when people are held accountable for living up to them.

Six—Ensure Ongoing Communication

Circulate drafts and invite users to make recommendations. Keep the development process visible through surveys and requests for suggestions. Remember the cardinal principle—"People support what they help create."

Seven—Train All Appraisers

Performance appraisal requires a multitude of skills—behavioral observation and discrimination, goal setting, developing people, confronting unacceptable performance, persuading, problem solving, and planning. Make appraiser training universal and comprehensive. Performance appraisal requires supervisors to do something they've always been told not to do—be judgmental. Include the need for courage in the training.

Eight—Orient All Appraisees

The program's purposes and procedures must be explained enthusiastically in advance to all who will be affected by it. Specific training should be provided if the performance management procedure requires self-appraisal, multi-rater feedback, upward appraisal, or individual development planning.

Nine—Use the Results

If the results of the performance appraisal are not visibly used in making promotion, salary, development, transfer, training, and termination decisions, people will view it as merely an exercise.

Ten—Monitor and Revise the Program

Audit the quality of appraisals, the extent to which the system is being used, and the extent to which the original objectives have been met. Provide feedback to management, appraisers, and appraisees. Train new appraisers as they are appointed to supervisory positions. Actively seek and incorporate suggestions for improvement.

So Why Does Performance Appraisal Go Wrong?

Complaints about performance appraisals—for instance, bad forms, low-quality data, and inept discussions—is only a small part of a much larger problem. The problem is that everyone involved with the performance management process—executives, assessors, recipients, and human resource management professionals—don't understand some of the most fundamental concepts underlying performance management. Worse, they believe a set of myths that actually prevent their performance management procedures from operating successfully no matter how well the managers have been trained and the forms designed. Only when these myths are brought to light and eradicated can performance management systems deliver what they are capable of and give organizations what they desperately need: valid, workable information that yields good business decisions.

One of the most basic causes of performance appraisal failure is that so few people understand what a performance appraisal is. Stated again: *A performance appraisal is a formal record of a manager's opinion of the quality of an employee's work.* Performance appraisal requires a manager to render his or her *opinion* about how well an individual performed. It is not a document that can be empirically tested and proven. It is not the end product of a negotiation between the manager and the individual. It is a record of the manager's judgment about how well a direct report has done his or her job over the past year.

Another myth of performance management is that the objective of the performance appraisal discussion is to gain the employee's agreement. It's not. If the manager has applied tough-minded, demanding standards, it is unlikely that the individual will agree. The tougher the manager's standards, the less likely it is that agreement will occur. The objective of the performance appraisal discussion is to get the individual to understand the rating and not necessarily to gain agreement.

The Infinite Capacity for Self-Delusion

While the individual's personal insights into the quality of his performance may be a useful data point for the manager in creating the formal performance appraisal, another common myth holds that asking the employee to complete a self-assessment using the company's form, or including the perspectives of others gained through a

360-degree feedback system, is a good idea. It's not. Research consistently demonstrates that individuals are notoriously inaccurate in assessing their own performance, and the poorer the performer, the higher (and more inaccurate) the self-assessment. Research by Lominger, Inc. affirms "In our last round of studies, the overall correlation between self-ratings and performance was .00, with the boss being the most accurate rater by far in predicting long-term performance and promotion" (Lombardo and Eichinger 2003).

In July 2007, *BusinessWeek* surveyed 2,000 Americans in middle management positions and above, asking them "Are you one of the top 10 percent of performers in your company?" Eighty-four percent of all middle managers reported that they were in the top 10 percent of performers in their company. Executives provided a "Yes" response in 97 percent of those surveyed.

Finally—Why Bother?

Performance appraisals are usually associated with compensation. If we believe in pay-for-performance, then there must be some mechanism to evaluate that performance so that rewards can be fairly meted out. But if organizations see the primary function of a performance management system as serving as the handmaiden of the compensation system, then performance appraisal results will be skewed to serve the manager's desire to support his or her troops. Many organizations build disincentives to honest assessment directly into the system. For example, if the performance management system links the amount of the individual's salary increase with the rating on the performance appraisal form, managers will be tugged between honesty and generosity.

While the performance management system provides vital information for use in making compensation, promotion, development, and termination decisions, the ultimate reason for doing performance appraisals is that it is an ethical obligation of leadership. The fundamental reason for conducting performance appraisals is that we owe it to all employees to let them know what we expect and how they're doing. Since performance management is an ethical obligation of leadership, we have an obligation to get it right.

References

Lombardo, M., and R. Eichinger. 2003. *The leadership architect: Norms and validity report*. Minneapolis: Lominger.

Chapter 6

Performance Measurement for All Employees

Mark Graham Brown, President
Mark Graham Brown & Associates

THERE IS NO SURER WAY TO ALIENATE TALENTED EMPLOYEES THAN TO MICROMANAGE them and hold them accountable for ludicrous performance metrics. Organizations take great care in recruiting, screening, and hiring the brightest employees and then measure their performance once a year via some totally subjective performance appraisal system that requires a lot of time to administer and gives almost everyone the same ratings. Everybody needs feedback, and regular feedback does more to improve and maintain good performance than just about anything else an organization can do. However, most organizations do not develop good performance measures for their people.

One of the main reasons "balanced scorecards" do not lead to improvements in performance is that scorecards are focused on strategy and vision, and they are only for senior management. While it is true that senior managers are the people most responsible for executing the vision and delivering on the strategy, most work in an organization is done by the people below the management levels, and all levels of employees need scorecards. Scorecards for employees and for leaders should be a mix of strategic or vision-related metrics (20 percent to 30 percent) and metrics that link to the mission or overall responsibilities of the organization (70 percent to 80 percent). Sharing management scorecards with employees is not the answer either! Employees at all levels need their own scorecards that link to their individual job performance.

This chapter explores the five most common measurement mistakes I have observed and the five best practices for measuring employees at all levels from the CEO to individual contributors.

Common Measurement Mistake #1: Too Many Team Metrics

Teams are currently in vogue. Every project is assigned a team, and every initiative or problem is addressed by a team. Some companies even refer to their employees as team members. Measures of how a team performs are important and belong on the scorecards or dashboards (same thing, different analogy) of all employees working in teams. In sports, the main team measure is winning. However, business is inherently more complex. For example, a team may be responsible for managing a big account or for completing a big project. Team measures might include metrics like customer satisfaction, key dates/milestones met, or staying within budget. The team measures should drive balanced performance as opposed to a singular focus on one dimension. Even for a team of salespeople, landing a big sale or winning a big proposal would not be a good team measure by itself. You might also measure the desirability of the new account, its potential profitability, and other factors.

The problem with all team metrics is that often employees cannot see a link between their individual efforts and the team measures. A team member can exhibit outstanding performance, but because the project was late and over budget, the team measures show poor performance. This scenario can demotivate a team member. Or conversely, the team measures look great, but everyone on the team knows certain team members have not contributed to the successful outcome. An individual employee scorecard that includes only team metrics can inadvertently reward poor performance and punish good performance

A good general rule to follow when developing scorecards for team members is to have about 60 percent of the metrics based on individual performance and 40 percent on team performance. On any team there are players that contribute more than others, and that should be reflected in the scorecard. However, you don't want team members to be competitive with each other and you want to encourage them to help out teammates, when needed, so the 40 percent team measures need to be there as well. The individual and team metrics might be different measures or the same measures and 40 percent of an employee's evaluation is based on how the team performs and 60 percent on how the individual performs. For example, a call center has three metrics on the scorecards of all customer service representatives: customer satisfaction—50 percent; call efficiency (includes call time and hold time)—30 percent; courtesy—20 percent. The behaviors driven by this combination of metrics ensures that the customer problem is solved, the telephone conversation with the customer is effectively and quickly handled, and the customer is treated with respect.

A team of employees responsible for managing a major customer account is another example for multi-metrics. Team measures on all scorecards can include profitability of the account, customer satisfaction, sales/growth, and operational measures such as on-time delivery. Within the team, each person has different responsibilities and each has his or her unique performance measures and targets to supplement the team metrics. One person on the team is responsible for operations and is measured by a number of operational metrics that look at factors like inventory turns, stock-outs, errors in orders, and other similar metrics. Another individual is responsible for all contracts and billing on the account, so the metrics focus on rework needed on paperwork, cycle time for processing invoices and checks, and ensuring that company policies are followed. Each person on the account team has four to six individual metrics focused on his or her role, and each one has partial responsibility for the four team metrics that track sales, profits, customer satisfaction, and operational excellence.

> Look at employee scorecards and ensure that no more than half of the metrics are based on team performance. A good guideline is 60 percent metrics evaluate individual performance and 40 percent team performance.

Common Measurement Mistake #2: Superstitious Process or Behavior Measures

Scorecards for CEOs and senior leaders tend to include measures of outcomes such as growth, profits, stock price, company valuation, risk, and brand strength. As measures are cascaded down to lower-level employees, there tends to be fewer broad outcome metrics and more process or activity measures. Overall company profitability is an inappropriate gauge on a first-line supervisor's scorecard, because there may be hundreds or thousands of employees that contribute to or detract from the company's profitability. The problem with most behavior or process metrics is that they rarely can be linked to outcomes or even outputs. This is particularly true when the job task involves some creativity. Landing a 777 airplane requires that the pilot performs the same tasks in the same sequence almost every time, with adjustments made for factors such as weather. However, when a salesperson conducts a demo of new software for a potential customer, following the company script may jeopardize the sale. Yet following company directions is often the type of unproductive behavior that is measured. If the company had clear cause/effect data showing that the salespeople who followed the script when doing demos closed more deals than those who did not, it would be a good measure, but they probably do not. I worked with a software firm that had a salesperson who never followed a script when doing a demo. In fact, she did each demo differently, depending on the prospect's interests and type of organization. I have watched her do more than 20 demos over the last 10 years, and each one was different. Yet she closed most deals and was able to quickly build trust with prospective customers. However, her scorecard indicated that she did not do a good job on demos because she did not follow the company script.

The key to establishing valid process or behavior measures is to study your best performers and look for subtle differences in what they do compared to their more average performing peers. These differences are often so slight that they are difficult to detect, and interviewing these high performers is rarely revealing because they are innately competent and often cannot explain their superior abilities.

Creating a culture of high performers means taking great care in measuring activities or processes that are predictors of good performance. Most process or behavior measures on employee scorecards are based on logic or opinions of managers who may have done the job at one time and have theories or opinions about how to be successful. They are usually wrong. I recall working with a company that designs and manufactures fabrics. They had a team of five designers whose job was to conceive new fabrics every year. Andrea, one of the designers, created top-selling fabrics consistently. The other four designers had about a 40 percent success rate compared to Andrea's 85 percent success rate. The company management insisted on measuring and managing the designers' behaviors so that they could perform better. Some of the metrics suggested by management were as follows: hours spent per week with customers, training attended, trade shows attended, number of rough designs submitted, thoroughness of manufacturability and profitability analyses done, and hours per week spent interacting with other designers.

None of the above measures led to more successful fabric designs. In fact, Andrea had the lowest score on these activity measures and still had the most successful designs. After much study, it was concluded that Andrea was more talented than the other designers. The company should have been focused on the selection process for designers rather than on micromanaging behaviors after hiring. Measuring and managing the activities of creative people is a guaranteed way to reduce their outputs or cause them to leave.

> Process or activity measures are important. However, before you start tracking them and holding people accountable for them, ensure that you can validate the link between the behavior or process and the outputs or outcomes.

Common Measurement Mistake #3: Infrequent Measurement

The most common way for most employees to get feedback on their job performance is the dreaded annual performance evaluation. Once a year the employee sits down with his or her boss and reviews a form he or she filled out on strengths, weaknesses, and overall job performance. These sessions are dreaded by both parties involved, and usually both employee and supervisor leave the meeting feeling depressed and unmotivated. Most companies have a 1 to 5 assessment scale, but few employees receive 1, 2, or 5. Even the worst slackers do not typically get a 1 or 2 rating because that requires the manager to document the low assessment and provide a corrective action plan. A low rating might also lead to a grievance or lawsuit and is typically perceived by the supervisor as "not worth the trouble." Ratings of 5 are rare as well, due to supervisors fearing being perceived by HR and managers as lenient assessors.

Annual metrics are not limited to performance appraisal. Many scorecards for everyone from the CEO down to the lowest level of employee have annual metrics. *Annual metrics have no place on anyone's scorecard.* Many organizations measure variables like customer satisfaction and employee satisfaction once a year. By the time you wait 12 months for another data point, your company can be in big trouble. Some performance dimensions like market share or your brand image may take a long time to move, and infrequent measurement could be sufficient. However, most other dimensions move and change on a daily basis. Even image can go from green to red in a single day after a bad news story or significant drop in share price. The most useful performance measures are those that change on a daily basis. By tracking performance daily, performance can be adjusted to keep all the measures in the green zone. For example, a medical devices client has a 15-minute meeting every morning at 8:00 where they review yesterday's performance on about 15 key metrics. When an individual metric appears yellow or red, analysis is done and an action plan is put into place immediately to correct the poor performance. This is a much better process than the typical quarterly management review meeting with 150 PowerPoint charts and spreadsheets, and a lot of time spent questioning the data and the targets that were set.

> Metrics for all levels of employees should be tracked at least quarterly (monthly, weekly, or daily is better) or they do not go on the scorecard. Save the annual metrics for the annual performance review.

Common Measurement Mistake #4: Metrics That Cannot Be Influenced or Controlled

Another common mistake on employee scorecards is metrics that the employee cannot influence. For example, an employee is one of over 40 people working on a project. The employee completes her tasks on the project done on time and under budget but still not be rated highly because the overall project metric shows red. Another common mistake is to put overall company metrics like profit, sales, or even overall employee satisfaction on employee scorecards. This was one of many mistakes Sears made in developing its scorecards. Sears was one of the pioneers in adopting a balanced scorecard approach to performance measurement. They put overall employee satisfaction on all employee scorecards and even linked part of employees' bonuses to this metric. Employees united and decided they could get a bigger bonus if they all said they loved their jobs at Sears. Sears' balanced scorecard was leading it to near business failure before the company was purchased by Kmart. The test of whether or not a metric should go on an employee's scorecard is the employee should be able to individually influence performance on the metric. This does not mean control. A CEO cannot control stock price or profitability, but can certainly exert a strong influence over it.

> Scorecard metrics should focus on important outputs and outcomes, but only those outputs and outcomes of individual employees' job, not the organization's outputs/outcomes. The less influence an employee has on a performance metric, the less feedback on this measure will drive behavior.

Common Measurement Mistake #5: Failing to Weigh the Importance of Metrics

The logic of the balanced scorecard is that it is important for organizations to focus on balancing performance on a number of metrics versus a single one like profits. Banks and insurance companies in 2008 and 2009 focused on profits and growth and failed to pay attention to risk. Retailers are measured on sales versus the previous year, so they heavily discount merchandise to hit sales targets and consequently fail to meet profit goals. Focusing on improvements in one area or single metric usually leads to problems in other areas. To prevent this, many organizations create a balanced suite of metrics to better drive good performance in all areas. While this is great in theory, and leads to what appears to be balanced scorecards, what usually happens is that employees view one performance metric as significantly more important than any of the others. A multilateral bank focuses on getting loans approved, a warehouse focuses on turning the inventory, a hospital focuses on getting patients discharged, and a Navy shipyard focuses on getting repair work done on time. All of these organizations have balanced sets of metrics, but the rewards and focus are all on a single metric which drives the wrong performance.

A better approach to drive balanced performance is to assign weights to each metric depending on its importance. For example, some of the outcome measures like loyal customers, profits, or engaged employees might be weighted as 20 percent each, and leading metrics might be weighted the remaining 40 percent. Assigning weights should be done based on importance and data integrity. As a general rule, each section of the scorecard should be weighted approximately equal so as to drive balance. That is, don't assign an 80 percent weight to the financial metrics and 20 percent to the remaining 12 measures. Scorecards for FedEx employees include three types of measures relating to people (employees), service (customers), and profits (financial). Each is given an equal weight. Individual metrics within each of the categories are then weighted differently, depending on its importance. An aircraft repair company has a project management metric that includes three sub-metrics: budget/cost, schedule, and quality. The customer is asked to assign a weight to the importance of each of these three factors at the start of every repair project. Some customers want the job done quickly, putting a heavy weight on schedule and a lower weight on cost. Another customer may have a limited budget and puts a heavy weight on cost. What this weighting accomplishes is informing the repair teams the priorities for each project. This enables them to make appropriate decisions if only two of the three metrics can be done to perfection.

> When an importance weight is assigned to each metric on a scorecard, employees don't have to guess about what is most important. Priorities and tradeoffs are specified on the scorecard so that the employee can assess how best to do his or her job.

Best Practice #1: Select a Reasonable Number of Metrics

No one can manage more than 15–20 performance metrics well. Research on scorecard best practices conducted by the American Productivity and Quality Center suggest that 12 to 15 metrics are ideal for a scorecard, and below the management level even fewer are recommended. This is a reasonable number of metrics to track, and the three gauges provide feedback on how well the employees are helping the company make a profit (billable hours), creating customer satisfaction (project management index), and improving internal efficiency and productivity (cycle time).

Numerous metrics on a scorecard forces employees to prioritize them and only concentrate on a few. This has the same effect as having fewer metrics. Save the time and money of tracking and reporting many useless measures, and concentrate on identifying the vital few.

> Limit the number of metrics to no more than 20 for any level of employee. Lower-level employee or supervisor scorecards typically have fewer than 12 metrics. Pay attention to balancing the number of metrics that address your major outcomes and customers/stakeholders.

Best Practice #2: Develop Meaningful Process Metrics by Studying Master Performers

The difference between mediocre and exceptional performance is often not a result of merely talent. In fact, some suggest that talent is overrated, and that practice is more closely linked with success than raw talent. We all know some highly intelligent and talented individuals for whom success is elusive. Yet others with average talents are very successful. Ongoing practice produces lessons that successful individuals internalize. The key to good scorecard process metrics is to find the subtle activities successful people are doing that make their performance so good and to teach these "tricks" to others and measure their compliance with these process steps. For example, successful men's suit salespeople always slip the most expensive jacket on customers to determine their size. Once customers see how good they look in the top designer jacket, they will unlikely be satisfied with a less expensive line. Finding these meaningful process measures does not come from interviewing the master performers. Most high performers are innately competent. These process performance metrics can only be determined by careful observations and comparisons to other more typical performers.

> Identify meaningful process metrics to put on employee scorecards by studying how master performers do their jobs and compare their approach/behavior with the process of more typical performers.

Best Practice #3: Use Technology to Provide Frequent Feedback

Do not wait for a monthly or quarterly report or meeting to give performance input. Leading companies use scorecard software to provide employees with real-time performance information. Most make use of desktops or laptops to display performance data on employee scorecards, but some use mobile devices like BlackBerrys or iPhones to provide employees with updates. Scorecard software is available at all price ranges. The ideal performance measurement system would feature daily feedback provided to employees via their computers or smart phones. One client installed 42-inch flat-screen televisions around the plant to display the previous day's performance on eight to ten key metrics. Employees can use the monitor and keyboard to drill down to their individual performance. Most employees review their performance every day, and report liking the daily feedback that the system provides.

> Use scorecard software and PCs or smart phones to communicate performance data to employees on an ongoing basis.

Best Practice #4: Set Targets Realistically and Use Comparative Data

The process of establishing targets or objectives for each of the metrics on a scorecard is rarely scientific or well thought out. The most typical approach is to review last year's performance and make next year's target slightly higher. There are several problems with this approach. First of all, last year may have not been a typical year. Many businesses experienced a downturn in 2009, while the same business had a profitable 2008.

If 2010 targets were based on 2009 or 2008 alone, they would probably be quite unrealistic. Targets should be based on requirements passed down from higher levels. Most big companies and government organizations develop broad objectives or targets as part of the strategic planning process. These need to be considered when setting lower-level targets. Industry and economic conditions also need to be considered. Finally, consider links between the metrics when setting targets. Achieving an aggressive cost-cutting target may result in lower employee satisfaction and lower levels of quality and customer satisfaction.

> Low, median, and high targets should be established for all scorecard metrics based on higher level targets, comparative data, and links to other metrics on the scorecard.

Best Practice #5: Link Metrics at All Levels

In the minority of organizations I work with that have scorecards for all employee levels, I find that the employee metrics are rarely connected to higher-level metrics. Often these metrics are developed by the employees themselves, without consideration of the company goals/strategy, or even the metrics on their direct boss's scorecard. Ideally, scorecards should be developed in a top-down fashion, starting with the CEO or the highest executive officer and cascading down in layers to the individual employee level. At the senior management level, most metrics focus on outputs and outcomes, and many tend to be indices or analytics that are composed of lower-level sub-gauges. Cascading to the employee level, some of the metrics might be the same as on the CEO scorecard, but the data shows individual employee performance compared to all employees' performance for the CEO. For example, both the CEO and hourly employees in an aircraft repair company track billable hours. The CEO tracks billable hours for all direct labor employees. Workers track only their own billable hours, and supervisors track billable hours for their entire team.

In other cases, the metrics for employees are connected to the senior management metrics but are different metrics. For example, a metric for salespeople might be leads generated. The sales manager might track leads as well. However, the sales vice president might not have leads as a metric and focuses only on bids or proposals submitted and win/loss ratio.

When evaluating organizational scorecards, assessing alignment among metrics across the different levels in the organization is necessary. Ideally, if all individual contributor employees achieve targets on their scorecard metrics, this should lead their supervisors to have positive results on their scorecards, and so forth.

> Scorecards should be developed in a top-down fashion, ensuring linkage of metrics at all levels.

Summary and Conclusions

Regular feedback is a key ingredient in a performance management system. Hiring smart and talented people and leaving them alone will not allow an organization to achieve lofty performance goals. Providing employees with annual feedback via a subjective performance appraisal system is a poor way of generating good performance and is probably worse than not giving feedback at all. Employees at all levels need scorecards that relate on a regular basis how well they are performing their job. Scorecards should have a reasonable number of metrics (12 to 20) and be a mix of input, process, output, and outcome metrics. Assigning importance weights to each of the metrics takes the guesswork out of establishing priorities and helps employees focus their behaviors on achieving the organization's goals.

Chapter 7

Conducting Performance Reviews That Improve the Quality of Your Talent Base

David Insler, Senior Vice President
Angelita Becom, Senior Consultant
Sibson Consulting

HIGH-PERFORMING ORGANIZATIONS KNOW THAT EFFECTIVE PERFORMANCE MANAGEMENT plays a critical role in the successful development of talent. The problem is that while performance management processes are critical to talent development, conducting a fundamental performance review is probably one of the most dreaded management tasks. In many organizations, the following comments are all too common:

- "Our performance review process does not work. It takes too long and I get very little value from it."
- "What is the point of our performance review process? It's just a check-the-box activity."
- "Why should we do performance reviews anyway? They're not linked to any decisions related to my pay or career advancement."

Several recent articles in the HR press have suggested that performance reviews are "dead" and should be eliminated, yet once readers get past the catchy headlines, two things emerge. First, criticism is aimed at bad processes and the lack of integration with other talent management activities. Second is the need for employees, particularly high performers, to receive objective feedback, understand the organization's career paths, and have a sense that the established performance management process or program truly differentiates the high performers from average to low performers and that the performance management process aims to improve talent at both the individual and the organizational level.

There are ways to improve and enhance performance management so that it not only improves the quality of the organization's talent base but also helps it achieve business success. This chapter is designed to provide direction and offer several key lessons:

- How to improve the execution of performance reviews through better conversations and calibration.
- The effective performance management framework and why performance management is a critical business process that leads to talent improvement.
- What leadership must do to promote a high-performance and a talent-development culture.
- What makes the performance management process work.

Improving Performance Reviews through Better Conversations

Conducting effective performance conversations is where the rubber meets the road. These conversations give employees the opportunity to learn about their development strengths, opportunities for improvement, and how their role links and aligns to the organization's goals. Without successful performance conversations, performance differentiation is not likely to occur, nor will development become a strong cultural characteristic. The organization's leaders and high performers will be left wondering what, if any, value performance management brings to the organization.

Sibson Consulting has developed the "Five Conversations" framework as content for basic management training. They provide a set of guidelines and a structure that managers and employees can use to

- Think about how to develop effective relationships.
- Promote meaningful dialogue and minimize ineffective one-way communication.

This framework will make it easier for managers to deliver performance messages, the most critical aspect of performance management.

The five conversations are as follows:

1. *Establishing the relationship.* The goal is to institute and reinforce the coaching and development relationship. Following are key steps:
   - Establish role accountabilities. Who is responsible for what in the relationship? How can each party show this commitment?
   - Discuss goals for the relationship. What are the goals and how can they be attained?
   - Agree on frequency of check-ins. How often will the manager and the employee meet or at least talk with each other? In what setting will that take place (e.g., scheduled monthly meetings, ad hoc, or on an as-needed basis)?
   - Identify potential challenges in the relationship and ways to overcome them.

2. *Setting expectations.* The goal is to clarify and develop a mutual understanding of performance expectations based on requirements of the role, development, and business needs. Key steps are as follows:
   - Clarify departmental and organization objectives. How can individual goals and accountabilities link to these objectives?
   - Review current job accountabilities. Do they support expectations? How do they align to expectations?
   - Discuss desired results for the year. How will they link to goals and expectations?
   - Discuss resources and evidence of expectation fulfillment. What resources may be required to meet goals and expectations? How will the manager and employee know that expectations have been met?
3. *Coaching for improved performance and career development.* The goal is to exchange performance and development information more effectively and define shared actions that enable the employee, with the supervisor's support, to improve performance in his or her current role and plan for desired and appropriate career progression. Key steps are as follows:
   - Use the Feedback Framework (see Figure 7-1 below) to work through an effective coaching conversation.
   - Restate expectations (as discussed in Conversation 2).
   - Describe observations, the facts of what actually occurred.
   - Provide assessments, the interpretations or evaluations of the stated observations. It is important to remember that most people develop from strengths and that performance improvement can focus on areas of deficiency and missed expectations.
   - Discuss consequences (positive and negative) and the results of continued performance without improvement. Ultimate consequences should be linked to processes beyond just performance management.

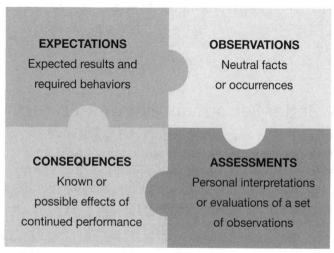

Figure 7-1 Feedback Framework
Source: Sibson Consulting

4. *Intervening during a crisis.* The goal is for the manager to become involved proactively in situations where the employee may not demonstrate the expected performance expectations. Key steps are as follows:
   - Gain an understanding of the situation from the perspective of the employee and other parties involved.
   - Discuss the risks to quality, performance, customer and colleague relationships, team effectiveness, and individual well-being.
   - Develop a plan for action including what will occur, with what support, from whom, by whom, and by when.
5. *Realizing potential.* The goal is to plan for more effective career development that balances an employee's career aspirations with business needs and requirements. Key steps are as follows:
   - Gain an understanding of the employee's interests and goals.
   - Discuss the business trends or marketplace events that may impact career decisions.
   - Determine professional development and support available for use by the employee.

By following these key points, managers and employees will ensure that each conversation focuses on development and guidance. Although the primary direction of the conversation is from the manager to the employee, employees should be prepared to actively participate.

Making the conversations about expectations and exchange will help establish "what's in it for me" for the employees. While the managers will know and communicate business needs and the organization's performance criteria, the employees will know and should be encouraged to communicate what commitment they will make, what they need to accomplish results, and where they may need development. Experience and research show that when the performance criteria includes career development plans, employees show more interest in the feedback and accept more guidance from their manager.

The five conversations will establish a framework to help managers and employees create trusting relationships. The stronger the trust, the easier it is to communicate effectively.

Executing a Better Performance Review Process

Another important factor in executing better performance reviews is an organization's ability to calibrate performance messages and ratings across its various functional groups, departments, or employee types. Calibration of performance management works to make the process visible throughout the organization. By making the proposed ratings, messages, and actions visible among peer managers, calibration helps ensure that standards, actions, and message delivery are handled with consistency.

Figure 7-2 demonstrates how calibration can work. It moves an organization from the old assumption that the subject of performance management and pay is between a manager and an employee to a new and enhanced assumption that these decisions are too important to be made individually and without visibility. It opens the curtain and forces an organization's leaders to support decisions around pay and any other processes tied to performance management.

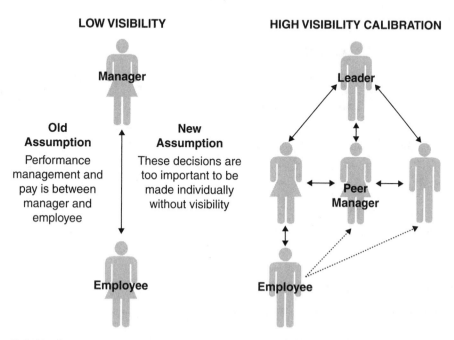

Figure 7-2 Performance Management Calibration

Source: Sibson Consulting

Integrating calibration into an organization's current performance review process can pose challenges, but there are ways to address them. Calibration can be done at various levels within an organization, from a specific department or function to across the entire organization. The calibration process can start with a small department and work its way up the organization by rolling up to the next level each time the process is used.

How a calibration session is conducted is also important. The goal is to make the process and information visible at appropriate levels to facilitate open and honest evaluation and developmental planning. Doing something as simple as projecting group or department ratings onto a screen can help lift the curtain on areas where ratings are applied more evenly and those where they are skewed in one direction or another. The example shown in Figure 7-3 would make these two departments visible to each other and force peer managers to discuss performance standards and messaging. The idea is to understand the standards used by managers to rate performance and to create norms around what is expected within an organization.

As an organization adopts calibration sessions, it may take a while for managers and leaders to become comfortable with the openness, but they will quickly begin to

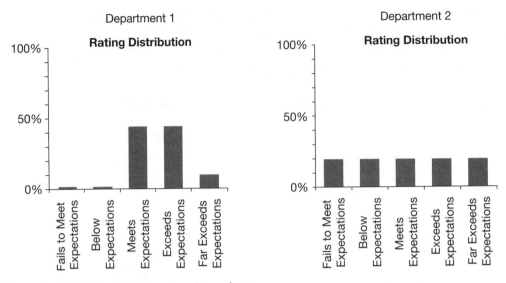

Figure 7-3 A Calibration Session Snapshot

Source: Sibson Consulting

appreciate the outcomes. By the second or third time, the process should become ingrained as a critical part of making performance management work.

Effective Performance Management

So far, this chapter has discussed ways to improve performance reviews to focus on talent development through better individual conversations and organization calibration. As an integrated business process, conducting performance reviews should be part of an overall effective performance management (EPM) model that encompasses leadership, program design and program execution. (See Figure 7-4.) Each element

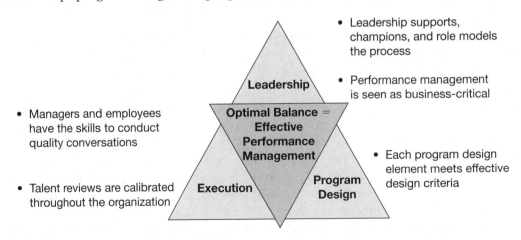

Figure 7-4 The EPM Model

Source: Sibson Consulting

plays a critical role in making performance reviews and performance management an effective business process for improving an organization's talent base. All three need to be in balance to create EPM.

The "Five Conversations" coaching model, described previously, enables managers to address the critical process steps. EPM design should include these objectives:

1. Aligning goals between and among organizations and individuals
2. Setting individual performance expectations so job requirements, goals and objectives, performance improvement, and career development plans can be met to increase individual and organizational capability
3. Providing feedback through ongoing coaching opportunities to continually improve and develop employees; setting a schedule to summarize the performance evaluation, document conclusions, and establish plans for the next period
4. Planning a career path with employees to further support their goals, improvement, and development
5. Defining how pay and other reward opportunities, such as position and promotional opportunities, will align with and reinforce performance

EPM is a critical business process that aligns expectations between organizations and individuals, ensures there are regular discussions to guide behavior and performance, and identifies changes in performance or expectations based on results and changes in business conditions. EPM includes both formal and informal performance reviews. The periodic formal reviews, which include evaluation and feedback that drives talent development, must be supported and reinforced with informal reviews for ongoing coaching and career planning.

If the objectives described above are addressed, an EPM process will achieve the following:

For the business:

- Align strategic, operational, and individual priorities and goals.
- Identify opportunities for improving business unit, group, and individual performance.
- Develop organizational capability and the talent of employees.
- Allow for determining future talent needs.
- Establish performance results as the basis for pay and rewards.
- Use performance to determine other critical talent management and development aspects such as promotions and advancements.

For the individual:

- Ensure efforts and capabilities are focused on business needs.
- Allow career interests and developmental needs to be considered in meeting future talent requirements.
- Define where resources and support are needed to improve results.
- Increase career and job satisfaction.

• Demonstrate commitment from an organization to individuals, particularly high performers and critical talent.

Further evidence that EPM is a critical business process can be seen in Figure 7-5, which compares the results of a poorly executed performance management program with those of an EPM.

A poorly executed performance management program results in:	EPM results in:
• Lack of direction and weak mobilization of resources	• Clear direction and strong, agile mobilization capability
• Lack of integration and alignment across the company	• Full integration and support by management
• Reduced motivation and retention	• Motivated employees who thrive in a culture of excellence
• Disincentives for teamwork or collaboration	• Rewards that recognize and encourage desired behaviors
• Perceived/actual inconsistent and unfair treatment of employees	• Consistent and fair treatment of employees relative to their role
• Political vs. fact based decisions regarding individuals	• A clear understanding of and connection to the strategic, long-term vision of the organization
• A dissatisfied and untrusting workforce	• Open and honest multi-way communication
Sub-optimized organizational results and talent	**Improved productivity, talent development, and organizational success**

Figure 7-5 Comparison of a Poorly Executed Performance Management Program with EPM

Source: Sibson Consulting

Leadership Support

An organization's leadership and its support of performance management and performance reviews are critical to the success of an EPM program. The role of leadership is to set and constantly reinforce the desired performance culture. CEOs and other executives are under great pressure to perform, and boards of directors are being strongly encouraged to manage, evaluate, and reward executives accordingly. This reinforces executives' desire for strong performance management and reviews throughout the organization. Research has shown that communicating expectations, providing regular and constructive feedback, and coaching employees toward their career aspirations will increase the level of engagement within the organization. This, in turn, improves performance and develops talent. For example, Sibson Consulting's *Rewards of Work Study* shows that employees who have a favorable view of their employer's performance management program are more engaged and satisfied with their work.

One example of a high-performing organization with a performance culture that is embraced by leadership is one of the most successful, multi-facility, casual-dining companies in the United States. The CEO and founder has inscribed a simple message that appears on the start-up screens of all employees' computers: "Do something today that adds value to our company." Periodic training programs emphasize the importance of questioning activities that do not add value. While this may not be part of the performance management process, this simple message instills a fundamental performance expectation.

Another successful tactic is to make "high performance" an operating principle, embedded in every aspect of the company's management and business process. The experience of successful companies (those with higher-than-average financial results over a specific time period) supports the idea that employees at most levels respond better to leadership than to management. Leaders who provide clear vision, values, and business objectives are far more likely to have highly engaged employees than are those who direct activities in a prescriptive manner.

In setting these operating principles, leadership must define the purpose and objectives that underlie the performance process. They must then align performance and business processes. Although this may sound simple, leaders should ask themselves whether business planning (creating annual revenue and budget plans) at their organization is a collaborative effort or a negotiation between top-down and bottom-up management styles. Building a trusting relationship is critical to setting realizable expectations.

Too many organizations align performance planning and evaluation around pay cycles rather than the business cycle. While this may be acceptable at the nonexempt level, it is not effective for establishing a high-performance culture among professionals and management.

Answering these questions within the organization will clarify and align processes:

- How do leaders model and support performance management and reviews?
- What tools and resources could they use to better espouse EPM principles?
- Is the performance review cycle linked to the business planning cycle?

Sometimes a fix as simple as changing the start date of the performance-management cycle can have a significant effect in making the process business-critical and help it lead talent management and development.

Making the EPM Process Work

This chapter has provided critical steps and program design objectives to improve performance reviews and talent development. Following these seven criteria can help make changes and process redesign work:

- *Criteria 1.* Process is clear and responsibility is understood by leaders, managers, and employees.
- *Criteria 2.* Goal alignment is clear and links the company, the organization, and the individual.
- *Criteria 3.* Performance management consequences help differentiate compensation actions; pay and performance are linked.
- *Criteria 4.* Performance management is linked to other HR and talent management processes, such as organization talent assessment and succession, and not just compensation.
- *Criteria 5.* Performance management and other business-critical process calendars are aligned.
- *Criteria 6.* The performance management system is user-friendly and technology-enabled with intuitive forms that are easy to use.
- *Criteria 7.* Rating scale is clear and applied appropriately by managers with calibration across appropriate organizations.

Testing for these criteria will allow an organization to determine whether its performance management program is working appropriately and set priorities for design improvements that will yield measurable results.

When considering the design of an organization's performance management program, remember that different roles and job levels have different performance expectations that require different performance management processes. These processes may also vary by type of industry. A basic model depicts the organization as a set of concentric circles, with performance expectations increasing in complexity, breadth, and depth the closer they are to the center (see Figure 7-6).

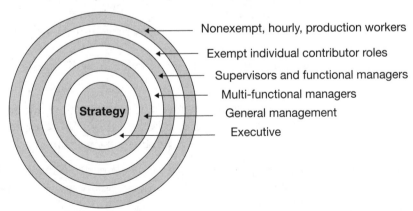

Figure 7-6 Performance Expectations Increase as They Near the Center of the Circle

Source: Sibson Consulting

To be most effective and ensure the organization is developing its talent correctly, differences in performance criteria, methods for measurement, frequency of direct feedback, and emphasis on direct communication should be tailored to each level during program design.

Using Performance Reviews and EPM Effectively

EPM and its imbedded performance review process should be the cornerstone of an overall effort to improve and engage an organization's talent base. EPM must not stand alone as a separate HR process but must be integrated into how the organization makes all talent and performance decisions.

It is important that EPM is linked to other key processes—including compensation differentiation, promotions and advancements, transfers, succession planning, and organizational goal setting—providing the input organizational and HR leaders need to make decisions. Without this linkage, EPM will become just another "check-the-box" activity without the weight of real decisions and results.

Chapter 8

Appraising Executive Talent

James F. Reda, Founder and Managing Director
James F. Reda & Associates, LLC

THE PERFORMANCE APPRAISAL PROCESS PROVIDES AN OPPORTUNITY TO CAPTURE THE attention of every individual in a company and point each individual toward the goals set for the organization. Every performance appraisal should foster an open, honest dialogue between employee and manager. Since executives are the most expensive resource in an organization, this resource needs to be protected through regularly scheduled appraisals to provide feedback and encourage improvement.

Performance appraisals of executives are not a ubiquitous process, and even when performed, often there is not a solid system in place to evaluate and encourage improvement. Considering that the potential gains from a performance appraisal process are greatest for high-level executives, it is surprising that appraisals become less structured and regulated as one moves up in the organization.

A number of factors can inhibit the effectiveness of an appraisal. Common inhibitors to a solid executive performance appraisal process include the following:

Discomfort. Some executives performing the evaluations find the process neither enjoyable nor comfortable. The majority of executives being appraised feel the same way.

Misunderstood purpose. Some executives misuse the evaluation to find fault rather than provide feedback for constructive purposes.

Ambiguity. This is a major impetus to implementing an effective executive evaluation process. Ambiguity can come from a "squishy" statement of the organization's strategic goals, the executive's job description and goals, process design, or the way that evaluation results are shared with the executive.

Low priority. Some managers have the impression that there will be a lack of time and energy to allow for an effective evaluation process.

Difficulty in rating the executive on qualitative factors. Factors such as the executive's ability to develop the leadership pipeline should not be included because sometimes the board does not directly observe these activities, and they can be difficult to objectively measure.

New source of criticism for the executive. Some companies fear the loss of an apparently good executive by the possibility that the executive may feel overly criticized

Despite this long list of inhibitors, when done properly, CEO and executive officer evaluations can create a sense of teamwork, mutual respect, and direct, clear lines of communication that are needed when moving forward with corporate and business goals (Reda et al. 2005).

The information presented in this chapter will assist in designing, implementing, and refining an executive performance appraisal process that will motivate leadership to optimize the organization's competitive advantages, manage talent, and improve economic performance.

Executive Categories

When discussing executive performance evaluations, we must make a distinction between the CEO, executive officers (those executives with broad policy making authority that typically make up the executives listed as the top 5 named executive officers, or NEOs, in the company's proxy statement) and all other executives (collectively referred to as the "executives"). As discussed later in this chapter, the process and oversight of each group of executives are different.

The Official Word on Executive Performance Appraisal Guidelines

The New York Stock Exchange (NYSE) requires that a CEO performance evaluation be created and that a system be in place for it. Boards are not required to disclose the results of the evaluation, nor does the evaluation have to be administered in written form. Since CEO performance evaluations are required as part of the listing requirements of the NYSE, more and more companies are evaluating the performance of executives; however, the details of how the appraisal system is designed and implemented are left unregulated.

On the other hand, NASDAQ listing requirements remain silent about CEO evaluation. Most NASDAQ companies have CEO evaluations in place because they commonly refer to the rules of both exchanges to discern appropriate governance practice.

The U.S. Securities and Exchange Commission (SEC) only requires that CEO compensation be clearly outlined and justified in the Compensation Committee's Report section of the annual proxy statement, and makes no mention of the appraisal process or its implementation (Reda et al. 2005).

So, although executive performance appraisal is a cornerstone of good corporate governance and is widely implemented in larger companies, the information it produces is highly confidential and carefully guarded. At the present time, the results of such evaluations are not publicly available unless disclosure is required by subpoena or other imposed process (Reda et al. 2005).

All of this begs the question: If the performance appraisal process tends to unravel at the top level of the organization, can increases in compensation of executives continue to be justified? Many share the criticism that executive compensation is excessive. Those in favor of lucrative compensation argue that it is necessary to compete with other companies to attract the best talent and that the return that this talent provides to shareholders is more than enough to justify their compensation packages (Hunt 2007). Given this debate and the threat of legislation to regulate top executive pay, the need for organizations to design and implement an effective executive performance appraisal process is obvious.

An effective executive evaluation system is composed of two main components: the evaluation criteria and the evaluation process.

Developing Executive Evaluation Criteria

Performance evaluation criteria have evolved in the modern corporation from trait-based, personality-centric measures to more specific, results-oriented metrics, which include financial and nonfinancial criteria. Until recently, performance appraisals were based on annual "trait" ratings. Certain character traits such as degree of initiative, personality, maturity, judgment, or appearance were assessed because of their supposed relation to executive performance.

Over time, executives became more hostile, defensive, and critical of the system as boards grew more critical in their assessments (Crystal 1968). This "trait-based" appraisal system was soon replaced with the "overall performance rating." This system, though more comprehensive, was so heavily subjective and lacking in structure that appraisals were easily influenced by insignificant factors such as personality and low golf handicap instead of more relevant factors such as growth and financial performance (Crystal 1968).

Out of the shortcomings of the "trait-based" and "overall performance rating" came "management by objective." This appraisal system was based on established long-term and short-term objectives or goals that CEOs were expected to achieve in a specified period of time and it measured the degree to which a CEO met, fell short of, or surpassed these objectives (Crystal 1968). This appraisal system, in comparison to the previous models, was more effective because it was: Simple; focused on actual work—and not personality; aligned executive objectives with overall company goals; accepted by many more CEOs. If the executive participated in the establishment of his or her objectives, it was even more motivating. Management by objective is still the most used and most accepted performance appraisal system used by many organizations.

All organizations need to have a well-designed and focused executive perform-ance plan. The performance plan process aggregates individual goals into larger over-lapping, collective goals that focus the organization to do more than it would have. A well-designed performance plan describes the preferred results, how results tie back to the company's results, weighting of results, how results will be measured, and what standards are used to evaluate results.

Executive Performance Measures

As part of the performance plan, executives should set objectives that align with the company's culture, business strategy, and compensation philosophy. The objectives set are used to define the performance measures that will be used as evaluation criteria during the performance evaluation.

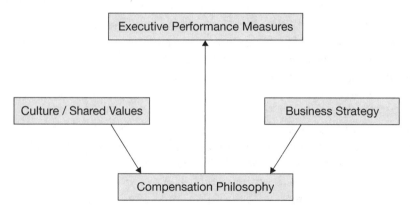

Figure 8-1 Factors that Determine Executive Performance Measures

Before executive performance measures can be defined, each of the three contribut-ing factors needs to be defined and understood so that objectives can be developed from each.

Compensation philosophy provides the overall framework from which the com-pany's compensation program is designed, and takes into account the culture/shared val-ues and business strategy. A compensation philosophy consists of four main components:

Peer group comparisons. Who should the company compare itself against for salary and short- and long-term incentive opportunities?

Pay positioning strategy. How should the company pay its executives in relation to the market levels of pay?

Internal vs. external pay equity. The culture/shared values are factored into this part of the compensation philosophy. How much weight should the company place on the internal relationships among executives (internal) versus the market (external)?

Performance alignment with business plan. Specifically, how is the compensation system aligned with the business strategy, particularly the incentive strategy with
emphasis on the performance measures?

The compensation philosophy should be reviewed when determining performance goals, as it takes some parts from the culture/shared values (internal vs. external
pay equity) and some parts from the business strategy (performance alignment with
the business plan). It is also important to determine the peer group that the company
competes with for products/services as well as talent.

Culture and shared values are naturally included while the manager is deciding
what criteria will be considered during the appraisal process. These values may
include open communications, reward for competence, preservation of integrity, openness to change, internal talent development, loyalty, and the belief that goals should be
results-oriented and not process-oriented. Identifying a culture and shared values will
be of great value when considering how to weigh both quantitative and qualitative
measures in the appraisal process. The culture and shared values will vary from company to company along with the executive performance measures.

Business strategy should be taken into account by the board of directors and CEOs
when developing a performance appraisal system. It is important that these strategies
are set and then made clear to the executives so as to guarantee cohesion and unity of
ideas and perspective over the course of the year. The appraisal process should assess
how successful the executive has been in moving forward with the pre-established
business strategy for that year. Midyear reviews allow for the company to reassess
these strategies and alter them if they are proving to be inadequate. Business success
factors should be an extension of the existing business strategy; these tend to be more
concrete and narrowly focused annual goals. The executives' ability to contribute to
the success in achieving these goals should be considered in the appraisal process.

Executive performance measures are those factors which compose each company's
background or identity and will determine the route the company will take to assess
the executive. It will also determine how much weight each area is given based on its
relative importance or value to the company.

Because a larger portion of executive compensation has been shifting to variable
pay plans, which are linked to performance, companies are placing more emphasis on
selecting performance measures that actually have an effect on the "bottom line"
(Schneier and Shaw 2000). The most obvious measurable financial results are the principal attributes of profit, total shareholder return, return on invested capital, cash flow,
earnings growth, and earnings stability.

Quantitative measures should work in concert with qualitative measures as
appraisal criteria (Schneier and Shaw 2000). There is no question that qualitative data
can be useful during the evaluation process; however, too heavy of a reliance on it can
lead to a loss of valuable resources such as time, money, and energy. This fact alone
would defeat the purpose of conducting an appraisal, since its main objective is to
ensure productivity and success.

Every goal specified should be quantified to the extent possible so that a third party could review the goal during an evaluation and determine if the executive had indeed achieved the goal. Qualitative information by nature is subjective, and quantitative data by nature is objective and less subject to evaluator bias. The mix of financial and nonfinancial measures is critical. If the executive evaluation is decoupled from the annual incentive plan (e.g., the bonus is paid independent of the evaluation), then nonfinancial measures should be the predominant part of the evaluation. However, if the executive evaluation is the sole determinant of the bonus, the use of quantitative data should be the main determinate of the bonus paid to the executive.

	Quantitative	**Qualitative**
Financial	• EPS growth • ROIC • TSR	• Better understanding of company strategy in investment community • Achievement of IPO/spin-off/restructuring
Nonfinancial	• Employee turnover • Diversity • Employee satisfaction (survey results)	• Milestones • Leadership skills • Strategy implementation • Communication effectiveness

Table 8-1 Qualitative vs. Non-Qualitative Measures

Typically, the most effective incentive measures are return on invested capital and total shareholder return (TSR). However, these financial measures may not be appropriate for all levels of executives as they may not be directly related to the executive being evaluated.

While there are ad hoc comments made by consultants and others that the achievement of the right nonfinancial goals (i.e., customer satisfaction, customer retention, employee satisfaction, brand recognition, or customer loyalty) will improve corporate profitability, there is no definitive proof of such claims. In addition, there are no good metrics as to the relationship between the achievement of nonfinancial goals and financial success. However, the application of nonfinancial goals is just as important as financial goals, particularly lower in the organization. Nonfinancial goals need to be simple, direct, and measurable. The goals should be results-oriented and not process-oriented—the goal should be expressed in achieving a result that will directly help the organization achieve short- and long-term objectives.

If the performance appraisal is closely linked to compensation, then extreme caution should be exercised on the selection of nonfinancial goals. In this case, a strict financial formula should be used to fund the program to avoid wasting corporate assets for overpaying executives.

Executive Performance Evaluation Process

While most companies have an executive performance appraisal process, more needs to be done to improve the process. When designing a performance appraisal process, consider who will be performing each appraisal and how the evaluation is to be administered including timing, the form the evaluation will take (written or oral), and finally, feedback to the executive.

Representatives Performing the Evaluations

As stated earlier, the executive evaluation process needs to be segregated into three categories: the CEO, the executive officers (NEOs), and all other executives. Typically, the board of directors evaluates the CEO and the CEO evaluates his or her direct reports, and so forth, with all evaluations being summarized and reported upward. There is also a typical "two-up rule" that the executive's manager performs the evaluation with the manager's manager reviewing the evaluation before it is completed.

Regarding the CEO performance evaluation, the entire board has the final say in most matters, although other entities participate in gathering and presenting data, such as the compensation committee. Other executives take almost no part in the CEO evaluation process, whereas outside advisors have some influence. Note that the corporate governance committee sometimes conducts the evaluation of the CEO, but for the purposes of illustration, we show the compensation committee.

As you can see from the charts that follow, there is a distinct difference in who evaluates which level of executive. Executive officer evaluation is handled chiefly by the CEO with the aid of the compensation committee and executive officers. The board also has some influence, but other executives usually do not have input.

The evaluation of all other executives is quite different from the CEO and executive officer evaluations. The board does not address the assessment of the other executives, nor does the compensation committee usually get involved. The evaluation is almost entirely in the hands of the CEO with the assistance of the other executive officers. For this level of executive, self-evaluation is prevalent as well as the participation of outside advisors.

Timing

The evaluation process should generally include three main stages: the establishment of the evaluation goals at the beginning of the fiscal year, the midyear review, and the end-of-the-year performance assessment and approval of the compensation package. Ideally there should be multiple evaluation sessions during the year. A meaningful CEO evaluation should contain regular board executive sessions, culminating in a formal annual evaluation. It should be well planned and objective and ultimately be tied to the executive's pay package. The executive officer and other executive processes are similar, except that their manager (most likely the CEO in the case of the EO) takes the place of the board.

Group*	Design System	Determine Measures, Set Targets	Gather & Present Performance Data	Appraise Performance	Provide Feedback	Determine Consequences
Entire Board	●	●	○	●	●	●
Compensation Committee	◐	◐	●	◐	◐	◐
CEO	○	○	○	○	--	--
Executive Officers**	○	○	○	--	--	--
All Other Executives	--	--	--	--	--	--
Outside Advisors	○	○	○	--	--	○

* Members of some group categories overlap.
**Includes Top-5 NEOs.

Key: Approve ● / Recommend ◐ / Influence ○ / No Role --

Table 8-2 Typical CEO Evaluation Process

Group*	Design System	Determine Measures, Set Targets	Gather & Present Performance Data	Appraise Performance	Provide Feedback	Determine Consequences
Entire Board	○	○	--	○	--	○
Compensation Committee	●	●	--	○	--	●
CEO	◐	◐	●	●	●	●
Executive Officers**	○	○	○	◐	◐	○
All Other Executives	--	--	--	--	--	--
Outside Advisors	○	○	○	--	--	--

* Members of some group categories overlap.
**Includes Top-5 NEOs.

Key: Approve ● / Recommend ◐ / Influence ○ / No Role --

Table 8-3 Typical Executive Officer Evaluation Process

Group*	Design System	Determine Measures, Set Targets	Gather & Present Performance Data	Appraise Performance	Provide Feedback	Determine Consequences
Entire Board	--	--	--	--	--	--
Compensation Committee	○	○	--	--	--	○
CEO	●	●	●	●	●	●
Executive Officers**	◐	◐	◐	◐	◐	◐
All Other Executives	○	○	○	○	○	○
Outside Advisors	○	○	○	--	--	--

* Members of some group categories overlap.
**Includes Top-5 NEOs.

Key: Approve ● / Recommend ◐ / Influence ○ / No Role --

Table 8-4 Typical Evaluation Process for All Other Executives

At the beginning of the fiscal year, the short-term and long-term objectives that will be part of the executive evaluation should be agreed upon. The establishment of objectives is discussed in the "Evaluation Criteria" section of this chapter. In addition to their creation, it is important that objectives be given relative weights and that the executive is aware of which objectives are of greater importance.

The midyear review provides an opportunity to assess progress toward performance targets, isolate and address problems, and determine if the executive is on the right path to meeting or exceeding the objectives. In some cases, it may make sense to adjust performance targets if they are no longer relevant to the company. However, it is not recommended that performance targets be changed unless there are unforeseen, unusual, or extraordinary circumstances. In a more volatile or dynamic industry (such as fashion or apparel), these intermediate reviews may need to be done quarterly or even on a monthly/weekly basis.

The end-of-the year assessment is the most thorough and time-consuming part of the evaluation process. Performance results must be compared to the set targets, and the appropriate compensation package must be determined. The final evaluation typically takes place two to three months after the end of the fiscal year, since it usually takes that long to finalize the financial statements. It is important and prudent that the financial statements be audited and signed off on before the evaluation is completed to ensure that performance data is correct. There have been recent examples of financial restatements that have highlighted situations where the bonus amounts paid should have been much lower based on the restated financial results.

This final evaluation is the formal executive performance appraisal and should contain the following components:

- Written self-evaluation
- Questionnaire completion by all evaluators
- Collection of internal and external data/information
- Preparation of recommendations by the compensation/governance committee
- Meeting between evaluators to discuss evaluations before approving final compensation package

Delivery of the Evaluation

Though it is highly recommended, there is no tax, accounting, security, or legislative rule that requires the evaluations to be in written form, which allows for the option of an oral evaluation. Like the written evaluation, the oral evaluation should also be very detailed, have outlined goals and objectives, and involve a feedback component. The oral evaluation should be conducted by the full board. Oral evaluations eradicate several of the problems with written evaluations but tend to be less thorough. Oral evaluations are much more prevalent in smaller organizations and when evaluating the CEO, particularly in larger organizations that are concerned about the misinterpretation of a CEO evaluation and the discovery of the evaluation in an adverse legal proceeding. Following are the advantages and disadvantages of oral evaluations:

Advantages of Oral Evaluation

- No written comments to be misinterpreted and misused
- May help some directors articulate their opinions
- Takes less time than written evaluations

Disadvantages of Oral Evaluation

- Very vocal directors (in the case of the CEO and in some cases executive officers) and executives (in the case of executive officers and other executives) can more easily influence others.
- Directors and executives can tend to be less objective and fair if the evaluation is oral.
- Tends to be a less in-depth review.
- It is very difficult to implement the "two-up" rule.
- There will not be a good record to assist in career development and promotional opportunities.

Written, documented evaluations are preferred, since a written evaluation allows for tracking of performance over multiple years; this is not as effective with the oral evaluation process. However, CEO evaluation materials are sometimes destroyed because there is no real career development once you are CEO, and records are destroyed to avoid a plaintiff's counsel using these documents in adverse lawsuits of various types.

Feedback to the Executive

Clear communication with the CEO and executives is necessary. At least two directors should deliver the CEO evaluation. Ideally, the chairs of the compensation and corporate governance committees would meet with the CEO in private immediately after full-board discussions. The two-person rule is also a good practice to follow with the other executives. The immediate manager should be present during the feedback session as well as a representative from human resources or the manager's manager.

It is paramount that confidentiality be preserved during the evaluation process. The issue of confidentiality is somewhat more difficult in the case of the CEO, as the evaluation process involves the completion of evaluation forms by each director. Evaluation of other executives are typically completed by the manager and reviewed by their manager.

In the case of the CEO evaluation, all completed evaluation forms by board members and other sources should be returned solely to the primary director or other designated person (often it is an outside advisor or in some cases the corporate secretary or lawyer working in the legal group) in charge of collecting the evaluation forms and disposed of after the data is summarized. The CEO and other executives should never see the raw data, since it is easy for data and responses to be misused or misinterpreted. A summary of the data is all that the evaluated executive should see. It is highly recommended for further security and confidentiality that outside consultants be utilized to manage the evaluation process.

Outcomes of the Performance Appraisal

Higher qualitative success is often accompanied by a higher profit margin, which is the ultimate goal of any company; therefore, qualitative criteria should be used in the executive evaluation process. Unfortunately, IRS Code Section 162(m) does not allow qualitative measures to be used when setting bonus amounts for the Top 5 Executives listed in the proxy statement. We recommend that the evaluation process be used as a "negative discretion" element. In other words, the annual executive appraisal can be used to lower the bonus for the NEOs. The treatment of the other executives can vary and may include adjusting the annual incentive upward or downward depending on the executive performance appraisal.

The last, and possibly most important, part of the evaluation process is to tie the evaluation process into the executive's pay package. This is especially important when corporate success is not synchronous with executive pay. For example, care should be taken to avoid large stock grants, bonus payments, salary increases, and other perceived compensation windfalls when there is an employee layoff, stock slump, or earnings drop.

One of the main objectives of assessing the performance of an executive is to ensure that the executive is being paid fairly, to gauge whether the salary for the performance is justified, is excessive, or should be raised. It is important that executives be monitored regularly to ensure that progress is being made. The outcome of the assessment will correlate directly to the salary of the executive. Meeting expectations, whether quantitative premeditated ones or goals set in relativity to competition, should be rewarded.

The current CEO evaluation process is typically de-linked from the CEO bonus decision. In the cases of the NEOs this is somewhat true, and it is less true for all other executives. The bonus is typically determined using quantitative financial criteria such as EPS growth, or EBITDA (earnings before interest, taxes, depreciation, and amortization). The CEO evaluation form, as shown in the example at the end of this chapter, is almost entirely based on nonfinancial measures in such areas as leadership, communications, board relations, and management development; however, companies are beginning to link these two evaluation processes.

Once performance has been appraised, the results will be considered and then used to make decisions. CEOs are often compared and evaluated in relation to the CEOs of other companies, the reason being that even if the CEO does meet financial goals, other companies may be doing better. If a CEO does not meet specified goals or is falling behind in comparison to other companies, he or she can be put on probation or more regularly monitored. If the CEO continues to fail to perform in the appropriate ways, then a case can be built against the CEO with records from multiple past appraisals and he or she can eventually be fired. If, on the other hand, the CEO meets or exceeds goals and has put the company in a good place in the market, he or she may be rewarded with a bonus or other incentives

The board alone should have the authority to adjust the CEO's salary and long and short-term incentive award. In several companies, HR typically gives guidelines as to salary increases. This places HR and management in an awkward position, as it may signal an action if the increase is below the recommendation. We recommend that the committee rely on outside advice for recommendations as to the range of the salary increase and LTI (long-term incentives) award.

The salary should not be adjusted as drastically as the LTI award, as it is important the CEO be paid according to general market levels with respect to base salary. There is ample room to adjust the LTI award opportunity based on the evaluation results.

In Conclusion

Executives should be evaluated regularly using a clearly defined process and measurable evaluation criteria. There are many factors to consider when designing, implementing, and operating an effective executive performance system. The performance measures (both quantitative and qualitative) are crucial to the success of the organization. The goals, as set by the board and the executive team, are created, ultimately, to grow the company and in turn add value to shareholders. Collectively, the board of directors, the CEOs, and the executive officers are focused on adding shareholder value. Formal appraisals of executive performance are crucial to establishing and ensuring an appropriate balance of power between the board members, the CEO, and the executive officers. By making a portion of executive compensation packages contingent upon the results of this evaluation, executives are held accountable for poor performance (Crystal 1968).

References

Crystal, Graef S. 1968. The performance appraisal process and its relation to compensation. *Compensating executive worth*. Russel F. Moore (ed.). American Management Association, Inc., 91–105.

Reda, James F., Stewart Reifler, and Laura G. Thatcher. 2005. *Compensation committee handbook*. 2nd ed. Hoboken, NJ: John Wiley & Sons, Inc., 54–76.

Hunt, Albert R. (2007, February 18) Letter from Washington: As U.S. rich-poor gap grows, so does public outcry. *International Herald Tribune: Americas*. Retrieved August 7, 2007, from http://www.iht.com/articles/2007/02/18/news/letter.php?page=1.

Conger, Jay A., David Finegold, and Edward E. Lawler III. 2000. Appraising boardroom performance. *Harvard Business Review on Corporate Governance*. Harvard Business School Press, 105–134.

Schneier, Craig E., and Douglas G. Shaw. 2000. Measuring and assessing top executive performance. In *The compensation handbook*, 4th ed. Lance A. Berger and Dorothy R. Berger, eds. New York : McGraw-Hill, 496–8, 500.

Chapter 9

Selecting the Right Performance Appraisal

Martin G. Wolf, Ph.D., President
Management Advisory Services

T HE IMPORTANCE OF MEASUREMENT IN SHAPING BEHAVIOR IN AN ORGANIZATIONAL SETTING is well known. Dr. Mason Haire, an industrial-organizational psychologist, said, "What gets measured gets done . . . If you want to change how an organization behaves, change the measurement system." Bill Gates said the same thing much more succinctly, "People behave as they are measured." The goal of this chapter is to help readers select, and implement, the type of measurement system that will have the most positive impact on their organization's performance.

Choice of Appraisal System

Appraisal systems can be categorized by what they assume and on what they focus measurement:

> *Trait based.* Assumes that certain traits drive performance; measures personal characteristics of the position incumbent.
>
> *Behavior based.* Assumes that certain behaviors drive performance; measures what the position incumbent does.
>
> *Knowledge/skill based.* Assumes that certain knowledge/skills drive performance; measures what the position incumbent knows/applies.

Results based. Assumes that achievement of objectives equals performance; measures what the position incumbent achieves.

Determining what type of appraisal system best fits your own organizational and business needs depends primarily on your objectives—that is, what you are trying to accomplish with the system. Is your priority remedying a performance shortfall, increased job understanding on the part of the incumbent, individual growth and career development, or performance planning and control?

Following are other important factors to be considered:

- The business environment
- The strategy and objectives of the business
- The organization's size and the management levels considered
- The corporate climate
- The values and style of the senior management group
- The resources available

Further, not all appraisal systems can be utilized effectively with all types of employees. Appraisal systems are best suited to employee types as follows:

- *Trait based.* All employees
- *Behavior based.* Supervisors and below
- *Knowledge/skill based.* Production workers, clerical workers, and some professionals
- *Results based.* Administrators/managers, most professionals, and executives

Table 9-1 presents a comparison of the general characteristics, advantages, and disadvantages of the four systems. Table 9-2 presents a different type of comparison of the four types of performance appraisal systems, focusing on the utility of each for different performance appraisal program objectives.

In Table 9-2, an X in the box indicates that that type of measurement has utility for that objective. Two Xs in the box indicates a high degree of utility for that objective, while a blank box indicates that type of measurement lacks utility for that objective.

System Type	Characteristics	Advantages	Disadvantages
Trait-Based	**Assumes that certain traits drive performance** • Emphasis is on personality/style/values • Traits are generic – one size fits all • Evaluation based on perception • Rating tied to degree/frequency trait is exhibited	• Simple to conduct evaluation • Can apply to different employee groups • Communicates important traits up front	• Not job-specific • Tends to be very subjective • Tenuous link between traits and accomplishments

Table 9-1 Comparison of Performance Measurement Systems (continued on next page)

System Type	Characteristics	Advantages	Disadvantages
Behavior-Based	**Assumes that certain behaviors drive performance** • Behaviors are specific to the work environment • Evaluation based on demonstrated actions • Rating tied to degree/frequency behavior is exhibited	• Can be tailored to specific jobs • Helps employees understand specifically how job is to be done • Behaviors help reinforce culture/values • Behaviors prove the presence of the related competency	• Time-consuming to develop and evaluate • Must be able to observe and measure discrete behaviors • Behaviors may not produce desired results
Knowledge- or Skill-Based	**Assumes that certain knowledge/skills drive performance** • Emphasis on employee capabilities • Tailored to each knowledge/skill area • Evaluation based on acquisition of knowledge/skills • Rating tied to degree/diversity of competencies achieved • Knowledge tied to organizational objectives	• Measures only the specific competencies required on each job • Reinforces cross-training and flexibility • Takes a strategic view, paying for competencies required both now and in the future	• Assumes link between knowledge/skills and results • Employee may have, but not need to use, certain knowledge/skills • Difficult to measure diverse skills
Result-Based	**Assumes that achievement of objectives drives total performance** • Objectives tied to job or organization goals • Objectives by which performance is measured are specific to the individual/group • Evaluation based on degree of achievement of specified results	• Tailored to specific jobs/organization • Emphasizes results • Direct linkage to the pay system • Encourages dialogue and employee buy-in if goals are jointly established	• Time-consuming to develop and evaluate • Works only where specific objectives can be established and measured • Debate between short-term and long-term emphasis

Table 9-1 Comparison of Performance Measurement Systems (continued)

	Type of Measurement			
Program Objective	**Trait-Based**	**Behavior-Based**	**KN/Skill-Based**	**Results-Based**
Increasing Job Understanding		X	X	XX
Remedial Performance Improvement	X	XX	XX	XX
Career Development/ Increasing Competencies	X	X	XX	X
Focusing Employee's Efforts on Specific Tasks	X	XX	X	X
Increasing Output	X	X	X	X
Talent Planning	XX	X	XX	X
Linking Pay and Performance		X	X	XX
Improving Teamwork	X	XX	X	X

Table 9-2 Utility of Different Performance Measurement Systems for Different Objectives

Designing a Performance Appraisal Program

Appendix A, at the end of this chapter, presents a detailed checklist of the many issues to be considered and the decisions to be made when designing a performance measurement program. Most are straightforward and need no discussion. A discussion of two key issues that are not so straightforward follows.

Choice of Appraiser

The person chosen as the appraiser *must* have the opportunity to observe the employee's performance on an ongoing basis. The most obvious choice as the appraiser is the employee's immediate superior (EIS), but often the EIS does not have the opportunity to observe the employee during the most important aspects of performance.

For example, a maintenance supervisor may have infrequent contact with maintenance personnel when they are performing repairs at various locations. Systems analysts may spend much of their time with users, far from where the EIS is working. Sales reps may be several states away from the EIS most of the time.

In such cases, evaluation by the EIS alone is inadequate. Additional inputs are required to fully and fairly evaluate the employee. (See Table 9-3.) Several solutions are possible:

Peer ratings
Evaluation by subordinates
Client/customer/supplier ratings
Use of outside experts
Some combination of the above

Rater	Advantages	Disadvantages
Peers	Excellent opportunity to observe performance Good knowledge of job requirements	Low rating may create resentment Possibility of collusion (everyone gets rated high or low) May weaken group cohesion/group trust Competition for jobs may cloud judgement
Subordinates	Excellent opportunity to observe performance Good knowledge of job requirements	They may distort ratings to curry favor or to get even They may be afraid to be negative when it is deserved May weaken the supervisory relationship
Clients/ Customers/ Suppliers	May observe the most critical aspects of performance	May not see some important aspects of performance May distort the proper business relationship Possibility of collusion (Employee does favors for rater in return for high rating)
Outside Experts	May possess excellent appraisal skills High degree of objectivity due to lack of personal relationship with appraisee	Limited opportunity to observe performance May not understand all aspects of the job Can be expensive

Table 9-3 Choice of Raters

The so-called 360-degree multi-rater feedback, using the first two or three of the above groups, has been widely used. Careful consideration must be given to the advantages and disadvantages of each alternative in each instance where the EIS needs assistance. Particularly in the case of peer ratings or evaluation by subordinates, care must be taken to keep the focus on performance and to avoid a "popularity contest."

It is particularly difficult to ensure that "performance" as defined by these groups is consistent with the organization's definition. For example, subordinates may rate their supervisor high on a dimension such as "Understands my job and helps me perform it better" if the supervisor bends policy to facilitate the subordinate's performance of specific subtasks. Customers may rate a sales rep high on a dimension such as "Understands my business needs and supports me in accomplishing my objectives" if he violates policy and clues them in to upcoming price increases in advance of their public announcement.

Method of Measurement

Each of the following sections presents detailed information on the design of one of the four types of performance measurement. While each of the four is different in various ways, there is some commonality.

Each trait, behavior, skill, or result constitutes a **dimension** of performance for that job. Dimensions communicate what traits, behaviors, skills, or results the organization considers to be important. Not all dimensions are created equal—some clearly are more important than others. Each dimension of performance must be assigned a weighting factor specifically for the job at hand. This weighting factor reflects the relative importance of the traits, behaviors, skills, or results to one another and to the job; it is not simply an indication of time spent by the incumbent in these areas.

When assigning percentage weighting factors, apply the following rules:

1. No single trait, behavior, skill, or result can be weighted more than 20 percent. If a trait, behavior, skill, or result warrants more than 20 percent, this indicates that it is complex enough to be broken apart into more specific aspects.

   For example, if making sales is felt to be 70 to 80 percent of the performance of a sales rep, then sales should be broken apart into four or more aspects. These might be as follows: repeat sales of existing products to old accounts; sales of existing products to new accounts; sales of new products to existing accounts; sales of new products to new accounts; average margin on sales.
2. No single trait, behavior, skill, or result can be weighted less than 5 percent. If a trait, behavior, skill, or result is less than 5 percent, it should be incorporated as a sub-part of another trait, behavior, skill, or result.
3. Avoid using fractions of a percent. It is impossible to determine such small differences. Many organizations prefer to stick to three or four weights—5, 10, 15, and 20 percent, for example. These then would correspond to important, quite important, extremely important, and critically important.

4. The total of all percentages must equal at least 95 percent and must not exceed 100 percent. (The use of less than 100 percent is allowed to indicate that there are other small but important elements to the job.)

Then, for each dimension, one or more **measures** must be established. Measures communicate how the organization will assess that dimension. The term measure refers to an index against which the dimension can be assessed; it does not specify the desired level (i.e., how much is "good", how much is "excellent", etc.).

Finally, for each measure, **standards**, the definition of the levels of that dimension, must be developed. Measures are always meaningless unless a standard is developed, and that is where the subjectivity enters in. How much is marginal, good, excellent? Basically, there are only three sources from which one can develop standards: the individual's history, peers, or management's wish based on hopes or pressures.

The latter is all too common, but not worthy of further comment herein. It is necessary to extrapolate from either of the first two to develop the projections that will form the coming year's standards. These projections must consider both internal limitations (financial and human resources, capacity, etc.) and external forces (macroeconomic conditions, competitive activity, technological changes, market trends, etc.). This process of extrapolation is the most critical part of the performance measurement process.

If the individual's history is used as the basis for standards, care must be taken to recognize not just the period to period change, if any, but also the baseline level of the prior period(s). The author once won the "most improved average" award in a bowling league by going from double digits to the still abysmal low 100s! On the other hand, it is unrealistic to expect continued improvement from someone already a top performer.

Similarly, when using peer performance as the basis for standards, care must be taken to recognize the group's overall level. All astronauts were well above the general population average mentally, physically, and educationally. However, as astronauts, some did not measure up and never received a mission, while others made multiple flights.

Rank ordering, paired comparisons, forced distribution, and other peer to peer scales that lack external criteria are inherently flawed. Depending on the talent pool in the organization, you identify either the cream of the crop or the cream of the crap, without the ability to tell which you have!

Trait-Based Performance Appraisal Process

As noted previously, a trait-based appraisal process rests on the assumption that certain traits drive performance, so it measures certain personal characteristics of the position incumbent. Therefore, the first step in developing a trait-based appraisal process is identifying the traits to be measured. There are two possible approaches.

One is to select different traits for different jobs from a "pool," based on those characteristics considered to be important for that job. The other is to use a common set of traits for all positions, weighting them differently for each position based on their relative importance to each position.

The former approach allows for the best fit between the selected traits and the job requirements. However, it is time-consuming to develop. The latter approach not only is quicker and easier to develop, but it has the advantage in human resources planning, as it allows any employee to be compared to any job.

The following are illustrative traits:

Relationships with others. Works in cooperation with others to achieve result.
Communication. Transfers ideas and thoughts by speech and writing
Planning/organizing tasks. Develops and arranges activity to achieve a result
Judgment. Evaluates job situation to arrive at sound decisions
Autonomy. Works with minimal supervision required by job
Work accuracy. Works within error standards
Work quantity. Meets work volume required within designated time frames

There are some elements which may or may not be separate/measurable traits. For example, is *leadership* a free-standing trait, or is it a function of the interaction of the traits of *relationships with others, communication,* and *planning/organizing tasks*? Should *intelligence* be a measured trait? *Loyalty?* What about the Boy Scout traits: *brave, thrifty, clean, and reverent?*

Sometimes the lines between traits, behaviors, skills, and results are blurred. Are *communication, planning/organizing tasks,* and *judgment* traits, or are they skills? Are *work accuracy* and *work quantity* traits, or are they really behaviors? Results?

Behavior-Based Performance Appraisal Process

As noted previously, a behavior-based performance appraisal process rests on the assumption that certain behaviors drive performance, so it measures what the position incumbent does. Therefore, the first step in developing a behavior-based appraisal process is identifying the behaviors to be measured, selecting different behaviors for different jobs from a "pool," based on those characteristics considered to be important for that job. See Figure 9-1.

One of the main problems with all performance appraisal ratings is rating inflation, and this is especially true of trait-based ratings. It is not only in Lake Woebegone that everyone is above average. Behavior-based scales attempt to reduce this type of creep by providing specific definitions of the levels of performance. Figure 9-1 illustrates one type of behavioral anchoring. Selected points on the scale are explicitly defined, and in between points on the scale are defined by implication. Other approaches to behavioral anchoring explicitly define every point on the scale (see Figure 9-2).

The use of behaviorally anchored rating scales offers several options as to the number of rating levels and as to whether or not a middle point is available (i.e., an odd or

5 - High	Accurately identifies employees' strengths, weaknesses, and potential; makes some job assignments based on experience needed for promotability; ensures that development plans consider correcting performance deficiencies as well as building proficiencies; communicates expectations; keeps direct reports appraised of their performance; immediately confronts problems; deliberately lets subordinates wrestle with solutions rather than making decisions for them.
4 -	
3 - Medium	Recognizes individuals' strengths; may be unaware of developmental needs or hidden potential; appropriately places individuals in positions compatible with qualifications; may neglect to challenge good performers sufficiently; identifies and informs others of unsatisfactory performance, requests improvement but may not offer suggestions for change; at times, neglects to offer deserved praise.
2 -	
1 - Low	Inability to recognize or evaluate strengths and weaknesses of individuals; places subordinates in positions incommensurate with qualifications and experience; fails to view others as possessing unique talent and potential; stifles growth by confining people to predetermined roles; subordinates are confused about what is expected; sets up subordinates for failure; allows problem performance to continue unabated; fills job vacancies on personality alone.

Figure 9-1 People Development

7 Excellent	Develops a comprehensive project plan, documents it well, obtains required approval and distributes the plan to all concerned.
6 Very Good	Plans, communicates, and observes milestones; states week by week where the project stands relative to plans. Maintains up-to-date charts of project accomplishments and backlogs and uses these to optimize any schedule modifications required. Experiences occasional minor operational problems but communicates effectively.
5 Good	Lays out all the parts of a job and schedules each part; seeks to beat schedule and will allow for slack. Satisfies customers' time constraints; time and cost overruns occur infrequently.
4 Average	Makes a list of due dates and revises them as the project progresses, usually adding unforeseen events; investigates frequent customer complaints. May have a sound plan but does not keep track of milestones; does not report slippage in schedule or other problems as they occur.
3 Below Average	Plans are poorly defined; unrealistic time schedules are common. Cannot plan more than a day or two ahead; has no concept of a realistic project due date.
2 Very Poor	Has no plan or schedule of work segments to be performed. Does little or no planning for project assignments.
1 Unacceptable	Seldom, if ever, completes project because of lack of planning and does not seem to care. Fails consistently due to lack of planning and does not inquire about how to improve.

Figure 9-2 Planning, Organizing, and Scheduling Project Assignments and Due Dates

even number of levels). Typically, four to seven levels are used. Many behaviorists feel that seven to nine levels represent the maximum number of distinctions that can be reliably made, but it is not unknown for some organizations to use a 100-point scale. I have encountered a number of these, and I typically ask the organization for a definition of the difference between a 91 and a 93, or a 7.2 and a 7.4. To date, I have yet to receive a satisfactory answer to these questions.

Knowledge/Skills-Based Performance Appraisal Process

As noted earlier, a knowledge/skills-based process rests on the assumption that certain knowledge/skills (competencies) drive performance, so it measures what the position incumbent knows/applies. Therefore, the first step in developing a knowledge/skills-based process is identifying the knowledge/skills to be measured, selecting different knowledge/skills for different jobs from a "pool," based on those considered to be important for that job.

The first challenge is to define the level of specificity to be used when defining knowledge/skills. Is leadership the skill to be measured, or is it to be broken down into more specific skills. Figure 9-3 presents one approach to defining the component skills involved in leadership.

---

a. **Creates Shared Vision:** Defines, communicates, and reinforces a common sense of purpose and set of values that are adopted by subordinate employees,

b. **Motivates and Empowers Others:** Influences, convinces, directs, and persuades others to accomplish specific objectives; provides sufficient latitude to allow subordinates to achieve specific objectives,

c. **Credibility:** Engenders the respect and confidence of others based on personal influence and reliability or organizational authority.

d. **Integrity:** Demonstrates consistency in beliefs, words, and behaviors,

e. **Sensitivity:** Alert to the motivations, attitudes, and feelings of subordinates and using this knowledge positively to direct behavior and achieve desired results,

f. **Develops People:** Identifies and addresses principal developmental needs of subordinates; provides frequent, effective feedback about accomplishments, strengths, and development needs,

g. **Group Skills:** Plans, conducts, and participates in meetings in which the collective resources of the group are used efficiently.

Figure 9-3 Leadership Skills

The positive value of such a breakdown is that it allows for a much more exact assessment of leadership than is possible if it is measured as a single skill. For example, a given individual may have average leadership skill if it is evaluated as a single entity. However, if evaluated on the components of leadership, the individual may be excellent in some and deficient in others. This more precise assessment has obviously greater utility for performance enhancement and career/talent development.

The problem with such a breakdown is that leadership is but one of a number of skill areas necessary for job performance. If each is broken into its component parts, the total will easily exceed 20 and may even exceed 30, depending on the position and the fineness of the breakdown. It is impossible to work effectively with that many elements of performance, both for administrative purposes (developing an overall rating) and for performance review (how do you focus the interview when you have 20-plus ratings to discuss).

Even assuming that the proper number and fineness of knowledge/skills have been identified, there is still the question of how to measure them. The link between possessing a certain knowledge/skill and its application to performance is at issue here. If you define possession of a skill by its application on the job, you are essentially measuring results, not the skill per se. If you define possession of a skill other than by its application on the job, you are getting into complex, technically difficult measurements. Depending on the skill involved, this may require special skill tests or even getting into the individual's psyche.

For example, look at sensitivity, one of the components of leadership in Figure 9-3. An individual may appear to be "alert to the motivations, attitudes, and feelings of subordinates," but it is impossible to know if he/she really is "alert" except by actions that demonstrate this ("using this knowledge positively to direct behavior and achieve desired results"). Even if one treats leadership as a unitary skill, how do you assess it except by either its application (which is behavior) or its outcome (which is results)?

Results-Based Performance Appraisal Process

In any sound management system, an important element is some procedure, preferably quantitative, to determine the degree to which results are being achieved. For example, a budget is a plan for spending money over a period of time. Periodic review of actual against planned expenditures provides an important check to control and correct negative variances or permit reallocation of resources in the event of an unpredictable event.

The measurement of results is what most people think of when they think of performance appraisal. Indeed, most people equate performance with results: Good performance is that which leads to desired results; poor performance is that which does not. Over a 30-plus year career as a management consultant, I have met thousands of managers, each of whom believed that he or she could easily recognize good performance. Yet few of them could appraise performance effectively. Their failure was rooted in the lack of proper definition of what constituted good performance.

The first step in results-based performance appraisal is to determine the **dimensions** of performance for that job. Dimensions may be permanent aspects of the position (i.e., making sales), specific one-time objectives (introducing a new product to the XYZ company), or a mixture of the two. Organizations that use a management by objectives (MBO) approach can fit these objectives in to the performance appraisal process as dimensions if they so choose. Some may prefer to keep the annually developed MBO dimensions separately, perhaps tied in to a bonus program, and use the permanent dimensions for a performance appraisal program that is tied in to base salary administration (pay for performance) and/or for development purposes. Then, for each dimension, one or more **measures** must be established.

Measurement of Results

It must be recognized that all performance measurement is subjective; there is no such thing as objective performance measurement. What many people call objective measurement (sales volume, number of units produced, percent of products meeting quality standards, etc.) is just as subjective as what those same people would call subjective measurement (customer relationships, communication, product knowledge, etc.). The differences between the two categories are in the degree of quantification and when the subjective judgments are made.

So-called objective measurements are those that are highly quantifiable and that allow for putting the subjectivity at the beginning of the measurement period rather than at the end of it. For example, sales volume is generally considered an objective measure of sales performance. Sales volume can be measured to two decimal place accuracy.

Suppose Sales Rep A sells $1,003,234.65 in a year, while Sales Rep B sells $1,534,201.32. What is A's level of performance—marginal, good, excellent? What is B's? Sales volume alone is meaningless for assessing performance. Clearly B has sold more dollars' worth of product than A, but has B performed at a higher level than A? Not necessarily, depending on such things as the products A and B each were selling (if A sells specialty items and B sells commodity items, A may represent a higher level of performance than B) or the territory in which they were selling (B may be in an established territory with little competition, while A may be in a new territory with well-established competition). Relative sales volume alone is meaningless for comparing performance.

Measures are always meaningless unless a **standard** is developed, and that is where the subjectivity enters in. How much is marginal, good, excellent? In which territories, for which products? Why is $xxx,xxx good? Why not 20 percent less, or 20 percent more?

It is necessary to develop standards for every measure. These are usually developed at several levels—**acceptable** (just enough to get by), **good** (target or expected), **very good** (clearly better than expected), and **outstanding**. (Feel free to pick your favorite term for each of these four conceptual levels of performance.)

The development of the standards for each measure *in advance of the performance period* is critical to performance enhancement. As the saying goes, "If you don't know where you are going, you will never know when you get there." Many otherwise excellent performance appraisal programs fail because standards were not properly developed and communicated to the employee in advance of the performance period.

Comparison of Types of Results Measures

When thinking about the results measurement process, keep a number of important points in mind. First, in establishing indicators, we need to direct our efforts toward finding the most quantifiable measures of performance. As we do this, we increase the chances that, regardless of who makes a performance assessment, the judgment will be the same. That is, there will be a high agreement among independent observers or evaluators.

In those cases where measures must be less quantifiable (and these are common), it is possible to increase accuracy by using either more than one measure or more than one observer or evaluator. Since the use of multiple observers is limited, multiple measures are often used. As a rule of thumb, no more than four indicators should be used to measure achievement against any one dimension of performance. More than this tends to confuse people. (See Figure 9-4.)

Least Quantifiable

General Descriptions - judgments used to indicate end results achievement. For example:
- Satisfaction expressed by supervisor
- Satisfaction expressed by customers
- Favorable publicity
- Quality of report or analysis

Judgmental Scales - measurement based on rating of results on a scale, say of 1 to 7, with 1 representing worst results and 7 representing best. For example:
- Perceived value of data processing services, low to high on 1-7 scale
- Level of personnel support, low to high on 1-7 scale
- Adequacy of drafting services, highly inadequate to highly adequate on 1-7 scale

Ratios - these use quantified, numerical results - they match actual performance to available opportunities. For example:
- Employee turnover ratio
- Labor hours per unit of production
- Market share

Direct Counts - these are completely quantified. Measures dealing with physical objects, specific occurrences, and other objective data. For example:
- Dollars of sales
- Cost of goods purchased
- Cost of operations
- Number of units produced or sold

Sometimes it is easier to count the exceptions than to count the normal occurrences. For example:
- Number of errors
- Number of complaints

Most Quantifiable

Figure 9-4 Types of Results Measures

Given our preference for quantification, we may find certain highly quantifiable measures that we cannot use. Why? They may be quantifiable but irrelevant—of marginal importance to the measurement process or even downright trivial. Body count, readily available and fully quantified, was used as a measure of performance in Vietnam. It increased steadily even as the area of population control diminished continually, resulting in withdrawal under pressure. Quantification should be valued, but not at the cost of relevance, practicality, and common sense.

Finally, there is the problem of the appropriate "cost/benefit ratio" for any specific measure. We may believe we can develop an unusually sound and highly quantifiable performance measure. However, further analysis may show that the cost of developing the measure (time, energy, money) is so high that the benefit (relevance, practicality, objectivity) is not worth it. We may achieve a tour de force by developing and using the measure—but it surely is not good business practice. Better to use a couple of rough-and-ready measures that are useful and inexpensive.

Developing Results Measures

In some cases, measures are directly suggested by the dimension of performance, and they are fairly easily specified and quantified. In those cases where this is not so, it is often helpful to ask two basic types of questions about the job:

1. What are the concrete signs of outstanding performance on this dimension? Often it is not too difficult to come up with the hallmarks of the real standout performance, and these signs should lead to measures of end results.
2. What are the concrete signs of poor performance on this dimension? It is often easier to bring to mind the things that represent an unsatisfactory performance. These, too, can be helpful in deriving useful measures.

The task is to identify the possible measures and narrow the choice to a few which capture most directly the nature of any end result which the position is to achieve.

The selected measures should meet the following criteria:

Relevant. They should relate directly to the major results, rather than activities or less important results. Measures should focus on, rather than divert attention from, the result.

Specific. The measures should accurately reflect performance the employee can control or directly affect with his or her job or organizational unit. For example, a manager of manufacturing might be measured on production costs, or "value added," but not on profit, since he or she has no control over the material costs or the selling price per unit, both of which also impact directly on profit.

Obtainable. Wherever possible, use measures that now are, or can easily become, available; avoid the need for major new and/or complex tracking mechanisms.

Practical. In most performance areas, many measures are already in use as common means of setting goals, controlling operations, and reporting results. Use these whenever possible because they represent the organization's business focus.

Reliable. Other raters will come to the same conclusions about level of performance from the measurement data.

Timely. Data must be available soon enough after the end of the performance period to affect most of the following performance period.

Appendix B presents some sample measures for line and staff jobs. This list is not all-inclusive, but it should provide further clarification of the types of measures that can be used to assess performance.

Results-Based Performance Appraisal Process

Once the dimensions are identified and weighted, and the associated measures and standards developed, results-based performance appraisal is simple. Performance is defined as the attainment of the specified results as defined by the standards. Performance appraisal is simply the comparison of the results achieved versus these specified results.

Appendix C presents an illustrative results-based performance appraisal form.

In summary, if the dimensions are well stated, and if realistic measures and standards of performance are formulated, there will be little question what has been accomplished. While many of the measures may be qualitative, the process will be reliable in that any evaluator who knew the relevant facts would give the same rating to the employee.

Appendix A

Performance Appraisal Diagnostic

Appraisal Issue	Key Questions	Decision Options
Philosophy	What is the primary need to evaluate?	A. Accountability B. Performance improvement/maintenance C. Career development/ increasing competencies D. Support of other systems (e.g., rewards, values)
Objectives	What specifically do we want to achieve?	A. Detailed evaluation B. Summary evaluation C. Combination
Type of Criteria	What makes employees/teams effective?	A. Knowledge or skill-oriented criteria B. Process-oriented criteria C. Output-oriented criteria D. Combination
Method of Measurement	How can we actually tell whether the employee/team is effective?	A. Trait-based B. Behavior based C. Knowledge or skill based D. Results based E. Combination

Appraisal Issue	Key Questions	Decision Options
Data for Measurement	What type of information is available for assessing effectiveness?	A. Quantitative B. Qualitative
Choice of Appraiser	Who should evaluate performance?	A. Supervisors B. Peers C. Subordinates D. Clients/customers/suppliers E. Outside experts F. Combination
Number of Appraisers	How many people should evaluate performance?	A. Single appraiser B. Multiple appraisers
Appraisal Instruments	What kind of documents should be used?	A. Checklists B. Narratives C. Rating scales D. Goal-oriented instruments
Performance Reviews	How should information be fed back to the employee/team?	A. Interviews B. Other (e.g., written document)
Appraisal Training	How should training in the conduct of the appraisal be provided?	A. Internal staff B. Consultants C. Combination D. Other (e.g., self-paced)
Assessment Period and Timing	Should timing be fixed or based on need?	A. Scheduled appraisals B. Appraisal in response to problems C. Both
Frequency of Data Collection	Is evaluation a continuous or discontinuous process?	A. Day-to-day data collection B. Periodic data collection C. Varies
Congruence of Outcomes with Objectives	Is appraisal going to do what we wanted to achieve?	A. Quality B. Timeliness C. Credibility D. Cost E. Accountability
Interactive Appraisal Design	Should the subordinates' appraisals be linked to the supervisor's appraisal and others in the value chain?	A. Separate appraisal systems B. Linked appraisal system

Appendix B

Sample Measures
of Performance

Sample Measures for "Line" Jobs

Cost Effectiveness
Actual/budget (by category and/or time period)
Net income/net sales
Forecasted/actual (by month/quarter)
Gross margin or gross operating profit (by profit center, product line, etc.)
Return on capital/risk
Break-even point as a percent of capacity
Average collection period
Return on investment
Return on assets
Earnings before taxes

Productivity
Dollar cost/unit of product or service provided
Actual/standard cost (by category)
Currency of manpower planning
Currency of work methods
Bottlenecks in work flow
Downtime of equipment
Absenteeism
Length of time for employees to meet performance standards
Turnover of above average performers

Relationships

Promptness of problem notification to others
Understanding of other functions' objectives and plans
Minority employees percent/percent in available workforce
Grievances (employee, community)
Agreement on schedules
Adherence to schedules
Peers' and superior's reactions

Staff and Organizational Development

Use of objectives by staff
Completion and application of job-related study
Number and type of decisions delegated
Number of conflicting objectives
Number of conflicting action plans
Results of career discussions
Job sequencing plans
Job enrichment plans
Results of attitude surveys

Quality

Internal reject percent
Complaints from customers
Results of internal/external audits
Employee commitment to standards
Actual/standard (errors, reject rate)
Warranty costs
Accuracy (production reports)
Raw material quality
Results of work sampling

Marketing

Knowledge of end-user requirements
Number of new products (programs) developed
Actual/forecast (sales, operating expenses
Market penetration (share)
Percent net income in R&D
Results of market research and advertising (public information) programs
Number of noncreative duties performed by sales staff
Timeliness of forecast submissions

Cost Control

Actual/standard (by cost category)

Actual/forecast (by cost category)

Worker's compensation costs

Unemployment compensation costs

Lost work hours due to absenteeism, accidents, tardiness, etc.

Direct/indirect labor ratio

Use of electric power

Cost of telephone service

Travel and per diem expense

Sample Measures for "Staff" Jobs

Some performance dimensions, such as those found in certain staff positions, are difficult to review. In some cases, it is best to use a measure that indicates what has not occurred rather than what has. For example, "unscheduled downtime" might be the most reliable indication of the incumbent's performance on a dimension involving the effective utilization of EDP equipment. The reviewer can assume that the most likely thing is for the end result (effective utilization of equipment) to occur. So rather than counting or describing what has happened, he or she focuses effort by considering only those times when the desired result was not accomplished. This amounts to keeping track of "unscheduled downtime."

Measures for staff positions must deal with end results that are to be accomplished by the staff unit. The vital question is—"What is the output of the position?" Following are some common measurements:

- Number of occasions on which schedules were missed
- Number of proposals implemented per number of proposals made
- Quality of service as rated or described by "client" or user
- Number of complaints (or commendations) regarding services provided
- Audits of effectiveness of services provided (internal or external)
- Number of "exceptions" found by outside sources—e.g., customer complaints, outside audit
- Number of person-hours (or budget) spent per service area versus plan
- Number of units of output per employee
- Descriptions of kinds of service provided relative to kinds of service requested
- The organization's record in an area (e.g., accident frequency, EEO data, worker's compensation rates) compared to industry average
- Descriptions or ratings of the relevance and quality of innovations or new services developed

Appendix C

Illustrative Results-Based Performance Enhancement Program

NAME_____ DATE_____

POSITION_____ DEPT._____

PERFORMANCE PERIOD: FROM_____ TO_____

I. PERIOD PERFORMANCE

Dimension: Weight_____ percent

Measure(s) and Standards:

Description of Performance:

===

Dimension: Weight_____ percent

Measure(s) and Standards:

Description of Performance:

===

Dimension: Weight_____ percent

Measure(s) and Standards:

Description of Performance:

II.   OTHER COMMENTS (Optional)

Use this space (and attach additional sheets if desired) to make any statement you feel will further explain and clarify this employee's performance.

III.   IMPROVEMENT ACTIVITIES FOR THE NEXT PERIOD

This section should contain an improvement plan to correct any difficulties noted in Sections I and II. These should be spelled out as to who will do what, by when, with specific behavioral objectives to be achieved.

IV.   OVERALL EVALUATION OF PERFORMANCE

V.   PERFORMANCE PLAN FOR THE NEXT PERFORMANCE PERIOD

FROM_____ TO_____

Establish the dimensions, measures, and standards for the next performance rating period.

Dimension: Weight_____ percent

Measure(s) and Standards:

===

Dimension: Weight_____ percent

Measure(s) and Standards:

===

Dimension: Weight_____ percent

Measure(s) and Standards:

===

Chapter 10

Improving Performance through the Employee Value Exchange

Jim Kochanski, Senior Vice President
JP Elliott, Senior Consultant
Sibson Consulting

WHY DO SOME COMPANIES ATTRACT SIGNIFICANTLY MORE THAN THEIR FAIR SHARE OF talent, have lower levels of turnover, and enjoy the admiration of their competition for the superior results they deliver time and time again? The answer lies in how highly successful organizations like Google, Southwest Airlines, and IBM have differentiated, redefined, and communicated their unique Employee Value Proposition (EVP) to their employees.

Many organizations would argue that they have well-defined EVPs. What is novel is the way top-flight companies are broadening this traditional concept to drive the exceptional performance of their people through what Sibson Consulting calls an Employee Value Exchange (EVE).

How We Got Here

Prior to exploring how forward-looking companies are moving to create stronger employer/employee relationships based on mutually beneficial value exchanges, it is important to review the history of the EVP and define what is working and what needs to be improved to drive high levels of organizational performance.

The concept of an EVP rests on what researchers and academics call a "psychological contract," which is the set of beliefs, perceptions, and informal obligations held by individual employees about the terms of the exchange agreement between themselves and their employer (Rousseau 1989). Unlike formal written contracts of employment, psychological contracts are based on perceptions and, therefore, an employee's interpretation of the terms, agreements, and obligations of the contract may not be shared by his or her employer. Further, research suggests that employees who are satisfied with their current employment relationship have lower levels of turnover intent and exhibit more commitment and organizational support (Shore and Barksdale 1998). On the other hand, employees who think their organization has failed to fulfill its end of the contract are less likely to give discretionary performance and more likely to have higher turnover intentions and exhibit a lower level of commitment to the organization.

Line managers and HR professionals have long understood the business impact that results when key employees leave the organization because of what they perceive as breaches in their psychological contract. The negative consequences of losing key talent was heightened during the talent shortage that began in the late 1990s—a situation that was captured in a study by Sibson Consulting and McKinsey and Company that became known as the "War for Talent." Frustrated by high turnover, an abundance of skilled employees who had more career options than ever and a limited understanding of what was driving people to leave, organizations began to ask their employees what elements of the psychological contract they *value* the most. This led HR professionals and academics to begin researching employees' needs and wants much like a marketing function would research its customers.

HR not only borrowed some of the marketing department's tools—including conjoint analysis and focus groups—but also specific language, especially the concept of a "value proposition." This term generally refers to what customers can expect or actually get for their time and money. From here, the academic concept of a psychological contract was transformed into the more marketing-friendly EVP. As the idea of the EVP took hold, more organizations, researchers, and consulting firms conducted research that provided both multiple definitions of the concept and linked an effective EVP to critical employee outcomes, including attraction, engagement, retention, and, ultimately, to business outcomes, including profitability, productivity, and customer service.

One of the most widely used definitions of the EVP comes from the Corporate Leadership Council (CLC), which defines it as "the set of attributes that the labor market and employees perceive as the value they gain through employment in the organization." Another popular definition describes it as "the value or benefit an employee derives from his or her membership in an organization." The main issue with the CLC's definition and others like it is that they focus solely on the employee side of the value equation. While this is understandable, given the strong empirical evidence that demonstrates how an organization's EVP influences key employee outcomes (i.e., employee engagement) and, ultimately, critical business outcomes (Heger 2007), it is also limiting. By neglecting to articulate the value that the employer expects in return for providing a particular set of rewards, these definitions ignore the most critical element of the employer-employee equation: the value exchange.

Beyond the EVP—the EVE

For this reason, Sibson has redefined the traditional definition of the EVP into the EVE, to include the expectations of the employer. Simply put, the EVE examines the *balance* between the rewards employers offer and the expectations they set in exchange for those rewards. This is done using Sibson's Rewards of Work model (see Figure 10-1), which examines the proposed suite of rewards an employer offers its employees.

Figure 10-1 The Rewards of Work Model

There are five types of rewards:

1. *Affiliation.* The feeling of belonging to an admirable institution that shares the employee's values

2. *Compensation.* The money employees receive for their work and performance
3. *Benefits.* Indirect compensation, including health insurance, retirement programs, and time off
4. *Career.* Employees' long-term opportunities for development and advancement
5. *Work content.* The satisfaction employees receive from the work they perform

Each factor affects current and potential employee decisions concerning their employment, especially whether to move to a new job or stay at an existing one.

While having the right mix of these rewards is essential in ensuring that employees think their needs are being met, it only speaks to one side of the value equation and provides little if any information about what level or type of performance is required to attain those rewards. On the other side of the EVE are the employer's expectations concerning what each employee must contribute to achieve the organization's goals. While these will vary by industry and organization, most companies want these five things:

1. *Performance.* The specific levels of discretionary efforts required and the desired objectives needed to achieve the organization's stretch goals and deliver superior performance.
2. *Three Cs of Teamwork.* The coordination, collaboration, and communication of organizational performance that is expected of individuals within and across business units and teams.
3. *Engagement.* The knowledge of what the priorities are and the motivation to attain them.
4. *Behavior.* The acceptable/desired behaviors required of individuals to support the desired culture and achieve results.
5. *Retention.* The level of retention that is desired of individuals and required to support the overall business strategy. (See Figure 10-2.)

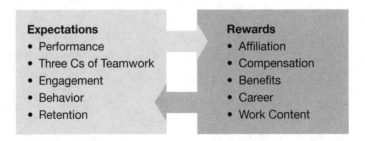

Figure 10-2 The Employee Value Exchange

For most organizations, defining the rewards they will offer prospective and current employees is much easier than identifying and gaining internal alignment on what they expect for those rewards. When attempting to operationalize less tangible concepts like performance, teamwork, engagement, and the like, you should begin with the end in mind.

In the case of developing clear expectations as a part of an effective EVE, the beginning and end is an understanding of the desired organizational culture—one that supports the strategic imperatives of the organization. What type of stretch goals does the organization consistently expect of its employees? Does it expect employees to work across silos, functions, and organizational levels to accomplish their work? What behaviors are consistently rewarded, reinforced, and expected on a daily basis? All these questions speak to both the type of culture and expectations an organization provides its employees in exchange for the rewards it offers. High-performing organizations usually demonstrate alignment among business strategy, employee expectations, the organizational culture, and the rewards that employees receive.

Southwest Airlines

Over the past four decades, Southwest Airlines has established itself as an example of an organization that drives high performance by developing a distinctive and compelling EVE. Long known for its unique and fun-loving culture, Southwest has come to dominate one of America's toughest industries.

One of the secrets to the organization's success is its ability to articulate what it expects of its employees in the key areas that have real business impact—efficient operations and superior customer service. Southwest truly "walks the talk" when it comes to teamwork. It is part of the company's core values and employees are encouraged to be "passionate team players." Moreover, Southwest effectively translates its values of being a passionate team player into specific performance expectations that help the company keep its edge in the marketplace. This includes establishing, communicating, and reinforcing the idea that all employees are responsible for keeping planes in the air, on schedule, and at the gate for the shortest time possible. Anyone who flies Southwest will notice that the entire flight crew, including the pilots, helps clean the plane after landing. This exceptional level of teamwork translates into lower operating costs, more efficient operations, and highly satisfied customers.

In exchange for being a high-performing team and going beyond what other airlines require of their flight crews, Southwest rewards its employees with a free-spirited culture and environment that encourages them to "bring their personality to work." Flight crews are encouraged to wear shorts, tell their own jokes, sing songs, and generally be themselves. As a result, Southwest has created a high-performance, team-oriented environment that is both good for business and is often cited as a key driver of employee attraction and retention.

The Expectations-to-Rewards Ratio

Unfortunately, most companies are not as explicit as Southwest in defining their unique EVE, and many have a value exchange that is significantly out of balance. The place to start assessing whether an organization's EVE is weighted too heavily on either the employer or the employee side is what Sibson calls the expectations-to-rewards ratio. This is a measure of the value exchange between an organization and its employees.

With the table in Figure 10-3 below, it is easy to determine whether an organization's culture is one of disengagement, "churnover" (high levels of churn and turnover), entitlement, competitiveness, or high performance.

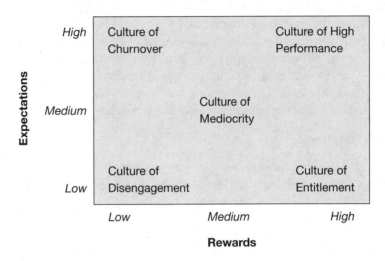

Figure 10-3 Determining an Organization's Culture

Attributes of High-Performance Cultures

A high-performance culture is the holy grail of the corporate world. Google, IBM, and many other organizations have discovered that the key to sustaining high performance levels is having the right balance in the EVE. High-performing organizations start by having elevated expectations of their employees and rewarding them accordingly. This balance ensures that employees feel they are being rewarded appropriately when they assess the level of effort they are putting into their work. In turn, employers are not afraid to ask for a high level of performance due to the level of rewards they provide.

Google is an example of a high-performing organization that, unlike many other dot-com companies, has managed to ensure that its many perks, including catered lunch and dinner, on-site dry cleaning, and the like, do not become entitlements. Google accomplishes this by keeping its expectations for performance extremely high and by ensuring that the perks employees most value are tied to their delivering on these high expectations. As an example, Google allows employees to spend 20 percent of their time on a personal project of their choosing. Although it has been reported that every employee gets this benefit, Google gives it only to those who have met a desired level of performance. By raising the bar on what they expect to receive in return for such unique rewards, Google has protected itself against a culture of entitlement while challenging employees to raise the level of their performance.

Creating an Effective EVE

While the benefits of establishing an effective EVE are great, many companies struggle to identify, develop, and communicate a model that will reduce the existing inequity between their expectations and the rewards they provide. Implementing an effective EVE requires that companies commit to moving through a series of steps that range from identifying the ideal future state of the organization, taking an inventory of current state, and beginning to use the new EVE to solve key organizational challenges. (See Figure 10-4.)

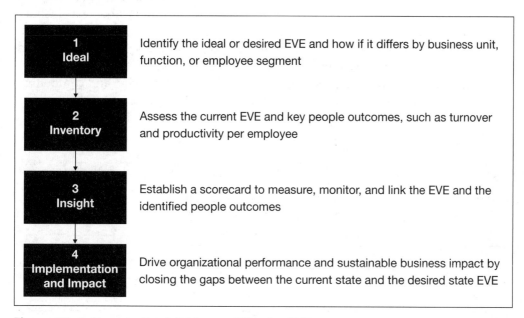

1 **Ideal**	Identify the ideal or desired EVE and how if it differs by business unit, function, or employee segment
2 **Inventory**	Assess the current EVE and key people outcomes, such as turnover and productivity per employee
3 **Insight**	Establish a scorecard to measure, monitor, and link the EVE and the identified people outcomes
4 **Implementation** **and Impact**	Drive organizational performance and sustainable business impact by closing the gaps between the current state and the desired state EVE

Figure 10-4 Steps to Establishing an Effective EVE

1. *Identify the ideal or desired EVE and how it differs by business unit, function, or employee segment.* Before an organization can begin the journey of transforming its current EVE, it must understand where it wants to go. The first step in this process is to examine the current business strategy and determine the ideal EVE that is needed to support the organization and the attainment of its goals.

   Two things are critical at this stage. The first is engaging the organization's leadership. Their input, actions, and support will be required to give the effort the momentum needed to alter the current EVE. Because the value exchange is a two-way street, employee involvement is also essential. The employees will have a clear perspective of what is working and what can be improved in both the current and the desired state.

   The best way to solicit feedback and engage both leadership and key employee populations on this important topic is to

- *Conduct a kick-off meeting with leaders.* The objective is to generate a robust discussion of how the current EVE is influencing the organization's performance. Exploring key topics—such as business results, productivity, employee engagement, and how overall levels of performance could be improved by altering the current expectations placed on employees and the rewards they are provided—should be enough to get the conversation started.
- *Gather leadership's vision of the future.* Interview each leader separately to uncover what he or she thinks would be the ideal desired state for the organization's EVE. This involves going through each area of the organization's expectations and the rewards provided to determine where each leader thinks the company needs to be to deliver superior results. In addition, leaders must help identify their main expectations and rewards focus areas and how each of these would differ from the current state. Gaining clarity on these factors will ensure the organization's EVE is distinctive and compelling when compared to its competitors' EVE. Figure 10-5 offers a simple template for the type of questions that leaders should be asked in conducting this assessment.

Expectations	Desired State?	Rewards	Desired State?
Goal stretch	_____	Compensation	_____
Teamwork	_____	Benefits	_____
Engagement	_____	Work Content	_____
Behaviors	_____	Career	_____
Retention	_____	Affiliation	_____
Main expectation focus? _____		Main reward focus? _____	
How different from current state? _____		How different from current state? _____	

Figure 10-5 Value Exchange Discussion Guide

- *Gather input and feedback from select employee populations.* Understanding how employees perceive the expectations placed on them and the rewards they receive is important to creating a complete vision of the future. Similar to the leadership interview process, employees need to be engaged to understand what their desired state would look like for areas such as goal stretch and affiliation. Since it would be impossible to speak with all employees, organizations would be smart to select only those employee populations that are seen as strategic to the organization's future. Their engagement and retention will determine if the organization reaches its goals.

- *Conduct a leadership working session.* With an understanding of both the leadership and key employees' perceptions of the desired state, it is time to define formally the ideal EVE. The output of this session will describe what will be expected from employees and the rewards the organization will provide for meeting these new expectations. It is important that the organization does not expect too much and provide too little or provide too much and not expect enough. While there is only one expectations-to-rewards ratio that will deliver a culture of high performance, it is the strategic choices on particular focus areas and how the organization implements those choices that will determine if it achieves the ideal state.

2. *Assess the current EVE and key people outcomes, such as turnover and productivity per employee.* With the ideal EVE in hand, an organization's next task is to determine the gap between what is currently being delivered and where it needs to be. At this time, it is important to move beyond strategic employee populations and understand, as much as possible, the perceptions of the organization in aggregate.

   The key steps in this process are drafting an EVE survey, testing the survey online, inviting a wide sample of employees to participate, compiling the results, reviewing them with leadership, developing an initial action plan, and communicating the survey results and next steps in the process to the organization. While there are many elements that go into each step (which are beyond the scope of this discussion), it is important that the assessment of the current state is not rushed. Ensuring the leadership accurately understands how employees perceive the current state and building buy-in for taking the appropriate actions to move to the future state are key objectives of this phase of the process.

3. *Establish a scorecard to measure, monitor and link the EVE and the indentified people outcomes.* Peter Drucker could have been speaking about transforming an EVE when he said, "What gets measured gets done." For many organizations, the gap between where they currently are and where they want to be is so great that without a way to monitor their progress they would surely fail.

   The focus of the insight phase is to establish, monitor, and begin holding leaders accountable for the metrics on an EVE scorecard that ensures focus and keeps the organization's eyes on the prize. Regardless of the metrics used by an organization, it is critical that an EVE scorecard is established. Without one, the effort is sure to lose leadership support, focus, and the needed accountability to realign the balance and create a high-performing culture.

4. *Drive organizational performance and sustainable business impact by closing the gaps between the current-state and the desired-state EVE.* With a clear vision for the future and the Employee Value scorecard as a compass to keep the organization on track, leadership must turn its focus to implementing a distinct expectations-to-rewards ratio that will drive results and sustain performance. Although this

step will vary greatly according to the gaps that have been identified in the current EVE, most organizations will probably need to

- Revise their rewards, career, and work systems to better align with the desired performance levels.
- Align their pay structure to the desired career path and work system. For example, adding or reducing levels in the pay system to increase the sense of career and/or team camaraderie.
- Launch a campaign to differentiate the organization's mission, values, and goals to encourage more employees to connect with the organization's leaders and its overall vision of the future.
- Revise employee benefits and enhance internal/external communication programs to ensure certain aspects of the benefits programs are perceived by current and would-be employees as truly distinctive and compelling.
- Realign the current performance evaluation process to make it more than an annual event and ensure that performance feedback and development conversations are a part of the fabric of how the organization operates.

While each organization's actions and investments will vary widely according to their business strategy, industry, and current culture, one thing is clear: High-performing organizations do not rest once they have firmly engrained their desired EVE into their culture. They use this foundation to gain further insight, increase organizational performance, and improve competitive impact.

Beyond the One-Sided EVP

The EVE is a dynamic framework against which to diagnose, implement, and communicate a mutually beneficial relationship between an employer and its employees. The EVE represents a better approach than the typical employee-focused value proposition because it clearly communicates what the company expects of employees in areas that can drive performance and what employees will receive in return for their dedication and hard work. Creating and maintaining an organizational culture that can sustain the needed expectations-to-rewards ratio is essential for all companies that want to achieve superior performance. While some organizations will likely lack the management courage to raise the bar on both their employees' performance levels and the rewards they receive, those that do will put themselves on the road to high performance.

References

Rousseau, D. M. 1989. Psychological and implied contracts in organizations. *Employee Responsibilities and Rights Journal* 2:121–139.

Shore, L. M., and K. Barksdale. 1998. Examining degree of balance and level of obligation in the employment relationship: A social exchange approach." *Journal of Organizational Behavior* 19:731–744.

Heger, B. (2007). "Linking the Employee Value Proposition (EVP) to Employee Engagement and Business Outcomes: Preliminary Findings from a Linkage Research Pilot Study." *Organizational Development Journal* 25, volume 2. 121–131.

Chapter 11

Integrating Succession Planning and Career Planning

William J. Rothwell, Ph.D., SPHR
Professor of Workforce Education and Development
Department of Learning and Performance Systems, College of Education
The Pennsylvania State University, University Park

A S THIS CHAPTER GOES TO PRESS, THE U.S. ECONOMY REMAINS IN THE THROES OF WHAT some economists call the worst downturn since the Great Depression. Unemployment rates are nominally around 10 percent, though experts note that the official unemployment rate does not include discouraged workers who have given up on finding jobs, the underemployed, and those who are working part-time. The college graduates of 2010 face the toughest job market in many years (Yousuf 2009). Despite the economy, "young people are more optimistic about the future, with 38 percent of 18 to 24 year-old workers feeling more positive about their career. . . . For the over 55s who work, the figure is 15 percent" (Woods 2009).

Despite these broad labor market issues, succession planning and career planning remain topics of keen interest to many senior executives (Paton 2008). Years of downsizing, coupled with the expected retirements of the baby boomers, have some far-sighted executives worried about who will replace today's generation of aging leaders. Despite high unemployment, many organizations are implementing programs to get ahead of an expected uptick in retirements in the future. These programs can be called variously succession planning, leadership development, talent management, or career planning.

How can leaders understand the specialized nomenclature associated with succession planning and related fields? What reasons account for growing interest in them?

What best practices are evident in succession planning and career planning programs? Why and how can such programs be integrated? This chapter addresses these questions.

Defining Special Terms

It is easy for managers and workers alike to grow confused over a dizzying array of special terms used in the succession planning, career planning, and related fields. It thus makes sense to begin this discussion with a few choice definitions to clarify these terms:

- *Replacement planning* is the process of identifying emergency backups for key people or key positions. When individuals are listed on replacement charts, they are not guaranteed promotions; rather, they are identified to serve in an acting capacity long enough for an organization's leaders to conduct a proper search, from inside and outside the organization, to find a qualified candidate.
- *Succession planning* is the process of developing the talent already existing in the organization for future deployment.
- *Succession management* is the daily process of cultivating future talent through coaching, mentoring, feedback, counseling, and development.
- *Career planning* is the process individuals go through to clarify their future career goals and aspirations and establish strategies to achieve them.
- *Career management* is the process organizations go through to clarify the relationships of jobs to each other.
- *Talent management* is the process of attracting, developing, retaining, and deploying the best people.
- *Human capital management* involves managing the organization's people, but it also implies the growing financial importance of the creativity and innovation that human beings bring to achieving and sustaining competitive advantage for their employers.
- *Workforce planning* is the process of comparing the match between the collective talents available to an organization (supply) and the talents needed by the organization (demand) to achieve its strategic objectives.

Note that some conceptual overlap exists among these terms. It is this overlap that sometimes confuses leaders.

Reasons for Growing Interest in Succession Planning and Career Planning

Over the next 20 years, about 10,000 people per day in the United States are expected to reach retirement age (Drenner 2008). That works out to about 416 people per hour, or 2.5 per minute. These people are typically called the baby boom generation, defined as those born between 1946 and 1964 and numbering about 76 million people. While often associated with western nations, the United States, the United Kingdom,

Canada, and Australia, baby booms also existed in other countries involved in World War II, namely, Russia, China, Germany, Italy, and France. Taken together, they represent the largest employed group in the world today, and their pending departure from the workforce poses dramatic challenges for many nations.

Another reason that prompts business leaders to consider succession planning programs is that the threat of terrorist attacks has left many wondering how well equipped their organizations would be if terrorists succeeded in destroying a corporate headquarters or the city in which the headquarters is located. How well prepared are businesses and government agencies to survive after a strike that could conceivably wipe out a corporate headquarters or even a city? Good information on that question is not readily available. But some contend that 67 percent of organizations do not have a systematic approach to succession (Cutting Edge Information cited in "Succession Planning: Current Trends," 2006).

Nor is terrorism the only threat facing today's modern, globalized companies. Kidnappings of executives, managers, and even workers are on the rise. Consider this: In Colombia alone, "more than 4 thousand kidnappings occurred and $250 million in ransom payments were collected over the past few years" ("Kidnappings for Ransom on the Rise," no date). In the United States each year, the FBI "investigates 350 to 400 domestic kidnappings, with ransom involved in one-third of the cases" ("Kidnappings for Ransom on the Rise," no date). Suicides have peaked as well, affecting the wealthy and successful as never before due to volatile business changes (Turse 2009). Prudent succession planning requires some attention to the risk of loss of key people due to crime or depression.

While the loss of baby boomers from the workforce is a reality in many organizations that can drive compelling interest in succession planning, the recent financial crisis has many boomers rethinking their retirement plans and careers after retirement. Many of them had their retirement funds invested in a stock market that has proven to be volatile. As authors Johnson, Soto, and Zedlewski (2008, 1) note, "the slumping stock market, falling housing prices, and weakening economy have serious repercussions for the 94 million Americans age 50 and older who are approaching retirement or are already retired. Older Americans have little time to recoup the values of their homes, 401(k) plans, and individual retirement accounts—all important parts of their retirement nest eggs." The result is that many older Americans are postponing their retirements, resigned to working until they are unable to.

Other factors can mitigate the prospective loss of people to retirement. One is downsizing, which can reduce the number of available positions. A second is immigration, which can reduce the number of available openings for all citizens. Consider that "an analysis of Census Bureau data shows that the nation's foreign-born or immigrant population (legal and illegal) reached a new record of more than 35 million in March of 2005. The data also indicate that the first half of this decade has been the highest five-year period of immigration in American history" (Camarota 2005). A third is outsourced offshoring, which can also reduce available positions in the United States and in other high-wage countries. It is nearly impossible to calculate the exact impact of offshoring, but it is clear that both high- and low-wage jobs have been outsourced to lower-cost venues such as China, India, Thailand, Malaysia, and other nations.

Against this backdrop, it is small wonder that many people speculate about the future. Will they be prepared to meet the challenges in their careers? If they are employed, will they have a job tomorrow; if they are unemployed, what it will take for them to find and keep a job.

Why and How Succession Planning and Career Planning Programs Should and Can Be Integrated

Succession planning helps to build the bench strength of the organization to meet future talent needs. Career planning gives individuals the ability to compare their current competencies to those needed for the future. The same model that works for succession planning can also guide career planning (Rothwell et al. 2005). The key difference is *who makes decisions*. In succession planning, the organization's leaders make decisions about future talent needs of the organization and how to develop people in line with those needs. In career planning, individuals make decisions about their future goals and aspirations inside (or outside) the organization. Both programs require clear descriptions of current job duties, competencies, performance requirements, future competency requirements, ways to assess potential for future responsibility, methods of developing talent, and evaluation strategies.

Launching both succession planning and career planning at the same time can help to establish a "what's in it for me" for individuals while helping the organization to build bench strength in line with future talent needs. A particular selling point of doing both is that career planning creates pressure from the bottom up to offset leader complacency in addressing talent needs. While leaders may not be aggressive about preparing their successors because they may wish to "ride it out to retirement with a minimum of fuss and bother," they tend to find that their most talented, aggressive reports may demand proper grooming—or may look for more promising opportunities elsewhere.

Best Practices in Succession Planning and Career Planning Programs

What should be the components of an exemplary succession planning and career planning program? The answer to that question depends on what organizations are benchmarked, of course, and some variations do exist by industry, by national cultural context, and by organizational size. But it is safe to say that most best-practice organizations do use a strategic model or roadmap to integrate the program components of succession planning and career planning. An example of such a model or roadmap is depicted in Figure 11-1. The model is described in the section that follows.

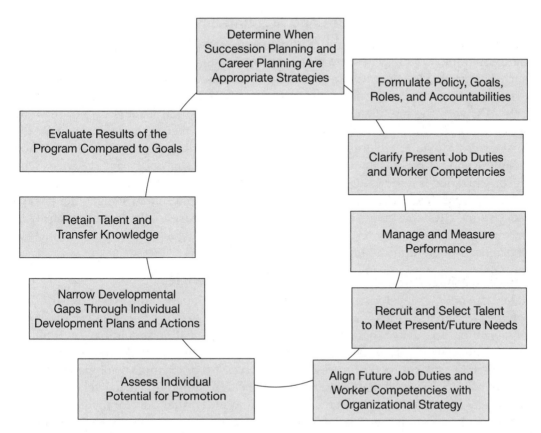

Figure 11-1 A Model for Integrating Succession Planning and Career Planning

Determine When Succession Planning and Career Planning Are Appropriate Strategies

It is worth emphasizing that neither succession planning nor career planning is a panacea. Managers sometimes request succession planning programs when they are worried about the loss of experienced staff. While succession planning can help to focus attention on the systematic development of internal staff, it is not a one-stop strategy for all talent issues. Organizational leaders are better advised to ask the question "How can the work be organized and accomplished best?" In short, there are many alternatives to internally developing talent. They include changing how the work is done by relying on temporary or contingent workers, outsourcing the work, changing the responsibilities of leaders or workers, simplifying the work, and many other such approaches (Rothwell 2005). Succession planning and career planning are components of, but not substitutes for, comprehensive work and workforce planning.

Formulate Policy, Goals, Roles, and Accountabilities

Inexperienced people who set out to implement succession planning and career planning programs too often assume that executives are of one mind on why they want such programs. However, that is usually not the case. A major reason is that senior executives wear two hats: one as leaders of their own units and another as team members to govern the organization. It sometimes happens that leaders do not separate these responsibilities, thinking only of what is good for their units rather than for the business as a whole. For this reason, an excellent starting point for any succession planning and/or career planning program is to write a clear policy that describes why the organization is undertaking the programs, what specific measurable goals are to be achieved from them, what roles should be expected from different stakeholder groups (such as the HR department, senior leaders), and how stakeholder groups will be held accountable for achieving results in line with measurable goals. An important aim is to crystallize leadership thinking.

Clarify Present Job Duties and Worker Competencies

Talent can only be developed when it is clear what work people are expected to do and what characteristics are apparent and desirable in the existing talent inventory of the organization. To clarify what work people do, the organization should have current job descriptions. To clarify what kind of people should do the work, the organization should clarify the competencies essential to successful or exemplary job performance. It is, of course, assumed that the core competencies required for each level of management may be related but different. To determine individual development needs, the organization's leaders need some objective way to assess individual promotability against the requirements at higher levels.

Manage and Measure Performance

A performance management system is essential to hold people accountable for what their job descriptions, and the competency models at their current levels of responsibility, require. The best performance management systems measure individuals on results (outcomes) and behaviors (linked to required competencies). In view of recent scandals, some organizations are also experimenting with measuring people on how well they behave ethically when compared to the requirements of the organization's code of conduct and on how well they behave compared to the organization's stated values.

A performance management system is essential to ensure that people who are eligible for promotion are at least performing their current jobs in a satisfactory manner. After all, nothing destroys the credibility of a promotion system more than promoting those who are failures at their current work. But, by the same token, outstanding performance at one level is no guarantee that individuals can meet the challenges at higher levels of responsibility. As a consequence, an effective performance management system is necessary to give people feedback on their current performance but is not robust enough by itself to measure potential for promotion.

Recruit and Select Talent to Meet Present/Future Needs

An organization cannot always rely on internally developing talent as the sole means by which to find the right people for the right work at the right times. For this reason, recruiting and selecting talent from inside and outside the organization is also necessary. Job posting, a common method of sourcing internal talent, should be aligned with the succession and career planning programs of the organization by ensuring that the same criteria are used to recruit and select people inside and outside the organization. At the same time, the organization should use a range of approaches to recruit and select people from outside.

Align Future Job Duties and Worker Competencies with Organizational Strategy

Neither job duties nor competencies are static. Both will change to accommodate efforts to execute business strategy. It can be argued that one reason so many strategic plans fail is that they do not sufficiently articulate the results/behavior requirements at all levels and in all departments to implement those plans. For that reason, both job descriptions and competency models should be reconsidered in light of what work and workers will be needed over time to implement strategy. Of course, it also takes time to develop people. While many organizations attempt to use acceleration pools or other methods by which to expedite talent development, it must be clear what people will do and what kind of people will be needed in the future to implement the organization's strategy successfully. Such information must also be communicated to workers so that they have sufficient information to plan career goals and initiate their own career-enhancing strategies.

Assess Individual Potential for Promotion

It is not enough for an organization to have a workable performance management system if the goal is to assess individuals objectively for possible promotion. After all, success at one level, or in one's current job, does not guarantee success at higher levels. To believe otherwise is to fall prey to the so-called *Peter Principle* (Peter and Hull 1969), which states that people are rewarded for their success with promotions and continue receiving them until they reach a level where they fail to live up to the requirements. They are then plateaued at their level of incompetence.

Organizational leaders are well advised to try *a combination of assessment methods* to explore possible promotability (sometimes called by the vague term "potential"). In doing so, one factor to consider is the required future work and competencies needed to implement the organization's strategy.

Many approaches can be used to assess potential for promotion to the next level or beyond. Among them (Rothwell in press):

- *Global manager ratings*. Managers rate the promotability of individuals on special forms or on performance reviews.

- *Manager ratings with criteria.* Managers are invited to rate the promotability of individuals against the competencies and behaviors required at higher levels on the organization chart.
- *360-degree assessments.* Individuals are rated by a superior, peers, and subordinates on competencies and behaviors required at higher levels of responsibility.
- *Assessment centers.* Individuals are subjected to simulated challenges like those faced at higher levels of responsibility and are rated by trained people at or above the targeted levels.
- *Psychological tests.* Individuals are rated using robust, five-factor personality tests.
- *Portfolio assessment.* Individuals are invited to supply work samples like those prepared at higher levels of responsibility, and the samples are "graded" against measurable standards prepared in advance.
- *Step-up assignments.* Workers are invited to assume responsibility for a duty normally carried out by a superior; the workers are then coached and rated by that superior.
- *Internal or external rotations.* Workers are rotated temporarily to see how they could perform at a higher level of responsibility. Rotations may be inside the organization or else to nonprofit or community organizations. Ratings are used to assess potential.
- *Realistic job previews.* The immediate reports of supervisors are invited to rotate into the job of their boss while he or she is on vacation or out sick. A review is performed upon the boss's return to assess how well the worker performed the job and to pinpoint areas needed for future development.

Of course, culture does play a part in deciding how to evaluate promotability or potential. In some developing economies, for instance, an individual's status and perceived promotability hinges not on individual performance but on family relationships or political affiliations.

Narrow Developmental Gaps through Individual Development Plans and Actions

A *development gap* exists when individuals are objectively rated against the work expectations and competencies/behaviors necessary for higher-level responsibility. To narrow these gaps, many organizations use Individual Development Plans (IDPs) to pinpoint developmental strategies to close the gaps. While sending people for training often occurs to managers first, the reality is that most development occurs on the job and results from the work experiences to which individuals are exposed. For that reason, managers play a critical daily (sometimes called *tactical*) role in cultivating the organization's talent (Rothwell 2010). IDPs help narrow developmental gaps, providing a basis for accountability of managers and workers.

Retain Talent and Transfer Knowledge

Effective programs address both the retention of talent and transfer of knowledge. Talent retention is often the least developed of succession or talent management strategy. While the reasons for that may be debated, the reality is that few organizations do as much as they could to retain talent. HR practitioners sometimes feel that it is the operating manager's responsibility to retain the best people, while operating managers sometimes blame HR for not maintaining competitive pay rates or monitoring working conditions that may prompt the best workers to leave. As many as 100 research-based best practices exist to retain talent (Rothwell 2007a).

Knowledge transfer, sometimes called *technical succession planning* (see Rothwell and Poduch 2004), focuses on retaining institutional memory and proprietary knowledge that can be lost when experienced workers depart organizations for retirement or for other reasons. It is technical because it centers on issues unique to the organization. Institutional memory means what the members of an organization have learned from experience as a direct consequence of living through experiences and participating in decision making. Proprietary knowledge stems from the lessons gained from experience that are unique to serving the organization's customers or building the organization's products. While some people regard the issue as an element of knowledge management, the fact remains that "what people have learned from their experience" is not always easily recorded or transferred. While computer-assisted knowledge management systems can help, they are not the only ways that knowledge can be transferred. Effective succession planning programs include knowledge transfer and guiding individuals to mentors who can help with knowledge transfer. Mentors can also be helpful in transferring professional contacts, an issue sometimes called social relationship succession planning (Rothwell 2007b).

Evaluate Program Results Compared to Goals

It is common for many managers to ask "What is the return on investment from succession planning or career planning programs?" Better questions are "What measurable results did the organization set out to attain based on business needs?" and "How did the outcomes match the targets?" For instance, one concern of business leaders is meeting the needs resulting from pending retirements (in Western countries) or from explosive business growth (in Eastern countries). A second concern is the time it takes to fill positions, which can be measured by the so-called *time-to-fill metric* (the elapsed time between the posting of a position and the first day that a successful applicant arrives on the job). A third concern is the quality of the match between posted requirements and the qualifications of the successful applicant. In short, the goals established for the programs should be measurable. It is then easy to monitor results. But if leaders are unclear about what results they want, it will be difficult to show results when the time comes.

Organizations need both strategic and tactical models to guide the integration of succession planning and career planning programs. Strategic models focus on the "big picture," while tactical models guide managers on what they should do every day to cultivate talent while also getting the work out. Use the rating sheet in Figure 11-2 to compare your organization against best practices in integrating succession planning and career planning programs.

Directions: Use this rating sheet to compare your organization against best practices in integrating succession planning and career planning programs. For each item listed in the left column below, rate your organization in the right column. Use the following scale for your rating: 1 = **Not effective**; 2 = **Somewhat effective**; 3 = **Effective**; 4 = **Very effective**. When you are finished with your rating, add up the scores in the right column and interpret the scores according to the guidelines below.

How well has your organization integrated succession planning and career planning by:	Rating			
	Not effective	**Somewhat effective**	**Effective**	**Very effective**
	1	2	3	4
1 Determining when succession planning and career planning are appropriate strategies	1	2	3	4
2 Formulating program policies	1	2	3	4
3 Formulating measurable program goals	1	2	3	4
4 Formulating roles of key program stakeholders	1	2	3	4
5 Formulating accountabilities of all stakeholders	1	2	3	4
6 Clarifying present job duties	1	2	3	4
7 Clarifying present worker competencies	1	2	3	4
8 Managing present work performance	1	2	3	4
9 Measuring present work performance	1	2	3	4
10 Recruiting/selecting talent to meet present needs	1	2	3	4
11 Recruiting/selecting talent to meet future needs	1	2	3	4
12 Aligning future job duties with organizational strategy	1	2	3	4
13 Aligning future worker competencies with organizational strategy	1	2	3	4
14 Assessing individual potential for promotion	1	2	3	4
15 Narrowing developmental gaps through individual development plans and actions	1	2	3	4
16 Retaining talent	1	2	3	4
17 Transferring knowledge	1	2	3	4
18 Evaluating program results compared to goals	1	2	3	4
Total (*Add up the scores in the right column and place the sum in the box at right*)				

Figure 11-2 A Rating Sheet for Comparing an Organization Against Best Practices in Integrating Succession Planning and Career Planning Programs (continued on next page)

Scores	
72–55	Congratulations. Your organization is closely aligned to best practice.
54–37	Your organization is on the right path. Focus attention on improving items with lower scores.
36–19	Your organization is far from best practice. Consider improvements.
18	Your organization is far below average. Take steps to improve your organization's commitment to preparing bench strength.

Figure 11-2 A Rating Sheet for Comparing an Organization Against Best Practices in Integrating Succession Planning and Career Planning Programs (continued)

References

Camarota, S. 2005. Immigrants at mid-decade a snapshot of America's foreign-born population in 2005. Retrieved January 19, 2010, from http://www.cis.org/articles/2005/back1405.html.

Carafano, J. 2007. U.S. thwarts 19 terrorist attacks against America since 9/11. (November 13). Retrieved January 19, 2010, from http://www.heritage.org/Research/HomelandDefense/bg2085.cfm.

Despite competitive labor market, one-in-five workers plan to change jobs in 2010, new careerbuilder survey reveals. (2010, January 7). Retrieved January 19, 2010, from http://www.prnewswire.com/news-releases/despite-competitive-labor-market-one-in-five-workers-plan-to-change-jobs-in-2010-new-careerbuilder-survey-reveals–80890002.html.

Drenner, D. 2008. First baby boomer receives 1st Social Security payment. (February 15). Retrieved January 19, 2010, from http://www.usatoday.com/money/perfi/retirement/2008–02–12-boomer-social-security_N.htm?loc=interstitialskip&POE=click-refer.

Johnson, R., M. Soto, and S. Zedlewski. 2008. How is the economic turmoil affecting older Americans? (October). Retrieved January 19, 2010, from http://www.urban.org/UploadedPDF/411765_economic_turmoil.pdf.

Kidnappings for ransom on the rise. nd. Retrieved January 19, 2010, from http://didyouknow.org/info/kidnappings.htm.

Paton, N. 2008. CEOs passing the buck on talent management. (March 5). Retrieved January 20, 2010, from http://www.management-issues.com/2008/3/5/research/ceos-passing-the-buck-on-talent-management.asp.

Peter, L., and R. Hull. 1969. *The Peter Principle: Why things always go wrong.* New York: William Morrow.

Rothwell, W. 2005. *Effective succession planning: Ensuring leadership continuity and building talent from within.* 3rd ed. New York: Amacom.

———. 2007a. Organization retention assessment. In *The 2007 Pfeiffer annual: Consulting.* E. Beich (ed.). San Francisco: Pfeiffer, 177–188.

———. 2007b. Social relationship succession planning: A neglected but important issue? *Asian Quality* 2(4):34–36.

———. 2010. *The manager's guide to maximizing employee potential.* New York: Amacom.

———. In press. *Effective succession planning: Ensuring leadership continuity and building talent from within.* 4th ed. New York: Amacom.

Rothwell, W., R. Jackson, S. Knight, J. Lindholm, J. et al. 2005. *Career planning and succession management: Developing your organization's talent—for today and tomorrow.* Westport, CT: Greenwood Press.

Rothwell, W., and S. Poduch. 2004. Introducing technical (not managerial) succession planning. *Public Personnel Management* 33(4):405–420.

Succession planning: Current trends. 2006. Retrieved January 19, 2010, from http://www.insala.com/Articles/succession-planning/succession-planning-current-trends.asp.

Turse, N. 2009. The financial crisis is driving hordes of Americans to suicide. (January 29). Retrieved January 19, 2010, from http://www.alternet.org/workplace/123563/the_financial_crisis_is_driving_hordes_of_americans_to_suicide/?page=entire.

Woods, D. 2009. Employees feel less optimistic about job prospects in 2010 than they did for 2009. (December 7). Retrieved January 21, 2010, from http://www.hrmagazine.co.uk/news/972341/Employees-feel-less-optimistic-job-prospects–2010–2009.

World faces escalation of terrorist attacks since 9/11: analysts. (2006, September 11). Retrieved January 19, 2010, from http://english.people.com.cn/200609/11/eng20060911_301712.html.

Yousuf, H. 2009. Job outlook for 2010 grads: Still stinks. Retrieved January 20, 2010, from http://money.cnn.com/2009/11/17/news/economy/college_graduates_jobs/.

Chapter 12

Determining Every Employee's Potential for Growth

Murray M. Dalziel, Ph.D., Professor of Management and Director
University of Liverpool Management School

GROWING EMPLOYEES AND DEVELOPING A CULTURE OF SUCCESS GO TOGETHER. As organizations grow, they often need more people, new skills, and different perspectives. This generates a dynamism that fuels growth. But depending on outside hires for your next growth spurt is fraught with danger. This tactic produces great headlines for sports teams but does little for business.

Consider the CEO, most popular role that companies feel compelled to hire from the outside. There is evidence that *insiders* produce superior returns to outsiders. In an extensive time series analysis of corporate performance of all U.S. public firms from 1985 to 2005, James Ang and Gregory Nagel demonstrate that not only do inside hires produce consistently better performance when all factors are taken into consideration but outside hires were more likely to detract from performance (2009). In view of these results, boards should be forced to show why they have a need to go external. Of course, many companies need to find outsiders because they have failed to grow their internal leadership .

How do you determine every employee's capability for growth? In this chapter we will start with the key ingredient: learning agility. Focusing on this ingredient will enable a company to be successful in a wide variety of situations. However, this will not be enough to predict who can lead the company in the future and therefore who should be developed to take on leadership roles. Combining these elements in the company's leadership development strategy will increase the odds for success.

In this chapter we will address three key propositions:

a) All employees should display "learning agility."
b) Employees with potential to grow start displaying this trait quite early in their career, but you need to look carefully for signs of learning agility, since these indicators are not always correlated with performance.
c) Successful leaders do not have to be perfect, but they do need a balance of attributes at the right level across three critical areas: deciding an agenda, taking others with them, and leadership presentation.

How Organizations Typically Spotted Talent in the Past

In the past, where structures, strategies, and even markets were relatively static, leadership was less complex. One model for leadership was all most organizations needed. Those who fit the model were groomed over years—in the days when employees stayed with one organization for their entire career—and eventually were moved into leadership roles

Today, the days of a single leadership model are gone. Even within a company, a variety of leadership models are needed and those models are constantly evolving. To add to the complexity, today's organizational leaders must hit the ground running and immediately produce results.

Why Every Employee Needs to Show Capacity for Growth

Consider Alison, an HR director of a large publishing and media company. With a new CEO and a bright young executive team, she is sure they have the talent to lead the company through a tumultuous time when their publishing models are rapidly becoming obsolete. The management team established business units for each new product introduction, with each unit responsible for developing plans. Alison worries whether the employees can grow into this challenge. She recognizes that to be successful, she depends on the ability of people throughout the organization to adapt to different scenarios but also to take the initiative for optimal success.

A useful concept for Alison and her organization is *learning agility*. Employees with learning agility are more likely to be successful and to adapt to change. The concept and associated measures developed by Eichinger, Lombardo, and colleagues focuses on four areas where employees need to be adaptable (2004):

- *People agility*. People who know themselves well and respond positively and resiliently to pressure around them
- *Results agility*. People who get results under tough conditions and inspire others to do likewise
- *Mental agility*. People who can think afresh about ideas and are comfortable explaining complex, often ambiguous notions

- *Change agility.* People who are curious and like to build and experiment with new cases as well as constantly strive to develop themselves

These factors are shown to be independent from either personality or IQ measures but have greater predictive power as to who will be successful. These will help predict who will grow within the organization.

Learning agility alone will not predict who will have the capability to perform the critical leadership roles in the future. What makes executive leadership different? There are at least three areas that need to be considered:

- The time horizon of executive decisions is often significantly longer than in other roles. A salesperson is expected to choose the right customers to call on depending on the current product line, but executives need to decide the product, segment, pricing, and a host of other factors that will last for some period of time.
- The impact of executive decisions is normally broader. The sales manager will affect his or her salespeople in a particular territory. Senior executive decisions will cross territories and divisions.
- The context in which executives make decisions is more complex with the solutions less obvious or well known. A plant manager may improve working practices through introducing innovative productivity improvements. The plant has to produce a given product, and the problems are defined. Positioning a company causes executives to face a good deal more uncertainty.

Spotting Talent Early

Because executive leadership has dramatically different demands than managerial or professional leadership, it is more difficult yet essential to spot talent early. Consider George, CEO of a mega health-care company. Although the company had achieved renown through mergers and great products, it lacked the high-potential managers required to move to the next level. "Frankly, I'm not as concerned about the next 24 months," George confided to his senior team. "It's who has the potential for our growth. I wonder how our brightest team leaders and our best product managers will fare when they're running the new companies we will create. I wish I had a crystal ball."

We will provide George with his crystal ball. Spotting future potential involves answering two questions: At what level can the person operate? Do they have the right combination of competencies to make them successful in future roles?

A useful way to obtain clues about what level a person is able to operate is to think about the essence of a job. At the heart of all jobs are a set of problems and a scope. But people also make jobs different. People redefine the problems they encounter in their role. Problems are redefined more broadly and innovatively by high potential talent. How people define problems and the scope present clues to the level at which a person can operate. Look specifically at the scope of three areas: management, problem solving, and impact.

The scope of management refers to whether the person manages strictly within a self-contained team or across a wider scale. Here, looking beyond the prescribed or stated role is required since frequently high-potentials move beyond that standard. Consider, for example, two regional sales managers in the same technology firm. Manager A leads ten sales managers. He is very active in his territory and has built a high-performing sales team. Manager B also leads a high-performing team of ten. But unlike his counterpart, she is in continual contact with regional sales managers in different territories, exchanging ideas and practices. Manager B is aware of what is going on in corporate marketing and understands how she can influence and use it to her advantage. In short, Manager B has broadened her scope so that she does not drive a defined business in a bounded business unit, but works across boundaries to better understand and react to the implications of potential broader decisions. Regional Sales Manager A does what the role prescribes. He solves problems that are required for his people to perform their role, using a prescribed body of knowledge. There is little originality and creativity in his approach, but he meets his objectives. Regional Sales Manager B also follows the prescribed body of knowledge, but also demonstrates originality and creativity. She is continually expanding the body of knowledge for future sales managers.

The scope of impact of these regional sales managers varies. Manager A impacts his team and their goals. His decisions will have a relatively short effect in terms of scope and time. Manager B impacts her team, and, in addition, she makes decisions that impact the wider organization and are longer lasting.

There may be a potential downside to operating beyond what the role requires. It may impact day-to-day performance but more often leads to frustration as the person tries to work beyond set parameters but often sees him- or herself blocked.

Successful Leaders are not Perfect but they Do Need to Display Attributes in Each of the Critical Areas

Paul, CEO of his family's fast-growing company, had once again been reminded by his board that even though he was in his early 40s, the day would come that he would have to pass the reigns to a new leader. Paul had little idea how to select his replacement. Of course, there were family members who could take over. But did they have what it takes to lead the firm? Paul also would like a crystal ball.

Of course, there is no single magic solution that will help Paul and other senior executives predict with absolute accuracy the leaders of the future. Three proven areas for identifying possible leaders and ascertaining whether they have the right leadership attributes exist: How a person thinks, how a person works with other people, and how resilient they are.

While the characteristics that enable people to perform well in these arenas are not tangible, they can be identified and, over time, developed or modified. It is evident that many popular methods for assessing leadership potential have their limits. Some fall into the Peter Principle trap, others fail to take into account major shifts in leadership scope, and others overlook possible candidates. Add to these that no one, including leaders and potential leaders, is perfect, and it is understandable why executives go begging for some magical answer—and why we recommend not one but three crystal balls. The good news is that potential great leaders don't have to be perfect. They don't even have to meet a lengthy laundry list of characteristics or competencies that form the preferred leadership model in many organizations.

Our research into competencies shows that the best predictors of leadership success are a handful of key competencies that, in various combinations, frequently lead to outstanding performance. The three crystal balls address these key characteristics by answering three questions that are important no matter what assessment process or rating system is used. Ball 1 asks: "How does this individual set his or her business agenda?" Ball 2 asks: "How do they take others with them?" Ball 3 queries: "How do they present themselves as leaders?"

Crystal Ball 1: How do High Potential Leaders Set Their Business Agenda?

To examine the first crystal ball, let's look at how two very different leaders, Anna and Tony, set their agendas. Anna, the marketing manager of a fast-paced consumer goods company, is frustrated. Her mission of launching the company's global brands in the Eastern European country to which she recently moved has been effectively thwarted by a large competitor who has launched an intensive campaign that dwarfs the efforts of Anna's predecessors. "There has to be a better way," she thinks. She notices cases of milk cartons being delivered to the apartment complexes in her neighborhood. Unlike milk cartons in major Western cities, these have little print on them. This led to a revelation for getting her company's message across every morning to millions of consumers by persuading the cooperatives that distribute milk to allow their cartons to become advertising space.

Tony is also a creative business developer who spots potential product ideas for his global health-care company and negotiates licensing arrangements. He is intrigued with science but is certainly no researcher. Rather, he enjoys matching his scientific knowledge with know-how about customers, markets, and trends. He has an uncanny way of seeing product possibilities that others have overlooked. "What I enjoy," he says, "is seeing how things come together after I talk with physicians, read the latest research reports, and discuss trends with my team."

When we look into our first crystal ball, we find both Anna and Tony have potential. What to look for here is where people get their ideas, their direction, the reasons that they want to act as a leader. Anna and Tony represent two basic thrusts that predict how high-potential leaders set their agendas. Tony primarily uses intellectual reasoning, while Anna's decisions spring from a deep motivation to achieve, improve, or excel. Of course, Anna must think through her ideas, but the source of decision making comes from a feeling that there is a better way. Tony also thinks about finding a better way. But his primary motivation comes from a fascination with ideas. Some leaders will drive their agendas from both these sources, although either one will predict potential. Intellectual reasoning is seldom about pure logical thought. Instead, it is usually demonstrated in behaviors such as Tony exhibits: perceiving possibilities, quickly grasping complex concepts, and seeing their implications.

Achievement motivation arises from a deep need to improve and to exceed standards of excellence. In leaders we often see this as a driving force that comes from the "gut" rather than intellect.

While either intellectual reasoning or achievement motivation can come into play when setting the agenda, they only become predictors of performance when they are deployed at certain levels. High-potentials using intellectual reasoning, for example, should be able to simplify complexity to the point of forming new concepts that lead people in a compelling way.

Achievement in high-potentials should be motivated by a driving need for making improvements or exceeding standards of excellence that is channeled into forming larger business concepts. People operating at this level start to look at the cost-benefits of moving in different directions, for example. They also channel their dissatisfaction or desire to exceed standards into real business projects, and they persist in these efforts no matter what the obstacle. The presence of these two drivers of agenda at lower levels may predict raw capability in this area, but not potential.

A lack of either of these drivers to create an agenda should raise a red flag. Consider, for example, the person who develops an agenda to impress rather than for results. Such individuals sometimes go far on the basis of the impressions they initially create. Eventually however, when results fail to materialize, they will fall.

Crystal Ball 2: How do high potential leaders take others with them?

Here, too, Anna and Tony are quite different but equally effective. Anna is a very persuasive individual but uses a thoughtful, low-key manner to influence groups, especially those outside her usual scope of leadership. As one of her subordinates states, "She is not charismatic, but she is determined. There is no mistaking what she wants, but she does this in a way that makes you feel good working for her. You feel she hears you and respects you and she also trusts you to get it done."

Tony, on the other hand, is seen as very charismatic. As one of his direct reports remarks, "He knows how to get a team going. We work together well because he is very clear about what he wants. He also enjoys the big stage and can be very persuasive with large groups. People in the industry know him and respect him."

As in setting an agenda, there are a number of approaches to gaining support that are equally effective. Some leaders are very empowering with individuals, others with their team, and others at forming influence agendas across a whole organization. These influence strategies are often fueled by empathy for others. Empathy grows into political or organizational smarts, commonly referred to as organizational awareness. At the heart of both of these attributes is the pleasure some people gain from having a positive impact on people and organizations.

One or both of these characteristics is necessary to predict potential. As with the agenda, it is the level at which leaders deploy their skills that is critical to assessing their potential. While most leaders can be personally persuasive, the higher you rise, the less time you have to personally persuade. Strategizing how you influence others indirectly or how your presence might spread through an organization reflects a higher level of both empathy and organizational awareness, and consequently, higher leadership potential.

Crystal Ball 3: How do High Potential Leaders Present Themselves as Leaders?

Three important attributes should be sought in high-potential leaders. The first is self-confidence and self-awareness. Are they willing to take on challenges to achieve goals? Are they aware of their strengths and weaknesses in getting there? Anna, for example, is on assignment in an Eastern European capital because she wanted the challenge of establishing programs in an environment where the art of marketing was less developed than in her home territory. She thrives on the challenge even though the obstacles are great.

The second attribute is an ability to objectively assess the strengths and weaknesses of others. These leaders avoid snap judgments by thinking through the issues and not immediately reacting. Tony is good at selecting people to work for him because he does not rush to judgment. Instead, he takes the time to develop a sense for their strengths and weaknesses and how others will complement him and his team.

The third attribute is the emotional fortitude to deal with high-pressure situations in an even-handed way. Anna, for example, works long hours but is careful not to allow her frustrations with her new environment get the best of her. She often takes quick breaks from work to revitalize herself. The key here is balance and consistency. High-potential leaders need at least two out of three of these attributes to contribute in consistent, positive ways that help drive performance.

Potential leaders with higher levels of these characteristics integrate them into their persona. Self-confidence, for example, expresses itself not in the challenges that a leader takes on but rather in the intuitive self-confidence they express in the face of a tough decision. Over time they know themselves better and integrate better judgment into their behavior. They see situations more objectively and, despite the pace and the pressure, exhibit resilience in tough situations.

Some Methods Companies Are Using To Select Their Leaders

Using the following methods enhances what organizations typically do to select their leaders. One common method that can be dangerous is past performance. Up to a point, it's valid. One has only to look at business headlines to see a "rogue's gallery" of failed business rock stars, individuals who rose to greatness, only to be dethroned as their market, their company, or the scope of their role shifted.

A critical issue for companies is to determine how far into the future to look. A company adopts a predictive process based on one successful in other organizations. Each year as employees are reviewed, their manager's manager is asked to rate how far each of the people in their business unit can move. "High potential" applies to people able to move a position two levels above their present position in less than 36 months, "promising" people are those who could take a position two levels above their own in 36 to 60 months, and "promotable" people are those who can move one step but perhaps not further. This enables a good discussion about the person's current level of effectiveness as well as his or her future potential for growth. There is usually a spirited debate over the assessments, since these ratings have to be defended at a company's executive committee session.

The debate in the executive committee often hinges on what it is the person is doing in his or her current role and how it prepares them to successfully move ahead. Comments such as "I really know that Mark can move into a Regional VP role. Look at what he has done in consolidating the two properties we just merged with his and the innovations he has encouraged" are often countered with observations such as, "Yes, but he has not had much exposure to finance and alternative ways of financing acquisitions. Can we help him develop those experiences?"

If the obstacles are too daunting, the person probably doesn't have the potential. If the obstacles can be removed with time and effort, he or she probably has the capability but not yet the potential to contribute at the higher level. Only if the person can overcome the obstacles in a reasonable time frame should they be classified as having potential.

This approach works well when the career paths and role requirements are quite similar. It also works well in organizations where there are multiple interactions across the organization so that members of the management team know people two or three levels from their position. However, it takes a tremendous amount of management time and commitment when the organization is more diverse. Even in a self-contained organization, there are obstacles, since employees tend to be regionally based with little interaction across groups.

Difficulties also exist in using this process in large organizations where the concept of levels varies. Consider the role of regional sales manager in a large pharmaceutical company with both animal health and primary care divisions. Regional sales managers in the flat animal health division may be only two levels away from the divisional CEO. Primary care regional sales managers, on the other hand, could be levels away from their divisional president. While both roles have the same demands, high potential means very different things. To circumvent such confusion, some organizations, such as a global health-care organization, focus only on people who can take on general management roles. Each year, along with reviewing employees' performance, the manager's manager is required to nominate people in their business unit who can take on general manager roles within the next 36 months. At this level, the requirements for leadership can change in general management roles. Often this is the first level where the transition from managerial to executive work becomes apparent.

Decisions must be made on the basis of information from several sources, some of which the general manager will not have adequate experience to make. Also, general managers frequently have to lead a diverse group of people often at a distance. The key question is whether the person can deal with these levels of complexity.

The advantage of these methods is that they involve executives and managers. Having managers understand not only how people perform but what causes them to perform well is a necessary condition for the organization to make good judgments about people and potential. Some organizations rely on external assessments, and, indeed, there are a range of formal methods to build an understanding of the level a person is performing and also the attributes which they demonstrate. But managers would do well not to rely on these in a mechanistic way. These external assessments should be giving them insights into what causes a person to perform. If the manager has doubt or sees some areas of ambiguity, a formal assessment may help to clarify. But as in all managerial judgments the executive has to live with the consequences of their decisions. Being informed is good. Delegating critical judgment is bad management.

Conclusion: Creating Crystal-Clear Assessments

Without resorting to lengthy leadership models and complex assessment processes, the three crystal balls developed through our research of high-performing leaders can give accurate insight into identifying high-potential candidates. By gazing into these globes and selecting leaders who appear in all three orbs, you can increase the probability of leadership success in your organization and take a huge step forward in improving talent management.

References

Ang, James, and Gregory Nagel. 2009. *Inside and outside hired CEOs: A performance surprise.* Financial Management Association Annual Meeting. Reno, Nevada. October.

Eichinger, Robert W., and Michael M. Lombardo. 2004. Learning agility as a prime indicator of potential. *Human Resource Planning* 27:12–15.

Chapter 13

Designing a Succession Planning Program

Doris Sims, SPHR, Founder and President
Succession Builders, LLC

THE BOARD OF DIRECTORS WANTS TO SEE A SUCCESSION PLAN FOR YOUR EXECUTIVE TEAM immediately. A potential client wants to know if the company has a succession plan in place for the leadership team before they agree to a contract with your company. The CFO announces her pending retirement and the VP of recruiting is asking you for a slate of internal successor candidates for this position. The company is planning growth into a new geographic area and the VP of operations is asking for a list of managers who are open to relocation to the new area. The mergers and acquisitions team is asking you for the profiles of the senior leadership team to include in their due diligence documentation. And now you are thinking, "How do I put together a valid succession planning strategy and process?"

With any of the scenarios described above, the good news is that you have at least one motivational force driving the support and accountability you will need as you implement a succession planning strategy. The other good news is that when a succession planning strategy is well planned, it will provide significant value and cost savings to the organization in a short time period. So, what are the five basic steps involved in designing and planning a succession management strategy?

Step One: Identify Your Talent Management Business Goals

Before you can create a valid talent management strategy, determine the one to three primary reasons you are implementing (or updating) a talent and succession management program in the first place, because the way you will design and measure the program will be very different based on your business goals, as shown in Table 13-1.

If Your Key Talent Goal Is...	Your Program Will Focus On...	You Will Want to Monitor...
Identifying and developing executive successors to fill pending retirement positions over the next five years	Developing executive competency models Top-tier succession plans Developing executive high potentials through strategic job rotations, executive mentors and job shadowing, executive coaching, etc. Identifying external candidates proactively if no prepared successors are identified for a critical position	The percentage of leaders who will reach retirement eligibility each year Other vacancy risk factors for the senior leadership team and the retention of executive high potentials The progress of development plan actions and readiness levels of each executive successor
The retention of experts in the organization	Identifying critical positions and experts Implementing a retention program (i.e., stock options, special recognition, etc.) for experts in the organization Ensuring experts develop successors, and provide training and mentoring to others in the organization to pass on their knowledge Ensuring the processes and procedures developed by experts is well documented	The retention rate of experts, and the exit interview information from any experts who do leave the organization The succession plans of experts and the development progress of successors
Developing store managers to prepare for growth and expansion	Obtaining current relocation ability, leadership ability, and career interest levels of store manager successor candidates to potentially fill these growth positions Creating and implementing a store manager development program to prepare multiple candidates for these positions	The percentage of these internal store manager successor candidates who successfully fill the growth positions as they become available The cost savings of filling the store manager positions internally versus externally The retention rate of the store manager successor candidates

Table 13-1 Business Goals and Focuses

To identify and validate your primary succession planning goals, you will want to work with executives, line managers, HR business partners (especially the recruiting and organizational development professionals in the company). To begin planning a successful succession planning strategy, some organizations form a talent steering committee, composed of business leaders and HR professionals, to work together to create the strategy, to monitor the progress of the program, and to provide feedback, review results, and make continuous improvements.

Step Two: Establish Metrics and Baseline Data

It may seem odd to establish metrics as a Step Two phase of the process, but in order to be able to demonstrate the business results and cost savings of your succession planning process, this is the time to identify the metrics to be used and to gather "before" baseline metrics, to create a comparison starting point. Before starting your succession planning process, you will want to gather the following baseline data:

- *What is the current internal fill percentage of open leadership positions?* For example, currently open leadership positions are filled with internal candidates 25 percent of the time and with external candidates 75 percent of the time. You might then set a goal to increase the internal fill of leadership positions by 10 percent over the next 12 months as one of your succession planning metrics.
- *What is the current percentage of leaders who will be eligible to retire each year?* For example, 10 percent of your leaders will reach retirement eligibility in the next 12 months, 5 percent more will be eligible to retire within two years, and 25 percent more will be eligible to retire within three years, then you know the time period to prepare and develop successors, and you can look at the lines of business with the highest retirement eligibility percentages in order to focus efforts in the areas with the highest vacancy risk issues.
- *How much does it cost to replace a leader with an external candidate at the manager level, at the director level, at the vice president level, and at the executive level?* This information is needed to calculate the cost savings to be achieved through your succession planning program.
- *What is the current turnover rate of employees in leadership positions in the organization?* Compare the retention rate of high-potentials, successors, and experts identified through your talent review and succession planning process to the overall retention of leaders across the organization to ensure top talent is retained at the highest possible rate. It is important to obtain this basic measurement to compare retention changes over the coming years as succession plans and high potential development programs are executed.
- *What are our basic leadership statistics?* Gather and document all the basic information about your leadership population, such as the ratio of leaders to employees in each department, in each geographic region, at each organizational level, and so on. This basic information may be needed at a later point in conjunction with one of your other metrics in order to formulate business results and conclusions.

- *What will our leadership staffing needs look like in the next year, in two years, and in three years?* In addition to replacement planning to address vacancy risk issues, a succession management strategy should factor in the leadership staffing changes and/or growth needs expected within the next few years, at minimum.

As part of your metrics and planning process, you will want to interview leaders and work with the recruiting management team to understand the workforce staffing strategy and the leadership competency and position needs for the future of the organization.

Step Three: Develop Your Scope, Criteria, Definitions, and Policies

Formulate at least a three-year plan to define the scope of your succession planning efforts and to define successors and high-potential categories and selection criteria. This action will set appropriate expectations and create a workable plan that fits the most urgent talent and business needs.

Even though it would be ideal to be able to create succession plans for every leader in the organization within the first year, for most companies this type of goal is too large to accomplish successfully. It is more important to implement a smaller scope succession strategy in the first year, allowing sufficient time to develop plan actions for these successors.

A sample three-year plan might look like that in Table 13-2 (depending on the size of your company and the talent management resources, budget, and staff available).

Your Succession Plan Strategy Will Focus On...	
Year One	– Developing your succession planning strategy, processes, tools, definitions, and policies – Identifying metrics and gathering baseline measurements – Communicating the new talent and succession management strategy to the executive team – Identifying successors for all vice presidents and above – Creating development plans for the executive successor candidates – Obtaining feedback from executives to make year two improvements
Year Two	– Updating your succession planning strategy, processes, tools, definitions, and policies based on year one feedback – Calculating and reporting year one metrics compared to baseline data – Communicating the new talent and succession management strategy to the director-level leadership team – Identifying successors for all directors and above through a talent review meeting process – Following through on development plan actions for executive successors

Table 13-2 Three-Year Plan (continued on next page)

Your Succession Plan Strategy Will Focus On...	
	– Creating development plans for director successor candidates
	– Obtain feedback from directors to make Year Three improvements
Year Three	– Updating your succession planning strategy, processes, tools, definitions, and policies based on Year Two feedback
	– Calculating and reporting Year Two metrics compared to baseline data
	– Communicating the new talent and succession management strategy to the entire leadership team
	– Identifying successors for all leaders, and identifying high-potential leaders through the organization through a talent review process
	– Following through on development plan actions for executive and director successors
	– Creating a high-potential development program
	– Obtaining feedback from all leaders to make Year Four improvements

Table 13-2 Three-Year Plan (continued)

Notice how the scope of the succession planning strategy (and the amount of work, budget, and resources involved) increases each year. Many organizations make the mistake of thinking that they can hire one talent management professional to handle the succession planning and leadership development strategy for multiple years. In reality, as successors and high- potentials are identified, more demands are placed on the talent management professional to not only complete talent review and succession planning processes but also work with internal recruiting professionals for internal placement and work with leaders and organizational development professionals to develop the successors and high-potentials. It is important to identify the budget, tools, and people resources needed within the three-year plan to ensure the program continues to be successful and sustainable.

During this phase of the planning process, it is also time to identify the categories of successors by readiness level and/or by leadership level, and creating behavioral definitions for each category to enable leaders to accurately identify successors based on valid performance and potential factors. If high-potentials or experts in the organization will be identified, you will need to create (or purchase) behavior definitions, assessment tools, and criteria for leaders to use as they are nominating individuals for these talent categories.

Documenting and communicating successor categories and definitions also increases the consistency of your processes and provides a fair and legally defensible succession planning strategy. All leaders in the organization will be referring to the same definitions and criteria as they are selecting successors, resulting in the identification of successors and high-potentials that will also be more successful moving across the organization rather than just moving and growing in a silo fashion within one department or division.

Qualified Successor	Employees who currently possess and demonstrate all of the required qualifications for the incumbent's position. This does not mean that a candidate who is ready today for the position has *every* competency of the incumbent leader, but he or she must have the required competencies *and* the potential to obtain the additional preferred competencies for the position.
	To help identify valid qualified successors, ask yourself, "If the position were open today, which employees in the company would be qualified to interview for the position now?"
	In our organization, a qualified successor must also
	– Have completed at least one year of employment with the company.
	– Have an overall annual performance appraisal rating of 4 or 5.
	– Be able to relocate if required for the incumbent's position.

Table 13-3 Behavior Definitions

An example of a successor category with a behavior definition is shown in Table 13-3.

Don't forget during this phase to also discuss and update your internal recruiting policies with business leaders and the recruiting department to help avoid issues and misunderstandings after your first succession planning cycle is complete.

For example, once successors for leadership positions have been identified, will you still post these positions to all employees when they become vacant or will the successors have the first opportunity to interview and fill the positions? To avoid a "cherry-picking" problem where managers start to directly recruit individuals who have been identified as high-potentials, does your current internal recruiting procedure require managers to talk with each other before contacting the internal candidate directly? These are the types of policies you will want to either create or update to align with your new succession planning design.

Step Four: Creating Tools for Assessment and Successor Tracking

During the preparation phase, either create or purchase tools and systems to assist leaders with the talent assessment and successor identification process, and create or purchase tools and systems to store the successor information, along with talent profiles and the development plans for the selected successor candidates. Your decision to create or purchase these tools will depend on your budget, your company size, the complexity of your organization, and the geographic spread of your organization. As another option, you can use either an internal technical team or an external software development designer to create custom tools that specifically meet your needs. Even if assessment and tracking tools consist of basic spreadsheets, you will need to design these tools and determine the best method of delivering the tools (along with instructions and Help information) to the business leaders.

There is the school of thought that you should first create your succession planning design and wait to purchase a talent and succession planning and tracking system to match your design. There is another school of thought that it is much easier to purchase a talent and succession system that already provides much of the structure, tools, and definitions needed for your succession planning design. The right decision for your organization will depend on your budget, previous experience in succession planning, the complexity of your organization, and the urgency level of your succession planning needs.

Step Five: Communicate and Launch! You Cannot Communicate Too Much!

Put together a documented communication plan that includes online tools and information, opportunities for training and presentations for leaders (virtual sessions or in-person meetings), and hardcopy materials as applicable to your culture and needs. A sample communication plan is shown in Table 13-4.

Tools	Objectives	Timeframe
Live Presentations	To provide a time to communicate and train leaders on the strategy, process, and tools. To provide a time for leaders to ask questions and to express any concerns they have about the strategy. To hand out any hardcopy materials, talking points, etc. business leaders need to implement the plan.	All presentations will take place during the month of April. Five "in-person" presentations and two virtual sessions will be provided.
Succession Planning Web Site	To provide one online location for leaders and the HR team to access assessment tools, talent profiles, etc. To create a marketing tool to increase buy-in and understanding of the succession planning strategy, with a URL link that can be easily e-mailed to leaders as the program is updated.	The Web site will be ready by March so the tool can be discussed in the April Live Presentations.
Hardcopy Leader's Guides	To provide a hardcopy Help Guide that includes our definitions, policies, and procedures, to be used as an "on-the-desk" reference tool as the leader is working in the succession planning system. The Guide will include blank succession worksheets for leaders to create draft succession plans before entering a final draft succession plan on the system.	The Leader's Guides will be ready for distribution by March. Extra copies will be provided to the HR team.

Table 13-4 Communication Plan

A common mistake in the succession planning design process is to forget the importance of the communication plan and tools that can result in confusion, inconsistencies, and even suspicion of the succession planning strategy. Allow four to six weeks just to implement your communication and training plans.

Ready to Go!

Now that you have completed a thorough design process, you are ready to implement your strategy and procedures with confidence. Although it may seem a lot of time is spent on the planning process, creating a solid foundation before launching your succession planning program will enhance the reception from business leaders, the consistency of procedures, and the results achieved.

Chapter 14

Practical Discussions for Sweet Success

Kevin D. Wilde, Vice President
Organization Effectiveness and Chief Learning Officer
General Mills

FORMAL TALENT REVIEWS, AN EVENT FOR BRINGING ORDER AND STRUCTURE TO THE informality of talent planning and development, are necessary because sometimes the daily press of business overwhelms the need for well-considered talent decisions. Formal talent reviews offer a timeout periodically to engage line leaders to be more disciplined, to think strategically about talent management, and to apply many of the tools presented in this book.

My 17 years at General Electric taught me the magic of line leaders who see the powerful connection between talent and business results. That same belief in talent—and the same practical approach to managing it—exists at General Mills. At General Mills, our annual, top-level talent review takes place over a period of three days. About 14 people attend, including the CEO and the company's highest-ranking functional executives. The conversations focus on the top 500 positions in the company—mainly officer and director-level jobs. Furthermore, during these discussions, a thousand names might come up as potential or future candidates for those roles.

A few of the questions on the table are likely to include

- What are the talent implications of our long-range plan?

- What is the succession plan for our senior team, and are we happy with it? (For obvious reasons, parts of this conversation do not include the people who attend the main meeting.)
- Who are the highest-potential people in each of our main functions? How do we intend to retain and develop them?

That's a snapshot of a talent review meeting. What makes these reviews work? Here is my cookbook—an eight-part recipe for finding sweet success in conducting talent reviews follows.

Playing Four Dimensional Chess

How do we know who are the thousand or so highest-potential people in our global company? The answer, of course, is that the top-level talent review is not the only such meeting that occurs. Information gathered at other levels "rolls up" to the top.

As a complex game of chess can be played on a multiple-level board, there can be four different types of reviews. Many parts of my recipe apply to all of them. But in setting the agenda for a talent review meeting, it is helpful to consider the nature of the review. The four types are as follows:

Functional reviews where the pipeline of leaders and organization capabilities being considered is limited to a single function, such as manufacturing or finance. While the other types of reviews serve as very useful forums for dialog and planning, I see the functional review as the richest for truly identifying and building talent.

In most cases, functions tend to "own" talent over the longest stretch of time. A high-potential marketing person is more likely to change business units than to change functions (from marketing to manufacturing) over the course of a career. For that and other reasons, functional executives usually are in the best position to see the full pipeline of available talent, identify the important capabilities to be developed, and select the best "stretch" roles.

Geographic reviews where talent is rolled up and analyzed based on location. The most dramatic illustrations are seen in highly diversified global companies where multiple lines of business may sit in one country or region. These reviews usually focus on how to grow talent within the region by moving people into stretch roles in other lines of business. Depending on the degree of enterprise-wide collaboration (the willingness of an executive to "lose" talent to another division), this can be a clever idea or frustrating work.

Business reviews where the talent census is multifunction but single business. Within General Mills' Big G cereals business, there are functions such as manufacturing, marketing, and finance, each with high-potential people. I find business-unit leaders to be very good judges of current performance through a business lens but less able to judge future potential or to determine development needs for people in various specialties. For that, it is wise to give business leaders some input from functional leaders, such as the director of marketing or finance.

Top team review, usually chaired by the CEO, is the meeting that takes a full enterprise-wide view of the top talent in the organization. It looks only at higher-level roles. It takes place after the other types of meetings and uses data rolled up from them.

Regardless of the type of talent review, one caution is to keep the meeting simple. Beware of adding unnecessary complexity. Also, there must be a way to integrate the findings from these various reviews into a coherent picture. One way to do that is to build in a common set of questions to each review. For example, Are we stronger than last year? Did we recruit better? Did we keep the best? Did we accelerate the development of the best? Did we invest sufficiently to position our talent for the challenges of the next five years?

Recognize What Is Set in Motion

Talent review meetings at the functional, geographic, and business-unit levels usually are ordered to take place by the CEO and other senior executives, the people who will attend the final, top team review. As the organizer of that final meeting, you need to recognize that the power of agenda setting at the top of the organization causes either good things or bad things to happen down below.

In my early years as a head of talent development, I fell into two bad habits. One was to add more administrative work to the process than necessary. The other was to surprise the HR generalists with unexpected topics and requests.

Good business decisions are made based on facts and relevant information. Likewise, talent review discussions must be based on accurate, relevant calibrations of people's performance and potential. In other words, you need good data. Information systems have replaced mountains of paper data. Unfortunately, they have not eliminated much of the human effort necessary to input, maintain, and report the online equivalent. Gathering data is necessary, but it can become an onerous, time-consuming chore. Help HR people keep the roll-up meetings as simple, practical, and useful as you would like the top-level meeting to be. If what you want rolled up is 1,000 names of high-potential people, make it clear that you don't want 50,000 names.

Great talent reviews are all about great conversations. Great conversations are enabled by good data.

Get the Time Right

Since information from lower-level talent reviews will roll up to the top, the timing of the top team meeting will determine when everything else has to happen. Getting on the corporate calendar is the first step. The annual talent review meeting should be locked into the corporate calendar alongside the budget meetings, long-range planning events, and high-profile operational reviews.

At General Mills, the talent review occurs in November, soon after the long-range strategic planning is completed but before next year's budget-planning process begins. This provides a number of benefits. The leaders are still in a strategic mind-set coming off their long-range planning work. In fact, the long-range plan becomes one excellent basis for the review, as we ask, "What new people capabilities are needed to make the plan work?" Also, because the leaders will soon switch from a big-picture perspective to tackle the challenge of translating strategy into next year's operating plan, they are ready to consider specific talent actions in the coming 12 to 18 months. So the timing gives us the best of both worlds: People in the meeting are in a mind-set conducive to looking at talent needs through a wide, strategic lens, and also ready to make decisions about specific roles and particular people.

Enable the Influencers

Once the date is set, next comes the memo. This is the notice that announces the meeting and describes what will happen. Behind the memo lies the work of engaging the most senior leader involved in the meeting as sponsor and collaborator. I work hard every year to draw the CEO and other key executives into the planning process to ensure it's *their* meeting and *their* agenda.

Getting engagement starts with a working relationship with the top leader with whom your credibility is already established, and you can work together to design a talent review that furthers his or her priorities. If you don't have that strong a relationship, then slow down and find ways to build one. It also helps to leverage a good connection with a co-sponsor; the senior HR leader is a logical choice in many cases. I've found it useful to consult with the business development team and a few strategic HR managers to glean what is top of mind for the CEO and then go in with a proposal that covers the hot topics.

In a way, the upfront work feels like consultative selling with the influential leader. It requires that you do your homework, find ways to involve the top leader early, and listen hard for the issues that really matter. Of course, doing your homework also means that you bring your own good ideas to the table. But don't fall in love with your own thinking to the detriment of working toward a talent review agenda that the leader can own.

Once the senior leader is fully behind the plan, be sure to make that interest visible to the other team members and the wider organization. The memo that actually should go out is a letter from the CEO detailing the purpose, agenda, and expected outcomes of the top-level talent review and the functional, geographic, or business reviews that will lead up to it. This is often followed by more detailed communication from the senior HR leader covering materials needed, support offered, and so on. But that first letter from the CEO makes a huge difference in signaling the importance of the work.

Finally, if the CEO is really on board with the topics, you should see the interest play out in the meeting. What true engagement looks like depends to some degree on the CEO's style and the culture of senior meetings. But it is eye-opening to see a passionate leader come into a talent review meeting with a ton of questions and a wealth of opinions and ideas. If the CEO takes a lot of notes as well, you won't be the only one who realizes that concrete follow-up actions are going to be expected.

Watch What Happens in the Room

In an ideal world, all the work leading up to the meeting would guarantee a dynamic event, filled with sparkling dialogue that generates brilliant decisions and inspires high levels of commitment to strategic talent development. In the real world, the affair can be as boring and scripted as any meeting in a *Dilbert* cartoon. I have learned never to take the success of an event for granted. I've seen very important meetings derailed by overlooked details or faulty assumptions. So I live by some checklists when orchestrating each year's talent review. Here's a sample of my first checklist, which contains some standard items pertaining to any kind of meeting:

- *Notice to the participants*. Send out the right kind of communication ahead of time to everyone involved (purpose, agenda, preparation needed), and don't forget last-minute briefings for key players.
- *Get the room right*. Some rooms are distraction-free and conducive to good discussions. Others aren't. Fight to get the first kind. Also, check the details: audio-visual tools and support, meeting materials, lighting, temperature, and sweet snacks.
- *Start well*. The first few minutes of the talent review set the tone and direction. Whenever possible, the senior leader should kick off the affair with comments about why the meeting is taking place, what needs to achieved, and how everyone should contribute to make it successful. I meet with the key leader early to set this up and also swing by at the last minute to ensure that all is well.
- *Signal relevance and interaction early*. As the early topics are taken up, there is often a critical moment where an unspoken ground rule is established: Participants either decide to play it safe and disengage, or they decide to join in the fun. Try to manage this early by introducing an interactive topic or inserting questions that signal this is a working session for everybody.
- *Throw in a surprise*. Early on, I try to add something interesting and unexpected to the meeting. Anything unanticipated can work, though something relevant to the subject is best. Start the meeting with a slide show about the future. Present a new scorecard for the talent review process. Show a provocative, counterintuitive analysis of talent trends. All are ways to inject interest.

Another checklist I bring into the meeting contains reminders of some "in the heat of battle" tools to keep things on track. The items on this list represent talent development issues that often arise in meetings, but not quite all the way to the surface. You can miss them if you're not paying attention. Here are two examples:

- *Derailment up ahead*. Like speeding trains, high-potential talent can jump the track. The derailed-executive phenomenon has been well researched. I have augmented that research with internal studies of the main reasons why some of our most promising people fell short of their potential. So I listen hard to discussions that sound as if they might signal trouble ahead for a high-potential person. My checklist reminds me to probe further when I hear about the following:

○ *A technically excellent performer with poor people skills.* Results may overshadow interpersonal weaknesses, but those weaknesses create bigger difficulties as leaders advance. Does this person perennially leave team problems in his wake as he or she drives for those great results?

○ *Stars in their own universe.* A manager who shines in one job, in one set of circumstances, can become narrow over time. Does this person need to be stretched with new challenges in a new setting to achieve his or her true potential?

○ *Lots of experience but declining results.* Sometimes managers are in a role too long and lose their edge. They can't produce fresh solutions to new challenges. Maybe it's time to find a different, revitalizing job for this person and look for a stronger replacement.

○ *Looks like an executive so must be an executive.* When someone sings the praises of an up-and-comer but glosses over questionable results while emphasizing style and other intangible qualities, that may signal a weak performer who can talk a good game but lacks the strategic smarts or the execution savvy to be effective.

• *Greater potential to unlock.* Quite the opposite of confronting a derailment situation is digging for unappreciated or underdeveloped talent. Sometimes executives downplay the best managers in their units as a way of hoarding talent. Other times, potential goes unrecognized because a talented person has a style clash with a boss. How can you spot these hidden gems? I listen for evidence of certain attributes that signal higher potential than a rating might suggest. Three of my favorites:

○ *Can see around the corner.* This is the leader who receives high marks for getting out in front of an issue or opportunity before it is evident to others.

○ *Unusual organization savvy.* Some leaders have an uncanny ability to rally resources across organizational boundaries or cut through divisional barriers to produce results.

○ *Talent magnet/talent builder.* Special leaders tend to draw in talent. They also become launching pads for an unusual amount of the organization's high potentials. A careful look at nine-block data or other talent evaluation forms often points to leaders who both attract the best people and groom the next generation. In the short run, these leaders have teams that can produce extraordinary results. In the long run, they leave legacy talent for the organization.

Finally, as discussions unfold, I have a standard set of questions to pose at the right moments to bring fresh energy and new perspectives. Following are some of my favorites:

• Are we moving that person too fast? Has Susan really reaped the developmental value we wanted her to get from her current job? Has Bob sufficiently addressed our reservations about him?

• Is this an opportunity both to accelerate the growth of a high-potential person and to raise the diversity and/or performance standards of a department?

• Is our succession strategy for this position realistic? Would we really move our top candidate up or would we look for other options?

- Are there better candidates for the role in other parts of the organization? Is there a nontraditional talent move here that would make a stronger impact on the organization and demonstrate our commitment to company-wide development?
- Are we hesitating about this performer because of a risk that isn't being articulated?
- If we're leaving this high-potential person in his or her current job for now, can we build in more challenge and development opportunities in the next 12 months? A high-profile taskforce leadership role, for example?

Watch What Happens Out of the Room

It may seem counterintuitive, but I've found that holding a great talent dialogue with senior executives in a room also engenders useful conversations outside the room. Let me explain. You might think that the ideal state in a senior team would be total transparency and openness. The practical reality is that excellent teams don't air all their sensitive topics in group settings. Nor do team members spring sensitive topics on the CEO in front of their peers.

I am not advocating avoidance or self-serving political plays. Talent review meetings absolutely should bring the right issues to the table: Are key roles being filled by great leaders? Where should we upgrade talent? Is the next generation engaged, stretching, and ready to move up? Is the organizational structure well aligned to meet the strategic challenges of today and tomorrow? What needs to change? What must we do to bring about those changes?

That said, however, an executive may reasonably choose to brief the CEO ahead of time on a sensitive personnel matter, to garner advance support for a restructuring with a few peers, or to resolve a sticky talent issue surfaced at last year's review before it is brought up again at this one.

I believe these back-office dynamics are normal and legitimate. What I've learned to do is stay close to the topics discussed outside the room when possible and sometimes to intervene for a better outcome. For example, I have set up and run narrowly focused mini reviews in cases where some part of the discussion about a candidate for a high-profile position was best handled by a subset of senior executives rather than the full team. The caution, of course, is that if too much is offloaded from the main event, the review meeting deteriorates into a charade without substance or engagement.

Using Reviews to Share Talent

One sign of excellence in talent discussions is that they break down barriers to moving people around the organization. Sharing high-potential leadership talent across business lines is a challenge because it's asking a lot of executives to move their most promising people to some other part of the enterprise. Executives invest in high-potential talent and deserve to reap the benefits. Any rational business leader would balk at giving up his or her best in exchange for someone else's so-called rising star.

Leaders often dig in their heels and refuse to share. Worse, they sometimes hide their most promising performers lest corporate find out about them.

It isn't easy to break through these barriers, but I've found it worth the effort. There is much to be gained by sharing. Any business unit can offer a certain amount of job growth and stretch assignments—but often with slow progression and limited challenges for the best. On the other hand, new business circumstances, geography, and trials broaden leadership capabilities. Fresh high-potential leaders moving into a new group often raise expectations and performance standards to higher levels. Mixing the most talented leaders brings new thinking and spreads best practices faster because these people are change agents by nature.

Several ideas are helpful in the attempt to spread talent around the enterprise. One technique we've used in top corporate reviews is to declare that above a certain level, the leadership group is "owned" by the corporation and is not the sole property of the individual business units. Everyone has a notion of the top 100, 500, or 1,000 leaders throughout the enterprise. Establish that the career development of this cadre will take place from a corporate point of view.

It also helps to build into succession planning a robust process to identify and track the best talent. The CEO and senior team should know the up-and-comers—first, perhaps, via the annual talent review and the HR system, but then by building personal relationships with each division's high potentials to facilitate movement.

A natural way organizations manage the top group of leaders is through direct ownership of compensation such as merit pay, stock options, bonuses, and other incentives. This can be useful in moving talent across divisions because it reinforces the belief that the corporation has a say in the treatment of these leaders.

Training programs can not only help identify high-potential talent but also enable cross-business movement. Filling a corporate leadership development program with people from all corners of the organization is a smart way to identify the best divisional talent. The networking that follows after managers meet one another in training programs can help open up some movement. Add in direct and meaningful contact with the CEO and other corporate leaders to increase visibility and reinforce relationships. Finish by sending the message that the leadership development path to the top will be built with cross-business moves that broaden executive experience.

Once you establish that the corporate office will be involved in filling divisional leadership jobs, the actual role played by corporate can vary, from helping assemble the slate of candidates to reviewing the finalists. This is the critical time to nudge a division executive to consider a high-potential person from another unit or to "recruit" talent from another division to interview for the opening.

Afterwards, Do You Tell?

One of the most debated topics in talent management is the degree to which the people talked about in a talent review meeting should be told afterwards what was said. Any answer to the question carries risks. If you don't tell Sam, he may be romanced away by another firm because he doesn't know how bright his future may be at this one—and telling him while he's trying to resign lacks credibility. On the other hand, if you do tell Sam, he may start obsessing about his "fast track" label, which can be distracting and destroy his sense of teamwork. He may have inflated expectations of rapid advancement, and those expectations might prevent him from learning critical lessons in his current role.

I see three options to consider:

- *Darkness.* Stay mum on the question of potential, and keep employees focused on today's work.
- *Sunshine.* Be completely transparent with all employees about how the organization judges their potential and regards their future.
- *Partly cloudy.* There are two options here. One is to inform some people, but not all, of how you regard their potential: Tell fast-trackers who they are, but don't tell workhorses that aren't going to rise much higher. The second option is to tell all employees some things about their potential but stop short of full disclosure about advancement opportunities or the timing of intended moves.

In my experience, the policy on disclosure inevitably depends on the organization's culture. Every company must tell employees how they rate in their current jobs, but in some organizations it is perfectly acceptable to keep silent on judgments of future potential. In others, employees demand to know their standing, and managers are more than willing to disclose the latest call on their prospects.

Which of the basic attitudes toward "tell or don't tell" is right for a particular organization? I think it depends on three factors:

1. *Confidence in the call.* Can executives make quality judgments or calibrations about future potential? Regardless of the form those calibrations take, are they real assessments of who is capable of greater roles? Is the distinction between current performance and potential clearly understood? Is there a good handle on what the critical needs in future roles will be? Are succession discussions rigorous and regular enough?

2. *Do they want and need to know?* To what degree will employees benefit from knowing how their potential is rated? In an aggressive, performance-oriented culture, with a reward system weighted toward "stars," people need to know what their prospects are. Should their energy be spent getting ready to move up or move out? A team-oriented reward system, on the other hand, is undercut by a focus on "where do you rank?" A related consideration: Will the organization benefit most from a talent pool in a constant state of churn as a way of keeping fresh? Or does it see more value in retaining organizational knowledge and steady, team-oriented performers?

3. *Can the message be delivered well?* How good are executives at communicating exactly what the organization means when it rates people's potential? I once worked with an executive who was so bad at getting the right message across

that our best talent often left his office thinking their careers were coming to an end! We finally learned to schedule an automatic "recovery" meeting with HR every time a high-potential person went to visit this executive.

Conclusion: Memo for the Meeting

Line leaders spend their days thinking of things other than talent management. A bit of friendly coaching before the talent review meeting can be helpful. I have often found it useful to do something besides just circulate an announcement of the meeting and an advance agenda.

A few years ago, I wrote a fanciful memo to an imaginary executive who might need some help with "framing" the talent meeting. Here is a condensed version:

To: My Senior Exec Friend
From: Your Talent Management Coach
Re.: Getting Ready for the Talent Review Meeting

Next week you'll be attending the annual talent review meeting. I know that in the past you have had mixed feelings about spending so much time on such a soft topic. Your calendar is certainly overloaded with meeting requests, and we shouldn't waste time with a so-so meeting. Here are a few ideas to help us make the most of our time together.

Think of this meeting as one leg in the three-legged stool that lets us manage the business. First leg: strategic long-range planning, where we look at our business prospects and make choices to improve our competitiveness. Second leg: annual operating planning, where we set targets for the following year to support the long-range plan. Third leg: talent review planning, where we translate the business plans into organization and people capabilities.

Each process supports the other. For example, the business growth plans you put forth in our recent strategy meeting will require new people capabilities. Do you feel set on what is needed or should we talk?

Let me offer a few thoughts about what makes for a productive talent-review meeting:

- *It's not about the system or forms. In our recent operations planning meeting, I'll bet you found that the real value came from the discussion and collaboration, not from the ritualistic review of data roll-up and plans. The same is true of talent review. We've gotten pretty good at automating a lot of people data. But don't be distracted by the charts and graphs. Look for the insight and implications for action.*
- *When you talk about your own people, please go beyond superficial descriptions. Provide solid facts and real examples of accomplishments and competence.*
- *Remember that performance, potential, and readiness are not the same thing. A high-performance contributor is great but may not be the best option for a more senior role.*
- *Extra points are awarded for thinking about nontraditional development moves. We want to accelerate the growth of our "best bets." Could you champion a move to shift that promising sales leader over to operations to broaden her knowledge of the business and to test her leadership skills in a different setting?*

I have seen you inspire great thinking and dialogue by asking the right questions. I hope you will do that in the talent review meeting. Here are some thought-starter questions you might want to bring along:

- *If we were to put that person in the new role, what would be the reasons why he would succeed? What would be the reasons he would fail?*
- *What would be our other succession options for this job if the current plan doesn't work out?*
- *What would we need to do to support this person in this new role?*
- *Are we writing off a talented person here because her style may be outside our comfort level?*
- *What are the two or three most important things we can do to strengthen our leadership pipeline in the coming year?*

I'll see you at the talent meeting. Your role is critical. You bring your best thinking. I'll bring the sweets.

Chapter 15

Career Development: Encompassing All Employees

Beverly Kaye, Ph.D., Founder and CEO
Joyce Cohen, Senior Consultant
Beverly Crowell, Senior Consultant
Career Systems International

T HERE'S A NEW NORMAL THAT IS DEMANDED OF CAREER DEVELOPMENT PROGRAMS AND practices. It is required alongside reorganizations, downsizing, budget constraints, and flattening levels of leadership. The new normal suggests that career development must occur right here, right now, and right where you are. Consider that old saying, "There's no sense in waiting for your ship to come in if you haven't sent one out." Companies who are excelling in the war on talent are getting their ships out and getting them out fast—at the helm, the employee.

It's time to declutter past thinking about career development. In business environments where employees and leaders are operating faster and leaner, career development must be flexible and self-powered by the employee no matter where they are or what they are doing. The new attitude about career development places responsibility squarely on the employee. It may even mean that succession plans for a few are replaced with career growth plans that build on the strengths of all employees. It promotes the belief that all employees must learn and grow, not just those on the high-potential list. Opportunities are readily present to do so if, and only if, the organization can truly support an "up is no longer the only way" philosophy.

World-class businesses who embrace this new attitude are building wider and deeper bench strength, enhancing employer brand, improving workforce flexibility and resilience, developing employee self-advocacy and career accountability, engaging and retaining key talent, and increasing employee productivity.

The Changing Face of Career Development

The nature of work today is very different from what it was several years ago. Because of the unsettling economy, HR departments are charged with filling the talent pipeline, with limited or no budget, fewer resources, and less time to execute. At the same time, they are tracking regrettable losses, satisfaction indicators, and individual development plan (IDP) progress. Business leaders and busy managers are turning to HR for quick answers and even faster solutions to talent management challenges as they are being held accountable for growing the talent in their departments. They must put practices into place that align the talent of an organization with the strategic direction of the business. When careers are aligned with core business principles, employees take on greater self-accountability for career, and connections foster strength across the organization.

On the organizational level, HR leaders look to identify and align with the organizational mission and strategy, evaluate organizational change and how it impacts the workforce, and track and monitor emerging trends and understand their impact on both the industry and careers within the organization. In addition, they will need to educate the workforce to take responsibility for their own careers and be willing to coach one another.

Within HR there is a need to respond in a timely manner to evitable change as it occurs, ask for opinions, value and respect diverse points of view, create a brand reputation, market to wider career audiences, and develop enrichment options that support career choices. It also demands the creation of an infrastructure that supports self-motivated career development and growth plans.

A proactive and accountable career development process, when partnered with succession planning, can meet these challenges swiftly and head-on. To work, it requires leadership buy-in, systems and tools that support this model, managers equipped to career coach, and employees willing to take ownership for their careers as well as their own job satisfaction. Ultimately, a development-minded strategy is needed that

- Holds employees accountable for personal development.
- Wins confidence of customers, community, and suppliers.
- Gains commitment of internal and remote workforce.
- Propels teams forward with internal worker support and buy-in.
- Uses power of generational teams to work together as partners in unprecedented ways.
- Optimizes diverse skills, talents, and age differentials.
- Gathers new information and remains open to new options, ideas, and strategies.

The Tie That Binds: Career Development Links to Succession Planning

Succession plans have been the mainstay for organizations for many years as the way to develop the leadership pipeline and to ensure a healthy talent management program. Career development was often reserved for the high-potential employee on the fast track. We believe a development message is critical for a wider array of workers. Career growth plans (CGP) are needed to enhance the traditional succession plan. Change in today's work structure calls for self-advocacy on the part of all employees. The CGP could become part of the hiring process, describe a variety of paths to development, emphasize the need to focus on mastery of the current job, build relevant skill sets, and value contributions from all generational groups. A CGP could motivate all employees to learn from their experiences and daily work, while expanding reach and network, both social and professional.

All employees must learn to build their own individualized career plan. Each person creates a master plan with the help of managers and mentors and their own peers to promote the learning and personal development areas that needs to be addressed. This CGP continues to latter stages of one's career within an organization where experienced employees focus on "what's next," legacy development, mentoring younger workers, sharing expertise, and working on projects aligned to their experience and skills.

Each organization must grapple with how to create a healthy tie between the business strategy and the ever-changing workforce. Along with the strong need for flexible policies and procedures, there is an immediate need for upgrades in skills. During one's tenure, from on-boarding all the way through phased retirement, it is important to balance individual goals with the business needs of an organization.

New language, such as "zigzagging" career moves or lattice instead of ladders is needed to replace terms that have lost their meaning. An example of such verbiage is the search for a new word to replace retirement, the last phase of the career continuum. Many words have been recommended to take its place, such as refirement, rewirement, and protirement, but none have caught on to date. That debate still continues after a decade of realizing that a new paradigm has emerged without much clear direction.

Other gray areas and questions emerge. What about those not included in a succession plan? How can career development be made viable and important to all? How will the organization respond to the younger generation who is asking about their development? How can traditional succession plans integrate harmoniously with emerging career growth plans?

A New Model for Career Development

Career development and career growth plans have evolved to be a business imperative that can directly impact the success of any organization. Talent demands more than a job. They demand a satisfying career that meets professional, personal, and emotional needs.

The hand-holding days are long gone. Multiple jobs are the norm with constant re-skilling and networking to stay attuned to business needs. Consider Ben and Janis who are self-motivated and successfully managing their careers. Ben is married, 42, with three children, completed a bachelor's degree through the armed forces ROTC program, has held six jobs and is working full-time as a computer technician, and is taking courses in pursuit of a master's degree in organizational management through an accelerated adult learning program online. He has already conducted numerous informational interviews and is focusing on a next career move as an IT business partner liaison (drawing on his education, current interests, and previous IT expertise). He is also beginning to think about his next career after he retires from this current line of work. A combination of a career development plan, flex time at work, distance education, and ROTC is making Ben's career dreams possible.

Janis, on the other hand, at age 32, has already navigated four different careers in education, library science, and early childhood development. She is job-sharing a position with a colleague to spend more time with her young child and her elderly widowed father, who lives with them.

Each unique situation can be accommodated by providing work/life balance, strong career fit, appropriate education, and flexible hours. Both Ben and Janis say their career choices and decisions have been driven by developing a portfolio of transferable skills and competencies, concrete career planning, personal life circumstances, and taking advantage of the flexibility of today's workplace and educational options.

Research suggests that challenging work, flexibility, career development, and the opportunity to learn and grow are some top reasons employees choose to stay, and stay engaged, in an organization. It doesn't happen by accident. Worker's attitudes and expectations have changed—permanently.

What Keeps Them?

These factors influence job satisfaction and commitment:

Exciting, challenging, and meaningful work

Supportive manager, great boss

Being recognized, valued, and respected

Career growth, learning, and development

Flexible work environment

Job security and stability

Fair pay

Job location

Working with great coworkers or clients
Pride in the organization, mission, or product
Fun, enjoyable work environment
Good benefits
Loyalty to my coworkers or boss

Source: *Love 'Em or Lose 'Em: Getting Good People to Stay.* Berrett-Koehler Publishers; Beverly Kaye and Sharon Jordan-Evans; 4th edition. (January 1, 2008).

Organizations must think beyond the traditional models of career and expand their thinking to an overall career development and growth strategy that focuses on three critical groups: the organization, the manager, and the employee. To begin, ask lots of questions. Investigate what's happening in your organization to discover the truth about your development culture.

The Organization

Organizations are continually asked to reinvent themselves and are forced to juggle priorities that shift regularly. The result is a leaner organization with fewer resources, fast-paced work, expanded spans of control, and a new normal at work that demands flexibility and the ability to thrive when ambiguity and change are the order of the day. To remain competitive in business and attract top talent, an organization must provide the systems and structure that support the career development needs across all levels. Framing responses to the questions below will be an important first step to addressing the development of systems and structures that support career development needs.

- How can leaders and managers who work within the organization guarantee that the business strategy will work, the day-to-day tasks are updated and redesigned, and the workforce still remain engaged?
- How do we respond to the constant change in business today?
- What does a career look like in our organization today?
- Do our systems and processes support career development and succession planning for the next generation?
- How do we measure results and does our career development process support those results?
- How do we establish a foundation for employees to grow in areas that matter across the life continuum of the organization and the employee?

The Manager

While the company provides the systems and tools for career development, the development-minded manager provides the support and guidance. Most managers are trained in performance management, and some believe performance management and career development are the same. They're not. Managers must understand that building talent for tomorrow requires commitment to career development today and at every level. Development-minded managers create and implement developmental assignments, encourage risk taking, set stretch goals, and tap unused resources. They provide a professional safety net so that employees can experiment and learn on the job. They continually ask themselves some key questions:

- How do I serve as a career advocate for my employees?
- How often do I talk with my employees about their career goals and what matters most to them?
- Do I provide candid and frequent feedback to my employees about what they need to do to grow in their careers?
- Do I link employees to the resources and information they need in support of their careers?
- Do I take career growth plans seriously? What amount of time do I devote to planning?
- Do I provide information to employees about the future of the organization and look for opportunities for employees?
- Do I stay current and future focused in the above concerns for me and my career as well as the careers of my direct reports?
- What am I reading and discussing with colleagues to ensure the above?

The Employee

No longer can employees wait for career development to happen to them or for them. To be effective, employees must begin to manage their careers by knowing themselves, knowing what's out there, knowing what others think of them, and knowing whom to ask for help. They pave the way by *taking charge of their careers:* developing on the job, ensuring that their work has heart, and networking throughout the organization to engage with others and energize daily work. There are five critical areas that demand exploration by the individual:

Change. What trends are impacting my organization and how can I capitalize on this reality to benefit my career? How will I hold myself accountable? Specifically, what am I willing to do?

Interests. How would I describe my current values, skills, and interests on the job? How do I use them regularly at work? How do I ensure that I'll continue to learn, grow, and develop on the job?

Reputation. I received a 360-degree report about my performance/work style and said, "They got my number!" What were the main messages of my strengths and weaknesses? How will I ensure ongoing performance feedback?

Options. If I could do any job within the organization, what would I like to do and why? How can I explore multiple growth avenues? Do I view change as an opportunity?

Actions. What do I want to be doing in one or three years and what's my plan to get there? What actions will I put in place to ensure that I put myself in position to turn these dreams to reality? With whom can I talk about these issues and build a viable personal plan?

An Important HR Role

Given the environment of constant change and uncertainty, one thing is for certain: HR leaders must align with the vision of the organization by serving as strategic partners who can integrate business-driven solutions around a robust career development program. This means they must take stock of their existing career development processes to integrate new thinking, ignite new strategies and behaviors, and infuse it into the culture of the organization. They must examine key questions about policies, systems, and structures that are designed to support career development in the organization. The list of questions that follows is just some of the challenges for HR professionals to consider and implement as new processes take shape.

How are our policies, systems, and structures

- Aligned with development choices?
- Focused on future directions?
- Driving new positive behaviors?
- Creating partnerships that energize and engage while fulfilling valued services/products?
- Investing in broad talents and determining where those talents can best be utilized internally?
- Growing a new brand of worker who is fulfilled both personally and professionally?
- Building confident, cost-conscious risk-takers?
- Ensuring respect and inclusivity across the workplace?
- Providing opportunities for employees at all levels to learn, grow, and develop within the organization?

Generational Diversity: Gifts of the Ages

No matter the generation they represent, employees want work that provides satisfaction. Consider the generational group when developing career development and growth plans by valuing and utilizing the uniqueness of each. If attention is provided across generational groups, organizations have a head start in embracing the new meaning of career, alignment to business strategy, self-accountability, connectedness, sustainability, and attention to a future-focused business.

MATURES (Ages 65+)

Savvy, experienced workers who want to use their expertise and be integral to the job. Include them in training (they're often overlooked) where they can learn new technologies and emerging concepts. Involve this group fairly, investigate phased retirement options, and consider age-specific perks.

BOOMERS (Ages 46 to 64)

Boomers are confident careerists who are also natural subject matter experts, teachers, and mentors. They possess a strong work ethic. Help them explore new work options and utilize their talent, expertise, and skill sets on the job or specific special projects. Redesign their jobs to meet multiple life demands and encourage growth in place.

GEN Xers, GAMERS (Ages 29 to 45)

They are collaborative, value team approach, work/life balance, self-reliance, and applying new skills. They seek autonomy, love a challenge, and need opportunities to grow. Provide feedback on reputation and candor about how to leverage their entrepreneurial spirit. Want to win their hearts? Offer meaningful work, stakeholder status, food, and fun!

GEN Y, GEN WHY, DIGITAL KIDS (Up to Age 28)

These global, street-smart, green multi-taskers are driven by technology and social media such as blogging, twittering, absorbing 24/7 news, e-learning, and electronic gadgetry. They adapt easily, value learning, love working in teams, and thrive on being developed by experts. Ensure that learning, growth, group work, and development are high on their work agenda.

The Opportunity Environment

Opportunities for employees to learn, grow, and develop within any job is key to a successful strategy. For many years, opportunity was defined as a promotion. Now opportunities can manifest themselves in many different ways—most specifically through enrichment in the current job and keeping an eye focused on emerging trends. These opportunities can be somewhat elusive to the untrained eye.

Today, we operate in a new opportunity environment as organizations position themselves to embrace a culture of success. Career development is not for the chosen few, but for all. With that said, organizations may struggle to understand where all this development will happen. Understanding that each organization is an "opportunity marketplace" is a critical mind-set necessary to meet the learning and development needs of employees.

The organizational culture must nurture all talent and educate managers to understand the needs inherent in the professional lives of their direct reports. By looking wider and deeper for talent within internal ranks, organizations can develop a new understanding and sensitivity to backfilling jobs and promoting career ownership. How might an organization embrace this concept of an "opportunity marketplace?" Consider the following examples:

(A) Communicate select issues downward in the organization typically discussed "at higher ranks." Isn't it time that more people seriously take on important internal problems? Encourage internal talent to turn those issues into opportunities and to think strategically and innovatively.

(B) Redirect a portion of funds earmarked for high-potential development to challenge and mobilize talent in the middle. Initiate competition, and embed reward/recognition in the stakes.

(C) Coach managers to work with their talent and reward competitive innovative thinking aligned to an organization's strategy, vision, mission, and purpose.

(D) Unleash "innovation teams" across generational lines to take on real company issues.

(E) Challenge employees to think about talent that will be needed in their "future" departments" to deliver the business strategy. Conduct a gap analysis, and redesign jobs with a focus on the future. As needed, update skills and retrain.

(F) Who may retire in the near future? How will you ensure his or her knowledge is transferred and important intellectual capital doesn't walk out the door? Or if it does, how will it be replenished internally and cost-effectively. Think of it this way: Who would you sorely miss if they didn't come to work tomorrow morning? How will you capture that expertise and where should it reside? That's costly, irreplaceable talent unless you start now.

Generating Buy-In

HR professionals readily understand and accept the importance of a development culture to drive talent to greater performance, higher levels of engagement, and job satisfaction. In a time when senior leadership and managers are focused on the bottom line or doing more with less, placing a priority on the career development of its people is often lost in the shuffle. Creating a strong business case, developing a marketing and communications strategy, and branding the career development effort early on will increase the probability of leadership buy-in and sustained support.

Find a champion. Who in the ranks of senior leadership places a high priority on career development and actively models it in their organization? Creating a strong culture of development will require the resources and funding that only senior leaders can deliver.

Develop a business case. What is your "burning platform?" Link to employee or culture surveys, take a look at turnover, tie talent to organization vision, link to business metrics, and identify the cost of doing nothing or maintaining status quo. Bottom line: Develop a case that demonstrates the return on investment for the leaders signing the check.

Know your key stakeholders and influencers. Talk with them often and keep them updated on the progress of your career development strategy. Ask their advice, seek their support, tailor your communications to their priorities, and encourage them to share the how and why with their teams. On the other side, know who in the organization will seek to derail your efforts. Get them on board and get them on board early.

Use employees to tell the story. Look inside the organization for employees who embody the culture of development in your organization. Demonstrate through videos, posters, e-mail, intranet, and reward "real" employees who have self-powered their career for success.

Keep it simple. Busy managers and employees need career growth plans that integrate into existing systems and processes with minimal impact on time, the most valuable resources today. Provide training to help master the how and sustain the learning though coaching, career action teams, career development resources, messaging, and communications. Keep the momentum going and commit to a long-term plan.

The Challenge

In this era of self-accountability, every organization must take a leadership role in developing individual resiliency through a strategic priority on career development. There will be times of not knowing. Recession tested leaders must convey a message of solidarity. In the midst of uncertainty, it is critical to reach out to all levels and work together to achieve deadlines and solutions. In developing a more robust career development process and ultimately transforming a culture, everyone is a stakeholder. So, here's the challenge, "What step(s) will you take *now* to build career development and growth in your organization?" Organizations, managers and employees alike, want a career culture where employees are in charge of their own destiny, feel more in control, and seek to do meaningful work. To make that happen, it will take new flexible career options, future-focused thinking, and professionals at all levels who are committed to their own learning. The time is now to launch—right here, right now, right where you are!

Chapter 16

CEO Succession Planning

Marshall Goldsmith, Executive Coach
*Leadership Development and
Behavioral Change*

A<small>S</small> CEO<small>S</small> <small>NEAR THE END OF THEIR CAREERS, THEY MUST NAVIGATE THE SUCCESSION</small> process in a way that is beneficial for themselves, their successors, and their organizations. It can be difficult to navigate this course and to pass the baton of leadership, and not every CEO does it successfully. I am a behavioral change expert. I do not advise leaders in the strategic and technical issues of succession. My expertise is on the human or *behavioral* elements of transition. This is the focus of this chapter.

Let's begin with an overview and then delve into the particulars of each topic. There are four basic steps of successful transitions:

1. Prepare for the transition.
2. Choose a successor.
3. Coach the successor.
4. Pass the baton.

From my experience, much of what has been written about succession has been academic, while little has been written about the drama that occurs at every step of this process. CEOs, like the rest of us, including their successors, are human beings. During the transition process, many of the soft issues of humanity—relationships, ego, self-interest, and feelings—come into play. As humans, we may find the steps outlined above are strategically simple concepts to grasp in the objective, but they can be emotionally difficult to navigate in the subjective.

Not alone in this identification, CEOs are very personally identified with their jobs. It's not just what they do; it is a very large part of who they are. This makes the transition process very personal. Further, it is not only personal for the CEO; it is personal for the successor, the other executives, the board, and the stakeholders whose lives will be impacted.

So how do CEOs proceed through the transition process with dignity and perhaps even pleasure? How do they ensure that their successor is in a good position right from the start? Let's go back to the steps outlined above.

Prepare for Transition

Transition is challenging and very few leaders realize how difficult it will be. If the CEO has done a great job of carrying the baton of leadership, the organization may last long after he or she is gone. This longevity is highly dependent on the success of the leadership baton pass between CEO and successor. Both leaders must be ready for the pass or the organization will suffer.

During the process of succession, the rest of the world will continue revolving. Competitors will compete with the organization; short-term and long-term results will need to be produced. In addition, the rest of the world will be watching as the CEO slows down and the successor speeds up and the handoff is made. If the handoff is successful, the CEO will quickly disappear from view as everyone cheers the next baton carrier. The CEO has to be prepared for this. It can be hard on the ego.

In preparing to depart, leaders might ask themselves, "What legacy do I want to leave?" "Do I want to be remembered as someone who did a great job of developing my successor?" and "Who worked to ensure that the organization would be successful after I departed?" While still carrying the baton and preparing for his or her departure, these considerations will help focus the process in the right direction.

Sometimes people don't want the CEO to quit. When this happens, it can be nearly impossible to let go. Sometimes the CEOs competitive drive won't let him or her leave; this person wants to stay just a little longer to put the organization over the top.

These are traps that CEOs fall into when facing the final challenge of great leadership: passing the baton. Is the CEO ready for succession? The answer to this question may be the determining factor in the organization's success after he or she departs.

Why is letting go of the CEO position so difficult? Simple. In addition to the adoration and accolades that success brings, there are a few basic reasons that this position is so hard to let go.

1. *Wealth.* Money can easily become a personal scorecard. It may not seem hard to walk away from making money, but when making much less as "civilians," some CEOs feel as though they are failing.
2. *Perquisites.* Perks like private jets, sporting events in the company box, and a dedicated staff of professionals are hard to give up.

3. *Status*. Being a CEO brings with it status, and a fear of successful people is becoming a "used-to-be CEO." It just isn't the same—and people know it.
4. *Power*. The sudden loss of power, the potential to influence and achieve big results, that accompanies leaving this position can be hard to take.

Leaders throughout history have had difficulty letting go of money, status, perks, and power. Without making peace with letting go, the CEO will not be able to hand off the position to his or her successor.

Then there are the softer perks that can be so hard to give up:

1. *Relationships*. CEOs enjoy most of their close coworkers, or they wouldn't be close coworkers. These people are practically family, and the more they have been through together, the harder it can be for the CEO to leave.
2. *Happiness*. The CEOs I have met love being CEOs. They love everything about the job, from the people to leading to the challenges. CEOs will have to find new ways to achieve the happiness they felt as CEOs.
3. *Meaning*. CEOs are important. With direct impact on people and products, their work is not trivial. CEOs who pass the baton will need to find meaning in other ways after they leave the organization.
4. *Contribution*. CEOs develop people, create jobs, and generate economic benefit. They are most proud of these things. Not making a contribution can lead to emptiness. CEOs may crave contribution and will probably need to find another way to contribute when they are no longer CEO.

Choosing the Successor

One of the most important accomplishments any CEO can achieve, the development of a great successor, starts with an important decision: Should the successor be chosen from inside or outside the organization? Hiring from outside can be very expensive, especially if the new CEO fails. And while the damage outside the organization can be severe when an external CEO fails —in negative press, company embarrassment, and so on—it is worse inside the company. The dismissed employees and cut resources that happen in order to pay off the external bad hire only reinforce the growing perception that CEOs are overpaid and board members are self-interested. The reputation of the former CEO, likely a major part of the selection process, will be tarnished by this failure, and that is not a great legacy to leave.

Another reason to hire from inside the company is that it sends a strong message about the organization's leadership development program. It says that leaders are developing their people. It says that there are strong possibilities to grow into positions of leadership at the company, and that those supporting chosen successors will have opportunities for promotion as well.

CEOs who develop internal successors can be more assured that those successors will carry on their company vision—with a fresh perspective—as they may have spent months or years understanding and working within the current leadership vision.

Yet sometimes it isn't possible to hire from inside the company. For whatever reason, the business environment may eliminate this possibility. For instance, the board may need to send a message to investors and customers that the organization is headed in a new direction, and they choose to do so by hiring an external CEO with credibility in the new area that no internal successor can match. Or perhaps the CEO must exit immediately and there isn't time to develop a high-potential candidate quickly. Sometimes there just isn't time to wait for the internal leader to develop.

Coach the Successor

When the succession process requires an external coach, the CEO should be involved to make sure the coaching process is successful. Before starting the coaching process, the CEO should ask him- or herself three qualifying questions:

1. Does he or she really want this person to be the next CEO? If there are any doubts, if the CEO doesn't really want this person to have the job, then he or she will not be very helpful in the coaching process and the transition will probably not be successful.
2. Will this person be given a fair chance by key stakeholders? The CEO may think this person is perfect for the job, but if the board doesn't think so, it won't matter. If the answer to this question is no, the time spent coaching and developing this person will have been wasted.
3. Does the person want to change? The motivation for change has to come from inside the successor; it will *not* happen because the CEO is a great coach. No one gets better because of the coach; they get better because they are willing to and work toward change.

Hiring an external coach is fairly simple. The CEO should ask the coach to describe his or her area of specialty and then analyze whether it fits the coaching needs of the successor. Is the successor in need of development in strategy, tactics, or behavior, or is the need in personal development or productivity? The coach should specialize in the area in which the successor requires development.

It's important to involve key stakeholders in the coaching process and in determining the successor's strengths and areas for growth. These are the people who will be involved with the successor long after the CEO has passed the baton, so it's important that they be on board for a number of reasons.

1. The new CEO will need their support to turn the succession into a success; help, especially early on in the position, to ensure a graceful transition will be required .
2. Stakeholders have ideas and perceptions of the company and what the next leader should be like that the current CEO may not have considered. These ideas will offer the incoming CEO a more well-rounded view of his or her role.
3. The CEO is not the only one whose input matters. The successor will learn a lot more when he or she gets coaching from key stakeholders. Stakeholders should

represent a variety of different perspectives—board members, peers, direct reports, and in some cases customers and suppliers. The CEO should list the relationships most important to ensuring success in leading the company, and then make sure that these names are on the feedback list for a successor

4. Stakeholders who are involved in the coaching process are more likely to become psychologically invested in helping the new CEO succeed. In addition, it helps the successor and stakeholders build effective relationships that will be in place long after the previous CEO departs.

5. Positive indications of change from many key stakeholders are much more valid than a positive indication of change from one person—even if that one person is the CEO.

When reviewing feedback, which is often in the form of 360 assessments, the CEO should look for trends. If areas of improvement show progress, the candidate may be a person who will work to get better. If the scores don't improve, the person may not be the best candidate.

The CEO should consider the business environment when these assessments were taken and feedback given. Was it during a difficult turnaround when decisions had to be made that didn't please employees? In these cases, 360-degree feedback scores may well suffer.

The CEO should look for key patterns. What areas of strength and areas for improvement will make the most difference in bringing the candidate into the best position to become a great CEO?

Personality tests and organizational surveys can be useful. Anecdotal feedback can also be used, though a very common error CEOs make can be over-reliance on this type of feedback. The CEO should consider the source when accepting this type of feedback and be careful not to let one event negate years of evidence.

After gathering feedback and suggestions, the CEO may start the coaching process with a goal-setting session. Working together to determine key areas for behavior change will help make the most of the transition and will help the successor candidate develop the skills and build the relationships for becoming a great CEO.

The most important variable in achieving positive, lasting change is follow-up. And the most important follow-up is not the CEO following up with the successor; it is the successor following up with key stakeholders (Goldsmith and Morgan 2004). The successor will acknowledge areas of development and then ask stakeholders for ongoing suggestions for future improvement. The CEO coach can reinforce these ongoing dialogues by asking the successor who he or she talked with, what he or she learned, and what he or she is going to do about what was learned.

Pass the Baton

When the successor is ready to move into the role of CEO, the CEO will finally have to go. The CEO may be tempted to stay on the board or in some other capacity. It is best to just go if the successor is going to be successful. Hanging on is not helpful.

The best thing the CEO can do is show integrity on the way out by doing everything possible to ensure that the next CEO is successful. That means not talking with the press disparagingly about the successor, especially if he or she ultimately is not successful. It's best to exit gracefully, and even if other people don't recognize it, the successor will. In turn, this fortunate person will have been taught one final lesson from his or her predecessor: How to pass the baton of leadership smoothly and successfully when the time comes.

References

Goldsmith, M., and H. Morgan, 2004. Leadership is a contact sport. (Fall). *Strategy + Business*.

Chapter 17

Ensuring CEO Succession Agility in the Boardroom

Dennis Carey, Vice Chairman
Korn/Ferry International
Marc Feigen, Founder
Feigen & Company
Kevin Cashman, Senior Partner
Korn/Ferry Leadership and Talent Consulting

O N APRIL 19, 2004, JAMES CANTALUPO, THE CEO OF MCDONALD'S, DIED OF A HEART attack. The next day the board of the McDonald's Corporation announced that Charlie Bell would succeed Cantalupo. Although the board and employees of McDonald's grieved for James and his family, the company didn't miss a heartbeat.

On October 2, 2009, in the midst of a financial crisis, Ken Lewis, CEO of Bank of America, announced his resignation. The board had ample warning, since Ken was under pressure to move on for months. But the board had no successor. Instead, they searched frantically. Some executives whom the Bank of America board asked to be their CEO refused the position practically on the front page of the *Wall Street Journal*. Excellent candidates that were brought forward were unsure of the board's process. The question of who would lead Bank of America riveted the business and financial community. In the meantime, the company was leaderless for months during the financial storm, and its stock price fell. The board with warning was caught off guard; the board without warning replaced its CEO overnight. What accounts for the difference? Board preparedness, or what we call "succession agility in the boardroom."

The hiring and the firing of the CEO is the number one role of the board of directors. Boards that have strong CEO succession management practices, such as McDonald's, Procter & Gamble, and Pfizer, offer other boards a reservoir of best practices that can be adapted and shaped to fit most companies.

Ten best practices of succession agility that we have distilled from boards with world-class CEO succession capability follow.

1. CEO Succession Planning Is a Process, Not an Event

CEO succession planning begins the day a new CEO takes the helm and continues until the next CEO takes over. At P&G, the board works with the new CEO during the first year of the CEO's tenure to develop a plan for his or her succession.

CEO succession is not a one-off event that happens every seven to ten years, nor is it just a transaction in which a search committee is formed and an executive recruiter retained. Rather, it is a systemic process integrated into a company's talent management approach. When done well, a company has multiple internal candidates, as well as younger up-and-comers with recognized future CEO potential, and has tailored development plans to fit. At Amgen, the board is directly involved in reviewing the senior leadership team annually, and CEO succession is an integral component of this work.

At well-run professional service firms, during review, young associates are asked the question, "Could you be a partner one day?" The same should be true of good senior leadership development processes, where the question should be, "Could you be our CEO in 5, 10, even 15 years?" Waiting until the incumbent CEO announces he or she is ready to move on is too late to begin.

2. CEO Succession Is a Strategic Move

The board's single greatest ability to influence the strategy of the company is through the CEO they hire. However, too few boards see CEO succession as a strategic event, an opportunity either to reshape strategy or to heighten a company's ability to execute strategic goals. The best processes start with the current strategy, or a clear sense of where a company's strategy must evolve, and then hire to drive the strategy. It is surprising when some otherwise knowledgeable boards write a set of leadership characteristics without either a deep rooting in strategy or significant input from management.

It is human nature for each board member to have two or three key attributes in mind and to test for those. But this often leads to dysfunctional discussions. Properly done, boards develop a strategic-driven, management-informed set of leadership competencies and the entire board works off the same page. It is important that these competencies be developed in an inclusive process involving the entire board, the current CEO, the head of HR, and often outside advisors.

Management reports to the CEO, but only the CEO reports to the board. Therefore, the board, in a sense, exercises strategic execution through the CEO. The leader chosen by the board must be properly geared to develop and implement the strategic direction the company must take.

3. Assess Character and Fit

How many WorldComs or Enrons could have been avoided had boards not only dug deep into CEO competencies but also clearly understood the values, character, and integrity of the leaders they have evaluated and entrusted? It is self-evident that the more self-focused the CEO, the more potential danger to the enterprise. The more enterprise-focused the CEO (on both people and performance dimensions), the more enduring value is created. But too many boards have failed to go beyond evaluations of competencies, drive, and achievement to develop a picture of a candidate's character. Doing so requires time, judgment, and the willingness of boards to listen to (and encourage) perhaps a minority of board members who speak up and say, "I'm uncomfortable." Of course, outside references are essential, and the board members chosen to lead this process must be of the highest character themselves.

Though the spectacular business failures of recent years were often driven by flawed individuals, most leaders are of good character. A larger and more important issue is "fit." Excellent leaders still fail. Often the problem is one of "organ rejection," or lack of fit. Boards may choose someone who is an intentional "non-fit" and who will shake up the organization and transform it. This can be good, but it must be purposeful. When a transformation is not required, a lack of fit can doom an otherwise excellent leader and bring dire consequences to the organization.

Evaluating fit can be tricky; management's and the current CEO's view is required. When done well, boards openly discuss the relative importance of fit and test for it.

4. Foster an Abundance of Candidates

Leading companies seek to have more than a handful of possible successors. Two or three successors should be the minimum number of inside "ready now" candidates in well-run companies.

5. Ensure That the CEO Is Leading the Process

Many CEOs, especially those early in their tenure, are understandably uncomfortable leading a process to select a replacement. Nevertheless, the age of the imperial CEO has past, and today it is part of the CEO's job description to create a fertile field of able candidates.

Boards will often pressure the CEO to narrow the list and declare a choice. But CEOs should resist naming a candidate too early. As one CEO told us, "I want all horses to run past the finish line." If the CEO chooses too early, the pressure is off and performance could suffer too. The job of the CEO is to present facts and information and candidates, and to let the board decide. As a member of the board the CEO should indicate a preference only later in the game, after the board has the time, exposure, and quality information to genuinely assess the lead candidates.

The quality of a CEO succession planning capability must be part of the current CEO's goals, and he or she should be reviewed accordingly on an annual basis.

6. Create Leadership Development Plans to Groom Internal Candidates

It is imperative to help key talent understand the requirements to become CEO. Candidates should not be left to wonder. A comprehensive, challenging, and actionable development plan needs to be established for each candidate. One critical component of the plan is to identify enterprise-wide initiatives that each candidate can lead to demonstrate his or her strategic, collaborative, and silo-breaking leadership competencies. Research has demonstrated that "stretch assignments" can account for up to 70 percent of leadership development impact.

Whether it is international, cross-functional or cross-business unit exposure to broaden a candidate's understanding of the entire business, the best training for the CEO role is often leadership away from headquarters, where the business unit leader has the opportunity to captain the ship. Companies such as Northrop Grumman have moved successor candidates into staff roles. For example, Wes Bush became CFO, moving in and out of the line with a purposeful, board-driven mission to broaden his experience, before being anointed Northrop Grumman's next leader.

7. Ensure the Board Knows Personally Key Candidates

Board exposure with candidates should include one-on-ones, visits to the candidate's business, and social interactions. For some current CEOs, this can be unsettling or intimidating, but many recognize the value. Board members need to invest the necessary time, outside of board meetings, to get to know the candidates. Some boards arrange overseas trips for directors and candidates to rub shoulders, as the proximity of travel is often a good way to build rapport. GE, for example, encourages board members to mentor candidates, walk the floors, and get to know in depth the operations and the leaders. The board members benefit from the education, the leaders/candidates benefit from the mentoring and experience, and the CEO succession process is strengthened.

8. Know the Outsiders

Many companies, especially those facing disruptions in their business, a marked increase in competitive pressure, or a failed CEO and management team, will not have a pool of inside candidates to draw upon. In these cases, the board should know the outside leadership community well and have their eyes on potential successors, even if from a distance.

The board should maintain a quiet "stable" of outside candidates. Of course, the identification of capable outsiders is best conducted without formal contact with the potential candidates until the board "pulls the trigger" and moves quickly on a CEO transition. This screening is most helpful when in response to the company's evolving business strategy and business climate, and therefore it needs to be an ongoing process.

In some cases, there will be no insider or ready outsider, or no warning of a CEO firing or death. In this case, the board should have an acting CEO in mind, and often a member of the board, such as Ed Whittacre, who took the helm of GM, adding the CEO title to Chairman when Fritz Henderson was asked to resign. This can be risky, as the new leader must be more than a caretaker and must not be seen as political choice or a usurper. In best cases, the acting board member enjoys the support of the board and moves quickly to find a permanent leader.

9. Have a Clear, Disciplined, Data-Driven Process

Once CEO succession shifts into high gear, a board search committee is named, often led by the lead director or non-executive chairman. The effectiveness of these committees varies. The best committees develop a CEO competency model, evaluate candidates, seek candidates from a wide pool, integrate the search with the company's strategic goals, and leverage executive recruiting. The worst committees are unclear of their process, force candidates through multiple interviews, thereby turning off high-quality people, and are aggressive or episodic.

The better processes are data-driven. For example, GlaxoSmithKline developed assessments of internal candidates with inputs from a variety of trusted executives in the organization who worked directly with the candidates, ensuring against favoritism and other biases such as a lofty title or a long term of service. This approach led GlaxoSmithKline to choose Andrew Witty, a dark-horse late entrant, who won an internal race against two long-serving executives. At WellPoint, the board ran a review of insiders and outsiders over six months, comparing both candidate pools on the same data-driven criteria.

Boards, having done the above, are now in a position to calibrate insiders against outsiders, and importantly follow a process that improves the company's chances of retaining talented inside candidates who were not chosen, but nonetheless feel they were well treated and are willing to serve under a new command.

10. Ensure the Retiring CEO Onboards the New CEO

Regardless of whether the new CEO selection is internal or external, it is too soon for boards to declare victory and hand the new leader the keys. CEO retention is an increasing issue in corporate America, and the first year is crucial. CEOs need to develop too, and care needs to be taken to their onboarding. This is best directed by the retiring CEO in partnership with the board. The new CEO will be evaluating the existing team, and care must be taken to ensure that onboarding does not become political. Nor is this an invitation for boards to meddle; the new CEO needs a free hand, but he or she also needs partners in the boardroom ready to offer a helping hand. The board must ensure that the current CEO is motivated and focused on an effective transition.

When the retiring CEO stays on for a limited time as chairman, as Bob Lane at Deere, there is time for an orderly passing of the baton. At the same time, all symbols must change: The new CEO is the CEO, and the chairperson must immediately assume the role of non-executive chairman of the board.

Conclusion

Boards will thrive or perish in direct proportion to their succession agility. Choosing the right leader at the right time is the board's most important role, and one that enables a board to create an enduring legacy of value creation through their carefully chosen appointment of a CEO.

References

Carey, Dennis C., et al. 2000. *CEO succession: A window on how boards get it right when choosing a new chief executive*. Oxford: Oxford University Press.
Cashman, Kevin. 2010. CEO succession. *Leadership Excellence*. Warren Bennis, ed. (February).

Part II

Formulating Coaching, Training, and Development Approaches that Drive Talent Management Processes

Chapter 18

Training and Development: A New Context for Learning and Performance

Dale E. Kunneman, Vice President Human Resources, Global Products
Francesco Turchetti, Director Talent Management
Sharon L. Cresswell, Talent Management: Competencies and Curriculum
Catherine M. Sleezer, Competencies and Curriculum Supply Chain
Baker Hughes Corporate

T HIS CHAPTER DESCRIBES RESOURCES THAT TRAINING AND DEVELOPMENT (T&D) professionals utilize to achieve results in four areas of responsibility: (1) target learning and developing efforts, (2) manage content development and administration, (3) deliver learning content efficiently, and (4) assess the value proposition of training and development efforts. Together, these responsibilities and the newly available resources for carrying them out create an expanded role for T&D. In the past, T&D professionals were responsible for disseminating instruction. Today the role includes analyzing, supporting, and managing learning at all levels of an organization to better impact business results. This chapter also describes how the T&D function contributes to business results at Baker Hughes, a global oilfield services company with operations in over 90 countries.

T&D Responsibility #1: Target Learning and Development Efforts

In the early days of T&D, critics recognized that workplace training efforts offered potential, but often criticized them for being inconsistent, unorganized, time-consuming, and costly. By contrast, today's training and development efforts are just-in-time, specific, and laser-focused on employee expertise that will

- Achieve the organization's strategic goals.
- Build deep levels of expertise that differentiates the organization from its competitors.
- Develop leadership expertise in high-potential employees, the Superkeepers™, who will lead the organization in the future.

This targeted approach produces better strategic decisions regarding the use of T&D resources. In the past many organizations used a general and egalitarian approach to allocate T&D resources. However, an organization's resources for T&D can be allocated more effectively by using a decision-science approach that is data-based and reflects the organization's strategic goals (Boudreau and Ramstad 2005). With a decision-science approach, T&D resources are allocated to those segments of employees who are most critical and who are expected to have the largest impact on the organization's success. Competencies and curricula are important mechanisms for targeting T&D efforts toward achieving the collective expertise that is critical to organizational success. Indeed, they bridge organization strategy, T&D policies, and employee learning.

Competencies

Competencies can be used to create a framework for growing and developing talent that is aligned with the organization's strategic business goals. The closer a competency framework is aligned to the organizational strategy, the more responsive an organization becomes to meeting the business needs.

Competency frameworks are often mistaken for skills, qualifications, and certifications. These can all be part of the underlying supports and tasks that define a competency but are not to be confused with the competency itself. A competency is a set of measureable, performance-related characteristics that are critical to driving the organization's strategic goals. A competency should be targeted and behaviorally performance-driven to meet strategic organization needs. It should be written at a high level and be more general in nature than specific skills, qualifications, or certifications.

As a company becomes more mature with using a competency framework, the value proposition of this type of targeted learning becomes more transparent. Mature competency-based organizations can differentiate themselves from their competitors by using a specific set of developmental opportunities and learning events that are targeted, are just-in-time, and enable faster employee growth and development for targeted roles.

Curriculum Development

Curriculum development is a process that leverages a competency framework to define a specific set of targeted learning events and development opportunities for a particular group of learners. A curriculum is a sequenced set of formal and informal learning events. Each learning event is composed of specific learning objectives and content.

Curriculum development should not be owned by human resources, but by a business partner who has deep knowledge about the curricula. The business partner ensures that all the learning events are strategic, just-in-time, and critical to the employee's current role and responsibilities. Participants in the curriculum development process include key business stakeholders, operations leaders, content developers, and the competency developers.

After the competencies are developed, needs assessments identify—for specific groups of employees—the gaps between the actual learning and performance and the desired learning and performance (Gupta, Sleezer, and Russ-Eft 2007; Robinson and Robinson 2008). Learning content can then be developed to meet the identified needs. The learning content, when aligned to specific roles and responsibilities in a job progression, creates learning paths that employees can use to guide their career development. Learning paths are evergreen and continue to change as the business strategies for new, emerging, and existing markets are defined and prioritized.

T&D Responsibility #2: Manage Content Development and Administration

Today's software systems make it easier to systematically develop learning content and to manage the logistics and record maintenance associated with registering for training, obtaining supervisor approval for employees to participate in learning activities, delivering online learning, and documenting the learning process and results. Software for managing learning includes learning content management systems (LCMS) and learning management systems (LMS).

Learning Content Management System

LCMS software provides a centralized, online repository for training content. An LCMS enables digital learning content to be collaboratively developed, stored, reused or repurposed, and distributed online. With an LCMS, T&D professionals and subject matter experts avoid creating from scratch each piece of content for a learning activity. Instead, they search the LCMS for the appropriate authoring tools and the learning objects, and quickly reuse or repurpose their finds. If no appropriate content exists, they may develop it. They then store the new learning objects in the LCMS database for future use.

An LCMS has many advantages. All learning objects are stored in one place. Increased efficiency and cost savings are gained when T&D professionals build on previous work.

Challenges with using this resource include the cost and the complexity of implementing a unified data management strategy. Issues to address include the following:

- Ensuring that the data is consistently created, managed, and disseminated
- Managing the range of technologies required to deliver content in the various formats
- Altering the view of content (i.e., from content viewed only as a course or book to content that can be used in many places without affecting the context)
- Learning new software for authoring and managing content

Learning Management Systems (LMS)

LMS software is an online tool that enables T&D professionals to systematically and efficiently administer, manage, and report learning events. For example, employees might click the online LMS links to access a catalog of training opportunities, individual learning requirements, training course registration forms, and employee transcripts of training activities. In addition to clicking on a list of required learning activities or searching the online catalogue, an employee might choose to register for a learning activity. When the registration process is completed, an employee can be placed on a wait list for the learning activity until the supervisor responds to the request for training approval received via e-mail. After approval, the employee can access an online computer-based learning activity via the LMS, complete the activity, and see the results posted on a transcript. At every step of this process, the LMS automatically updates and manages information.

Supervisors can use the LMS to monitor learning activity records for their employees. T&D leaders can use the LMS to view real-time reports that show patterns of learning within the organization (e.g., whether compliance requirements were met to satisfy government or other regulatory agency regulations).

Challenges in implementing an LMS include managing user expectations; the effort required to gain stakeholder agreement on the processes for administering learning activities should not be underestimated.

T&D Responsibility #3: Deliver Learning Content Efficiently

The responsibility of delivering the learning content, regardless of the delivery channel, stipulates that the learners acquire new knowledge, skills, attitudes, and experiences that they then transfer to the workplace to improve performance on the job with results accruing to the organization. To meet this responsibility, T&D professionals integrate knowledge about the following:

- Trainees and the training goals
- Learning and performance research
- Channels for delivering training

Knowledge about the Trainees and Training Goals

Consider the differences between the best training approach for orienting employees to new learning content and the best training approach for developing the skills of highly knowledgeable employees to make consistent judgments based on situational demands. As these two applications of training illustrate, the trainees' level of expertise and the training goal interact to influence the training delivery approach. Clark (2003) identified four instructional architectures that can be used to inform training delivery decisions. Following are brief descriptions of each architecture and some applications for it:

- *Receptive architecture.* The delivery of content with little opportunity for participant interaction. Use this architecture for building awareness and for briefings.
- *Directive architecture.* The delivery of content in short lessons with corrective feedback and avoidance of errors. Use this architecture when learners must acquire the skills to accurately complete procedural tasks or tasks that must be performed consistently each time and by each person.
- *Directed discovery architecture.* The delivery of content using problem-centered tasks where learners have opportunities to learn from mistakes. Use this architecture when learners need to build problem-solving skills and when learners will make judgments about applying their skills based on situational demands.
- *Exploratory architecture.* The delivery of content by providing training participants with learning resources and navigational interfaces. Use this architecture when teaching concepts, when learners have content knowledge and good metacognitive skills, or when learners will make judgments about applying their expertise based on situation demands.

Knowledge of Learning and Performance Research

Common sense is no longer sufficient for making training delivery decisions. Instead, T&D professionals increasingly rely on research findings. For example, research studies describe how to minimize cognitive overload so learners remember the content longer, how to best structure job aids, and so forth. To keep up with the latest research, we participate in professional research communities, such as Bersin & Associates, and monitor professional journals, such as the *Human Resource Development Quarterly, Human Resource Development International, Human Resource Development Review, Adult Education Quarterly,* and *Performance Improvement Quarterly.* We also monitor the competencies and standards created by the *International Board of Standards for Training, Performance, and Instruction.*

Knowledge about the Channels for Delivering Training

Training delivery channels can be grouped into three main categories: (1) formal instruction, (2) informal learning, and (3) instruction embedded in the work. Blended learning involves using channels from at least two of the three categories.

Formal instruction. For decades, instructor-led training (ILT) in a classroom was considered the ideal way to provide training content to groups of learners. ILT continues to be a predominant channel for instruction. The benefits of classroom instruction include the following:

- The training method is familiar to learners (i.e., most learners and instructors are experienced in classroom learning).
- Group training can be less expensive than training one-on-one.
- All participants are presented the same content.
- The presence of a trainer emphasizes the importance of the content to the organization's decision makers.
- Interactions among participants during the class can influence the acquisition of expertise and its application on the job.

Following are disadvantages of classroom instruction:

- It may be inconvenient for learners to participate at a specific time and place.
- It involves costs of the facility, transportation, and learner time away from the job.
- Some learners associate classroom learning with schools and teachers who lectured, which creates a barrier to their learning.
- Transfer of learning from the classroom to the job must be managed or it is unlikely to occur.

In addition to ILT, formal instruction can be delivered via electronic media (e.g., computers and cell phones). Learners can participate in structured classes via the Internet, intranet/extranet (LAN/WAN), satellite broadcast, interactive TV, and CDs or DVDs.

Formal instruction can be either synchronous or asynchronous. In synchronous instruction, the presentation of content and the learners' responses occur in real time. Synchronous instructional delivery channels via electronic devices include online chat sessions, audio and video conferences, and webinars. In asynchronous instruction, a time delay occurs between the content delivery and the learners' response. Examples of asynchronous instructional delivery channels include e-learning and e-mail.

Whether formal training is delivered in person or through electronic devices, T&D professionals recognize that the level and kind of interactivity affects learning. Interactivity refers to the learner's ability to affect, direct, and change the learning experience. When training is interactive, learners engage in the instruction and alter it through their choices about the content and the direction of the learning experience. Interactivity occurs through active, two-way dialogue between the learner and the instructor, the learner and peers, and/or the learner and instructional materials. Incorporating interactivity in instruction is challenging because predesigned graphics, audio recordings, video clips, and slide shows do not provide true interactivity.

Informal learning comes from acquiring new knowledge and skills both from daily experiences and from the resources in their environment. Whether intentional or unintentional, informal learning influences performance. For example, an employee who received a low rating on conflict management skills may intentionally read a book on the topic and practice the recommendations. Or that same employee as part of daily interactions with direct reports may incidentally realize that the team's many ongoing disagreements lead to poor performance.

Today's T&D professionals do not leave informal learning to chance; they facilitate it to ensure that it contributes to the organization's strategic goals and objectives. Informal training delivery channels include training libraries, rotational job assignments, communities of practice, mentoring, coaching, and social networks.

Training libraries are collections of learning resources that employees can access on demand. Libraries can include such resources as books, articles, self-study courses, and employee directories. Training libraries usually support informal learning; however, they can support formal instruction when each library resource is mapped to competencies and curricula and then systematically assigning to targeted groups of learners.

Rotational job assignments involve placing employees in a series of jobs and monitoring their performance. During each job assignment, the employee performs the work, is evaluated on performance under pressure, and learns firsthand the job's challenges and rewards. Because rotational job assignments have the advantage of providing employees with immediate stimulation and networking, they are often used to improve employee retention. In addition, rotational assignments can provide the organization's high-potential and high-performing employees with the front-line experiences and networks that become the foundation for leading the organization in the future. Often Superkeepers™ report out on their rotational experiences to executives in meetings that provide opportunities for review, feedback, and networking.

Communities of practice (CoP) provide a venue for a group of people who have similar interests to share information and experiences. A CoP can focus on a set of issues and problems. Members of a CoP learn from each other, increase their visibility, and develop a network of relationships. CoP meetings can take place in person or online via newsgroups, workspaces, or discussion boards. Some CoPs are informal, self-organized, and independent (i.e., they form when the experts gather to discuss or solve a problem and dissolve when the experts disband). Organizations are increasingly integrating CoPs into formal management structures where they can contribute to achieving organization goals (McDermott and Douglas 2010).

Mentoring and coaching have taken on an interesting mystique in the T&D field. While some people use the terms interchangeably, in practice, mentoring and coaching are different.

Mentoring occurs when a more experienced person (the mentor) guides a less experienced person (the protégé) in acquiring competencies for professional development. A mentorship is interactive and collaborative, with both the mentor and the protégé providing topics for learning. The mentor models behaviors and provides expertise and networking opportunities. The protégé acquires expertise, applies it on the job, and reports the experiences to the mentor. Mentorships vary in terms of their time span; some focus on a specific job, and some continue throughout the protégé's career. Outcomes of mentorships include the following:

- The transfer of specific knowledge and skills between the mentor and the protégé
- Relationship building, networking, and the creation of social capital
- Transmission of the organization culture as the mentor explicitly guides the protégé by sharing perspectives and views about "how things are done here"
- The development of new mental models, as the dialogue between the mentor and protégé produces new insights about how to better frame various situations
- Psychological support for both the mentor and the protégé

Mentorships can be structured or unstructured; however, T&D professionals increasingly rely on structured mentorships to ensure that the organization receives the maximum benefit from the informal learning. The book *Structured Mentoring for Sure Success* (Rousseau 2008) contains useful information on establishing a structured mentoring program.

By contrast, coaching as an employee development strategy (as compared to coaching in sports) tends to be short-term and to focus on specific issues or projects. Over the course of their careers, Superkeepers#™ rely on many coaches. Moreover, their coaches can be peers, supervisors, or subordinates—and the coaching often takes place on the job.

Social networks are composed of people who share interests and exchange information and knowledge. Employees can use digital social networks to share their applied knowledge, to self-manage, and to be responsible for the performance and management of various organizational processes (Hasgall and Shoham 2007). Such networks provide efficient avenues for employees to expand their business contacts by working through others.

Web 2.0 tools are used to manage access to knowledge and to ensure that knowledge is automatically updated. Web 2.0 also enables new ways to foster knowledge exchange (e.g., wikis/blogs, collaborative calendaring, photo sharing, presentation sharing, etc.). As an example, employees can upload information from the work site with the click of a cell phone camera for review by the relevant persons in their network. Moreover, the photo may be shared on the social network as a resource for other employees. To review additional examples of how organizations use social media, check out the Web site *Social Learning Examples: In the Workplace* (www.c4lpt.co.uk/handbook/corporate.html).

Learning embedded in the work can be extremely efficient. The boundaries between learning and performance are blurring. People gain much of their expertise while performing their work, and they perform their work while gaining expertise. A major advantage of learning that is embedded in work is improved learning transfer: Employees immediately apply the expertise they gain from learning on the job. Delivery channels for embedded training include performance support, on-the-job training, and new projects.

Performance support includes decision aids, content summaries, flow charts, advice, software, information, expert advice, data, visuals, tools, and more that employees use to guide their work. These tools can be available via computer networks that provide online access and also include self-monitoring systems. With performance support, employees access instruction when they need it and perform their work to the expected standard with minimal assistance from others.

Performance support is especially useful in potentially risky situations. For example, a pilot uses preflight checklists to confirm that the aircraft is ready for flight. By following a checklist, even expert pilots ensure that they do not inadvertently skip a critical step. Performance support is also useful for jobs with high turnover or jobs with processes that are performed infrequently.

On-the-job training (OJT) can be either structured or unstructured. Unstructured OJT is the most common delivery channel for training, especially for small groups of employees. However, unstructured OJT is costly. Have you ever been taught to perform a job by working with a veteran employee who was unorganized, emphasized the wrong information, and skipped critical steps in the process? Although those organizations avoided the costs of developing instructional materials, the instructional results of poor OJT included learning bad habits, using inefficient work processes, and, ultimately, producing inconsistent products and services.

By contrast, structured OJT incorporates a systematic instructional process, training lessons or guides, documentation, and trainee assessment (Jacobs 2003). While structured OJT offers an efficient, low-cost channel for delivering instructional content, implementing it requires management support and the investment of resources.

Projects, which can be assigned while employees perform their regular work, produce benefits for the organization. Projects also enable employees to develop expertise that later provides a scaffold for future learning and development.

Training and Development Responsibility #4: Assess the Value Proposition of T&D Efforts

T&D leaders rely on data to ensure that their efforts achieve the intended results, are implemented efficiently, support other talent management efforts in the organization, and provide for continuous improvement. Bersin (2008) offers a useful framework for evaluating training as an essential aspect of talent management.

Dashboards are easy-to-use visual displays that enable organizational decision makers to evaluate and drive business results. They present summary data for various measures that are important for business success. Decision makers can drill down into the data to gain additional insights. Dashboards also focus employees on the T&D measures that matter to the organization's decision makers.

T&D Success at Baker Hughes

T&D at Baker Hughes is structured to support the enterprise, which is composed of:

- Three oilfield services business segments that develop, manufacture, and support their industry-leading technologies.

- Operations organizations that render assistance to customers (i.e., the independent, international, and national oil companies). The operations organizations are organized into nine geographic regions composed of 26 geomarkets.

The T&D function has approximately 140 fulltime employees who work across the globe in such roles as competency manager, curriculum manager, content developer, training manager, instructor, facility manager, and learning administrator. Also supporting the T&D function is a network of internal instructors composed of over 200 subject matter experts, certified to deliver instructional programs related to company technology, processes, and culture. The corporate Talent Management Center of Excellence provides strategic direction for the global HR organization.

T&D efforts within Baker Hughes address the four responsibilities described above. To ensure that employee learning is targeted to the strategic needs, T&D professionals work with their business partners to stipulate the required competencies for specific jobs, develop curricula, and specify the learning and performance needs. This information provides the basis for developing training content and recommending other solutions to address the learning and performance needs. Learning content is delivered via formal instruction, informal learning, and/or instruction embedded in the work. T&D professionals are implementing and improving the LMS and LCMS for administering and managing learning content, and the value proposition for T&D is assessed. T&D employees actively work to improve the T&D process by participating in communities of practice where they gain additional expertise, develop toolkits that community members use to do their work, and engage with professionals from other organizational functions on shared issues. Outcomes of the T&D process at Baker Hughes include increased effectiveness in meeting business needs, increased credibility with stakeholders, more efficient and less costly training delivery, increased transfer of learning to the job, and T&D accountability.

An example of a T&D Baker Hughes success story is the Field Engineer Career Development Program. This structured competency-based program promotes and accelerates the development of field engineers. Those who complete the specified sequence of competency-based development steps can advance early in their careers. The program's learning activities include formal training through participation in the Baker Hughes Engineer Development Program (EDP). The courses in this program, which are designed to help newly hired field engineers gain the experience and knowledge needed to be effective leaders at Baker Hughes, involve both theoretical and hands-on learning, and are flexible and adaptable to different job requirements and work environments. The goal of EDP is to accelerate the development of competent and versatile people, enhance teamwork, and improve service quality.

The Field Engineer Career Development Program also relies heavily on informal learning through mentoring and learning what is embedded in the work via structured on-the-job training and performance/competency reviews. Candidates must successfully complete a structured review process every 12 months, and progression through grades is achieved only if requirements are met.

As this example highlights, T&D at Baker Hughes is integral to performing the organization's work and to developing employees and future leaders. Activities related to the four T&D responsibilities provided the foundation for this success.

Conclusion

The context for T&D has changed over the last decade. To meet current expectations for contributing to talent management and to organizational strategic goals, T&D professionals today must use resources that enable them to better focus their learning and development efforts, manage content development and administration, deliver learning content efficiently, and assess the value proposition of those efforts for continuous improvement. By combining resources, T&D professionals can create exciting opportunities to change the way learning and development efforts are viewed, carried out, and managed in their organizations. Ultimately, they will maximize T&D's benefits in their organizations.

References

Bersin, J. 2008. *The training measurement book: Best practices, proven methodologies, and practical approaches.* San Francisco: Pfeiffer.

Boudreau, J. W., and P. M. Ramstad. 2005. Talentship and the evolution of human resource management from "professional practices" to "strategic talent decision science."

Clark, R. 2003. *Building expertise: Cognitive methods for training and performance improvement* (2nd ed.). Washington, DC: International Society for Performance Improvement.

Gupta, K., C. M. Sleezer, and D. Russ-Eft. 2007. *A practical guide to needs assessment* (2nd ed.). San Francisco: Pfeiffer.

Hasgall, A., and S. Shoham. 2007. Digital social network technology and complex organizational systems. *VINE* 37(2):180–191.

Jacobs, R. L. 2003. *Structured on the job training: Unleashing employee expertise in the workplace.* San Francisco: Berrett-Koehler.

McDermott, R., and A. Douglas. 2010. Harnessing your staff's informal networks. *Harvard Business Review* 88(3).

Robinson, D. G., and J. C. Robinson. 2008. *Performance consulting: A practical guide for HR and learning professionals* (2nd ed.). San Francisco: Berrett-Koehler.

Rousseau, M. 2008. *Structured mentoring for sure success.* Tulsa, OK: Pennwell.

Social Learning Academy. 2010. *Social learning examples in the workplace.* (April 2). Retrieved April 3, 2010, from http://www.c4lpt.co.uk/handbook/corporate.html.

Chapter 19

Developing Your Workforce: Measurement Makes a Difference

Jack J. Phillips, Ph.D., Chairman
ROI Institute, Inc.
Lisa Edwards, Senior Director for Talent Management
Corbis

Introduction

The 2008 global financial crisis forced many organizations to rethink the way they manage and develop talent. After organizations responded to the initial crisis by making significant cost and head count reductions, many talent management professionals scrambled to demonstrate the value of talent management related programs to the organization. More importantly, executives recognized the urgent need to quickly innovate after cutting costs in order to retain market share and speed ahead of the competition. The role of the talent management professional emerged as an important piece in the organization's ability to survive the recession and thrive beyond the crisis to succeed in the future. Talent management professionals continue to be faced with a challenge to demonstrate the monetary value of talent development investments targeted to the right people, at the right time, and for the right reasons. The key to success is in measurement.

Without measurement, talent management professionals are at risk of failing to demonstrate value. For example, consider the organization development (OD) leader of a large health-care provider whose entire team was eliminated because the leadership was unable to see the contribution this team made to its competitive advantage or the bottom line. Or think about the training leader of a regional nonprofit whose role and team were under consideration for elimination because the head of the organization had no data about how the work of this team made a difference to the operational efficiency of the organization.

Moreover, as training budgets are reduced and competitive pressures continue to increase, the demand for a targeted focus on specific talent groups has become equally important. In 2008, organizations slightly reduced average expenditure per employee from $1,110 in 2007 to $1,068, reflecting a decrease of 3.8 percent and likely to be reflected in 2009's data (ASTD 2009). Now is the right time for talent management professionals to adopt a strategic accountability approach to developing its workforce. This chapter illustrates the key steps in developing such an approach.

A Strategic Accountability Approach

The approach to developing the workforce has evolved since the origination of the corporate university concept. This evolution is likely to continue as more executives demand to see results and organizations must continue to get more with less in order to remain competitive in the global marketplace. In the past, training and development activities were assumed to work. Reporting was focused on a number of participants in attendance, number of programs offered, and reaction and satisfaction data.

Today things have changed. There is a need to develop the Superkeepers™, the employees who greatly exceed expectations, so that their performance is reflected in bottom-line outcomes as well as other intangible measures. Programs must be linked to business strategy, and there are greater expectations to provide a comprehensive approach to measurement and evaluation. This shift from a focus on activities to results is illustrated in Table 19-1.

Activity-Focused	Results-Focused
No business need for the program	Program linked to a specific business
No assessment of performance issues	Assessment of performance effectiveness
No specific measureable objectives	Specific objectives for behavior and business impact
No effort to prepare program participants for results	Results expectations communicated to participants
No effort to prepare the work environment to support the application	Environment prepared to support application
No efforts to build partnership with key managers	Partnerships established with key managers and clients
No measurement of results or ROI analysis	Measure of results and ROI analysis
Planning and reporting is input-focused	Planning and reporting is outcome-focused

Table 19-1 Activity-Focused vs. Results-Focused Approach

Balanced Scorecard

Much of this change is reflected in the way top-performing organizations run their talent management function. For example, the American Society for Training and Development (ASTD) has tracked the characteristics of the BEST, award-winning organizations since 2003. Award-winning companies are identified by their previous year's financial and operational data such as customer satisfaction, quality of products and services, cycle time, productivity, retention, revenue, and overall profitability. The 2009 BEST Award winners continued to validate the same eight characteristics as identified in 2003, which include clearly defined processes to link learning strategies and initiatives to increases in both individual and organizational performance. Additionally, the BEST organizations indicated that they used a balanced scorecard to assess learning's impact on individual and organizational performance metrics by gauging key performance indicators or performance objectives (ASTD 2009).

Why a Scorecard?

A scorecard is an effective way to provide critical information to client groups, including senior executives. The scorecard also provides a useful way for talent management staff to track success and ensure their approach is focused on the key objectives of the business.

   While there are many stakeholders of the scorecard, there are two primary groups: consumers and clients. Consumers are the individuals who participate in the program; clients are those who fund, support, request, or approve programs. Both groups have a vested interest in the scorecard, and a recent survey shows that 22 percent of CEOs say they have a learning scorecard (Phillips and Phillips 2010).

Consumers

To ensure that programs are effective, the talent management staff must have feedback in the form of data from the consumers of the programs. Not only do they need to know to what extent the participants believed in the program, but they must also know that the participants learned new information and applied that new knowledge to their work situation. Ideally, the talent management staff must also understand which programs are making an impact on the business and to what degree. Finally, talent management staff should gain insight on the return on investment (ROI) of the programs. All of this data combined gives the talent management team important information they can use to develop, refine, and improve their approach.

Clients

The client group is interested in knowing how participants changed their behavior, the business impact of those behaviors, and the resulting ROI of the program for the organization. They are also interested in knowing that there is a clear linkage between what the business needs and the program outcomes. More often, senior executives are looking to see actual return on investment to ensure the programs have an important payoff for the organization.

The needs of both the consumer group as well as the client group can be met through a scorecard. Collectively, the needs from these different target groups create a demand for a measurement system that will collect, distribute, and interpret the necessary data on a routine basis.

Developing the Scorecard Data

There are three considerations in developing the scorecard:

1. Measuring effectiveness at five levels of evaluation
2. Utilizing a strategic approach to the measurement and evaluation framework
3. Following a standardized set of guiding principles in monetizing data

Five Levels of Scorecard Evaluation

The first consideration in developing the scorecard is based upon the work of Kirkpatrick (1975) and later enhanced by Phillips (1995). This approach includes evaluating programs at five levels represented in Table 19-2.

Level	Description
1. Reaction and satisfaction	Measures participants' reaction to the program and stakeholder satisfaction with the program and the planned implementation.
2. Learning	Measures skills, knowledge, or attitude changes related to the program and implementation.
3. Application and implementation	Measures changes in behavior on the job and specific application and implementation of the program.
4. Business impact	Measures business impact changes related to the program.
5. Return on investment	Compares the monetary value of the business impact with the costs of the program.

Table 19-2 Phillips' Five Levels of Evaluation

Scorecard Measurement and Evaluation Framework

In addition to the five levels of evaluation, it is important to utilize a framework which allows for a way to plan, collect, and categorize the data. This framework, illustrated in Figure 19-1, is the ROI Methodology™ and allows for the collection of good data and a comprehensive approach to analysis. Through the application of this process, six types of measures are generated:

1. Participant reaction and satisfaction
2. Learning application
3. Implementation
4. Business impact
5. ROI

6. Intangible benefits, such as improved engagement, productivity, customer satisfaction, and so on.

This approach ensures a balanced set of measures.

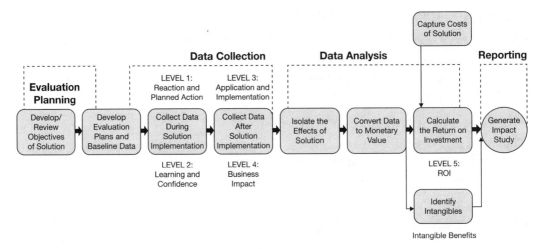

Figure 19-1 ROI Methodology Framework

Source: Phillips, Jack J. *Return on Investment in Training and Performance Improvement Programs*, 2nd Edition. (Boston, MA: Butterworth-Heinemann, 2003).

Scorecard Guiding Principles

Finally, to ensure that the scorecard is credible with senior executives, the following Twelve Guiding Principles must be followed:

1. When conducting a higher-level evaluation, collect data at lower levels.
2. When planning a higher level evaluation, the previous level of evaluation is not required to be comprehensive.
3. When collecting and analyzing data, use only the most credible sources.
4. When analyzing data, select the most conservative alternatives for calculations.
5. Use at least one method to isolate the effects of the program or project.
6. If no improvement data are available for a population or from a specific source, assume that little or no improvement has occurred.
7. Adjust estimates of improvements for the potential error of the estimates.
8. Avoid use of extreme data items and unsupported claims when calculating ROI calculations.
9. Use only the first year of annual benefits in the ROI analysis of short-term solutions.
10. Fully load all costs of the solution, project, or program when analyzing ROI.
11. Intangible measures are defined as measures that are purposely not converted to monetary values.
12. Communicate the results of the ROI methodology to all key stakeholders.

Building the Scorecard

Traditionally, a talent management scorecard would reflect the inputs and include budget, spend per employee, number of participants, and so on. While this information is important to include in the overall scorecard, it is not the only data to include. The scorecard should also include learning, application, impact, and ROI.

The first step is to determine how many and which programs will be evaluated at the various levels. Ideally, as many programs as possible will be measured at the ROI level. Then the data from each of the programs must be integrated to present an overall picture at the macro level. The end result will be a scorecard that represents seven major categories to include indicators, each of the levels, and intangible benefits.

Following are descriptions of each of the categories.

Indicators and Inputs

Indicators and inputs are the traditional input data. These data are indicators of organizational commitment and investment. It is important to clarify the most important indicators, as it is easy for this section of the scorecard to contain too much irrelevant data. The data that are included must be important to the executive team and are likely to include the following:

1. The number of employees participating in the programs
2. The number of hours of learning activity per employee
3. Enrollment statistics such as demographics of participants, participation rates, completion rates, and so on.
4. Investment in learning reported as total cost, cost per employee, direct cost per participant, and cost as a percent of payroll
5. Cost recovery if there is a charge-back system, which is typical in many corporate universities
6. Status of alternative delivery programs

Additional inputs may include the use of technology, on-the-job training, trends, volume, and efficiencies. Indicators demonstrate the degree of the executive leadership's commitment to talent management.

Reaction, Satisfaction, and Planned Action (Level 1)

Level 1—reaction, satisfaction, and planned action—is the most popular level of measurement and is typically used in 100 percent of all talent management programs. Some argue that 100 percent is not needed and that a sampling is sufficient. However, if planned action is a part of the data collection at this level, it is important to capture planned action from all the participants. Additionally, many participants want to be able to give their feedback—especially if they had an exceptionally satisfying or extremely disappointing learning event.

While specific items can vary with the programs offered, following are eight recommended items:

1. Relevance to the job
2. Usefulness of the program

3. Amount of new information
4. Likely to recommend to others
5. Importance of information
6. Intention to use skills/knowledge
7. Effectiveness of the facilitator
8. Effectiveness of the delivery method

These items represent useful Level 1 data. Additionally, six of the eight have been found to be predictive of learning and application outcomes (Warr, Allan, and Birdi 1999; Alliger and Tannenbaum 1997; APQC 2000).

Learning (Level 2)

Measuring the extent to which participants acquire new skills and knowledge offered in the program is a greater challenge. The first step is to determine the number of programs that will be evaluated at this level. Typically 60 percent of programs will be evaluated at the learning level.

Methods for collecting Level 2 learning data include formal methods such as tests, simulations, and structured skill demonstrations. Informal methods include self-assessments, facilitator assessment, and team assessment. Some organizations distinguish between formal and informal data collection methods and report it as such.

In order to compare learning changes from one program to another and integrate the data into a macro view, it is essential to have only a few identical measures and should include:

- Understanding of the skills/knowledge
- Ability to use the skills/knowledge
- Confidence in the use of skills/knowledge

A final technique for measuring learning effectiveness of the program is a pre- and post-test and is reported as percent improvement. Reported in the scorecard as an average measure for similar programs, it provides insight into the extent of learning change for all of the programs measured at Level 2.

Application and Implementation (Level 3)

At this level, change in behavior is measured. As in the previous step, the first issue is to determine the number of programs that will be measured at this level. Typically 20 to 50 percent of programs are measured at this level.

When assessing change in behavior, you should evaluate the following:

- The importance of the skill/knowledge in the work as applied on the job
- The frequency of use of the new skill/knowledge on the job
- The effectiveness of the skill/knowledge as applied on the job

Additionally, the next recommended measures can be critical to the success of the program:

1. The percent of planned action plans completed by the desired follow-up time, which indicates the extent to which participants apply and complete their assignments from the program.
2. The barriers and enablers to the skill and knowledge application on the job as well as management support, which indicates what helps or hinders the application of the knowledge and skills learned through training.
3. The data collection technique utilized, which shows whether subjective or objectives data was collected.

Business Impact (Level 4)

The connection to the business measure is easily tabulated when impact studies are conducted to show business impact or when follow-up questionnaires are utilized to capture application data. Typically 10 to 20 percent of programs are evaluated at this level. This percentage can be increased through interviews, questionnaires, and focus groups to capture business impact data.

Sometimes it is useful to present the investment perception from the viewpoint of the participant. In this instance, participants provide input about the expected ROI with simple questions about their perception of the quality of the program and its monetary contribution. These questions are included in follow-up questionnaires and can be a simple question such as "Was this program a good investment for the organization?" The summary of responses is reported in the scorecard.

An important element to be reported on the scorecard is the method of isolation used to isolate the effects of the program. There are several ways to isolate the effects of the program:

- Using a control versus an experimental group
- Trend line analysis of performance data
- Use of forecasting methods of performance data
- Participants estimate of the program's impact
- Supervisor's estimate of the program's impact
- Management's estimate of the program's impact
- Use of previous studies/experts
- Calculating/estimating the impact of other factors
- Use of customer input

Finally, Level 4 data is important for improving the performance of all employees and in particular for the Superkeepers™.

Return on Investment (Level 5)

The ultimate level of evaluation is the actual ROI, in which the monetary benefits are compared with the cost of the program. Generally only 5 to 10 percent of programs should be measured at this level. An ROI study is reported to specific target audiences and only summary data are needed on the scorecard. A brief paragraph showing the nature of the study and the actual results, including the ROI percentage along with information on how to obtain additional details, should be included in the scorecard. To ensure credibility, it is important to illustrate how data was converted to monetary values. Typical techniques for converting data to monetary value include the following:

- Converting output to contribution
- Converting the cost of quality
- Converting employee's time
- Using historical costs
- Using internal and external experts
- Using data from external databases
- Linking with other measures
- Using participant's estimates
- Using supervisors' and managers' estimates
- Using talent management staff estimates

The cost per participant can also be included, and at this level represents fully loaded costs. Cost items include, but are not limited to, needs assessment cost, program development and delivery costs, facilitator as well as participant costs, travel and facilities costs, administrative costs, and the cost of the evaluation. This cost is then divided by the number of participants in the program and reported in the scorecard.

Intangible Measures

The final category to report is intangible measures. These measures can be included in the business impact category as a subcategory or mentioned in a separate section. Intangible measures are defined as those that have not been converted to monetary value but are important to the program. Examples include customer satisfaction, employee engagement, and job satisfaction. Keep in mind that although each of these measures *could* be monetized, doing so is not always practical or desired. Sometimes intangible measures are reported voluntarily by participants, while at other times they are tracked throughout the organization.

Communicating the Scorecard

The primary target audience for the scorecard is the executive team as well as the talent management team. Additionally, supervisors of program participants as well as participants are interested in the scorecard. The elements of the scorecard are shown in Table 19-3.

Scorecard
Indicators
1. Number of employees involved
2. Total hours of involvement

Table 19-3 Scorecard (continued on next page)

3. Hours per employee
4. Training investment as a percent of payroll
5. Cost per participant
Reaction and Planned Action (Level 1)
1. Percent of program evaluated at this level
2. Ratings on seven items vs. target
3. Percent with action plans
4. Percent with ROI forecast
Learning (Level 2)
1. Percent of programs evaluated at this level
2. Types of measurements
3. Self-assessment ratings on three items vs. targets
4. Pre/post average differences
Application (Level 3)
1. Percent of programs evaluated at this level
2. Ratings on three items vs. targets
3. Percent of action plans complete
4. Barriers (list of top 10)
5. Enablers (list of top 10)
6. Management support profile
Business Impact (Level 4)
1. Percent of programs evaluated at this level
2. Linkage with measure (list of top 10)
3. Types of measurement techniques
4. Types of methods to isolate the effects of the programs
5. Investment perception
ROI
1. Percent of programs evaluated at this level
2. ROI summary for each study
3. Methods of converting data to monetary values
4. Fully loaded cost per participant
Intangibles
5. List of intangibles (top 10)
6. How intangibles were captured

Table 19-3 Scorecard (continued)

Scorecard Challenges

Three main challenges must be addressed in moving to a comprehensive scorecard to measure and track success. The first challenge is to allocate appropriate resources for measurement and evaluation. The scorecard can be developed and implemented for 5 percent of the total talent management budget. However, cost savings can be realized when effective measures reveal programs to be eliminated so that budgets can be utilized more effectively.

The second challenge is to approach the task in a disciplined, methodical method. This is difficult when not required by senior management. However, the responsibility for ensuring the process is utilized appropriately rests on the talent management team.

The final challenge is the actual use of the data. While the data reveals successes, it potentially also reveals programs which are not effective. Treating the scorecard and the methodology as an approach to process improvement alienates the fears that some may have with this approach.

The good news is that developing a scorecard of program success, based on outcomes rather than activities, provides evidence that developmental opportunities for the Superkeepers™ are working within the organization.

References

Alliger, George, and Scott I. Tannenbaum. 1997. A meta-analysis of the relations among training criteria. *Personnel Psychology* 50 (2):341–358.

American Productivity & Quality Center. 2000. The corporate university measuring the impact of learning, Houston.

Kirkpatrick, Donald L. 1975. Techniques for evaluation training programs, McGraw-Hill Education (India) Pvt Ltd.

Phillips, Jack J. 1995. Corporate training: Does it pay off? *William & Mary Business Review* (Summer) 6–10.

Phillips, Jack J., and Patricia P. Phillips. 2010. *Measuring for success: What CEOs really think about learning investments*. Alexandria, VA: ASTD Press.

Warr, Peter, Catriona Allan, and Kama Birdi. 1999. Predicting three levels of training outcome. *Journal of Occupational and Organization Psychology* 72:351–375.

Chapter 20

Developing Top Talent: Guiding Principles, Methodology, and Practices Considerations

Karol M. Wasylyshyn, Psy.D., President
Leadership Development

TWO CATALYTIC EXPERIENCES SIGNIFICANTLY INFLUENCED MY BELIEFS AND PRACTICES regarding the development of top talent.[1] One occurred in the mid-1980s with a global manufacturer of chemical and electronic materials and will be discussed later in this chapter with a view toward conveying potential best practices as related to top talent development. These potential best practices will be considered through the guiding principles, methodology, and practices considerations that drove this work. The other catalytic event occurred in the early 1990s with a global pharmaceutical company. The chapter begins with this experience—one that provides clues about the possible traps to avoid in top talent development initiatives.

Catalytic Experience 1

In this experience, I was one of a cadre of external consultants involved in a leadership development program focused on a company's top 400 high-potential managers. In the full-day orientation to the program, we were briefed on the design that placed multi-rater feedback as its core element. These were early days of the data-gathering tool now known as "360 feedback," so considerable time was spent on the leadership competencies as well as on the electronic data-gathering process—also innovative at the time (Bass 1995). Participants represented every global sector; and given some lingering concern about confidentiality, a significant number of them had requested external feedback consultants. Another concern, raised by company HR professionals based in Asia about the difficulties associated with getting meaningful multi-rater feedback from Asians, went unanswered.

Regarding action planning, the expectation was that participants were all smart enough to complete their own development planning. Within a year or so, this initiative was abandoned. A former HR professional of the company confirmed the reason: Talent development initiatives cannot maintain traction or credibility absent action planning and follow-up. Such initiatives must also be connected to a company's broader talent development strategy.

Catalytic Experience 2

The second catalytic experience was significantly more influential in that it involved one of the longest continuous top talent development initiatives in a global organization, Rohm and Haas Company (now Dow). For nearly 25 years, I worked in close collaboration with the CEO and other C-suite executives, particularly the leader of the HR function, to ensure the development of its top 70 senior executives and high-potential managers (top 5 percent of the company).

In 1985 the then-Chairman of Rohm and Haas Company Larry Wilson concluded that the growth of his company necessitated the focused development of top business and functional leaders. He needed leaders who were more globally minded, entrepreneurial, and market-facing, and who would drive business growth faster. Wilson charged his Corporate Head of Human Resources, Mark Feck, to design and implement an initiative that would deliver on this objective.

After a series of discussions about competencies, Wilson determined the initial set[2] and Leadership 2000[3] was launched in 1986. In brief, this was conceived as a top talent development *process*—not a program. The four phases of this process will be described under "Methodology" later in the chapter.

Guiding Principles

See Table 20-1.

CEO makes business case for top talent development/internal-internal partnership
Conveyance of executive wisdom
Internal-external partnership—holistic approach
Fostering trust—maintaining boundaries of confidentiality

Table 20-1 Developing Top Talent—4 Guiding Principles

CEO Makes Business Case for Top Talent Development/ Internal-Internal Partnership

High-impact top talent development work evolves best when initiated by a CEO who makes the business case for its necessity. Such efforts can also be initiated by a senior HR professional who provides the business rationale and enjoys a collaborative relationship with the CEO. Ideally, the CEO is maintained as an overt champion of the initiative and along with other C-suite executives actively participates in the work. Further, such initiatives take hold and thrive in the presence of a strong strategic (internal-internal) partnership between the CEO and senior HR officer who is a member of the CEO's leadership team.

Conveyance of Executive Wisdom

The ongoing engagement of the CEO and other C-suite executives in rigorous and thorough follow-up phases ensures the necessary motivation and commitment of all involved. *Leadership 3000* participants wanted to "show well," and senior executives wanted to convey their lessons learned in ways that would accelerate business success. Often these lessons involved the less obvious tactics, interpersonal dynamics, and grittier "political" aspects of effective leadership in a global business world in which factors like customer intimacy were assuming greater importance (Wiersema 1998). Further, the candor that typified action planning and follow-up meetings gave C-suite executives a closer look at top talent individuals, and often ignited unexpected possibilities such as ex-pat assignments or function-to-business management role rotations.

Internal-External Partnership—Insight-Oriented/Holistic Approach

Feck believed there was a talent pool "waiting to be released." He also believed Wilson's objective was steep given potential barriers, most specifically what was commonly referred to as "Rohm and Haas polite." This culture factor, coupled with his desire to give participants an insight-oriented and holistic experience, influenced his choice of me, a clinically trained consultant, as his design and implementation partner. In Feck's words, "We need to go inside-out. We need to assess the whole person, not just one's profile of leadership competencies. We need to have real relationships with these people, and they need to know themselves and understand what influences their behavior in good times and bad. Their accurate self-awareness is essential for continued learning and personal growth. Continued learning and personal growth are essential for the development of world-class leaders" (Wasylyshyn 2003, p. 322). This interdisciplinary (business, HR, and psychology) partnership ensured the project's holistic and insight-oriented intent. Equally important, it helped to maintain a focus on business priorities and to link me with other key HR stakeholders in the organization.

Fostering Trust

Fostering trust that was grounded in clear boundaries of confidentiality was another— and perhaps overarching—guiding principle of *Leadership 3000*. This was accomplished in numerous ways, commencing with the invitation to participants that stressed its *developmental* (versus evaluative) intent. This meant that each *Leadership 3000* participant was considered the "client," the company was the "sponsor," and each client owned her or his data (Tobias 1990). Through the action-planning and follow-up phases, the sponsor received detailed information about participants' strengths and development areas, but this was quite different from their having access to actual psychometric and/or multi-rater data. Surely it was appropriate for Feck to weigh in on key personnel decisions involving these participants, but he did so in a manner consistent with his HR role versus *Leadership 3000* process owner.[4] Finally, I was never asked—or expected—to "vote" on candidates as related to C-suite succession planning activities.

Methodology

See Table 20-2.

| Identification of participants |
| Four-phase model |
| Multifaceted data gathering |
| Synthesized feedback |
| Comprehensive action planning and follow-up |
| Optional spousal module |
| Fostering "total brain leadership" |

Table 20-2 Developing Top Talent: Methodology Factors

Identification of *Leadership 3000* Participants

Participants in *Leadership 3000* were identified through an annual talent review process that included the specification of activities that would yield rapid developmental mileage. For top talent, this meant nomination into *Leadership 3000*. This linkage between the company's overall talent management strategy and the specialized *Leadership 3000* development process was key in socializing its purpose and place in the array of human resource development activities.

While there was a concern at the outset about fostering a "crown prince/princess" dynamic ultimately, the retention benefit of sending the "top talent" message far outweighed any adverse effects. Further, this process was also used in the onboarding of newly hired C-suite executives. In this instance, multi-rater feedback was gathered after the individual had been in role for several months. Initial feedback to these executives focused on the company culture norms, the individual's behavioral preferences, and opportunities for leveraging quick "wins," as well as avoiding early faux pas.

Four-Phase Model

The *Leadership 3000* four-phase model consisted of data gathering, feedback, action planning, and follow-up. On the surface this appears similar to other insight-oriented leadership development methodology (Kilburg 2004), but there were two notable differences. The first was the ongoing engagement of the CEO and other C-suite executives in the action-planning and follow-up phases, as described above under "Guiding Principles." The second was the optional Spousal Module. More will be said below about this uncommon development tool.

Multifaceted Data Gathering

Given the holistic principle of *Leadership 3000*, its data-gathering phase was multifaceted and began with gathering a full life-history. Core life themes were then integrated with the psychometric data in an attempt to provide participants with deeper insights about their motivations, aspirations, behavioral preferences, and quality of both personal and work-related relationships—particularly as related to leadership style.

A broad array of psychometric tools[5]—appropriate for use in the workplace—were used to engage participants rapidly and to cause relevant leadership information to surface. On an optional basis a projective technique, the Rorschach, was also included in an effort to provide participants with even deeper insights about their personalities (de Villemor-Amaral 2007). Of note, given the confidential nature of all testing data and the innate curiosity of these high-potential individuals, every participant elected to include the Rorschach. Feedback discussion of deeper issues such as the individual's potential for transference reactions,[6] behavioral hot buttons, and points of particular vulnerability often provided breakthrough insights.

In addition to the company competencies, a set of Essential Leadership Behaviors[7] provided the basis for the multi-rater data gathering. This information was gathered face-to-face initially and then electronically with follow-up conversations to ensure full understanding of each rater's input, as well as of pertinent contextual factors.

Synthesized Feedback

The goal of two lengthy feedback sessions (one for the psychometric data and one for the organization-based multi-rater data) was to synthesize all the information and identify both strengths to leverage and development needs. In the last wave of *Leadership 3000* (2000–2008), participants' most frequently occurring strengths were bias for action, strategic focus, creative thinking, business acumen, and courageous leadership. In this same population the most frequently occurring development needs were emotional fortitude, persuasion and influence, developing people, courageous leadership, and strategic focus.[8]

Comprehensive Action Planning and Follow-up

Participants prepared a *preliminary action plan (PAP)* based on their strengths and development needs. This document provided the basis for the action planning meeting that would be attended by members of her/his development "brain trust."[9] Participants then integrated meeting content into what became the *Master Action Plan (MAP)*. Participants' MAPs, consisted of specific actions and included timelines for progress. While they could include familiar development vehicles such as business school executive education programs, job rotations, task force assignments, short-term mentoring, and executive coaching, they were also distinguished by the pursuit of "lessons learned" (conveyance of executive wisdom) as provided by C-suite members.

Regarding the essential leadership behaviors, *emotional fortitude*,[10]. emerged as a particular development need. As top talent, they represented what I saw in other companies: unilateral cognitive strength (IQ) but less strong in terms of emotional intelligence (EQ).[11] Through *Leadership 3000* participants focused on the development of "total brain leadership"—that is, the integration of left and right brain functioning. In a global business climate, right-brain capabilities particularly as related to cultural understanding and other relationship challenges need to be on a par with left-brain analytical and problem-solving strengths (Wasylyshyn 2008).

In the words of former General Electric CEO Jack Welch, "No doubt emotional intelligence is more rare than book smarts, but my experience says it is actually more important in the making of a leader. You just can't ignore it" (2004, p. A14).

Numerous researchers emphasize the importance of emotional intelligence as a fundamental leadership competency (Goldman 1998; Goldman, Boyatzis, and McKee 2002; Brienza and Cavallo 2005). Further, ongoing research in this realm of leadership has produced the construct of social intelligence. Goleman and Boyatzis wrote, "The salient discovery is that certain things leaders do—specifically, exhibit empathy and become attuned to others' moods—literally affect both their own brain chemistry and that of their followers" (2008, p. 2).

And from the C-suite, we hear the all-encompassing importance of this leadership dimension captured in a comment from Haemonetics CEO Brian Concannon, "Leadership is about connecting the longest distance in the world—the one between the head and the heart"[12] (personal communication, 2005).

Regarding the *Leadership 3000* follow-up phase, all members of a participant's development brain trust attended a mandatory MAP review meeting approximately eight to nine months after the action planning meeting. This gave participants sufficient "real world practice" time to work their MAPs (Hicks and Peterson 1999). For this meeting, participants provided annotated versions of their MAPs to indicate progress made and/or the need for additional guidance.

Optional Spousal Module

The optional Spousal Module was designed in response to the holistic intent of *Leadership 3000*. It was grounded in the following rationale: top talent individuals do not usually seek assistance with personal issues, however difficult they may be. Giving them a confidential opportunity to explore and, in some instances, to assist in resolving marital or other family issues in a constructive and problem-solving manner could help reduce personal distractions, thus fostering greater focus on work.

For those who included this optional component in their *Leadership 3000*, I gathered data from each partner using a customized interview protocol. A subsequent three-way planning meeting focused on a broad array of personal issues, as well as work-related concerns including the stress of ex-pat assignments, repatriation, dual careers, and chronic work-family integration[13] issues.

Practice Considerations

See Table 20-3.

Commitment to one program/one external partner over time
Positioning the initiative as a "pilot"
Fierce truth-telling
Relationship-based commitment—meeting participants where they need to be met

Table 20-3 Top Talent Development: Practice Considerations

Commitment to One Development Model and One External Partner

The importance of Rohm and Haas's commitment to *one* leadership development model for its top talent, as well as its 24-year partnership with the same external consultant, enabled the company to leverage numerous longitudinal effects. These effects included (1) participants' accelerated preparedness for bigger roles, the building of a new business platform, and expansion into Asia; (2) the establishment of a clear and sustained set of leadership competencies for top talent; (3) a clear semantic regarding the behavioral norms as related to leadership effectiveness; (4) the culture and C-suite relationship "archeology" I could bring to each new *Leadership 3000* participant; and (5) and an unexpected top talent *retention* benefit. (More will be said about this under "Relationship-Based Commitment" later in the chapter.).

Positioning the Program as a "Pilot"

The decision to position *Leadership 3000* as a "pilot" had effects beyond the obvious grace period for identifying constructive changes.[14] Given the absence of a major program rollout, outcome expectations were managed, and concerns about costs were minimized. By choosing the potential best "ambassadors" for the initial "pilot" group, participants themselves established the credibility of the process.

Further, since the first wave of participants included top talent from regions other than North America, there was time to fine-tune the methodology and create a viable long-distance approach for future non-U.S. participants. For example, American and Asian HR professionals based in Asia were enlisted as feedback resources for competency-based data gathering versus holding the expectation that direct reports or even the peers of Asian top talent participants would be comfortable enough to provide candid feedback

Fierce Truth-Telling

It is only in recent years that the leadership clarion call for transparency has helped break through business culture totems, turf struggles, unproductive competitive dynamics, and the silo mentality that can block honest performance feedback and candor generally (Olegario 2006). *Leadership 3000* tackled this potential barrier by (1) using the multifaceted data-gathering phase to illuminate inescapable development themes, (2) holding firm on the guiding principle of data confidentiality, and (3) leveraging the trusting relationships that formed between participants and both the internal (HR) and external (myself) members of their *Leadership 3000* brain trust. It would appear that the fierce truth-telling that characterized this work chipped away at the "Rohm and Haas polite" dynamic.[15] Specifically, in the early days of the Dow acquisition (2009), Dow executives described Rohm and Haas top talent as "considerably more aggressive and direct" as compared to their Dow peers.

Relationship-Based Commitment: Meeting Participants Where They Need to be Met

In the first catalytic experience cited above there were two fundamental problems with the program developers' contention that participants should be smart enough to craft their own development plans. First, sound development action planning is not about being smart. In fact, we know that for smart people developmental learning can be difficult due to their tendency for defensive reasoning (Argyris 1991). Second, objective and targeted action planning is not easy—hence, the just-in-time, step-wise collaboration between participants and consultant in framing good PAPs and MAPs.

More importantly, from an authentic, relationship-based perspective, was the immediate assistance participants received in the wake of difficult, sudden life events such as accidents, deaths, and illnesses. For example, a French participant was provided a bilingual bereavement counselor when his father died.

The consideration of love—that is, the place of affiliative love in top talent development—is beyond the scope of this chapter. However, meeting *Leadership 3000* participants where *they needed to be met* involved many acts of attunement and committed caring that could be considered a way of loving. It is possible then that on a deeper, psychodynamic level such caring and/or loving was part of the "glue" in these close, development-oriented relationships.

Of particular note was the unexpected top talent retention benefit of *Leadership 3000*. Participants were often contacted by executive recruiters luring them with opportunities that were both appealing and anxiety-provoking. In the safety and candor of *Leadership 3000* brain trust relationships, they were helped to weigh the pros and cons of outside roles objectively. In nearly 25 years, the company only lost three of its Superkeepers™.

Implications for the Future

Was *Leadership 3000* successful in developing top talent at Rohm and Haas Company? This will be impossible to assess fully in light of its purchase by Dow. However, in the wake of the purchase, Rohm and Haas CEO Raj Gupta wrote, ". . . *Leadership 3000* resulted in the development of a highly diverse group of global leaders and ensured a smooth leadership transition at the CEO level. Further it helped deepen the self-confidence and preparedness of key business leaders who drove two of the company's boldest initiatives—the building of its Electronic Materials business and its presence in Asia" (Gupta and Wasylyshyn 2009, p. 37).

An assessment of over half of the *Leadership 3000* participants conducted by an outside evaluator hired by Dow found them to be "significantly above the industry benchmark" especially in terms of customer and marketplace focus. While these assessments of success cannot substitute for empirically based research, they are nevertheless positive indications of the potential value of a CEO-sponsored, insight-oriented, holistic development process delivered over an extended time (Gupta and Wasylyshyn 2009, p. 37).

Further, beyond the impact such a process can have for the development of top talent, there are potential systemic effects with implications for building vibrant learning and success-oriented cultures. Bennis (1999) in summarizing his research on a number of global companies that had invested in leadership development initiatives concluded, ". . . leadership development programs have made significant influence on the culture of organizations. The shift in culture may have eased an important organization transition, helped anticipate pressures of globalization, or toughened an organization to compete" (p. xviii).

Conclusion

Turning to the future there are global economic, technological, environmental, political, ethical, and societal forces that will test the stamina and talents of even the best business leaders. The psychological effects of the unknown, relentless change, and continued threats of terrorism will further intensify their leadership challenges. They will also have to create new models of working in order to corral an increasingly nomadic workforce and to compensate for a general lack of local talent. Therefore, in the face of these and other issues yet to come, whatever companies are doing now to develop top talent will need to be bolder and faster to fully equip business leaders for the rest of the twenty-first century.

There are global economic, technological, environmental, political, ethical, and societal forces that will test the stamina and talents of even the best business leaders. The psychological effects of the unknown, relentless change, and continued threats of terrorism will further intensify their leadership challenges. They will also have to create new models of working in order to corral an increasingly nomadic workforce and to compensate for a general lack of local talent. Therefore, in the face of these and other issues yet to come, whatever companies are doing now to develop top talent will need to be bolder and faster to fully equip business leaders for the rest of the twenty-first century.

References

Argyris, C. 1991. Teaching smart people how to learn. *Harvard Business Review* (May–June): 99–109.

Bass B. M., and B. J. Avolio. 1995. *The multifactor leadership questionnaire*. Redwood City, CA: Mind Garden.

Bennis, W. 1999. Foreword. D. Giber, L. Carter, and M. Goldsmith (Eds.). *Linkage Inc.'s best practices in leadership development handbook: Case studies, instruments, training.* Burlington, MA: Linkage Press.

Boyatzis, R. and D. Goleman. 2008. Social intelligence and the biology of leadership. *The Harvard Business Review* (September):87–92.

Brienza, D., and K. Cavallo. 2005. *Emotional competence and leadership excellence at Johnson & Johnson: The emotional intelligence and leadership study.* The Consortium for Research on Emotional Intelligence in Organizations. Retrieved July 9, 2008, from http://www.eiconsortium.org.

de Villemor-Amaral, A. E. 2007. Executive performance on the Rorschach comprehensive system. *Rorschachiana* 28:119–133.

Goleman, D. 1998. What makes a leader? *Harvard Business Review*, (November–December): 93–102.

Goleman, D., R. Boyatzis, and A. McKee. 2002. *Primal leadership: Realizing the power of emotional intelligence.* Cambridge, MA: Harvard Business School Press.

Gupta, R. L., and K. M. Wasylyshyn. 2009. Developing world class leaders: The Rohm and Haas story. *People and Strategy Journal* 32(4):37–41.

Hicks, M. D., and D. B. Peterson. (1999). The development pipeline: How people really learn. *Knowledge Management Review* 9:30–33.

Joiner, B. 2009. Creating a culture of agile leaders: A developmental approach. *People and Strategy Journal* 32(4):29–34.

Kilburg, R. R. 2004. When shadows fall: Using psychodynamic approaches in executive coaching. *Consulting Psychology Journal: Practice and Research* 56:246–286.

Maslow, A. H. 1943. A theory of human motivation. *Psychological Review* 50:370–396.

Olegario, R. 2006. *A culture of credit: Embedding trust and transparency in American business.* Cambridge, MA: Harvard University Press.

Peterson, C., and M. E. P. Seligman. 2004. *Character strengths and virtues: A handbook and classification.* Washington, DC: American Psychological Association and Oxford University Press.

Rosier, R. (ed.) 1994–1996. *The competency model handbook.* vols. 1–3. Burlington, MA: Linkage Press.

Tobias, L. 1990. *Psychological consulting to management: A clinician's perspective.* New York: Brunner/Mazel.

Wasylyshyn, K. M. 2008. Behind the door: Keeping business leaders focused on how they lead. *Consulting Psychology Journal: Practice and Research* 60 (Winter): 314–330.

———. 2003. Coaching the SuperKeepers. Chapter 29 in *The talent management handbook: Creating organizational excellence through identifying, developing, and positioning your best people.* L. A. Berger and D. A. Berger (Eds.) New York: McGraw-Hill.

Wiersema, F. 1998. *Customer intimacy: Pick your partners, shape your culture, win together.* Publisher: Knowledge Exchange.

Welch, J. 2004, January 23. Four e's (a jolly good fellow). *Wall Street Journal*, A14.

Notes

1. In this chapter, the term "top talent" refers to those already successful business managers and/or functional leaders who are capable of handling assignments of greater scope and responsibility and who may also become candidates for C-suite roles.

2. The initial competencies were (1) ability to earn trust and support among superiors, colleagues and subordinates, (2) ability to form a realistic vision for the organization, (3) ability to communicate vision and inspire commitment/quality performance, (4) toughness and drive to overcome obstacles, (5) ability to size up opportunities/problems and take effective action, and (6) managerial and administrative competence. Several years later these were revised to (1) market-aware & customer-driven, (2) strategic focus, (3) global perspective, (4) bias for action, (5) adaptive to change, (6) creative problem solving, (7) professional credibility, (8) business acumen, (9) persuasion and influence, (10) safety and performance, (11) people and performance management, and (12) interpersonal effectiveness.

3. This top talent development program was initially named Leadership 2000. Given its sustained value and credibility, in the year 2000, Wilson's successor, CEO, Raj Gupta, renamed it *Leadership 3000*. In the remainder of this article, it will be referred to as *Leadership 3000*.

4. Since Feck's death in 2000, I have worked with three other corporate HR heads building on the original intention of *Leadership 3000* and preserving its guiding principles, methodological rigor, and practice commitments.

5. The psychometric battery used for *Leadership 3000* included the following; Myers-Briggs Type Indicator, Watson-Glaser Critical Thinking Appraisal, Life Styles Inventory 1, Revised NEO Personality Inventory (NEO PI-R), BarOn Emotional Quotient Inventory (EQi), Rorschach, Hermann Brain Dominance, Guilford-Zimmerman Temperament Survey, and PRF-Form E as well as the participant's life history.

6. A "transference reaction" is a psychological phenomenon whereby emotions related to past experiences (often repressed childhood events) are triggered—a deep emotional nerve is struck, and an individual transfers those past feelings onto someone in the present. Often the personal insight that a particular person may be eliciting a transference reaction can be helpful in understanding and adjusting a difficult work-related relationship—particularly with peers and authority figures.

7. The Rohm and Haas Essential Leadership Behaviors consisted of courageous leadership, emotional fortitude, enterprise thinking, pragmatic optimism, steel trap accountability, truth-telling, and tough on talent.

8. Courageous leadership and strategic focus were either a strength or a weakness for participants. Therefore, short-term peer mentoring was a common action step, i.e., linking individuals with others who were strong where they were not.

9. The *Leadership 3000* "brain trust" of every participant consisted of his or her boss, the CEO or another C-suite executive, the corporate head of HR, and the external consultant who facilitated the action-planning and follow-up meetings. Since there was no ceiling placed on access to members of one's development brain trust, participants could call on them for years thereafter, as well as through the four phases of the *Leadership 3000* process. Often these relationships continued for years, and I became a "trusted advisor" to many.

10. This Essential Leadership Behavior was defined as: the ability to use self-awareness (of strengths and weaknesses), self-management (focus, discipline, tact, and diplomacy), attunement (empathic understanding of others), and relationship-building skills (relating to people in ways that are deeper than transactional need) to drive business results. Emotional resilience (can deal well with ambiguity, crises, and adversity in all forms). Stays cool under pressure.

11. Emotional intelligence (EQ) is defined as the awareness of one's own and others' emotions and the ability to discriminate among them, and the ability to use that emotional awareness to achieve work and personal objectives. Emotional intelligence consists of four dimensions—self observation, self management, attunement to others, and relationship-building.

12. A graduate of the United States Military Academy, Concannon became president and CEO of Haemonetics Corporation, the global leader in blood management solutions, in 2006. This comment was made in a conversation we had that spanned a number of leadership considerations.

13. I use the more apt term "work-family integration" instead of the popular "work-family balance" terminology. For top talent individuals, work-family balance—if considered literally as a balance between the two domains of work and family—is an impossible objective to achieve. On the other hand, everyone should strive to find his or her version of work-family integration.

14. *Leadership 3000* maintained its "pilot" status for approximately five years when CEO Wilson acknowledged its success, and it then became integrated into annual talent review discussions and targeted development actions for top talent.

15. It was in the course of this top talent development work that I acquired the professional nickname, "The Velvet Harpoon."

Chapter 21

Coaching for Sustained, Desired Change: Building Relationships and Talent

Richard E. Boyatzis, Ph.D., Professor in the Department of
Organizational Behavior, Psychology, and Cognitive Science
Melvin L. Smith, Ph.D., Professor in the Department of
Organizational Behavior
Ellen Van Oosten, Department of Organizational Behavior
Weatherhead School of Management
Case Western Reserve University

T HE DRIVING CHALLENGE FOR ORGANIZATIONS CONTINUES TO BE TO ATTRACT, RETAIN, and motivate their key people. Surveys in the United States and Europe consistently illustrate that the primary reasons that people choose to join and stay in organizations is the degree to which they are stimulated and challenged (Boyatzis and Skelly 1995; McKinsey 1998). As a result, attracting, keeping, and motivating the best employees become an important responsibility of every leader and manager. This is where the practice of coaching becomes a key ingredient for effective talent management.

In this chapter, we offer two fundamentally different ways to approach coaching with vastly different implications for the person being coached (Boyatzis, Smith, and Blaize 2006; Smith, Van Oosten, and Boyatzis 2009). They are "coaching to the Positive Emotional Attractor (PEA)" and "coaching to the Negative Emotional Attractor (NEA)."

The former leads to learning, change, and adaptation, while the latter leads to compliance, conformity, stress, and the loss of openness and learning potential. These dynamics are rooted in the psycho-physiological arousal of each type of encounter.

Before delving into these ideas, try this two-part exercise. List all of the things about you and your behavior that you should change to become more effective at work and a more engaging family member. Now add to the list the feedback you have received from others about areas you should change. Lastly, add to the list the things you have heard that people say behind your back (not to your face) that are negative characteristics about you or your behavior—things they laugh or complain about to others.

Pause and ask yourself, "How do I feel after compiling this list? Do I feel deflated, elated, glad, sad, happy, guilty, joyful, depressed, or what?" Take a few deep breaths. Now let's go to the second part of the exercise. List all of the things you do that people enjoy and that makes them feel good. List your strengths that others have mentioned to you or you have overheard. Think of moments when you have been at your best at work, at home, with friends, in professional settings, and at leisure. For each of these moments, add to the list those things that you said or did that were most effective. Now pause and ask yourself, "How do I feel after compiling this second list? Do I feel deflated, elated, glad, sad, happy, guilty, joyful, depressed, or what?"

If you're like most people, you may have experienced two somewhat distinct sets of feelings. In the first example, you probably experienced a generally negative feeling and in the second, a generally positive feeling. Our relationships and interactions with others often fall into similar positive and negative camps. In this chapter, we explain what happens physiologically in those instances, describe what we mean by coaching to the PEA and coaching to the NEA, and offer an approach to engaging positive feelings when coaching others.

Coaching to the PEA versus to the NEA

We define *coaching to the PEA* as "helping others in their intentional change process (i.e., achieving their dreams or aspirations or changing the way they think, feel, and act)" (Boyatzis, Smith, and Blaize 2006).

When you coach others for their personal development and growth, it's different than coaching in response to an organization's desire or a boss's mandated objective. The latter can be seen as directive and more instrumental, which we call "coaching to the NEA" or compliance with someone else's wishes. Coaching to the NEA may be aroused when a manager or coach cares more about the team's performance than the aspirations and well-being of their employee.

Coaching may involve both caring for the person's development *and* serving an organizational need. In such situations, the instrumental utility of the coaching act does not necessarily preclude the PEA experience. It also appears, however, that many in helping roles are not invoking empathy and caring but may instead be serving their own desires or goals—coaching to the NEA. This is seen in the extreme and often hostile acts of those parents who, when watching their children's sports competitions, get too involved and start yelling obscenities at the children, the coaches, or the umpires. In such a situation, they are motivated by their own competitive needs, not the desire to watch their children grow and develop. Similarly, a college coach, who is part of the staff of an educational institution, may forget that his or her role is to develop players as students and athletes, not merely to win games. In the process, such coaches may regress to behavior that expresses predominant concern over winning and not development of the players' talent or character.

A benefit of coaching to the PEA is that the coach will be less focused on him- or herself (Boyatzis and McKee 2005). This decrease in self-preoccupation could help alleviate some of the tendency toward self-aggrandizement that comes with the power associated with being in leadership, management, or consulting positions.

Coaching others to the PEA can be a partial antidote to narcissism, we believe, because people in positions of responsibility would be genuinely focused on others. At the same time, the improved quality of the relationship with others could result in a better flow of disconfirming, negative, or even critical reactions. Put in a more positive way, coaching to the PEA could result in both parties (i.e., the coach and the person being coached) being more open to others and their ideas. It allows or invites more self-awareness by moving into a relational world in which you get feedback and have to look at it.

It is important to note that coaching or mentoring others does not always involve the PEA (Raggins and Kram 2008). Instrumental coaching occurs when the coach is offering or providing help to another person for a purpose other than the person's own desire to develop, which can feel like being coached to the NEA. An example is helping someone fill an organizational need or making an introduction to facilitate a person's career progress. If these acts are done without caring about the person's development, then we believe it would not invoke the PEA and therefore not arouse the psycho-physiological response beneficial as an antidote to the chronic stress nor the learning and health benefits of parasympathetic nervous system (PNS) arousal. Providing advice to someone, or trying to convince him or her to accept a particular assignment, or putting pressure on him or her to "fit in" or act more consistent with organizational norms appear to be focused on influencing the person to do something—coaching to the NEA. As with the instrumental focus, we believe this will not result in arousal of the PNS. Instead, we contend that it is likely to arouse the sympathetic nervous system (SNS).

A Process for Coaching to Achieve Sustained, Desired Change

We consider the ultimate pursuit of coaching to be helping another individual change in ways that he or she most deeply desires and for those changes to "stick"—meaning that they become sustainable over time. So how does one do that? In this section, we will offer a theory and a process as a starting point.

First, sustained, desired change often appears discontinuous over time (Boyatzis 2006). While to an observer it appears as emergent or catastrophic change, to the person changing, it is more likely experienced as an epiphany or discovery. Intentional Change

Theory (ICT) describes the essential components and processes that encourage sustained, desired change to occur in a person's behaviors, thoughts, feelings. and/or perceptions (Boyatzis 2006). The model includes five phases or discontinuities, called "discoveries." Boyatzis observed that the moments of emergence for deeper self-discovery include (1) discovering one's Ideal Self, (2) confronting one's Real Self, (3) creating a learning agenda, (4) taking action in service of one's desired change through practice of new behaviors, and (5) development of trusting relationships to support the person through his or her change process, as shown in Figure 21-1.

The starting point is the discovery of who the person wants to be and occurs through a moment of emergence into a person's consciousness. This is known as the *Ideal Self* and includes an individual's deepest aspirations for his or her career and life. The outcome of exploring one's ideal self is the creation of a personal vision statement, which is where the coach can play a pivotal role. Boyatzis and Akrivou (2006) reported that, in practice, vision appears in many forms for a person. Theoretically, they contend that it needs three major components to emerge from a person's Ideal Self. Like other strength-based approaches (Roberts, Dutton, Spreitzer, Heaphy, and Quinn 2006), it

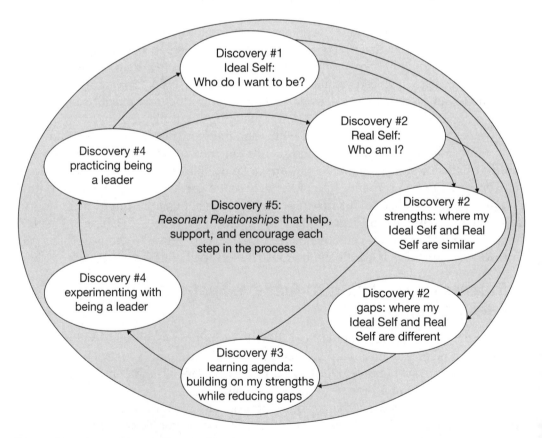

Figure 21-1 Intentional Change Theory

needs an awareness of the person's strengths. Boyatzis and Akrivou (2006) call this a person's Core Identity. They go on to add that a person also needs two other crucial components of a Personal Vision to be effective: an image of the desired future and a sense of hope that it is attainable.

Positive visioning is an important technique for creating new neural circuits that help to guide future behavior, as shown in sports psychology (Loehr and Schwartz 2003; Roffe, Schmidt, and Ernst 2005). Engaging in positive visioning seems to arouse hope (Groopman 2004; Curry, Snyder, Cook, Ruby, and Rehm 1997). Ironically, teachers, coaches, trainers, and often managers know the importance of the Ideal Self, yet they often don't take the time to articulate its formulation. When parents, spouses, or bosses tell a person something should be different, they are describing the person *they* want. This is called the Ought Self and often causes conflict with the Ideal Self (Higgins 1987). As a result of these factors, people often get anesthetized to their dreams and lose sight of their deeply felt Ideal Self. Some managers encourage people to explore growth and development by focusing solely on deficiencies. Organization-based coaching and mentoring programs and the tradition of managers conducting annual reviews often make this mistake. They "leave well enough alone" and focus on the areas that need work. This is what we are calling coaching to the NEA.

The third emergence is the articulation of a way to get to the desired self, using strengths and building on some weaknesses. The most critical element of this emergence is that it is a type of plan for things the person's wants to try and explore. The openness to new activities and experiences is in contrast to the often felt obligatory nature of fulfilling to-do lists, or complying with an agenda for the future that a person's boss, spouse, or others want for him or her. A learning agenda focuses on development and novelty.

The next emergent awareness comes in the form of experimenting and practicing the new behaviors. This may be reinforcing some behavioral habits that have been effective in the past, or trying new ones. The experimentation and testing of the new behaviors must be followed by a period of practicing them until they become second nature, or unconsciously enacted.

Given the difficult nature of personal change, enlisting the help of others often makes the difference between a person staying focused on his or her ideal and trying new behaviors and resorting to the status quo. This suggests the importance of building trusting relationships with others, who can serve as a source of compassion, a mirror, and a sounding board, and describes the fifth discovery in ICT. Relationships with others are an essential part of our environment. Our relationships create a context within which we can interpret our progress on desired changes and consider the utility of new learning. Through their observations and feedback, but mostly through their support, a person develops a sense of safety to explore new thinking and behaviors and confidence to take a step forward toward his or her ideal. They may also be the most important source of protection from relapses or returning to earlier forms of behavior (Boyatzis 2006).

Physiological Implications: The Experience of the Positive and Negative Emotional Attractors

At the heart of the difference between these two approaches to coaching, and possibly your experience in the opening exercise, are two distinctive psycho-physiological states. These two states have been described as the human response to stress (Sapolsky 2004) and renewal (Boyatzis and McKee 2005). But they have also been described as a Positive Emotional Attractor and a Negative Emotional Attractor (NEA) within an individual (Boyatzis 2006).

The NEA is the state that arouses stress and stimulation of part of the human autonomic nervous system called the sympathetic nervous system (SNS), which helps the individual to deal with stress and threat and protect itself. When aroused, the NEA pulls a person toward defensive protection. There are four situations that are known to provoke stress more than others:

1. Situations that are perceived to be uncontrollable.
2. Those involving social evaluation (i.e., others observing and judging).
3. Those in which commitment to reaching important or salient goals or tasks is a stretch.
4. Anticipating events; in fact, merely anticipating events invoking these perceptions and feelings seems to provoke stress more than other types of situations (Dickerson and Kemeny 2004; Sapolsky 2004).

The repeated arousal of stress is called chronic stress, with the possibility of periodic episodes of acute stress adding to the experience. Acute stress includes the occasional episode when you feel as if you want to "tear your hair out" and also moments like those that occur when someone cuts you off in traffic. When combined, these events create a condition of chronic stress (Dickerson and Kemeny 2004; Segerstrom and Miller 2004).

The experience of chronic stress, in arousing the SNS, initiates the classic fight-or-flight physical response (LeDoux 2002; Sapolsky 2004; McEwen 1998). Individuals experience an increase in systolic and diastolic blood pressure (DeQuattro and Feng 2002; Sapolsky 2004). Meanwhile, even neural circuitry is reallocated, in the sense that the brain appears to focus on those circuits deemed necessary for survival while closing down other neural circuits (LeDoux 2002). This arousal of the SNS has been shown to be related to emotions, such as fear and disgust (Davidson et al. 1990) and feeling depressed or anxious (Tomarken et al. 1992).

But the most damaging aspect of chronic stress for the prospect of helping a person change through coaching is that in this arousal the person's range of perceptions are limited and therefore his or her openness to new or different emotions and ideas is constrained. Also, the person's cognitive functioning is limited and the potential for neurogenesis is inhibited, thus decreasing his or her ability to learn (Erikson et. al 1998).

While the SNS is responsible for the body's ability to react quickly and effectively to physical or emotional provocation, the PNS is responsible for recovery from such excitement and for keeping the body functioning when at rest (McEwen 1998; Sapolsky 2004). The PEA arouses the PNS (Boyatzis, Smith, and Blaize 2006). Once the PNS is aroused, the person experiences more perceptual openness to others and new ideas and emotions. With particular regard to coaching, this is the condition that allows people to explore and consider change, new ideas and emotions, openness to others, and learning.[1] A recent study has shown that each of these coaching approaches stimulate different regions of the brain associated with the two states described above (Boyatzis, Jack, Cesaro, Passarelli, and Khawaja, in review).

Coaches are often called upon to help others who are different than the coach in background, experience, or visible differences. This can affect the rapport or relationship building that seems so important. Studies have also shown that arousal of the emotional states we include in the PEA are directly linked to openness to people who are visibly different in conditions where prejudice may exist (Crisp and Turner 2009; Schmitz, De Rosa, and Anderson 2009).

Caring relationships cause a decrease in SNS reactivity via oxytocin that has been shown to reduce blood pressure and reduce stress reactivity, reducing the chemical response elicited by stress and reversing its harmful effects on the body (Insel 1997; LeDoux 2002). Social interactions can therefore down-regulate an individual's SNS response to stress, both in the presence and absence of the caring figure by increasing the basal level activity of the PSNS (Diamond 2001; Sapolsky 2004).

The different components of the PEA and NEA aroused states are shown in Table 21-1, classified in terms of the stages of Intentional Change Theory. Specific questions that can be used in coaching to the PEA are shown in Figure 21-2.

Stage of ICT	PEA Components	NEA Components
Ideal Self	Personal vision, efficacy, hope, dreams, values	Ought Self, preoccupation with one element
Real Self	Strengths	Weaknesses
Learning Agenda	Things you are excited about learning or are eager to try	To-do lists, performance improvement plans
Experimentation/Practice	Trying new things, exploring, getting positive reinforcement and feedback from others about one's new behavior, thoughts, or feelings	Repetitive activities such as skill building seen as somewhat tedious
Trusting Relationships	Trusting support, encouragement for the pursuit of one's dreams	Reminder of progress on one's learning plan, constructive or negative feedback on behavior or attempted new behavior

Table 21-1 Intentional Change and the Positive and Negative Emotional Attractors

Preparation

1. Do I know elements of the person's Ideal Self and Personal Vision?
   a) Do I know his/her dominant values?
   b) Do I know his/her operating philosophy?
   c) Do I know his/her life and/or career stage, or point in his/her life/career cycle? Is he/she approaching or in a mid-life crisis?
   d) Do I know aspects of his/her dreams, fantasies, and aspirations for the future?
   e) Do I know what he/she considers his/her passion and calling?
   f) Do I know what he/she considers his/her strengths?
   g) Do I know the level of his/her optimism?
   h) Do I know the level of his/her efficacy?

2. Do I care about him/her?

3. Am I tuned into how he/she is feeling today?

Coaching Discussion

4. Have we discussed his/her dreams about the future?

5. Have we discussed his/her Personal Vision or elements of his/her Ideal Self?

6. Have we discussed who helped him/her the most to become who he/she is or get to where he/she has?

7. Have we discussed his/her strengths that can help them move closer to or maintain their Ideal Self.

8. Have we discussed his/her weaknesses that may inhibit that movement? Which of those are close to a tipping point, suggesting that they can be developed?

Post-Coaching Discussion

9. Was the person's awareness of his/her Ideal Self or Personal Vision enhanced as a result of our conversation?

10. Was the person able to make discriminating choices or identify priorities within those things discussed as to which are the most salient?

11. Did we cover a comprehensive array of relevant topics in the person's life and work?

Figure 21-2 Guide to Coaching to the Positive Emotional Attractor

Emotional Contagion and Relational Arousal

As a result of certain neural properties of the brain, humans are hard-wired to mimic the emotions of other living things around them (Goleman and Boyatzis 2008). This results in an emotional contagion of people who are exposed to each other (Hatfield, Cacioppo, and Rapson 1994). In dyadic relationships, this exposure is often more intense than in other relationships because of the focused attention on the other person. This carries implications for coaching relationships because an aroused PEA or NEA state in one person, whether it is the coach or the person being coached, will stimulate a sympathetic or similar state in the other person that is often unconscious.

Conclusion

Managing or leading is a relationship. Coaching is a relationship. These two types of relationships can enhance each other. If these relationships arouse the Positive Emotional Attractor, they help a person open to new possibilities, grow, and renew themselves. It does this by engaging a set of neural and endocrine processes that enable the human organism to rebuild itself. Coaching to the PEA invokes compassion, because it involves the coach feeling compassion toward the other person.

Unfortunately, often in our desire to help another, we focus on the aspects of the person or their behavior that need to be changed. Coaching to the NEA can be called "coaching for compliance." It arouses the Negative Emotional Attractor, which results in the person becoming defensive, closing down mentally, and not learning. Sustainable, desired change does not occur from such relationships.

The good news is that when people develop these positive relationships, the coaching is quite effective. We hope that by explaining the internal processes and emotional contagion that occurs in coaching relationships (for better or worse), a coach can build more sustainable relationships and more effectively build talent in organizations.

References

Boyatzis, R. E. (in press). Coaching teams to use emotional, social and cognitive intelligence for sustainable, desired change. In *Beyond coaching: Creating better leaders, teams, and organizations*. Manfred Kets De Vries and Laura Guillen (Eds). Harvard Business Press.

Boyatzis, R. E. 2006. Intentional change theory from a complexity perspective. *Journal of Management Development* 25(7):607–623.

Boyatzis, R. E., and K. Akrivou. 2006. The ideal self as a driver of change. *Journal of Management Development* 25(7): 624–642.

Boyatzis, R. E., A. Jack, R. Cesaro, A. Passarelli, and M. Khawaja. (in review). *Coaching with compassion: An fMRI study of coaching to the positive or negative emotional attractor.* Cleveland: Case Western Reserve University.

Boyatzis, R. E., and A. McKee. 2005. *Resonant leadership: Renewing yourself and connecting with others through mindfulness, hope, and compassion.* Cambridge, MA: Harvard Business School Press.

Boyatzis, R. E., and F. R. Skelly. 1995. The impact of changing values on organizational life: The latest update. In *The organizational behavior reader* (6th edition). D.A. Kolb, J. Osland, and I. Rubin (eds.). Englewood Cliffs, NJ: Prentice Hall.

Boyatzis, R. E., M. Smith, and N. Blaize. 2006. Developing sustainable leaders through coaching and compassion. *Academy of Management Journal on Learning and Education* 5(1):8–24.

Curry, L., C. R. Snyder, D. Cook, B. Ruby, and M. Rehm. 1997. The role of hope in academic and sport achievement. *Journal of Personality and Social Psychology* 73:1257–1267.

Davidson, R. J., P. Ekman, C. D. Saron, J. A. Senulis, and W. V. Driesen, 1990. Approach-withdrawal and cerebral asymmetry: Emotional expression and brain physiology I. *Journal of Personality and Social Psychology* 58(2): 330–341.

DeQuattro V., and M. Feng. 2002. The sympathetic nervous system: The muse of primary hypertension. *Journal of Human Hypertension* 16:S64–69.

Dickerson, S. S., and M. F. Kemeny. 2004. Acute stressors and cortisol responses: A theoretical integration and synthesis of laboratory research. *Psychological Bulletin* 130(3), 355 –391.

Erikson, P. S., E. Perfilieva, T. Bjork-Eriksson, A-M Alborn, C. Nordburg, D. A. Peterson, and F. H. Gage. 1998. Neurogenesis in the adult human hippocampus. *Nature Medicine* 4:313–317.

Frederickson, B. L., and M. K. Losada. 2005. Positive affect and the complex dynamics of human flourishing. *American Psychologist* 60:678–686.

Goleman, D., and R. Boyatzis. 2008. Social intelligence and the biology of leadership. *Harvard Business Review* 86(9):74–81.

Gottman, J. M., J. D. Murray, C. C. Swanson, R. Tyson, and K. R. Swanson. 2002. *The mathematics of marriage: Dynamic nonlinear models.* Cambridge, MA: MIT Press.

Groopman, A. 2004. *The anatomy of hope: How people prevail in the face of illness.* New York: Random House.

Hatfield, E., J. T. Cacioppo, and R. L. Rapson. 1994. *Emotional contagion.* New York: Cambridge University Press.

Higgins, E. T. 1987. Self-discrepancy: A theory relating self and effect. *Psychological Review* 94:319–340.

LeDoux, J. 2002, Synaptic self: How our brains become who we are. New York: Viking.

Loehr, J., and T. Schwartz. 2003. *The power of full engagement: Managing energy, not time, is the key to high performance and personal renewal.* New York: Free Press.

McEwen, B. S. 1998. Protective and damaging effects of stress mediators. *New England Journal of Medicine* 338:171–179.

McKinsey & Company. 1998. *The war for talent.*

Roberts, L., J. E. Dutton, G. Spreitzer, E. Heaphy, and R. E. Quinn. 2006. Composing the reflected best-self portrait: Pathways for becoming extraordinary in work organizations. *Academy of Management Review* 30:712–736.

Roffe, L., K. Schmidt, and E. Ernst. 2005. A systematic review of guided imagery as an adjuvant cancer therapy. *Psycho-oncology.* DOI: 10.1002, 889.

Sapolsky, R. M. 2004. *Why zebras don't get ulcers.* (3rd edition). New York: New York: HarperCollins.

Segerstom, S. C., and G. E. Miller. 2004, Psychological stress and the human immune system: A meta-analytic study of 30 years of inquiry. *Psychological Bulletin* 130(4):601–630.

Smith, M., E. Van Oosten, and R. E. Boyatzis. 2009. Coaching for sustained desired change. In *Research in organization development and change* (Vol. 17). W. Pasmore and R. Woodman. (Eds.).

Tomarken, A. J., R. J. Davidson, R. E. Wheeler, and R. C. Doss. 1992 Individual differences in anterior brain asymmetry and fundamental dimensions of emotion. *Journal of Personality and Social Psychology* 62(4):676–687.

Notes

1. Studies of women suggest a slightly different response to stress, but one that still involves arousal of the SNS (Taylor et al. 2002). But the positive effects of arousal for the PNS are similar for both genders.

Chapter 22

Developing Leadership Competencies through 360-Degree Feedback and Coaching

John W. Fleenor, Research Director
Sylvester Taylor, Director, Assessments, Tools, and Publications
Craig Chappelow, Global Portfolio Manager, Assessments
Center for Creative Leadership

AS TALENT MANAGEMENT HAS BECOME A CRITICAL CONCERN FOR ORGANIZATIONS, 360-degree feedback has gained increasing popularity and importance (Silzer and Church 2009). In order to develop an accurate analysis of leadership potential, the 360-degree process takes into account the collective judgments of multiple coworkers, including peers, and subordinates (Fleenor and Brutus 2001).

In addition to assessing potential, 360-degree feedback is useful for soliciting the input of employees to determine if the organization's plans for them match its own developmental goals (Gutteridge 1986). By integrating 360-degree feedback into the talent management system, the organization can successfully assess leadership potential, identify employee strengths and weaknesses, and recommend developmental activities.

Best-practice organizations have a clearly articulated, well-implemented, and widely accepted description of effective leaders. These descriptions often take the form of a leader competency model that outlines the competencies that contribute to leaders' effectiveness. Best-practice organizations use the same competency model across various talent management processes including 360-degree feedback. This approach reinforces the importance of the organization's view of effectiveness and provides employees multiple opportunities to use and better understand the competency model.

The 360-Degree Feedback Process

Most 360-degree feedback processes share similar characteristics:

- Multiple individuals (bosses, peers, direct reports, the employee himself or herself, and others such as customers, boss's boss) provide ratings for the employee. The raters assess the employee's on-the-job behaviors and other attributes using a numerical rating scale. The ratings are usually collected anonymously with the exception of boss ratings. That is, the employee cannot tell who provided the ratings. Because most people have only one boss, it is usually not possible to keep boss ratings anonymous.
- Feedback is provided to employees in reports that itemize the results of the assessment. With the assistance of a professional feedback coach, employees examine their high ratings (strengths) and low ratings (weaknesses), as well as differences between their own and others' perceptions of their performance.
- Employees create a development plan and work with feedback coaches to identify ways they can change their behavior to become more effective.

Evaluating Potential

Probably the most common use of 360-degree feedback is to assess organizational competencies. Some 360-degree surveys are appropriate for assessing the potential of employees to perform in roles with greater responsibility. The Center for Creative Leadership (CCL) has developed a 360-degree survey called *Benchmarks*® (CCL 2004) that focuses on what executives can learn from experiences on the job. *Benchmarks* is based on research on how successful executives develop and why they sometimes derail. To assess leadership potential, *Benchmarks* has a section, "Meeting Job Challenges," that contains competencies measuring (a) the resourcefulness needed to cope with the demands of the job, (b) the drive and attitudes necessary to be successful, and (c) the ability to learn and make decisions quickly. *Benchmarks* also has a section, "Problems that Can Stall a Career," that contains scales that assess an employee's potential for derailment. The derailment scales include (a) the failure to build relationships and to negotiate well, (b) problems with interpersonal relationships, (c) difficulties changing or adapting, and (d) having too narrow of a functional orientation.

Several potential issues in identifying high-potential employees through 360-degree assessment must be considered. Assessing leadership potential is not an exact science, and the results could turn into a self-fulfilling prophecy. Additionally, individuals who are not selected as high-potential employees may become disgruntled. Furthermore, organizations may fail to follow up the 360 assessment with appropriate developmental activities such as training or job assignments.

Competencies

When each component in the human resources system (talent management, leadership development, and performance management) is built around a common set of competencies and rating scales, the entire system becomes more efficient and effective

(Byham 2004). The competencies should be built on examples of behaviors that are required for successful job performance. Once a comprehensive competency model has been developed, these competencies can be incorporated into a 360-degree feedback survey. This ensures that the leadership competencies that are considered important by the organization are measured by the 360-degree process and that employees receive feedback on these competencies (Fleenor, Taylor, and Chappelow 2008).

A leader competency model requires detail. For example, behaviors that indicate low, moderate, and high levels of a competency are outlined, providing a picture of what the competency looks like at different levels in the organization. Generally, three levels are used, corresponding to executive, middle, and supervisory employees. This approach may dictate multiple 360-degree feedback models that align with organizational level.

Organizations use different methods to arrive at a 360-degree feedback competency model: (1) they adopt an existing competency model that comes from a reputable source, has been used successfully across organizations, and has high face validity within the organization; (2) they create a model "from scratch," involving numerous stakeholder groups within the organization to arrive at some agreement about the most important leader competencies in their organization; or (3) they begin with an existing framework (e.g., a set of organizational values or strategic priorities) and derive a set of competencies needed to deliver on that set of values or priorities. Whatever process is used, the goal is to arrive at an integrated set of competencies that are relevant, meaningful, and understood across the organization.

Mone, Acritani, and Eisinger (2009) recommend framing the competencies into three major categories: foundational, growth oriented, and career specific. Using this framework will help managers understand that some competencies are good predictors of long-term potential but may not necessarily be predictive of immediate promotability (Silzer and Church 2009). There may be other competencies that are more useful for immediate promotions to meet specific business needs. Using this framework will help managers better understand the nature of potential and how to assess it, and to realize that some competencies are more static and some are more developable than others. The framework will also help to determine the competencies necessary for long-term potential decisions and to distinguish the competencies needed for promotion from those necessary for the development of potential.

It is usually necessary, however, to provide training for the participants and the raters before implementing such a process. Managers must be educated about the competencies and how to use them, and implementation of a competency model may involve modifications to the organization's current processes.

Bridging the Leadership Gap

Organizations are discovering that their leadership pipelines are filled with employees who are deficient in the skills and capacities necessary for long-term success. How profound is this "leadership talent gap"? To find out, researchers at the Center for Creative Leadership (Taylor 2010) surveyed more than 2,000 executives from the

United States, India, and Singapore to explore which factors are most critical for present and future success and to see how today's leaders measure up. In this study, participants were asked to rate the importance of 20 key leadership competencies that are used on CCL's 360-degree feedback surveys. The findings were consistent across country, industry, and the organizational level of the respondents. Executives from businesses, government agencies, nonprofits, and educational organizations agreed that they need leaders who can effectively navigate complex, changing situations and get the job done.

The following eight key competencies were found to be particularly critical to future success (in order of importance): (1) leading others, (2) strategic planning, (3) managing change, (4) inspiring commitment, (5) resourcefulness, (6) doing whatever it takes, (7) being a quick learner, and (8) participative management.

The survey respondents reported that their employees were lagging behind on all 20 of the competencies. These findings suggest that today's leaders lack the skills needed to effectively manage common challenges. Among the biggest skills gaps were managing change, developing employees, planning strategically, and managing one's own career. The leadership gap was found to be greatest in high-priority, high-stakes competencies. The four future skills that were ranked the most important by survey respondents were found to be among the weakest: leading people, strategic planning, inspiring commitment, and managing change.

Conversely, the results indicated that many leaders possess strengths in areas that are not vital for future success. Organizations report their greatest bench strength in building and mending relationships, compassion and sensitivity, cultural adaptability, respecting individual differences, composure, and self-awareness. Only four competencies were found to be on track with the current level of strength matching the level of importance: being a quick learner, resourcefulness, participative management, and doing whatever it takes.

The most effective organizations will use research such as the leadership gap study to adapt and refocus their talent management efforts. Steps that organizations can take to bridge the chasm between current leadership talent and future leadership needs (Taylor 2010) include:

- Perform a needs assessment for the organization that evaluates the challenges the organization faces and identifies the specific competencies that leaders need to meet these challenges, both today and in the future.
- Implement a 360-degree feedback process that assesses these competencies.
- Create a talent strategy to identify, develop, and retain leaders who possess the capabilities the organization needs. Leadership gap data can be used to determine if the organization needs to transform its culture, modify its leadership development processes, or change its talent management practices. This strategy can serve as a catalyst for developing an HR system that links talent management to performance, hiring, compensation, and leadership development.

- Develop specific goals and tactics for individual leadership development to determine how to spend energies and investments. For example, organizations may provide training on strategic skills, define and encourage rotational job assignments, and create a forum leaders can use to exchange ideas and solutions.
- Determine whether the organization has in place the underlying systems and processes needed to excel at identifying and developing talent, retaining top employees, and managing performance. In addition to implementing a 360-dgree feedback process, this may include revamping job descriptions, changing recruiting practices, and/or developing a new incentive plan more closely aligned with the organization's strategy.
- Routinely evaluate how talent management efforts are paying off across the organization. What additional resources are needed? What metrics are in place to assess impact?

Coaching and Development

A recent survey of 152 coaches in 68 organizations found that, after face-to-face interviewing, 360-degree feedback was the most popular tool used for talent coaching purposes (Nowack 2007). When 360-degree feedback is used for coaching and development, a private feedback session is held with a trained coach who is experienced with the survey being used and, if required, is certified in its use. In this one-on-one session with the feedback recipient, the coach provides a brief introduction to the background of the survey, an interpretive session on the recipient's data, and assistance with developmental planning. Recipients usually appreciate the opportunity to discuss their feedback with a dispassionate third party. One-on-one feedback sessions are particularly important for individuals receiving 360-degree feedback for the first time (Fleenor et al. 2008).

One CCL client, a large global biopharmaceutical company, sets up four separate debrief sessions. The goal for the first session is to help the feedback recipient decipher the data—how to read the report, understand the scoring, and gain preliminary insights about trends and patterns. The second meeting is to help the participant narrow the focus and begin to create a development plan. The third meeting is to review the final development plan with the boss. The fourth meeting occurs six months later as a first check of the individual's progress towards goals.

The feedback coach should be someone outside the recipient's chain of command. When no one but the recipient and the coach sees the feedback report, it reinforces the confidential nature of the data. When delivering 360-degree feedback, the coach helps the recipient draw conclusions about the data. The coach ensures that the recipient fully understands the process and helps him or her to get past the data to the meaning of the feedback.

It is important to give the recipient time to analyze the data before the feedback session takes place, and best practices suggest that the participant have at least one night to "sleep on" the data. If some of the feedback is negative or surprising, the recipient will need this time to deal with emotional reactions to the data or to the raters. The coach should allow from one to four days between the delivery of the feedback report and the coaching session. When a recipient has a chance to digest the data in advance, he or she will understand it better, have time to deal with immediate emotional reactions, and be more open and positive in the feedback session.

The coaching session should be held in a private area. The coach prepares for the session in advance by thoroughly reading the feedback report and making notes. The coach should suggest to the recipient to audio record the session to allow for full engagement rather than note taking. An audio recording will serve as a useful tool later when reviewing progress against development plans.

Facilitating the Coaching Session

A good feedback coach tries to understand not only the data but also the work context for the particular individual. The following questions will help to facilitate the coaching session (Fleenor et al. 2008).

- How will the data be used? The recipient who is seeking a promotion to the next level in the organization has an entirely different framework for feedback than does a person who is happy in his or her current role.
- What is happening in the present job situation? There may be something occurring within the organization that is having an impact on the feedback (e.g., downsizing).
- Is the recipient surprised by any of the feedback? Disappointed? Pleased? Sometimes these questions alone are enough to get people talking about their reactions to the data.
- What overarching themes emerge from the data? Perhaps the most valuable thing experienced feedback coaches can do is to help recipients make connections in the data that they do not initially see.
- How can the data be summarized? What are key strengths? What are key development areas? Helping the recipient to summarize and focus the data is critical. The session should progress from the general to the specific.
- What changes is the recipient motivated to make right now? In the future? The most critical decision the recipient makes about the data is choosing the areas on which to focus and work.
- While experienced feedback coaches should leverage their expertise with the feedback survey, they should resist any temptation to act as an expert on the individual recipient's data. The recipient should decide what to pay attention to and how to make meaning of the feedback. Effective coaches see themselves as guides to the feedback, asking helpful questions and helping the recipients to make connections in the data they have received.

Steps for Ensuring a Successful Coaching Session

The following steps should be followed by coaches to ensure a successful feedback session:

1. Clarify purpose, goals, and expectations of the feedback process.
2. Briefly discuss the research that supports the 360-degree feedback survey being used.
3. Provide a context for receiving feedback, including the following points:
   - First, feedback is data, and data are neutral. Data cannot make decisions about an individual—the individual makes decisions about the data.
   - The feedback represents a snapshot of the recipient. It does not define him or her as a person. It is important to put this snapshot alongside others to see what overarching patterns emerge.
   - Recipients often make one of two common mistakes when they receive 360-degree feedback: they accept the information too quickly or they reject it too quickly. Encourage recipients to carefully consider and think over their data.
4. The recipients know who they asked to fill out their questionnaires, and they know their work situations. Help them understand the data, but the recipients must decide themselves what the data mean.
5. Explain how to read and interpret the feedback report.
6. Allow time for individual reflection on the data, and for answering questions.
7. Introduce any guides or other materials that will help the recipient with developmental planning.

Summary

To create an effective talent management process, a leadership development program that includes 360-degree feedback should be integrated into the HR system. The following best practices for creating an integrated talent management system should be followed (Groves 2007):

- Develop mentor networks.
- Identify high potential employees using 360-degree feedback.
- Develop high-potential employees through on-the-job developmental experiences.
- Establish a flexible and fluid succession planning process.
- Create organization-wide forums for exposing high-potential employees to multiple stakeholders.
- Establish a supportive organizational culture.

An integrated talent management system, as opposed to stand-alone developmental activities, will become a core part of the organization's value proposition by attracting future leaders and establishing bench strength to execute critical strategy. (Cohn, Khurana, and Reeves 2005).

References

Byham, W. C. 2004. *Developing dimension-/competency-based human resource systems.* Pittsburgh: Development Dimensions International.

CCL. 2004. *Benchmarks facilitator's guide.* Greensboro, NC: Center for Creative Leadership.

Cohn, J. M., R. Khurana, and L. Reeve. 2005. Growing talent as if your business depended on it. *Harvard Business Review* (October): 1–10.

Fleenor, J. W., and S. Brutus. 2001. Multisource feedback for personnel decisions. In *The handbook of multisource feedback.* D. Bracken, C. Timmreck, and A. Church (Eds.). San Francisco: Jossey-Bass, 335–351.

Fleenor, J. W., S. Taylor, and C. Chappelow. 2008. *Leveraging the impact of 360-degree feedback.* San Francisco: Pfeiffer.

Groves, K. M. 2007. Integrating leadership development and succession planning best practices. *Journal of Management Development* 26: 239–260.

Gutteridge, T. 1986. Organizational career development systems: The state of the practice. In *Career development in organizations,* D. Hall (Ed.). San Francisco: Jossey-Bass.

Mone, E. M., K. Acritani, and C. Eisinger. 2009. Take it to the roundtable. *Industrial and Organizational Psychology* 2:425–429.

Nowack, K.M. 2007. *Using assessments in talent coaching.* Retrieved January 20, 2010, from http://www.talentmgt.com/includes/printcontent.php?aid=483.

Silzer, R., and A. H. Church. 2009. The pearls and perils of identifying potential. *Industrial and Organizational Psychology* 2, 377–412.

Taylor, S. 2010. Bridging the leadership gap. *Chief Learning Officer.* Retrieved February 4, 2010, from http://www.clomedia.com/business-intelligence/2010/February/2857/index.php.

Chapter 23

Using 360-Degree Feedback for Talent Development

Michael Haid, Senior Vice President, Global Solutions
Right Management

T HE PRACTICE OF USING MULTI-RATER FEEDBACK SYSTEMS—USUALLY REFERRED TO AS 360-degree feedback—has long been popular with training professionals and human resource departments. However, the business world is now subject to shifting workforce demographics, a rise in both employee sophistication, and use of technology—all of which can impact the way in which 360 evaluations need to be conducted.

Used as a tool for supporting the development of management and leadership skills, 360-degree feedback is an important element in an organization's talent management strategy, helping to assess the strengths and weaknesses of employees and providing a basis for training or coaching plans. Its versatility makes it an effective way to assess employees who greatly exceed or exceed organization expectations, as well as those who merely meet expectations. But, perhaps more important, these assessments can transcend these benefits, impacting retention, engagement, and performance—and even permitting a stronger link of key behaviors and competencies to bottom-line business results.

Nevertheless, as is the case with many good tools, 360-degree feedback is often subjected to misuse or less than effective implementation, which nearly always yields disappointing results. The opportunities to misuse or misapply 360 surveys and the subsequent feedback have multiplied as increasingly companies need to deal with more complex communication plans, multicultural workforces that have different values and norms relative to this type of assessment, and technological advances that can either expedite or inhibit the survey rating, scoring, and report generation process.

The actual scope and breadth of application for a 360 evaluation can also be too narrow, creating another missed opportunity to leverage the power of the information generated by the evaluation more fully. For example, multi-rater instruments are often used for single-event interventions, rather than as an integrated feature of human resource management systems. In these cases, time constraints can lead frequently to inadequate design and administration of the instrument, ineffective presentation of feedback, and missed opportunities for follow-up.

With careful attention to the following fundamentals of this potentially powerful tool, however, you can dramatically increase the level of its effectiveness in your organization.

Current Considerations for 360-Degree Feedback Assessments

Multi-rater assessments were designed as a way to address capabilities and competencies that could be observed by others. While 360-degree feedback is still employed for that vital purpose, some organizations now take its use one step further as one piece in a larger effort to identify and strengthen key competencies needed to accelerate performance and meet organizational goals. For example, one current approach uses 360-degree feedback as a before-and-after measure of a development program that includes a variety of elements. In effect, it provides a pre- and post- snapshot of an individual's performance that serves as a validation of an integrated development program.

Trends Impacting the Use of 360-Degree Feedback

A number of key trends are affecting the use of multi-rater assessments:

Engagement levels. Through global research conducted by Right Management, we know that both senior leaders and immediate supervisors have a significant impact on engagement levels. No longer do only immediate supervisors exert the dominant influence on employees. With that in mind, 360-degree feedback, as one of the most effective tools for evaluating behaviors associated with engagement, takes on more importance.

Succession planning. Boards increasingly are being held accountable for making sure the organizations they represent are using evaluations and assessments like 360-degree feedback for succession planning purposes.

Building a leadership pipeline. In many fast-growing countries, such as Korea, China, and Thailand, there's an urgent need to develop managers for senior positions quickly. In these regions, the efficient introduction and use of 360-degree feedback as a tool for assessing and developing important management behaviors is crucial.

Innovations in technology. The use of technology has transformed the way 360-degree feedback assessments are administered. More automation allows for a reduction in communication error and a high degree of consistency in not only the way communications are phrased but also the efficiency with which evaluations are sent out to raters.

Selecting the Feedback Instrument

Before investigating feedback instruments available on the market, it is important to develop a clear sense of what you are trying to accomplish. What do you want participating individuals to be able to do differently once the process is completed? Answering these questions means finding out about the model on which each instrument is built, in order to know whether it is compatible with your organization's model of leadership and management effectiveness.

If you learn that an instrument is based on a particular theory or study or on someone's idea of the qualities that constitute leadership competency, be sure that the items in the instrument seem appropriate for your organization and your objectives. For instance, do individual survey items have what is called "face validity"—that is, do they make sense to you and will they make sense to a manager filling out the survey? Have the items been worded clearly and unambiguously?

You also need to make sure the 360-degree feedback assessment is the best instrument for your needs. For example, 360-degree feedback tends to be most useful for measuring observable behaviors. If you're more interested in issues related, for example, to meeting corporate values, you might consider a different instrument.

Beyond this, your investigation should find that each item passes the following tests:

Validity. Every survey question should measure a behavior that has been proven to relate directly to managerial effectiveness. Knowing that the survey is valid, based on accepted validation methods, will increase participants' willingness to take the process seriously and to make good use of the feedback provided. Validity data, which should be contained in a technical report obtainable from the authors of any instrument, will attest to the survey's integrity. That means it measures what it claims to measure and that what it measures correlates directly with effectiveness on the job. Sometimes this validity will be based on evidence of survey scores related closely to the metrics of another independent source, such as performance appraisals, or scores on a separate instrument developed by other authors. When this type of corroboration is not available, look for data indicating that raters using this instrument also rated the same managers similarly when using a different scale of effectiveness. In either case, the report should describe at least one study demonstrating strong relationships between scores on this instrument and some other measure of actual managerial effectiveness.

Reliability. Similarly, the technical report should show that survey items have three types of reliability. Test-retest reliability refers to stability over a period of time—that is, would those rating the individual in question respond to the survey items in the same way if they answered them again after a few days or weeks—assuming there is no change on the part of the one being rated? The technical report should indicate a test-retest rating of at least 0.4 for each scale in the instrument.

The second type of reliability is internal consistency. This refers to the requirement that all the items in a given survey scale measure the same thing and that there be enough items in the scale to measure it accurately. Consequently, managers who score well on one behavioral item in the scale should also tend to do well on the others. A low internal consistency coefficient indicates that the items do not have enough in common or that more items are needed to provide the needed cohesiveness. This coefficient should be between 0.65 and 0.85.

The third type of reliability is called inter-rater agreement. This is a measure of how similarly raters with a similar perspective on the manager respond to items in the instrument. Raters within a group, such as direct reports, should generally demonstrate moderate agreement in their responses. Low agreement would indicate that the instrument lacked stability or was hard for respondents to interpret clearly. Nevertheless, inter-rater agreement cannot be expected to be as statistically strong as the other measures of reliability, because raters are human observers of the behaviors they are evaluating and will respond to them in individual ways. Inter-rater reliability of 0.5 is considered to be high.

Wording. The way a survey item is worded has a lot to do with how successfully it will measure what you intend to measure, and this will naturally impact validity and reliability. In addition to examining the technical report data, you can do your own gut-level evaluation of survey items by considering several criteria:

- Is it positively phrased? Behaviors referred to in survey items should be expressed in positive terms rather than negative. If an item says, "Fails to communicate about key decisions that affect me," this will discourage some raters, especially direct reports, from being honest in their assessment. Instead, wording like "Regularly keeps me informed of decisions made that affect me" will permit the rater to indicate whether or not the manager does this effectively, without seeming critical or negative. Furthermore, the manager will be more inclined to accept feedback that rates behaviors against positively worded criteria.
- Is it sensitive to the needs of a culturally diverse population? This might require adding, deleting, or modifying some items. For example, it might be necessary to include questions that address competencies needed to accommodate cultural differences in leadership and cultural sensitivity. You also will have to evaluate questions to look for items that might be culturally unacceptable to some raters. In certain cultures that discourage people from voicing criticism directly, for example, questions have to be worded in a way that avoids alienating raters.

- Is it appropriate for a virtual workforce? In many cases, raters may have worked with the individual, but may have done so long-distance, communicating via e-mail and telephone for much, or all, of their working relationship. Therefore, the wording needs to take into account the fact that there may not be direct observation of the individual. Specifically, you need to examine questions to make sure they are logical for employees, colleagues, and superiors who may, or may not, work virtually with the subject.
- Is it put in personal terms? A survey item that says "Treats me with respect" will be more effective than one that says "Treats all staff members with respect." An individual rater can respond on the level of his or her individual experience, but should not be expected to generalize to the point of speaking for the manager's treatment of a whole group. If a manager does, in fact, behave differently with different people, a well-worded survey item will uncover this fact and add value to the feedback data.

Flexibility and customization. Many organizations want or need to adapt an existing questionnaire to suit the requirements of their individual leadership or management models more closely. Most important is the need to ensure that there is a definite relationship between identified competencies, performance improvements, and business results.

Many 360-degree feedback assessments are customized to fit a very specific competency model or set of behaviors that have been identified as being tied to performance. To that end, multi-rater assessments tend to be somewhat narrowly focused, using a precise series of questions to create an alignment between key organizational objectives and behaviors needed to achieve those objectives.

There are many other potential situations that could call for adapting existing questionnaires. For example, a company with a large union presence would have to develop an instrument that reflects and measures against leadership profiles developed by and for management and union groups, as well as the behaviors associated with good working relations between them. A company seeking a culture change initiative that requires developing new leadership skills might need a 360-degree feedback tool that assesses those competencies.

Making the Instrument Work with Your People

Timing. When you introduce a 360-degree feedback assessment, the timing of the evaluation is also an important element in its successful implementation. It's vital to consider what other events are happening that might inhibit employees' embrace of the assessment. For example, if a restructuring is imminent, participants might become suspicious of leadership's motives, fearing the instrument will be used as part of a punitive screening process. In general, managers need to ensure that the tool is introduced during a relatively stable period. That way the context for the assessment will support the message that it's a development initiative and there's no other management agenda.

Choosing raters. Managers taking part in 360-degree feedback are usually asked to select those who will complete the questionnaire relative to their behavior on the job. While there might be some concern that the managers could pick primarily those whom they believe will provide positive feedback, experience has shown that even the closest acquaintances will give honest answers if they are sure these will be kept confidential.

It is important, however, that each participating manager select individuals who have a relationship with him or her that permits them to give accurate feedback on issues of effectiveness. Selected raters should have had a chance to observe the manager's behaviors on the job for at least four months.

Increasingly, companies are limiting the group asked to provide assessment, instead focusing on more segmented populations such as peers and supervisors, without using direct reports, depending on what behavior is being assessed. In addition, not all raters will have had the opportunity to observe the person directly. For example, a manager of a virtual workplace may spend little time in physical proximity to employees asked to participate.

Communication issues. Asking one worker to assess the behavior of another, especially if the one being rated is in a superior position, presents some delicate issues. Without careful handling of communications, organizations risk a low response rate from those selected to complete the questionnaire or responses that are less than fully forthcoming.

Perhaps the most important element is consistency. For example, all too often, organizations unwittingly send out conflicting messages by failing to ensure that the wording is the same in all communications. "This is for development only" and "This is primarily for development" may seem to say the same thing, but the implications, in reality, are quite different. One solution is to assign a manager to the role of "continuity contact"—someone who not only checks each communication for consistency but also keeps his or her ear to the ground, to make sure the right messages are being heard.

Raters need to feel that they understand the process in which they are being asked to participate and to believe that their answers will never be connected to them personally. Communications should include an explanation of the nature of the process, the importance of their honest feedback, the purposes for which it will be used, and the assurance of complete confidentiality of all responses. Confidentiality can be further ensured through the use of an outside, third-party consultant who will receive all completed questionnaires and who will process the results and produce the feedback report.

Another key to success is that top management demonstrates genuine support of and involvement in the 360-degree feedback process. Senior leaders should be given the responsibility for setting the tone and oversight of the development process. A visibly committed and engaged leadership will ensure that the rest of the organization sees the importance of getting involved and the value of fully participating.

An especially critical message that needs to be communicated is the feedback's goal: that it will be used solely for developmental purposes. If a rater understands the input provided will assist the individual to create a development plan to address identified weaknesses and further develop strengths, and will not be used as a formal performance appraisal or as a factor in compensation decisions, then he or she will be more inclined to make direct and useful observations regarding the on-the-job behavior of the manager in question.

Last, good communications can help prevent or minimize some common problems that occur in the rating process. For instance, "attribution error" is the result of a rater's decision, conscious or unconscious, to rate the individual based on his or her good reputation, rather than on actual observed behavior. When this happens, the rater may give high ratings in areas potentially relevant to manager effectiveness simply because the individual being rated is widely known to be effective. This phenomenon tends to blur the distinctions between specific behaviors, which, if properly observed and identified, could serve to point out areas needing improvement.

Similarly, a "halo effect" can occur when a rater responds to the questionnaire more on the basis of his or her own general positive or negative feelings about the person, instead of on the basis of observed behavior. As with attribution error, this has the effect of painting a manager with a broad brush and reduces the amount of helpful information collected for feedback. Pre-program communications can alert all participants to these potential pitfalls and encourage them to base their responses on real behaviors they have witnessed on the job.

Delivering the Feedback

In addition to providing written feedback reports, there is much to be said for also providing the opportunity for managers to work with an outside facilitator to explain the feedback, help to interpret it correctly, and assist managers in using this information profitably. In general, it's best to use group sessions for delivering results to lower levels of management and individual one-on-one interaction for higher levels.

Content of feedback sessions can vary, but certain key elements have proven to be especially helpful. Among these are the following:

- *Explaining the model the survey is based on.* Normally the questionnaire would have been developed around a particular theory or model of effective management and leadership. This may have been a model of the survey author's choosing, or it may be a model specific to the organization, if the questionnaire was custom-built to be fully integrated with the company's other related development initiatives. In either case, the better managers understand the model operating behind the survey, the better prepared they will be to interpret and benefit from the feedback they receive.
- *Engaging managers in interpreting their feedback.* Managers who have substantial responsibilities in the organization may not appreciate forms of feedback that smack of a cookie-cutter approach, such as may be the case with some computer-based 360-degree feedback instruments. Skilled facilitation can elicit from the managers valuable perspectives and interpretations that can reveal insights leading to

needed behavioral changes. Also, managers who have been involved in the process of interpreting their own feedback are more likely to accept the implications of the feedback and to pursue a follow-up plan for self-development.

- *Keeping a balance of positive and negative.* A facilitator should present feedback on strengths as well as weaknesses identified in the 360-degree feedback process, keeping in mind that people are more receptive to criticism when they believe it to be well-balanced. The session can demonstrate that the feedback process shows managers what they are doing effectively and should continue doing, as well as what they might consider changing.
- *Encouraging managers to develop an individual action plan.* If participating managers are permitted to exercise a measure of control over the process, they usually will decide correctly what course is needed to improve. The action planning process, coupled with an understanding of the leadership or managerial model being used, will lead participants to design a personal development plan that will address their individual needs and lead to more effective leadership behaviors.

Making the Most of Follow-up Activities

Most organizations using 360-degree feedback systems understandably place a lot of emphasis on the individual's own commitment to making improvements over time, based on the plan developed. As critical as this element is to successful outcomes, additional activities can accelerate and reinforce the developmental steps needed for a manager to make the desired progress. Activities can include the following:

Skills training. If the feedback identifies needed improvements involving behaviors or skills for which the recipient is inadequately trained, this training or developmental experiences must be provided. Whatever the skill, the individual may be unable to make much progress without help. For best effect, follow-up should emphasize on-the-job experiential training with performance tools to support these activities. That would include assigning projects with a real business purpose that allow skills and abilities to be developed.

Coaching. Providing support and coaching at the individual level can make a significant difference in helping managers make practical use of the feedback they receive. After some reasonable interval of time, a follow-up session can be scheduled with the manager's boss and/or a human resource manager or an outside consultant, to review progress made against the development plan and challenges that may have arisen and to provide any other specific encouragement or coaching support appropriate to the individual need. This coaching should focus on applying lessons learned to real situations on the job.

Revisiting raters. One of the most useful ways to get the most out of the 360-degree process is to resurvey the original raters for a specific manager after a period of time—usually about 12 to 18 months—to determine how the individual's behavior has been altered. In addition to providing critical information on the manager's progress, this method can also help quantify the organization's return on its investment in the program

In fact, long-term commitment is vital to success. Indeed, while collecting feedback is relatively easy, ensuring that people change their behavior is more difficult. But while such commitment involves significant investment of time and effort, not to mention expense, it is an investment that pays off and provides benefits far superior to other top-down one-on-one reviews.

We firmly believe that careful attention to the principles explained in this chapter—relative to selection/design of the survey instrument used, survey administration and communications, feedback delivery, and follow-up development opportunities—will help to reinforce the enormous potential of this tool—a powerful instrument that serves as an invaluable source of data for measuring and developing key behaviors linked directly to business performance success.

Case Study: Using the 360-Degree as a Before and After Assessment of a Development Program

After experiencing a significant downturn, a global high-tech company knew it needed to transform from its growth-oriented focus—where stock options motivated employees—to a more mature profit-oriented company. The goal was to create a culture in which people development was continual and company-wide collaboration ensured profitable growth.

Right Management designed and facilitated a significant organizational change process aimed at mobilizing an emerging leader base capable of and committed to leading the company to success. To that end, Right developed a three-phase program with a learning assessment conducted before and after that objectively and accurately quantified a new leader's mindset as it aligned with the company's model for emerging leaders, measuring how effectively participants were able to change. A central part of that before and after assessment was conducting 360-degree feedback assessments on all leaders.

The program received extremely high participant ratings, strong executive support, and highly successful results. For example, a study conducted by an independent evaluator indicated a $3 return for every $1 invested in the program.

Case Study: How 360-Degree Feedback Was Used to Develop Coaching Capabilities

A wireless telecommunications services provider wanted to boost organizational performance by improving coaching capabilities of all its leaders, from front-line to CEO. Doing so was crucial to the successful repositioning of the company's consumer brand. Right Management partnered with the firm to create an assessment and leadership development experience that provided all levels of leaders with critical insights and skill building.

To that end, consultants designed, developed, and implemented custom online 360-degree feedback surveys based on the new competency model, followed by classroom training. Central to the process was a tiered coaching approach. For strategic leaders, 25 coaches worked with the top 85 leaders, using the custom 360 and other assessments as needed. Thirty-five coaches facilitated development planning for 270 operational leaders. And about 2,000 call center and retail store leaders received coaching from their immediate supervisors, who were assisted by Right Management consultants in interpreting 360 results and coaching basics.

Over a two-year period, turnover was reduced by 20 percent in over 800 retail stores, in exit interviews, the ranking of managers as "the reason for leaving" moved from second to tenth place, employee satisfaction increased significantly, and the top 15 percent of call center leaders had 66 percent less turnover.

Chapter 24

Coaching Leaders for Corporate Social Responsibility

Deb Jacobs, Partner
Axiom Consulting Partners
Mayra Hernandez, CEO
Impactomb

"Integrity is the essence of everything successful."

Richard Buckminster Fuller

I N ARTICLES ON CORPORATE SOCIAL RESPONSIBILITY (CSR), IT IS CONSISTENTLY PORTRAYED AS: "a company's active and voluntary contribution towards social, economic, and environmental improvement. Together these actions serve to improve the company's competitiveness and value-add, for the creation of a socially, economically, and environmentally sustainable planet."

Despite all the agreement about what CSR *is*, there remains, however, a sizable debate about what CSR *is not*. This debate takes place in the minds of leaders who are being held accountable to bring CSR to life within their workplaces while simultaneously being measured by short-term gains in shareholder value. The question on the minds of CEO's and their counterparts in the C-suite is not whether their organization's active and voluntary contributions can improve social, economic, and environmental concerns, but whether those actions will also directly improve the business performance for which they are accountable.

Consider Walmart's cost-cutting efforts as described in a seminal article on sustainability, "Green is Good for Business" (BusinessWeek 2006). Walmart requested

Kid Connection, a private toy brand, to reduce its packaging size. Kid Connection complied and 497 shipping containers were eliminated, with the following results: 1,000 barrels of oil were eliminated, 2.4 million dollars in fuel expense were saved, and 3,800 less trees were involved in the packaging process.

Leaders of CSR initiatives often ask valid questions about these statistics:

1. "Were the savings a result of a primary focus on cost cutting, with the added bonanza of being good for the environment?"
2. "Would any company act in a significant way that is good for the planet or good for people that was not first and foremost a source of greater corporate profitability?"
3. "How is CSR fundamentally different from traditional efforts to keep operational expenses to a minimum?"
4. "Was the real impetus for change driven from a quest for cost cutting and operating more 'lean'? Was the real story spun by publicists to focus on CSR as a way to improve the company's image or strengthen its brand?"
5. If a business is rapidly depleting the precious natural resources of a region and consequentially interfering with sacred rituals or customs yet replacing those resources with new commerce that results in economic improvements for the region in the form of new jobs and community infrastructure, how does a leader reconcile the polarities?
6. How did the CSR cost-cutting impact other parts of the supply value chain; whose business performed less well because of decreased orders for packaging materials and how did the changes in that business' performance impact society, the economy, and the planet?

There is so much positive momentum about the value of CSR, most leaders are careful to publicly express enthusiasm. In our work, we have found that despite the fact that CSR is perceived to be a clear and achievable path to greater profitability, top leadership commitment to the development of a fully integrated CSR strategy remains an anomaly in American business. CSR champions (a leader with some formal accountability for figuring out how CSR will be realized in their organization) remain confused about how CSR can be realized while maintaining and even growing a robust bottom line.

CSR champions ask the following valid questions: Is CSR here to stay? Does the board really care about a sincere approach to CSR or one that shows on a checklist that there is a CSR platform? Should the CSR strategy be bold or should be taken slowly based on competitors' commitments?

CSR champions are engaging coaches to help guide them. In these coaching relationships, CSR leaders have a safe place to express and expand on their beliefs and concerns. They also have a partner to help them develop change strategies that will tap into both stakeholder CSR ideals and alleviate fears, evaluate various CSR platforms, and collaboratively drive an integrated CSR strategy throughout the business.

To explore the mechanics and principles of how coaching for CSR works, this chapter is based on an actual coach-leader relationship.

Preparing for Coaching

Step 1: Is the leader ready for coaching? (one session)

Before agreeing to work with the leader, the coach evaluated the leader's coaching readiness. The coach used The Renewable Enterprise Self Assessment to get a sense of the leader's interest in thinking systemically, leading complex change, expanding business acumen, valuing interpersonal relationships, and self-awareness (Figure 24-1).

Deb Jacobs, Axiom Consulting Partners

SCALE:	4: Very much like me	3: Somewhat like me	2: Not very much like me	1: Not at all like me	
Lens 1 Global Thinker	Gathers information about problems and opportunities from diverse resources. 4 3 2 1	Identifies new patterns in information. 4 3 2 1	Avoids getting self or others trapped by "old-think" assumptions or boundaries. 4 3 2 1	Recognizes the enterprise-wide implications of actions. 4 3 2 1	Applies an enterprise-wide perspective to local problems. 4 3 2 1
Lens 2 Future Designer	Understands the success factors associated with leading organization change. 4 3 2 1	Inspires others to navigate through the heart of complex challenges using shared values and principles. 4 3 2 1	Encourages the transfer of learning from the past and the present to help ease the way to the future. 4 3 2 1	Promotes giving up sacred rituals and habits to make room for new thinking and possibilities. 4 3 2 1	Appreciates the disruption and discomfort that leads to new innovation. 4 3 2 1
Lens 3 Business Value Driver	Searches for the key drivers of business value and the associated business priorities. 4 3 2 1	Mobilizes others to achieve business results. 4 3 2 1	Develops fresh, whole system approaches to realizing shared goals. 4 3 2 1	Sticks to the big picture value drivers and does not get lost in the mechanics of execution. 4 3 2 1	Communicates strategies and provides support so others can succeed. 4 3 2 1
Lens 4 Relationship Focuser	Balances inquiry with advocacy when exploring points of view. 4 3 2 1	Empathizes and connects with the unique socialization and experiences with others. 4 3 2 1	Recognizes and appreciates both the bold and nuanced contributions of others. 4 3 2 1	Demonstrates compassion and caring for others in ways that are authentic to self. 4 3 2 1	Uses own voice to directly communicate and inspire needed change and truth telling and encourages others to do the same. 4 3 2 1
Lens 5 Self Awareness	Seeks new learning and insight about self. 4 3 2 1	Monitors own ego and self-interest seeking. 4 3 2 1	Develops and shares new personal practices with transparency and openness. 4 3 2 1	Operates with authenticity and integrity, honoring own dreams and goals. 4 3 2 1	Asks for help and is comfortable inviting others to support own development. 4 3 2 1

Figure 24-1 Renewable Enterprise Thinking: Self Assessment

The coach used this self-assessment to engage in a dialogue with the leader about his beliefs about CSR, how he or she was thinking about approaching the task, and how he or she had been successful in the past when handling similar challenges. This discussion helped the coach to get an idea of the leader's ability to engage in an effective partnership. A summary of the coach's assessment follow:

1. Encourage intellectual curiosity and wonder about the paradoxes and polarities of CSR. (*High curiosity and wonder*)
2. Stimulate fresh insight and new ways of thinking about problems. (*Moderate, but can be cultivated*)
3. Engage in the process of innovating to achieve elegant solutions that serve a variety of stakeholders. (*Low, but open to thinking differently; not rigid, a bit fearful about making mistakes*)
4. Remain resilient and courageous in the face of resistance and adversity. (*Low, easily discouraged; need to test assumptions about consequences associated with managing resistance and expand skills to influence and persuade others*)
5. Act with consistency and commitment to values and strategic imperatives, over time. (*High in personal life, other-centered and integral*)

Step 2: Establish a foundation of clear roles and guardrails. (one session)

At the onset of the coaching engagement, the leader confided that he was particularly interested in how the coach would interact with his manager, the CEO. The coach clarified that the leader will be having all communications with his manager. The coach would be happy to help plan communications with the CEO and coach on how to successfully report plans and progress. Other topics discussed in this step are as follows: bind decision and communication responsibilities to the leader; clarify the coaching protocol and revise to reflect the needs of the leader; discuss the difference between content and process, emphasizing the coach's role as process consultant; identify practices that are important to both leader and coach such as frequency of communication, accessibility, methods of giving and receiving feedback, methods of supporting and redirecting, interactions with third parties; select and prioritize goals.

Engaging in Coaching

Coaching Phase I: Establish with the leader a shared understanding of CSR and his role as a champion (can take weeks or months).

Coaching Principle: Balance the use of advocacy and inquiry through a combination of initiating communication, being direct, listening with empathy, and showing respect for the point of view of the leader.

For example, in an early coaching session, the leader shared that in the past, his organization demonstrated magnanimity by writing a check to its chosen charity. It didn't hurt that the donation was a tax write-off. The coach listened without judgment or criticism.

The coach helped the leader conduct a stakeholder analysis to identify the various entities that would be connected with the CSR initiative. The leader was surprised by the number of stakeholders needed to be considered. He and the coach pinpointed where they thought each stakeholder was in terms of blocking, allowing, helping, or driving a CSR initiative. Next they discussed where each stakeholder needed to be relative to blocking, allowing, helping, or driving the CSR initiative and what it would take to nudge each stakeholder closer to the ideal.

Coaching Principle: Continually conduct new stakeholder analyses. Remember to consider stakeholders from these sectors: Government and nonprofits; opinion leaders including traditional media and academics; investors and shareholders; risk assessors including insurers and banks; business partners including industry associations, suppliers, and buyers; and competitors.

The coach asked the leader to gather information about the stakeholders and what they had in mind when they considered the organization's CSR contributions.

The coach shared with the leader an article about myths associated with CSR to help broaden thinking and stimulate discussion at their next session. The major takeaways of the article are in Figure 24-2.

Coaching Principle: Help the leader get started.
The following CSR Strategy Roadmap has proven useful in helping leaders to fine-tune an approach.

- CSR is repackaged philanthropy or charity.
- CSR is simply a marketing campaign.
- CSR is only necessary when there is outcry from a special interest.
- CSR does not provide direct benefits to the company.
- CSR provides no real ROI.

Courtesy of Mayra Hernandez LLC

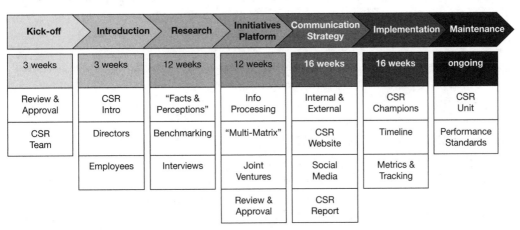

Kick-off	Introduction	Research	Initiatives Platform	Communication Strategy	Implementation	Maintenance
3 weeks	3 weeks	12 weeks	12 weeks	16 weeks	16 weeks	ongoing
Review & Approval	CSR Intro	"Facts & Perceptions"	Info Processing	Internal & External	CSR Champions	CSR Unit
CSR Team	Directors	Benchmarking	"Multi-Matrix"	CSR Website	Timeline	Performance Standards
	Employees	Interviews	Joint Ventures	Social Media	Metrics & Tracking	
			Review & Approval	CSR Report		

Figure 24-2 Myths Associated with CSR

Part I. Project Kickoff

Begin with an easy-to-understand work plan. Each phase should include timeline, deliverables, project owners/roles, and budget. Present the work plan to a CSR committee or team that should include CEO, CFO, Marketing, Human Resources, Operations, Legal (ad hoc), and IT (ad hoc).

Part II. Introduction

1. Introduce CSR as a new and key initiative of the company.
2. Share point of view concerning CSR as a concept and its relevance in today's world.
3. Improve communication.
4. Use examples that relate to various functionalities so each sees the relevance to their work.

Coaching Principle: Help the leader to get everyone aligned. Introduce to the company not only the work plan but also the concept of CSR across the whole organization. This is the time to stress higher ideals such as making the world a better place. It is essential to establish a common organization-wide language about CSR. These practices will help create a compelling and uniting vision.

Part III. Research and Benchmarking

The primary goal of this part of the work plan is to gather as much relevant data as possible to clarify facts and perceptions. This data is gathered through interviews and surveys. Competitive data and internal CSR-related activities are cataloged. The overall scope of this research depends on the company's size and CSR objectives. Perceptions about CSR including its potential and its elements collected from key internal players can be very helpful to a CSR champion as he or she completes the ever-growing stakeholder analysis. By learning about best-in-class practices within the industry, the leader is able to gauge his or her efforts and use their experiences to frame his or her decisions and commitments.

Coaching Principle: Help the leader to avoid getting lost in the data and to concentrate efforts to building positive relationships with those who would be endorsing or implementing the plans.

Part IV. Initiatives Platform

Once all the research has been synthesized, organized, and classified, the process of data analysis begins. Ideally, information is entered in a "multidimensional matrix" so that a wide range of relevant factor analyses can be completed. Exploring the meaning of this data with the CSR team leads to the exploration of possible decisions concerning CSR costs, time to achieve goals, risk, where the work takes place, what CSR pillars will be impacted (social, economic, or environmental), and other relevant factors.

Coaching Principle: Help the leader to stay with the process. Insist that the leader stay with the work plan and not put "the cart before the horse" at any juncture

V. Communication Strategy

The purpose of a communication strategy is to

- Ensure the right stakeholders get the right information at the right time through the right channels (efficiency and effectiveness).
- Ensure alignment and consistency of key messages to minimize misinterpretation of plans (both internal and external).
- Ensure ongoing information sharing and engagement of key stakeholders in a style and form that fits with the business culture.

At this stage, the leader should share what is established and use various communication channels to further shape the CSR strategy. The communication strategy should consider the needs of both internal and external stakeholders. All senior leaders should be prepared to communicate an aligned and consistent story about the company's commitment to ethics, the environment, and society. More importantly, the story has to be meaningful to all stakeholders.

Internal: Use tools managed by HR such as bulletin boards and newsletters; tap into the power of the intranet and utilize mass communication events to promote knowledge transfer, integration, and development.

External: In addition to including CSR messaging in strategic marketing efforts, a social media plan must be developed, since it can play a key role in how the business shapes its CSR strategy while also presenting information that positions the organization as a good corporate citizen. Develop a CSR Web site to communicate progress on sustainability initiatives and as a hub for the social media initiatives underway.

CSR report: A CSR report is a strategic document that offers an assessment of an organization's nonfinancial performance. The Global Reporting Initiative (GRI) provides a reporting framework that sets out the principles and indicators that organizations should use to measure and report their economic, environmental, and social performance. CSR reports based on the GRI framework are now the standard.

Coaching Principle: Help the leader to create a comprehensive communication plan. The coach helps the leader understand how a flawed communication strategy impacts a CSR platform. Through powerful questions and examples from the research, the coach is able to help the leader see how town halls, e-mails, newsletters, campaigns, press, and leader-cascaded key messages could work together to create positive momentum and commitment.

VI. Implementation

Successful CSR strategy implementation is about discipline and focus. The following considerations will help the leader construct a strong platform for implementation.

1. *Clarify the objective.* Stipulate the intended result or accomplishment.
2. *Provide a rationale.* Explain the purpose.
3. *Identify the benefits.* Provide a brief list of the CSR pillars—economic, social, and environmental benefits expected.
4. *Publicize the metrics.* Simplify the indicators and identify the milestones that will enable others to know the objective is on track or has been realized.
5. *Performance goals.* Explain performance targets and how these will be established and cascaded for each metric.
6. *Blueprint or design strategy.* Review steps and means to achieve the objective and tighten up as needed.
7. *References.* Ensure appropriate references, materials, and information to the people and areas involved.

VII. Maintenance

Once the initiatives linked to the CSR strategy are underway, it is time to ensure the strategy is protected and fueled over time. Budgets must be allocated, resources, procured, training and development arranged, and progress tracked. In addition to measuring the success of various initiatives, the leadership effectiveness of the CSR strategy must be evaluated and continuously improved. This can be achieved either by the original CSR team or by creating a CSR business unit.

Coaching Principle: Help the leader gather feedback about his effectiveness. This input can be helpful during the leader's annual performance review and when the leader passes the CSR initiative on to the next champion. While the leader is gathering information about his effectiveness, he can also use the opportunity to pinpoint ways to improve CSR strategy and maintain enthusiasm.

Coaching Phase II: Select learning priorities and agree on specific action learning goals (ongoing coaching over many weeks or months).

As the leader continues to lead and develop a meaningful and workable CSR strategy, many coaching opportunities arise. The leader may find it difficult to resolve conflict among factions that have strong points of view about what initiatives should receive funding or other resources, and also may need help with how to best communicate with each faction. It is likely that the leader will need to reflect on some of his or her assumptions about actions and their relative value. The coach helps the leader be more strategic "in the moment" by encouraging him or her to slow down, stick to the plan, examine the process carefully, and integrate learning about effective change leadership into actions.

This is a good time to keep success factors out front and center as outlined in the following:

Success Factors

- Board-level oversight
- Top management leadership and commitment
- Business units' ownership/support
- Employees engagement (grass roots)
- Metrics and tracking
- Accountability
- Long-term commitment
- Emphasis on creating new value

---

1. Formalize areas of focus and learning and link to strategic imperatives.
2. Discuss and agree on what success looks like and how it will be measured.
3. Remind leader that this work is a new paradigm and to stay patient.

Coaching Phase III: Use real business issues and challenges to fine-tune the leader's ability to successfully implement the CSR strategy.

Most leaders who are asked to take the lead on CSR or serve as a member of a CSR strategy team are also responsible for a business unit or function. The leaders "day job" challenges provide opportunities to integrate learning about CSR to the workplace.

Coaching Phase IV: Continually stretch and expand the skills of the leader to move the organization toward emerging CSR goals (begins midway and continues through the coaching transition).

At the onset, the leader wanted to focus only on sustainability. The idea of moving from green to blue (see Figure 24-3) seemed too far afield. However, over time, the leader began to consider "blue" CSR and to see how it might be incorporated as a new phase of the strategy. The coach encouraged the leader to keep learning about blue and thinking about the best timing and communication to ensure it would get a fair hearing. They agreed that it made sense to wait until the first work plan was successfully in place and maintenance in progress before exploring ways to raise the bar. In some organizations, a blue approach may be the most appropriate way to commence. In this phase of CSR coaching the coach is prompted by the leader's interest in innovating and creating breakthroughs.

Blue is the New Green

More than just a new color trend or a simple communication concept, it's a philosophy based on the principles of authenticity, integrity, commitment, dialogue, transparency, transformation, and constant evolution.

The "Blue Innovation" is the second generation, in terms of strategic sustainability, with a social media scheme. It was presented last year by Saatchi and Saatchi, in the Sustainable Brands International Conference, and adopted by major companies.

- In terms of opportunities, it's strategic and flexible.
- It seeks to generate emotions through brand power.

"A Blue Ocean of Opportunity": "Blue thinkers" attract different interest groups: shareholders, employees, clients, suppliers, and communities.

Instead of focusing on a pessimistic environmental and economic view, they focus on generating inspiration and, through brand power, they awaken emotions "using the power of emotion to drive innovation."

Figure 24-3 Think Blue: A New Paradigm to Capture the Power of CSR

Coaching Phase V: Coaching Transition

As the leader becomes comfortable with the role as CSR champion, the coach establishes closure. The timing of this transition depends on a number of factors including the terms of the coaching contract, the perceived value of the coaching, and the coach's assessment of the leader's ability to move forward alone. Part of the closure includes the following:

1. Encourage the leader to find opportunities to share new skills with others.
2. Coach the leader to act with commitment.
3. Help the leader develop a CSR toolkit to share with future champions.

Conclusion

Coaching leaders to be effective in their championing of CSR is an important new role for executive coaches. This type of leadership development combines elements of strategy, leadership, and change coaching. CSR coaching entails a clear understanding of CSR and an in-depth knowledge of the internal conflict associated with bringing a new social innovation and conceptual framework to a politically, socially, and environmentally charged workplace. Engagement in leading the development of a CSR platform frequently takes more time and effort than leaders and their counterparts might envision. Much of the effort is focused on both hearing out and communicating with the CSR skeptics. Coaches are very valuable to a leader when trying to find the right way to navigate organizational roadblocks.

CSR coaching isn't for everyone. Many leaders are not interested in taking on a significant new role. However, enlightened leaders will step up and enter an uncertain space, eager to explore a more holistic approach to doing business in the fundamental belief that doing the right thing will ultimately lead to greater profitability and sustainability.

Chapter 25

Integrating Coaching, Training, and Development with Talent Management

Kaye Thorne, Founder and Managing Partner
Talent Perspectives

Introduction

Talent development should not be about a few special people; it should be about maximizing everyone's strengths, championing diversity, and encouraging creativity and innovation. Above all, it should be about working to create an environment where the organization buzzes with energy and people come to work anticipating a positive experience. "Talent is not a rare commodity; it is simply rarely released" should be the premise behind coaching, training, and development.

Organizations often try to set up talent management processes, but true success comes with the engagement of its employees' hearts and minds. The organizations that achieve optimal engagement are those where vision and values are aligned with individual needs.

Fundamentally, talent development needs a holistic approach. There has to be a belief and a commitment to make it happen from the CEO and the executive right through line management to the newest recruit.

Organizations can convince themselves that talent management is being carried out when they create a system to define the steps or outline a process. However, talent development only happens when a culture, based on shared values and beliefs, is created, thinking and emotions are engaged, and the leadership demonstrates its commitment through its behavior and attitudes.

Individuals within an organization need to feel that they are valued and that their contribution will make a difference. It is easy to say that this is happening, but far harder to have concrete evidence of its application.

In any discussion about talent or high-potential development, it is important to emphasize the development of all individuals. No organization should focus its attention solely on developing only part of its human capital. What is also essential is recognizing the needs of different individuals within its community.

Talented people do not necessarily fit into an easy system of classification. People are talented in many ways: Some may have a particular aptitude that may be primarily skill based, others may be gifted artistically, and others may demonstrate their talent in more nontraditional ways and may be viewed as maverick in their approach. How does an organization recognize and develop an individual's abilities? It is also about matching individual needs and organizational requirements.

HR/OD/L&D training professionals should be asking: How do we manage our pool of talent to suit our evolving business need? How much of what we need have we currently got? How much of what we need can be developed from what we have already? How much of what we have cannot be used by us effectively over the next one to three years? How much of what we need is external, where are they, and how do we attract them?

Responding to these questions creates a cross-company, integrated learning strategy. In this chapter, I will identify solutions that are applicable in the broadest context of talent development.

Creating a Learning and Development Plan for Talented Individuals

There is much talk about employee engagement, but learning engagement goes much deeper; it goes to the very heart of an individual, what inspires him or her, what interests the individual, how he or she learns best. Without learning, engagement much investment in training and development will be wasted. Individuals will attend, but their hearts and minds will be elsewhere. With learning engagement, individuals are energized, committed, and want to take the next step in their development.

Increasingly organizations are moving from menu-driven training to competency-based learning. This can provide an opportunity for more individualized learning. In the best competency-based learning, the learner is encouraged to ask themselves questions and to reflect on their experiences as part of their learning. This self-assessment and reflective learning needs support from either a line manager or coach.

As previously mentioned, talented people vary in their development requirements and no one approach suits all. Furthermore, talent is not age driven. Currently the emphasis is on attracting young talent, but ignoring experience can be perilous to an organization. The organization should focus on *all* employees.

This process should start at the recruitment stage and continue throughout the organizational lifetime of an individual, and in many cases beyond that. Real talent is in such short supply that if you identify someone who is particularly talented who is leaving your organization, you may want to "keep the door open" for his or her return in the future. Equally if someone applies who does not fit a particular role now, ask to keep his or her details on file for a potential role in the future. Search and recruitment businesses build their reputations on keeping track of talented people, and HR functions should do the same.

Consistency of approach is also important, as is honesty in performance feedback. Once you raise the expectations of talented people, it is important to follow through. There are far too many talented people who become disillusioned because their expectations were raised either during their initial interview or in ongoing appraisal discussions only to find that their manager or the organization reneges on commitments or promises. Succession planning processes are a case in point. Many talented people are attracted to an organization on the promise of rapid promotion or increased responsibility only to find that the opportunities do not exist or evaporate.

Money or promotions are not the only motivators. For a number of years, I have had an ongoing talent tracking process, interviewing different generations of talented people about their hopes and aspirations and what they look for from an organization. This research has quite conclusively shown that recognition, praise, and feedback are equally important motivators. What demotivates talented people is being ignored or, even worse, being trapped in one role in one business function when they have the capability to contribute across a number of areas. People in traditional roles or with a narrow perspective often fail to understand a talented person's breadth of capability and the need to demonstrate it.

How we learn is one of the most individual and personal activities that we undertake, and yet many organizations put individuals together in group or classroom training environments that allow little opportunity for individual coaching and support. Especially for creative people, this dynamic presents a challenge. They crave feedback, they need time to reflect, and they want specialized coaching to help them develop what they believe they need. Unlike many of their colleagues, they often have a purpose to their learning and they get frustrated with what they may perceive as trivia or irrelevant information.

In creating a learning and development strategy, focus on:

- Accurately analyzing the talent that exists and the gap between the talent base and desired talent
- Base-lining competency based criteria for all roles and ways of identifying and developing talent
- Reviewing current learning and development opportunities offered to employees
- Creating criteria for talent development
- Devising a development plan for growing talent
- Identifying opportunities for talented individuals
- Creating a method and template for succession planning across the organization for expert and leadership roles

- Identifying the key roles that need succession plans
- Establishing a process for tracking talent and identifying successors/talented individuals for those roles

Coaching

One of the key ways to support the development of talented individuals is through coaching. To develop a coaching landscape and maximize the effectiveness of coaching, focus on the following areas.

1. Identifying Organizational Readiness for Coaching

This is an essential first step. While organizations may decide to introduce coaching, it is also important to prepare for it, to identify the individuals who will be responsible for coaching delivery, and to determine where coaching fits in the people strategy. Some organizations choose to train line managers as coaches, while others choose to use external coaches, and still others use coaches only for remedial purposes when dealing with underperformance issues. All approaches can work, but it is important to define where the support from a coach fits in the overall strategy.

2. Identifying Potential Coaches

Linked to the organization's decision about the role of coaching is the decision about who should be the coaches. Just as managers need to be trained to manage, training them to be coaches is equally important. All the important points about confidentiality, recognizing when people need additional specialized support, and the important difference between coaching and counseling need to be addressed. If coaches from outside the organization are used, all the above points apply, along with the need for them to have recognized qualifications and accreditation.

3. Clarifying the Role of the Coach

Talented individuals often have a passion to make something work, to find a new way of doing things, and often want to "make a difference" not just within their working environment but by contributing to the greater good of the organization or humanity. In pursuit of this, they can be frustrated when others do not have the same passions. For example, when investing energy and time in an embryonic idea, it can be hard for a creative person to wait for a decision while the idea languishes in a bureaucratic process.

A difficulty of being driven by creative thoughts is controlling this process and channeling it into the working environment. Here a coach can help a talented individual manage his or her creativity and give guidance to the organization about how best to support the individual. Helping talented people recognize the best way to use their talents is an important aspect of motivating them. Unfortunately, many people get frustrated by the lack of opportunities to demonstrate their talent and move on to other organizations or channel their creativity through self-employment.

4. Developing the Right Attitudes and Behaviors and Equipping the Coaches with the Right Skills and Knowledge

Key stages in the coaching process and some of the skills, knowledge, and attitudes/ behaviors required follow:

Creating the Climate

This stage relates not just to the initial meeting but also subsequent meetings. Often when people are being coached for the first time, they are unsure what to expect or they have limited experience with coaching. For the new coach, too, particularly if it is in the workplace, the surroundings may not naturally be conducive to creating the right learning environment. However, a good coach can, with experience, create the feeling of intimacy even in the most hectic conditions. What is important is the attention to the individual and the application of coaching behaviors. A good coach needs to help the learner create his or her vision and is able to work in partnership with the individual to build an infrastructure to support coaching. They should also be able to contextualize the learning—helping them to develop the right skill in the right context.

Building Relationships

To be able to build relationships is at the core of being a good coach. The need for enhanced interpersonal skills and the development of emotional intelligence is critical in the development of the coach. The coach's ability to develop a natural coaching style while using different interventions can be invaluable.

In the context of learning and development, transferring knowledge while understanding how people learn can make the learning experience much more effective. Equally, structuring the learning so that the needs of the learner are taken into account and adapting coaching style to suit the learner are all-important stages in building a relationship. Being open and responsive, and expressing a genuine interest in the learner can also help to build a relationship. Using the right interventions at the right time is another important skill to develop.

In a coaching relationship, a coach is often accompanying a learner on a journey. It could be a journey toward developing a particular skill, or toward achieving a particular ambition or the completion of a specific action plan. Tuning into learners and identifying how they may be feeling, knowing when to check on progress, or simply calling them just to remind them of ongoing support are all important parts of the coach's role.

The ability to inspire is another important ingredient in a good coach that can make the difference between success and failure. The significant difference in the coaching relationship is the intuitive ability to say the right thing or take the action that elevates the learner into achieving self-belief.

Being Open to Experience

Ambitions are often capped because of the perceptions of others. Teachers, parents, partners, and managers are often responsible for limiting an individual's belief in his or her ability to achieve. Therefore, it is imperative for the coach not to make the same mistake. Coaches must listen to the learner's ideas with an open mind and react appropriately. Coaches must recognize their own limitations and may need to identify other colleagues who may be able to offer alternative suggestions, advice, or support. If the learner's previous experience has resulted in low self-esteem, a coach can help avoid self-fulfilling prophecies of failure.

Being a Solution Partner

A coach needs to be able to rise above the issues, to be able to help a learner to work through opportunities and challenges, and to act as a sounding board. Coaches work at many levels within an organization. To be taken seriously as a business partner, it is important that the coach understand the organization's goals, vision, and strategy. Coaches do not necessarily have to have the same professional skills and knowledge as their learner, but they do need to know how to coach toward solutions. It is important to have productive conversations, offer meaningful advice, use problem-solving tools and techniques, and help the learner generate alternatives/solutions.

The coach should also help the learner manage risk appropriately. A good coach encourages the learner to make an accurate risk assessment. Ultimately, the decisions are made by the learner, and he or she must own the consequences. A coach's role is to help the learner in moving forward and to offer support when falling back.

Being a Collaborator

Learners are part of a larger organization, and helping them make the appropriate connections with others is an important part of the coaching role. A good coach can link people either individually or in teams to share information and best practices.

Identifying Appropriate Closure

In a coaching relationship, it is important to understand the point at which to pause and to encourage the learner to put his or her ideas and discoveries into practice. When people find a supportive coach, like a thirsty plant, they often drink up the attention and may be reluctant to stop the session. The learning will be more effective if a cycle of input, practice, and feedback is formed.

Maintaining the Relationship

In any coaching relationship there will come a time when the coaching relationship has run its course and the coaching should end or be passed on to a new coach. Identifying this point and handling it appropriately is important. The learner must be reassured and confident that the coach is available if the need arises.

5. Using Coaching to Support the Talent Management Process

Good motivators lead by example. Delegate authority to people, empowering them to make decisions while supplying the support and information they need. Give people recognition, show they are valued, and encourage them to take responsibility. Monitor performance and give constructive feedback.

6. Learning from the Experience and Sharing the Wisdom.

Any new learning initiative must be contextualized and clearly introduced, with endorsement from the CEO and senior management and supported by line management.

Conclusion

In summary, training, development, and coaching have a vital role in the talent management process. Key concepts are as follows:

- Coaching presents the opportunity for leaders to share wisdom and knowledge, and to create a culture that values the contribution of each and every employee.
- Managers who coach have the opportunity to inspire, excite, and develop motivated employees.
- Individuals who are coached and who coach have the opportunity to embark on a voyage of self-discovery and fulfillment.

The more collaborative and forward-thinking organizations recognize that a motivated workforce does not need to be "managed" in the traditional sense. What employees need, in order to fulfill their promise, is guidance, coaching, and the sharing of wisdom.

Part III

Making Compensation an Integral Part of Your Talent Management Program

Chapter 26

Driving Success through Differentiation: Compensation and Talent Management

Andrew S. Rosen, Executive Vice President
Jodi L. Starkman, Executive Vice President
ORC Worldwide

WHETHER CONFRONTED WITH THE CHALLENGE OF GLOBALIZATION, DEMOGRAPHIC shifts, emerging markets, changing business models, or global economic crises, successful organizations look to their employees as a critical source of differentiation in the market. In fact, research shows that the performance of top performers almost always exceeds the performance of average performers by a significant differential (Sullivan 2004). Hence, the ability to attract, develop, motivate, and retain high-performing talent is a key driver of corporate performance and competitive advantage.

The theme of differentiation is an important one in today's successful business. The hyper-competition and pace of change in business means that competitive advantage needs to come from every part of the organization. The investments that are made in human capital need to be evaluated and managed as strategically as any other investments made in an organization. This suggests some great opportunities for compensation professionals to more effectively contribute to business results. However, it requires a shift in thinking and willingness among compensation staff (and line managers) to reject the "one size fits all" natural tendency to spread rewards around the organization and, instead, invest where the greatest returns are.

Although every employee contributes to the success of an organization, high-performing employees who consistently demonstrate superior accomplishments contribute higher levels of value. Similarly, certain jobs or roles contribute higher levels of value to the overall achievements of business objectives. And, lastly, different segments of the candidate and employee population have different preferences when it comes to the things that attract, engage, and motivate them. So the notion of differentiation is one we will examine from multiple angles as we explore the role of compensation in talent management.

Defining a Model for Differentiation: Start with the Jobs

The most essential or valuable jobs in an organization vary depending on the company's business model. For example, in a company that is high-volume/lower-cost driven, some of the most important jobs are more likely to be in the supply chain management or distribution area. Consequently, the most valuable jobs might not be the most senior or even the most "competitive" from a labor market perspective. But if the job is one that has a differential impact on business results, an organization would be well served by putting its best talent into those roles and by making a larger investment in the incumbents, an element of which is compensation. In fact, companies that utilize this kind of approach to compensation often wind up paying a premium to people in critical jobs because the market value for the job doesn't reflect how important the position is for that particular company.

Interestingly, when HR professionals are asked to prioritize jobs that are most critical to an organization's success, they frequently begin by looking at the positions near the top of the organization chart. But "when forced to really think about what positions in the organization have the ability to immediately impact a firm's time to market or quality of goods or services being offered, the list of critical positions looks a lot different" (Henneman 2005). A position is labeled critical based not on who holds it but on its importance in achieving business goals.

Do You Want the Market to Determine Who Is Most Valuable to Your Business?

For most organizations, looking at compensation in the context of the jobs that are most critical to the company's success represents a shift from the typical focus on skill gaps and external market conditions. But *differentiation involves making choices that have strategic consequences* (Becker, Huselid, and Beatty 2009). So how might a company tackle this? The first step is to describe your organization's strategy or profit model and the capabilities that are most critical to executing that strategy. One tool for accomplishing this is a strategy map, a graphical depiction of the strategy of an organization, which illustrates the cause-and-effect relationships between different strategic objectives (Kaplan and Norton 2001).

Whatever approach or process is used to identify the positions that have the most strategic impact on business results, it is an activity that will require an investment of time among managers in order to thoroughly understand the strategic capabilities and the jobs most critical to delivering them. Once that is done, most organizations utilize their talent review process to decide who gets those jobs.

Consistent with a model of valuing jobs based on alignment with business imperatives is the notion that the value of a job may change as business strategy is updated from year to year. Hence, a job might be critical at one point in time but less critical in a subsequent year. But identifying critical jobs is just one element in a talent management-driven compensation strategy. Another piece is identifying key talent.

Defining a Model for Differentiation: Segment the Talent

Increasingly in companies that seek to execute business strategy through people, the models for attracting, developing, motivating, and retaining talent are taking a lesson from the way companies manage their customer relationships. For years, companies have prioritized customers by segmenting the market and placing emphasis on high-value customers with large and/or repeat-spending patterns, recognizing that a high-value customer or group of customers can make or break a business. This recognition is used to inform the design of products and services that appeal to particular customer segments. Inherent in this strategy is the fact that the return on marketing, product, and service investment is different depending on the customer.

In HR, this truth is often lost in an effort to be "fair," "equitable," and "evenly spread," when it comes to investments in employees. HR professionals and line managers are often reluctant to take a more segmented approach to investing in employees; it's a more complex process, and it requires a willingness to explicitly recognize the inequality of employee contributions.

Talent segmentation can be accomplished in multiple ways, utilizing programs and processes that are already in place but, perhaps, not being rigorously pursued in the context of an integrated talent management strategy. For example, most companies utilize some method of identifying high-potential employees and nearly all companies assess performance and assign performance ratings to their employees. Companies that do these well recognize that it is not sufficient to look at high levels of performance in a current position. The "high potential" marker that identifies longer-term potential is also based on looking at talent in the context of ideal attributes for future positions and business capability needs.

The piece of the puzzle that is often missing is how well integrated these processes are with compensation and other reward decisions. Do those employees with the best performance ratings and the highest levels of potential consistently receive the best compensation? Are they always the first people considered when an innovative project opportunity arises? When a strategic position needs to be filled? When an expatriate assignment becomes available? If not, these are missed opportunities for rewarding the best talent in ways that are typically most valued by high performers and high potentials.

The Employment Value Proposition

Historically, the focus of compensation tended to revolve around financial rewards, including base salary, short- and long-term variable pay, and certain wealth-creating and security-building benefits, such as health insurance, life insurance, savings or retirement plans, and profit sharing programs. As the cost (and value) of non-cash rewards increased, and the talent marketplace became more competitive, it became more common to include such non-cash reward elements in the design and valuing of "total reward" packages for employees.

More recently, the practice of total rewards has further evolved into the notion of an "employment value proposition" (EVP). The EVP typically includes a broader set of elements that characterize the employment relationship and are designed to attract job candidates and engage, motivate, and retain employees. In short, the EVP answers the question, "Why would a talented person want to work here?" There are many EVP models, but they share some common elements, as depicted below.

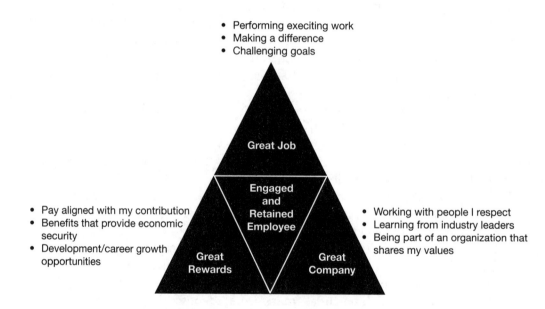

While they share some common themes, "winning EVPs are designed to appeal to the needs of specific talent segments. . ." (McKinsey 2001). There is much research to support the assertion that different talent segments do, in fact, value elements of the EVP differently. Such variations may be the result of differences across geographies, generations, performance levels, and other segment characteristics. Hence, to be effective, organizations must consider the implications of different HR investments for different segments of the workforce.

Building an Effective Compensation Foundation

Developing an effective approach to compensation (and by effective, we mean a reward system that is aligned with an organization's mission; supports the organization's business strategy and key objectives; helps ensure that the talent needed to deliver on those objectives is in place, engaged, and achieving at high levels; is understood and per-ceived as fair by most of the employee population; and has a cost structure that is con-nected to the financials of the company) is *conceptually* simple. But making the system actually work as planned is not so easy. Why is that?

Often compensation is viewed as a technical exercise led by compensation engi-neers, as opposed to a tool to manage business performance and the talent needed to operate the business, and hence the focus may be more on the elegance of the design than on the strength of its impact on target employee populations. To help make this shift in focus, HR leadership will want to ensure that compensation metrics, which may start with *efficiency* (how good, fast, and cost-effective we are at market pricing, survey participation, allocating and distributing cash, responding to questions from managers, etc.), also incorporate *effectiveness* (to what extent we are generating the kind of individual, business, and organizational successes leadership expects to have as a result of the investments we are making in people).

Further, in many cases there is hope that the compensation program will be all the motivation that employees need, allowing managers to do their "real jobs." But one of the critical measures of a manager's effectiveness as a business leader is his or her ability to help employees succeed and, in doing so, help the company succeed; and compensation is a tool (but only one tool) that can and should be used in the service of that goal.

And lastly, the tangible elements of compensation—salary, bonus, equity—are often divorced from the more qualitative (and often more engaging) elements of the EVP pyramid discussed earlier.

Addressing all of these questions would turn this chapter into a broad treatment on compensation design, so we will cover two simple principles that can guide the development and maintenance of effective compensation:

- Identify the right people and reward them in the right way (be competitive, emphasize performance, pay fairly, and use the entire total reward toolbox).
- Make certain that managers do more than just "administer" compensation.

Identify and Reward

In terms of what kind of compensation design works best, the answer is a resounding "it depends." The goal is to create a total work offering that is magnetic, flexible, clearly communicated, and, in particular, compelling in the employee's mind. Such an inte-grated, values-aligned approach to rewards is often one of the things that separate the top places to work from just places to work.

Most companies don't need to set up separate reward systems for their key per-formers. What they need are structures and decision-making processes that are flexible and targeted enough to allow *well-trained* managers to provide the necessary totality of rewards to their people overall and to each person in particular.

The result of an effective system is that the most talented employees, "A talent," will (1) tend to be in the bigger and/or more central roles (hence at higher pay levels),

(2) be paid in the upper end of a particular salary range (or be promoted frequently and, hence, not have the time to penetrate very far into each range), (3) most likely be receiving above-target bonuses (if incentives are well-designed and performance is managed effectively), (4) be recognized in multiple ways for their contributions, and (5) have a clear understanding of the close link between how they perform and how the organization performs, and between their personalized rewards and what the organization receives in return. At the same time, "B talent" will still be treated as valuable members of the community and rewarded accordingly.

It's Not Only about Administration

If managers view pay decisions as primarily administrative in nature, those decisions will be divorced from considerations of talent. How can we move beyond an administrative mind-set?

First, the organization has to commit to a holistic approach to rewards in which compensation is only one of the key components, and is communicated as such. This is consistent with the EVP model in which the success of the employment relationship depends not only on tangible compensation and benefits offerings but also on those elements that help employees feel that they have a great job in a great company supported by those great rewards, and in which a one-size-fits-all compensation approach is not optimal for companies that have taken the time to identify their talent segments and to figure out what motivates people in those segments.

Second, managers need to be properly trained in how to use compensation as a tool in managing their people. Finally, these well-trained managers need to be given sufficient flexibility to make the necessary informed decisions on allocating pay to the right people at the right time.

Let's look at how flexibility can be manifested in the area of salary structure.

Structure

Some companies do not have minimums and maximums on their salary ranges, which is counter to typical practice. The rationale is to assign managers accountability for determining salary adjustments that deliver pay levels appropriate to performance, experience, business impact, labor market scarcity, and so on. While at first glance this may seem frightening (visions of runaway salary budget overruns), this approach can work if budgets are communicated and maintained and if managers understand the relationship between salary ranges, the market, and the organization's competitive philosophy. In some cases, even though minimums and maximums are not defined explicitly, next-level or HR management review may be required if someone's pay exceeds market by more than a certain amount or is below some defined threshold. So there are well-defined parameters and guidelines even without the absolute constraints of minimums and maximums.

Other companies with strong performance emphases use only performance as the criterion for determining salary adjustments and do not consider position-in-range.

In such performance-only situations, having a well-designed and carefully implemented and maintained performance management process is absolutely essential.

Another approach is to do away with the ubiquitous midpoint or control point. While midpoints are useful constructs for building ranges, once used, they often serve either to unnecessarily constrain pay or to showcase the failure of the employer to meet its compensation philosophy targets.

Concerns that people express over the use of midpoints often include some of the following: "No one can get over midpoint here. Even though it's just the middle of the range, management treats it like a maximum." "We're supposed to hire at minimum or at least below midpoint unless the candidate literally walks on water. This makes it hard to bring good people in, since we can't offer them competitive salaries." "HR says that it should take about four years for someone in my grade to get to midpoint, but I've been in this job seven years, and I'm nowhere close!" "We know high performers in nanotechnology engineering. They get offers every week for $15,000 over their current salaries, but I can't pay them more than 110 percent of midpoint because of our salary policies."

There are a number of alternative approaches to midpoints that work in the right environments:

- A focus on the extent to which an individual's pay has progressed into the range, sometimes called "point-in-range" or "range penetration." "Often range penetration is a preferred tool because it does not focus on one number alone, the midpoint. Instead it refers to how far into the range a particular individual's salary has penetrated" (WorldatWork 2007). Some practitioners also feel that this is more "intuitive" than the midpoint.
- The use of zones, sometimes overlapping, instead of specific points. Often these are seen in thirds, with the first zone reserved for new employees and/or those coming up the learning curve, the middle zone for those who are fully experienced and performing competently, and the highest third reserved for top performers who are typically highly experienced and may be in jobs that are in high demand in the labor market. While zone approaches have a reasonable degree of structure, the use of overlapping range segments does allow for some flexibility on the part of managers and HR to position pay appropriately.
- Organizations interested in creating an explicit relationship between compensation and advancement may want to consider career-based structures. While traditional salary structures based only on quantitative measures, such as points or market values, are used successfully in many organizations, typically they are not especially useful for career movement purposes, since the advancement from one grade to another is usually more of a "black box" than a decision-making process using well-defined criteria. Career structures, whether based on job families or career ladders (dual or otherwise) or both, can help facilitate both lateral and vertical moves and can help employees better understand both current and potential opportunities and the roadmap to pursue those opportunities.

Market Pay Segmentation

The market must be considered when segmenting and rewarding talent. Nearly all organizations test the compensation market and use market values as an essential basis for developing salary structures and delivering pay. Many, in fact, set their ranges based solely on market values in recognition of the importance of paying competitively. But let's be clear: pay competitiveness is a ticket to play and not a differentiator. While it's always important to understand the best practices among your top competitors and not fall behind in the area of rewards, if your organization only mirrors other organizations, it will fail to create a competitive advantage. To create that advantage, employers should be willing to be a bit creative in the way they approach the *design* or *structure* of compensation, which must build a foundation for the effective *delivery* of pay to the people in the organization.

Much research indicates that premier organizations tend to target and/or provide compensation that is highly competitive (typically in the 3rd quartile). It is our experience that a highly competitive strategy is often more a function of the company's goals and values than it is a driver of competitive advantage.

Many organizations establish overall market targets (e.g., 50th percentile base, 75th percentile incentive) which typically apply across all or most areas of the company. Fewer decide to segment these targets based on the extent to which certain functional areas, job families, or specific jobs are core to strategy or revenue generation or interact with pay in a different fashion.

Some organizations start their segmentation exercise with a focus on particular jobs, regardless of function, that are essential to strategy and business success. This is typically a fluid process that is often updated annually, especially as business models, business strategies, and labor markets shift. Metrics used at Edwards Lifesciences include ensuring that key jobs are not open longer than 50 days, having successors in place for every critical job, and keeping turnover to less than 6 percent (Bingham and Galagan 2007). While the discussion focuses on jobs, note the people-oriented metrics as well. Clear-eyed leadership recognizes, of course, that a program focusing on key jobs will go nowhere if it doesn't translate the reward structure into the pay delivered to employees. For that reason, organizations that are successful in segmenting and rewarding talent often define a market target or a "pay floor" for key talent, such as not allowing the pay for identified individuals to fall below, say, 75th percentile or targeting pay at or about the 90th percentile.

Segmentation based on performance is the most typical and widely used approach, though it is also, unfortunately, frequently not utilized effectively (for example, by focusing only on individual merit pay, by allowing salary review and/or performance review to become administrative procedures rather than talent management ones, or by concentrating only on pay and not on other EVP components as well).

It will be very hard for an employer to maximize return on investment in its talent if it relies only on the traditional "look back," merit approach to pay-for-performance. Why?

- In many organizations, merit pay ends up being a procedural activity in which managers and employees spend a great deal of time distributing a relatively small amount of money in a generally undifferentiated kind of way, often resulting in a serious disconnect between the evaluation of performance and the size of the award.
- Even the best-designed programs with adequate funding tend to have a "what have you done for me lately" focus, as opposed to taking into account sustained contribution or future potential.

Some possible solutions to these common challenging situations include:

- Developing a target pay approach to salary levels, in which the focus is not on what kind of increase the employee should get in a given year, but instead on an appropriate pay level based on sustained performance/contribution, experience, and perhaps other criteria the organization may have identified. In such an approach, the company can take a coordinated look at the relationship between an individual's overall contribution to an organization and the amount of money an individual is receiving (establishing a more direct quid pro quo), as opposed to looking only at the amount of increase the individual should receive (Rosen 2007).
- Ensuring that compensation is viewed, at least, in a total compensation framework (salary, bonus, and long-term incentive or equity) and, at best, in a total reward framework. In the former case, we are taking a coordinated look at the tangible offerings for each employee and, working each of the "levers" and the overall compensation mechanism in an effective fashion: salary and its progression connected to doing one's job and contributing to the company's success on an ongoing basis; cash incentives to reward contributions that are "above and beyond" the norm and help the company achieve, or progress toward, its goals; and longer-term incentives for those who have an impact on results that affect the longer-term value of the organization.

   In the latter case, we hearken back to the EVP, through which we achieve our goals by having a well-stocked and finely tuned toolbox that may start with cash compensation and equity participation but also takes into account other more qualitative motivators.

The Reward-Performance Challenge

As noted earlier, while studies show that top performers often exceed the performance of average performers considerably, the typical difference in pay levels between these same performers is relatively insignificant. At the same time, researchers have been coming to the conclusion that focusing solely on top talent can, in fact, be detrimental to the culture and success of an organization. "The impact of top talent on corporate performance hasn't diminished, but what's much clearer today . . . is that organizations can't afford to neglect the contributions of other employees. Several authors in recent years have rightly emphasized the contributions of B players: capable, steady performers who make up the majority of any workforce . . . Experience suggests that an exclusive focus on top players can damage the morale of the rest of the organization and, as a result, overall performance (Guthridge, Komm, and Lawson 2008).

How can employers create a winning balance between what may seem like competing priorities: paying top performers a lot more than average performers but not dividing talent cadres into the haves and the have-nots? In truth, these two priorities don't need to be in opposition. If we consider salary to be the *only* method for rewarding performance, then we would certainly expect to see a much greater difference in pay levels between those groups. If, however, we take into account other elements of tangible rewards—incentives and equity—and couple those with the Great Job and Great Company components of the EVP pyramid, customized to the needs of the different cadres, total reward differences could, indeed, be much more aligned with the extent of performance/contribution differences.

The bottom line is that high performers should have, compared to average performers, an earnings delta closer to the performance delta than we see at present. Companies might have a better shot at achieving that parity via several different tactics:

- Using the target pay approach discussed earlier versus the more typical year-to-year salary increases.
- Implementing a career-based structure that helps integrate decisions on pay, performance, and advancement and that is also tied into target incentive opportunities.
- Establishing performance-based competitive targets for both total compensation and for each component of pay.
- Having in place a robust performance management system as the basis for making pay decisions.

Conclusion and Key Points to Remember

Effective talent management is really about optimizing talent in the service of both individual employees and the organization. One of the best ways to be successful in this area, at least when considering rewards, is to segment talent, first, on a macro basis (focusing on different talent populations) and, second, on a micro basis (or individually), which is realized in the interaction between employee and manager and the manager's understanding of what motivates his or her staff members. To be successful at the macro level, organizations will work to understand their own employee segments, develop and offer rewards that are geared to the motivations of people in those segments, test the effectiveness of those linkages, and continue that loop in order to keep strengthening the bond between the company and the employees and the achievements that flow out of that bond. To be successful on a micro basis, one must keep in mind that the individual, not the organization, determines the value of any rewards.

References

Becker, Brian E., Mark A. Huselid, and Richard W. Beatty. 2009. *The differentiated workforce.* Cambridge: Harvard Business School Press.

Bingham, Tony, and Pat Galagan. 2007. Finding the right talent for critical jobs. *Training + Development* (February).

Guthridge, Matthew, Asmus B. Komm, and Emily Lawson. 2008. Making talent a strategic priority. *The McKinsey Quarterly*, no. 1.

Henneman, Todd. 2005. The jobs you can't do without. *Workforce Management* (December 12). Quoted in article by John Sullivan. San Francisco State University.

Kaplan, Robert S., and David P. Norton. 2001. *The strategy-focused organization: How balanced scorecard companies thrive in the new business environment.* Cambridge: Harvard Business School Press.

McKinsey & Company, Inc. 2001. The war for talent. (April).

Rosen, Andrew S. 2007. Salary structures and administration. In *The compensation handbook.* Lance Berger and Dorothy Berger (Eds.). See chapter for a graphic representation of this model.

Sullivan, John. 2004. End "equal treatment" today! Focus on top performers. *HR Magazine* (June 15).

WorldatWork. 2007. *The WorldatWork handbook of compensation, benefits, and total rewards: A comprehensive guide for HR professionals.* WorldatWork.

Chapter 27

Rewarding Your Top Talent

Mel Stark, Vice President
Mark Royal, Senior Consultant
Hay Group

REWARDING TOP TALENT IS, OBVIOUSLY, A CRITICAL ELEMENT OF EVERY ORGANIZATION'S talent management and business strategy. This fact has been made even more apparent in the recent past where the business recession has put a lot of stress on payrolls, salary increases, and other human resources expense and management concerns, such as retention.

While professional sports is not always the best place to look for compensation comparability and logic, given the "entertainment" nature of that business, all one needs to do to understand the importance of rewarding top performers and star power is to look how sports franchises actively manage their staffing and payroll in getting ready for each new season. You can argue with their generally perceived excesses but not with the concept of rewarding top talent—they do it to enhance their ability to outpace and one-up the competition, which is good business under any circumstances.

However, you cannot isolate the idea of rewarding your top talent from how you reward all others. There needs to be a "system," an overarching philosophy as well as practices that articulate the how, what, and why of your organization's approach to rewards across the board. Rewards should be considered in the broadest terms and should include elements that can be assigned a monetary value as well as the intangible rewards that are provided, as both are key to retention of top talent. Many might argue, and rightfully so, that the intangible rewards actually carry more weight in talent retention. So, we'll start there, with an overview of rewards.

Total Rewards

When most people think of "compensation," the first thing that comes to mind is what they see each payroll period: their net paycheck. Beyond that, some may also include any variable-pay opportunity (i.e., incentive or bonus) they may earn. While these amounts are real and tangible, the concept of reward is much more far-reaching.

"Reward" signifies different things to different people, and its meaning depends on the context in which it's used. Consider, for instance, those "Reward" posters on old TV Westerns. In the context of business, however, while things can often feel like the Wild West, rewards are traditionally interpreted as an employee's pay (base salary, incentives, or bonuses) and the value of benefit plans. Yet the concept of "total rewards" goes beyond these tangible elements. Total rewards also includes intangible elements that are harder to see and touch but are real enough to affect an employee's level of engagement and satisfaction while contributing to attraction and retention of key staff. A working definition of rewards is "anything that the organization provides that is of perceived value to employees." So, in the spirit of rewarding your top talent, you have to be aware of and pull on all the available levers to maximize your offering and the messages you want to send.

		Common Examples	Reward Elements	Definition
Internal value or motivation	**Intangible**	• Career development • Work-life balance • Safety and security	Nonfinancial rewards	Total **reward**
Rewards to which an objective dollar value can be assigned	**Tangible**	• Social security	Statutory benefits	Total **remuneration plus**
		• Retirement provision • Death/disability/medical • Cars • Benefit allowances/loans	Non-statutory benefits	Total **remuneration**
		• Executive share options • Restricted/performance share • Long-term cash schemes	LTI	Total **direct compensation**
		• Sales commission • Annual bonus • Annual incentive	Annual variable	Total **cash**
		• Basic salary • Fixed payments • Near cash allowances	Guaranteed cash	

Figure 27-1 Total Reward Elements

Figure 27-1 highlights these distinctions. Base salary forms the foundation for all other tangible reward elements. Beyond that, there can be bonuses, long- and short-term incentives, and, of course, a variety of considerations that contribute to the benefits plan. The message here is to move beyond the obvious, yet important, elements of pay, benefits, and perquisites to explore all the intangible aspects of an employee's work experience that compose an organization's total rewards offerings. When properly orchestrated, these offerings can be synergistic and a true competitive advantage that cannot be easily duplicated. As Herb Kelleher, founder of Southwest Airlines, has said, "It's the intangibles that are the hardest things for a competitor to imitate. You can get airplanes, you can get ticket counter space, and you can get baggage conveyors. But the spirit of Southwest is the most difficult thing to emulate. If we ever do lose that, we will have lost our most valuable competitive asset" (Jensen, McMullen, and Stark 2007).

You cannot effectively consider or make good on how best to reward your top performers if you're only looking at the most obvious pieces of the puzzle. It will take more work and creativity, and it will demand more of the organization, its managers, and HR leaders. But isn't that comparable to what you expect of your top performers?

Return on Investment

It is often said that people are an organization's greatest asset, but they are also one of its greatest expenses. Remuneration tends to be one of the worst-managed parts of an organization's cost structure. Yet with 10 to 70 percent of total costs wrapped up in it, reward cannot be ignored, particularly in challenging economic times.

Most organizations wouldn't purchase a $10,000 copier without calculating its ROI, but many will spend hundreds of millions of dollars on their compensation programs without considering an ROI analysis. In recent research conducted by Hay Group, WorldatWork, and Loyola University Chicago, we found that approximately 62 percent of employers in a general industry survey reported that they don't even attempt to measure ROI of the compensation programs. Of the 38 percent that do, most do so informally by talking with managers and employees about their perceptions of program effectiveness. The balance of organizations that measure ROI (18 percent) use formal measures such as employee opinion surveys and comparisons of the investments in people and their productivity.

You have probably heard the saying, "If you don't know where you are going, any road will get you there." That's especially true when it comes to reward programs. Rewards, whether tangible or intangible, are tools for increasing organizational effectiveness. The employment relationship involves an exchange of organizational "carrots" for employee contributions. A well-designed reward program focuses those offers to attract and retain the talent the organization requires and incent employees to act in ways consistent with business objectives. Accordingly, a total reward approach should be both about organizational needs and employee wants.

Figure 27-2 highlights Hay Group's Total Reward Framework. As the graphic illustrates, a well-designed reward program needs to focus first on developing a

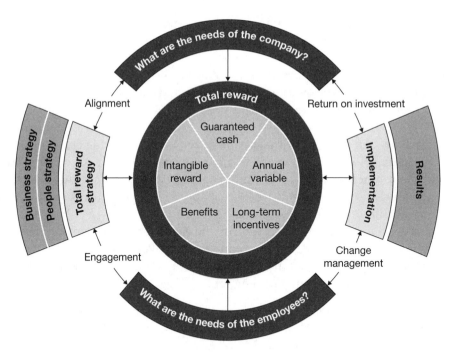

Figure 27-2 Hay Group Total Reward Framework™

total reward strategy that is aligned with and designed to support the organization's business strategy and people strategy. Equally important, reward programs need to maximize employee engagement levels in the organization. In addition, changes to reward programs must be carefully managed and communicated during implementation to ensure adequate understanding of rationales and implications behind decisions.

When considering the motivational impact of reward programs, the manager must note that one size is unlikely to fit all business and employee groups. What motivates a late-career manager, for example, may not be the same as what motivates a newly hired entry-level employee. What motivates employees in a start-up entrepreneurial technology organization may fail in a highly regulated public services organization. Critical to the ROI of total reward programs is tailoring those reward offerings to the unique interests of particular employees or employee groups.

Promoting High Levels of Employee Engagement

Retaining top talent is a key concern in both good times and bad, given the importance of these employees to a company's success and competitive edge. Many organizations turn primarily to compensation for the answer. But dissatisfaction with pay is generally not what leads employees to begin exploring job alternatives, although the prospect of better compensation elsewhere may solidify the decision to leave. To keep and motivate their talent, organizations should focus on increasing employee engagement and developing systems that provide better support for employees' success.

Engagement refers to the commitment employees feel toward the organization (e.g., their willingness to recommend it to friends and family, their pride in working for it, and their intentions to remain a part of it). But it's also about employees' discretionary effort—their willingness to go the extra mile for the organization. As organizations need to do more with less and strive for greater efficiency, tapping into the discretionary effort of employees is all the more essential. And in the rapidly changing environment where roles and responsibilities are continually evolving, organizations must count on employees to act on their own in ways consistent with organizational cultures, objectives, and values.

We have conducted extensive research on the characteristics of work environments that promote high levels of engagement among employees. While we see some variability from industry to industry and organization to organization, common themes of high-engagement work environments emerge.

- *Clear and promising direction.* Ensuring that the practical implications of organizational directions are clear to employees is essential to effective execution. But connecting employees with the big picture is equally important from a motivational perspective. In their work, most employees are looking for an opportunity to contribute to something larger than themselves, a chance to make a difference. Appealing to this sense of purpose is the essence of transformational leadership and critical to promoting high levels of employee engagement.

- *Confidence in leaders.* If faith in the direction of the organization is critical for fostering high levels of employee engagement, so too is ensuring that employees have confidence that there are strong hands on the wheel at senior levels that are capable of executing strategic objectives. Today's employees recognize that their prospects for continued employment, career development, and advancement are dependent on their companies' health and stability. They cannot be expected to bind their futures to those of their employers unless they are confident that their companies are well managed and well positioned for success.

- *Quality and customer focus.* Demonstrating to employees that the organization is focused on its customers, delivers high-quality products and services, and is innovative in developing new offerings is critical to building employee confidence in the direction and future market position of the organization. For any employees in customer-facing roles, there is no more important dissatisfier than the sense that the organization doesn't "get it" when it comes to what customers require.

- *Respect and recognition.* Employee engagement involves striking a new employment bargain with employees. Organizations invest in creating the conditions that make work more meaningful and rewarding for employees. And employees, in return, pour discretionary effort into their work and deliver superior performance. Employees cannot be expected to take a personal interest in organizational objectives unless organizations make a reciprocal commitment to employees as more than factors of production. Instead, it is critical that organizations demonstrate a basic respect for employees as individuals.

- *Development opportunities.* Employees are increasingly aware that they are responsible for managing their own careers and that their futures depend on continuous elevation of their skills. If employees are not expanding their capabilities, they risk compromising their employability—within their current organizations or elsewhere. Accordingly, opportunities for growth and development are among the most consistent predictors of employee engagement.
- *Pay and benefits.* With today's organizations operating increasingly lean, employees are being asked to do more with less. In high-workload environments, employees are generally sensitized to compensation issues. Acutely aware of all that they are contributing, employees are inclined to pressure their organizations to balance rewards and contributions. In this context, it is more important than ever that organizations ensure compensation systems are perceived to recognize employee efforts adequately. Clarifying the equity of pay systems both internally and externally is critical to building employees' confidence that they are receiving an appropriate return on their investments in the organization.

Where the Rubber Meets the Road

Though we've called out the importance of total rewards as the right means to rewarding your top talent, there's an old adage that "cash is king." Employees may not remember all of the objectives in their organization's incentive program or be able to recite their employer's core values. But they do know their base salaries and likely their variable-pay opportunities, they understand what relative fairness and competitiveness are, and they probably have strong opinions about why their last raises weren't big enough.

Base pay is the foundation of any compensation program and the most visible component to the vast majority of employees. Every paycheck is a reminder of the link between their efforts over the last pay period and how the organization perceives their value. Clearly there is a critical need to "get base pay right" and to use it as one important means of rewarding top talent. But there are a number of core elements that must work together to manage base pay and overall cash compensation effectively and that contribute to your ability to deliver effective and meaningful rewards to your top talent.

The first core element is having a philosophy and a set of guiding principles that highlight the organization's intent regarding reward. Examples include where the company targets its pay—base and total cash—and why, how it balances and mixes the various reward components, and its perspective on pay for performance—and how all these factors are intended to impact on individual employees, what they're expected to do every day, and, ultimately, how they contribute to the organization's success. But it's not sufficient to only have a sense of one's philosophy; it has to be effectively communicated and understood. Hay Group research has shown that while almost 90 percent of surveyed companies say they have a compensation philosophy, only two-thirds acknowledge that it has been committed to writing. However, and this is the point of primary concern, when asked about communication to staff, only one-third believe they have effectively communicated about compensation.

The second core element in cash compensation management is allocating salary increases relative to performance. Organizations need to ensure that performance ratings translate into differentiated rewards. Many organizations spend an agonizing amount of effort to ensure that managers comply with some sort of a distribution curve of performance ratings. But what value is this if the highest performer still receives only marginally more rewards—whether in merit pay, variable pay, or options—than the average performer? The ratings are merely a means to an end. And the end is higher rewards for the highest performance, not just a perfect distribution curve.

Most managers and employees agree that rewards should be differentiated based on performance (and the best organizations make this happen), leading to better execution and employee behaviors. At many organizations, managers want to give their stars bigger increases. But many see it as a zero-sum game. Providing larger increases to certain employees means that other employees get less, which requires managers to make some difficult decisions. Many managers choose to take the path of least resistance, giving employees roughly the same increase, rather than confronting and addressing poor performance. This can be avoided by having an ongoing dialogue with employees throughout the year and truly differentiating rewards. Ongoing dialogues eliminate the element of surprise, which can lessen the impact of giving a smaller increase. Managers weak in conducting performance-oriented discussions should seek coaching to improve their skills. This type of management "courage" can go a long way to improving the climate of the organization. Nearly a third of workers surveyed by Hay Group agree that poor performance is tolerated in their organization.

The "merit increase matrix" provides a tool to allocate a merit budget based on individual performance and the position of an employee's salary relative to the overall salary range and can be used as a reference for competitive market pay. But the tool itself will prove insufficient and merely a crutch if managers are not prepared with the right information and tools to tell employees about the company's reward program as well as to effectively counsel them about why they earned the increase they did and what needs to change to improve future opportunities.

The other component which is also frequently awarded as cash is variable pay, often referred to as a "bonus" or an "incentive." However, we think use of these terms interchangeably is lazy and reduces the organization's quiver of reward offerings. For clarity, we suggest you consider the following distinctions. "Incentives" should be predetermined, communicated, and known by the employees. The measures should be clear and trackable so that at different points of the year the company and employees get a sense of how they're doing and at year end there are few surprises. Employees may know about "bonuses," on the other hand, but bonuses are typically determined after the fact and are highly discretionary. Accordingly, using these terms interchangeably limits the organization's ability to offer bonuses; however, they may be described and awarded, in addition to an incentive.

Beyond the definition of these two approaches to variable pay, in order for the programs to be effective (i.e., motivating, if so intended, and as a way to offer a simple thank-you in recognition for something well done), they should be rooted in the organization's overall compensation philosophy and operating culture. In addition, their amounts should be meaningful and relevant to that philosophy and culture. There's a disconnect and a lack of logic if, on the one hand, the organization promotes itself as fiercely competitive with a take-no-prisoners approach to business development but then offers an incentive plan without much upside. For those who worked hard and got good results, what will be the message and the motivational intent in subsequent years?

Similarly, what's the message you're communicating if overall the organization has a "passable" year and employees don't really see their work connected to the end result but then the organization makes lavish bonus payments? We're sure it will be well received, but what signal are you sending about future expectations? And are you running the risk of creating an entitlement mentality?

Help Me Help You

Identifying top talent is critical to driving performance. Using research-based competency assessment and modeling with a more direct line of sight to the characteristics of those who truly make a difference in the organization is one approach that can help. Assessments can be seen as another way to reward your top talent. It's clear that not every organization offers, and certainly not every person gets, the opportunity to have a professional assessment of his or her skills and development needs. Done well, it is often seen as a gift by those who participate. The process can yield some revealing information and needs to be managed in the most professional way, especially as it relates to feedback that can be quite sensitive. Still, there is a wealth of applications to fit a variety of needs and budgets. Hay Group has developed and makes extensive use of some very effective tools in this domain such as the Inventory of Leadership Styles, Organizational Climate Survey, and the Emotional and Social Competency Inventory.

Assessment information is a way to help those invited to participate ("help them") to determine the best way to contribute on a higher level for the company ("help you"). And if you choose to focus this type of opportunity on top performers, it can be promoted and seen as a piece of their total reward offering. They get the chance to obtain insights that otherwise would have gone unnoticed and use those to enhance their self-awareness and focus their development efforts. It's also happened that after involvement in an assessment process, people determine that "this is not the right place for me." But is it not better for all concerned to have this epiphany earlier in their career or at least before time and money is spent on a less-than-desirable situation and employment track? This could be the best gift of all.

Further Enabling Employees to Succeed

The assessment process outlined above is an example of what Hay Group would describe as one element of enablement. Our research shows that employee engagement alone does not guarantee an organization's effectiveness. Studies we have conducted in the last five years involving hundreds of companies in diverse industries worldwide confirm that many companies enjoy high levels of engagement yet still struggle in terms of performance. What's missing is real "employee enablement" to position motivated employees to succeed. In an enabled workforce, employees are effectively matched to positions such that their skills and abilities are put to optimal use. Likewise, employees have the essential resources—information, technology, tools and equipment, and financial support—to get the job done. They are able to focus on their key responsibilities without wasting time navigating such obstacles as procedural restrictions or nonessential tasks in the work environment. A cross-industry analysis we conducted in 2009 involving over 400 companies represented in our global employee opinion database suggests that while organizations in the top quartile on engagement demonstrate revenue growth 2.5 times that of organizations in the bottom quartile, companies in the top quartile on both engagement and enablement achieve revenue growth 4.5 times greater.

To get the most from engaged employees, organizations must position them to channel their extra efforts productively. That is, motivation to contribute has to be matched with the ability to contribute. Unfortunately, most organizations employ a sizable number of "frustrated" workers—individuals who are highly engaged but are not sufficiently enabled to be fully effective and successful. Frustration is a significant problem for organizations and employees. In the short term, these motivated but poorly enabled employees may suffer in silence. But over time many can be expected to turn off and disengage—or tune out and leave.

Bottom Line

A common dictionary definition of "reward" is "something given in return for some service or attainment." We believe that reward is considerably more than "some thing"; in fact, rewards that the organization should provide are numerous and come in various forms—monetary and otherwise. In order to be effective, responsible management should be aware of all such reward opportunities and actively manage the money, mix, and message in order to make rewards the dynamic management tools they are meant to be.

References

Jensen, Doug, Tom McMullen, and Mel Stark. 2007. *The manager's guide to rewards: What you need to get the best for—and from—your employees.* New York: Amacom, 61.

Chapter 28

Using Long-Term Incentives to Retain Top Talent

Paul Conley, Consultant
Towers Watson
Dan Kadrlik, Stock Plan Consultant
Executive Pay and Benefits
Target Corporation

T O ATTRACT AND RETAIN TOP TALENT, ORGANIZATIONS NEED TO UNDERSTAND THE WANTS and needs of these people and provide the right combination of reward elements to ensure top performers remain focused and committed to the organization. Our research suggests that offering the right financial incentives to key talent is an essential ingredient in the equation. Appropriately designed, long-term incentives can be especially powerful in promoting retention and aligning the interests of top employees and their organizations. This chapter provides an overview of current trends in long-term incentives and offers some advice for maximizing the impact of these programs.

The Big Picture

While tangible rewards, such as pay and benefits, often attract high performers to an organization, often, intangible rewards drive engagement and encourage talented people to stay. Key intangibles include the caliber of a company's top leaders and their ability to inspire loyalty by showing a genuine interest in employees' well-being, along with factors such as developmental or career advancement opportunities and the organization's culture.

Towers Watson's ongoing employee research at leading organizations world-wide sheds light on the aspects of the rewards program and work experience most important to top talent. For purposes of our research, top talent is defined as a combination of three categories of employees: Those whose performance ratings place them in the top tier groups for their organizations, those chosen to participate in specific leadership development programs, and those identified as top performing by their managers.

Comparing survey responses from more than 12,000 top-talent individuals at 19 companies in a broad range of industries to responses from over 150,000 other employees in the same organizations reveals some interesting differences in what engages and motivates these different groups of employees:

- Employees in the top-talent categories have significantly more favorable views of their work environment than others, particularly with regard to their company's performance management practices and the degree of open, two-way communication with management.
- Conversely, top-talent employees are more critical than others of their companies' competitiveness, efficiency, innovation, and ability to mobilize/act in response to market changes.
- Like other employees, those in the top-talent groups require strong leadership and career development opportunities to be fully engaged. More than other employees, however, top talent also needs to *buy into* the company's vision, values, and strategy in order to be fully engaged. Ensuring that these employees embrace (and are guided by) company values is important to keeping them committed over the long term.
- Top-talent employees who are at risk of leaving their organizations can be frustrated for a number of reasons, including a lack of recognition/rewards and management's inability to prioritize, act quickly, and set clear objectives. Beyond advancement and reward opportunities, top-talent employees require clear communication about company priorities and strategy.

The finding that dissatisfaction with rewards is common among at-risk employees isn't unique to top talent, of course, although it provides important context for any discussion of the role of long-term incentives. Notably, our research shows that top talent who pose the greatest retention risk have significantly less favorable views of their incentive opportunities than other high performers (i.e., those who have no plans to leave their current organizations).

Ultimately, companies that understand the needs of high performers tend to do a better job of engaging them in the business, linking performance with rewards, and differentiating rewards for top and average performers. Over the past few decades, long-term incentives have become an increasingly important part of the rewards mix, especially for senior leaders in certain parts of the world (e.g., the United States).

Role and Types of Long-Term Incentives

A long-term incentive provides an opportunity to realize a financial gain for the achievement of specific performance results, typically over a multiyear period. Long-term incentives have been prevalent in the United States for decades, although they were originally granted primarily to senior executives. These programs are designed to align employee performance and compensation with longer-term business objectives and, ultimately, results. Another significant design consideration is the way these programs can be used to promote retention of senior executives and other employees critical to the business. As long-term incentive programs have evolved, they are no longer being reserved solely for upper management but are being provided to high performers and key contributors at lower levels. During the dot-com era, a growing number of companies, especially in the technology industry, offered stock options, a form of long-term incentive, to broad-based employee groups, both to align employee and shareholder interests and to enhance the company's ability to attract and retain scarce talent in a highly competitive market. However, the trend toward more broad-based option programs has largely reversed in recent years as a result of a change in accounting treatment. With companies now incurring an accounting expense at the time options are granted, eligibility for stock option grants has steadily narrowed.

Companies use different long-term incentive approaches to achieve varying objectives. The primary categories of long-term incentives are stock options, restricted stock, and long-term performance plans.

Stock Options

A stock option is an award that provides the right to purchase shares of stock at a predetermined price, most commonly the price of the stock on the date the option is granted. To ensure a long-term focus, options typically vest, and become exercisable, over a period of three to four years from date of grant. The value of stock options depends upon the appreciation of the company's stock price over the option term, typically ten years with employee options. Value is realized based on the spread between the market price of the stock at the time the option is exercised and the grant price.

Organizations have long used stock options to reward employees for the creation of shareholder value—their contributions relative to driving up the price of company stock. Stock options are particularly effective for young, high-growth organizations and remain an effective motivational tool in rising stock markets. They may be less effective as a mechanism for producing value to retain/engage top performers for mature companies, especially in times of stock market uncertainty.

As mentioned, in recent years, stock options have gradually decreased in prevalence due to a number of factors, including the change in accounting treatment. Additionally, recent stock market losses have left many outstanding stock option grants with little or no current realizable value, engendering negative employee views and, in some cases, prompting companies to conduct option exchange programs that give employees the opportunity to exchange "underwater" options for new at-the-money options. Such exchanges can meet with resistance from company shareholders.

Restricted Stock

Restricted stock is an award in which actual shares of stock (or units representing shares) are granted to employees subject to a vesting period. The recipient must remain employed by the company until the vesting period is satisfied to earn the award. When the vesting schedule lapses, often within three to five years, the recipient receives the shares (or units). Recipients normally have voting and dividend rights even while shares are subject to restrictions.

Restricted stock is used primarily for retention purposes and generally does not have forward-looking performance provisions. However, restricted stock is increasingly being used as a reward mechanism for high performers at lower levels of organizations to provide an equity reward in recognition of their efforts and accomplishments. This in turn provides an incentive to remain with the organization.

The use of restricted stock has been increasing in recent years as companies' reliance on options has declined. Unlike options, which can become worthless even as the recipient stays with the company, restricted stock is always "in the money." Even if the value of the shares declines, they still retain some monetary value, barring a company bankruptcy.

Performance Plans

A performance plan is an award that is contingent upon the achievement of specified organizational goals over a given performance cycle, typically three or more years. Most companies using performance plans grant new award cycles annually. These plans pay participants in shares, stock units, or cash at levels typically pegged to organizational or business unit performance against predetermined goals.

Performance plans are designed to reward executives and other high performers for their level of achievement against performance metrics deemed critical to the organization's (or business unit's) success. Examples of performance metrics range from operating measures, such as growth in revenue or sales, to financial measures, such as earnings before interest, taxes, depreciation, and amortization (EBITDA), return on invested capital, or total shareholder return. The focus is on the achievement of long-term business objectives.

Since performance plans align actual participant award levels with the achievement of long-term organizational goals, they are quite effective in advancing "pay for performance." Two points are critical to the success of these plans:

- It is pivotal that employees receiving these awards clearly understand the goals to be met and the levels of achievement necessary to receive them.
- Employees must understand their roles in achieving the pre-established goals. It's critical for plan participants to have a clear line of sight between the plan measures and how they can influence performance against those measures.

If communicated correctly, performance plans effectively align pay with performance. If communicated poorly, performance plans can confuse recipients and create a distraction that hinders them from focusing on the company's core business objectives.

Key Issues to Consider

Designing a long-term incentive program that helps in attracting, retaining, and motivating top talent goes beyond understanding market practices and plan prevalence. To optimize the program's impact, each organization must give careful thought to a number of fundamental issues:

What are your organization's critical business objectives? Understand how long-term incentives can communicate the objectives of your organization. Is your organization concerned primarily with retention of top talent? Are you looking to reinforce a strong pay-for-performance philosophy? Do you want to advocate equity ownership among your leaders? It's important to know how long-term incentives fit into your overall corporate strategy.

How do you recognize talent? The process of identifying and recognizing your top talent has as much—if not more—impact on talent retention and engagement than the specific incentives you offer to focus your best people on key business results. The recognition associated with incentive eligibility is an important outcome for high performers. They need to understand that the organization recognizes and is willing to invest in their talents. Long-term incentives are only one aspect of this recognition, but an important one.

Who can participate? In addition to your leadership team, consider introducing long-term incentives deeper within the business—selectively—for your high performers. Perhaps it's time to forget internal equity and ensure that superstars understand how important they are to the organization's success, both in the short and the long run. Top performers aren't born in top management positions; they often rise from lower levels within the organization. Who are your next generation of leaders? Use selective awards of long-term incentive opportunities to connect them more deeply to the business.

What do employees value? Our research underscores that it is imperative to understand what your employees value and how they view various aspects of the work experience, including rewards. If your organization is growing rapidly, employees may place a high value on the opportunity to profit from anticipated stock price appreciation. If your organization is in a mature industry, the stocks value as an incentive may be less than in a growth industry. Know your organization and what your employees value.

How should incentive opportunities be determined? Even if you currently provide long-term incentives below the executive level, consider providing additional long-term incentive opportunities to your top talent. Thoughtfully differentiating the size of incentive opportunities can help boost morale and engagement—and reinforce a sense of fairness that superior performance is rewarded.

What is your organization's performance horizon? Long-term incentives can help shift the focus of your top talent to long-term organizational objectives and the creation of sustainable shareholder value. Understand your organization's long-term strategic plan. Carefully align all incentive pay with the achievement of goals that will help your company achieve its long-term objectives.

The Bottom Line

Retaining and motivating top talent involves connecting leaders and other key people to the business and giving them a meaningful stake in the outcome. But be aware that there is no silver bullet in this regard, and long-term incentives are likely to be only part of the answer. Whatever your talent and reward strategy, be certain to identify and reward your high-performing and high-potential employees in a way that

- Leverages their needs and desires (talk to them!).
- Reflects what they offer your organization and their fellow employees.

Ultimately, harnessing the energy and contributions of an ever-evolving group of exceptional people may require some out-of-the-box thinking and changes to your current approach to performance and rewards. Don't be afraid to think creatively.

Chapter 29

Fostering Employee Involvement and Engagement through Compensation and Benefits

Gerald E. Ledford, Jr., Ph.D., President
Ledford Consulting Network

EMPLOYEE INVOLVEMENT AND ENGAGEMENT ARE AMONG THE MOST WIDELY EMBRACED concepts in current thinking about human resource management. This chapter explores how compensation and benefits can foster employee involvement and engagement. Nearly all organizations offer compensation and benefits to their employees, and these rewards clearly play a critical, and sometimes unexpected, role in determining the level of employee involvement and engagement. The focus on compensation and benefits does not imply that these practices are the only way to promote employee involvement and engagement. Clearly, a great many other management tools play critical roles as well. However, compensation and benefits play a powerful role in determining the level of involvement and engagement, and if badly designed, these tools can undermine other approaches.

We begin by exploring the meaning, measurement, and effects of employee involvement and engagement. Next, we consider the linkage between these concepts and business outcomes. Finally, we consider how different compensation and benefits practices can foster involvement and engagement in the workforce as a whole and with different segments of the workforce.

What Is Employee Involvement?

Employee involvement is a set of management practices that extend decision-making power, business information, technical and social skills, and rewards for performance to the lowest levels of the organization (Lawler 1986). Employee involvement is thus a property of organizational systems and not individuals. Each set of practices is integral to the definition. Without the power to make decisions, employee participation is superficial. Without adequate business information, involvement is naïve and potentially harmful. Without skills, employees will not have the technical and social knowledge they need to participate effectively. Without rewards for performance, worker motivation and organizational objectives will not be aligned.

This concept of employee involvement as a set of practices distinguishes it from participation and empowerment. Participation, especially as studied in academic research, often involves a relatively trivial degree of decision-making authority. Empowerment is different from involvement because it is a feeling that results from employee involvement. It is an attitude that can be measured by an employee survey, not a set of management practices.

There are three types of employee involvement. *Suggestion involvement* entails the power to make suggestions for change, but not the power to make decisions. It typically makes use of special structures such as participation groups or quality circles that are parallel to the formal organization and are dependent on it for implementation of changes. This is the most limited and the most common form of involvement. Management can install it without making major changes to the key design elements of the normal organization.

Job involvement makes changes in the design of work so that employees have more control over day-to-day decisions relevant to their jobs. Job enrichment or work teams (also called self-managing teams, autonomous work teams, etc.) are the means for this change. This approach automatically provides the power to make decisions, but information, skills, and rewards may or may not be changed.

Finally, *high involvement* encompasses the other two types but goes further, to include employees in the management of the business. It uses a wide variety of mutually reinforcing elements, including a whole range of innovative power sharing, information sharing, skill building, rewards, and other human resource practices. The most prominent examples are high-involvement manufacturing plants pioneered by Procter & Gamble and many other companies. This type of plant has become commonplace in such industries as food processing, chemicals, paper, and metals. Procter & Gamble, General Mills, and others that have used this approach indicate that high-involvement plants have better quality and 25 percent to 35 percent higher productivity than traditional plants. In the last 20 years, this form of organization has spread to many different types of settings, including back-office operations, call centers, retail, and professional work.

A series of six surveys of Fortune 1000 firms from the late 1980s to the early 2000s by the Center for Effective Organizations (for example, Lawler, Mohrman, and Ledford 1995; Lawler, Mohrman, and Benson 2001) explored the use of employee involvement practices. The surveys found that nearly all firms used some employee involvement practices, and the use of these practices increased during the 1990s until reaching a plateau near the end of the studies. The 1995 study classified companies by their level of involvement. Some 38 percent were characterized as low in employee involvement, with less than half of employees covered by a pattern of involvement practices; 37 percent focused on suggestion involvement; 6 percent focused on job involvement; 6 percent focused on high (business) involvement; and the remainder could not be classified. In other words, the most complex and advanced forms of involvement were heavily used by fewer firms than suggestion involvement. The studies further found that users overwhelmingly (over 80 percent) reported that their employee involvement efforts were successful, and almost none reported failure. Similar percentages reported that employee involvement had positive effects on measures related to employee engagement and to a wide variety of organizational performance indicators, and very few reported negative effects.

There is a growing body of research on the positive effects of employee involvement practices on objective indicators of firm performance. The 2001 study by Lawler and colleagues, for example, found that return on sales, return on assets, return on investment, return on equity, and total return to investors were consistently higher in firms that made extensive use of employee involvement practices. Similarly, a detailed study of the steel, apparel, and medical device industries (Appelbaum, Bailey, Berg, and Kalleberg 2000) found that high-involvement systems were associated with higher engagement (higher job satisfaction, higher organizational commitment, higher trust, and less stress) and higher organizational performance (higher efficiency, quality, and productivity) on a set of measures specific to each industry.

Most available studies have a shortcoming: The direction of causality cannot be determined definitively. If employee involvement and organizational performance are correlated, is that because employee involvement increases performance or because high-performing companies are more likely to adopt employee involvement practices? Considerable research indicates that better-performing companies are more likely to adopt human resource innovations of all kinds, including employee involvement practices.

What Is Employee Engagement?

One might expect that the mountain of publications about employee engagement would have generated clarity about the term. This is not the case. Macey and Schneider (2008) note the commonalities in typical definitions of engagement: Engagement is a desirable condition, has an organizational purpose, and connotes involvement, commitment, passion, enthusiasm, focused effort, and energy. This focus implies an emotional connection between employee and employer that is far stronger than simply satisfaction. The strong emotional bond implied by engagement is the basis for claims that it is something new, different, and important.

Practitioners might be surprised to learn that the definitions and survey measures of employee engagement overlap heavily with three very old concepts in the research literature: job satisfaction, organizational commitment, and job involvement. The concept of "job satisfaction" has been assessed in survey research for almost 60 years. Job satisfaction implies satiation, a cerebral evaluation of one's feelings about the job, and a focus on the employee's connection to the job rather than to the organization as a whole. "Organizational commitment" was proposed over 30 years ago. It implies attachment to the organization as a whole, including feelings of loyalty and pride as well as shared values. "Job involvement" dates to the mid–1960s and indicates an intensity of feelings, with a focus on the job rather than the organization.

There is a great deal of conceptual and measurement overlap between each of these terms and engagement (see Figure 29-1). Survey respondents do not make fine distinctions between these concepts. They are highly correlated and are best thought of as different reflections of a more general concept—something like employee morale, to use the oldest term of all (Harter and Schmidt 2008; Harrison, Newman, and Roth 2006). Despite the claims that engagement is something new and different, it is old and familiar.

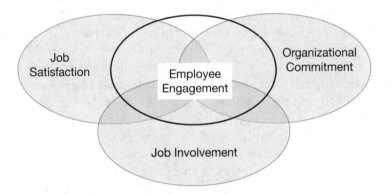

Figure 29-1   Concepts Related to Employee Engagement

The measurement discussion raises a very important practical issue for managers: What exactly do we want employees to be engaged *to*? Their jobs, their work groups, their local work units, or the organization as a whole? This is a basic decision with no obvious answer. The answer may also be different for different segments of the workforce. Certainly, we want senior executives to feel attachment to the entire corporation, not only a part of it. For front-line employees, however, building engagement to a large organization may be a much tougher and more complex task than building engagement to a job, team, or work unit. Focusing on the organization as a whole requires practices including rewards that lift employee attention to the entire company. Rewards such as profit sharing and broad-based stock options might make sense if engagement with the company is the goal; these have too long a line of sight to be effective if the goal is to improve the performance of the local work unit.

A final issue is whether more engagement is always a good thing. At what point does the organization ask for too much engagement? Several studies link high levels of job involvement to neuroticism and burnout. In practice, this is not as serious a problem as it might appear. The usual emphasis is on increasing the engagement of those who are low on the measure, not asking ever more from those who are already high.

Relationship between Employee Involvement and Employee Engagement

The evidence very strongly indicates that high employee involvement leads to high employee engagement. Indeed, the relationship between employee involvement and employee engagement is probably stronger and more certain than the relationship between employee involvement and organizational performance. Many factors can cause employee involvement or engagement to be disconnected to performance, but employees so widely embrace employee involvement that it almost always is associated with improved attitudes.

Employee Engagement and Business Outcomes

The relationship between employee engagement and organizational outcomes is more complex and varied. Figure 29-2 suggests that three types of outcomes that matter to employers: increased job performance, increased citizenship behavior, and decreased withdrawal behavior (absenteeism and turnover). Each of these is potentially valuable to the organization. Clearly, job performance matters because organizational performance is largely the sum of the performance of individual employees. Organizational citizenship behavior represents things that an employee does that are necessary but not formally a part of the job. All firms depend on employees who take initiative, are proactive, go above and beyond their formal role, and conscientiously do what needs to be done. Withdrawal behavior (absenteeism and especially turnover) is far more expensive than is commonly realized. An incident of turnover typically costs one 0.5 to 2 times annual salary, depending on employee skills.

Organizations always want greater job performance and greater citizenship behavior, but they do not always want less turnover. Turnover rates vary inversely with

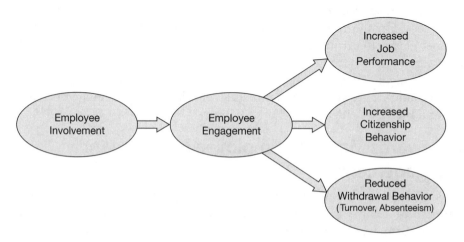

Figure 29-2 Employee Involvement, Employee Commitment, and Organizational Effectiveness

unemployment rates; when employees have few job opportunities, they stay put. At such times, organizations do not need to reduce voluntary turnover and they may welcome it when they need to reduce staffing.

How strong is the relationship between engagement and business outcomes? The contemporary practitioner literature is filled with claims that employee engagement is a key to business results. A sampler of such reports:

- Gallup Consulting (2008) claims that disengaged employees cost the U.S. economy over $300 billion in lost productivity and that the difference between organizations in the top quartile of engagement on its 12-item survey measure show 18 percent greater productivity, 12 percent greater profitability, 27 percent less absenteeism, 51 percent less turnover, and 62 percent fewer safety incidents than organizations in the bottom quartile on engagement.
- A Corporate Leadership Council study (Buchanan 2004) surveyed over 50,000 employees in 39 companies worldwide and concluded that increased engagement can lead to a 57 percent improvement in discretionary effort, a 20 percent individual performance improvement, and an 87 percent reduction in turnover intentions.

The findings from academic research, spanning decades and thousands of studies, are not so consistent or dramatic as in the popular literature. Early reviews found small, almost inconsequential correlations between morale and performance. More sophisticated recent meta-analytic reviews indicate that morale accounts for between 9 percent and 14 percent of the variance in employee performance (Judge et al. 2001; Harrison et al. 2006)—enough for a significant competitive advantage. A limitation of the available research is that there are not enough direct tests of the hypothesis that performance improvement follows increases in employee engagement. High organizational performance may cause high engagement rather than the other way around. Successful organizations offer more pay, more career opportunities, more security, more good feelings that come with working for a winner, and more feelings of personal success. On the other hand, there is strong evidence showing that reducing engagement leads to turnover.

Overall, there is strong evidence that employee involvement practices foster employee engagement, relatively good evidence that employee engagement promotes job performance, and strong evidence that employee engagement decreases withdrawal and increases citizenship.

Why Rewards Matter to Employee Involvement and Engagement

Decades of research on employee motivation confirm that well-designed reward systems are critical to linking employee involvement, employee engagement, and organizational performance. The reward system specifies the behaviors and performance that the organization values, and reinforces them through compensation and benefits. Without good reward systems, employee engagement and involvement will lack focus and may not improve performance.

This is not the popular view. The popular belief is that "a happy worker is a productive worker," and if management just showers employees with the things that make them happier, performance will follow. Considerable evidence demonstrates that this is not the case. Both happy and unhappy workers can be either productive or unproductive. Ensuring that employees see a linkage between rewards and performance creates the condition in which employee involvement and engagement generate organizational as well as individual returns.

Impact of Rewards on Involvement, Engagement, and Organizational Outcomes

We next consider the most important types of compensation—base pay, short-term incentives, and long-term incentives—and benefits. Earlier, we defined performance-based rewards as an element of employee involvement. Here we consider how other elements of employee involvement are reinforced or undermined by rewards, and how they affect employee engagement and organizational outcomes.

Base Pay

Base pay, the largest component of compensation, usually is determined by the market value of the employee's job. Research has long established that pay level has a great deal to do with employee withdrawal behaviors. A more recent finding (Mulvey et al. 2002) is that pay process, which includes systems for determining pay levels and communicating how those are set, is a major problem for employee engagement. Knowledge of pay process and satisfaction with pay process on average is actually worse than satisfaction with pay level. Moreover, pay process has strong effects on employee engagement and retention. This suggests that management has a great deal of work to do in helping employees understand the pay system.

The most important base pay innovation for increasing employee commitment and performance is skill-based pay (also called pay for skills and competency pay). Skill-based pay plans can take many forms, including bonuses, but the most common form is a base pay system that rewards skills, knowledge, or competencies. Skills are acquired and observable expertise in performing tasks, knowledge is the acquired information that is applied to task performance, and competencies are generic skills and traits. Skill-based pay systems are used extensively for manufacturing workers, teachers, scientists and engineers, and military personnel.

There is considerable evidence that skill-based pay increases both employee engagement and organizational performance (Ledford, Heneman, and Salimäki 2008). Skill-based pay can increase employee engagement in several ways. First, employees tend to prefer the logic of earning more by learning more, and they typically can earn a premium of 10 percent to 15 percent of wages in return for learning more skills. Second, cross-skilling helps employees gain a better understanding of how their job fits into the whole, increasing their focus from the job to the organization as a whole. Finally, skill-based pay reinforces other employee involvement practices including power sharing, training, and communication of business information. For this reason, skill-based pay has long been considered a standard part of high-involvement manufacturing plant designs. A variety of survey and case studies also indicate that skill-based pay tends to produce a smaller, more capable, more highly paid workforce, with increases in productivity and decreases in staffing and turnover offsetting higher average costs.

There are many potentially difficult issues in the design and administration of skill-based pay systems. Poorly designed plans can increase costs without generating off-setting benefits. Certain types of employees (senior employee near retirement or those with low needs for personal growth) may reject these pay systems. Overall, however, the track record for pay for skills plans appears to be a good one.

Short-Term Incentives

Short-term incentives pay out at least annually, usually as cash bonuses. The use of performance-based bonuses has increased markedly in the past two decades, especially for rank-and-file employees. For most of the U.S. workforce, individual incentives are difficult to design and in fact would be counterproductive to work unit performance. That has led to increased use over time of group incentives. The basic choice in rewarding unit performance typically is between approaches that reward unit performance (gain sharing and goal sharing plans) and plans that reward corporate performance (profit sharing). Ultimately, the choice between these approaches depends partly on whether management wishes to have employees who are engaged in the entire corporation, business unit, or their work unit. There is reasonably good evidence that corporate profit sharing can increase employee engagement, decrease turnover, and possibly increase citizenship behavior by increasing compensation and by giving employees a stake in the performance of the entire corporation. Such plans have the additional advantage of varying wages with the firm's ability to pay. However, employees lack line of sight to the profitability of the corporation in a firm of any size, so these plans probably have little effect on corporate performance. Gain sharing and goal sharing focus on productivity, quality, cost, and customer service metrics that offer greater line of sight, in work units that are not too large for the employee to understand and influence. There is considerable evidence that these plans have the advantages of profit sharing but a much stronger effect on unit performance.

An additional issue in short-term incentives is the increasing use of unit engagement scores as a criterion for management bonuses. Zingheim and Schuster (2007) found that fully 50 percent of a sample of fast-growing technology companies did this. Such incentives pose a serious threat to the validity and value of surveys. Managers can encourage, cajole, or threaten employees to give high scores without doing anything that really increases engagement.

Long-term Incentives

Long-term incentives include stock grants and options, restricted stock, and "phantom stock" arrangements that mirror equity value in organizations that are not publicly traded. Clearly these incentives pay out based on the performance of the organization.

As such, they appropriately are a critical component of compensation for senior executives. In the last 20 years, they have become increasingly important in executive compensation.

Programs to provide broad-based stock options to all employees surged during the 1990s. As changes in tax laws made these plans more expensive, their use has receded sharply in recent years. Certainly there is merit to the argument that individual rank-and-file employees cannot affect organization performance and therefore stock price directly. The motivational arguments are the same as for corporate profit sharing. However, some research indicates that equity programs are highly valued by employees and that providing a modest level of stock options to all employees can increase engagement, possibly influencing citizenship behavior and withdrawal behavior. The Sibson Rewards of Work Study (Ledford and Lucy 2003), based on a random sample of the U.S. workforce, found that stock grants were more powerful at inducing employees to quit their job for a similar position with another employer than time off, bonus opportunities, salary increases, career opportunities, or extra retirement benefits. Fully 50 percent of the U.S. workforce would quit their current position for a similar job that offered 100 shares of a $10 stock (total value of $1,000) that they would not be able to sell for four years. The same 50 percent would quit for a salary increase of $7,500 (an average of 24 percent increase for this sample) or a one-time retirement plan contribution of $20,000.

Benefits

Benefits are a large slice of the rewards pie, currently representing over 40 percent of wages on average in private-sector firms. The most expensive benefits are health care, paid leave (vacation and holidays), and retirement. Typically, all or most employees receive benefits by virtue of employment, not their performance. As a result, benefits play an important role in attracting and retaining employees, but there are few ways to link benefits and performance.

Paid leave is among the most highly valued rewards by U.S. employees. The Sibson study (Ledford and Lucy 2003) found that fully half of a random sample of the workforce would leave their current position for another employer if they were offered an additional two weeks of paid vacation per year. Given the average wage of the sample, this would have cost an employer $1,400 per employee. By contrast, retirement benefits tend to have low value for most employees. Retirement plans have the most value to older employees, who are more likely to see retirement approaching. On average, it would take a $20,000 one-time contribution per employee to the company retirement plans to achieve the same effect. In other words, time off is 14 times as powerful as retirement benefits in retaining the average U.S. employee.

There have been just a few transitory experiments with basing some retirement benefits—for example, the level of 401(k) match—with individual performance. Perhaps more common in the future will be varying retirement benefits based on firm rather than individual performance.

One of the most prominent developments in the benefits arena has been the widespread attention to "work/life benefits." Given that these programs are typically aimed at creating balance between work and non-work lives, it is ironic that such programs are often advocated as an employee engagement tonic. Because the wide range of work/life benefits are almost never tied to performance, they have little motivational value, and in the view of this author, there is little convincing evidence that such programs affect job performance or citizenship. They can reduce withdrawal behavior, but the corporate emphasis on such programs tends to ebb and flow with the economy and the need to attract and retain employees.

Rewards for the Contingent Workforce

Current estimates are that a staggering one-fourth of the U.S. workforce is part-time, an independent contractor, or a temporary employee. This poses a tremendous challenge for involvement, engagement, and rewards. Clearly the contingent workforce helps companies avoid the costs of full-time employment. Contingent employees usually receive less compensation than full-time regular employees, and no performance bonuses or benefits. Employers are often unconcerned about high turnover in this workforce segment. As this segment grows, there will be an increasing need to develop rewards that focus the effort and talents of contingent workers, and we expect to see more experimentation with rewards for such employees. A key design issue is the level of engagement desired. The company typically does not want contingent employees to be highly engaged with the firm; the emphasis is on engagement with a job or work unit, or in many cases only with a project. However, it is possible to create incentives that support unit-level engagement.

Conclusion

Employee involvement and engagement remain core ideas in contemporary human resource practice, and there is much excitement about their promise. Our argument has been that the benefits of increased involvement and engagement depend on well-designed reward systems that create motivation for employees to meet organizational as well as personal goals. A wide variety of compensation and benefits tools can be used for this purpose.

References

Appelbaum, E., T. Baily, P. Berg, and A. Kalleberg. 2000. *Manufacturing advantage: Why high-performance work systems pay off*. Ithaca, NY: Economic Policy Institute.

Buchanan, Leigh. 2004. The things they do for love. *Harvard Business Review* 82(12):19–20.

Gallup Consulting. 2008. *Employee engagement: What's your engagement ratio?* Gallup: Washington, D.C.

Harrison, D. A., D. A. Newman, and P. L. Roth. 2006. How important are job attitudes? Meta-analytic comparisons of integrative behavioral outcomes and time sequences. *Academy of Management Journal* 49(2):315–325.

Harter, J. K., and F. L. Schmidt. 2008. Conceptual and empirical distinctions among constructs: Implications for discriminant validity. *Industrial and Organizational Psychology* 1:36–39.

Judge, T. A., C. J. Thoreson, J. E. Bono, and G. K. Patton. 2001. The job satisfaction-job performance relationship: A qualitative and quantitative review. *Psychological Bulletin* 127:376–407.

Lawler, E. E. III. 1986. *High involvement management.* San Francisco: Jossey-Bass.

Lawler, E. E. III, S. A. Mohrman, and G. Benson. 2001. *Organizing for high performance.* San Francisco: Jossey-Bass.

Lawler, E. E. III, S. A. Mohrman, and G. E. Ledford, Jr. 1995. *Creating high performance organizations.* San Francisco: Jossey-Bass.

Ledford, G., R. L. Heneman, and Aimo Salimäki. 2008. Skill, knowledge, and competency pay. In *The compensation handbook* (5th ed.). Lance A. Berger and Dorothy R. Berger (Eds.). New York: McGraw-Hill, 143–158.

Ledford, G., and M. Lucy. 2003. *The rewards of work: The employment deal in a changing economy.* New York: Sibson Consulting, The Segal Company.

Macey, W. H., and B. Schneider. 2008. The meaning of employee engagement. *Industrial and Organizational Psychology* 1:3–30.

Mulvey, P. W., P. V. LeBlanc, R. L. Heneman, and M. McInerney. 2002. *The knowledge of pay study: E-mails from the frontline.* Scottsdale, AZ: WorldatWork.

Zingheim, P. K., and J. R. Schuster. 2007. Measuring and rewarding customer satisfaction, innovation, and workforce engagement. *WorldatWork Journal* 16(4):8–22.

Part IV

Using Talent Management Processes to Drive Cultures of Excellence

Chapter 30

Establishing a Talent Management Culture

David C. Forman, Chief Learning Officer
Human Capital Institute

ECONOMISTS, CEOS, AND THOUGHT LEADERS HAVE RECOGNIZED THAT WE ARE IN A different time, space, and context than companies in the Industrial and even Knowledge Ages. In the twenty-first century, success is based on the ability to innovate, be creative, connect across boundaries, and adapt to unparalleled change. When 90 percent of Hewlett Packard's and Medtronic's revenues are from products that did not exist a year ago, it is clear that you need to innovate or lose. Yet most current management and talent practices are based on a model of the company that is outdated and ensures that organizations will never be as capable as the people who work in them. The vestiges of the past are restricting the changes required to be successful now and in the future.

"The only unique asset that a business has for gaining a sustained competitive advantage over rivals is its workforce—the skills and dedication of its employees. There is no other sustainable advantage in the modern, high-tech, global economy." —Robert Reich

"Today's marketplace is incredibly competitive in every industry around the globe. The difference between success and failure is talent, period." —Indra Nooyi, CEO PepsiCo

Only those companies that win the hearts and minds of their top talent will be able to deliver value over both the short and long term. —Deloitte Research (2008)

These statements are not just theoretical banter or emotional chatter. The contribution of talent to the success of an organization is clearly established by more than a decade of research. Organizations that invest in effective talent management practices consistently outperform their industry peers. An even greater advantage is gleaned by those organizations that have more of an *integrated* approach in which various talent practices inform and influence each other (IBM-HCI 2008).

External factors have also driven the impetus for improved talent practices within organizations. In publicly traded companies, a key driver is the rise of the intangible value of an organization. In the 1980s most of the valuation of a company was determined by its tangible assets—equipment, facilities, technology, resources. Now these tangible assets account for less than 40 percent of a company's worth, and instead, it is the intangible assets of brand, relationships, talent, and ability to innovate and execute that can compose up to 85 percent of the market value of these companies.

With this new reality, a different set of stakeholders are interested in talent management: the financial community, investors, analysts, and the media. Since talent and intangible assets are now so vital, these stakeholders are looking for metrics and accountabilities to define which organizations are managing their human capital effectively.

In the government sector, an important impetus for improved talent practices has been the President's Management Agenda (PMA). One of the top five pillars of the PMA is Strategic Human Capital Management. Departments and agencies were directed to make progress in this initiative and to "go green." A critical new position, the Chief Performance Officer, whose job is to improve the productivity of government agencies, has been established.

Finally, there is a strong push for implementing talent practices from "The Best Places to Work" lists in both business and government. The criteria for the Malcolm Baldrige Award also have the same influencing effect: If organizations want to apply, they must have strong human capital practices. The result of these efforts is to create a "Culture of Envy" (Wright 2008) that differentiates recognized from unrecognized organizations. These lists then contribute to brand, credibility in the marketplace, and ability to attract top talent. Sullivan (2006) has said that getting on such lists is worth millions in free public relations coverage and exposure.

These forces have combined to reinforce the importance of talent to organizations in the twenty-first century. Winston Churchill predicted this likelihood decades earlier when he said: "The empires of the future will be empires of the mind." Among the critical questions that need to be addressed in developing a talent-driven culture are the following:

- How do organizations transform themselves to be aligned and synchronized so that talent can be leveraged more effectively?
- How can high standards of performance and accountability be established?
- How can organizations move beyond past practices where people are viewed as replaceable parts and as costs to be curtailed and controlled?
- How can people work together with greater collaboration and connection?
- How can cultures be challenging, demanding, and respectful at the same time?

- How can more flexibility, choices, and options be built into the workplace so that people choose to opt in rather than drop out?
- How can autonomy, mastery, and purpose be part of the workplace (Pink 2009)?
- How can the job be seen as a career and experienced as a calling (Conley 2007)?

The answers are not easy or quick, but patterns are emerging, and there do appear to be steps that can be taken along this journey to a talent-driven culture and organizational success.

The Talent Management Adoption Model

Organizations vary in their commitment to talent management practices and in building high-performance cultures. The specific attributes of a new talent-driven culture will vary depending on the organization's values, mission, and strategy, but it is difficult to change existing structures, traditions, and past ways of operating. The journey can be slow and arduous for those wanting to move to a culture that fosters and supports high performance and enduring talent-driven practices, and essential steps must be taken. These steps can be categorized in terms of the vision of leaders, the infrastructure provided, processes and people, and implementers who live and demonstrate the values of what Hamel refers to as "opt-in organizations—ones that people chose to associate with and commit to."

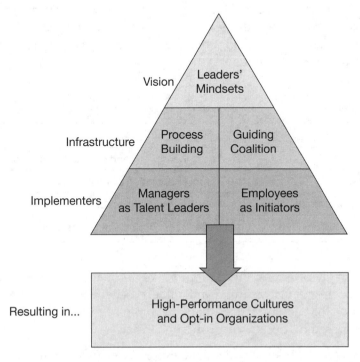

Figure 30-1 The Talent Adoption Model

Step 1: Enterprise Leader's Talent Mind-Set

McKinsey first formalized what many people already recognized: If the boss isn't supportive, big changes won't happen. In McKinsey's *The War for Talent*, the importance of the leader's talent mind-set was empirically established as the primary distinguishing factor between successful and less successful companies within industry cohort groups. This research resonated with well-publicized examples. Jack Welch lived and breathed talent practices, and GE reflected his passion. He taught a half-day class for new GE managers every two weeks for fifteen years, and never missed a class. Andy Grove taught all Intel managers how to spot change in the microprocessor market as a critical part of their ongoing development. Sam Walton infused an employee-first philosophy as Wal-Mart was getting started, and Herb Kelleher would show up in hospital rooms for Southwest employees (or even relatives) to show his personal commitment to them. Wayne Calloway at PepsiCo would spend weeks with key managers reviewing strategy and playing a key mentoring role in their development, and AG Lafley of Procter & Gamble spends 30 to 50 percent of his time developing future leaders.

These organizations have a great advantage over their competitors that view talent as costs and not assets. The real danger at this stage is that the leader says all the right things but doesn't follow through with tangible commitment and action.

Only when the leader has a talent mind can the journey begin; but what happens if the leader does not? In this latter case, the real question is this: Is the leader open to data and changing his or her mind? If the answer is no, then the best outcome is incremental and slow change. For the leader who can be influenced, a compelling case depends on the organization's *pain points* that the leader is trying to address, such as those listed in the table that follows.

Immediate Benefits	Enduring Benefits
1. Reduces risk.	Improves productivity.
2. Stems turnover.	Strengthens brand and competitive position.
3. Saves money.	Improves execution of strategy.
4. Improves ability to attract talent.	Builds deeper pipelines of critical talent.
5. Joins the "culture of envy."	Makes better business decisions regarding human capital.

Given this array of issues, the champion (key influencer) needs to address those issues that have the greatest meaning and highest cachet with the leader. A compelling case can be made for talent practices that ameliorate key issues through the following framework proposed by Condit and Forman (2008):

The alignment case. Link the value of talent practices to achieving strategic goals of the organization.

The business case. Calculate the monetary impact of improved talent practices.

The experiential case. Show the personal impact of changes because compelling cases include both the mind and the heart.

The comparative case. Demonstrate that others are taking similar actions through benchmark and comparative data.

The null case. Articulate the cost of doing nothing and losing momentum and morale.

The continual case. Keep making the compelling case and be able to respond to changes in both internal and external factors.

Step 2: The Division Leader's Talent Mind-Set

When the enterprise leader's talent mind-set is genuine, it influences his or her direct reports. The talent mind-set, then, has started to cascade down the organization and widen its path of influence. This is a critical step in infusing new values and behaviors into the culture. If the commitment just stays at the very top, it fails to impact the organization in any meaningful way.

More often than not, a few divisional leaders become ardent champions of what Lawler (2008) has termed a "human capital-centric organization." They see the opportunity to shape their division, group, or agency as a center of innovation and talent excellence, and be the "early adopter" within the larger enterprise. In organizations that do possess high-performing cultures, it is very clear which groups and people are excellent at developing talent. These talent laboratories (or some even call them "talent factories") are well recognized both informally and at the board level.

Because the division is smaller than the enterprise, a divisional leader can often impact the culture more quickly and directly than the CEO or general manager. Because culture change is incremental, the steady presence of a strong and dedicated talent champion and divisional leader can make significant progress at the local level.

Step 3: Process Building

Leaders supply the mind-set and direction, but infrastructure is needed to move the culture to a different level. This stage can occur in parallel with Steps 1 and 2 or follow in sequence. Among the processes and practices that should be built over time are the following:

Key Talent Management Processes
Workforce planning
Competency development
Recruiting

(continued)

On-boarding
Engaging talent
Performance management
Talent reviews
Succession management
Leadership development
Manager development
Employee development
Talent deployment and internal mobility
Knowledge and expertise management
Career development
Proactive retention programs

Some, or many, of these practices occur in most organizations, but their purpose is more for operational consistency than talent optimization. For example, many performance management systems have not dealt with the issue of ratings inflation and therefore serve little purpose in providing honest and direct feedback for employees. Many other organizations have a difficult time segmenting top talent and critical jobs so that resources and interventions can be targeted to the areas that will provide the greatest return on investment.

Process building is the domain of experts. A center of excellence in talent management often includes experts in the processes previously identified as well as technology and analytics. The purpose of this center is to provide proven tools, templates, and systems so that leaders, managers, and employees can be more successful in their talent management responsibilities.

The list of talent processes and practices is long and requires prioritization.

Priorities usually start where the pain is greatest. For example, for organizations that have a turnover problem, engagement and retention programs are paramount. For organizations that have a leadership depth issue, succession management is more essential. With this caveat in mind, consider some core processes that should form the baseline: talent acquisition, performance management, engagement, and learning and development. These provide the core functionality that the other talent practices can build upon.

Process building is absolutely essential. It forges processes and systems that work and drive effective talent practices throughout the organization. It provides the infrastructure for the next critical stages in adopting talent management throughout the enterprise.

Step 4: Strengthening Organizational Commitment through a Guiding Coalition

Just as processes have to be built to provide direction and credibility to talent management, further human technology also needs to be added. It is not sufficient for leaders alone to have talent mind-sets; others in the organization must understand and support the drive to a high-performance culture. The guiding coalition represents the next level of necessary organizational commitment, and as the influence of the coalition cascades down, together with strengthened processes, organizations begin to transform.

A guiding coalition consists of respected people from different levels and groups. While process building is the province of experts, the guiding coalition is not composed of these individuals. The coalition must represent *the line and core functions of the organization*. These individuals must have a rock-solid sense of the business, be highly respected, and have the ability to shape the future. There are numerous examples of meaningful guiding coalitions. A regional construction company has a human asset management (HAM) group to guide and monitor its human capital initiatives. These estimators, construction managers, and foremen meet regularly and report directly to the senior management team. McKinsey has its aptly named People Committee, and it looks over the talent needs and requirements of the firm.

Step 5: The Manager as Talent Leader

This step in the model has been achieved by less than 10 percent to 15 percent of organizations. To be at this level means the following: Talent practices have the backing of leaders; many effective talent processes are in place; new mind-sets and behaviors are percolating down the organization; and managers now recognize that they are a key "owner" of the talent imperative. The manager's most important role is now to be able to hire, engage, develop, and retain talented employees.

Organizational rewards and incentives must reinforce the talent leader role of the manager. If these systems still value the individual contributor role and reward achievement of operational targets to the exclusion of talent goals, then the organization is out of alignment and a talent-based culture will be stalled.

Typically, managers do not initially have the requisite skills to become talent leaders. Traditional management training has been anchored in past perceptions of what managers do, and not how to know, grow, inspire, involve, and reward talented employees. Coaching and further development are required.

This step takes at least several years to accomplish. The cultural shifts are huge, and a great deal has to be aligned and synchronized for line managers to become talent leaders. The organizations that have crossed this barrier accomplish this transformation by using proven change management processes and tools.

Step 6: The Employee as Initiator of Talent and Career Development

Probably 5 percent of organizations currently inhabit this stage. In Step 6, individuals take responsibility for directing and running their own careers. They have access to all the information and tools they need to chart their own course, and their managers are there to support them and do minor course corrections. The locus of ownership now shifts to the individual.

The psychological adjustments to this stage are not nearly as significant as Step 5. Most people want to be in charge of their own destiny, but they have not had the information, tools, and organizational authorization to do so. Employees increasingly recognize that their greatest security is to continue to drive their own professional bus forward by learning new skills, having unique experiences, expanding professional networks, and stretching into the learning zone.

It is the organization that must provide these choices, and be committed to unleashing and not micromanaging talent. Employees now should be able to chart more of their own course. They can use the organization as a learning laboratory, take greater responsibility for their own development and performance, and come prepared to talk to their managers about what *they want to do*. They become real investors in themselves and the organization. They make choices and have more "skin in the game" than simply obeying orders or taking traditional paths. It's all about creating more choices, options, and paths for individuals. When people are responsible for their choices, engagement goes up and productivity increases.

With the locus of control shifting to individuals, greater flexibility and choice need to characterize the workplace. EDS publishes the results of its workforce plan and encourages employees to develop new critical skill sets. IBM Blue Opportunities not only allows employees to promote their own personal brand and publishes internal jobs but also proactively informs employees of new opportunities that match their competencies and interests. Technology allows for vibrant talent marketplaces and the sharing of expertise and knowledge more pervasively than ever before.

The New Talent Management "Academy Companies"

The organizations that have gone through the six steps of the talent management adoption model are known as "academy companies." Many academy companies have been developing their practices not for years, but decades. They have overcome past barriers, mind-sets, and traditions, and have changed their cultures to reflect the new desired values and mores. They now have an engine for sustainable competitive advantage if it is properly serviced and calibrated. Their names are familiar: GE, IBM, PepsiCo, Procter & Gamble, Johnson & Johnson, Hewlett Packard, Intel, Southwest Airlines, Cisco, Microsoft, FedEx, and Nordstrom's, among others. These corporate giants are no longer the only organizations to deliver on the promise of talent management. The message is being heard in small and medium-sized firms, in government agencies, and in different types of organizations. Just as new companies are not having to follow the traditional path for going global—from domestic to regional to global to multinational organizations—but rather are "born global," the same path is true for what Gary Hamel (2007) has called "opt-in" organizations. These are organizations that people want to work for and have been founded with that principle in mind.

The 2010 *Best Companies to Work For* list from *Fortune* magazine (and the Best Places to Work Institute) provides some interesting insights into this generation of organizations. Thirty four of the first fifty companies have fewer than 6,000 employees. Among the types of companies presented, there are 14 hospitals, 5 retail markets, 7 law firms, and 6 construction/engineering companies. Ten years ago, hospitals, construction companies, and law firms would be outliers on the Fortune list: Hospitals were too bureaucratic and departmentalized, construction companies were too gruff and command- and control-driven, and law firms were piranhas. But now many of these organizations play by a different set of rules; they have to or they will not compete for talent and thrive in the twenty-first century.

There is an advantage to being a small to medium-sized organization. The goal is not economies of scale anymore, but rather it is to create an opt-in, high-performance culture, and this is inherently easier in a community where lines of sight and connections are strong. As Gary Hamel (2007) has said, "When it comes to mobilizing human capability, communities outperform bureaucracies." W. L. Gore & Associates, a frequent member of the Fortune list, is a company of 5500 employees, but intentionally limits the size of groups and departments to 200 people or less. This guideline guards against the type of hierarchy and bureaucracy that squash new ideas and lead to a much less engaging place to work.

Another excellent example is Tony Hsieh, the CEO of Zappos and number 15 on Fortune's 2010 list. Hsieh is a very successful businessman and now part of the Amazon family. He will pay people $2,000 after their first week in the company if that person does not believe that Zappos is the best place to be. The result is a highly productive and engaged workforce with a fraction of the turnover of other customer service call centers.

Summary

A diverse set of organizations are moving through the talent adoption model in larger and larger numbers. This is no longer just the province of the well-heeled, tradition-rich corporations. A democratization is occurring that spreads the opportunity and promise of "opt-in" organizations that can attract, engage, develop, and retain top talent.

There are necessary steps that organizations go through to reach the state in which a talent-based culture is established. The process starts with the mind-set of the leader that talent is a key differentiator for success. Then this talent mind-set must go beyond the leader to other influential people within the enterprise. As "talent laboratories" get established in key divisions or groups, the culture starts to shift and adapt to these new values and messages. Substance needs to accompany mind-set to change behavior, so process building must occur. Infrastructure needs to be built by scientists and domain experts, whether internally or borrowed.

The hardest step in the process is the transition of line manager to talent leader. When organizations go through this transformation, the journey to a high-performing culture is close at hand because many barriers have been overcome. The final step is to have employees really drive and own the process. This is when talent-centric beliefs and practices become embedded into everyday activities and organizational culture, and when talent becomes a sustainable competitive advantage.

In some cases this journey can take decades, and in others it is the platform on which an organization is founded and grown. The steps to pursue a talent management culture will be climbed slowly or in a rush depending on history and context; but regardless, they will have to be climbed.

References

Condit, R., and D. Forman. 2008. *Compelling cases for change*. Washington, D.C.: Human Capital Institute.

Conley, C. 2007. *Peak*. San Francisco: Jossey-Bass.

Deloitte Research Series. 2007. *It's 2008: Do you know where your talent is?* Deloitte Consulting.

Hamel, G. 2007. *The future of management*. Cambridge: Harvard Business School Press.

Hewitt-HCI Research Study. 2008. *The state of talent management*. Hewitt Human Capital Consulting.

IBM-HCI Research Study. 2008. *Integrated talent management*. IBM.

Lawler, E. 2008. *Talent: Making people your competitive advantage*. San Francisco: Jossey-Bass, 2008.

Michaels, E., H. Handfield-Jones, and B. Axelrod. 2001. *The war for talent*. Cambridge: Harvard Business School Press.

Pink, D. 2009. *Drive*. New York: Riverhead Books.

Sullivan, J. 2006. *Rethinking strategic HR*. Chicago: CCH Incorporated.

Wright, Thom. 2008. Conversation with author.

Chapter 31

Linking Culture and Talent Management

Andy Pellant, Managing Partner
Emergentedge

MUCH HAS BEEN WRITTEN ON ORGANIZATIONAL CULTURE AND TALENT MANAGEMENT, but rarely are these areas linked in the literature. This chapter seeks to establish a natural law and common-sense link between culture and talent and will also seek to offer a framework that establishes a more empirical and metric-driven approach to the creation and management of this vital interrelationship. The dynamics of culture and talent are applicable to organizations of every size, sector, and stage of development.

Defining Culture and Talent

Many businesses leaders that I meet look sincere and earnest when they say that their business "doesn't really have a culture." Of course it does; along with every family, brand, church group, political party, and sports team. If you cannot describe the culture of the organization that you lead or operate within, chances are you don't have the culture that is required for success.

Culture is the way that we behave; it's in the behavior that we *permit* and the attitudes that we *promote*. It exists in the way that we treat each other, our suppliers, and customers. Culture is all about the atmosphere that we work within, and as we will see later in this chapter, it is the atmosphere that enables or undermines the creation of a coherent talent environment.

Culture is not defined by the words that are printed on the laminated piece of paper in each of your meeting rooms, nor is it defined by the mission or the vision or the values that is expounded by your organization, and it is certainly not defined by posters hanging in your offices that try to inspire teamwork, leadership, trust, excellence, and winning—meaningless pieces of cardboard. If you already have an inspiring culture, you don't need the posters, and conversely, if your culture doesn't induce these positives, then the posters are reminders of an unfavorable environment. In either case, remove the posters!

Culture is everyone's responsibility; it is not only the domain of the executive suite, nor the responsibility of the HR team. Everyone needs to confront the following questions:

- If I think that the culture is right for now and the future, then what have I done to promote and ensure it?
- If I think that the culture is ineffective or divisive in some way, then what have I done to confront and change it, or have I sat back, believing that there's nothing I can do?
- Am I comfortable being in this culture? Does the culture support me in achieving excellence?

Most people carry on managing the consequences and symptoms of the culture rather than working through a model to make a meaningful contribution toward improving it.

One of the aspects of culture that needs exploring is the role of a leader and the "shadow" that leadership casts across the organizational landscape. Good or bad, this shadow defines a view of what is and what isn't acceptable in the organization; the trick is to make that shadow deliberate and positive; accidental cultures do not lead to success. The only successful cultures are the result of clarity, dedication, and discipline.

To link culture and talent, I propose a model based on the work of Virginia Satir (see References at the end of the chapter), one of the world's first "functional" psychologists, who originally attempted to describe the dynamics of successful families. We have applied this architecture to organizations, teams, and even individuals. Her assertion is that culture is so complex that people feel they are unable to address the entire issue, so they abandon change and development. The model is shown in Figure 31-1.

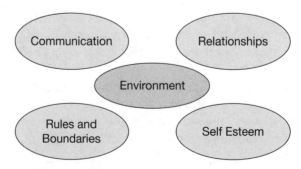

Figure 31-1 Culture/Talent Link

It is a cultural map that is broken into five component parts to be used as a diagnostic and planning tool to induce cultural change in a manageable, implementable, and measurable way.

We'll look at each of the components and the questions the organization should ask in addressing each one.

Communication

Consider: Who communicates? What is communicated? How and when and with what effect? What is heard and how does that vary from what is said? How does bad news get around so fast? How much communication is two-way?

Relationships

Consider: Who controls the relationships? How are relationships formed? On what basis are these relationships managed? What is the "currency" within the relationship (obedience, money, effort)? How are relationships described? Are these relationships "toxic" or "nurturing"?

Rules and Boundaries

Consider: What are the explicit and implicit rules? How are these rules set and by whom? Who polices the rules? Is there one set of rules for "us" and another set for "them"? How can these rules be renegotiated? Are these rules necessary, effective, appropriate, helpful?

Self-Esteem

Consider: How do we talk about ourselves? How do we write about ourselves within the corporate literature? How do we describe our competitors and customers? How do we talk about our staff, our managers, and our leaders?

Environment

Environment is an often overlooked aspect of culture. Consider: Can we effectively and successfully do our jobs in this environment? Does this environment provide us with the tools and equipment necessary to be successful? Do we have an environment that reflects our brand and image? Do I feel good at my desk? Are we aligned with our clients and competitors?

Answers to these questions can act as a *current-state* checklist and provides a map of the current culture. In large organizations you need to ask these questions at both the global and local levels. The term for this state is the Horizon One Picture.

A different mapping exercise emerges when asking the same questions in the future tense: What would the picture look like if everything were as we wish to achieve goals and objectives? This provides a blueprint for the future state. The term for this state is the Horizon Three Picture

By reviewing the gaps between the Horizon One and the Horizon Three Pictures, scenarios that deliver a plan of migration from current state to future state can be created. This plan is defined as the Horizon Two Picture and provides a measurable and shareable implementation of change.

The answers to some of the questions begin to link culture and talent.

Defining Talent

There are many definitions of talent management. Our definition: "A meaningful, shared, conscious, and deliberate approach undertaken to attract, develop, and retain people with the aptitude and abilities to meet the defined current and future organizational needs in terms of capability, behavior, attitude, knowledge, and style."

Figure 31-2 depicts this talent management definition.

Figure 31-2 Talent Management Definition

Linking the Satir Culture Model and the Authentic Organization Talent Model

The imperative is to design the *best* talent management system to deliver the current and future needs of your organization. To do this, consider the following:

> **Can a talent management system create a talent culture?** No. Grafting a talent management system onto a poor culture cannot work. Elements of the culture react to the talent management system, but unless the performance management culture

and the reward and recognition systems are updated, then the organizational "antibodies" work to reject the talent "invader." Recruiting external talent to bring about culture change is not a panacea. It can only work when the new hire is in the most senior position.

Does the creation of a talent culture lead to the development of more talented people? If the dynamics of the Satir Culture are aligned with the strategy of the organization, then the answer is an unqualified, "Yes." This means that the future state culture is consciously designed to deliver the climate that supports the attraction, recruitment, identification, development, deployment, and promotion of talented individuals. The main inhibitor to this "updraft" is the capability of the senior middle managers who must be developed early and supported intensely if this approach is going to work.

How do you use the Satir Culture Mapping Process to change culture? At the core of failed attempts at changing culture is a lack of honesty and integrity when establishing a consensus for a starting point for change. The plans for change, although robust and thoughtful as to desired destination, are doomed without a stated starting point.

What are the phases of culture change? By considering the earlier questions, several "documents" should result: an assessment of the current culture, the desired culture, and the plan to move into the desired state. In addition, a refreshed view on the business strategy and some aspects of a people plan that includes behavioral and capability specifications should emerge.

The Five Stages of Culture Change

Culture change evolves through five phases:

1. *Unfreeze—Break with the Past.* Set the direction and explain the benefits of arriving in the "new place." Create desire and overcome inertia through senior management's obvious and vocal commitment.

2. *Mobilize—Build the Energy.* Gather momentum and begin to lead in the same direction, using common language to describe the journey. Trial early changes and gain confidence.

3. *Realize—Performance Lift-Off.* Recognize progress and celebrate shifts in metrics. Shift language from "what we need" to "what we have achieved." Secure full commitment to the journey.

4. *Reinforce—Embed the New Culture.* Underpin the shifts with new and supportive enhancements to systems and processes; be aware of the need to "stop" those elements of infrastructure that support the old and unwanted behaviors and attitudes.

5. *Sustain—Maintain Momentum and Push the Limits.* Strive for continuous performance and identify those aspects of the environment that now need to be given the "unfreeze" treatment.

New Leaders

We have been developing an alternate structure, titled New Leaders, offering a description of behaviors, attitudes, and approaches that we have seen in successful organizations. They are not essential in every situation, but their presence seems to create a climate that fosters excellence, increases performance, ensures discretionary contribution, maximizes learning, and leads to strong aspects of employee branding. The competencies in this structure are as follows.

- *Self-awareness*. Knowing what they believe in and value, and what motivates them
- *Spontaneity*. Living in and being responsive to the moment
- *Vision and values led*. Acting from principles and deep beliefs
- *Holistic*. Seeing larger patterns, relationships, and connections
- *Compassion*. Feeling empathy
- *Celebration of diversity*. Valuing others for their differences
- *Field independence*. Standing against the crowd when appropriate and having one's own convictions
- *Humility*. Having the sense of being a player in a larger drama, of one's place in the world
- *Tendency to ask fundamental questions* Needing to understand things
- *Ability to reframe*. Standing back, seeing problems in a wider context
- *Positive use of adversity*. Learning and growing from mistakes, setbacks, and suffering
- *Sense of vocation*. Feeling called upon to serve, to give something back

Conclusion

There exists a linkage between the most successful organizations, their approach to talent, and their commitment to culture. Embedding the culture and talent "language" within every team, business unit, brand, and aspect of the organization is essential to the creation of momentum, and this must be modeled by the senior staff and echoed throughout the leadership ladder. The leadership shadow can impede or enable shifts in culture and the talent management systems benefit from consistent and guiding leadership.

Find ways of measuring your organization's culture, using some of the tools in this chapter or building your own. Create a metric and a description that helps everyone in the organization recognize talent. A range of behavioral and attitudinal profiling systems that can be tailored and contextualized for use within a variety of scenarios and can also be used to run "excellence studies" are available.

References

Satir, Virginia. 1988. *The new peoplemaking*. Palo Alto, CA: Science and Behavior Books.
———. 1991. *The Satir model: Family therapy and beyond*. Palo Alto, CA: Science and Behavior Books.

Chapter 32

Creating a Culture of Success: What Every CEO Needs to Know

Owen Sullivan, Chief Executive Officer
Right Management

I N TODAY'S HYPER-COMPETITIVE GLOBAL MARKETPLACE, BEST-IN-CLASS ORGANIZATIONS NEED to embrace a strategic mind-set for how they manage talent. Doing so will ensure the successful execution of their business objectives.

Led by the CEO, organizations must apply the same rigor used to create an overall business strategy that is used to create a workforce strategy—not just a workforce plan. This strategy requires a comprehensive understanding of how complex trends and shifting business realities will impact your business—now and in the future.

The resulting strategic blueprint provides line of sight into understanding the talent choices available today that impact an organizations' ability to deliver on their business strategies in the future.

Key components that every talent strategy must leverage include the following:

1. Assessing talent
2. Developing leaders
3. Implementing and aligning strategy
4. Engaging employees
5. Redeploying and/or transitioning employees

Each component is supported by success stories from the clients we have served.

Building an Exceptional Workforce

In the changing world of work, the one constant is the need for an exceptional workforce. This is regardless of the economic environment, your industry or geography, your size or your earnings. Undoubtedly, your most valuable asset continues to be your workforce. How you manage this asset spells the difference between success and failure.

Increasingly, the demands and composition of the workforce are shifting in response to economic, social, and demographic trends. The need for more specific skills is creating a growing talent mismatch and scarcity of leadership talent. Multiple generations and cultures in the workplace have resulted in changes in motivations and preferences, profoundly impacting individual choice. Technological developments allow new ways of getting work done. It has never been more challenging to manage your workforce effectively.

Despite their varied implications, these trends revolve around one central theme: the need to empower the right people, in the right places, in the right ways. This requires a sustained commitment to and a strategic investment in talent. The company that pays the most attention will rise to the top. Your talent assets need to be managed as aggressively as the fine-tuning you apply to other organizational assets. Everything else fails if you don't have the right talent in place.

This requires an alignment of talent strategy with business goals. Talent is the number one impediment or success factor to executing your business plan. Led by the CEO, a talent strategy must

1. Articulate a comprehensive vision of where the company wants to go, what unique value it delivers, and what effects it wants to have.
2. Organize work structures to unleash the knowledge, innovation, and creativity of every employee in order to achieve that vision.
3. Examine, understand, and deliver what your employees want from their employer and work environment.

You can't change what is happening relative to the external world of work trends or today's economic reality. But you can change your "people strategies" in order to respond to those trends and position your company to gear up for growth in this context.

It's not a matter of having "bodies" in your organization. It's a matter of having the "best bodies and minds" available in the market. Those who are committed and enthusiastic, and provide advocacy. The best talent always has choices no matter what market conditions exist. If your high-value talent is not engaged with you, they will walk out the door at the earliest opportunity.

You have many options for talent acquisition, retention, development, redeployment, and transition. The key is to align the right talent approaches to your business strategy.

What follows are five practical components of an integrated talent management plan that will help you build the exceptional workforce you need to execute your business strategy.

Five Key Components of an Integrated Talent Management Plan

When integrated, each of the following five key components leads to a comprehensive approach to talent management—one that is sure to build a culture of success.

1. Assess Talent

Your workforce is the critical ingredient to delivering business objectives and sustaining competitive advantage. The ability to strategically assess the talent you have—and the talent you need—underpins the ability to meet and exceed the goals of your organization. With the right workforce in place, you can build your brand more effectively, achieve your goals more consistently, and deliver higher competitive value to customers and stakeholders.

From a CEO perspective, it is important to assess where you are today and where you want to be—before you can even start to build the bridge between the talent strategy and the business strategy. Assessing talent enables you to evaluate your current workforce and forecast future needs; the resulting gap analysis provides a roadmap for sourcing, onboarding, developing and accelerating talent, and aligning performance with your business direction.

Assessing talent includes a number of different steps:

- *Competency Modeling*
  Every organization has a strategy, but not all have people with the competencies to execute it. Competency modeling identifies the knowledge, skills, abilities, experiences, motivations, and personality traits an organization's workforce must develop to realize present and future strategic goals and enhance company agility, innovation, engagement, and retention. Well-designed competency models provide organizations with accurate criteria for optimizing performance management as well as talent assessment, hiring, development, redeployment, succession management, and promotion systems.

- *Organizational Assessment*
  In today's do-more-with-less business environment, higher productivity is often the single most important determinant of business success. An organizational assessment provides you with a clear understanding of how factors such as an organization's strategy, communications, leadership skills, employee processes, engagement levels, retention rates, and cultural alignment drive productivity. With accurate organizational assessment and value-added analyses, you better know how to increase employee engagement and retention, improve productivity, and realize business goals.

- *Individual and Team Assessment*
  The road to better business performance runs through the individual. The entire organization can benefit when individuals are recruited, onboarded, developed, and promoted, based on accurate, in-depth assessment. Individual assessment helps align your workforce with the organization's strategic imperatives by

evaluating the capabilities of individuals and their potential fit with the culture and climate of the organization. Team assessments increase employee engagement, improve team productivity, and help teams meet their objectives when linked with business strategy. These types of assessments help teams execute strategy and drive organizational performance.

Case Study

How do you ensure that culture becomes part of a talent strategy?

Business need:

- Leaders needed to be aligned to new business opportunities due to shifting industry dynamics and changing market needs. Provide top leaders with the skills needed to shape the strategic approach required to fulfill the firm's vision and goals.

Solution:

- We implemented a culture assessment to identify talent priorities for achieving business goals. This resulted in shaping a robust new talent strategy including branding, recruitment, and onboarding.
- We provided executive-level team alignment and leader coaching.
- We provided change management services that led to the first employee recognition program, creating a critical link to the firm's guiding principles.

Result:

- Business success factors included 300 percent expansion of desired client base, record financial growth, 150 percent growth in staff, and significant positive "press" in the community and within the firm.
- The Managing Partner was invited to join a prestigious firmwide leadership council.
- This successful process is being adopted by other business units.

---

2. Develop Leaders

To build global leadership capacity that is both deep and wide, you must continually identify, develop, nurture, and retain leaders as part of an ongoing talent development strategy.

Do you know where your next generation of leaders will come from? As organizations de-layer to contain costs, as demographic trends continue to shrink the pool of talent, and as the need for global leadership mind-sets and skills increase, the "leadership agenda" is ascending the scale of pressing business challenges. Building a pipeline creates the bench strength to fill leadership positions throughout the organization. Development is the first step in ensuring a steady flow of leaders to continue to grow the company over time.

Coaching as part of leadership development must be provided. The best coaching uniquely integrates the needs of the leader, his or her manager or sponsor, and the organization, to achieve the desired performance outcomes. As the challenges confronting organizations proliferate, such as globalization, economic turbulence, new business models, transformational technologies, changing demographics, and virtual working, bringing leaders to the peak of their potential with maximum efficiency assumes increasing urgency. Coaching can accelerate leader development and delivers performance improvements that lift the entire organization.

Case Study

How do we develop high-potential leaders more quickly?

Business need:

- A U.S. sales and distribution division of a global automotive company was concerned about sustainability and effectiveness of its leadership development initiatives. With 30,000 employees and a competitive marketplace, the company needed to identify and develop near-future leaders at a faster rate to outpace the competition.

Solution:

- Coaching for leaders.

Result:

- Nearly 40 percent of participants in each year's program have been promoted at or near the end of the program.
- More than 70 percent of participants achieved or exceeded their individual goals.
- Return on investment exceeded 5:1.

The next step is to start planning for succession. The value of this process is to focus not merely on who is next in line but also how to ensure a smooth, seamless transition from one leader to the next. Not merely the right skills but also the right commitment and demeanor are essential. Reacting quickly to change, restructuring for growth, and sustaining competitive advantage into the future are the outcomes of effective succession management, where both critical positions in the organization and key talent needs are addressed simultaneously. A growing number of company boards and executives are viewing succession management as an essential business process.

Ultimately, performance is the only metric that matters. Performance management ensures that your managers have the processes, tools, and skills needed to set goals, provide ongoing feedback and coaching, and evaluate performance effectively. In a volatile economy, the lean organization is the desired model more than ever. But it truly succeeds only when employees maximize performance. People perform better when they understand what is expected of them, participate in establishing performance goals, and receive continuous feedback and coaching. They perform best when their efforts are linked to the organization's strategy.

3. Implement and Align Strategy

Winning organizations create sustainable competitive advantage by aligning the workforce with business strategies. These companies pursue a well-articulated strategic direction in terms of execution, performance, and workforce management. Having a strategy is only half the challenge: Strategy implementation requires a sustainable, proactive process to effect a smooth transition that ensures employees understand and execute strategic imperatives and are operationally supported in doing their jobs.

There are three main components to implementing and aligning your workforce with the organization's strategy:

- *Implement strategy effectively.* Mergers, acquisitions, restructurings, and dynamic market conditions can all necessitate strategic change. You can execute strategic change by first understanding the complexities of the change and facing the realities of the external forces putting pressure on your business. Prioritize critical issues, analyze root causes of performance inhibitors, and identify capability gaps. Once strategy has been clearly articulated and agreed upon, clarify fit-for-purpose structures and roles, deploy people systems and processes, communicate with authenticity and regularity, and assign capable leadership at all levels. And finally, make sure you measure for impact on actual business performance.
- *Put strategy to work.* A winning strategy is no guarantee of successful results. Your workforce needs to be aligned with strategic objectives. Identify employee and workforce issues impeding strategy implementation. Prioritize workforce management strategies and align them with broader strategic goals. Use diagnostic tools to build executive team alignment around the organization's greatest strengths and needs. Identify top priorities, gain team consensus around priorities, analyze gaps between the organization's current state and the state of benchmark organizations, and then build collaborative approaches with the workforce to get the job done!
- *Manage change effectively.* More than half of the respondents in our recent employee engagement research[1] did not believe their senior leaders managed change effectively. You and your leaders need to take a greater role to ensure change is communicated and implemented effectively. Communicate openly and honestly, keep employees informed, solicit feedback from those impacted by change, and commit to meeting expectations. From the senior leader on down, the messaging must be consistent.

Case Study

How do you achieve organizational effectiveness when implementing a change initiative?

Business need:

- Significant cultural changes were necessary for an administrative organization due to the enactment of a new policy that would change their operating environment. It needed to form an effective strategy and approach to build an organization that could thrive in a new environment.

Solution:

- Using an effectiveness framework where core elements act as levers for cultural change, the discovery process at the onset was essential for uncovering workforce planning challenges and issues critical to the organization's success.
- To drive change from the top, a leadership engagement and alignment process helped the executive team build an organizational effectiveness strategy and implementation plan which included performance metrics and a process for engaging the next level of leaders in the plan.

Result:

- As the implementation process neared completion, the employee opinion survey showed that key staff engagement measures had exceeded first-year goals and had actually achieved the second year's goals as well.
- Client satisfaction scores reached 80 percent—a 13.6 percent increase over the previous year.

---

4. Engage Employees

Do your employees view working for you as a job or as a career? Are they aligned with corporate goals and strategies? Do they take pride in their work and ownership of their projects? In short, are they engaged?

The more employees know, the better they can perform. As leaders and human resource professionals, we need to clearly and effectively articulate business strategy, vision, mission, and purpose to the entire workforce. This will result in optimum engagement and employee contributions.

First, create a communications plan. Fluid strategies reflecting today's dynamic business conditions can make communicating business objectives very difficult. Yet a workforce that better understands your strategy is better able to execute it. Equip senior leaders and managers to convey clear, consistent messaging that links every employee to strategy and drives engagement, productivity, and success. Develop a comprehensive communication plan to carry employees at all levels from awareness and understanding to commitment and enhanced performance. Deliver messages in a clear and compelling manner and monitor the effectiveness of the delivery and its impact on strategic goals.

Invest in engaging and retaining your workforce. Employees need to feel they have a stake in the company's success. Help employees understand the significance of their role and how they directly participate in achieving the company's business objectives and performance goals—today and in the future. In a competitive environment, engagement can make the difference between an organization that thrives or barely survives. An engaged workforce is 50 percent more productive than a disengaged workforce and displays retention rates that are 44 percent higher.[2]

Case Study

How do you define and leverage the drivers of employee engagement?

Business need:

- A company of more than 1,200 cafes, employing 6,000 associates, needed to link its employee and customer metrics to key business drivers that improved performance.

Solution:

- We helped the company refine its "people metrics" with our measure of employee engagement as well as 360-feedback tools to identify key metrics impacting customer satisfaction.

Result:

- Based on our work, senior leaders can establish a direct link between high employee engagement scores and favorable customer experiences at the cafes.
- We have been able to isolate "key drivers" of employee engagement, thereby allowing the company to develop programs aimed at employee engagement that boosts customer satisfaction and, in turn, profits.

---

5. Aligning Your Workforce with Business Needs

Competitive market conditions and changing business objectives can necessitate the need to reassess workforce needs. It is about strategically mobilizing and sizing your workforce to meet the needs of your business, minimize turnover, and maintain employee productivity.

Assisting employees affected by organizational change to make the transition to a successful career outcome delivers real business value. Outplacement support must be provided to departing employees. Organizations offering effective outplacement support solidify their reputation for valuing employees and enhance the morale, engagement, and productivity of employees who remain.

Consideration should be given to redeployment before layoffs. Sooner or later, every business has to reinvent itself and every workforce has to adapt. Organizations that manage workforce transition successfully retain top talent, sustain productivity and employee engagement, and align workforce competencies with new organizational needs. Redeployment contributes to successful transitions by helping you to identify and reassign talented individuals to new roles or departments.

Redeployment also optimizes the benefits of change. Individuals make positive career moves without having to leave the organization. You retain talent, reduce severance costs, and reduce the costs of recruiting and training new talent to staff new departments. Demonstrating the organization's commitment to employees also improves employee morale, engagement, and productivity. Familiar with the ways of the organization, redeployed talent will have a shorter learning curve than new hires and will remain unavailable to be hired by the competition.

Employees should be provided with support to make informed career decisions. Offer employees access to resources to help them to better make career decisions. Allow individuals to explore what they want and what they offer the organization, and empower them to make considered decisions about the future of their career, whether inside or outside the organization.

Invest in ongoing career development. Encourage employees to develop skills and competencies aligned with organizational needs. Provide assessments and coaching to help employees create a detailed career map and action plan to take control of their careers. Helping high-potential employees develop their careers offers your organization a powerful engine for driving workforce engagement, retention, and productivity.

Case Study

How do you build a leadership framework to increase capacity and capability and meet growth targets?

Business need:

- A U.S.-based medical equipment and testing company needed its leaders to make strategic decisions faster, increase cross-functional and cross-business collaboration and synergy, and continue to improve their ability to engage and motivate a growing employee population in order to meet growth targets.

Solution:

- We helped the company build and implement an intensive, high-impact leadership program to build bench strength through accelerated development of top talent. During five rigorous sessions over 14 months, Fast Forward Leadership focused on participants' ability to drive organizational performance through improved skills. It helped leaders to: assume greater accountability for business results; increase ability to think/act more strategically and systemically; build "human capital" with improved attraction, retention, and development of key talent; lead the business and its people through significant change; and provide consistent and accurate clarification and direction.

Result:

- The business unit's revenues more than doubled in the first three years. Based on their success, this business unit is viewed as the growth engine for the enterprise.
- Over 60 percent of graduates from the first program were promoted or took on roles with greater levels of responsibility and influence—including several promoted to significant enterprise-level roles.
- A large percentage of succession charts for key positions across the enterprise are populated by program graduates.
- Past participants come back to co-teach/facilitate, sponsor action learning projects, and coach peer learning teams.

Creating a Culture of Success

A culture must be created that reflects values with which employees can identify. An organization's culture has a life of its own. No leader or group of leaders can control it entirely. However, leaders can influence a culture in ways that will drive engagement. The most effective leadership behavior is to show that you value employees. You must do more than simply say you value employee contributions. Make it real and demonstrate it. To maximize employee contribution, top management must be aligned and show employees that they really count. This includes continually acknowledging employees' ideas, contributions, values, and commitment.

Many options for talent acquisition, retention, development, redeployment, and transition exist. To evolve a culture of success, the key is to align the *right talent management* approaches to *your business strategy.*

Notes

1. Right Management's research into employee engagement was conducted in 2009 and included responses from 28,000 participants in 15 countries.
2. Weir, J. HR.com. 2003. Reporting findings of *First, Break All the Rules*, by Marcus Buckingham and Curt Coffman (Simon & Schuster, 1999), and *Now, Discover Your Strengths*, by Marcus Buckingham and Donald Clifton (The Free Press, 2001).

Chapter 33

Using Onboarding as A Talent Management Tool

David Lee, Principal
HumanNature@Work

What Is Onboarding?

Onboarding is the process of helping new employees become fully integrated, contributing members of your organization. Effective onboarding accomplishes the following objectives:

Makes new employees feel welcomed and valued.

Helps new employees feel connected to their peers and the organization's mission.

Provides new employees with whatever they need to become productive as quickly as possible and excel at their jobs.

Helps new employees understand and adopt cultural norms of excellence.

Communicates clearly what they need to do to become successful.

Inspires them.

Onboarding includes the initial orientation process and the ensuing 3 to 12 months, or however long it takes to get an employee up to speed in a particular company or discipline.

Why Is It Important to Get Onboarding Right?

Both common sense and research speak to why it is important to create an effective onboarding process. First, from the common-sense perspective, think of how much it costs your organization to recruit, screen, hire, and train new employees. Doesn't it make sense to protect this investment by ensuring you don't push your new hires overboard? Furthermore, doesn't it make sense to get a return on this investment as quickly as possible by helping new employees achieve 100 percent productivity as quickly as possible?

Benefits of Upgrading the Onboarding Process

It reduces turnover.

New hires make the decision to stay or look for a better employer rather quickly. A survey of HR professionals revealed that the 86 percent of new hires have made the decision on whether they will leave their new employer within the first six months of employment.

Improving onboarding can make a huge difference in turnover. When Hunter Douglas improved its onboarding process, turnover dropped from 70 percent at 6 months to 16 percent. The relationship between effective onboarding and turnover is especially critical among the Generation Y or Millennial workers who are less likely to tolerate an unpleasant or unsatisfying work experience.

It shortens the time new hires take to become productive and revenue-positive.

Every month a new hire performs below baseline productivity levels is a month of revenue lost. When Randstad, an international staffing company, upgraded the onboarding process for its account executives, it achieved an almost 500 percent increase in revenue generation per new employee.

It increases employee engagement.

A poor new hire experience can quickly extinguish the flame of enthusiasm most people bring to their new job. Conversely, a well-executed onboarding process can fan this flame, resulting in a passionate, proud, and determined employee. A 2003 study by Hewitt Associates demonstrating the connection between effective onboarding and engagement revealed that organizations that invested the most time and resources in onboarding enjoyed the highest levels of employee engagement (Hewitt Associates 2003).

Not surprisingly, employee engagement impacts the bottom line, according to a number of studies. Research by Towers Perrin, involving over 35,000 employees employed at dozens of companies, revealed that employee engagement affected sales growth, cost of goods sold, customer focus, and turnover. Companies with highly engaged employees surpassed the revenue growth of companies in the same sector with average engagement by 1 percent, while companies with low engagement were behind their sector's revenue growth by an average of 2 percent (Towers Perrin 2003).

Interestingly, employee engagement has an even more significant impact during difficult times, according to a study by Watson Wyatt Worldwide. In a study of 12,750 workers, Watson Wyatt found that employers with highly engaged employees outperformed their competitors by 47 percent during an up business cycle and by 200 percent in a down economy (Watson Wyatt 2002).

It affects management's credibility.

One of the under-recognized effects of poor onboarding is how it reflects poorly on an employer's leadership. Few factors affect a leader's ability to bring out the best in his or her workforce than trust. Whether the leader is trying to rally workers to embrace a new initiative, quell fears during a difficult time, or ask for even greater effort, leadership effectiveness is largely dependent on whether employees trust that their managers are truthful, have employees' best interests in mind, and know what they are talking about and what they are doing.

Because of the power of first impressions—and their intractability—it's imperative that the new hire experience evoke the above perceptions. If new hires get negative messages that this is a poorly run organization, one that doesn't recognize that helping employees succeed makes sense, future actions and decisions by management will be viewed with skepticism.

Guiding Onboarding Principles

Everything Matters

The concept "everything matters," an important tenet understood by world-class brand managers, should be adopted when you are developing an onboarding initiative. Every communication, decision, and interaction matters because it will have an effect—for better or for worse. There are no insignificant "moments of truth" in creating a strong brand, and the same can be said about onboarding. Everything you do—or don't do—in your onboarding process will affect new hires' perceptions about their jobs and employers.

Think "Experience"

Using another lesson from successful brand managers, organizations need to consciously design experiences that generate a strong positive response when developing new hire programs. Onboarding should be about consciously creating experiences that lead to positive emotions and perceptions, not just efficient transactions.

Emotional Take-aways

Every onboarding experience will leave an emotional impression—for better or for worse. Each step of the onboarding experience should leave the new hire with positive emotions such as feeling welcomed, comfortable, secure ("If I have a question, I know where to get the answer," or "I know enough to not feel in the dark"), valued, important, proud, excited, inspired, and confident.

Perceptual Take-aways

Designing positive employee experiences also involves consciously considering what perceptions you want to create in your new hires' minds. Desirable perceptual take-aways include these: "This is a well-run organization," "I'm part of an organization that is doing good things in the world," "They care about their people," "I can make a difference in this company," "This will be a fun place to work," and "I'm lucky to be working for this company."

Onboarding Is Everybody's Business

Onboarding isn't just "an HR thing." Since everything matters, everybody who comes into contact with new hires has an impact on their experience. Thus, all employees must be enlightened as to their role in onboarding and take accountability for their part in making onboarding successful.

Ask the Right Questions

Rather than trying to force-fit another employer's onboarding processes or an off-the-shelf solution into your organization, use questions that get at the "differences that make a difference." This will help create a tailor-made process that fits your organization.

In the next section, 11 questions will be posed that can guide your onboarding development and refinement processes. While it is important to ask yourself and your management these questions, it is even more important to ask your new hires.

11 Questions to Guide Your Onboarding Process

The following questions will help you shape your new hire process:

1. **How can successful onboarding processes be designed from a new hire's perspective?** Design your new hire experiences by viewing them through the new employee's eyes. If you want to create an employee-friendly work experience, new hire input must play a major role. Solicit input from new hires at ongoing intervals early in their employment so specific details are not lost through the passage of time. You need the particulars of each "moment of truth" if you are to intelligently design and refine your onboarding process. Find out what information is needed during each time period (i.e., surveyed at day two, week one, week two, one month of employment) and whether the new hire received it, and if so, whether it was readily available. Ask new employees what could be done to remove anxiety. Get their feedback on each of the questions in this chapter.

2. **How can new hires be made to feel welcomed and valued?** This is one of the most important goals of an onboarding process, especially in retaining and engaging Millennial workers. Practices that achieve this goal include the following:
   - Receiving a welcome letter or phone call from the hiring manager and future team members

- Meeting the hiring manager and team on the first day
- Receiving an e-mail with a link to a new employee portal that includes welcome videos from senior management and coworkers
- A sign in the company's lobby welcoming new employees
- A poster in the orientation room with welcome messages from team members
- Inviting senior-level executives to speak at orientation to inform new hires of their importance to organizational success

    Ask your new employees what can be done to create an even more welcoming message. Ask them about what their previous employers did—and didn't do—and what that meant to them.

3. **How can the orientation program be made more inspiring?** One of the critical roles of orientation is to communicate "What we do in this organization matters and what you do will help make that happen." By doing this, your orientation will address one of the most fundamental human needs: the need for meaning and purpose. When employees believe they are part of something great and that what they do matters, it unleashes a willingness to go the extra mile and a passion for excellence left untapped by people who feel like their job is just a paycheck. Orientations can be made inspiring by

- Sharing stories of how your products or services change lives.
- Presenting videos of appreciative customers talking about why they love your product or service.
- Discussing the organization's community involvement and contributions to worthy causes.
- Presenting examples of the great things employees do, especially of employees "going above and beyond" in both working hard, giving great service, or being resourceful.
- Offering examples of how employees have made a difference in your organization by coming up with innovative breakthroughs, process improvements, and so on.
- Having senior-level executives present and available for questions.

4. **How can new employees' understanding of the big picture and their role in accomplishing it be clearly communicated?** A study by Harris Interactive involving 23,000 employees revealed that only 37 percent of employees interviewed had a clear understanding of what their employer was trying to achieve and why (Covey 2004). It is no wonder that numerous studies reveal the dismal level of employee engagement both in the United States and abroad. How can employees be excited and committed to something they know little about? How can employees maximize their contribution if they don't know what matters most to their employer and how they can provide the most value? Thus, an onboarding program should help new employees understand the organization's

- Business and how the pieces fit together
- Mission in understandable and concrete terms
- Success factors

- Cultural norms and valued behaviors
- Current marketplace factors

In addition, the new employee needs to understand how his or her department or team, and his or her position contribute to the big picture, as well as how his or her department affects other parts of the organization.

Given the complexity of many organizations, covering all of these items might be best accomplished with a mixture of live lectures, online learning, and one-on-one coaching.

5. **How can the orientation program be made more fun and interactive?** This is important for two reasons: First, people learn more effectively if they are not passive recipients of data, and second, delivering a fun, interactive orientation program elicits positive emotional and perceptual take-aways. Fun and interactive orientations communicate: "This place is different," "They know what they're doing," and "This is going to be an enjoyable working environment."

Adding fun and interactivity also improves learning, thereby increasing the effectiveness of the orientation program. To make your orientation more fun and interactive, you can

- Use a game show format and divide new hires into teams.
- Use a "scavenger hunt" approach to learning about different departments, key resources, and so on.

For more ideas on how to enliven an orientation program, conduct an Internet search for training games and accelerated learning.

6. **Should the orientation program be digested in small chunks?** Orientation marathons are ineffective. When people are expected to digest large chunks of information in long sessions, very little is retained. Furthermore, lengthy orientations leave new hires with engagement-damaging emotional and perceptual take-aways.

An excellent example of breaking down a long orientation comes from Northeast Delta Dental, a New Hampshire company and winner of multiple 25 Best Small Companies to Work for in America awards. Evaluations revealed that new hires were overwhelmed by Northeast Delta Dental's one-day orientation program, so they spread the material over two days. However, evaluations of this approach revealed that new hires were still overwhelmed. So, based on a suggestion from a new employee, the company conducted the program in four half-days. This proved to be ideal.

7. **What information is best delivered to new hires through the intranet or other means?** Subjecting new hires to information they don't need during the early phase of employment or that could be better digested by reading on their own is a waste of valuable time for all involved. It also creates the perception that "This is an employer that doesn't know what it is doing." Involve your instructional designers and learning specialists to sort through orientation and training content for what needs to be taught in person and what would best be delivered in a self-study and as-needed mode. For

example, Southwest Airlines created an online "pre-orientation video" for new hires. This opened up time to cover topics that were best discussed in a live setting.

8. **How can new employees be prepared to be proficient and productive more rapidly?** At the most obvious level, the better you are at preparing new hires for success, the quicker you achieve a positive ROI. The impact, though, goes deeper. Your ability to set new hires up for "the thrill of victory" dramatically affects their level of engagement, inspiration, and job satisfaction. Furthermore, providing new hires with the tools, knowledge, and training needed to excel creates very different emotional take-aways than carelessly allowing them to flounder. The following questions can help frame an action plan:

   - What knowledge does the employee need?
   - What skills need to be developed?
   - Who are the people/mentors who can help?
   - What experiences would help? (e.g., interactions with other departments, shadowing a seasoned sales rep)
   - What activities should he or she be able to perform?
   - How will the company provide ongoing feedback to help the new employee evaluate his or her progress and accomplishments?

   Ask these questions of your hiring managers for each position they supervise and include time frames. Then translate this into checklists and protocols.

9. **How can new employees be encouraged to solicit help or to give feedback?** Most employees are conscious of not wanting to appear as if they are "high maintenance" or anything but "can-do people." Furthermore, most managers are busy—and often overwhelmed. This combination is a recipe for new employees developing an "I'll just suck it up and make the best of it" attitude. Smart employers make it clear to employees—new or otherwise—that they desire feedback about anything that compromises the employee's ability to perform his or her job well. Thus, at every stage of the onboarding process, explicitly communicate that you want and need your new hires to speak up and let you know how the onboarding experience can be improved, and how you can do a better job helping them excel.

   The impact of making it easy for new hires to speak up cannot be overstated. At Designer Blinds, an Omaha-based company, HR Manager Deb Franklin discovered that most of their new employees were leaving between the second and sixth month. Rather than waiting for the exit interview to find out why, they created an "entrance interview" just prior to the second month of employment. This procedure and the resulting actions enabled the company to reduce turnover from 200 percent to 8 percent.

   Besides including an employee interview within the first 90 days as part of the onboarding process, successful employers also provide checklists soliciting feedback from new employees for hiring managers, as well as a checklist of questions new hires should be asking their manager.

10. **How can the mentoring program be made more effective?** Whether the term "mentor," "buddy," "sponsor," or some other label is used, you want to link your new hires with a veteran employee or multiple employees. A mentor is more often a highly experienced employee who can help the new hire grow professionally, while the role of a buddy or sponsor is to help in navigating the new organization. You don't want to haphazardly throw together a mentor or buddy program. How well mentors and buddies are selected and prepared will have a profound impact on the emotional and perceptual take-aways created. It will also make a big difference in whether seasoned employees view being a mentor or buddy as just another task or as an honor and professional development opportunity.

11. **How can managers be prepared to do their part well?** Because the hiring manager plays a central role in the success and happiness of the new hire, it is imperative that they

    - Understand the crucial role they play.
    - Receive the training and coaching necessary to do their part well.
    - Be held accountable for doing their part well.
    - Receive logistical support in the form of systems and template processes so they can do their part well.

Without managers having the commitment and ability to do their part, the onboarding program will be marginally effective. This is why it is important to communicate "onboarding is everybody's job."

3M is an example of an employer that helps their managers do their part well. Prior to their new hire coming on board, managers receive an e-mail from the onboarding team containing a link to an online module, *Preparing for a New Employee*. Two days prior to the new employee's arrival, managers receive another e-mail with a link to the online module *Welcoming the New Employee*. After that, hiring managers receive e-mails with links to other online modules corresponding to their new employee's onboarding phase. At 3M, communicating to managers the critical role they play in onboarding has been a significant component of their onboarding upgrade. This message, along with the "how to" has been integrated into 3M's three-day supervisory development course. Preparing and supporting their managers' important role in onboarding has paid off, as evidenced by employee feedback reporting significant improvement in new hires' perceptions of their managers and employer.

Summary

Utilizing the 11 suggested guidelines can result in an upgraded onboarding process for your organization. Your organization can also reap the following benefits:

1. Shortening the time for new employees to become productive and revenue generating
2. Minimizing the cost of poorly trained new hires, in terms of substandard quality and customer service

3. Reducing turnover
4. Increasing engagement
5. Establishing leadership credibility

References

Covey, Stephen, R. 2004. *The eighth habit: From effectiveness to greatness*. New York: Free Press.

Hewitt Associates. 2003. Best employer to work for in Australia. Available at http://was2.hewitt.com/bestemployers/anz/pdfs/bereport2003e.pdf.

Towers Perrin. 2003. Working today: Understanding what drives employee engagement. The 2003 Towers Perrin Talent Report. Available at http://www.towersperrin.com/tp/getwebcachedoc?webc=hrs/usa/2003/200309/talent_2003.pdf.

Rana, Eila. 2002. When employees go the extra mile, does the bottom line benefit? *CFO Magazine*. Feb 8, 2008. http://www.cfo.com/article.cfm/10610786/c_2984355/?f= archives

Watson Wyatt Worldwide. 2002. WorkUSA 2002. Weathering the Storm: A Study of Employee Attitudes and Opinions.

Chapter 34

Employee Engagement and Talent Management

Deborah Schroeder-Saulnier
Director of Marketing, Senior Vice President, Global Solutions
Right Management

Synopsis

Among talent management issues, none is, perhaps, more essential to building a culture of organizational success than employee engagement. A direct line can be drawn through engagement to retention, productivity, customer satisfaction, and financial performance. Yet research by Right Management and others suggests that engagement levels at many organizations worldwide are disturbingly low and may have been falling for many years. Drawing for the most part on evidence gathered by a Right Management study of organizational effectiveness involving nearly 30,000 representative employees globally, this chapter will consider the nature and importance of engagement, the challenges that engagement poses for many organizations, and the key drivers that must be addressed if these challenges are to be met. It concludes with some best-practice advice on how organizations can reverse the trend and make engagement a cornerstone of their success.

Engagement Matters

Employee engagement needs to be understood as more than a simple matter of satisfaction or commitment. While it includes these elements, it also encompasses pride and a willingness to advocate on behalf of an employer—speak highly of the organization's products and services and recommend the organization as a highly desirable place to work. It must also be understood as involving attitudes connected with both the job and the organization. It is possible to feel engaged by the job but not by the organization, in which case the employee may be making an important contribution to organizational performance but is essentially a "free agent" primed to move to perceived greener pastures. Alternatively, it is also possible to feel engaged by the organization and not the job, in which case the employee is essentially a "benchwarmer" content to cheer the organization from the sidelines without making a contribution to meeting its performance goals. Satisfaction, commitment, pride, and advocacy in relation to both job and organization constitute the essential elements of engagement.

When organizations address these essential elements, good things follow. Intuition alone suggests that engaged employees are more likely to be loyal and productive. A large and growing body of research has confirmed this.[1] Our study of organizational effectiveness found strong correlations between employee engagement and retention, productivity, customer satisfaction, and organizational performance. For example, engaged employees were

- 6.5 times more likely to identify their organization as one of the best-performing organizations in its sector than to identify it as a below-average performer
- 1.5 times more likely than disengaged employees to indicate that they would stay with their organization for at least 5 years
- Nearly 2 times more likely than disengaged employees to say that customers think highly of their organization's products and services

While our study recorded employee perceptions, it isn't unreasonable to assume that these perceptions have a basis in fact and that engagement is an essential building block of organizational effectiveness.

The Engagement Challenge

Even as our study supports this conclusion, it also reveals a troubling lack of engagement among the 28,810 employees we surveyed across 10 sectors in 15 countries worldwide. Testing for engagement understood as satisfaction, commitment, pride, and advocacy in relation to both job and organization, we found that only about 34 percent of employees globally could be defined as fully engaged. Nine percent indicated that they were benchwarmers—those engaged by their organization but not their job. Seven percent indicated that they were free agents—those engaged by their jobs but not their organization. And 50 percent indicated that they were engaged by neither their organization nor their job.

This picture is no more encouraging when results are considered by country. While levels of engagement exceeded the global average in several countries, no single country showed levels above 50 percent. The highest levels of engagement were recorded in India at 45 percent, the United States at 44 percent, and New Zealand at 43 percent. European engagement levels were at or near the global average, with France and Germany at 30 percent, the UK at 33 percent, and Sweden at 34 percent. The lowest scores came from Asia, with China at 29 percent, South Korea at 18 percent, and Japan at 11 percent.

The engagement figure for the United States (44 percent) is consistent with a Conference Board study of 5,000 U.S. households, which found that only 45 percent of U.S. employees are satisfied with their jobs. While job satisfaction constitutes only one of the essential elements of engagement, the Conference Board finding, nevertheless, provides valuable evidence corroborating the results of Right Management's survey. Even more importantly, it offers some historical perspective on U.S. job satisfaction and, by extension, engagement, since it is only the latest contribution to an ongoing Conference Board initiative that has been monitoring job satisfaction since 1987. This initiative has recorded a significant, steady, almost uninterrupted decline in U.S. job satisfaction for more than two decades. During this period, job satisfaction has fallen by 16 percent, from 61 percent in 1987 to 45 percent today.[2] Clearly, if these historical findings are representative, low and/or declining engagement cannot be understood as a cyclical issue tied to a given set of economic or business conditions. The issue is structural.

The Drivers of Engagement

How can organizations meet the engagement challenge and improve their performance? Identifying the drivers of engagement is a necessary first step. Our study of organizational effectiveness provides significant insights into what these drivers are. We designed our study to cohere with—and, in effect, to test—a conceptual model of organizational effectiveness that sees (1) employee engagement as the key determinant of (2) customer satisfaction and, from there, organizational performance.

Figure 34-1 Organization Effectiveness Conceptual Model

This model posits that engagement is, in turn, determined by (3) leadership; (4) structure, roles, and capability; and (5) people systems and processes when aligned with (6) strategy, and embedded in (7) a positive work culture.

Our study asked respondents to indicate their level of agreement or disagreement with 100 statements addressing these 7 essential elements of organizational performance. Some statements pertained to customer experience and engagement, and others to strategy; culture; leadership; structure, roles and capability; and people systems, and processes. Leadership statements were further divided into those addressing (3a) senior leaders and (3b) immediate managers, while people systems and processes statements were further divided into those addressing (5a) communications, (5b) recognition and reward, (5c) learning and development, and (5d) work processes.

The 100 statements, in other words, were grouped into 11 different categories and subcategories connected with organizational effectiveness. The responses to these statements were then analyzed to test for statistically significant correlations between responses indicating full engagement and positive responses to (i.e., agreement or strong agreement with) statements belonging to the 10 other broad groupings. While correlation should never be confused with causality, the existence of a strong correlation provides reasonable grounds for concluding that the elements in question are causally related. Our analysis revealed just such statistically strong correlations between engagement and the aggregated responses of statements in each of the other categories of organizational effectiveness.

A Broad Systemic Approach

The first, most general insight our study offers is that our model of organizational effectiveness is supported by empirical evidence. The responses of nearly 30,000 employee participants suggest that engagement can be optimized when leadership, structure, roles and capability, and people systems and processes are aligned with an appropriate strategy and embedded in a positive work culture. Maximizing levels of employee engagement requires a broad, systemic approach. Any organization adopting and executing such an approach can be reasonably confident of realizing the predicted effect.

Group Drivers of Engagement

Beyond this general insight, our study also provides a more discriminating view of what drives engagement. Not every element of our model impacts engagement equally. From most to least, the 10 categories and subcategories already mentioned correlate with engagement in the following order:

1. Work processes (a subcategory of people systems and processes)
2. Learning and development (a subcategory of people systems and processes)
3. Culture
4. Senior leaders (a subcategory of leadership)
5. Communication (a subcategory of people systems and processes)

6. Structure, roles, and capability
7. Recognition and reward (a subcategory of people systems and processes)
8. Customer focus
9. Strategy
10. Immediate managers (a subcategory of leadership)

While all of these factors should be considered group drivers of engagement, some of these group drivers are more significant than others. Ensuring that good work processes govern the workplace and that employees are provided with effective career development opportunities will do most to promote engagement, while ensuring that strategy and immediate managers are engagement friendly will do least. Work processes and learning and development belong to the people systems and processes category. It only makes sense that process or system designed to enable productive performance and behaviors among individuals should have a greater impact on engagement than strategy, which is more distant from people's everyday work experience. Three of the top five group drivers are within people systems and processes subcategories.

The correlation between engagement and customer focus deserves special consideration. To an extent, it seems plausible to regard customer focus as an engagement driver. Consisting of such statements as "our customers think highly of our products and services," customer focus can be seen as contributing to an employee's pride in his or her job and organization. Pride is, of course, an essential element of engagement. On the other hand, it also seems plausible, perhaps more plausible, to interpret the engagement-customer focus correlation as indicating that engagement drives customer focus. An engaged employee is more likely to focus on meeting customer needs than is a disengaged employee. The relationship between engagement and customer focus may be dialectical: Engagement drives customer focus and customer focus, in turn, drives engagement.

Another correlation deserving special notice is that between engagement and reward and recognition. This correlation ranks only seventh on the list. While reward and recognition are important to engagement, they are by no means most important. Simply increasing rewards and recognition for employees is unlikely to help an organization meet its engagement challenges in any meaningful way.

Individual Drivers of Engagement

As well as providing insight into group drivers of engagement, our study also reveals the most important individual drivers. We tested for correlations not only between engagement and broad groups or categories but also between engagement and the individual statements composing these categories. Of the study's 91 statements not part of the engagement category, the following 10 show, in order, the highest correlations with engagement:

1. I am committed to my organization's core values (strategy).
2. Our customers think highly of our products and services (customer focus).

3. My opinions count (people systems and processes: communications).
4. I have a clear understanding of what is expected of me at work (structure, roles, and capability).
5. I understand how I can contribute to meeting the needs of our customers (customer focus).
6. I have been fairly rewarded (people systems and processes: recognition and reward).
7. Senior leaders value employees (leadership: senior leaders).
8. Everyone is treated with respect at work regardless of who they are (culture).
9. I can concentrate on my job when I am at my work area (people systems and processes: work processes).
10. My personal work objectives are linked to my work area's business plan (strategy).

Respondents who identified themselves as fully engaged were more inclined to agree or strongly agree with the statement "I am committed to my organization's core values" than with any other. While responses to the strategy statements considered as a whole showed a relatively low correlation with engagement (strategy is the ninth-place group driver), this particular strategy statement ranks first among 91. Responses to individual statements provide a slightly different perspective on engagement than the group drivers do. They show, for example, that, if organizations can take only one step to drive engagement, this step should be to pursue a business strategy reflecting core values employees can identify with. Organizations pursuing strategies that conflict with the values of their employees do so at their own peril.

Several of these top individual engagement drivers are clearly related. Ensuring that the opinions of employees count is one way that senior leaders can show that they value employees. Valuing employees and attending to their opinions are both, in turn, ways in which organizations can treat employees with respect regardless of who they are.

While several of the statements listed suggest the relative complexity involved in driving engagement (just how do you ensure that employees are committed to the organization's core values or that employee opinions count?), others imply fairly clear, concrete prescriptions. Enhancing engagement can be as simple as ensuring that employees are assigned work areas where they can concentrate, are informed of what is expected of them, and are fairly rewarded.

Best-Practice Recommendations

Some best-practice recommendations have already been offered, the most important being that organizations can do most to increase engagement by adopting a systemic approach in alignment with our organizational effectiveness framework. The following six additional recommendations are closely tied to group drivers.

Promote Wellness in the Workplace.

Work processes, a subcategory of people systems and processes, is identified by our study as the top group driver of engagement. Of the 13 statements composing the work processes section of the study, 7 can be interpreted as addressing in some form the physical and psychological wellness of employees:

- I have an appropriate workload.
- The amount of pressure I experience in my role is reasonable.
- Processes and procedures in my work environment promote safe working conditions.
- I work in a safe and healthy environment.
- You can balance work and personal interests at my organization and still progress.
- My organization actively promotes health and well-being.
- My organization allows me to maintain a reasonable balance between my family and work life.

Creating safe working conditions and procedures should be an obvious imperative for any responsible employer. Less obvious is the counterintuitive suggestion that demanding less of employees can actually lead to more. Employees, our results show, are likely to be more engaged and therefore more productive if their workload is appropriate, if the pressures they face are reasonable, and if they are allowed to maintain some form of balance in their lives.

Organizations can realize even higher engagement gains if in addition to creating these wellness-inducing processes, they also promote health and well-being actively. Formal wellness initiatives, especially when shaped by the strategic goals of the company, can have a strong impact on engagement. Our study shows that employees are eight times more likely to be engaged when well-being is a priority in the workplace. In organizations perceived as actively promoting health and well-being, 55 percent of employees reported being engaged. In organizations not so perceived, by contrast, only 7 percent of employees reported being engaged.

Provide Career Development Opportunities

Learning and development, a subcategory of people systems and processes, is the second most important group driver of engagement behind work processes. "There are career opportunities for me at my organization," a statement grouped under learning and development, is the 15th highest individual driver of engagement. Yet our study reveals that globally only 48 percent of employees feel that their organization provides them with career development opportunities. It also reveals that employees are six times more likely to be engaged when such opportunities are provided. Fifty-four percent of employees who responded favorably to the statement, "There are career opportunities for me at my organization," reported being engaged. That figure compares to an engagement rate of only 9 percent among employees who responded unfavorably to this statement.

Make Engagement a Leadership Priority.

Among items grouped under senior leadership, valuing employees, communicating organizational strategy to employees, and leading by example are key engagement drivers. So too are the following items grouped under immediate manager: Provide the support employees need to do their job well, facilitate discussions about career development, and explain the link between the employee's role and the organization's strategy. Helping leaders and immediate managers develop and refine the competencies enabling them to perform these tasks will go a long way toward meeting the engagement challenge.

Create an Engagement Culture

Creating a positive work culture, according to our study, is the third most important group driver of engagement. Statements in this category stress not only treating people with respect (the eighth-highest individual driver of engagement) and valuing diversity but also empowering the individual. Engagement is positively impacted when people are encouraged to make appropriate changes to the way things are done, to come up with new and better ways of doing things, and to pursue creativity and innovation.

Stress Effective Communication

Employees want to work for successful organizations and to feel that they are contributing to that success. They need to know that their opinions count, to be clear about what is expected of them, to understand their organization's strategy, and to see how their work objectives are linked to their work area's business plan. Clear and meaningful communication from leaders to employees but also from employees to leaders (how can employee opinions count unless employees are encouraged to voice them?) should be a primary engagement priority.

Conclusion

Organizations around the world face a structural crisis of engagement and productivity transcending any particular turn in the business cycle. Only 34 percent of employees globally report being fully engaged, and there is evidence to suggest that engagement levels have been falling for over two decades. Tackling this crisis to greatest effect requires a systemic approach involving strategy; leadership; structure, roles, and capability; people systems and processes; and culture. Leadership, culture and people systems and processes governing work processes, learning and development, and communication have a special role to play, as do individual drivers of engagement such as ensuring that strategy reflects appropriate values and that employee opinions count. When the systemic, group, and individual drivers of engagement are addressed on their own and in concert, an organization can expect to see marked improvements in retention, productivity, customer satisfaction, and financial performance.

Notes

1. See Holbeche, L., and N. Springett. 2003. *In Search of Meaning in the Workplace*, Horsham, Roffey Park; Harter, J. K., Schmidt, F. L. and Hayes, T. L. (2002), "Business-Unit-Level Relationship Between Employee Satisfaction, Employee Engagement, and Business Outcomes: A Meta-Analysis," *Journal of Applied Psychology*, 87, 268–279; Maslach, C., Schaufeli, W. B., and Leiter, M. P. (2001), "Job Burnout," *Annual Review of Psychology*, 52, 397–422; Kahn, W. A. (1990), "Psychological Conditions of Personal Engagement and Disengagement at Work," *Academy of Management Journal*, 33, 692–724; May, D. R., Gilson, R. L., and Harter, L. M. (2004), "The Psychological Conditions of Meaningfulness, Safety and Availability and the Engagement of the Human Spirit at Work," *Journal of Occupational and Organizational Psychology*, 77, 11–37; Schaufeli, W. B., Bakker, A., and Salanova, M. (2006), "The Measurement of Work Engagement with a Short Questionnaire: A Cross-National Study," *Educational and Psychological Measurement*, 66, 701–716; Gonrig, M. P. (2008), "Customer Loyalty and Employee Engagement: An Alignment For Value," *Journal of Business Strategy*, 29, 29–40; Seijts, G. H., and Crim, D. (2006), "What Engages Employees the Most, or the Ten Cs of Employee Engagement," *Ivey Business Journal*, March/April, 1–5; Attridge, M. (2009), "Employee Work Engagement: Best Practices For Employers," *Research Works: Partnership for Workplace Mental Health*, 1, 1–11.
2. Lynn, F., J. Gibbons, and L. Barrington. 2009. I can't get no . . . job satisfaction, that is: America's unhappy workers. *The Conference Board*, 3.

Chapter 35

Crafting a Culture of Creativity and Innovation

Fredericka K. Reisman, Ph.D., Professor and Director
Drexel/Torrance Center for Creativity and Innovation
Theodore A. Hartz, MBA, Executive Director of Customized Learning Solutions
Drexel University Goodwin College of Professional Studies
Co-Director, *Drexel/Torrance Center for
Creativity and Innovation*

WHY IS AN UNDERSTANDING OF CREATIVITY AND INNOVATION IMPORTANT FOR TALENT managers?

Talent managers are active participants in making strategic decisions that directly impact the creative work environment. They are actively involved in an organization's effort to build a structure or process to support creativity and innovation: to help ideas to be generated, vetted, resourced, and championed, and to eventually become innovations. This has many different names at various organizations. For this chapter it will be referred to as the "innovation process," the pathway from creativity to implementation.

The results of a 2007 Ipsos Public Affairs Poll indicated the existence of a "Creativity Gap" in the United States. Employees believe they are creative (88 percent), but they do not find their positions at work (63 percent) or their companies (61 percent) to be creative. The same poll indicated that 27 percent of employees would change jobs, even if it meant less money, to be more creative at work, and this was especially true for Millennial employees (ages 18 to 34), where 37 percent were willing to make the change. Twenty-nine percent of those surveyed indicated they would change where they live if it meant being part of a more creative community (creativeeconomics.org). Talent managers need to develop strategies to address the creative needs of all workers and especially the younger generation. Talent managers stand at the front line of the battle to fill the creativity gap at their organizations. Although these results demonstrate an important challenge, many companies have changed to embrace the creativity of their people, resulting in increases in creative output and reductions in employee turnover. It can happen in any organization, in any industry.

An organization's sustainable success in the future will derive from its ability to leverage the creativity generated from the minds of its employees. It's time to go beyond the slogans, ("Our people are our most important asset") and realize the future depends on the ideas created, the designs originated, and the innovations implemented from the brain power of our employees. Having a solid understanding of creativity theory, research, and best-practice cases is invaluable. It allows talent managers to "influence change through knowledge" to help establish novel yet useful approaches. It becomes a solid foundation to guide human resource policy setting and provides a better understanding of employee behavior. This chapter is an introduction, to the role of talent management in crafting a culture of innovation and creativity.

Informal discussions were held with 20 leaders from a variety of different types of organizations in support of this chapter. They answered questions concerning creativity and how it relates to talent management in their companies and industries. A number of Industry Concern Points emerged from the discussions and they form the framework of this chapter. A discussion is presented for each point providing research results followed by Best Practice Notes, which present practical implications of the research and some best-practice examples. Two attachments are included: first, Table 35-1 is a Creativity Theory Toolkit which provides a brief description of various theories and some practical implications for talent managers, and, second, Appendix A, Creativity Tools and Techniques, introduces ways to implement creativity in the workplace

Creativity Theorist	Main Ideas	Relevance to Talent Managers
	**1. What are the creative processes used by creative people?**	
Graham Wallas (1858–1932)	Graham Wallas model contains five stages for creative thinking: 1. Preparation—Focuses on the problem and explores the problem's dimensions 2. Incubation—Subconscious mulling of the problem 3. Intimation—Inkling that a solution is on its way 4. Illumination—Discovery; "Eureka!" 5. Verification—Focus on practicality, effectiveness, appropriateness	Provides a structured approach to creative problem solving. Understanding this is essential especially when considering the development of a creativity and innovation structure or process in your firm. The structure needs to provide time and involve a variety of employees. Today's knowledge management systems are greatly beneficial to this process.

Table 35-1 Creativity Theory Toolkit and Relevance to Talent Managers (continued on next page)

Creativity Theorist	Main Ideas	Relevance to Talent Managers

Sid Parnes (1922–) and Alex Osborn (1888–1966)	Creative problem-solving model focused on using creativity in advertising. Component stages included both divergent (d) and convergent (c) processes:
	
	  I. Understanding the problem
	  II. Generating ideas
	  III. Planning for action
	  IV. Acceptance finding
		Provides another look at the creative problem-solving process. See http://creatingminds.org/tools/brain storming.htm. A solid understanding of the difference between divergent and convergent processes is important.

Mihaly Csikszentmihalyi (1934–)	Focus is on the interplay among the creative person (the individual), the domain (the discipline), and the field (the experts/gatekeepers).	The individual is the talent manager, the domain is the discipline of creativity, and the field is composed of the gatekeepers, e.g., CEOs whose decisions either allow or inhibit individual and/or group innovation. This may help you influence change in your organization.
	Also, discussed "flow" experiences.	Flow involves energy that focuses attention and motivates action.
Teresa Amabile (1950–)	Motivation is central to Amabile's research: intrinsic motivation is more apt to generate creativity than extrinsic motivation.	Establish diverse teams, perhaps from different company departments, to foster different perspectives, exploration, and debate. Teams should comprise variety in expertise, creative-thinking styles, and cognitive abilities. This leads to divergent ideas and innovative solutions.
	**2. What does a creative person look like?**	
Ellis Paul Torrance (1915–2003)	Building on Guilford's work, Torrance developed the Torrance Tests of Creative Thinking	Managers of creativity facilitate original thinking, fluency and flexibility of ideas, elaboration, smart risk taking, tolerance of ambiguity, resistance to premature closure
Robert J. Sternberg (1949–)	Presented two ideas: 1. Triarchic Theory of Human Intelligence. Creativity is balance among three forms of thinking: analytical, creative, and practical.	Talent managers often deal with training on *analytical* thinking that includes having to analyze, critique, judge, compare/contrast, evaluate, assess. *Creative* tasks deal with the ability to invent, discover, imagine, suppose, predict; *practical* intelligence is involved in everyday problem solving.

Table 35-1 Creativity Theory Toolkit and Relevance to Talent Managers (continued on next page)

Creativity Theorist	Main Ideas	Relevance to Talent Managers
	2. Sternberg compared creativity to investment activities of buying low and selling high.	Investment theory highlights perseverance in selling one's creative idea(s); talent managers need to do this both within their discipline and also to the field (see Csikszentmihalyi).
Abraham Maslow (1908–1970)	Hierarchy of Human Needs 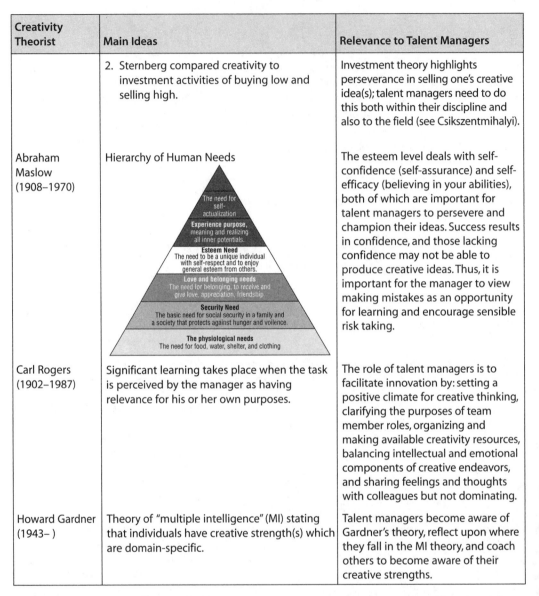	The esteem level deals with self-confidence (self-assurance) and self-efficacy (believing in your abilities), both of which are important for talent managers to persevere and champion their ideas. Success results in confidence, and those lacking confidence may not be able to produce creative ideas. Thus, it is important for the manager to view making mistakes as an opportunity for learning and encourage sensible risk taking.
Carl Rogers (1902–1987)	Significant learning takes place when the task is perceived by the manager as having relevance for his or her own purposes.	The role of talent managers is to facilitate innovation by: setting a positive climate for creative thinking, clarifying the purposes of team member roles, organizing and making available creativity resources, balancing intellectual and emotional components of creative endeavors, and sharing feelings and thoughts with colleagues but not dominating.
Howard Gardner (1943–)	Theory of "multiple intelligence" (MI) stating that individuals have creative strength(s) which are domain-specific.	Talent managers become aware of Gardner's theory, reflect upon where they fall in the MI theory, and coach others to become aware of their creative strengths.

Table 35-1 Creativity Theory Toolkit and Relevance to Talent Managers (Continued)

Industry Concern Point 1: Creativity versus Innovation

How does creative thinking differ from innovation? Creative thinking generates the creative novel ideas; innovation is the process of implementing these creative ideas. Many believe that creative thinking is synonymous with divergent thinking, which involves elaboration and thinking of diverse and original ideas with fluency and speed (e.g., brainstorming). But this is only one component of creative thinking; convergent thinking also is involved. Convergent thinking includes narrowing ideas by evaluating the previously generated ideas that emerged in the divergent portion of the sequence (e.g., settling upon an idea from a selection of ideas).

Graham Wallas in 1926 depicted creativity as a process with five stages:

1. Preparation (preparatory work on a problem that focuses the individual's mind on the problem and explores the problem's dimensions)
2. Incubation (where the problem is internalized into the unconscious mind and nothing appears externally to be happening)
3. Intimation (the creative person gets a "feeling" that a solution is on its way)
4. Illumination or insight (where the creative idea bursts forth from its preconscious processing into conscious awareness, sometimes referred to as the Eureka moment)
5. Verification (where the idea is consciously verified, elaborated, and then applied)

Sometimes the Wallas model is shown as four stages with intimation incorporated into the incubation stage. This model is used as a problem-solving tool and has provided structure to many innovation processes implemented by organizations. Sundgren and Styhre support the process view of creativity and argue that creativity does not occur at a single point in time (hire the right consultant or buy in special talent) but is rather the outcome from a series of interconnected events and undertakings (planned strategies). A process-based view of creativity can thus escape the misplaced concreteness that the mythology of creativity postulates. Drucker defines innovation as "the effort to create purposeful, focused change in an enterprise's economic or social potential."

Best Practice Notes: Creativity versus Innovation

Not allowing adequate time for incubation causes many firms to be less innovative. It is very important to provide opportunities for teams to move away from projects for a time and return with fresh thoughts. Some organizations have various types of activities to allow team members to divert their minds to other areas and eventually bring a renewed perspective to their primary project. Firms, including Pixar Animation Studios, have interdisciplinary team members working on a primary film project but also play a smaller role in others. This mishmash of tasks allows them to focus and refocus during the creativity process. Demanding creativity by the clock, a "brains to the grindstone" approach is very problematic. Many people feel they are most creative when faced with tight time constraints, but research does not support this view (Amabile, Hadley, and Kramer 2002). Obviously, projects have timelines, movies do need to hit the theaters, and "innovation needs to ship," but too much emphasis on time can lead to "the pressure trap"; the drop in creative thinking becomes most apparent when time pressure is the greatest.

Industry Concern 2: Characteristics of Creative Individuals

Many leaders thought of creativity as a domain reserved for a small segment of their workforce—the CEO or C suite team, the talented ones, the R&D group, the eggheads, or even outside consultants.

"Whether it's farming, the production of automobiles, or hair cutting, every job has a creative component, and every person is creative" (Florida 2010). Although every person is creative, and anyone with normal intelligence can thrive in an innovation process, there are some individuals who are more creative than others. The creativity literature points to certain traits that distinguish highly creative individuals from colleagues. These traits include a high level of curiosity, willingness to learn from experience, preparedness to take risks, persistence in situations of failure, high levels of energy, and distinctive goal orientation. Creative people typically tolerate contradictions, ambiguities, and uncertainties in their work. Many terms represent creativity, such as original, relevant, influential, innovative, out-of-the-box, fluent, flexible, divergent, open, generative, nonjudgmental, and courageous. Other descriptions include "is a risk taker," "resists premature closure," and "tolerates ambiguity." Three currently prevalent descriptors of creativity are *novel,* which refers to something original and unique, *appropriate* or suitable, and *useful,* which means serving a purpose.

Highly creative workers ask more questions; they thrive on inquiry and discovery. Sometimes the questions do not seem to be to the point. They seem to take longer to get ready to solve problems and may see problems as more complex. Sometimes this is referred to the "mountain out of a molehill" challenge, but they are more perceptive and notice more possibilities. They embrace change and prefer to create new things rather than just improve on the old. They bring to the process knowledge from a wide variety of fields beyond their "specialty." They are more self-critical and will question criticism, which is sometimes interpreted as defensive behavior. They have a very low sense of associative fear and are willing to look for connections in many areas sometimes out of their perceived field of excellence.

Best Practice Notes: Characteristics of Creative Individuals

Some of the characteristics of highly creative people may be challenging for talent managers. They are very serious about their work, and even the process of reviewing performance evaluations may be difficult because it is hard to measure creative success. Know that they may question everything. If the standard practice at your company is to hire "PLUs" (People Like Us), then you, as talent manager, will be in the middle of a major struggle to recruit and retain creative employees, who thrive in organizations that embrace diversity in every sense including cross-disciplinary abilities. They want to work for a company where creativity is part of its mission and is inherent in its culture, an exciting place where employees are motivated in every way to innovate. Talent managers need to serve as catalysts for cultural change within their organizations. They must have total "buy-in" to the innovation process and serve as a creative team member themselves. "Creativity has to have the right conditions to survive. It has to be valued and then employees can feel free to be creative. Businesses attracting and retaining the best knowledge workers have a mix of creativity and focus (Jackson 2008). We need to break down the silos and create a "silo-less," whole-minded company that employs the collective brain power of all employees.

Industry Concern 3: Importance of Building an Innovation Process

There were mixed views of collaborative decision making and development in the workplace. Some saw it as too expensive, impossible to control, too slow to market, and not related to ROI. A few remarked how could they afford to pay people to daydream and what would they do with so many "pie-in-the-sky" ideas?

Peter Drucker describes the "fallacy of individual creativity," which is if you just put people together and leave them alone, they'll come up with "far better, more advanced, far more productive answers than the experts."

> Drucker used a wonderful analogy, shoveling sand, to demonstrate that the proper design of work is not intuitively obvious and the people closest to the work are the least likely to properly redesign their own work. He said people have been working day by day, shoveling sand for thousands of years and if design is intuitively obvious then those closest to the work would have redesigned their tools long ago to make the work more productive and less back breaking. Instead they select the biggest shovel with the longest handle—exactly the opposite of the design that is more efficient and less fatiguing (Drucker 1986).

In reality, senior management and talent managers have a role to play in designing an innovation process because; the "best" ways of doing work are never obvious; they require information, analysis, and knowledge. A continuous role is reinforced by the research of Sethi, Smith, and Park (2002), who found that "within limits, close monitoring by senior management signals to team members and the rest of the company that their project is important. This is a powerful motivator, enhancing the team's creativity. It also makes organizational resources more available to the team because it's hard not to cooperate with a team that is visible on management's radar."

In regard to organizational level, another form of product innovation is *social innovation*. Collins (1997) gave the following examples of social innovation that relate to the changing role of talent managers:

> . . . what was Thomas Edison's greatest invention? Not the lightbulb. Not the phonograph. Not the telegraph. . . . His greatest invention was the modern research-and-development laboratory—a *social innovation*. . . . The builders of 3M . . . never came up with a single product innovation themselves but instead invented a perpetual-innovation machine, fueled by social inventions like "bootleg time" (which gives 3M employees 15 percent free time to tinker around) and an internal venture-capital fund . . .
>
> Great companies are early adopters, if not outright inventors, of progressive management methods. They are among the first to try the outlandish, the different, the radical. They are like Procter & Gamble, which experimented with employee stock ownership and profit sharing in the late 1800s, 100 years before such practices became commonplace. They are like Nordstrom, which

encouraged salespeople to use their discretion in serving the customer 50 years before the word empowerment showed up in the popular business press. They are like W.L. Gore, which experimented in the 1950s with Abraham Maslow's self-actualization concepts and a loosely coupled "lattice organization" structure decades before those ideas became widely taught at business schools. . . . Boeing jets, 3M Post-it Notes, Federal Express, universal telephone service, the Sony Walkman, the HP 200LX pocket computer—none of those would have been possible without human organization and continual innovation in the practice of management.

Sundgren and Styhre (2007) proposed that a dominating view in the literature of organizational creativity is to treat the creativity as an ex post facto construct rather than a process that may be subject to systematic and thoughtful managerial practices. Drawing on Alfred North Whitehead's writing, their paper seeks to examine how creativity is conceptualized in the pharmaceutical industry. This study is based on a series of interviews with managers and scientists in three pharmaceutical companies. Although researchers and managers designate the role of organizational creativity as the most important strategic capability of the firm, they found that there is almost no communication about it. The respondents point out a gap between understanding and action in the innovation process (i.e., what precedes it in new drug development): Creativity is what makes the difference for the companies, but hardly anyone talks about it. From a talent management perspective, they conclude that organizational creativity can become a more actionable concept by capturing images and narratives relevant to the organizational reality—in this case, new drug development. This lack of communication or lack of process awareness is a major roadblock to innovation in many firms.

Best Practice Notes: Importance of Building an Innovation Process

It is true that creativity flows from employees, but the insightful development of an innovation process that stimulates the flow and provides a clearly understood structured pathway to implementation requires careful analysis and knowledge. It is hoped that the process will lead employees away from "big shovels with long handles," and although autonomy is an essential element in creativity, the ultimate objective is "innovation that ships." Successful firms strategically employ a structure or constrained process where winning ideas are encouraged, vetted, funded, and ultimately developed into innovations. American companies adopt about 38 percent of all creative ideas presented to them, as compared to Japanese companies who adopt about 90 percent (Robinson and Stern 1998). In reality, most American firms do not have an innovation process in place. The design and start of the firm's innovation process are two instances where outside consultants may be helpful to the firm. However, we believe that the capacity to sustain the process beyond startup is totally within the ability of the firm and the use of outside consultants may be counterproductive.

It's a lot easier to discourage creative ideas from developing—that's what most firms do now. Stop your firm from killing creativity and pushing creative employees out the door. We hire people to think and then provide them with almost no time to think. Companies cannot afford a "creative brain drain" where employees leave for more creative environs, including self-employment. The impact is much more than the high cost of turnover. It is the destruction or disruption of long-term team and knowledge-sharing relationships. The fact that firms whose survival depend on continuous innovation, including pharmaceutical companies, fail to support their innovation processes with thorough communications is startling. Talent management needs to have a much larger role in the development of the innovation process, building the support system, and communicating the process within the firm.

A lack of communication effort or skills can kill an innovation process at many levels. The innovation process requires the clear communication of ideas through the process to win acceptance in order to move forward. An unshared idea is worthless to the firm and may be a waste of company resources. Talent managers may need to offer communication courses because ideas will be pitched by more employees or teams as the innovation process becomes more effective. A communications strategy will need to be developed to make the employees aware of the process and to help alleviate concerns about its implementation. There are a lot of behavioral implications of creating an innovation process, and some employees may feel threatened by being asked to be creative ("that's not what I signed up for!"). They may not know what it means. They may not be able to accept so much change or the stress to create new ideas, or understand the necessity of having to work with others in other departments on projects.

Industry Concern 4: Compensation and Motivation Issues for Creative Employees

Amabile (1992) identifies three components of creativity: expertise, creative-thinking skills, and motivation. Her years of research indicate that various forms of motivation do not have the same impact on creativity. There are two categories of motivation: *extrinsic*, or outside, motivation, and *intrinsic*, or inside, motivation. Extrinsic motivators include money. "Money doesn't stop people from being creative, but in many situations, it doesn't help." Intrinsic motivation includes a person's passion and interest in their job. "When people are intrinsically motivated, they engage in their work for the challenge and enjoyment of it. The work *itself* is motivating." Amabile developed "the *Intrinsic Motivation Principle of Creativity*: people will be most creative when they feel motivated primarily by the interest, satisfaction, and challenge of the work itself—and not by external pressures." She stresses that leadership in an organization can have the most impact on creativity and innovation by concentrating on intrinsic motivation.

Best Practice Notes: Compensation and Motivation Issues for Creative Employees

Teresa Amabile's research reinforces the leadership role that talent managers need to play in innovative organizations. Not only should they be key players in the design of the innovation process, but they need to help build a workplace that eliminates roadblocks to the process and creates intrinsic motivators that drive creativity. The most successful innovative firms have stimulating work environments supported by advanced communications and knowledge management systems. They take care of the extrinsic motivation of the employees by providing wage and benefit packages but often go way beyond the norm in other positive psychology or fun areas.

Google is considered one of the best places to work and has developed an innovation process for its engineers where interesting ideas receive attention, even those not directly related to the company's business model. The company instituted the ITO (Innovation Time Out) policy that encourages employees to spend 80 percent of their time on core projects and 20 percent (or one day per week) on "innovation" activities that speak to their personal interests and passions. This resulted in the development of Gmail, Google News, AdSense, and Orkut, but more importantly, it keeps employees challenged and engaged, allows them the freedom of self-expression, which helps support professional development and retention. The 20 percent innovation program is a major positive for the firm's recruiting efforts. This is not an unstructured process. Innovation time is tracked, and managers know which projects are being pursued. There had been some criticism that the process was slowing and becoming bureaucratic, but in 2009, the firm decided to add more structure or discipline to the process by establishing "innovation reviews" where department heads share ideas with Google's top leadership, helping executives to focus attention and resources on promising ideas early (Anthony 2009). A similar program at 3M, the 15 percent bootlegging program, resulted in the development of Post-it Notes and Scotch Tape.

Google pays its employees very well, including stock options, and the company has an excellent benefits program (extrinsic motivation), but they have developed a very supportive work environment, with flex-time for all; casual dress every day; allowing employees to bring their dogs to work; on-site doctor and dental care; free massage and yoga; free drinks and snacks; free gourmet meals, including breakfast, lunch, and dinner; free recreation, including video games, foosball, volleyball, and pool tables; valet parking for employees; on-site car washing and detailing; near site child care center; a "no tracking of sick days" policy; an on-site gym; and so on.

How about incorporating some novel intrinsic motivators into your workplace to help stimulate cross-discipline learning or creative thinking? Why not try offering one afternoon off per quarter to enjoy an arts program if arts are important to an employee, or funds to support attending a seminar in a field not related to an employee's specialty (even the Federal Reserve Bank of Philadelphia provides this for its economists)? Or how about offering "creative thinking spaces," ideation rooms, or special software packages that facilitate online interaction or customized learning experiences?

Industry Concern 5: Low Tolerance for Failure in the Workplace

Sternberg and Lubart (1995) created the "investment theory of creativity," making an analogy between successful innovation and good investing. They believe successful creative people and organizations "buy low and sell high," realizing that major returns require sensible risks. Innovative firms know there is always risk in creativity. "To be truly creative, an idea must not only be novel, but also appropriate to the task. Too often, ideas we reject out-of-hand are the truly creative ones, so if you invent (or hear about) an idea that sounds ridiculous at first, you might profit by giving it another glance. Taking sensible risks, and letting others take them, means being prepared for failure; creative people inevitably make mistakes. Obviously, you should not reward mindless mistakes, but you must tolerate the mistakes that result from genuine attempts at creativity, because in the long run that's where the real returns will originate."

Farson and Keyes (2002) identified the characteristics of "failure tolerant leaders. These are executives who, "through their words and actions, help people overcome their fear of failure and, in the process, create a culture of intelligent risk taking that leads to sustained innovation."

Failure tolerant leaders break down barriers that separate them from their employees, avoid giving praise or penalize but analyze (less evaluation and more interpretation), encourage employees to make constructive mistakes by building empathy by sharing their failure experiences, build a work environment where internal competition is eliminated through collaboration including work groups, support the development of communication strategies to support idea sharing, and believe that a "good idea is a good idea" no matter where it originated.

A study of scientists producing innovative research was completed by Azoulay, Manso, and Zivan in 2009. Pierre Azoulay of MIT concludes that "if you want people to branch out in new directions, then it's important to provide for their long-term horizons, to give them time to experiment and potentially fail."

Successful firms establish innovation environments where employees have the freedom to develop new ideas and engage in cross-disciplinary exploration. They have the time to shepherd their discoveries through a disciplined process where the potential of failure is considered a normal part of innovation.

Best Practice Notes: Low Tolerance for Failure in the Workplace

The willingness to accept failure in the innovation process has led some firms to measure failure activity, and if the number of failures is too low, it is a negative sign. Zero tolerance may be their greatest barrier to success.

Consider these quotes from "The Failure Tolerant Leader" by Farson and Keyes in the *Harvard Business Review*, September 2002:

> "I have not failed. I've just found 10,000 ways that won't work."—Thomas Edison
> "We reward failure."—Jack Welch, explaining that to do otherwise would squelch daring
> "A good research man failed every time but the last one. He treats his failures as practice shots."
> "What every educated person needs to learn, is that it's not a disgrace to fail, and that you must analyze each failure to find its cause . . . You must learn how to fail intelligently. Failing is one of the greatest arts in the world. One fails forward toward success."—Charles Kettering, GM, considered second only to Thomas Edison as an inventor

"The fastest way to succeed is to double your failure rate."—Thomas Watson, Sr., IBM

"We do our best to make sure that people aren't afraid of the possibility of failure, and we do a lot of experiments."—Michael Dell, Dell Computers

"What prevents innovation? The dangerous brew of fear and complacency—staying where you are out of fear of failing, of blowing too much money, or of placing the wrong bets."—Betty Cohen, Turner Broadcasting System

Conclusion

Talent managers need to look at the way they spend their time—and the company's money. Are they hiring creativity consultants to help create their companies next great innovation, or are they creating an environment that stimulates innovation that is based on their own expertise in the theoretical and research foundation of creativity? Is focus on what to do when current product lines become obsolete, or is the focus on building a creative culture? The next wave of effective talent managers will take leadership in generating new ways of organizing and supporting human effort and creativity. This will require a departure from the status quo for, as Hillis (2002) puts it, "Maybe, in fact, the biggest risk in innovation lies in sticking too closely to your plans."

In summation, different perspectives of investigating creativity include a psychometric approach which focuses on assessing one's creative strengths (Torrance); a systems approach to understanding creativity (Csikszentmihalyi) which focuses on the individual, the domain (discipline), and the field (gatekeepers of an industry); the role of intrinsic and extrinsic motivation (Amabile) which states that intrinsic motivation yields more creative products; comparison with intelligence (Guilford, Sternberg); multiple intelligences (Gardner); humanistic psychology (Rogers, Maslow); and creative problem solving models (Wallas, Parnes).

Appendix A

Tools and Techniques for Enhancing Creativity

T ALENT MANAGERS CAN PROVIDE TOOLS AND TECHNIQUES FOR ENHANCING CREATIVITY. Due to space limitations here, we provide references to delve more deeply into the tools and techniques presented.

1. Torrance, building upon Guilford's work, suggested the following activities:
   - *"Unusual uses" task.* Participants are asked to generate unusual uses of an object such as a brick, tin can, or book. Company-related objects such as a pharmaceutical product, an engineering technology artifact, a blue print, and so on may be used;
   - *Impossibilities task.* Participants are asked to list as many impossibilities or improbable situations as they can.
   - *Consequences task.* Participants are asked to predict possible outcomes of a situation, for example, forecasting financial options for a company, considering possible results of modifying job descriptions, or determining many solutions to a situation (e.g., avoid negative impact on a community if a plant is in financial trouble).
   - *Improvement task.* Participants are given a list of common objects and are asked to suggest as many ways as they can to improve each object without regard to whether or not their suggestions are possible.
2. *SCAMPER* stands for Substitute, Combine, Adapt, Modify, Put to other uses, Eliminate, and Rearrange. This technique involves a list of verbs that you relate to a problem resulting in creative solutions.

3. *Six Thinking Hats* is used to encourage and generate different types of thinking, to alleviate individuals feeling inhibited, and to explore ideas when selecting which to take forward. (See DeBono 1999.) The following table shows how the activity works. Each activity is designed to provoke different types of thinking in individuals and groups.

Hat	Function	Example
White	Information	Asking for information from others
Black	Judgment	Playing devil's advocate. Explaining why something won't work.
Green	Creativity	Offering possibilities, ideas
Red	Intuition	Explaining hunches, feelings, gut senses
Yellow	Optimism	Being positive, enthusiastic, supportive
Blue	Thinking	Using rationalism, logic, intellect

4. *CATWOE* is an acronym for
   Customers (Who is on the receiving end? What problem do they have now? How will they react to what you are proposing?)
   Actors (Who are the actors who will carry out your solution? What is the impact on them? How might they react?)
   Transformation process (What is the process for transforming inputs into outputs?)
   World view (What is the bigger picture into which the situation fits? What is the *real* problem you are working on? What is the wider impact of any solution?)
   Owner (Who is the real owner or owners of the process or situation you are changing? Can they help you or stop you? What would cause them to get in your way? What would lead them to help you?)
   Environmental constraints (What are the broader constraints that act on the situation and your ideas? What are the ethical limits, the laws, financial constraints, limited resources? regulations, and so on? How might these constrain your solution? How can you get around them?)

5. *NUF Test* is helpful when you want to identify what to work on: being more creative, developing an idea, or getting something that you will be able to implement. The acronym stands for *New* (not been tried before), *Useful* (solves the problem), and *Feasible* (can be implemented in practice). Solutions to the following problem may be scored from 0 to 10 on these three characteristics: *An idea for keeping a door open.* One solution, which is scored below, may be to use a magnet attached to the wall and to the door. Each solution generated could be scored and the one with the highest score be given serious consideration.

Criteria	Rating	Assessment
New	2	Similar ideas have been used before.
Useful	7	Should work.
Feasible	3	Expensive to install on grand scale.
Total	12	

6. *Mindtools*™ provides a tool kit addressing the following skills that a talent manager can use: leadership tools, team tools, strategy tools, problem-solving techniques, decision-making tools, project planning skills, time management techniques, stress tools, communication skills, creativity techniques, learning skills and study techniques, and career development skills. The cost is very inexpensive.

7. *Mycoted* is a company dedicated to improving creativity and innovation for solving problems worldwide, they are a central repository for creativity and innovation on the Internet as a summary of tools, techniques, mind exercises, puzzles, book reviews, etc., that is open to all.

8. Another excellent resource offering a variety of tools and techniques for enhancing creativity is M. Michalko. *Thinkertoys: A Handbook of Creative-Thinking Techniques*, 2nd ed. (Berkeley, CA: Ten Speed Press, 2006).

References

Adams, K. (2005, September). The Sources of Innovation and Creativity. *National Center on Education and the Economy.*

Amabile, T. M. (1998, Sept-Oct). How to Kill Creativity. *Harvard Business Review.*

———. (1992). *Growing up creative: Nurturing a lifetime of creativity.* Buffalo, NY: Creative Education Foundation Press.

Amabile, T. M., C. Hadley, and S. Kramer. (2002, September). Creativity under the Gun. *Harvard Business Review.* p. 52–61.

Anthony, S. (2009, June 23). Google's Management Style Grows Up. *Harvard Business Online.* Retrieved on January 20, 2010 from http://www.businessweek.com/print/managing/content/jun2009/ca20090623_918721.htm

Bacon, J. (2006). *Cirque du soleil: The spark.* New York: Currency Doubleday.

Bilton, C. (2007). *Management and creativity: From creative industries to creative management.* Carlton, Victoria. Australia: Blackwell Publishing.

Breen, B. (2007, December 19). The 6 Myths of Creativity. *Fast Company.com.* Retrieved from *http://fastcompany.com/magazine/89/creativity.html*

Collind, J. C. and J. I. Porras. (1997). *Built to Last: Successful Habits of Visionary Companies.* New York: HarperCollins

Csikszentmihalyi, Mihaly. (1996). *Creativity: Flow and the psychology of discovery and invention.* New York: Harper Perennial.

De Bono, Edward. *Six thinking hats.* Back Bay Books, 1999.

Dougherty, D., and J. Tolboom. (2009). Creative Organizing to Enable Organizational Creativity. In *Handbook of organizational creativity*. (Zhou, J. & Shalley, C.E., Eds.). New York: Psychology Press, Taylor & Francis Group.

Drucker, P. (1986). *Management: Tasks, responsibilities, practices*. New York: Truman talley books / E. P. Dutton

———. (2002, August). The Discipline of Innovation. *Harvard Business Review*. p. 95–102.

Farson, R., and R. Keyes. (2002, September). The Failure-Tolerant Leader. *Harvard Business Review*. p. 64–71.

Florida, R. (2010). Managing Those Creative Types interviewed by J. Robinson. *The Gallup Management Journal*. Retrieved from http://gmj-gallup.com.

Gardner, H. (2006). *Five minds for the futures*. Boston: Harvard Business School Press.

Goodman, G. S. (2009, April 8). Scripting – Do You Have Enough Monkeys for the Job? Retrieved January 3, 2010, from http://ezinearticles.com/?Scripting-Do-You-Have-Enough-Monkeys-For-the-Job?&id=2197885.

Hillis, D. (2002, August). Stumbling into Brilliance. *Harvard Business Review*. p. 152.

Hirsch, J. (2009, December 9). MIT study: Scientific innovation is more likely with long-term less-restrictive funding. Retrieved February 1, 2010 from http://web.mit.edu/press/2009/creative-research–1209.html.

Jackson, M. (2008, June 23). May we have your attention, please? *Business Week*. Retrieved from http://www.businessweek.com.

Johansson, F. (2004). *The Medici effect: Breakthrough insights at the intersection of ideas, concepts, and cultures*. Boston: Harvard Business School Press.

Jones, R. (2009 October 15). Talent management in the new economy: Applying lessons learned from knowledge workers. Univ. of Maryland University College. Retrieved from http://www-apps.umuc.edu/blog/library/Talent%20management%20in%20the%20new%20economy.pdf.

Mauzy, J., and R. Harriman. (2003). *Creativity, Inc: Building an inventive organization*. Boston. MA: Harvard Business School Press.

McGregor, J., W. Symonds, D. Foust, D. Brady, and M. Herbst. (2006, July 10). How Failure Breeds Success. *Business week*. Retrieved February 1, 2010 from http://businessweek.com/magazine/content/06_28/b3992001.htm.

Noh, H. (2010). Micro-Fluidics Laboratory (MFL). *Modules and kits for undergraduate education*. NSF submission.

Osborn, Alex. (1953). *Applied imagination: Principles and procedures of creative problem solving*. New York, New York: Charles Scribner's Sons.

Parnes, S. J. (Ed.) (1992). *Source book for creative problem solving: A fifty year digest of proven innovation processes*. Buffalo, NY: Creative Education Foundation.

Pressroom. (2007). New Survey Points to Creativity Gap in U.S. Workplace. *Creativeeconomics.org*. Retrieved on November 18, 2009 from http://www.creativeeconomies.org/pr-sep21–07.asp.

Robinson, A., and S. Stern. (1998). *Corporate creativity: How innovation and improvement actually happen*. San Francisco: Berrett-Koehler Publishers

Rogers C. *Experiential learning*. http://tip.psychology.org/rogers.html (*accessed February 7, 2009*).

Sethi, R., D. Smith, and C. W. Park. (2002, August). How to Kill a Team's Creativity. *Harvard Business Review*. p 16–17.

Shartle, C. L. (1951). Studies of Naval Leadership. Part I. In Guetzkow, H. (Ed.), *Group, Leadership and Men*. Pittsburgh, PA: Carnegie Press, pp. 119–133.

Skeel, S. New working models. *Management Today*. London. May 1992. http://sorrel.humboldt.edu/~gjf2/mgmt311/8a/discussion/messages/19.html.

Sternberg R. J. *The nature of creativity*. Creativity Res J 2006;18(1):87–98.

Sternberg, R. J., and T. Lubart. *Ten Keys to Creative Innovation*. #148 from R & D Innovator Volume 4, Number 3.

Sundgren, M., and A. Styhre. (2007). Creativity and the fallacy of misplaced concreteness in new drug development: A Whiteheadian perspective. *European Journal of Innovation Management*, Vol. 10, Issue 2, pp.215–235.

Taylor, W., and P. LaBarre. (2006). *Mavericks at work*. New York: William Morrow.

Torrance E. P. The Torrance Tests of Creative Thinking streamlined (revised) manual. Figural A and B. Bensenville, IL: Scholastic Testing Service; 1984.

———. *The manifesto: A guide to developing a creative career*. Westport, CT: Ablex Publishing; 2002.

Wallas, G. (1926). *The art of thought*. New York: Harcourt Brace.

Whitehead, A. N. (1933). *Adventures of ideas*. (1967 paperback). New York: Free Press (Simon & Schuster).

Chapter 36

Building A Sustainability Culture through Employee Engagement

Max Caldwell, Managing Director
Denise Fairhurst, Senior Consultant
Towers Watson

LEADING ORGANIZATIONS RECOGNIZE THE POWER OF AN ENGAGED WORKFORCE IN delivering superior business performance. Our research over the past decade or more has consistently found a strong link between high levels of employee engagement and above-average financial and operational results (e.g., customer loyalty scores).

We define engagement as employees' willingness and ability to contribute to company success—the extent to which they put discretionary effort into their work and contribute more of their energy, creativity, and passion on the job. Our research shows that only a small percentage of the global workforce—about 20 percent—is highly engaged, although engagement levels vary from organization to organization, country to country (due to cultural differences), and even within the same organization at different times (e.g., during or following significant internal or external events, such as mergers, major recessions, etc.). Despite these variables, the one constant is that organizations and their leaders play a critical role in driving employee engagement. In short, they have the power to "move the needle" when it comes to making the critical connections that shape employee perceptions and behavior.

Organizations measure engagement to gain insights about employees' attitudes and behaviors that in turn inform decisions about operations support, leadership development, and workplace programs and investments.

Towers Watson's approach to measuring engagement is based on three dimensions: the rational (how well employees understand their roles and responsibilities), the emotional (how much passion and energy they bring to the workplace), and the motivational (the degree to which they are willing to go the extra mile in their work). Based on a statistical analysis of employees' responses to a core set of questions across these dimensions, we cluster the workforce into four groups:

- *Engaged.* Those with very high scores on all three dimensions willing to invest full discretionary effort
- *Enrolled.* Employees who are partly engaged, with higher scores on the rational and motivational dimensions, but less connected emotionally
- *Disenchanted.* The partly disengaged, with lower scores on all three components of engagement, especially the critical emotional dimension
- *Disengaged.* Workers who have disconnected from the organization and have very low scores on the rational, emotional, and motivational dimensions

Over the years, through studies we have done with tens of thousands of workers around the world, we've seen dramatic differences in how employees in each of these groups interact with their organization and their job. For example, in our *2007 Global Workforce Study*, which surveyed 86,000 workers worldwide, about 85 percent of engaged employees felt they could have a positive impact on the quality of their work and on customers' level of satisfaction with the company, compared with only 40 percent of the disengaged—an enormous (and disturbing) difference.

On the positive side, Towers Watson has found a compelling relationship between high levels of workforce engagement and top-performing organizations. In one of our studies, for example, we analyzed 50 global companies over a one-year period to correlate employee engagement levels to company financial results. As Figure 36-1 shows, the companies with high employee engagement experienced a 19 percent increase in operating income and a jump of more than 25 percent in earnings per share over this period, while those with low engagement levels saw deterioration in these key financial measures. Similar studies over longer time horizons have showed a similar pattern.

These studies, combined with our experience surveying many large, multinational organizations, underscore that employee engagement matters and is a foundation of strong organizational performance. In addition, there is an emerging body of social research growing out of employee health and wellness measurement that suggests that a more robust set of factors also comes into play in shaping employees' behavior, performance, and perceptions of their employers. Those factors collectively add up to a concept we refer to as *employee well-being*, which represents one way to ensure that high engagement can be enhanced and sustained in the context of a "healthy" work environment.

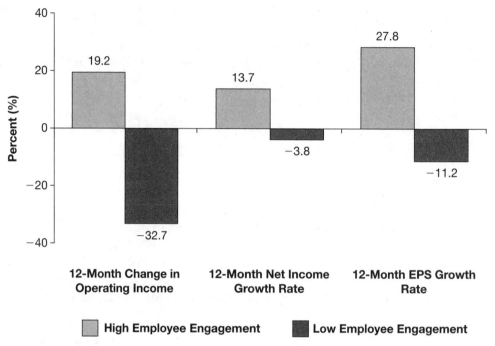

Figure 36-1 Engagement and Financial Performance

Defining and Measuring Well-Being

While organizations define well-being in different ways, it generally moves beyond physical health and wellness to embrace important psychological and social components. The World Health Organization today defines health as not only the absence of infirmity and disease, but also as a state of physical, mental, and social well-being. For example, are employees positive and enthusiastic about their jobs—or frustrated, stressed, and unhappy? Do people feel connected to a community of coworkers that provide support and emotional sustenance—or isolated from colleagues and alone to fend for themselves? For people to deliver peak performance, they need to not only be "well" and energized physically but also feel balanced, supported, and connected psychologically and socially.

There is an ongoing evolution in the way both private and public organizations approach the concept of health and wellness. In recent years, driven in part by cost concerns, companies have introduced more sophisticated health and wellness strategies. These include more extensive programs to sustain physical health, ensure workplace safety, effectively manage chronic health issues, deal with workplace stress, and balance the sometimes conflicting demands of work and life. A number of employers have also integrated incentives into their benefits programs, such as offering reduced health-care contributions for completing a health risk assessment. The focus, in short, is on enabling people to live a healthier, more balanced, more productive life, while at the same time managing costs for the company. In many organizations, employee well-being has evolved from focusing primarily on controlling the cost of serious disease, disability, and absenteeism to also focusing on enhancing the engagement and productivity of the workforce. Combined with a greater focus on corporate social responsibility and sustainability, wellness has been elevated to a C-suite and boardroom issue, not only an HR topic.

At Towers Watson, well-being is defined as the interplay between physical well-being (i.e., health and energy), social/relational well-being (such as work/life balance and respect), and psychological well-being (such as mood and sense of accomplishment), as illustrated in Figure 36-2. One advantage of this model is that it offers a more holistic picture of well-being and, as such, offers organizations more potential levers to drive improvements. Interventions are not limited to simply trying to influence intangibles such as mood or morale. Instead, the focus is on the more tangible and practical actions mentioned above, such as ensuring physical health, managing stress, balancing work/life demands, developing and growing on the job, working effectively with colleagues, and building a secure financial future.

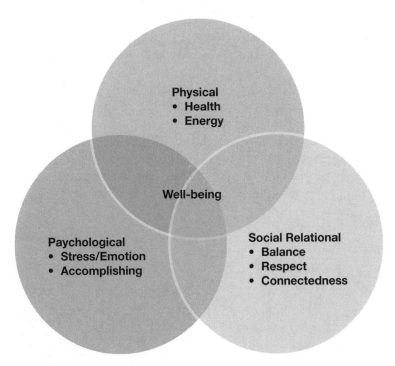

Figure 36-2 Critical Dimensions of Employee Well-Being

Changing Employee Perspectives

The backdrop for this new way of thinking about the workforce involves the evolution of employee perceptions and expectations regarding their employer and the work experience. In a highly competitive world where change is continuous (e.g., in business models, organization structures, and technologies), consistently strong individual performance is expected, and job security cannot be guaranteed, Towers Watson's research has revealed a subtle shift in the way employees value various aspects of their jobs. People increasingly look to their organization to contribute to their *sense of worth* in three areas:

- *Social worth*, which springs from employees' belief that they are performing meaningful work for an organization that demonstrates social, environmental, and community responsibility, and working for a manager who cares about their individual growth and success and for senior leaders who genuinely care about their well-being
- *Self-worth*, which combines psychological, physical, and social health with the capability to achieve work/life balance and manage stress with the aid of employer programs, resources, and tools
- *Financial worth*, which is supported both by traditional reward programs (e.g., pay, health care, and retirement benefits) and by the information, resources, and tools to help people make good financial decisions based on their needs and build for the future

Our research demonstrates that well-being and engagement are connected and interact in a number of ways, as show in Figure 36-3. When employee well-being is high but engagement is low, the organization is in a state of "Complacent Disengagement," where people are generally happy and satisfied but not motivated to invest extra effort; hence, productivity and performance suffer.

Conversely, when engagement is high but well-being is low, in what we label a state of "Unstable Engagement," there is greater risk of employee burnout and attrition, and potentially problems related to health, absenteeism, and even safety. In this environment, employees may be motivated to work long hours to achieve strong

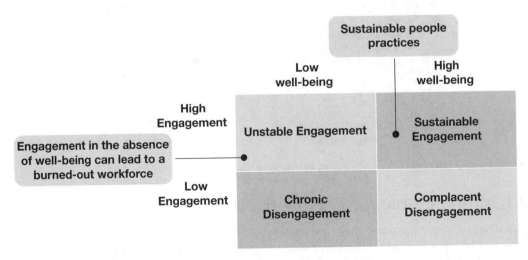

Figure 36-3 Engagement and Well-Being

performance, but their personal well-being—and therefore their ability to sustain this performance—may suffer. In the recent recession, Towers Watson observed a trend in some of the organizations we survey showing significant *decreases* in employee well-being together with *increases* in stress levels. Yet many organizations experienced relatively little change in engagement levels as employees remained motivated to do their best in the face of furloughs, layoffs, pay freezes, "de-layering," and other cost-reduction moves. The recession played a key role, as many employees were relieved simply to have jobs and had little choice but to accept unpleasant organizational changes and reductions in rewards that in other times might have prompted widespread discontent.

In such climates, while employees may believe in the goals of the organization, be proud to work for the company, and make the extra effort to deliver, they may forego healthy activities such as eating well, getting adequate rest, and spending time in the gym. Combined with the uncertainty and stress of seeing valued colleagues leave the organization, carrying heavier workloads, and having friends and family (perhaps even their spouse) lose their jobs, we would posit that engagement in these environments is at risk and unsustainable, and could lead to burnout and more serious issues.

The optimal state, "Sustainable Engagement," combines high engagement and high well-being. Employees who work in a physically, psychologically, and socially healthy environment that at the same time maintains a climate of high engagement are far more likely to be able to not only go the extra mile and be highly productive but to deliver this peak performance over the long term. "Chronic Disengagement," in contrast, is a state marked by low engagement and low well-being—the worst of all worlds from an organizational perspective.

The Critical Role of Local Performance Support

Employees can be highly engaged and have a great sense of well-being but still not be able to deliver their full performance potential if their workplace is missing one more critical ingredient: what we call "local performance support," meaning the resources required at a local team level to be effective and productive. These resources include having capable team members, efficient work processes, leading-edge technology, effective supervision, and sufficient scope of decision making to deliver what is expected. Towers Watson's research shows that organizations with highly engaged employees who also have strong local performance support can generate up to one and half times more profit (based on net profit margin) than organizations with comparable engagement levels but weaker local performance. Organizations with high engagement and strong local performance support outperform companies with low scores in both of these areas by more than four times. (See Figure 36-4.)

Like engagement and well-being, local performance support is critical to creating the connection between organizational culture/climate and performance. The sweet spot is where engagement, well-being, and local performance support combine to yield sustainable levels of enhanced employee performance.

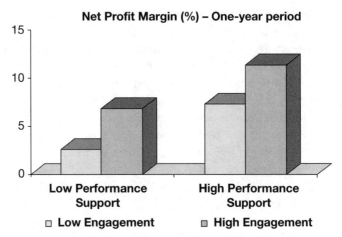

Figure 36-4 Impact of High Engagement and Local Performance Support on Net Profits

Source: © 2010 Towers Watson. All rights reserved. Proprietary and Confidential. For Towers Watson and Towers Watson client use only. www.towerswatson.com

Creating Sustainable High Performance

There is no one simple answer to how to improve employee performance. Towers Watson's global research over 35 years has demonstrated that the drivers of employee engagement differ by country, industry, organization, and even job function and level. Workplace well-being is no different—there is no one right recipe for all organizations. However, our research underscores that organizations seeking sustainable high performance need to understand the extent to which their work culture enhances—or diminishes—engagement, well-being, and local performance. Consider these examples:

- One global pharmaceutical company emphasizes the combination of personal relationships and professional support to address well-being. Supervisors are encouraged to build listening skills and be available to employees who want to open up on issues ranging from workplace safety to the social environment on the job. For issues beyond the supervisors' ability to address—such as a death in the family or mental health issues—employees are counseled to seek help from the company's Employee Assistance Program (EAP). While recognizing that the immediate supervisor may be the employee's closest opportunity to connect to the organization, this company knows that the supervisor can't do it alone, no matter how empathetic he or she may be. The organization's top managers also demonstrate their concern by sponsoring formal work/life balance programs, showing that they care about employees' lives outside the workplace.
- Another company, in the global gaming industry, offers a broad range of personal support to employees, including career development and tuition assistance, flexible scheduling, free fitness counseling, on-site child care, and smoking cessation programs. Taken together, these programs send a very powerful message to

employees who believe the organization not only understands and empathizes with their personal situations but is also willing to invest in enabling them to succeed at work and beyond.

How can organizations take action? A good start may be to rethink and expand the traditional employee survey to assess the organizational climate from these three perspectives and identify and address potential barriers to sustainable engagement. These barriers may include poor internal communication, supervisors who lack the time or skill to effectively manage teams, a lack of awareness of (or access to) health and wellness programs, or inadequate resources at the local level. The good news is that none of these barriers is insurmountable—all can be overcome with deep insight and practical action.

Chapter 37

Unleashing Talent in Service of a Sustainable Future

Jeana Wirtenberg, Ph.D., Director, External Relations & Services,
Institute for Sustainable Enterprise
Fairleigh Dickinson University

Introduction

> I'm going to be able to attract talent, because the talent wants to work with
> the best companies, and the best companies are those that not only get results,
> but do it in a way that creates a sustainable environment.
>
> —*C-suite executive from one of world's most sustainable companies*

Creating a sustainable future is the greatest challenge facing humanity today. Cries of concern emanate from every sector, industry, region, and profession, at every level of society—from the most local to the emerging global culture. There is a case for action and a burning platform. But who will lead the way? It is the talent who will make this happen, guiding the conversations, inspiring new ways of thinking, and creating the novel practices that will make this future a reality. This talent already exists. But it must be unleashed, aligned, and fully supported by the enterprise to rapidly shift its focus. Sustainability must be built into an organization's talent management plan, and in turn the talent must be imbued with a mind-set that will allow it to bring about a sustainable future.

Current research shows that people deeply care about poverty and inequity, climate change, species extinction, clean water, clean air, and other critical social and environmental issues, but because they believe they care more about these issues than do their companies, they are often "doing sustainability" in their personal lives but not living their values in the workplace. A corporate or organizational culture that doesn't encourage greater employee involvement not only makes for dissatisfaction and frustration, it cheats itself. The organization loses out when employees, feeling bound by the confines of traditional job descriptions, are afraid to stretch themselves, take chances, and work in creative ways to effect changes in the service of a sustainable future.

An organization's overall strategy, as well as its culture, systems, and structure, must encourage individuals to hone their unique skills in areas that engage their passions and ignite their highest level of thought and imagination. Along with explicitly aligning its strategies with sustainable goals, the organization must immediately take specific, practical steps to enable, incentivize, and support the talent that already exists and to reach out to the next employee generation. This work must be linked to the challenges of the twenty-first century as they pertain to people (governance, ethics, societal, and employee concerns), environmental stewardship (restoring the natural environment, biodiversity, climate change, etc.), and economic/financial profitability that will sustain the organization and its people for decades to come

The twenty-first century presents the enterprise, society, and the environment with particularly complex situations and problems. But in the right hands, these obstacles can be transformed into opportunities. Effectively overcoming the hurdles endemic to the twenty-first century and taking hold of the advantages requires a combination of seasoned, Generation X and Millennial generation employees.

Defining Sustainability in the Context of Global Human and Ecological Imperatives

> Meeting the needs of the present without compromising the ability of future generations to meet their own needs.
>
> —*Our Common Future, UN Brundtland Report*

Issues of *environmental sustainability* are foundational to any discussion of the future. Scientists agree that global warming alone threatens human existence and that human activities are contributing to it, with the consequence of daily diminishing the number of species on the planet. In his classic book, *The Ecology of Commerce*, Paul Hawkens introduced the term "the death of birth" to refer to this loss of biodiversity, with plant and animal species disappearing at 50 to 100 times the natural rate. Deforestation, as well as contributing to global warming and the extinction of species, is devastating huge areas of South America, Thailand, Indonesia, Sri Lanka, and Haiti, exacerbating the effects of such weather events as tsunamis and earthquakes. Throughout the planet, people are consuming resources at a level that far exceeds the planet's capacity for regeneration. By 2009, this use had outstripped the Earth's ability for renewal by 23 percent. Forty percent of the world's people (more than 2 billion) do not have access to clean water or sanitation.

Issues of *social justice* are inextricably linked to poverty and other systemic problems. One in five children worldwide is not formally schooled, while the United States spends more money building prisons than schools.

The global population has increased by 500 million people since 1999, to more than 6.5 billion, and is estimated to grow by almost 50 percent to 9.1 billion, by 2050, with almost all increases occurring in developing countries. Eight hundred thirty-four million people are undernourished in developing countries. More than 3 billion people live on less than $2 a day. Furthermore, 80 of the world's poorest countries are poorer now than they were 20 years ago.

What does this have to do with talent? The classic definition of sustainability from the UN Brundtland Report points to the obligation of each generation to take care of future generations. Yet we have just begun to think about how to address these formidable challenges in the context of empowering our next generations and equipping the talent to step up to the plate.

Why Integrate Sustainability into Talent Management: Moral Responsibility

> You can't ignore the impact your company has on the community and
> the environment. CEOs used to frame thoughts like these in the context
> of moral responsibility, but now it's also about growth and innovation.
> In the future, it will be the only way we do business.
>
> —*Paul Cescau, CEO, Unilever*

Concern for the planet and its inhabitants is a business as well as moral issue, with implications for all aspects of an organization's health and profitability. Increasingly, organizations are moving to infusing concern for people, planet, and profits into their core strategy, and in doing so are attracting the best, most highly qualified talent. No longer is sustainability a moral imperative that is the province of a few "do-gooders." It is becoming business as usual and necessary if a company is to secure, keep, and grow the most effective, productive, and proficient talent.

In a recent study, forty percent of MBA graduates rated a company's commitment to CSR (corporate social responsibility) as an "extremely" or "very" important measure of the company's reputation. Ninety-two percent of students and entry-level job seekers look to work in an environmentally friendly company. Eighty-three percent of employees in G7 countries say that a positive CSR reputation deepens their loyalty and increases their motivation.

Companies with strong reputations for having a triple-bottom-line or sustainability focus accrue benefits in several areas related to talent management, including reduced recruiting costs, reduced attrition costs, and increased employee productivity. Furthermore, 92 percent of employees "would feel better about themselves" if they worked for a socially responsible corporation, according to a national survey, and

96 percent would like to work at a "successful company that also aspires to do good." Respondents also believe that companies have an obligation to help the environment (93 percent) and that employers should support social issues (72 percent).

Making It Happen: Principles, Frameworks, and Tools for Integrating Sustainability into Your Talent Management Systems and Processes

> I'm always looking for an engineer that's thinking beyond building the structure, but understands that building that structure impacts the people around the community. So hiring those people is one of the greatest sustainability benefits HR can bring.
>
> —HR *executive in one of the world's most sustainable companies*

In this section, we offer ways to integrate sustainability into your organization's talent management systems. First, we propose four fundamental principles for making this shift. Second, we review a framework for building a foundation, creating traction, and engaging all the key stakeholders in the process of embedding sustainability into talent management systems and processes. Third, we suggest several tools.

Guiding Principles for Integrating Sustainability into Talent Management

I. Tie Your Talent Management Plan to Your Sustainable Business Strategy

The first principle is to ensure that your sustainability strategy is central to your business strategy. The sustainability strategy will not work if it is a "bolt on," or seen as a *program du jour*. Once the sustainability and business strategies are fused, you can begin to build your talent management strategy as a key enabler of your sustainable business strategy.

The talent management strategy needs to reinforce, support, and breathe life into your business strategy. Put the top talent in your organization to work on your sustainable business strategy. Identify opportunities to implement sustainability initiatives and to energize and reward key players.

II. Embrace the Qualities of a State-of-the-Art Sustainable Enterprise

The state-of-the-art sustainable enterprise can be identified by the following characteristics and activities:

- Reflects a long-term, collaborative, and "holistic," or systems-oriented, mind-set
- Adopts a triple-bottom-line focus in which the central strategy simultaneously embraces *social, environmental,* and *economic* factors for short- and long-term performance

- Emphasizes ethics-based business principles and sound corporate governance practices
- Promotes transparency and accountability
- Pays attention to the effects of its operations on the planet's five capital stocks—*natural, human, social, financial,* and *manufactured capital*—that is, it ensures that rather than depleting or decreasing these, it generates or regenerates them
- Considers rights and interests of all relevant stakeholders, not only company shareholders
- Gives stakeholders opportunities to participate in all relevant decisions that affect them
- Promotes meaningful systemic change among its peers, within its neighboring communities, and throughout its supply chain

III. Examine and Reinvent Your Values

Most companies have defined and articulated a set of corporate values for their employees, customers, shareholders, and other stakeholders. Sustainable enterprises embrace specific values that focus on particular issues, values associated with "equity, justice, freedom, honesty, humility, and peace, among others" (Twomey et al. 2010).

The focus on sustainability values provides a powerful and exciting opportunity for engaging your organization's top talent, encouraging them to stretch themselves and bring their most innovative and creative thinking to the table. It also affords the organization a chance to reexamine its core values in light of what appears to be an ever-increasing emphasis by the consumer on a company's values and its success in embodying them in its products or services, with the brand more than ever affecting the choices the consumer makes. In an online survey of 500 consumers, 58 percent responded that a product's environmental impact influences their purchase decision.

Within the organization, top talent's actions speak louder than words, as they must lead by example and make difficult but important choices in guiding the enterprise toward a more sustainable future. (For a deep inquiry into these issues, see Twomey et al. 2010.)

> *The popular green initiatives, while noteworthy and necessary in the company's overall sustainable operations, are not enough to transform the company to be fully sustainable. . . . An examination of the current values-in-use will begin a shift in both operations (tangible) and processes (intangible) as a first step on the path to sustainability.*

The authors recommend that HR can and should play a pivotal role in embedding the dialogue about values and sustainability into such traditional HR functions as recruitment, hiring, and training. "If HR attempts to move to the sustaining practices without changing the values-in-use, they will not only be 'swimming upstream,' but they will also not be laying the foundation for a larger organizational transformation" (Twomey et al. 2010).

Exhibiting an organization's values in one's work is also becoming essential to employee success. "People here don't get promoted if they don't have the values

. . . [and] a sustainable mind-set," said an executive from one of the world's most sustainable companies.

IV. Align Your Talent Management Systems, Processes, and Practices with Sustainability

Once these foundational elements are in place, it will be infinitely easier to align your talent management systems, processes, and practices with sustainable strategies and values. Like building a house, the foundation has to be solid, and it has to come first. There are two key systems to align. To be effective, they must be aligned in tandem: leadership development and performance management, which includes recognition and reward.

Leadership Development

Leaders in sustainable enterprises have a "way of being" that is distinctly different from the command-control hierarchical management styles prevalent in the twentieth century. They interact with the people inside the organization as if it were a living system, recognizing that it is operating in the larger ecosystem of the world. In addition, they work with all aspects of the organization to create conditions that encourage people to self-organize and to unleash their natural energy and creativity. The leaders, together with the staff, foster the principles and practices of a self-initiating culture, with the purpose of co-creating the future.

Key concepts for sustainable leadership are authenticity, trust, integrity, and mutuality. These are described in detail with case studies, tools, and examples in "Leadership for a Sustainable Enterprise" (Knowles, Twomey, Davis, and Abdul-Ali) in *The Sustainable Enterprise Fieldbook: When It All Comes Together* (Wirtenberg, Russell, and Lipsky 2008).

Pfizer, through its Global Health Fellows Program, sends 40 of its most talented people from every level of the organization to work on "high-impact capacity building projects" to developing countries to help address systemic health-care challenges and at the same time strengthen their leadership skills. This three- to six-month work assignment's focus is sustainability.

Organizations are creating models to help leaders make the transformation from a command-control culture to sustainability. In addition to developing models, companies are training leaders in sustainability practice. Alcoa, for instance, has adopted a program in its Brazil businesses in which leaders use an online training tool called Chronos to learn about the concept of sustainability.

Performance Management

Recent research found "some of the lowest scores for HR leaders related to helping other executives see the links between sustainability strategy and HR investments, connecting sustainability strategy to talent and performance management systems, and working across boundaries inside and outside the organizations. This was true even in organizations most deeply involved in sustainability" (Harmon et al. 2010).

It is our conclusion that while HR executives care deeply about most global issues, they do not find many incentives in their organizations for acting on their concerns. Thus, it is critical that recognition and reward systems become aligned with and supportive of sustainability initiatives, and equally important, that the human and financial capital be made available to translate these commitments into reality.

Frameworks for Engaging Top Talent in Building a Sustainable Enterprise

Building on these four principles, we now move to a framework for thinking about how to engage top talent in all aspects of building a sustainable enterprise. The "Seven Core Qualities of Highly Successful Sustainability Strategies," shown in Figure 37-1, were first identified in a study of nine of the world's most sustainable companies (Wirtenberg, Harmon, Russell, and Fairfield 2007), validated through a worldwide study commissioned by the American Management Association (AMA 2007), and expanded on more recently in a study of HR leadership and sustainability strategy (Harmon et al. 2010).

At the foundation level of the core qualities pyramid, the journey to sustainability must have top management's visible support; it must be guided by deeply held sustainability values, and sustainability must be central to the core business strategy. At the second level of this pyramid, building traction requires aligning all the hard and

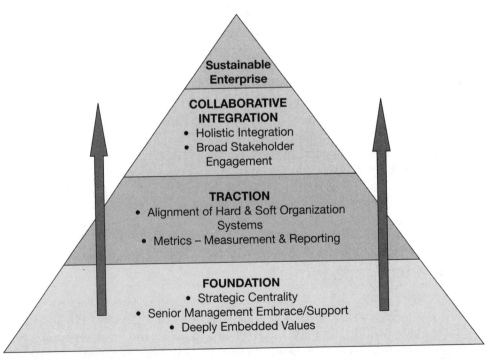

Figure 37-1 Seven Core Qualities of Highly Succcessful Sustainability Strategies

soft organizational systems, including your supply chain, IT, performance management, compensation, and other systems and processes. This traction is then reinforced through extensive metrics, measurements, and reporting systems. The most sustainable companies are extremely measurement-driven, helping top talent, and all employees, understand what's most important and rewarding them for meeting the stringent and ever-expanding goals and objectives that are being set around sustainability. These include specific sustainability key performance indicators (KPIs) on each of the social, economic, and environmental aspects of sustainability.

At the pinnacle of the core qualities pyramid is what we call collaborative integration, the state in which a broad spectrum of stakeholders work together to integrate many diverse initiatives and functions on behalf of sustainability. Since this tends to be the most difficult area for companies to accomplish when creating a sustainable enterprise, we recommend that teams of top talent be assigned to work together across the enterprise to address the cross-functional and broad stakeholder challenges and opportunities.

To achieve the highest degree of success, we recommend involving top talent at every step of the process. As shown on the right side of the "Sustainability Pyramid Framework" (Figure 37-2), top talent can be instrumental in formulating strategy, ensuring top management support, and developing leaders at every level of the organization. As noted above, top talent is critical in designing, embracing, and living the values through which sustainability comes alive in the organization. This talent is essential to the workforce engagement strategy, as they will be looked to for guidance and inspiration. Indeed, with the support of HR and organization development professionals, we recommend that the entire transformational change process be visibly led by top talent after they've been given the freedom, resources, and support necessary to ensure their success.

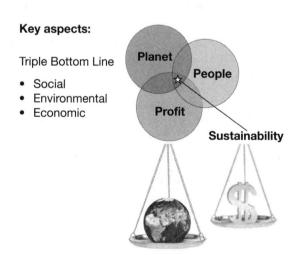

Figure 37-2 What Is Sustainability?

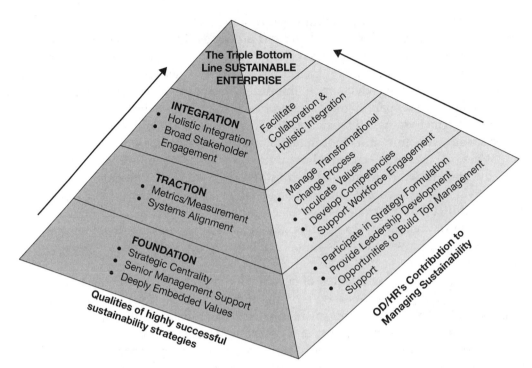

Figure 37-3 Sustainability Pyramid Framework

Source: © 2006. Institute for Sustainable Enterprises.

Key Tools for Integrating Sustainability into Your Talent Management Systems and Processes

I. The Power of Competency Models in Driving Sustainability

Several tools can be instrumental in helping infuse sustainability into talent management systems and processes. First, design and implement competencies that align with your sustainable business strategy. Once this is done, the competencies can readily be incorporated into each of your talent management systems, processes, and practices:

- *Recruitment and selection.* Design and deliver sustainability criteria for recruitment and promotion. Build the competencies into your behaviorally based interview guides.
- *Training and development.* Develop face-to-face and online training programs to educate managers and employees around sustainability. Top talent can be engaged as speakers and trainers wherever possible to demonstrate and heighten their commitment. They can also participate in employee orientation, focusing their remarks around the sustainability strategies of the company and associated competencies.
- *Coaching and 360 feedback.* The competencies can be embedded in 360 feedback tools and processes. Then leaders can be coached to ensure their mind-sets and behaviors are consistent with the sustainability strategic intent.

- *Performance management.* The competencies can easily be incorporated throughout the performance management system; goals and objectives for every employee can be set against them; development plans and career paths can be linked.
- *Compensation.* Structure compensation so it is tied to sustainability goals and make advancement and promotions contingent on demonstrated commitment to sustainability, including measurable results in moving your company forward on its sustainability journey.
- *Career advancement.* Turn sustainability leadership expectations into clear executive competencies and performance standards as a key element of the career advancement process.

II. Communications: Creating an Ennobling New Conversation for the Future

A second key tool top talent can deploy in service of sustainability is in the area of communications. The opportunity and the challenge is to craft a compelling and inspiring sustainability story. This story must be inclusive and widely shared inside and outside the organization. The idea is to engage the entire organization in a conversation designed to give rise to a vision of what's possible, with sustainability being the fuel that unleashes everyone's energy, exciting and ennobling them by giving new meaning to their work and bringing whole new possibilities into being.

III. Employee Initiatives and Opportunities to Engage Top Talent in Sustainability

A third set of powerful tools are employee initiatives and opportunities for employees to contribute at every level and in every function of the organization. For example, many companies are launching "Green Teams," sponsored and supported by top talent, to improve morale, encourage innovation and risk taking, reduce costs, seize opportunities, and enhance the company's reputation and brand.

Offering opportunities for employee volunteerism is a great way to engage talent in service of sustainability. This might include allowing employee participation in community volunteer programs during company time and offering other types of socially responsible activities. Similarly, from an environmental perspective, top talent can lead the way in reducing pollution by promoting conservation at home and in the office, encouraging telecommuting, biking, and the use of mass transit, and conserving electricity. Top talent should also be incentivized to develop "green" products and services wherever possible, green the supply chains, conduct life-cycle analysis of new products, and reduce the carbon footprint of the company (for related research and ideas, see Sroufe, Liebowitz, and Sivasubramaniam 2010).

Next Steps for a New Century: All Hands on Deck

Essential to a sustainable future is the movement to a green economy. This offers some of the most tantalizing occasions for introducing concrete practices, but as it is currently formulated, it does not go far enough. True sustainability requires profound shifts in our mind-sets and ways of living, demanding that we question the deeply embedded concepts of endless consumption and "growth" as the sine qua non of success and measurement systems of wealth based on gross domestic product as opposed to indicators that measure and value the quality of life. All this can and must be changed to ensure a sustainable future for us all. But that is a conversation for another book, albeit a very important one.

Infusing sustainability into our talent management systems means a lot more than dropping words into a competency model or putting a training course together. We each will need to look deep into our souls to determine the legacy we want to leave our children and grandchildren. And then each of us must do what is needed, wherever we are, with the talent we have.

References

American Management Association. 2007. *Creating a sustainable future: A global study of current trends and possibilities 2007–2017*. New York: American Management Association.

Ehrenfeld, J. R. 2008. *Sustainability by design*. New Haven: Yale University Press.

Harmon, J., K. D. Fairfield, and J. Wirtenberg. 2010. HR leadership and sustainability strategy: Missed opportunity? (Special issue: Transitioning to the green economy). *People & Strategy* 33(1).

Knowles, R. N., D. F. Twomey, K. J. Davis, and S. Abudul-Ali. 2009. Leadership for a sustainable enterprise. In *The sustainable enterprise fieldbook: When it all comes together*. New York: AMACOM Books, in association with Greenleaf Publishing Limited, UK.

Sroufe, R., J. Liebowitz, and N. Sivasubramaniam. 2010. HR's role in creating a sustainability culture: What are we waiting for? (Special issue: Transitioning to the green economy). *People & Strategy* 33(1).

Twomey, D. F., R. F. Twomey, G. Farias, and M. Ozgur. 2010. Human values and sustainability: Can green swim upstream? (Special issue: Transitioning to the green economy). *People & Strategy* 33(1).

Wirtenberg, J. 2010. (Special issue: Transitioning to the green economy). *People & Strategy* 33(1).

Wirtenberg, J., J. Harmon, W. G. Russell, and K. Fairfield. 2007. HR's role in building a sustainable enterprise. *Human Resource Planning* 30(1):10–20.

Chapter 38

The Role of Ethics in Talent Management: How Organizations *Ought* to Behave

Stephen F. Hallam, Ph.D., Professor of Management
Teresa Alberte Hallam, Ph.D., Senior Lecturer
University of Akron

THE TOPIC OF BUSINESS ETHICS AND HUMAN RESOURCE MANAGEMENT RAISES SEVERAL questions:

- Whose ethical values should we follow?
- Are business ethics significantly different from general ethics?
- Can ethics be taught?
- Should business leaders teach ethics to their followers?
- How can we go beyond talking the talk?

Whose Ethical Values Should We Follow?

Some argue that each person has an individual set of ethical values and it is impossible to create a set of ethical values for an organization—people have ethics, not organizations. What one person considers wrongful behavior, another may consider within ethical parameters. While these statements are partially true, our ultimate goal is a civilized society. In an organization, we must learn to cooperate and work together or it will eventually fail.

In Western culture, Socrates is considered the Father of Ethics. He defined ethics as the set of moral principles or values that defines right and wrong for a person or group and asserted ethics is about how we *ought* to live. Socrates believed that different persons or groups of persons could have different sets of values but, despite our differences, we need to live and work together to develop society and culture. (Plato and Scott 1963).

Leaders in business organizations have a special challenge because they must consider many diverse stakeholders. Stakeholders include investors, employees, suppliers, customers, local, state, and federal governments, as well as members of society. The most basic ethical principle of "Do unto others as you would have them do unto you" is complicated because there are so many "others" to consider.

There have been several attempts to create a set of principles, a code of ethics, which transcends the individual differences within an organization. In the field of human resource management, the Society for Human Resource Management (SHRM) has such a code of ethics, the *SHRM Code of Ethical and Professional Standards in Human Resource Management* (SHRM 2007). SHRM also provides *A Code of Ethics Toolkit: A Guide to Developing Your Organization's Code of Ethics* (Ethics Resource Center 2001). SHRM recommends giving a code of ethics a meaningful title such as the World Bank Group's *Living Our Values* (The World Bank Group 2010) or *The Way We Do Business* by PricewaterhouseCoopers (PricewaterhouseCoopers 2010).

For an even broader perspective that transcends nations, religions, and cultures, see *The Universal Declaration of Human Rights* approved by the United Nations in 1948 (United Nations 1948). This document has withstood the test of time in addition to the tests of many diverse nations that approved the principles over 60 years ago. It demonstrates that it is possible for diverse people within an organization to agree on many basic ethical principles.

Are Business Ethics Any Different from General Ethics?

According to writings by Socrates and other philosophers, ethics is how we *ought* to live (Plato and Scott 1963). Business ethics today can be defined as how we *ought* to perform our business responsibilities. The more general field of ethics considers such profound issues as euthanasia, human cloning, and justifiable versus unjust warfare. Business ethics deals with the more narrow issues facing business professionals such as balancing the need to make a profit for the stockholders while also respecting the rights of numerous other stakeholders. It is more narrow than the general field of ethics but broader than the field of law. To distinguish law from ethics, consider the field of general ethics to be like the ocean and the field of law like an iceberg floating on that sea of ethics. When a society decides a particular unethical action is so egregious it simply cannot be tolerated, society solidifies its position into a law with specific punishments for its violation. People caught violating that law must pay the penalty, usually in the form of a fine, imprisonment, or both. To be legal, a person or an organization must not get caught disobeying the law. In contrast, an ethical person or organization must obey ethical principles even when they know no one is watching. Business ethics address the highest standards of professional behavior in the conduct of business or how we *ought* to behave in our business life.

Human resource management ethics addresses how the HRM function *ought* to operate within an organization. As stated in the Society for HRM Code of Ethics, "As human resource professionals, we are ethically responsible for justice for all employees and their organizations." Further, human resource management should "create and sustain an environment that encourages all individuals and the organization to reach their fullest potential in a positive and productive manner" (SHRM 2007).

SHRM goes on to provide the following guidelines (2007):

1. *Respect the uniqueness and intrinsic worth of every individual.*
2. *Treat people with dignity, respect, and compassion to foster a trusting work environment free of harassment, intimidation, and unlawful discrimination.*
3. *Ensure that everyone has the opportunity to develop their skills and new competencies.*
4. *Assure an environment of inclusiveness and a commitment to diversity in the organizations we serve.*
5. *Develop, administer, and advocate policies and procedures that foster fair, consistent and equitable treatment for all.*
6. *Regardless of personal interests, support decisions made by our organizations that are both ethical and legal.*
7. *Act in a responsible manner and practice sound management in the country(ies) in which the organizations we serve operate.*

Can Ethics Be Taught?

Many of us conclude that we learned right from wrong from our parents, teachers, religious leaders, and others long before reaching adulthood. Some then mistakenly make the jump in logic that ethics cannot be taught to adults. They reason that all they need to know about ethics has already been learned and that further ethical education will not be effective. While all ethicists accept the concept that early education is important, it does not follow that childhood schooling in ethics will guarantee ethical decision making regardless of the level of problems and challenges we may face as business professionals. Your mother may have taught you that it is wrong to hit your sister, but what did she teach you about employee rights to privacy versus the organization's right to read employees' e-mail? Did she show you how to fairly and equitably reduce the organization's direct labor costs to avoid bankruptcy? What did your father have to say about the proper and improper use of background checks of job applicants?

Others will argue that "bad people" will be bad regardless of an organization's code of ethics or ethical education required in business school or on the job. Still others will take it a step further and assert, "Greed is good" (Stone 1987). That famous quote comes from Gordon Gekko, the fictional character in *Wall Street*, the 1987 movie. Gekko was his company's single largest shareholder, and he was complaining that the company had too many executives that were not major shareholders but merely bureaucrats getting fat salaries while making decisions not in the best interest of the shareholders. Gekko not only asserted that greed is good but "Greed is right. Greed works. Greed clarifies, cuts through, and captures the essence of the evolutionary spirit. Greed, in all its forms—greed for life, for money, for love, for knowledge—has marked the upward surge of mankind. And greed, you mark my words, will not only serve Teldar Paper, but that other malfunctioning corporation called the USA" (Stone 1987).

Gordon Gekko, for many, represents the norm for a business professional; executives are bad, greedy, heartless people, and no amount of ethics training will change them. In the real world, Milton Friedman, Nobel Prize-winning economist, appears to confirm that opinion but with one proviso. He stated, "There is one and only one social responsibility of business—to use its resources and engage in activities designed to increase its profits so long as it stays within the rules of the game, which is to say engages in free and open competition, without deception or fraud (Friedman 1970, p. 178). Friedman appears to be building a case for "all is fair in generating profits with the sole restriction of 'stay within the rules of the game'" (p. 178).

We witness a steady stream of news stories about greedy, unethical businesspersons who appear to be motivated by excessive greed and are void of any conscience about the harm they have brought to stakeholders and the shame they have brought on the business profession. Those who doubt the ability to teach ethics argue that such people would not have been persuaded to choose the high road by ethics training. However, those who teach ethics such as Dr. Bruce Weinstein are likely to reply the following (Weinstein 2002):

> . . . teaching ethics is not about turning bad people into good people. It is about helping good people make better decisions. It is about raising their awareness of ethical issues. It is about teaching people how to think—not as in 1 + 1 = 2, but as in what would an ethical person do in this situation.

People throughout life can benefit from learning more about ethics. As we mature, we move beyond learning to hit our little sister is wrong to dealing with budgets measured in mega dollars, employees in the hundreds or thousands, and stakeholders too numerous to count. In short, we need all the help we can get.

Should Business Leaders Teach Ethics to Their Followers?

Ethical business leaders must first set an example. As Robert Fulghum, author of *All I Really Needed to Know I Learned in Kindergarten*, warned, "Do not worry that your children do not always listen to what you say; worry that they always watch what you do"(1988, p. 102). Employees are likely to ignore the organization's printed code of ethics if they see management ignoring it. Managers can delegate many important responsibilities, but setting the ethical tone cannot be delegated. The spotlight is on the leader. You must be ethical yourself if you expect your followers to be ethical.

Beyond the necessary, but not sufficient, condition of being ethical yourself, business leaders must teach their employees what is considered right and wrong in the environs of their organization. You must teach them how business is done here; how we treat our customers, fellow employees, suppliers, investors, neighbors, and the public. These lessons begin in the job recruitment process. Do we say we value diversity but actually hire only those who look just like our previous employees? Do we say our employees are our most valuable asset yet implement massive layoffs the instant orders decrease? Do we profess to be family-oriented yet move employees without considering family upheaval? Do we claim to use a participative management style yet during times of high unemployment actually treat our employees as easily replaceable cogs in a machine? Do we increase the top executives' pay from $10 million to $20 million while negotiating with the union for our workers to accept a higher share of health-care costs and lower contributions to their pension fund?

How Can We Go beyond Talking the Talk?

We must go beyond talking the talk and actually walk the walk. To demonstrate the cynicism of merely talking the talk, consider Enron's Code of Ethics distributed to all Enron employees just months before the firm's collapse. Exhibit 1 in the eventual court case involving CEO Ken Lay contained the Code of Ethics and the July 1, 2000, memorandum from Ken Lay to all Enron employees telling them to "Please carefully review this booklet . . . [and] certify your compliance . . . " (Lay 2000, p. 2).

Employees will be especially observant of what happens when someone violates the organization's code of ethics. Are low-level employees immediately fired but upper-level managers given a slap on the wrist? Does the whistle-blower who pointed out the ethical breach get a pink slip while the employees that knew but kept still get promotions? Fredrick Taylor, author of *The Principles of Scientific Management* (1914), and other management experts have emphasized that control requires not only standards but also observation, measurement, feedback, and corrective action. Standards must be fairly and uniformly enforced if they are to be anything more than the source of employee cynicism.

Whistle-blowers must be protected. Imagine the difficulties that could have been avoided if Sherron Watkins, the former Enron accountant who sent a memo to Ken Lay warning of the potential consequences of Enron's unorthodox accounting practices, would have felt free to speak up much earlier and her warning had been heeded. Instead, a culture was created at Enron that it was best to keep quiet and pretend that everything was being handled according to generally accepted accounting principles and practices. In an organization as huge as Enron, there had to have been many accountants and others who knew, or at least suspected, that something was unethical about the way assets were so overvalued and liabilities so undervalued or hidden.

Some organizations may use threats to keep employees from speaking up, but others use "golden handcuffs." An employee may feel he or she is so richly rewarded that speaking up will kill the goose that laid the golden egg. Enron, for example, was famous for hiring only the best and the brightest from the top business schools, paying them big salaries, and richly rewarding them for getting major contracts signed. Each action, by itself, was a good thing. Collectively, the excessiveness of the reward system motivated good people to look the other way when unethical and, ultimately, illegal actions became commonplace. Professionals in HRM need to not only point out when some employees are underpaid but also when some are being so overpaid that the risk is high something is being covered up.

Summary

This chapter began with five key questions regarding HRM ethics: Whose ethical values should we follow? Are business ethics any different from general ethics? Can ethics be taught? Should business leaders teach ethics to their followers? How can we go beyond talking the talk?

HRM managers should look to the guidelines supplied by SHRM as a starting point for a set of ethical values to follow. Another good place to begin is with the UN Declaration of Universal Human Rights. Business ethics are a subset of ethics dealing with the ethical challenges faced by decision makers in the field of business. HRM ethics is a subset of business ethics concerning the responsibilities of HRM functions. Ethics can be taught, especially in HRM. We enter adulthood with basic values, but we must continue learning to deal with bigger and more difficult problems as we mature professionally. Business leaders must first demonstrate good ethical behavior and then teach their followers what is considered right and wrong in the particular environment of their area of responsibility. We can go beyond talking the talk by establishing standards of ethical behavior, observing the resulting behavior, measuring it, making corrections, and, when necessary, enforcing sanctions against those who violate the organization's code of ethics.

The history of American business abounds with examples of successful and ethical firms. Warren Buffett speaking to business students at Columbia stated, "In this country you can succeed magnificently with ethics. It is not a hindrance; it is a help sometimes—neutral sometimes, but never a hindrance"(CNBC 2009). In the long run, business is about relationships and trust, and the ethical way is the successful way.

References

CNBC. 2009. *Warren Buffett and Bill Gates: Keeping America great* [Television program]/ Transcipt retrieved from http://www.cnbc.com/id/33901003/CNBC_TRANSCRIPT_ Warren_Buffett_Bill_Gates_Keeping_America_Great.

Ethics Resource Center. 2001. Code of ethics toolkit: A guide to developing your organization's code of ethics (p. 23). Retrieved from http://moss07.shrm.org/about/ Documents/organization-coe.pdf.

Friedman, M. 1970. The social responsibility of business is to increase its profits. *New York Times Magazine* 32(13):122–126. Retrieved from http://www.springerlink.com/content/m2141pp14981487h/fulltext.pdf.

Fulghum, R. 1988. *It was on fire when I lay down on it.* New York: Ivy Books/Random House.

Lay, K. 2000. Enron's code of ethics. Retrieved from http://www.thesmokinggun.com/ graphics/packageart/enron/enron.pdf.

Plato, A., and W. Scott. 1963. *The Republic.* Retrieved from http://www.ucc.ie/academic/ appsoc/hdsp/THE%20REPUBLIC.pdf.

PricewaterhouseCoopers. 2010. Code of conduct: The way we do business. Retrieved from http://www.pwc.com/en_GX/gx/ethics-business-conduct/pdf/pwc-codeofconduct.pdf.

Society for Human Resource Management. 2007. SHRM code of ethical and professional standards in human resource management. Retrieved January 21, 2010, from http://www.shrm.org/about/Pages/code-of-ethics.aspx.

Stone, O. 1987. *Wall Street* [Film]. In E. R. Pressman (Producer). USA: Twentieth Century-Fox Film Corporation.

Taylor, F. W. 1914. *The principles of scientific management.* New York: Harper.

The World Bank Group. 2010. Living our values: Code of conduct. Retrieved from http://siteresources.worldbank.org/INTETHICS/Resources/World_Bank_Group_Code_Of_Conduct_11_06_09.pdf.

United Nations. 1948. The universal declaration of human rights. Retrieved from http://www.un.org/en/documents/udhr/.

Weinstein, B. 2002. Teaching business ethics [Television program]. On MSNBC (Producer), *Economy Watch.* USA: Newswatch Cleveland.

Chapter 39

Collaboration: Getting the Most Out of Informal Connections

Robert J. Thomas, Executive Director
Institute for High Performance
Yaarit Silverstone, Managing Director
Talent & Organization Performance
Accenture

COLLABORATION IS HUGELY VALUABLE BUT LARGELY INTANGIBLE. MOST MANAGERS TODAY understand the importance of collaboration to the success of their companies. In an era of globalization, proliferating technology, and the specialization of knowledge-based work, accomplishments of any substance require more than streamlined processes; they require people to work together in ways that aren't fully captured on formal organizational charts or standardized processes and procedures. Important outcomes—revenues, patent approvals, cycle time reduction, client retention—are associated with collaboration. But managers aren't the only ones who value collaboration: employees experience it as a vital ingredient to engagement and job satisfaction. Moreover, investors regard it as an asset that differentiates frontrunner companies from those in the middle of the pack.

Yet because collaboration is difficult to see and feel—much less to record on a ledger sheet—it constitutes a paradox in organizational life. Managers can never get enough but they often overlook the volume and variety of collaboration that's going on around them. The building blocks of collaboration—for example, the intense conversations and head scratching that are the preamble to defining (or discovering) a higher-order goal—demand time, attention, and presence (mental, if not always physical). Pressure to collaborate can kill the impulse to share. Employees exhibit a lot of collaboration, but much of it does not get recognized, and in some cases, collaboration is actually aimed at accomplishing ends that are at odds with formal corporate objectives. If not configured properly, technologies intended to enhance collaboration can turn work into a labyrinth of meetings, phone calls, videoconferences, e-mail, instant messages, voice mail, postings, and tweets.

In this chapter we suggest that before managers can determine whether they are getting (and/or promoting) the right level and kind of collaboration, they need first to understand that collaboration comes in many flavors, not all of which will suit the managerial palate. We offer a simple typology that takes into account the visible and invisible as well as the productive and unproductive features of collaboration.

Defining collaboration is important, but it only takes us part of the way to resolving its paradoxes. Equally important is the ability to see it and measure it. Fortunately, research on social networks has enhanced our ability to "see" collaboration at work and to measure its consequences. However, the more important contribution of social network analysis is that it forces managers to prioritize their quest for collaboration because the preconditions for productive collaboration—things like trust and respect—don't take root overnight.

Defining Collaboration

The dictionary defines collaboration as "working together." Strictly speaking, then, any work that relies on the cooperation of two or more people would qualify as collaboration. However, we want a definition that is useful to practicing managers. And we feel that it is essential to highlight the truly distinctive quality of collaboration: the unstructured and voluntary component of working together. Thus, we define collaboration as people working together on things that require negotiation of meaning and order. We use the term negotiation to suggest that there isn't an obvious process to follow in working together. An assembly line uses physical technology to organize how people work together; likewise, a standard operating procedure tells people what to do and when. To our mind, collaboration requires that people come to some agreement about what they're trying to accomplish and in what order each will contribute.

After reviewing the diversity of work activities one finds in organizations, we concluded that there are two defining characteristics to collaboration. The first dimension has to do with *purpose*, or why collaboration is initiated. Sometimes collaboration is instigated by an intentional search—for instance, someone is looking for the solution to a problem or a partner who can provide much-needed expertise. The initiator may not know all that she needs, but she knows that she's got to find people who have pieces to the puzzle. For example, someone who is responsible for organizing a departmental offsite goes out in search of others who have managed one successfully and finds partners willing to share agendas, location details, planning templates, and a list of potential caterers. In other instances, collaboration results from discovery of a shared interest in a topic; collaboration is therefore emergent, a by-product of a casual search.

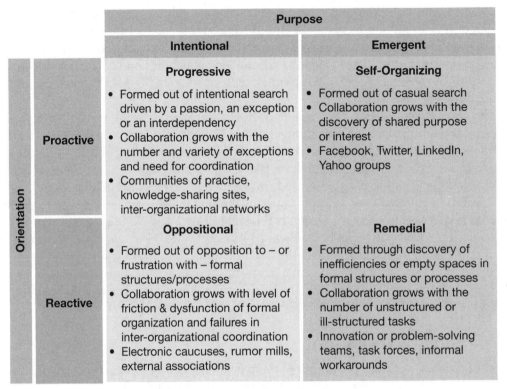

Figure 39-1 Proactive versus Reactive Collaboration

The second distinguishing characteristic of collaboration is its *orientation*—it can either be proactive or reactive. Sometimes collaboration is proactive: People assemble to pursue a common goal, usually one they consider to be constructive and aligned with or complementing a positive organizational objective. For example, employees mobilize informally to smooth the onboarding of new colleagues from an acquired company—even though the HR organization is effectively managing things like benefits enrollment. In other instances, collaboration may be reactive: It comes about in response to shortcomings in, or the failure of, a formal structure or process. For example, when problems arise in the switchover from one software system to another, people rally to keep things going until the crisis is resolved.

Four Types of Collaboration

Progressive collaboration often starts out as the product of chance encounters but grows into something purposive and durable as collaborators discover a shared need or passion and recruit others to it. Casual searches lead to richer conversations, a refined understanding, and a deeper appreciation of the complexities to be found in the object of common interest. Relevant examples include communities of practice and centers of excellence. The latter are often created with the explicit intent that they foster progress and knowledge-sharing among people who have invested in similar areas of expertise.

Self-organizing collaboration emerges out of the discovery of shared purpose or interest on the part of previously unconnected individuals. Social media and networking Web sites—including those that are part of a company's intranet—offer a place where people can post their interests and others can see them. Once a connection is made or a common interest is discovered, creation of a subgroup or alliance is possible. The underlying technology or platform allows for many possible connections.

Remedial collaboration occurs as a constructive reaction to elements of the formal organization that do not work completely or well. Rather than throw up their hands in frustration or wait for someone else to repair a broken process, people find workarounds that enable them to complete their tasks. For example, employees on a loading dock may improvise alternative approaches to make up for the fact that the software that determines shipping routes doesn't take into account roadwork or construction projects. In other words, remedial collaboration fills the empty spaces left untouched by policies, answers the questions that procedures manuals don't, and makes it possible for people to secure resources, get approvals, and negotiate ambiguity in places where there is no documented process.

Oppositional collaboration may seem a contradiction in terms, but it is a reaction triggered by the shortcomings, the failings, and/or the perceived injustices associated with a formal policy or process. Unlike remedial collaboration, oppositional collaboration does not seek to ameliorate or compensate for those shortcomings; it seeks instead to leverage them in order to strike a more attractive effort bargain and/or to grow a counterculture and a distinctive identity based in opposition. Creative energy that might be directed to fixing formal processes gets channeled into defensive routines, rate-setting, and dissent. For example, people may use advanced communications technology to spread rumors faster or to transmit potentially embarrassing information to competitors, regulators, or the media.

Having distinguished types of collaboration based on purpose and orientation—from chance encounter to intentional search, from desires to advance or to protect a set of interests—we can now refine our investigation of what it takes to establish and maintain these different types of collaboration.

Fostering Collaboration

Three of these four types of collaboration are attractive from a managerial perspective, but each poses unique requirements and challenges alongside the opportunities. Based on extensive research conducted by a team from Accenture's Institute for High Performance and the Network Roundtable at the University of Virginia, we have identified the distinctive opportunities, requirements and challenges for each type of collaboration (see Figure 39-2).

For progressive collaboration, a major challenge resides in finding ways to reduce the time and the energy required for people to find one another—i.e., to root out who has expertise or experience in a particular domain—and then to "qualify" (gain comfort or trust) in the information or expertise the other person has to offer.

Type of collaboration	Opportunities	Requirements	Challenges
Progressive	• Leveraging/re-use of existing intellectual assets • Increased organizational agility • Increased employee engagement	• Effective, continuously refreshed knowledge exchange • System of rewards that promotes both voluntarism and trust	• Reducing the time and energy it takes for people to find and qualify one another • Expense associated with administering databases/ portals and maintaining quality
Self-Organizing	• Unanticipated discoveries and breakthroughs • Increased employee engagement	• Accessibility to a large percentage of employees • Technology platform that supports peer-to-peer connectivity	• Appearance of unproductive time spent online • Difficulty of channeling activity to specific goals
Remedial	• Low-cost, informal solutions that complement the existing organization	• Effective, widespread use of problem-solving methods (e.g., six sigma) as a foundation for collaboration	• Avoiding collaboration overload • Reducing the time and energy it takes for people to find and qualify one another

Figure 39-2 Comparisons of Collaboration Types

In the ideal, self-organizing collaboration ought to enable a company to fluidly capitalize on new opportunities regardless of functional, hierarchical, geographic, or organizational lines. In reality, however, self-organizing collaboration challenges managers to accommodate themselves to the fact that success often involves high levels of uncertainty, non-linearity, and serendipitous advance. However, the process of search, particularly broad-based search, can appear to the untrained eye to be aimless time-wasting. In many organizations, and especially in those with managers unaccustomed to supporting broad-based search, it is common to hear complaints about people idly surfing the web or chatting on Facebook when, in fact, people may be scanning the environment garnering potentially valuable connections for the company.

While most commonly found in the case of remedial collaboration, the specter of collaboration overload—a close cousin to information overload—arises whenever managers fail to prioritize their efforts to foster collaboration. Remedial collaboration is highly valued because it addresses bottlenecks, breakdowns, and failures in existing processes. But, in the absence of a clear set of priorities—which repairs or improvements really matter—and lacking a shared methodology for analyzing and repairing breakdowns (such as six sigma or total quality management) it is common for people to find themselves inundated with requests for collaboration. Technology that allows for instant communication and cross-platform connectivity (e.g., presence-based applications that follow the subscriber from PC to smart phone to videoconference) can exacerbate problems they were meant to solve when all they do is multiply (and amplify) the number of calls for collaboration. As we've tried to show, a manager who wants to make the most out of collaboration needs to understand what type of collaboration he or she wants to foster and how. He also needs to be clear as to why he wants collaboration because it is expensive, requires distinctive supports and can easily consume the time and attention of some of the most valuable people.

What can't be seen often does not get measured, and what does not get measured rarely gets managed. We describe, in the next section, the utility of social network analysis for these tasks.

Seeing Collaboration in Action

Collaboration—of any type—is largely invisible without the right tools or lens with which to see it. Fortunately, social network analysis (SNA) has emerged as a powerful new way for managers to see the patterns of interaction—information sharing, problem-solving, and mentorship, as well as collaboration—that make up the less visible, often informal side of an organization.[1] By asking simple survey questions online and identifying the people with whom they most frequently interact, SNA makes it possible to depict (in a network diagram such as Figure 39-3 or in a matrix) the networks that underlie or exist in parallel to the formal organization charts and process diagrams. Repeated surveys will, over time, reveal changes in networks or in patterns of collaboration, making it possible to assess whether interventions such as reorganization or targeted efforts to improve collaboration (like off-site events, new software/communications tools, or incentive programs) actually have their desired impact. Moreover, targeted questions can reveal different types of collaboration.

To illustrate the utility of SNA, we present three short vignettes featuring examples of progressive, remedial, and self-organizing collaboration.

Progressive Collaboration

A very successful partner was tapped to lead a new business unit at one of the world's largest professional services organizations. Since the organization she'd been given had been composed out of several disparate units, she found herself leading people she did not know—many of whom had never worked together before. To make matters even more challenging, the group was tasked with achieving a significant increase in market share quickly so as to justify the reorganization.

To tackle her new challenge, she decided to approach collaboration systematically. Rather than rely on a few energetic collaborators or rushing to install a much-hyped technological solution, she elected to start by asking a few basic questions: What networks were in place that leveraged the expertise and project experiences within her business unit? How much did her employees know about the depth of skills residing in the group (and so whom to tap when certain opportunities appeared)? And what incentives were most likely to encourage value-added collaborations?

Knowing that she could not answer any of those questions by looking at the unit's organizational chart or even by reading people's job descriptions, she carried out a social network analysis to find targeted ways to enhance collaboration—particularly progressive collaboration—among experts in the group. She focused on progressive collaboration because her organization relied on teams of experts to solve client problems and to do so in a way that leveraged not just the immediate team's knowledge but the knowledge of the unit as a whole.

To get a sense of these patterns of collaboration amongst her employees, she asked each employee to rate all other employees on the following question: "Please indicate the extent to which the following people are effective in providing you with information that helps you to learn, solve problems, and do your work." She was concerned that a lack of awareness of "who knows what" and trust in other colleague's expertise was invisibly leading to missed sales opportunities and less than optimal delivery of services.

The SNA revealed barriers that were keeping the unit from combining expertise in key areas and differentiating itself from its competitors. A quantitative presentation of the network data (see Figure 39-3) helped her see the extent to which a pattern of recurring work assignments had created silos within and between key industry account groups and business units like hers. The table in Figure 39-3 shows the percentage of information-seeking relationships that existed within and between each function out of 100 percent if every person were collaborating with every other person at that network juncture (either within or across units). For example, if everybody in High Tech had effective informational relationships with one another, the figure 100 percent would appear in the top left-hand cell (instead of the actual 35 percent).

The table revealed several opportunities. Although she did not want to see high numbers in all the cells—everybody collaborating with everyone else would mean time was probably being wasted—she did want to see specific points of integration where fluid information flow was important to the success of the unit. Two things

	High Tech	Banking	Government	Consumer Products	Natural Resources	Strategy	Other
High Tech (11)	35%	0%	0%	1%	3%	10%	0%
Banking (3)	0%	100%	11%	0%	6%	4%	0%
Government (3)	9%	22%	50%	7%	17%	10%	11%
Consumer Products (9)	3%	0%	0%	13%	2%	1%	0%
Natural Resources (6)	0%	6%	11%	4%	23%	5%	22%
Strategy (26)	7%	3%	6%	1%	4%	36%	36%
Other (3)	6%	11%	0%	0%	11%	36%	0%

Figure 39-3 Collaborative Information Sharing Between Functions

stood out. First, looking *down the diagonal*, she hoped to see 25 percent to 35 percent connectivity within each group to ensure that best practices and synergies were being realized in groups that had similar expertise. Within Consumer Goods and Natural Resources, those figures were much lower. She knew that even though those functions were small, each had specialists who rarely worked together yet where collaboration could help to develop truly unique service offerings.

Second, she was keenly interested in building certain off-diagonal collaborations that could yield a competitive advantage with clients—especially where bringing together people from different functions produced a holistic solution to clients' problems. These key off-diagonal junctures represented the greatest opportunity to combine unique, tacit expertise in offerings to clients that competitors could not re-create. Collaborations often break down for simple reasons—two leaders don't like each other, physical distance between people gets in the way, incentive schemes are incompatible, or there is a lack of technical infrastructure. The figures in this kind of grid help locate those breakdowns that will undermine strategy execution

Remedial Collaboration

A small pharmaceutical company found itself ensnared in a paradox. It had enjoyed extraordinary success in the market with its initial products, but an annual employee climate survey revealed that people were feeling increasingly dissatisfied with the company as a workplace. They complained that the culture of openness and collaboration they had always valued had eroded precipitously and they were feeling increasingly bogged down by a lack of autonomy and glacial decision-making processes. The more successful the company was in the marketplace, the less happy employees seemed to be. Management was puzzled by the survey results but might have passed them off as a momentary blip on an otherwise clear radar were it not for the fact that they had ambitious plans for growing the number of products and adding even more new employees. They were wary of putting their plans for expansion at risk, but they lacked a way to test many of the hypotheses spurred by the survey. They decided to commission a social network analysis to assess the state of collaboration in the company.

One aspect of the situation particularly intrigued senior management: complaints about the slow pace of decision making. They were curious because as a group they felt busier than they had ever been and had been trying to decentralize decision making in order to avoid becoming a bottleneck. The SNA therefore focused specific attention on the patterns of activity that went into making decisions of various sorts (routine versus strategic, for example). People were asked to trace work processes in which they were engaged and to identify who in the organization they had to consult, inform, or seek approval from at various moments in the decision process.

The SNA survey and subsequent interviews revealed two important things. First (as depicted in Figure 39-3), the network analysis revealed that despite their professed efforts at decentralizing decision making, senior leaders (vice president and above) were right at the center of the organizational network, meaning that they were vital players in virtually everyone's depiction of decision making (routine as well as strategic). They were in such high demand that no matter how hard they worked, the organization slowed down. Second, the SNA, along with qualitative interviews, showed that rapid growth in the number of new employees and the absence of well-documented procedures actually encouraged enormous effort at remedial collaboration. Quite simply, people were inventing workarounds on a daily basis just to get things done. Rather than complain about the lack of process (except, indirectly, through the employee survey), collaborators created new ones.

Armed with these insights, management undertook a three-step enterprise-wide program to revamp decision-making processes. They first impaneled a team to draft guides on overall decision-making principles and practices, and produced optimal decision-flow schematics for two categories of decision types: the most common and the most important. By simplifying the decision-making network and effectively delegating and communicating routine decision-making roles and authority, the number of costly and time-consuming interactions of limited value was dramatically cut.

Second, senior leadership established a steering committee to reconsider governance principles and practices. One key action of this group was to quickly and dramatically reduce the number and size of committees. Those that remained involved in strategic initiatives were held accountable for being more timely and decisive.

Third, management began a cultural and behavioral change program to highlight individual accountability and reduce people's sense that they had to be consulted on even trivial decisions. This program included revised leadership training on decision making. Conflict resolution training was instituted to ensure that disputes didn't bog down the decision-making process.

Self-Organizing Collaboration

The R&D organization of a large food products company began ten years ago to experiment with communities of practice as a way to foster product innovation—a classic approach to progressive collaboration. But management grew concerned that the communities of practice were aimed several levels above the space where real breakthrough innovation was most likely to take place. For example, there were communities of practice around food groups and specialty products like snacks for people with diabetes but none around emergent topics in bioengineering and nanotechnology. If future products were likely to be built from new combinations of knowledge, then the communities of practice were not likely to take the company into the future.

An experiment with "smart" (electronic) name tags at an annual internal conference attended by many of the leading scientists provided a powerful example of how social networks thinking could enhance self-organizing collaboration in the company. The electronic badges had the ability to communicate with every other badge in the main conference hall and helped broker introductions. But not just any introductions. Two things were programmed into each tag: each person's existing network of collaborators and a listing of the skills that person needed to find in others if he or she was to collaborate effectively to spur innovation. The tags then helped broker very targeted introductions that held value for the organization rather than allowing people to simply connect with those they already knew or those that had similar expertise.

In practice, this meant that people would mingle until their badge indicated they were in the proximity of another person that was both outside their network and had expertise they should be connecting with. When that happened the badge would light up and flash a welcome to the other person to the effect: "Hi Bob. We should be talking about biochemistry." So the first function the tags served was to create potentially valuable introductions—not just a "more connectivity is better" approach. It also generated a great deal of energy and enthusiasm in the room. Further, if people stayed connected long enough to hold a deeper conversation, a network link between the two people would be logged with the name tags. This link was then transported to the front of a ballroom, where it appeared on two very large screens so that people could see the network being built in two-minute increments. This added to the sense of energy in the room. But more important, it gave management a baseline of potentially valuable connections and the ability subsequently to determine where innovative opportunities had been realized and where potential still lay.

Conclusion

In times like these—when increases in market volatility and complexity have delivered a one-two punch to many organizations—collaboration brings a richer and more diverse gene pool of interests, skills, and experiences to bear on a common topic. And, perhaps most importantly, it encourages initiative from people who might otherwise wait for direction.

But it is important to recognize that not all collaboration adds value, and not all value-adding collaboration is evident when it begins. Progressive collaboration produces value indirectly, largely by adding depth to the understanding of a process or an activity that directly creates value. Remedial collaboration helps achieve value when a system is incapable of monitoring and correcting itself. Self-organizing collaboration helps people discover the common interests that often serve as the precursor to value-creating activity. Oppositional collaboration usually destroys value or dissipates it.

Collaboration is most powerful when focused on the creation of intangible assets like ability to innovate, talent and human capital development, leadership development, reputation, and brand. Fortunately, tools like social network analysis are making it possible to do something more than "water and wait" when it comes to cultivating collaboration. By utilizing more effective ways to depict collaborative networks, to see change in them as a result of targeted interventions, and to distinguish among the types of collaboration possible, managers are finding that they can encourage collaborations that are likely to yield fruit for the organization.

Notes

1. For a more detailed discussion of the origins and varieties of social network analysis, see R. Cross and A. Parker, *The Hidden Power of Social Networks* (Boston: Harvard Business School Press, 2004); R. Cross and Robert J. Thomas, *Driving Results through Social Networks* (San Francisco: Jossey-Bass, 2008); M. Gladwell, *The Tipping Point: How Little Things Can Make a Big Difference* (Boston: Back Bay Books, 2002); R. Burt, *Structural Holes* (Cambridge: Harvard University Press, 1992); M. Granovetter, "The Strength of Weak Ties," *American Journal of Sociology* 78 (1973): 1360–1380; T. Allen, *Managing the Flow of Technology* (Cambridge: MIT Press, 1984); P. Monge and N. Contractor, "Emergence of Communication Networks," Forthcoming in ed. F. Jablin and L. Putnam, *Handbook of Organizational Communication*, 2nd ed. (Thousand Oaks, CA: Sage); E. Rogers, *Diffusion of Innovations*, 4th ed. (New York: Free Press, 1995).
2. See Cross, Thomas, Dutra, and Newberry 2008.

Chapter 40

Creating Competitive Advantage through Cultural Dexterity

Reginald F. Butler
Managing Director, Cultural Transformation Services
PricewaterhouseCoopers LLP

Cultural Dexterity—Key to a Company's Future Success

In the current business environment, diversity and inclusion matter more than ever to an organization's future success. Taken together, they result in cultural dexterity—a business skill that enables effective collaboration and communication among people across multiple dimensions of diversity. Cultural dexterity, in turn, leads to stronger and more agile organizations and broadens the ways that a company can identify talent potential.

The business environment is never static. Now is the time for forward-looking organizations to position themselves for the next business cycle—the time to harness the collective power of their people across the broadest spectrum. An organization's environment can enable or impede the success of its employees and itself, in that groups of diverse people who approach problems from different perspectives can improve corporate performance. Reevaluating the ways that an organization identifies talent potential may reveal untapped promise that had previously gone underutilized. As companies continue looking for ways to do more with less, this ability to better leverage the existing workforce is critical.

The Talent Pipeline—A Key Area of Focus

We are witnessing a significant labor shortage. Growth in the U.S. working-age population in the next four decades will drop more than 60 percent from that seen in the previous four (PricewaterhouseCoopers 2008). What's more, the population of Caucasians in the United States—currently about 70 percent—will drop below 50 percent by mid-century (U.S. Census Bureau 2008). Economic crisis or not, today's leaders must continue to anticipate future "people" needs and take steps now to groom tomorrow's leaders.

Keep in mind that high-performing individuals want to be part of a high-performing organization, and a company's commitment to diversity and inclusion is one of the dimensions they will evaluate when making career decisions. In our experience, the best talent actually searches for inclusive environments.

Keeping Up the Momentum

Forward-looking organizations have made good progress with their diversity programs over the years. Programs that began as token diversity programs have now become *strategic business imperatives*. But this is no time to rest on one's laurels. Savvy leaders recognize that relying on yesterday's progress is not enough to position the company for future success. They know that without constant attention—not just by the company's diversity officer but also by *all* its leaders companywide—progress can grind to a halt, or even reverse itself. In order to attract, groom, and retain the leaders that will carry the organization into the future, companies must effectively manage talent and embed diversity and inclusion into the very DNA of the company.

A Bird's-Eye View of Diversity Progress

- Recruiting programs designed to meet legal obligations have become recruitment *and retention* programs that reflect how demographic trends will impact the labor market in the future.

- What began as an effort to hire and promote minorities has led to a culture of inclusion that not only allows but indeed *encourages* all employees to contribute in different ways.

- A commitment to fairness and equality has become an understanding that cognitively diverse organizations often outperform those that draw on homogeneous talent bases.

- While diversity was once the exclusive domain of the human resources department, today it is the personal responsibility of *everyone*—corporate leaders and all employees companywide.

Morale—A Key Factor in Employee Retention, Particularly after a Riff

When companies are forced to jettison their highest-performing, highest-paid talent, the people who remain are typically expected to do their own jobs plus the jobs of those who left, while at the same time striving to meet their own individual goals for the year. As a result, pressure to produce increases, overtime becomes commonplace, work/life balance falls by the wayside, and morale takes a nosedive.

As we see it, employee engagement is critical to morale building, and too many employees across the country are unhappy with their jobs. A recent article in Associated Press underscores our point of view (2010). Author Jeannine Aversa writes, "Even Americans who are lucky enough to be working in the current economy are becoming unhappier with their jobs." She goes on to describe a recent survey of 5,000 households, conducted for the Conference Board, which shows that only 45 percent of Americans are satisfied with their work—the lowest level recorded by the Conference Board's research groups in the 22 years since they first began studying the issue. According to the author, economists are saying that if the job satisfaction trend is not reversed, it could stifle innovation and hurt America's competitiveness and productivity. From our perspective, growing job dissatisfaction will have a negative impact on the workforce of the future if companies do nothing to break this spiraling trend.

Diversity—A Talent Management Issue

So how can companies with a tired and demoralized workforce boost morale going forward? From our perspective, morale and employee engagement have a direct link to productivity output, and that circles back to place integration squarely into the talent management space. Why? Every company is going to have to figure out how to retain top talent, and top talent has no color. Top talent has no gender. Top talent is just top talent. Some of the best retention ideas come from a mix of people—not the people at the top but the people in the ranks who carry the day-to-day workload. When all of a company's people are alike—white males, for example—innovative ideas about boosting morale and retention don't usually show up. To effectively manage talent at all levels, you need to stir diversity into the mix to create an inclusive environment. Success means elevating diversity to the talent management space. Indeed, diversity and talent management are synonymous.

We believe that corporate America is trending toward viewing diversity as a talent solution. Consider this situation: Companies that are forced to let their highest-paid "superstars" walk out the door expect that the employees who remain will become the superstars of the future. But although those women and minorities who are left are *good* performers, they are not the *highest* performers. As a result, when business leaders look to the Office of Diversity for the best person for a specific function, there is typically a dearth of high performers available. All too often, the person assigned is unable to measure up to the specific job at hand. The company is then forced to look outside the organization for a top performer, and the diversity initiative loses credibility. What is the solution? It is critical for the Office of Diversity to build its diversity and inclusion infrastructure at a faster rate, so that the next time a request for a top resource comes in, it will be able to assign a fully capable person with the knowledge and skill set to fill that particular function.

Diversity? Inclusion? Is There a Difference?

You bet there is a difference. When we consider diversity, we look at the full range of human and organizational differences and similarities. Many organizations think of diversity in terms of attributes like generation, race, gender, ethnicity, and sexual orientation. But there are more than 20 dimensions of diversity at play. Acknowledging and even celebrating an organization's diversity are only starting points. The real payoff comes through creating an environment of inclusion—the process of leveraging each unique individual to strive toward a common goal and objective. When individuals believe that they're in an environment that is supportive and collaborative, and that their voices are being heard, then increased productivity and a greater sense of loyalty result. This is where transformation takes place, where the impact on your business and necessary competitive advantages are realized.

Diversity + Inclusion = Cultural Dexterity

From where we stand, it is a company's responsibility to create an environment that offers systemic opportunities equally to all employees.

And it is the responsibility of the company's leaders—*all* of its leaders, not just diversity leaders—to make themselves accountable for creating a diverse and inclusive culture—one in which all employees clearly understand what success is and how to achieve it, and are effectively encouraged to participate. This is the best time ever to elevate diversity to the talent space. But where do you start, and what does it take?

Four Considerations for Cultural Dexterity

1. Complementary skills add value; diverse groups have been shown to outperform those made up exclusively of members who share similar abilities.
2. Innovation is driven by a willingness to consider unique, or previously unconsidered, ways of thinking.
3. Reorganizing the value of a wide variety of abilities—and allowing those abilities to flourish—enable a company to draw the most out of its existing workforce.
4. Demographic trends will continue regardless of the economic environment; companies that develop cultural dexterity today will be more competitive—hence more successful—tomorrow.

Navigating today's challenges and anticipating tomorrow's opportunities require an expanded way of thinking. In that context, the diversity of an organization's talent base may be its greatest asset. In an increasingly tight and diverse labor market, companies will need cultural dexterity to attract—and *retain*—talent. The creation of an inclusive culture that encourages productivity, creativity, and loyalty among all employees does not happen overnight. Companies that begin today will be more competitive in tomorrow's market. But creating sustainable competitive advantage through diversity and inclusion takes hard work.

In our experience, successful leaders begin by accepting personal accountability for diversity—examining their own behavior and identifying their individual role in creating an environment of equal access and opportunity. Here are some action steps along the road to cultural dexterity:

- *Acknowledge your own blind spots.* Studies show that people make approximately 11 judgments within the first seven seconds of meeting someone new. Examine and neutralize any unconscious bias that may underlie your own decision-making process.
- *Start the dialogue.* Demonstrate that diversity and an environment of inclusion are important by initiating conversations. The more open and authentic the dialogues, the easier it becomes to promote change.
- *Search for behaviors of exclusion.* Whether exhibited by yourself or others, many exclusionary behaviors are unintentional—or even well intentioned—such as assuming a working mother would refuse a weekend travel assignment. Seek out and eliminate such behaviors.
- *Create an environment of advantages.* Small, unintentional inequalities can become pervasive. Establishing a culture of inclusion fosters an environment where small advantages are available to all—for example, candid feedback, special assignments, and invitations to contribute at meetings. Keep a record of those who are given such advantages and the impact that it has. Make a conscious effort to include everyone on your team.
- *Be a visible champion of cultural dexterity.* Show your commitment by what you say and do. Broaden your perspective by becoming involved with people and groups outside your normal personal and professional social circles.

What This Means to Your Business

PricewaterhouseCoopers recently convened a Diversity Leadership Forum where more than 700 business leaders participated in a discussion around strengthening diversity efforts. Here is the consensus that emerged: Those companies that cultivate cultural dexterity now as a tool for effectively managing diversity will be better equipped to weather today's many challenges and will have a competitive advantage in the marketplace of the future. Forward-thinking leaders recognize the need to invest in diversity and inclusion as part of their overall talent management practices, and to continually challenge their organizations to make the connection between those principles and their corporate performance. The payoffs for such investment are real.

Case in point: An increasing number of studies indicate a correlation between the number of women in management positions and corporate performance. A 2001 survey found that Fortune 500 firms with more female executives outperformed their industry medians by 34 percent in terms of profit as a percent of revenues, and by 69 percent in terms of profit as a percent of stockholders' equity (Tuhue-Dubrow 2009). A 2007 survey found that among European firms, those with higher percentages of women in management saw their stock price increase 17 percent more than the average in a two-year period (McKinsey & Co. 2007). These results suggest that the cognitive diversity brought by just one dimension of diversity alone may impact the bottom line, making the need to recruit, retain, and motivate a diverse talent base a business imperative.

Bottom Line

Companies that build a diverse and inclusive environment and achieve cultural dexterity position themselves to reap results that touch every area of the business— potentially resulting in greater agility, better market insight, stronger customer and community loyalty, innovation, and improved employee recruitment and retention. What company can afford to ignore competitive advantages such as these?

References

Associated Press. 2010. Survey says American workers can't get no job satisfaction; recession partly to blame. Jeannine Aversa, Associated Press economics writer. January 5.

McKinsey & Co. 2007. *Women matter: Gender diversity, a corporate performance driver.* [Report]. New York: McKinsey & Co.

PricewaterhouseCoopers. 2008. *American Perspectives.* New York: PricewaterhouseCoopers LLP.

Tuhue-Dubrow, Rebecca. 2009. The female advantage. *Boston Globe.* May 3 (Final Edition).

U.S. Census Bureau 2008.

Chapter 41

Building a Reservoir of High-Performance and High-Potential Women

Molly Dickinson Shepard, Chief Executive Officer
Nila G. Betof, Ph.D., Chief Operating Officer
The Leader's Edge/Leaders By Design

Preface

As *The Economist* reports, "Women's economic empowerment is arguably the biggest social change of our time" (The Economist 2010). Women in 2010 now represent half of the U.S. labor force in the United States and are slightly more than half of the managerial and professional labor force. However, women are still underrepresented in the largest American companies. Only 3 percent of the Fortune 500 CEOs are women. Women hold less than 16 percent of the board seats.

Even given the larger number of working women, retention continues to be a major issue for corporations. Female executives are leaving organizations at a significantly higher rate than their male counterparts. Because of this, a number of challenges exist for corporations concerned with attracting and retaining talented women. Given the aging population in the United States, the fact that women are getting advanced degrees in greater numbers than their male peers, and the "war for talent," women's participation in the economy is vital. Research discussed in this chapter addresses the reasons that senior women are abandoning their big companies, big jobs, and big money. Why should this trend be both important and alarming to corporations? There are clear reasons for companies to direct attention to their women executives. Research indicates that companies that are more diverse and have women in their highest executive ranks fare better financially. In addition, the inclusion of women creates a diversity of viewpoints, perspectives, and management styles, which in turn produces better business decisions that can generate additional profits. The benefits offered through the addition of women are vital and cannot be overlooked by business.

Loss of Senior Talent

So why is it that women are leaving their corporate jobs in droves? Where are they going? Research shows that many of the women cite frustration with their work environment, specifically that they feel out of sync with the corporate culture and see few opportunities for advancement. This leads them to the pursuit of entrepreneurial endeavors and positions with corporate competitors. Women are starting their own businesses in record numbers. The recently released Center of Women's Business Research Report (October 2009) reported that there are 8 million U.S. businesses that are majority women-owned. The economic impact of these businesses is $2 trillion annually and 23 million jobs, 16 percent of all U.S. jobs. They indicate that this shift is "due to the education, experience, and characteristics of women at different stages and the lack of opportunities and flexibility in major corporations and large businesses for women." Indeed, in light of the cultural obstacles many women face, their decision to leave and start a company of their own where they can establish values and have the flexibility they desire is logical.

The Business Case

This loss of a large percentage of the talent pool constitutes a unique challenge to corporations' ability to retain, develop, and advance their women employees. The associated business issues can have a significant impact on corporate productivity and profitability.

There is no question that the loss of high-level women in corporations results in a loss of intellectual capital and knowledge. It also affects employee morale and results in increased costs of recruiting and hiring replacements.

Recent national studies show a correlation between the number of women executives and profitability. Most recently, Catalyst completed two studies, both of which showed that companies had a better return on equity and return on investment if they had more women in senior roles. (The 2004 study looked at business results for 353 companies with the highest and lowest representation of women on top management teams.) McKinsey & Company also has linked higher operating margins (EBITDA) and valuation along with significant differences in performance on nine dimensions of leadership and accountability when there are more women in top management. (The 2009 study looked at data from 231 companies and 115,000 employees.) According to a study published by the *Harvard Business Review* and conducted by Pepperdine University in California, among Fortune 500 companies, organizations with higher percentages of female executives produced earnings far in excess of the median for other large firms in their industries.

Another study, conducted by a University of Michigan Business School professor Theresa Welbourne, analyzed over 1,400 companies and found that women in top management positions make for a healthier and wealthier company. Her research found that for rapidly growing companies, the initial stock price, stock price growth, and growth in earnings over three years was higher for companies with women executives. Professor Welbourne stated, " I don't think it's the women per se that's causing the positive effect. I think it's the diversity of the management team." As more of these studies are done, the business case cannot help but get stronger for ensuring that women have equal and fair opportunities to advance to the top of their organizations if they so choose. Most interesting is that the numbers haven't changed significantly for women in top jobs over the last decade in spite of the growing evidence that more diverse teams contribute not only more to the bottom lines of their companies but also to the richness of thought, innovation, and strategy.

The business case for this issue has been written by hundreds of Women's Initiatives and Heads of Diversity in this country, but still change has been slow. There are a number of potentially costly business issues to be faced by companies, either as a direct expense or in terms of potential revenue lost:

- *The need for women, as a key market segment, to be represented in leadership positions.* With women making over 80 percent of the buying decisions in the $5 trillion consumer product market in the United States ($12 trillion consumer market worldwide), there is significant potential revenue to be lost by eliminating or ignoring even a portion of the market. If a company's human resources are not matched to the needs of the market segment, opportunities will be lost. The woman consumer clearly responds to marketing and makes buying decisions in a different way than a man. In fact, women purchase 65 percent of all new cars and 53 percent of used cars, and they influence 95 percent of all auto purchases (Road & Travel Magazine 2009). Women influence the purchase of 92 percent of home furnishings and vacations. Women influence the purchase of 91 percent of all homes. Women influence the purchase of 51 percent of all consumer electronics (Cavallari 2008). Women own over 76 million credit cards, 8 million more than men, and use them! The list of women's buying power goes on and on, but in short, women are significant stakeholders in the long-term success of most businesses worldwide. Therefore, the optimal business decision is to have women actively involved in creating and implementing strategies, and designing and marketing products and services which appeal to the woman's market.
- *Creating diversity in senior positions within the corporation.* The unique perspective of female executives has been documented as leading to better business decisions, which translates to greater revenue and can produce better operating decisions that save the company money. Conversely, a homogeneous group may generate decisions with limited scope. With its narrow point of view, it is more likely to miss an option or creative solution to a problem. Further, if a company exhibits a pattern of exclusionary behavior, it risks the threat of costly litigation that can effect shareholder value and generate negative publicity. This type of behavior will ultimately affect the cost of recruitment because it will be harder

to persuade women and minorities to join a company without a demonstrated commitment to diversity. In spite of these known facts, Catalyst's figures for 2009 document that only 3 percent of the CEOs in the Fortune 500 companies are women and those same companies only have 15.2 percent female representation on their boards and 13.5 percent female representation in their officer ranks.

- *Retention of female talent, which composes half of the workforce.* The cost of replacing an executive is generally calculated at one and one-half times current salary, which includes recruitment costs, replacement salary, and possible severance and litigation costs. There are a number of soft costs as well, including loss of knowledge, client relationships, and morale of the other women in the company. Businesses that are serious about retaining women leaders should first determine the extent and cause of the problem and become active in making necessary changes within the culture of the organization so that it becomes more attractive. Women who are being recruited for senior positions will undoubtedly look at the success of the company they are interviewing with in retaining key talent and may decide not to pursue even the most attractive job if they will be in a distinct minority.

- *Integrity within the organization and the authenticity of its leadership.* Companies must articulate a cogent set of values and act on them in a consistent manner. For example, a leader who believes in diversity must ensure that the message is being reflected in the structure and composition of the organization and that there is consistency in the company's words, policies, and practices. When a company is perceived as inconsistent, sending confusing messages, or not being open and honest with employees, commitment is lessened. As anyone who has worked in Corporate America has undoubtedly observed, untold dollars are lost in wasted time spent by employees speculating at the water cooler or coffee pot, discussing rumors and complaining to others, as well as time spent looking for other jobs. Additionally, there is a lessening of morale, performance issues, and finally, attrition. Authenticity, the consistent alignment between action and values, is a frequently cited reason for women leaving an organization.

- *Accountability throughout the company, from the top down.* It is critical to the integrity of the organization that its leadership team is held accountable for carrying out the company's vision and meeting the goals that have been set forth. All members of the organization should get appropriate, ongoing feedback in order to determine if policies are being practiced at all levels. If leaders are viewed as exempt from accountability, it becomes clear to employees that the policy is not truly valued because there are no repercussions for failing to follow it. This behavioral gap between practice and policy is a key issue and one where many companies fall short. Whether it involves diversity goals, a respectful environment, or work/life balance, once employees, particularly women, no longer believe that the company is behaving authentically, there will be substantial costs involving commitment, retention, motivation, and recruitment of female talent.

What the Research Shows

A Leader's Edge Research™ study surveyed 100 hundred high-level women who recently left their companies voluntarily, and the stories they tell are compelling. The focus of the research was to determine why high-level executive women leave companies, what companies could have done to retain them, and what advice these women would give to Corporate America.

When asked about the reasons for leaving their organizations, a majority of respondents' answers fell into the following categories:

- *Culture.* The women felt that their "style" was criticized and that it was difficult to get their ideas recognized. They discussed integrity issues, and some said that it bothered them that the company philosophy had become more about profitability than client needs. Others cited a "closed" management style and felt a lack of trust. "Corporate America needs to know, accept, and respect the fact that completely different work styles from people, including women, are not only okay, they are valuable and productive," according to a former health-care industry executive interviewed.
- *Communication.* They felt that they were excluded from important meetings and pipelines of information, company information was not openly shared, and they were often "out of the loop." One consultant put it this way: "Key information was being held by just a few individuals, even if others needed it to do their job right."
- *Career development.* Respondents voiced concerns that no one took an interest in their careers and that they did not have a course charted. A number of women surveyed mentioned the lack of a career plan and strategy. As a partner in an international accounting firm said, "There was no real attention paid to my career path once I made partner—I was the only one who thought about it. There is no institutional path for career development."

Lifestyle issues were also mentioned as important in the decision to leave:

- *Flexibility.* Many women discussed the inflexibility of the work environment; they were not given the ability to work off-site or adapt hours to family obligations. "With all my travel, there was no official flexibility to allow me to work from home. I was finally told that the company would allow me to work from home, but that it couldn't be official because they didn't want to set a precedent," according to a former human resources director.
- *Life/family balance.* Women are clear that there is no such thing as "balance" between their personal lives and their careers. Women report that the juggling they need to do to manage their home and work lives leaves them feeling exhausted and unfulfilled in both parts of their life. To some women it seemed the message was that it was unacceptable to have a life apart from work and that time needed for family reasons was not seen as valid or important. A woman executive in the medical industry said, "We were expected to work 24/7. No one

in management had a home life." Women with children make less than either childless women or men. As they rise in their careers, the demands on their time become even greater. Many women report greater travel time away from their families, longer hours, and sometimes international assignments being required to move to higher levels. If they feel they can't, or choose not to, keep up the exhausting pace, they leave seeking either another, hopefully better, company opportunity or start their own businesses.

Respondents were asked what changes their most recent employer could have made to encourage continued employment. The answers were as follows:

- *Inclusion.* A more open, less secretive culture and a respectful environment were mentioned as positive elements of change.
- *Flexible environment.* Suggestions in this area included allowing options such as telecommuting, job sharing, and more flexible hours, which would provide a more family-friendly atmosphere.
- *Feedback and career planning.* Respondents want their contributions to be valued, and feel that the company should encourage and support their efforts. They want to feel that there is a system in place for career planning based on honest evaluations and feedback. It is difficult for any senior person to get reliable, open, and honest feedback, but even more so for the female executive. This is due perhaps to fear of litigation, but unfortunately, many women, absent the feedback, are unaware that their style or behavior is problematic until it is too late and bridges have been burned.

The survey asked women to recommend a global change that Corporate America could make to help retain senior executive women. They said the following:

- *Invite diversity.* They want to have their business style respected and the company to have an appreciation of the benefits of diverse thinking.
- *Create critical mass.* Respondents want to see increased numbers of women in all areas of the organization, specifically senior and board positions.
- *Level the playing field.* Women still tend to be directed into staff areas which do not lend them the kinds of opportunities that will put them in line for the most senior positions. The women surveyed recommend that women be exposed to more job areas and opportunities. They want to be certain that they are being given equal access to challenging assignments, clients, and new business opportunities. It is also important to them that there are no assumptions made about their interest in, or qualification for, new positions based on their gender, marital status, or age.
- *Establish flexibility within the corporate culture.* The women stressed the significance of an atmosphere of trust so that people can do their jobs within a more flexible and accommodating culture. This includes more flexibility in hours, ways of working, and amount of travel scheduled.

- *Offer mentoring opportunities.* Mentoring is seen as important, and it is emphasized that programs should be started at the early stages of women's careers and must be encouraged by the company. Women should be encouraged to engage multiple mentors at different points in their careers, men and women as well as external mentors where appropriate. Women can benefit dramatically from the access to their mentor's network of contacts and become more visible to others within an organization.
- *Provide ongoing career development.* Companies should not make the assumption that all employees are motivated by the same things, including compensation. Women want to know where they stand in terms of the organization and their opportunities for advancement.
- *Establish and support women's networks.* Women's networks not only provide support but can also provide opportunities for development and leadership. Many women's networks focus their programming on development issues so women can gain more leadership skills. Also, networks encourage women to look at the opportunities around them and seek new opportunities within their organizations.

The study underscores several issues of interest to Corporate America:

- *Women feel underutilized,* due in part to the fact that they do not feel they are assigned strategic and important work assignments.
- *Recognition of differences in the styles* of men and women, and appreciation of that diversity, is beneficial to an organization.
- *Flexibility can enhance productivity* and is plainly on the minds of senior women executives.
- *Providing new challenges in positions and assignments* is seen as motivational and can provide additional productivity to the company. It is also a key component to retention.
- *Consistency in words, policies, and practices is vital* to the senior women surveyed. If they sense a behavioral gap, there is a breakdown in the level of trust.

Diversity in Practice

Creating diversity within an organization changes its corporate culture. According to former Public Broadcasting System President and CEO Pat Mitchell, "When women are at the top, we can and do change the culture. As women have come into corporations at critical mass levels, things have changed." However, the majority of companies do not find that diversity comes to them without a concerted effort. In some industries, however, there is a more female-friendly culture which makes gender diversity easier to achieve. Examples of these industries cited by the National Association for Female Executives (2002) include insurance, consumer goods, and educational publishing. In other companies and industries, attracting female executives has required a significant endeavor. These companies have taken different approaches to changing the culture.

Some have created top-down programs using precise tools to measure the results. This can be a positive indicator of change to an organization if well thought out by those who understand the company's existing cultural barriers. However, according to Myrna Marofsky, a consultant on diversity topics, ". . . programs can exemplify the worst kind of window dressing if they're adopted with no understanding . . ." (Cleaver 2002).

Others promote programs that appeal to women, such as flexible hours and professional development, thereby taking a more long-term growth tactic in changing their companies' cultures. "The beauty of a steady, inside-out transformation is that the expectations of nearly everyone in the company start to realign, creating an entirely different culture," says Barbara Waugh, author of *The Soul in the Computer: The Story of a Corporate Revolutionary*. It has also been noted that in companies where a top male executive leads the initiative for change, he has often been influenced by a situation where he can observe work/family challenges faced by a female close to him such as a wife or daughter.

A number of different approaches and initiatives have been used by companies, according to a report in *The Economist* (January 2, 2010). Flexibility is seen as being the key to retaining women. Addleshaw Goddard, a law firm, has established a new role called legal director as an alternative to partnership for women. More companies have developed flexible work arrangements and/or provide day care for their employees. Another trend is to allow employees to work from home either on a full-time or part-time basis or work a set number of compressed hours over a period of time with greater time off in between. In some instances, we are seeing an increase of extended unpaid leaves or sabbaticals that may be helpful for women with children who want to return to work.

Strategies and Guidelines

In order to create a more effective workplace, and one which attracts, develops, and retains talented females, the company and its women employees should enter into an agreement on what steps each will take to improve the work environment. This new "employment contract" requires an acknowledgment that cultural improvement is necessary and recognition that it is a corporate priority. The accomplishment of this initiative involves a commitment from both sides of the equation confirming that each is responsible for contributing to its success. The "contract" entered into by the company is that it will take the necessary steps to address the needs of its female employees and support women throughout the organization. The women's portion of the contract is that they will be responsible for their own development and take advantage of the opportunities provided by their employer in order to be more effective business contributors. Following are some guidelines for the organization and its women.

Organizational Guidelines Checklist

Management

- Create a vision of the company as a diverse organization and share it with all employees.

- Conduct an assessment of the current situation, if not already completed.
- Prepare diverse slates for promotions and key assignments.
- Create a "respectful work environment" and have senior management participate in education for managers and employees around diversity. Management should lead this effort through their behavior.
- Identify opportunities for women to serve on outside boards and committees in representing the company.
- Support the creation of women's networks and other affinity groups.

Human Resources

- Establish business unit-specific diversity performance guidelines to attract and retain a diverse workforce at all levels of the organization and hold managers accountable.
- Link talent management reviews with diversity goals for identifying women and minority candidate pools.
- Monitor EEO/AA (Equal Opportunity Employer/Affirmative Action) and other employment-related data to identify and address diversity issues.
- Support flexible work options in situations where individual and department objectives can be met.
- Have the words from the top connect to policies that lead to practices that reinforce the goals of senior leadership to have a community of employees that mirror as best as possible the communities in which you live and work.

Development

- Create role models for identified leadership behaviors.
- Select high-potential women and minorities for coaching to develop or enhance the necessary skills for growth and advancement.
- Create information networks, supports, and resources for women to learn about leadership capabilities and opportunities.
- Identify and encourage mentoring opportunities that support the enhancement of critical leadership skills.
- Support networking groups.
- Create opportunities for visibility (taskforce leadership, presentations, etc.) for high-potential women.
- In the performance review process, give appropriate training to managers so that career development is truly discussed, as well as opportunities for lateral transfers, rotations, and new assignments, to give an individual the opportunity to increase and enhance skills.

Women's Guidelines Checklist

- Build open and more effective networks in order to become better known, make important contacts internally and externally, and gather competitive and/or helpful information for the company.

- Identify and communicate strengths by having a clear, realistic picture of one's talents.
- Study and refine communication skills with the understanding that men and women communicate differently in order to more effectively communicate ideas and strategies and be heard.
- Endeavor to be more risk taking and strategic in terms of career growth.
- Use mentoring effectively, choosing the right mentor for a particular situation.
- Enhance personal presence and understand your leadership style.
- Learn to be political savvy, to "play the game," and navigate the political arena.
- Become known internally and externally in order to gain credibility and clout.
- Self-nominate to serve on projects and task forces that will enhance your skills and introduce you to new people.
- Speak up and let management know of your career goals, qualifications for advancement, and desire to advance.

Summary

The case is strong for businesses to rethink their approaches for attracting women and incorporating them into the workplace culture. Indeed, it is well beyond merely accepting the addition of a few token women in order to improve internal and public perception, and it is of vital importance to the health of the organization. With half of the available talent being female and the market demographics increasingly diverse, attracting and retaining women will be a competitive necessity. Diversity brings new viewpoints, styles of work and management, solutions to problems, and links with the marketplace, adding positively to the company's bottom line. Responsibility is twofold: the company must acknowledge the importance of cultural improvement, and the women in the company need to take responsibility for their leadership growth and career development. Once the behavioral gap is closed and senior management is committed, diversity on all levels within the corporation should become a matter of course.

References

Catalyst. 2004. The bottom line: Connecting corporate performance and gender diversity.

Cavallari, Renie. 2008. *Working women statistics and what women want: Surprises?* Aspire Marketing.

Cleaver, Joanne. 2002. *The Top 25 companies for executive women*. National Association for Female Executives. May.

Desvaux, G., S. Devillard-Hoellinger, and M. Meaney. 2008. *A business case for women*. McKinsey & Company.

Donahue, K. B. 1998. Why women leave and what corporations can do about it. *Harvard Management Update*. June.

Foroohar, R., and S. Greenberg. 2009. The real emerging market. *Newsweek*. September 21.

Gurer, Denise. 2002. *Why are women leaving corporate America and where are they going?* CobolReport.com. July.

Hochwald, Lambeth. 2002. 10 best companies for women. *Health Magazine.* July/August.

Leader's Edge. 2002. *The Leader's Edge Research™ of 100 executive women.*

Pepperdine University study of Fortune 500 companies. 2001. *Harvard Business Review.* November.

Road & Travel Magazine. 2009. Women in the automotive world.

The Economist. 2010. We did it! January 2.

Waugh, Barbara. 2001. *The soul in the computer: The story of a corporate revolutionary.* Makawao, Hawaii: Inner Ocean.

Welbourne, Theresa. Research study of over 1,400 IPO companies from 1993–1999. University of Michigan Business School.

Part V

Using Talent Analysis and Planning Techniques to Enhance Your Talent Management Program

Chapter 42

Multiplying Talent for High Performance

David Smith, Managing Director, Talent & Organization Performance
Elizabeth Craig, Research Fellow
Accenture

ONE OF THE MOST IMPORTANT SOURCES OF VALUE FOR ANY ORGANIZATION TODAY IS ITS people, from current and future leaders to frontline employees. In a global knowledge economy, organizations depend more than ever on the capabilities, creativity, and engagement of their people. Competitive success is increasingly a function of an organization's ability to leverage each employee's unique talents while creating opportunities for people to interact, communicate, and collaborate. These new success factors have elevated the strategic importance of talent for virtually every organization.

Yet few organizations are managing talent strategically. Too many leaders view the endgame as simply a matter of attracting and retaining the best people, but that alone cannot ensure competitive success. Not only does the fierce competition for star performers make it hard to secure them, but a star-oriented strategy leaves the considerable talents of the rest of the organization more or less untapped-and those talents are too valuable to waste.

This is why a focus on managing stars or so-called "A" players is not the key to sustained success. Talented individuals certainly help their companies succeed, but organizations that rely primarily on the skills and abilities of top-performing individuals will not realize the full potential of their entire workforces.

The most successful organizations don't just add top talent; they multiply all their talent. They do this by combining and recombining knowledge, skills, and processes throughout the organization to generate superior levels of workforce engagement, creativity, learning, adaptability, and performance. What separates these high performers from lesser competitors isn't just the talent they have. It's what they do with it. Their ability to access, develop, and channel their collective talents gives them an advantage over their competitors.

Talent and High Performance

Companies seeking to achieve high performance through an advantage in talent must build a distinctive capability we call "talent multiplication." Accenture's High Performance Business research program has identified three primary building blocks of high-performance: market focus and direction, distinctive capabilities, and performance anatomy. Talent figures heavily in two of the three. First, talent multiplication is one of the winning mind-sets in the performance anatomy of high-performing businesses. But when organizations embed the multiplier mind-set and practices into their strategies, processes, and operations, talent multiplication becomes more than a competitive mind-set: It becomes an important source of competitive advantage—a critical element in a top performer's distinctive capability.[1]

In this chapter, we describe what talent multiplication looks like in practice and explain how it creates value for organizations. We also briefly discuss how organizations can build the capabilities that they need to be in a position to multiply their talent and thus to create sustainable long-term competitive advantage.[2]

What Talent Multiplication Looks Like

Talent is typically thought of as an attribute of individuals. It is admired in artists, musicians, and athletes. In business, we praise the talents of the exceptional leader, the brilliant strategist, the outstanding salesperson, the savvy marketer, the financial wizard. Consequently, most organizations' talent management strategies and practices focus on individuals. But an exclusive focus on leaders, stars, and high-potential employees misses the opportunity to identify and nurture collective talents that may yield a whole that is greater than the sum of the parts.

Consider an organization whose talent primarily consists of 12 individuals: a U.S. professional basketball team. In 2006, the Miami Heat won the NBA Championship, and they won it by multiplying their collective talents. Statistical analyses of individual player performances and the team's performance with different combinations of players on the court revealed that Shaquille O'Neal, one of the best basketball players ever, was not the driving force behind the team's success. In fact, he was not even part of the best five-player combination (based on point differential when players are both in and out of the game) (Reuters 2006). It was the Heat's ability to engineer the best combinations of players' talents that led them to victory.

The Power of Multiplication

To understand how talent multiplication works, consider this hypothetical example. Imagine that a team of 10 baristas in a busy coffee shop can make 1,000 cappuccinos each day (each barista makes 100 drinks). If a star barista joins the team and makes 50 percent more drinks than the other baristas (150 a day), the team's output is increased to 1,150 cappuccinos per day. However, if the organization has the ability to multiply talent, then the new barista will be able to contribute his or her talent toward improving the entire team's knowledge, skills, and processes in ways that increase everyone's performance. Even if the newly hired barista only makes 120 drinks each day, talent multiplication will help everyone to make 120 cappuccinos each day, so that the team's output becomes an impressive 1,320 cappuccinos a day.

From Stellar Players to Stellar Organizations

Now consider the real-life example of the New Jersey Devils, one of the best teams in the NHL during the 2007 season. The team's top goal scorer ranked only 48th in the league, but the Devils succeeded by developing highly integrated systems for defense and scoring that enabled them to create and deliver on strategic opportunities-high-percentage scoring chances. Each member of the team remained focused on contributing to the system and multiplying the team's talent for collective impact.

The ability to multiply talent requires more than talented people, effective teamwork, or inspired leadership. When talent is a key strategic resource, an organization's success depends on the effective management of people, relationships, and human capital. In today's talent-driven world, having the ability to unlock talent's collective potential may give a long-term sustainable competitive advantage.

How Talent Multiplication Creates Value

Talent multiplication creates extraordinary value by transforming individual talents into new human, relational, and organizational resources.[3] These new human capital resources generate superior returns by enhancing individual and collective performances. And the benefits of talent multiplication do not end there. A distinctive capability in talent multiplication also enables strategic change and expands value creation opportunities for the organization. The following examples show how.

Enhancing Individual and Collective Performance: UPS and Marriott

As they deftly combine and recombine employees' knowledge, skills, and abilities, companies that multiply their talent foster the kind of collaboration, knowledge sharing, and collective learning that can elevate the performance of all employees, as well as teams, work groups, and entire workforces.

UPS, one of the world's largest package delivery companies, routinely takes employees out of their regular departments and temporarily assigns them to problem-solving teams in different parts of the business. The goal is to stimulate new ideas and new solutions, share best practices and innovations, and encourage greater communication and collaboration throughout the organization. "They will pull people from any job all across the country to join a special assignment team," says Peggy Gardner, director of customer communications. "The teams are of short-term duration; [they] go in with a very specific mission and come back with recommendations. It allows a lot of people who aren't always working together and getting into that sort of group mindset to come in and put their heads together on an issue." (Thomas, Linder, and Pham 2006; Thomas, Linder, and Dutra 2006).

However, it is essential to note that UPS does not consider the job done when an individual or a team achieves a specific improvement. The job is not considered complete until the skills that individuals and teams acquire are spread to adjacent teams and processes. In the case of UPS, the secret of talent multiplication is that only half of success is improvement of a specific process; the other half is transferring the knowledge to other team members.

Marriott International has its own approach to increasing individual and collective performance. It develops managers and promotes innovation through internal internships and mentoring relationships that allow senior leaders to learn about and contribute to areas of the business outside their current areas of expertise. Marriott views the intern program as both a developmental tool that builds individual capabilities and an innovation lever that sparks new ideas.

For example, a marketing executive with little experience in hotel operations completed an assignment in the operations division. To help her get up to speed quickly, she was assigned both senior and peer mentors. Moreover, she wasn't the only one who benefited from the experience. During her assignment, she shared some of her marketing knowledge with her colleagues in operations, by suggesting ways to attract more customers, for instance. The internal internships pay off in two ways: The company's investments in interns' time is more than recouped in cost savings from the help they bring to new situations; and the interns leave behind enhanced capabilities (because they are expected to teach, as well as to learn) while taking with them to new assignments a better understanding of the enterprise (Thomas 2006).

By combining and recombining knowledge and skills from across the organization, Marriott generates superior levels of creativity, adaptability, and performance. Moreover, it retains this engaged and superior talent-Marriott has one of the strongest, most seasoned, and cohesive management teams in the industry.

Enabling Strategic Change: GE and Goldcorp

The ability to multiply talent also enables organizations to take new strategic directions and adapt more readily to changes in the business environment. GE is a powerful case in point. In the 1980s, GE dramatically enhanced the organization's ability to adapt with its famed Work-Out initiative. The effort brought employees and managers from different levels and functions throughout the organization to improve work processes and solve organizational problems quickly. It was effectively a large-scale investment in multiplying the talents of people in the organization to not only improve individual performance but to dramatically enhance the organization's ability to change-whether change was incremental (as most performance improvement efforts demanded) or transformational (as in the case of mergers, divestitures, or recombination of businesses).

At the core of Work-Out was a common methodology-often referred to as a change checklist-that was simple yet comprehensive and capable of being applied to a wide range of situations. The genius behind Work-Out rested as much in the way it prepared people at all levels and in all businesses for managing change as a continuous process as it was in the fact that it provided a common starting point and action plan for use by groups of people who were, at the beginning at least, strangers to one another. In the words of one observer, Work-Out made people with different backgrounds and experiences "plug compatible from day one."

In the 1990s, the Work-Out approach was used to both develop leaders and clarify GE's "leadership brand"—the expected values and behaviors of leaders—which completely transformed the organization's core values and culture in a few short years (Ulrich, Kerr, and Ashkenas 2002). By multiplying talent throughout the organization, GE built an adaptable workforce and a large pool of capable leaders that, in turn, make it better able to transform the organization or change strategic direction rapidly and confidently.

More recently, mining company Goldcorp multiplied its talent by reaching outside the organization to bring about strategic change. The company used "crowd sourcing" to find gold in a mine that was believed to be dead. For the "Goldcorp Challenge," the company posted geological survey data on the Internet and offered prize money to anyone who could identify likely veins of gold in its Red Lake, Ontario, mine. This innovative way of accessing talent not only led to the discovery of gold worth $3 billion but also introduced new capabilities to the company. More than 1,400 geologists and mining engineers, as well as mathematicians, military officers, and management consultants, introduced Goldcorp to a variety of new technologies and approaches to exploration and extraction (see Tapscott and Williams 2006).

Combining the organization's resources with new knowledge and skills from the outside enabled Goldcorp to increase the knowledge, skills, and performance of its workforce and expand its mining capabilities. Multiplying talent helped transform Goldcorp from a struggling USD $100 million traditional mining company into a USD $9 billion business. It also developed Goldcorp's ability to collaborate, learn, and solve problems in ways that will enable the organization to innovate and change in the face of future business challenges.

Expanding Value Creation Opportunities: UPS and Google

Talent multiplication can also expand an organization's opportunities to create new value by entering new businesses, markets, or sectors. These transformative business moves take an organization beyond its existing value chain. In this process, intangible resources such as know-how, networks, and proprietary processes are transformed into assets such as new product areas, lines of business, or ventures.

UPS actively exploits market "adjacencies" to make use of the company's most valuable resources, including its industrial engineering capabilities, IT infrastructure, and network of aircraft and facilities. Its philosophy of "growth with purpose" means that expansion into adjacent business areas is expected to complement the core business. For example, UPS managers elected to capitalize on the organization's core business and knowledge of the customer by moving into supply chain management for their customers-that is, providing not only shipment but inventory management and, in some cases, repair work. "We wanted to leverage that engineering prowess-the talents of our 3,000 engineers-externally," says Bob Stoffel, senior vice president of the Supply Chain Group.

The idea made sense in theory, but it wasn't embraced as a practice until a cross-functional team was assembled to experiment with it. In the early 1990s, 30 "UPSers" were brought together to develop and launch a new Service Parts Logistics business. The new initiative combined talent from across the organization and resulted in the creation of a billion-dollar business. The experience had huge benefits not only for the company but for researchers and employee teams: Both walked away better equipped to think broadly about the business and to bring a variety of perspectives to their assignments. The team members returned to their regular jobs with new knowledge and skills that they put to use to improve performance.

Google's foray into renewable energy also shows how companies can combine and recombine their human and organizational resources to create new value.[4] Google's cofounder, Larry Page, has said that the company has "gained expertise in designing and building large-scale, energy-intensive facilities by building efficient data centers"-expertise it will put to use in this new venture. Google's leaders believe their ability to bring together talented technologists, engineers, outside partners, and funding will allow the company to accelerate the development of renewable energy sources. It will use the talent management capabilities that built the creative, collaborative, and innovative workforce at the heart of the company's success in its core businesses for the challenge of launching the renewable energy venture.

Building a Distinctive Capability in Multiplying Talent

By studying high-performance businesses in many different industries and locations, we have gained some insight into what it takes to help build a distinctive capability in talent multiplication. At the core is what we call the "four Ds" of talent multiplication: define, discover, develop, and deploy. To multiply talent, leaders must first be able to clearly define the talent they need to execute business strategy. This means identifying mission-critical jobs and key workforce competencies in light of current and future strategic goals.

Second, companies must have the ability to discover new and diverse sources of talent inside and outside the organization. Third, organizations must be able to develop employees' individual and collective talents, building people's skills, knowledge, and competencies in ways that also expand the organization's collective capabilities. Finally, talent multiplication requires an ability to deploy the right talent in the right place at the right time. Organizations must engage and align employees by creating the best-possible match between peoples' talents and aspirations and the organization's strategic goals. Together, these capabilities help ensure that an organization has a capable, diverse, engaged, and adaptable workforce whose knowledge, skills, and abilities can be swiftly and strategically combined and recombined.

When these four capabilities are in place, aligned with each other and with the business strategy, and highly integrated into business operations, the true power of talent is unleashed, stimulating a "virtuous cycle" of talent multiplication. The organization can increase skills, adaptability, learning, flexibility, innovation, and performance. It has a more engaged workforce, which is equipped to deliver greater productivity, higher quality, innovation, and customer satisfaction. Employees are using their strengths to improve performance, and new talent is attracted to the organization. Individual and collective performance is improving; the organization is more adaptable and prepared for change; its strategic opportunities are expanding. Talent multiplication is creating extraordinary value.

Putting It All Together

Accenture research has shown that the development of a distinctive capability is one of the three building blocks of high-performance businesses. When companies master the four talent management capabilities discussed above, they can create a distinctive capability in talent multiplication that will set these organizations apart from their competitors in product and talent markets. It will also position them to obtain future growth, to seize strategic opportunities, and to achieve high performance.

But as with so many management ideas, the execution is not easy. From the start, leaders must provide the vision and communicate the passion for talent multiplication. After, they must use data and metrics to measure the return-on-talent investments and guide talent decisions. And the efforts of middle managers are critical: They must have the people management skills that will enable them to effectively define, discover, develop, and deploy talent. The importance of line managers and supervisors in engaging and multiplying talent cannot be overestimated.

Just as executives and employees had to become technology-savvy when information technologies became strategic, and just as they had to learn to think globally when the world's markets changed, they now need to become multipliers of talent. This task is crucial for those who want to create, and be a part of, a high-performance business.

References

Reuters. 2006. If computers ran the NBA, Shaq would be benched. October 23. Retrieved March 27, 2008, from http://uk.reuters.com/article/technologyNews/idUKN2335640120061024.

Thomas, Robert J. 2006. *Marriott: Building a winning mindset, brand, and organization.* Accenture Institute for High Performance Business.

Thomas, Robert J., Jane C. Linder, and Ana Dutra 2006. Inside the values-driven culture at UPS. *Outlook*.

Thomas, Robert J., Jane C. Linder, and Chi T. Pham. 2006. UPS: Mastering the tension between continuity and change. Accenture Institute for High Performance Business.

Tapscott, Don, and Anthony D. Williams. 2006. *Wikinomics: How mass collaboration changes everything* (New York: Portfolio Hardcover).

Ulrich, Dave, Steve Kerr, and Ron Ashkenas. 2002. Electric's leadership "work-out." *Leader to Leader*.

Notes

1. For more on the building blocks of high-performance businesses, see Tim Breene and Paul F. Nunes, "Going the Distance: How the World's Best Companies Achieve High Performance," *Outlook*, 2006.

2. When organizations nurture a distinctive capability in multiplying talent alongside the other distinctive capabilities that underpin their formula for success, talent power can propel the organization to high performance. For more on this topic, see Peter Cheese, Robert J. Thomas, and Elizabeth Craig, *The Talent Powered Organization: Strategies for Globalization, Talent Management and High Performance* (Kogan Page, 2007); and Peter Cheese, Robert J. Thomas, and Elizabeth Craig, "The Talent-Powered Organization: Leveraging Your Most Important Competitive Asset," *Outlook*, 2007.

3. For more on types of organizational resources, see John Ballow, Roland Burgman, Göran Roos, and Michael Molnar, "A New Paradigm for Managing Shareholder Value," Accenture Institute for High Performance Business, 2004.

4. See Google's press release: http://www.google.com/intl/en/press/pressrel/20071127_green.html. More information available at Google's Web page on green energy, "At Google, we're committed to helping build a clean energy future," http://www.google.com/intl/en/corporate/green/energy/index.html (accessed January 31, 2008).

Chapter 43

Workforce Planning: Connecting Business Strategy to Talent Strategy

Ed Newman, Founder
The Newman Group
Leader, *Futurestep, US*

T HERE IS NO QUESTION THAT WORKFORCE PLANNING HAS BECOME A HOT TOPIC IN TALENT management. It has garnered attention well beyond the borders of the human resources function, as business leaders and industry analysts grapple with the challenges of changing demographics, a choppy economy, and the globalization of labor markets.

Workforce planning initiatives have also proven to be very challenging for companies to get off the ground. Recent studies have shown that most companies conduct workforce planning in crisis mode and only in response to specific events such as mergers and acquisitions, layoffs, or restructurings. If you asked 10 different people the definition of workforce planning, you could quite possibly get 15 different answers. Despite the confusion, workforce planning is nothing new; it has been a function in business for decades and perhaps centuries. If this business process has been around for so long, why is it such a challenge for organizations today? A look back at some history might help us understand.

The main reason workforce planning is so much more challenging today is because of the changing role of labor and talent. Over the last two centuries, as we moved from the Industrial Age, through the Knowledge Age, and now find ourselves in the Age of Talent, determining talent needs has simply become much more complicated. In the

Industrial Age, the purpose of most jobs was to maximize the throughput and performance of machines and equipment. Equipment and infrastructure were considered assets, and labor was viewed as an expense to operate that equipment. Labor was required for a very specific function, and determining the number of people needed to operate the equipment required a fairly straightforward mathematical calculation. Workforce planning was more aptly called manpower planning in the Industrial Age.

As we moved into the Knowledge Age, the purpose of jobs shifted. Rather than simply making the machines run, people were needed for their intellect. While this made the planning process a bit more complicated, the paternal nature of company cultures and the concept of lifetime employment made forecasting the need for new employees relatively predictable.

In the current Talent Age, the average worker will hold more than ten jobs in his or her career. The paternalistic relationship of employers has been eroded by downsizing, rightsizing, and off-shoring. The majority of jobs are so dynamic that a worker's role, function, and responsibilities can change on a frequent basis. In the Talent Age, we are investing in deploying systems and equipment to get more from our workers, to help them think better, communicate more effectively, and become more innovative. Talent has become the valued asset that companies need for optimal business performance. In short, where companies in the Industrial Age were concerned about talent availability, those in the current Talent Age are focusing on talent *capability*.

With this focus on talent capability comes many planning implications. Workforce planning is no longer a simple matter of applying an equation to figure out the amount of labor needed to operate the equipment. Today, workforce planning is about determining the type of people and capabilities that will be required to drive business strategy. Combine this shift with changing demographics and the rapid pace of change in the global economy, and workforce planning is now a much more complex process than the manpower planning of the past. The workforce is no longer viewed as the operating expense required to run the equipment; instead, it is seen as the talent that drives the business strategy. As a result of this shift in perspective, workforce planning has become much more important.

What Does Workforce Planning Really Mean?

The history of workforce planning and the dynamics that make it so challenging are useful as background, but to truly understand workforce planning, it is important to apply a concrete definition to the concept. To set the stage for this, we will first start with the process. At a high level, the workforce planning process has not changed much over the years.

If you or your organization is embarking on a workforce planning effort, the first step is to define the objective. What exactly is it that you are planning for? Is it for a single business unit, perhaps a division that is growing or contracting? Is it for a certain role or function across the entire enterprise? Or is it for a specific geographic region? Additionally, what is the time span for which you are planning—is it for the coming year, or are you taking a longer-term view? (See Figure 43-1.)

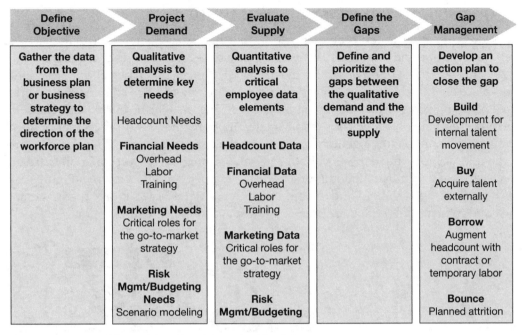

Define Objective	Project Demand	Evaluate Supply	Define the Gaps	Gap Management
Gather the data from the business plan or business strategy to determine the direction of the workforce plan	**Qualitative analysis to determine key needs** Headcount Needs **Financial Needs** Overhead Labor Training **Marketing Needs** Critical roles for the go-to-market strategy **Risk Mgmt/Budgeting Needs** Scenario modeling	**Quantitative analysis to critical employee data elements** **Headcount Data** **Financial Data** Overhead Labor Training **Marketing Data** Critical roles for the go-to-market strategy **Risk Mgmt/Budgeting**	Define and prioritize the gaps between the qualitative demand and the quantitative supply	Develop an action plan to close the gap **Build** Development for internal talent movement **Buy** Acquire talent externally **Borrow** Augment headcount with contract or temporary labor **Bounce** Planned attrition

Figure 43-1 Workforce Planning Maturity Model

Once you have defined the objective, the next two steps involve projecting the demand and evaluating the supply of resources required to meet the needs of the business. Forecasting demand tends to be challenging, because it involves predicting the future, and that requires some qualitative analysis. The tendency for many organizations is to jump past the demand planning step and focus more exclusively on the supply, looking at historical attrition rates and potential retirements to develop a forecast.

The results of the supply and demand analysis lead to the next step of identifying the gaps. Once gaps are determined, the final step in the process is to develop strategies to manage and close those gaps. These strategies may include developing existing talent, acquiring new talent, leveraging talent through a contingent workforce, or moving people through managed attrition. You might refer to these as the build, buy, borrow, or bounce strategies. What is interesting about the gap management step is that we are in essence developing strategies that intersect with each of the functional areas of talent management. In other words, the workforce plan should be the driver of talent management activities so that talent management programs align with the goals and objectives of the business. With this in mind, the following definition encompasses these key strategic aspects of workforce planning:

Workforce planning is the process that *provides strategic direction* to talent management activities to ensure an organization has the right people in the right place at the right time and at the right cost *to execute its business strategy.*

A Look at Workforce Planning Maturity

Workforce planning is the type of function that happens inherently, whether it is a well-thought-out and organized activity or simply a knee-jerk reaction to the challenges that are thrust upon us. Given the dramatic changes that have taken place in the workplace over the last several decades, some organizations have adapted their workforce planning processes to be very strategic, focusing on specific talent segments. On the other end of the spectrum, some maintain only the basic process of human resources planning, with a general view across the entire workforce. Finally, some are in the middle, applying aspects of both basic and strategic workforce planning. Based on research of workforce planning practices, the maturity model shown in Figure 43-2 has been developed to help understand the different types of workforce planning that exist and to identify where your organization stands along the continuum.

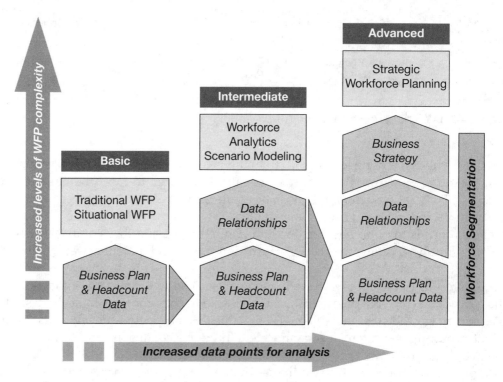

Figure 43-2 Workforce Planning Maturity Model

1. *Basic.* The basic level includes both traditional and situational workforce planning. Traditional workforce planning is most like the human resources planning processes of the past and is typically referred to as budgeted head count today. This type of planning normally occurs on an annual basis as organizations go through their budgeting process. Based on the projected revenue and growth goals of the business plan, a financial analysis is conducted to determine the net

incremental headcount across the organization that will be needed to achieve the organization's goals.

In many cases the budgeted head count is simply broken down by department, business unit, or location, and it may also include some categories such as sales, delivery, and administrative. Situational workforce planning is more of a tactical planning process that takes place for a specific event. For example, the opening of a new plant will require a very specific number of workers in different roles. In this case, there needs to be a plan to determine the sequencing, the training requirements, and other logistical aspects such as the movement and relocation of existing employees to the new location. In both cases, the planning at the basic level is relatively linear, focusing on determining the number of people that will be needed in a specified period of time.

2. *Intermediate.* The intermediate level involves the use of data relationships to produce workforce analytics or the development of scenario modeling. Workforce analytics can be used for a very specific analysis, or in a broader context to identify trends that warrant action.

   An example of scenario modeling can be seen with the well-known demographic data of the aging workforce. Many companies have been conducting analyses to estimate the pace of retirements and the subsequent impact on performance. Some companies find that more than 60 percent of their leadership will be eligible for retirement in the next three to five years. What would the impact be if a majority of them decided to retire upon eligibility? Running a scenario to answer this question helps planners identify potential risks to the business and develop specific strategies to mitigate them. Another commonly used analytical model at the intermediate level looks at attrition through various lenses of demographics. Many companies consider two types of turnover: voluntary and involuntary. From a workforce planning perspective, though, all attrition should be analyzed, because it influences the makeup of the workforce.

   If you are involved in this type of planning, the first step is to compute the overall average turnover in your company and then calculate turnover within a specific demographic, such as by performance level. Subtract the turnover percentage of the demographic from the overall average. If the result is a negative number, it means you are losing people from that category faster than average. If you have attrition in your higher-performance categories that is greater than average, you have a *talent leak* that should be addressed. This process and resulting data can also be referred to as a retention index. You can run a retention index on any demographic that is important or will help you make a business case. A retention index by department or manager, by tenure with the company, or even by job family could reveal interesting trends in your workforce that might warrant action.

3. *Advanced.* It is at the advanced level that we make the distinction of strategic workforce planning. At this level, workforce planning becomes an integral part of the overall business planning process, and the business strategy becomes a

focal point of the activity. There are several key differences between strategic workforce planning and more basic resource planning. Basic planning efforts typically attempt to look into near-term workforce needs, reaching anywhere from 6 to 24 months out. Strategic workforce planning takes a longer term view, looking forward as much as five to ten years. Scenario modeling is also a critical part of strategic planning, with forecasts that look beyond numbers and financial aspects to focus on people and capability. The result is a planning ability that can do more than control talent as a current asset; it can support decision making and prioritization that can change the shape of the workforce to adapt to changing needs.

A common feature at the strategic level is the activity of dividing the workforce into different talent segments based on their relative criticality to the goals and objectives of the business. Workforce segmentation allows planners to break down the population into smaller pieces and focus in on those that are most critical to the business first. For example, most organizations break out leadership roles for specific talent management activities such as succession planning and leadership development. This is most common because it is easy to see the relative impact on the business results for this category. But what about roles such as the front-line customer service representative or mid-level management roles that can have a broad and significant impact on customer or employee satisfaction? Workforce segmentation is typically implemented with two to four categories, where critical roles are divided into strategic and core positions, and non-critical roles are divided into necessary and non-core positions. The table that follows provides an illustration of this.

Workforce Segmentation by Criticality		
Roles	**Segment**	**Description**
Critical	Strategic	Critical to driving the strategy of the business, creates long-term competitive advantage
	Core	The positions that are essential to delivering the product or services of the business
Non-critical	Necessary	Positions that must exist but are not unique to the business; could be delivered through alternative approaches such as contingent workers or outsourcing
	Non-core	Positions that are no longer aligned with the direction of the company and could be eliminated

Depending on the circumstances and the overall direction of a business, a variety of roles could fall into the critical category. For example, if a company has recently experienced a shift where value-added services are required to differentiate a commoditized set of products, the sales roles will most likely become a critical and strategic segment. Specific strategies will be needed to convert a percentage of the existing sales team from product sales to solutions sales, and then determine the number of hires needed (drawn from either external hires or from internal talent) to effectively carry out this strategy. Another example is the business that has been impacted by the proliferation of online and electronic media. Moving from print media to electronic requires a whole new set of capabilities, and there will likely be several roles that fall into the non-core category.

Building a Workforce Planning Capability

In many organizations, all three types of workforce planning are being carried out today, even though they are not recognized as such. The work may not necessarily be organized and defined into a specific function, and it may not even be called workforce planning. The maturity model helps organizations understand the depth of their workforce planning and identify potential opportunities to expand and take it to the next level. With a better understanding of the complexities of workforce planning and the maturation model, the next step is to figure out how to get started.

One challenge to launching a workforce planning initiative is the fact that the demand typically comes from the top down in response to an urgent business need such as a major restructuring or the launch of a new line of business. When these requests come, there is little time to think about a workforce planning model, and planners respond as quickly as possible, only to be faced with the same challenge during the next emergency. It is always important to manage the top-down requests as efficiently as possible; however, to create a sustainable and repeatable process a workforce planning, practice must be built from the ground up. A few key building blocks will be instrumental to success, including data analysis, establishing a process, and HR capability.

1. *Data analysis.* The foundation of any workforce planning practice is a robust ability to access and analyze data. Many organizations are dealing with a fundamental data problem. Over the last two decades, automation and large-scale systems implementations took place with the promise of providing data to help make business decisions. There are two common problems. First, there may be too many systems. Data may reside in multiple locations. It may be collected inconsistently, and often the types of data simply do not match what is needed.

   Second, the integrity of the data itself may be in question. There has been so much change in the last ten years that often the data in ERP systems does not reflect the actual organizational structure. Information on employee competencies, experience, and development needs are almost always out-of-date, if populated at all. When the top-down requests come and data integrity is compromised, we are forced to manually tabulate information in spreadsheets. The result is a one-off analysis. Solving these data problems must be a high priority to make the workforce planning function scalable.

2. *Establishing a process.* The second building block is to establish the process. This does not necessarily mean defining the process from scratch. As mentioned earlier, the process is fairly well defined already. The challenge is to determine who

will be involved in the process, what role they will play, and what information needs to be collected and analyzed to make business decisions. In a recent study on workforce planning practices, one of the key findings was that most initiatives fail if they are perceived as simply HR projects. It is important to have the right stakeholders from the business leadership ranks, finance, HR, and IT all working together as an integrated team.

3. *HR capability.* The third building block involves adding the right skills to the HR team. Even though workforce planning will not be successful when viewed as an HR project, the HR function is the most appropriate group to facilitate the process. Workforce planning requires a slightly different skill set than traditional HR roles, although you may find you have some people who fit the bill. First and foremost there is a need for analytical skills and an inquisitive mind-set. An ability to manipulate data and look for trends is important. Developing forecasts and making estimates about what might happen in the future requires taking risks. There is also a need for a certain level of business acumen so that when talking with business leaders or other stakeholders, they can be prodded to think about the talent implications of what is going on in the business environment.

It is not necessary to make everyone on the HR team a skilled expert in workforce planning. One approach that has been effective is to create a workforce planning center of expertise (COE). This is where people can be added with the unique skills that don't exist in other parts of HR. Depending on the size of the organization, it could be one person or a small team. The COE becomes the driver of the process, although for certain activities the COE may leverage other resources. For example, one organization that was concerned with head count hired a statistician to focus on cleaning data and running analyses. The HR business partners possessed the business acumen to interact with the business stakeholders and talk about talent implications, and they used the statistician to develop the scenarios and models.

Getting started with workforce planning may seem daunting, and that is because it is. As with any large undertaking, it is usually a good idea to start out small and grow into it. If you spend a little time educating yourself and your internal stakeholders on the subject of workforce planning, it is generally not difficult to find a few opportunities to create a positive result. Try to think of a department or senior leader who might embrace the subject, and initiate a small pilot to get some experience. Once you develop experience and create success stories, it is much easier to get buy-in and expand from there.

Worth the Effort

One thing is certain: Change is inevitable. Often we hear comments like "why bother building the workforce plan, because when the economy tanks, or there is some other unexpected catastrophe, it will become obsolete." It is this kind of mentality that creates the overhiring and mass layoff cycles that occur during recessions. It is important to note that the purpose of workforce planning is not to "get it right" all of the time. It is to have a plan and know the workforce well enough so that when these instances occur we are prepared to take appropriate action. It does not mean that when the bottom falls out we won't have to make layoffs, but what it can do is give us the insights into our organization to make those decisions with precision and to limit any long-term negative impact on the business.

Workforce planning is also a continuous process, which means it is not simply something to do yearly. There should be periodic reviews to evaluate how closely you are tracking to the plan. When you identify discrepancies (and there will be discrepancies), you make adjustments accordingly. Workforce planning may be one of the more difficult initiatives to get off the ground, but in terms of strategic influence and impact on talent and business performance, the results are worth the effort.

Chapter 44

Using Workforce Planning as Part of a Talent Management Program

Robert Conlon, Senior Vice President
E. Michael Norman, Senior Vice President
Aaron Sorensen, Ph.D., Senior Consultant
Sibson Consulting

WORKFORCE PLANNING—THE ACT OF IDENTIFYING THE CHARACTERISTICS AND QUANTITY of human skills needed to accomplish a specific objective—has been practiced for hundreds of years. Whether it is armies preparing to invade foreign lands or corporations planning to launch a new product or penetrate a new market, to be successful an organization's strategic plan must include a plan for the human element. Workforce planning has received increased attention across all sectors of the economy. One recent study[1] found that 92 percent of companies use some level of workforce planning and 21 percent take a strategic, long-term approach to addressing the supply and demand of talent and the actions necessary to close the gap between the two. In addition, the federal government's Office of Personnel Management has established requirements for each government agency to maintain a current human capital plan and submit an annual human capital accountability report.[2]

Workforce planning, in its most advanced form, should be an integral part of an organization's overall approach to talent management. As such, it should be closely related to another critical aspect of talent management: succession management. There are, however, distinct differences between the two processes. First, succession management generally focuses on individuals, while workforce planning is concerned with roles, regardless of the number of incumbents. As such, workforce planning may be viewed as the critical macro-level talent management process, while succession management is one of the critical micro-level talent management processes. Second, workforce planning largely concentrates on the type and number of critical talent for the future, while succession management generally covers the replacement planning aspect of critical positions within an organization. Third, succession management, as typically implemented, is a hierarchical process in that it usually is limited to the top layers of an organization. Workforce planning, on the other hand, is largely independent of hierarchy. If a critical role exists in the first-line supervisory ranks, it should be treated identically to the most senior-level roles also deemed critical to organizational success.

There is, however, significant opportunity for linkage and integration between the two processes. Specifically, there is evolving thought that succession management need not be strictly hierarchical. While it may be true that succession management for the top few layers of an organization is a given, below that level, leading-edge thinking holds that succession management activities and resources may be best deployed on those strategic and critical roles identified through workforce planning. Similarly, there is emerging thinking that incumbents in those same critically important roles should be among those who would be included in succession planning and whose roles should be identified for particular attention to reduce unplanned turnover.

The Evolution of Workforce Planning

Workforce planning has evolved significantly over the past three decades, from traditional head count planning to workforce analytics to strategic workforce planning (SWP):

- *Traditional head count planning* (sometimes referred to as operational head count planning) is the practice of determining an organization's head count needs by using internal information—including the operating budget and turnover and retirement data—to calculate how many people the organization will need in certain jobs at a specific point in time. A key distinction of head count planning is that it typically is tied to an annual operational plan and budget. The organization derives the head count plan by determining how many employees it can "afford" to add and how many it will need to replace because of turnover or retirement. This type of workforce planning can be beneficial to a mature organization that is experiencing little change in terms of product type, competition, or other environmental factors.

  A disadvantage of head count planning is that most organizations must evolve and innovate to remain relevant, competitive, and profitable. Head count planning creates a workforce plan by "backing into" the head count from the budget rather than by strategically identifying the future talent need to execute the organization's strategy. Additionally, head count planning fails to take into account the supply of talent in the labor market when planning for head count needs. Perhaps the biggest problem with this method is the fact that there is often no dialogue between the workforce planners and business leaders on future organizational capabilities and the roles the organization will need in two, three, and five years. As a result, the planning process often is a mathematical exercise around head count targets rather than a strategic exercise focused on planning for the organization's current and future human capital needs and talent strategy.

- *Workforce analytics* (also referred to as human capital analytics) blends approaches from forecasting principles, scenario planning, and traditional head count planning to create current and future workforce forecasts for specific roles under various business scenarios. A key advantage of this approach over traditional head count planning is that it can produce a picture of future business scenarios.
- *Strategic workforce planning (SWP)* represents the most advanced approach to workforce planning. It allows an organization to generate data, analytics, and insights about the current and future talent it will need to achieve its strategic capabilities. This enables leaders to better understand, forecast, and manage future talent needs based on relative value to strategy execution. SWP builds on techniques used in traditional head count planning and workforce analytics to identify future talent gaps and determine what actions and investments are needed to close them before they limit growth and profitability.

A key distinction of SWP is that the workforce plan is a by-product of ongoing dialogue and analytics concerning the talent required to execute the organization's strategy. The workforce plan becomes the talent component of the business strategy, which aligns the talent needs with the business strategy. SWP also involves segmenting roles in the workforce according to their contribution to the organization's strategic capabilities and informs decisions about whether to "build" or "buy" talent. In summary, SWP provides the analytical rationale organizations need to optimize their workforce by integrating decisions around workforce investments—for instance, compensation, development, succession, and the Employee Value Proposition (EVP)[3] relative to the strategic capabilities the organization needs to succeed.

Five Steps to SWP

While there are many variations in how organizations approach SWP, in most cases, the following five-step approach forms the backbone of the process:

- Translate business strategy into organizational capabilities.
- Determine the talent needed to deliver on organizational capabilities.
- Confirm current talent needs and future talent forecasts.
- Conduct a talent gap analysis for current and future states.
- Identify actions and investments to close current and future talent gaps.

Organizations should tailor each step to their operating model and culture. In terms of the frequency with which the SWP process should take place, SWP typically occurs annually, although the process can be more frequent in organizations that are experiencing significant change.

Step One: Translate Business Strategy into Organizational Capabilities

The critical first step of the SWP process sets the stage by translating the organization's business strategy into organizational capabilities. This will identify the broad categories of collective skills the organization needs to execute its business strategy.

An organization's capabilities reflect its ability to manage people to gain a competitive advantage. Traditional sources of competitive advantage—offering better goods or services, pricing them lower than the competition, or incorporating technological innovation into research and manufacturing—must be supplemented by organizational capabilities.[4] Translating business strategy into organizational capabilities also makes it possible for an organization to convert concepts into actions by articulating the collective knowledge and skills it must apply to succeed.

Apple, Inc., for example, increased its share of the smart-phone market from 9.1 percent to 14.4 percent from 2008 to 2009 with the introduction of the iPhone. Although this can partly be attributed to the technological innovation of the product, Apple also leveraged its organizational capabilities of research and development, brand recognition, marketing, and distribution by acquiring the talent it needed to beat the competition.

Translating a business strategy into organizational capabilities requires the input of senior leaders who intimately understand the organization's strategic business drivers and can articulate the competitive levers it can use. A value mapping exercise can help. (See Figure 44-1.)

A value mapping exercise begins with an examination of the business strategy that clearly articulates and distinguishes its various elements. The next step is to identify the specific value drivers and the organizational capabilities required to implement them. Typically, the human capital requirements needed to execute the organizational capabilities are segmented into four categories: strategic, core, requisite, and misaligned. (A detailed discussion of the segmentation model is provided below.) Another important consideration in this step is to ensure the organizational capabilities do not just reflect the organization's current state but include its long-term goals.

In organizations where SWP fails to have an impact, one of the most common reasons is a disconnect with the organization's business strategy. As a result, the workforce plan becomes a numbers exercise that lacks a business rationale for the talent strategy. Left unaddressed, this can lead to a talent portfolio that does not align with the needs of the business.

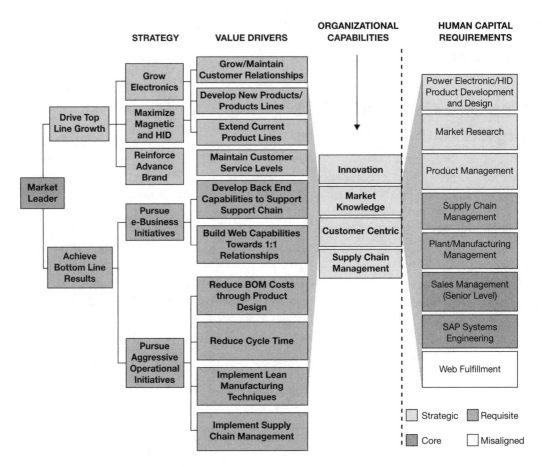

Figure 44-1 A Sample Value Mapping Exercise

Source: Sibson Consulting

Step Two: Determine the Talent Needed to Deliver on Organizational Capabilities

The next step of the SWP process is to establish the types of roles the organization will need over the next two, three, and five years and identify where it must acquire, build, or divest talent. This process is typically conducted by answering a series of questions that can help determine each role's impact on organizational capabilities. For example:

- What is the nature of the work required to achieve the desired organizational capabilities?
- Which roles are necessary to complete the work required to build the organizational capabilities needed to achieve the business strategy?

- Among these roles, which will contribute the most toward the organizational capabilities required to achieve the business strategy?
- Do these roles have a quantifiable impact on operations or on the top or bottom lines? If so, what is this impact?
- Which roles, if any, will no longer be required in the short- or long-term because of the business strategy?
- How does the time frame for a specific business strategy or objective increase the importance of a role?

The answers to these questions should create a clear picture of the importance of the various roles to the success of the organization.

Apply a talent segmentation technique to differentiate the roles according to the needed strategic capabilities[5]: Sibson has developed a practical model that organizations can use to apply segmentation and differentiation principles to their workforce. (See Figure 44-2.)

The talent segmentation model is based on four descriptors—strategic, core, requisite, and misaligned—that are used to categorize roles based on their relationship to the organization's strategic capabilities. These categories help focus the investments that the organization will direct toward these roles in the future. Sibson also has developed

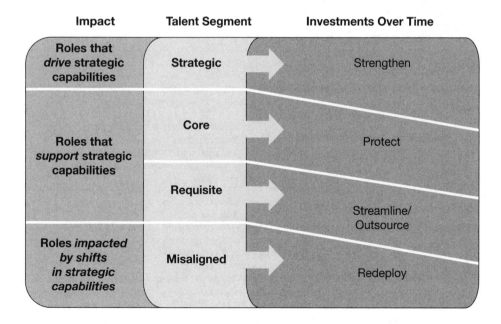

Figure 44-2 Talent Segmentation Model

Source: Sibson Consulting

a series of segment definitions and questions that can be used to determine a role's segment classification. (See Figure 44-3.)

Segment	Definition	"Yes" responses to a majority of these questions typically determine the segment classification	Typical Action
Strategic	Roles that are critical to driving long-term competitive advantage through strategic organizational capabilities. These roles often have specialized skills or knowledge that is in high demand.	• Does the role possess unique skills directly related to the strategic capabilities and competitive advantage of the organization? • Can this role be linked directly to top-line growth, innovation, and/or speed to market? • Is the training for this role related to the strategic direction of the organization? • Does hiring for this role generally focus on the specific knowledge, skills, or abilities that are directly related to the strategic direction of the organization? • If the strategy were to change, would the answers to the questions above likely change?	Strengthen
Core	Roles that are the "engine of the enterprise," unique to the company and core to delivering on its products and/or services. These roles often possess proprietary knowledge and skills that are hard to find or replace.	• Does the role possess capabilities that are directly related to the ongoing operations of the organization? • Does the role possess proprietary knowledge, skills, and abilities that cannot be outsourced, either strategically or practically? • Is the training for this role mostly independent of the strategic direction of the organization? • Does hiring for this role generally focus on the broad knowledge, skills, and abilities needed to sustain ongoing operations of the organization?	Protect
Requisite	Roles that the organization cannot do without, but whose value could be delivered through alternative staffing strategies (other than full-time head, count).	• Does the role possess capabilities that are directly related to the ongoing operations of the organization? • Does the role possess knowledge, skills, and abilities that can be outsourced, either strategically or practically? • Are there other roles like this role being transitioned to outside vendors or contractors? • Could this role be staffed differently to reduce costs while maintaining quality and consistency and privacy of corporate information?	Streamline/ source differently
Misaligned	Roles whose skill sets no longer align with the company's strategic direction.	• Does the role possess capabilities that are no longer related to the ongoing operations of the organization? • Would redeploying or eliminating the role have minimal negative impact to the organization (i.e., if the role is re-skilled, deployed, or eliminated, revenue or productivity will not decrease)? • Could resources (including time and money) saved in staffing, managing, and training people in this role be used to offset the cost of needed strategic and core roles?	Redeploy

Figure 44-3 Segments, Definitions, Questions, and Actions

Source: Sibson Consulting

Many organizations find it difficult to differentiate their workforce. The challenges they experience tend to fall into three areas:

- A focus on people as opposed to roles
- An inability to separate title from impact relative to a strategic capability (i.e., not all leadership roles are classified as strategic)
- An egalitarian culture that does not accept differentiated investment

It is important to understand these challenges when preparing for the implementation of SWP so they can be addressed before they derail the organization's segmentation efforts. In addition, using forced distribution approach where approximately 25 percent of the roles in the organization are identified as strategic, 60 percent are core, 10 percent are requisite, and 5 percent are misaligned can help facilitate the segmentation process.[6]

Step Three: Confirm Current Talent Needs and Future Talent Forecasts

The next step in the SWP process is to forecast the organization's future head count and the timing of any talent needs. Among the factors to consider are the internal dynamics of the current workforce, the external dynamics of the labor market, and staffing economies. Although detailed forecasts usually are conducted for strategic roles, these analytics should also be applied to other segments if the organization thinks its strategic capabilities may change.

The tools of workforce analytics are also helpful at this stage to derive the SWP program, especially if the organization wants to test various scenarios that require manipulating the underlying variables. (See Figure 44-4.)

Before forecasting for each role, it is helpful to understand the methods managers have used in the past and whether their assumptions led to accurate head count forecasts (i.e., did the business or function have too many or too few people in its roles?). There are a number of ways to forecast head count needs, which can be divided into two categories:

- *Quantitative staffing.* A formulaic projection based on economic, capacity, and/or other drivers (e.g., ratio staffing methods, such as one HR generalist to every 155 employees)
- *Qualitative staffing.* A logical projection based on the characteristics, distinctiveness, and/or contribution of the roles (e.g., a project typically requires one project manager, two applications developers, and two quality assurance analysts).

A traditional example of a role that uses a quantitative staffing method is a sales representative, since an organization can typically calculate the number of salespeople it needs to meet sales goals, based on average sales. An example of roles that typically use a qualitative staffing method are research and development roles, where there is no formula to determine the number of people needed to develop new processes,

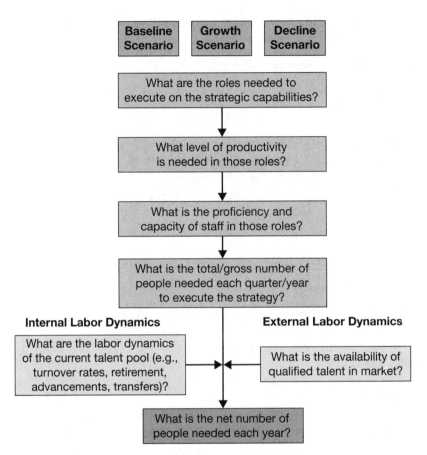

Figure 44-4 Using Workforce Analytics to Test Various Scenarios

Source: Sibson Consulting

materials, or products. In these cases, the organization should explore the contribution of the role with business or function leaders to help them articulate a successful staffing footprint to determine the needed head count. The organization must also identify specific events and scenarios that will determine the timing of head count needs (i.e., the sequencing of when employees are needed).

An often overlooked factor in SWP is accounting for the proficiency of the current workforce. Specifically, it is important to understand how many people in the role are proficient (capable of performing all skills required) and not proficient but can be trained to proficiency. The goal is not to get a precise number, but a reasonable figure with which to work during the planning process. Time to proficiency of new hires can also be used to estimate the average amount of time it will take to train an employee. This is an important component in training plans.

At this point, the organization will need to integrate the internal labor dynamics to model how factors such as turnover, retirement, advancement, transfers, and time to proficiency will affect the workforce forecast in the next two, three, and five years. Since these figures will be used to forecast, it may be appropriate to adjust the turnover, retirement, and redeployment numbers accordingly if the organization deems that recent circumstances or historical figures do not reflect projected rates. For example, external market dynamics, such as an improving economy, may increase turnover in the near future, or a new internal policy could positively or negatively affect retirement rates. External labor dynamics should also be factored in, as they will affect the time and cost of acquiring talent. The availability of talent in the external labor pool may also influence decisions about where and when to staff strategic initiatives. Workforce planning software applications can produce these analytics or custom Excel or Access tools can be built to model these workforce variables.

This step will reveal the total number of people needed by role and how many current incumbents are proficient. To validate the SWP process, the organization should identify potential staffing economies (duplicate roles included in SWP processes across enterprise objectives or within the business or functional unit) across objectives, and adjust (or validate) needed head count projections accordingly.

Step Four: Conduct Talent Gap Analysis for Current and Future States

The next step is to identify any talent gaps—differences between current and needed head count after considering all types of churn (turnover, retirement, advancement, and redeployment), proficiency rates, and staffing economies. Ultimately, this difference represents the number of employees the organization needs to acquire or develop to drive its strategy. Each talent gap should be assigned a priority. (See Figure 44-5.)

While this is never a simple calculation, Sibson's experience suggests it is important to consider three factors:

1. *Value to the strategic objective.* This is perhaps the most important factor because many organizations have a small group of roles that must contribute to a strategic objective before other roles can be brought on board. For example, a facilities engineer may have to open and test plant operations before production roles are needed.
2. *Time to proficiency (acquisition and training time).* This factor is critical to the priority analysis because it will help identify the lead time that is needed to bring on a role. For example, if a plant is ramping up capacity in the second year of a three-year plan, but it takes two years to ramp up a plant manager to manage the additional capacity, hiring must start now. Recruiting should be constant for strategic roles that are in high demand and have above-average churn and a time to proficiency of more than one year.
3. *Size of the gap.* The size of the talent gap (both percentage and raw value) should also be included in the priority analysis. A large talent gap in a role with high value and long time to proficiency will be a high priority.

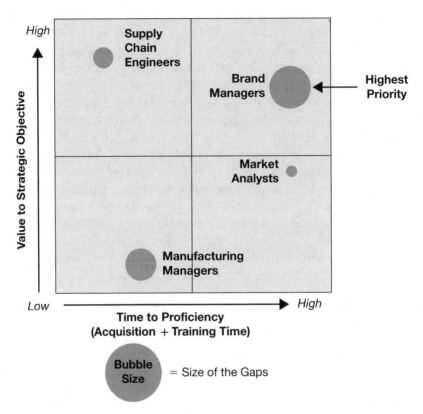

Figure 44-5 Prioritizing Talent Gaps

Source: Sibson Consulting

Step Five: Identify Actions and Investments to Close Current and Future Talent Gaps

The final step in the SWP process is to put in place a plan to close any gaps and better understand the financial implications of hiring and training required talent. Many organizations make the mistake of creating sophisticated SWP processes and work-force analytics but fail to invest the time and effort in documenting what actions and investments the organization needs to implement to make SWP a reality. The outcome of this step will be a completed SWP process as well as an HR operating plan to support the execution of SWP. Many organizations also use this output as the primary input to their talent strategy.

To integrate the actions and investments into SWP, HR will need to analyze options regarding "building" talent internally versus "buying" talent externally to close a talent gap. In addition, an organization may choose to "rent" talent through a contingent or temporary staffing model to address a talent gap. However, for roles that are strategic, "renting" talent is not advised.

When evaluating whether talent should be sourced internally or externally, the manager should consider the components of cost, timing, and successful placement rates for sourcing talent through these different methods. For example, for an internal hire, the ramp-up time may be shorter, successful placement rates may be higher, and costs may be significantly less than for sourcing externally. However, there are situations where the organization does not have resident talent or enough time to train and develop a group of employees for a role. In such cases, it will need to use external sourcing to execute an objective on time. What is important is that each organization decides whether the sourcing strategy of building its own talent or attracting it from outside strategy is most appropriate.

The Future Landscape of Talent Management and Workforce Optimization

The one-size-fits-all era is also over (if it ever really existed). A new era of fairly applied, but segmented, processes and applications will characterize contemporary organizations in the future. Those that can most effectively deploy leading-edge talent management with integrated succession management and SWP processes will be best positioned to succeed. They will be

- Better able to identify the skill areas that differentiate success from mediocrity
- Well positioned to retain critical talent because they recognize the need to differentiate the employment experience for those on whom success is dependent.
- Able to more effectively target their training resources, recruiting muscle, and compensation programs to outcompete for the talent necessary for success.
- Among the first to complement the idea of the differentiated workforce with the reality of a massively differentiated employer, and through this, their talent investments will be more likely to yield positive dividends for all stakeholders.

Notes

1. Bersin & Associates. *Modern Approach to Workforce Planning*. March 2009.
2. U.S. Office of Personnel Management.
3. The Employee Value Proposition describes the balance of the rewards and benefits employees receive in return for their performance. The EVP framework has five elements: affiliation, work content, career, benefits, and compensation.
4. See D. Ulrich, and D. G. Lake. 1990. *Organizational capability: Competing from the inside out*. Hoboken, NJ: John Wiley & Sons.
5. Brian E. Becker, Mark A. Huselind, Richard W. Beatty, The Differentiated Workforce: Transforming Talent into Strategic Impact, Harvard Business Press, 2009.
6. Note that these percentages should be used as guidelines only and may change as organizations go through periods of change.

Chapter 45

New Tools for Talent Management: The Age of Analytics

Haig R. Nalbantian, Senior Partner and Director of Global
Research and Commercialization
Jason Jeffay, Partner and Global Talent Management Leader
Human Capital business, Mercer

ALMOST EVERYONE AGREES ON THE IMPORTANCE OF TALENT AS A CRUCIAL ASSET TO BE managed in today's globally competitive business environment, but effectively managing talent has become a more strategic, less intuitive pursuit than in the past. A successful talent strategy needs to be multifaceted, aligned with business goals, prompted not by "gut" managerial attitudes and decision making but by *fact-based* decisions that reflect the hard realities of what drives critical business and workforce outcomes. And more than ever, making those fact-based moves requires solid analytic tools.

Let's also be clear that the multifaceted nature of talent management today extends beyond any superficial sense of mere alignment with business goals. For example, it's not enough for an engineering or a service culture simply to be well stocked with appropriately qualified talent. A talent strategy must also be actionable, nimbly responsive to changing needs within and without the organization. It must be specific to the organization, acknowledging the variety of skills, specialties, and nuanced capabilities that make for successful execution within a given business and organizational context. It must be impactful and consequential, so that talent decisions—whether deploying talent to various regions, building or buying talent, or addressing issues of succession—quickly and measurably answer business needs. It must be sustainable, relying on a talent pipeline that doesn't fall prey to gaps in skills or leadership. And it must be adaptable to changing market and business conditions.

Indeed, differences in context, internal and external, are often at the heart of why firms that compete with each other don't manage their talent in the same way. Thus, establishing key facts about internal and external circumstances is often one of the first tasks to perform when revisiting or creating a talent strategy, in order to ensure the new strategy is in sync with those realities—and thus has a chance of succeeding. Therefore, in this expanded—and expanding—conceptual universe of talent management, the role of analytics takes on increasing importance.

The Analytics Value Curve

Analytics is not just about data mining; at its best, it's a disciplined form of empiricism that draws on learnings from the relevant disciplines (organizational psychology, economics, business management, etc.) and growing experience applying analytical techniques in business practice. It allows decision makers to test specific hypotheses about talent management and its role in business performance and to project the likely consequences of specific actions, in order to produce actionable insights, prioritize and size the impact, and set the yardstick to measure progress—all of which we'd call "workforce intelligence"

There is a wide spectrum of analytics—from low to high sophistication, simple to complex, cheap to costly. (See Figure 45-1.) This spectrum of analytics comprises both qualitative and quantitative methods for eliciting workforce intelligence.

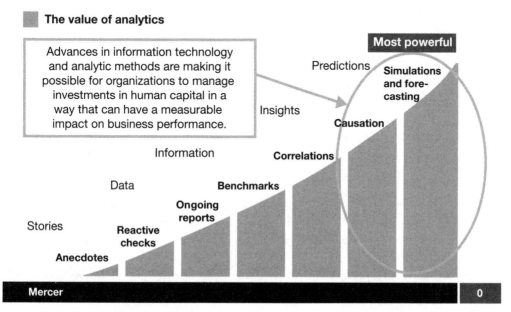

Figure 45-1 Spectrum of Analytics

A generation ago, HR departments were mostly operating at the lower left end of this curve, making workforce decisions based on anecdote, gut feel, reactive checks and simple ongoing descriptive reports. To the extent analytics were used, they were primarily qualitative in nature, largely survey driven. In the late 80s and 90s, the benchmarking craze took hold and many organizations moved up the curve to rely more on external benchmarks and so-called "best practice" comparisons.

Even as some benchmarking methodologies became more sophisticated, involving statistically based, cross-company comparisons, the results overall have been disappointing. Benchmarking inputs can be misleading and counterproductive; they can fail to recognize the unique strategic and operational context that influences how well talent and talent management practices will actually perform; and they are not sufficient to counter prevailing myths about talent that take hold in organizations and are not easily dislodged.

Currently, we are seeing signs of rapid evolution of workforce analytics, of movement up the value curve. More and more firms are deploying workforce analytics that offer deep-dive assessments of the dynamics of their own workforce and how they affect performance. The approach goes well beyond deployment of packaged workforce analytics modules in human resources information system (HRIS) or attendant systems. Top organizations are undertaking sophisticated, controlled statistical analyses aimed at surfacing cause-and-effect relationships and allowing them to project likely outcomes of policy measures to simulate and forecast future states.

Moreover, at the high end of the spectrum, organizations are combining perceptual and archival data in statistical models to better understand the interplay of perception and actual events as well as the mechanisms by which management practices influence results. And while many organizations may perceive barriers to moving up the analytics value curve—such as cost, complexity, and the capabilities of HR departments—easier access to data and statistical modeling packages are overcoming those barriers.

Using Analytics to Drive Strategy

A talent strategy comprises numerous elements of workforce management that influence the capabilities, behaviors, and attitudes of the organization's workforce. These elements would include factors affecting the talent "flows"—attraction, development, and retention—as well as specific practices (e.g., rewards, supervision) that influence them.

A talent strategy should be assessed in terms of its ability to help the organization secure the talent required to meet business goals, optimize the performance of that workforce, and establish a culture that facilitates high performance and adaptability to rapid market, business, and technological change. In addition, it must be measured against specific workforce goals relating to diversity, professionalism, social responsibility, and so on, which not only contribute to business results but are often workforce goals in and of themselves.

A good talent strategy can be developed by answering a series of questions. Following are some (but not all) of the main questions a talent strategy should address:

- What are the critical talent segments in which we need to be strong?
- What are the critical operational roles where the best talent matters?
- What are our leadership requirements and what kind of leaders do we need?
- What are our performance requirements?
- What is our Employee Value Proposition?

The following reviews some examples of how talent analytics can be applied to address these questions.

Critical Talent Segments

Some talent segments are more important to driving business results than others. This may be particularly important in times of change—a new strategy, changing technology, new sources of competition, and so on. And organizations with multiple business lines at different levels of maturity may need to deemphasize some segments and increase emphasis on others. This is especially important in times of limited or contracting budgets.

A case in point is that of a leading technology company that faced stronger competition from firms in Asia and the advent of new technology requiring wholesale changes in its business model and significant reorganization. It needed very different skill sets, experience, and capabilities in its workforce. Veteran analog-technology technicians, the mainstay of its historic cash cow business, were no longer as important as a new cadre of technicians and engineers with knowledge of digital, color, and network technologies.

For a culture that was team-oriented, with a one-size-fits-all approach to talent management, this was a challenge. The company needed to segment its talent carefully to enhance the ability to transform the workforce without undermining a culture that historically had been very effective and to which there was strong allegiance among employees and throughout the leadership ranks. To do this well, the company needed to know not only which segments were critical, but to what extent workforce segments differed in the way they responded to elements of rewards and other management practices. They also needed to determine whether current talent management practices supported or impeded the required workforce transition. In an environment where resistance to change was strong, nothing less than hard facts would enable senior leadership to make the business case for change.

Given the stark shifts in the business, it was quite obvious which talent segments were increasingly important. Interviews with corporate executives and line leaders on the directions of their businesses would suffice. But more quantitative analytics were required to address some of the other key questions, and in this case they ranged from simple descriptive information on the workforce to more sophisticated statistical analyses of the workforce impact of specific programs and practices. For example, a simple review of raw turnover data showed exceedingly low rates of turnover among low performers.

To what extent were talent management practices driving those outcomes? To answer this question, a more rigorous, holistic analytical approach was required, an approach we call Internal Labor Market (ILM) Analysis®. ILM analysis recognizes that an organization's workforce is the outcome of the three interrelated labor flows—attraction, development, and retention—that operate dynamically in an open system that is influenced both by management practices and external business and labor market conditions.[1] Briefly, the analysis comprises an integrated set of statistical models of talent flows and associated rewards to quantitatively describe these workforce dynamics and, more importantly, explain what drives them. Organizations that gain such understanding of their internal labor markets—understanding, for instance, what factors most influence promotion, development, and pay, or to what extent specific practices help retain high-potential talent, among other things—are in a much better position to effectively manage this internal market and shape its outcomes.

For the technology firm, one simple, purely descriptive analysis mapped the annual flow of compensation dollars to those in different performance quartiles. Astonishingly, it showed that the lowest performers were absorbing a larger share of bonus and other "pay for performance" dollars than all but the highest quartile of performers. In effect, the company was inadvertently valuing its low performers more than many other employees who delivered higher current and, quite likely, future value. With that kind of subsidy, was it surprising that turnover of low performers was so low?

ILM analysis also showed that the company's internal labor market was insensitive to labor market conditions. Specifically, all else being equal, changes in unemployment rates in the locations where the company operated had no impact on rates of turnover. So when labor markets tightened, there would be no additional flow of talent out the door, and vice versa. This could be explained in part by what was happening on the reward side. Statistical modeling of pay revealed employees' years of service to have a particularly strong influence on pay; indeed, it dominated other demographic, skill, and performance factors as drivers of individual pay. This result showed again that the company was not valuing, through its rewards, factors most essential to its future success.

But it told an even more important story: The strong emphasis on seniority (with back-loading of pay and benefits), characteristic of strong internal labor markets, effectively insulated the company from outside market forces. Historically, this had allowed the company to invest efficiently in the training and development of employees required to support its old business model—in other words, those trained could be counted on to stay and deliver a return on this investment. But now the company's strong internal labor market had become a liability. It prevented external market signals of price and value to influence how its internal labor market was functioning and induce accommodating changes in the flows and relative prices of talent required to deliver the new mix of talent the business required. Significant changes in talent management—emphasizing talent segmentation—would be necessary to remove these roadblocks to workforce transformation.

Critical Operational Roles

Certain roles are more important than others, and it is often difficult to estimate the value of specific roles within an organization. If markets are competitive, market pay should reflect the marginal productivity of specific jobs. But this may not capture the value of specific roles in a given firm or in relation to the unique production process of an organization. How else, then, would one know the relative value of a role within a company?

In the case of one banking organization, analytics helped reveal the answer by looking at the actual business impact of turnover in different jobs. The presumption is that the disruption, loss of continuity, and loss of firm-specific knowledge often resulting from turnover will be more costly to an organization if it occurs in more important roles. Therefore, one way to determine which roles are most important is to try and measure the actual impact of turnover on key business outcomes of turnover in different roles.

At its simplest, this might be examined by measuring the correlation of turnover in specific roles with the business outcomes associated with the units in which it occurs. So, for instance, looking across all branches in the bank, does turnover among branch managers correlate more strongly with outcomes such as customer retention or growth in accounts than, say, turnover among tellers or back-office personnel? If so, by how much? But the simplistic approach can be perilously misleading. Is the correlation meaningful, or does it reflect yet another factor that is correlated with both turnover and business results? Is higher turnover in a role causing worsening business results, or is it the other way around? And under what conditions does turnover influence these outcomes most? Without some level of response to such questions, simple correlation would not be a reliable basis for making a determination about the relative importance of different roles.

We know that many factors beyond turnover affect the business outcomes noted. Some are external to the branch—such as customer mix, proximity of competitors, location— and some internal, reflecting management practices. A more robust and precise approach needs to account for such other factors as well as how the relationship between turnover and business outcomes play out over time to provide a more credible basis for drawing empirically based conclusions. In the case of BankCo, a methodology we call Business Impact Modeling®,[2] was used to statistically estimate and quantify the effects of turnover in different roles on several key measures of financial and operational performance. This involved controlled statistical analysis of the running record of these performance measures, which allowed the organization to assess if turnover was correlated with the specified performance measures *even after* accounting for the effects of other key business, workforce, and external market factors. It also allowed the firm to assess if the changes in business results followed changes in turnover rates in different roles or if the relationships were the other way around. While no statistical method ever conclusively proves cause-and-effect relationships, a rigorous statistical modeling approach, using longitudinal workforce and performance data, can increase confidence in the interpretation of a causal relationship.

For BankCo, modeling results showed that turnover in customer-facing, front-line jobs was far more costly to the company than in back-office or even management roles. Whatever their level in the organization hierarchy, those routinely interacting with customers were demonstrably more important to retaining and growing customers, as well as delivering branch level profitability.

Leadership Requirements

What constitutes effective leadership may well differ across organizations. Often, leadership is associated with breadth of experience, which is acquired through mobility across different business units, functions, geographies, and so forth. But is mobility always the key? Many organizations are adopting the view that there are leaders at all levels who need to be developed and cultivated. They need to carefully consider what types of capability and experience are required for different types of leaders, and talent analytics can help.

A premier global hospitality organization uses planned movement of managers from smaller to higher and from lower brand to higher brand properties or units as a key pillar in its approach to developing managerial talent. Was the company meeting its leadership requirements through this approach? One measure of effectiveness certainly would be how managers themselves responded to these kinds of opportunities. Did they have a favorable view? Did opportunities to move laterally help the company attract and retain its better managers? Of course, simple surveys, exit interviews, or focus groups could be used to inform the answers to this question. That's how many organizations proceed. But this organization went further. It wanted to see if there was direct evidence of positive impact and know *how much* of an effect there was.

The company undertook an Internal Labor Market analysis to determine if lateral moves were helpful in retaining its managers. The answer was a resounding yes. Managers with more opportunities to move were significantly more likely to stay and grow with the company than those who remained in place longer. Of course, what is good for the manager is not necessarily good for the organization. Could it be that such mobility undermined the performance of the properties that exported or imported managerial talent due to instability in operations or lack of sufficient knowledge of local conditions and requirements among the incoming managers? The company used analytics to address this question as well. Using Business Impact modeling, it found no negative effects on either financial performance or customer value measures. All in all, the company developed strong evidence that its approach to leadership development, relying on progressive steps to build breadth of experience, was working well and had become a significant asset for the company.[3]

Performance Requirements

Assessing performance in organizations is always a challenge. Sometimes it's easy to identify and measure individual performance, sometimes not. And sometimes individual performance may show up more in group outcomes, reflecting high interdependencies among employees. Depending on the context, how you measure performance and how much you differentiate between individuals in their assessments as well as in their pay may have very different effects on business outcomes.

In one example, a global media organization with a number of different businesses—we'll call it MultiCo—sought individual performance data to help guide its rewards structure. Company management was determined to create a "performance culture" among its employees and was concerned that laxity in its performance management system was standing in its way. A first step was simply to review the distribution of ratings to assess the extent of differentiation across its five-point ratings scale. Not surprisingly, it found ratings skewed to the higher end. Fifty percent of employees received one of the top two ratings. What about the value of ratings themselves? To what extent did earning a higher rating translate into higher pay and other rewards for individual employees? As part of the assessment, MultiCo modeled the relation between pay and ratings, accounting for multiple other factors (age, tenure, education, job family, location, etc.) that also influence base and total compensation. In this way, it was possible to assess the incremental effect on individual pay of raising a performance rating and a subsequent return on higher individual performance. MultiCo found that the value of improving one's rating was relatively small. Overall, all else being equal, raising one's rating from the "meets expectations" rating to an "exceeds expectations" rating was worth about $1,000, rather small relative to average compensation levels. Most interestingly, however, MultiCo found that the value of higher ratings tended to differ substantially across businesses within MultiCo. One unit in particular differentiated higher- and lower-rated employees by pay far more than others, especially at the lower end of the performance scale. Clearly, MultiCo had significant work to do to align the performance management system with the overriding concept of a performance culture.

In the case of a midsized regional bank, analytics showed that rating and pay compression actually worked better to drive branch performance than did highly differentiated individual ratings and rewards. In this case, leadership had been convinced that it needed to focus on individual performance, get tougher in evaluating performance, and distinguish higher and lower performers far more aggressively. But the facts showed otherwise, dispelling an organizational myth, and helped leadership better understand that it had to build a team culture to better serve itself. The easy temptation to exercise a muscular, individualistic approach to performance management lost out in a confrontation with facts. In both of these cases, high-end analytics helped inform major talent management issues with significant economic consequences—and proved well worth the cost.

Understanding the Employee Value Proposition

For companies, the Employee Value Proposition, or EVP, whether explicitly stated or not, expresses the terms of employment—what is expected of employees and what they can expect to derive from employment with the organization. In effect, it is the employee counterpart to a talent strategy, but the essential point is that it derives from the talent strategy, which itself reflects the human capital requirements for accomplishing business goals.

Some organizations can easily articulate an EVP, but does that EVP materialize in the constellation of practices and conditions that employees actually experience at work? Is it reflected in the perceptions of employees as captured in engagement, satisfaction, or other types of employee surveys? Does it match well with what employees value in the employment relationship? These are critical questions, and good analytics are key to answering them.

A variety of tools are available for these purposes. Perhaps the most common and direct way to determine what employees perceived to be the EVP in place, what they themselves value most, and how they respond to different elements of the EVP is to ask employees directly through some form of employee sensing, surveys, or focus groups. Employee engagement surveys are good barometers of the state of employees and can capture what it is about an EVP that is most important to employees. To avoid the pitfall of everything being reported as equally important, some organizations have turned to more sophisticated ways of eliciting and handling perceptual data, such as conjoint analysis. This methodology, in essence, forces choice among alternatives through a series of grouped comparisons and helps assess the degree of consistency across those choices.

Of course, what employees say they value and what, in fact, they act upon may be different. It is therefore prudent to augment traditional sensing methods with an analysis of the predictive antecedents of actual behavior to measure hard realities.

For example, MultiCo *asserted* a "high-performance culture" as the basis of its EVP. But was it really? MultiCo used a combination of quantitative and qualitative analytics to assess perceptions and practices relative to what would be expected in a high-performance culture. The company realized what employees actually perceived and experienced were in fact far removed from their preferred model. For example, extremely low spans of control, reflecting strict governance and hands-on supervision, belied all the talk about the value of entrepreneurial initiative and risk taking. And MBA recruits from top schools entering the organization through a special "high-potential" program did anything but thrive: Even though they were paid a premium, their performance ratings and career progression were indistinguishable from their less pedigreed counterparts, and they were about 25 percent more likely to leave. These patterns, like the ones observed regarding performance ratings, were hardly markers of a performance culture.

Modeling Internal Labor Market dynamics can reveal an underlying culture at work that is not consistently perceived by leadership and provide clear quantitative markers for the organization to track. In the case of a large banking organization, ILM analysis revealed the dominance of what might be called a "career culture" with opportunities for advancement, growth, and learning emerging as most salient to employees. For instance, these career factors, far more than pay, influenced employee retention. Drawing on this strength, the bank determined to make that implicit culture more explicit in its EVP. The challenge of maintaining this EVP came to fore when the bank acquired another major regional bank. Applying the same analytics, it found the acquired bank to have far more of a "pay culture." Understanding the stark contrast in implicit EVPs for the two entities made it possible for them to anticipate potential barriers to integration and work proactively to mitigate them. Without talent analytics, they could not have done so effectively.

Talent Strategy and Human Capital Dashboards

For companies that take advantage of a strong, fact-based talent strategy driven by analytics, the importance of ongoing measurement can't be overstated. Timely, efficiently updated, and accessible measurement of talent data is vital for renewing, revisiting, and adjusting strategy, and human capital dashboards are among the most effective tools that put information at the fingertips of decision makers. Web-enabled or desktop-based, the best dashboards are customized to display information of unique importance to an enterprise and its workforce. Dashboards also serve other functions, such as enabling easy data querying and issuing ready-to-distribute reports.

Mainly, the dashboards help management command of two types of information essential to effective workforce management: One set of facts consists of accurate and timely descriptive information on outcomes, such as head counts, turnover ratios, promotions, and pay changes. These are crucial for monitoring progress and providing leading indicators of an emerging problem. The second set of facts concerns the drivers or causes of critical outcomes, determined from statistical modeling. These are facts that explain important outcomes and also show the pathway to improving them. They are critical for making decisions about what to change and why and for tracking whether policy initiatives are, in fact, taking hold and changing realities.

The monitoring function of human capital dashboards includes internal and external reporting, tracking progress toward strategic objectives, and responding to queries from business and human-capital partners—performed on an ongoing, frequently updated basis. The analytic function extends the dashboard's range to strategic planning, forecasting, proactive management, and problem solving—performed on an as-needed basis, with appropriate updates.

Conclusion

These observations and strategic examples underscore some basic requirements in utilizing and optimizing the value of analytic tools for talent management. For one thing, the talent strategy to which the tools will apply must be aligned with business goals and built around fact-based decisions—taking into account the larger context of external and internal business factors. And while there is a wide spectrum of analytics—from low to high sophistication, cheap to costly—and while many organizations may perceive barriers to moving up the analytics value curve—such as cost, complexity, and the capabilities of HR departments—easier access to data and better modeling packages are overcoming those barriers.

Beyond the tools and technology, though, modern talent is about a mind-set—one that (a) recognizes the singular importance of talent and how well-managed talent contributes to the success of an enterprise and (b) insists that decisions about talent, as with other critical assets, be based on the hard facts, the kind that can only emerge from the disciplined application of workforce analytics and measurement tools.

The authors would like to thank Mercer's Rick Guzzo, Matt Stevenson, Bill Sipe, and Pete Foley for their helpful input, and Matt Damsker and Ann Egan for their editorial support.

Notes

1. For a full discussion of the ILM concept and analytics, see Nalbantian, Guzzo, et al., *Play to Your Strengths* (New York: McGraw-Hill, 2004).
2. For a fuller description of Business Impact Modeling, see Nalbantian, Guzzo, et al., *Play to Your Strengths* (New York: McGraw-Hill, 2004).
3. See Nalbantian and Guzzo, "Making Mobility Matter," *Harvard Business Review*, 2009.

Chapter 46

The Role of Line Managers in Talent Planning

Rick Lash, Ph.D., Canadian Leadership and Talent Practice Leader
Tom McMullen, North American Reward Practice Leader
Hay Group

OUR RESEARCH AND OUR EXPERIENCE IN WORKING WITH ALL SIZE ORGANIZATIONS AND IN all industry sectors suggests that "best practice" is often not so much about sophisticated and unique design but about effective alignment and execution. Sports teams rarely win based on new plays. They win with great players, coaches, and the ability to execute as a team.

Line managers perhaps have the most impact on performance within the organization. In fact, Hay Group research has shown up to 30 percent of variance in business results can be explained by differences in work climate and talent management processes created by the manager. They set the tone for a particular work unit, group, or department and employees in positive environments and are more likely to engage in discretionary effort in support of their individual work units. Managers who are attuned to this get the performance gains that others don't come close to achieving.

This chapter is a practical guide designed to better understand the role of line managers in the talent management process and what they can do to better manage their talent. This chapter will focus on line manager's role in the following areas:

- Assessing and selecting talent
- Performance planning
- Coaching and developing talent
- Reviewing and rewarding

There are no "silver bullet" talent management programs. There is no one best approach to talent management that is right for all organizations and for all employees. Many managers tried to replicate Jack Welch's approach to rewards as outlined in his book *Jack: Straight from the Gut*, but most failed. Why? Because they adopted the mechanics of the GE reward system but didn't have the underlying capability and cultural alignment to support it. For talent management programs to be effective, managers need to be clear in understanding, identifying, and leveraging what drives value in the organization and then relentlessly and consistently manage the talent in their organization to achieve desired outcomes.

The Changing Role of Line Managers in Managing Talent

Gone are the days when managers could delegate talent management to the human resources function. Managers today are expected to be intimately involved in all aspects of people management, including hiring, onboarding, and ongoing coaching and development of staff. For example, line managers are developing their skills in the interviewing and hiring process, learning sophisticated techniques like Behavioral Event Interviewing, which has traditionally been the domain of HR or external consultants. Many managers now develop their own innovative talent management tools and more often see themselves as working in partnership with HR to create workable solutions to their ongoing talent management needs. Organizations have recognized that line managers have the most direct impact on the largest segment of people in an organization. The stronger the pool of talent, the more engaged front-line staff will feel and the more competitive and successful the organization will be.

Line managers need to understand and use talent management tools and processes to close the gap between the talent they will need in the future and what they currently have today. Answering the following questions and leveraging the best practices implied can help line managers prioritize those talent management actions that have the greatest impact on the performance of their team and ensure a sustainable flow of qualified talent to meet future business needs.

1. *Defining the future.* What kind of talent will you need to execute your strategy? How is your organization changing today and in the future? Will certain roles become more important? What skills and leadership will your team need in the next three to five years that you don't have now?
2. *Attracting talent.* What is your employer value proposition? How successful are your current approaches to making your organization or team an attractive place to work? Should you look for talent in different places than you normally do?
3. *Selecting.* Do you differentiate between high performance—those who excel in their current role—versus high potential—people who may be successful in future roles? Are competencies used in selecting staff, and if so, are they aligned to your future business needs?
4. *Developing.* Are staff assessed for their capabilities, and do they receive ongoing coaching and feedback? Are there opportunities for staff to develop their technical

skills as well as their interpersonal and leadership capabilities? Are "stretching" job assignments made available to high potentials? Are leaders expected to participate as teachers in development programs?

5. *Engaging.* Are your current reward practices aligned to the current values, individual needs, generational differences, and demographics of your employees? Do you provide a range of both monetary and nonmonetary rewards to high performers? Do you have the flexibility to adapt your reward practices to the needs of individuals and teams?

6. *Deploying.* Do line managers collaborate in discussing talent and movement of high potentials for ongoing development? Are candidates identified as potential successors for key positions? Do you have a robust succession plan? Are development plans in place for high potentials to ready them for future roles? Are lateral movements valued as highly as upward promotions?

Line Managers' Talent Management Issues

Each organization has a unique combination of business strategy, culture, and talent, so its strategy for talent management should also be unique. There are, however, some best practices that can benefit all organizations—the most important being the alignment and clarity needed for people in the organization to deliver on the organization's strategy. And line management's ability to motivate and engage employees is central to all effective talent management practices, including assessment, providing feedback, coaching, developing, and rewarding staff.

Assessing and Selecting Talent

Once you have defined the "demand" part of the talent management equation—the critical roles, competencies, and skills that will be needed to support the organization's future strategy—it's time to determine the "supply" side: How do current capabilities match up to those demands and then, through the right selection, coaching, development, and rewarding of staff, how best to close the gaps? Assessment is the foundation of any effective talent management process. A robust assessment process will include several objective and valid tools that will provide line managers and HR with the data needed to make effective hiring, deployment, and development decisions.

The most important criteria for assessing and selecting talent is to ensure that each approach, whether a self-scoring survey or 360-degree feedback tool, assesses the critical competencies and capabilities that define superior performance in the role being selected against. Using the right assessment tools will provide more accurate data to help make informed decisions on who will be a best fit for future roles and what development will make the most difference to their long-term growth and success.

Typically, assessment tools fall into several broad categories:

- *Cognitive ability measures.* These assessments measure critical thinking, an essential capability required for managerial and executive roles where problems are often ambiguous and require the ability to quickly analyze data and draw inferences with limited information.

- *Personality measures.* These assess key personality traits that indicate longer-term patterns in behavior and personal preferences. Combined with other sources of data, they can provide an important insight into an individual's overall fit within a role and the challenges he or she may face over the long term.
- *Competency-based assessments.* Competency-based assessments can come in several varieties. These include self-assessment, multi-rater, or 360 or Behavioral Interviews by a trained assessor, each providing an individual with feedback on his or her performance against the behaviors that define superior performance for the role.

Accurate, objective assessment data linked to the requirements of roles are an invaluable tool to assist line managers in identifying development needs and designing training and other learning opportunities.

Performance Planning

Performance planning sets the expectations between the manager and the employee. It's during this phase that the "what" and the "how" of the job are discussed and agreed upon. It's critical that the manager ensures there is both clarity and commitment to the performance goals that are established. This may be via an initial meeting in an annual cycle, or it may be discussed throughout the year if goals, strategies, or conditions change. It is key that this performance planning process be a dialogue between manager and employee.

One trap that many line managers fall into during the performance planning phase is the failure to communicate the linkage between the individual employee's accountabilities and the team's and organization's goals. A recent Hay Group study of performance management design and administration practices indicated that while 72 percent of organizations have clear strategic objectives, only 30 percent believe that there's a clear linkage between the strategic objectives and individual performance criteria. Helping employees understand the contribution their work has toward the organization's larger goals helps to provide a sense of belonging to something greater than their individual selves.

Coaching and Developing

Best-in-class organizations recognize coaching as a critical talent management skill. A coach can be a manager or peer who works with someone—either an individual or in some cases a team—to foster long-term development and growth in others. Coaching usually involves formal feedback from assessments (such as those described above) and direct observations of an individual's behavior.

As Dick Brown, EDS's former chairman and CEO, states, "Coaching is not a once or twice a year activity reserved for the annual performance review. A leader should be constructing his or her performance appraisal all year long." You have numerous opportunities to share your observations and give honest performance feedback. If at the end of the year someone is truly surprised by what you have to say, this is a failure of leadership.

Coaching involves developing capability in a range of skill areas. These can include the development of technical, managerial, and interpersonal skills. Effective coaching will touch upon all of these areas. To be most effective, coaching begins with understanding the key requirements of the job role and then determining where the primary skill gaps lie. Coaching looks different depending on the level of manager you are coaching:

- *Coaching for technical skills.* Coaching for technical skills involves the development of specific knowledge and skills for a particular area of specialty, ensuring that direct reports have the right skills so they can properly perform the technical tasks of their job. Coaching activities can include giving corrective feedback or detailed task instructions, arranging for job-specific training, or showing others "how it's done."
- *Coaching for managerial skills.* Managers of other managers need to ensure they are developing the leadership, managerial, and administrative skills in their direct reports. First-level managers require coaching in areas including planning, organizing, executing, coordinating, and evaluating, as well as developing their leadership skills and sharpening their insights on the impact of their behavior on the motivation and engagement of their teams. Multi-rater assessments that provide feedback on their leadership from their teams as well as deeper insights on their personal motivations and fit with their job role are powerful tools a coach can use to help grow management and leadership skills.
- *Coaching for interpersonal skills.* These skill sets are often referred to as emotional or social competencies. It includes four key areas: emotional self-awareness, self-control, social awareness (including empathy), and managing relationships with others. Developing interpersonal skills begins with building self-awareness through multi-rater feedback and helping others perceive differences between their self-perception ("I think I'm an empathetic listener") versus the perception of others ("She never listens and spends more time telling me what to do").

Coaching Competencies for Line Managers

Coaching is an ongoing process of dialogue and feedback throughout the performance management cycle. Effective coaches do not necessarily need to be deep experts in their technical area, but they do need to possess a wide range of interpersonal skills.

- *Creating trusting relationships.* Establishing open, mutually respecting relationships that empowers others to act
- *Emotional maturity.* Knowing one's own strengths and weaknesses and managing emotions, making balanced, effective judgments of others
- *Integrity.* Acting in ways that are consistent with one's values and beliefs and acting on them in the face of difficult or challenging situations
- *Empowering others.* Acknowledging strengths in others and inspiring them to take actions to improve

- *Empathy.* Accurately hearing and understanding other's thoughts and feelings and probing for deeper understanding
- *Accurate feedback.* Providing constructive and/or difficult feedback in a way that others can understand it, see common patterns and the implications, and make appropriate recommendations

Contrary to popular notions that managers should focus on strengths, a growing body of research suggests that this may not be the best strategy for developing future leaders. Strength in one role, for example, may turn out to be a weakness in the next. In fact, research in how the brain learns and grows throughout adulthood indicates that deliberate, focused, and sustained practice in areas where one is weaker may be the most effective way of accelerating leadership capabilities.

In a pivotal scene in the movie *Invictus*, the story of the South African rugby team, Matt Damon's character says to his players, "We are more than just a rugby team," as they prepare to take their practice sessions out into the community to involve the entire country in their quest for victory. All good coaches help others see themselves in a larger context, engaging them to have an impact beyond their limited roles.

A newly promoted manager may struggle with leaving behind his old self-image as an individual contributor, continuing to do the tasks that give him a sense of self-confidence and self-esteem but get in the way of his ability to delegate and build his network. Helping leaders establish an expanded self image for their role can be one of the most important contributions a line manager can provide. It is the equivalent of building a strong core upon which other leadership competencies are built and sustained.

Reviewing and Rewarding Performance

While reviewing performance is an integral part of coaching (managers need to monitor performance all the time and use that information wisely and strategically), it also includes a formal performance period review (typically quarterly, semiannually, or annually). In ensuring a "no surprises" philosophy, managers need to ensure they not only use the performance feedback data they've gathered throughout the year but also carefully balance all the different data points they've collected when coming to their formal evaluation.

When it comes to the performance review phase of talent management, there are two potential pitfalls for managers: giving away high performance ratings when they're not earned and using the meeting only to look back and not for forward planning purposes. Because they are human and perhaps not adequately trained, managers often have a tendency to avoid the difficult conversations that accompany poor performance assessments. When it comes time to assign a final performance rating for the year, the same patterns apply. Employees need to understand and appreciate the difficulty in achieving high ratings. Providing them with the necessary information needed to excel will help to challenge them continually and raise the standard of excellence across the organization. The second challenge in the reviewing phase lies in using this final review as a starting point for the next cycle. Many managers, finding themselves overwhelmed with the administrative burden of the process, simply stop once they come to a final rating (some even opt out of communicating the rating) and thereby miss an opportunity to look forward and begin the planning phase of the next performance management cycle.

When most people think of performance rewards, they immediately jump to monetary rewards, incentive plan payouts, year-end bonuses, and base salary increases. However, this is a limited perspective considering the breadth of tools available to line managers for recognizing employee contributions. While the rewarding phase usually does include year-end monetary rewards, it also includes recognizing and rewarding employees throughout the year for work well done and delivering performance that exceeds expectations. This view is especially important given that our research indicates that for a majority of organizations, there is little differentiation in pay between top and average performers. Less than one-third of organizations provide salary increases that might be considered "differentiated" between top and average performers (at least a two-times difference in increase size between top and average performers). To increase differentiation, managers should reward their employees as often as their performance demands and shouldn't think it all comes down to a year-end base salary increase or incentive reward.

Line managers actually have a broad range of nonmonetary reward vehicles at their disposal to reward employee performance, such as future career development opportunities, the opportunity to do meaningful work, new project opportunities, training, public recognition, increased exposure to the senior leadership, and greater empowerment in making key decisions. Recognizing and rewarding employees can have a significant impact on employee motivation. Unfortunately, when the rewards are poorly communicated and misunderstood, they can be equally demotivating. It's critical to link these rewards directly to individual performance and organizational goals. As a line manager, you'll need to ensure that employees perceive there is a clear differentiation in the perceived "value" of the reward that is directly proportional to performance. Without this perception, high-performing talent will likely feel disengaged—and no one will understand what high performance means because everyone's treated the same.

The Role of Human Resources

In building and sustaining the organization's talent management capabilities, one must not lose sight of the vital role played by the organization's human resources function. While line managers are the lynchpin of the talent management process, HR must take the strategic position and perspective that many individual managers are ill-placed to see. For many organizations this means the HR function, working with senior leadership, is the catalyst and steward of the organization's talent management processes. They are there to support and equip line managers with the tools and processes to support their management of talent.

Hay Group research indicates that there is a great opportunity for many organizations in improving their talent management processes, as well as HR's support to managers in their execution of these processes. Many HR functions are inadequately supporting their line managers in this regard. Figure 46-1 summarizes data from the study concerning the perceived effectiveness of line management from the perspective of HR and line management themselves in terms of selected talent management and reward processes.

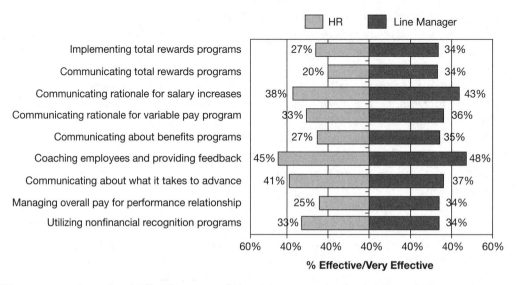

Figure 46-1 Perceived Effectiveness of Line Management from HR and Line Manager Perspective

Source: Line Managers Impact on Reward Effectiveness (Hay Group: 2007)

It is troubling that the effectiveness ratings are below 50 percent for all categories—indicating that there is substantial work to do to better equip and support line managers in these core talent management processes. In order to be effective, HR needs to be focused on developing and leveraging the right talent management practices across the organization and equipping line managers in leveraging these tools.

Summary

Effective talent management is about ensuring an ongoing focus of a two-way dialogue between manager and employee about what is important and how to improve. This idea, while simple, takes a lot of energy from line managers to execute. We believe the principles embodied in this chapter, if incorporated into ongoing management practice, will lead to greater success both for the manager and the employee, and if practiced broadly, a healthier, more successful organization.

Chapter 47

Making Recruitment Part of Your Talent Management Process

Randy Jayne, Ph.D., Managing Partner
Global Aerospace, Defense, and Aviation Practice
Heidrick & Struggles

The What and Why of the Recruitment Challenge

This chapter examines the bottom-line business importance of executive recruiting in businesses today, treating both the substance of recruiting and its value to the organization, and the trends that make recruiting both more important and more challenging to today's executive and human resources leadership. We define "executive recruiting" as applying to senior management positions, and do not treat in this discussion the recruiting strategy and process for lower-level management and staff of typical corporate structures. The discussion that follows seeks to help organizations position recruitment as a priority corporate strategy at the same level as it treats other performance-driving strategies.

We will discuss executive recruitment as a talent management strategy, perspectives on the corporate environment today regarding this recruitment requirement, observations about issues in some company cultures and approaches, dos and don'ts for successful recruiting strategy and execution, and finally, some current marketplace trends that represent both further reasons to improve organizations' executive recruiting and challenges to success in those efforts.

Recruitment as Strategy: A Proactive Approach

For the world's highest-performing businesses, the great majority of the decisions that deliver financial benefit and competitive leverage are truly strategic in nature. As we address recruitment here, we are focused at that strategic level, and not on the "this week's emergency" recruiting challenge generated by a previously unexpected need to replace a key executive.

That recruitment capability can and will be needed even in the best of company cultures. Often at the most inopportune time, a company experiences the reality of a new leadership need, based on new strategy, product, market location, acquisition, or divestiture, and so on, or the unanticipated loss of a key executive when the best of succession plans simply suffers a "gap." When these executive recruitment situations arise, they demand prompt and efficient approaches by the company and its leadership. In our view, a strategic perspective and long-term plan for such processes is a genuine competitive discriminator in the world marketplace.

Today's Corporations "Get It" Regarding Recruitment

Few companies today in highly competitive markets lack for strategy and process for new product development, operational performance improvement, supply chain excellence, information technology, and the like. One might imagine, therefore, that we would see the same strategic focus and skill in the marketplace regarding executive recruitment. In fact, many otherwise high-performing organizations seemingly "don't get it" and are surprised and not at their best when faced with the reality of the kind of new leadership need. Often, otherwise high-performing companies manifest one or both of two equally dangerous modes.

"Executive Recruiting Isn't a Priority Here" Syndrome

My colleagues and I are surprised by situations where the executive search client interaction leaves much to be desired regarding the company's grasp of the basics of the search process, and of the market realities that define the current environment. The most prevalent aspects of this lack of awareness include the following:

- Lack of understanding of the overall market, particularly for highly skilled functional or business unit general management executives. This can lead to over optimism or overconfidence as to the time required or degree of difficulty for a specific search. An example of this in the past decade has been the failure by some larger public companies to recognize the degree of attractiveness and "pull" generated by the literally hundreds of executive opportunities in businesses acquired by private equity funds. The opportunity for subsequent wealth building through the equity component of compensation for these private equity situations was and continues to be a substantial draw for talent, and some companies seem not to appreciate that trend, and its negative manifestations of lost leadership from their own ranks.

- Insufficient appreciation and factual knowledge of the market levels of compensation—base, bonus, equity participation, fringe benefits—for each category of executive sought. Again, the equity element of private equity or venture capital-owned opportunities has impacted the market, as have tighter "golden handcuffs" in the form of deferred equity earn-outs for many executives.
- Uncertainty or inflexibility regarding "desired" or "nice to have" versus "must have" executive characteristics. Things as simple as "more than 15 years in this function" or "technical masters degree" can have significant impact in a particular search if they are made to be "essential" as opposed to "desired."
- Inflexibility regarding "already done it" and "ready to step up to the next level" judgments about specific candidates. Here, the company in search of a new executive sometimes insists on assessing only candidates who have "been there, done that." In some markets and for some roles, this is quite reasonable, given the availability of talent with that qualification. Even then, though, this posture has a sort of inherent logical inconsistency. The inconsistency is found often in the very best of corporate cultures that prepare and hire from within. These organizations are generally able to promote from within, and in doing so, advance dozens of executives each year into demanding new levels of responsibility where the new person has not done it before at that level—for example, new CFO, new business unit P&L general manager, and so on. Top companies, and the executive recruiting profession in general, always strive to identify, assess, and consider the best available candidates in both logical categories—for example, the person who has already been a corporate CFO and the person who has excellent financial background and accomplishment and is clearly ready to be a CFO. To *not* approach searches this way can and does lead to less optimal search outcomes for some companies.
- Unrealistic or over optimistic perceptions on the company's part regarding their organization's comparative and competitive attractiveness in the recruiting marketplace. Every opportunity has pluses and minuses, and the most effective recruiting is characterized by open and balanced communication to candidates, as opposed to overselling the opportunity and avoiding negatives. Issues of less desirable locations, team and leadership situations where excessive conflict is evident, poor market position versus other companies, below-market executive compensation levels, or financial problems that affect ability to invest properly in the business are all unfortunately common and need to be addressed proactively and honestly by companies.
- Excessive reticence in considering outstanding candidates who are at the moment not employed, or involved in unusual career situations. Our own natural comfort with executives who are currently working in a role similar to our own search need is certainly normal, and understandable. However, they greatly increase corporate churn of acquisition, divestiture, roll-ups, private equity transactions, and venture capital situations for exciting new organizations result in a number of excellent candidates being on the sidelines at any given time.

Add to that the huge corporate downsizings driven by sector crises (think automotive, the tech crash of 2001, or the financial markets more recently) or global recessions such as we have seen too frequently in the past two decades. While hiring organizations should carefully question why an executive is not currently employed, the fact is that the market always has truly outstanding candidates in this transitional circumstance. These people can be and are excellent hires in many situations.

"Executive Recruiting Isn't a Priority Here" Syndrome—Version Two

Another frequent and clearly suboptimal situation that reflects lack of company priority on executive recruitment can be given the tongue-in-cheek label of "Human resources is supreme" or "Even though the new hire will be my direct report, I'm too busy to lead the search process." Following are some specific characteristics of this syndrome:

- Highly bureaucratic human resources style and approach to executive recruitment, with little or no real partnership with others in the organization, or with external search resources
- Absence from the recruiting process, or high indifference to it, by the executive—often the CEO or COO—who will be the person to whom the newly recruited executive reports
- Inflexibility regarding either or both search process or substance—from development of the position specification to selection of candidates to interview, to the interview process, to the checking of references and generation of the offer letter, and finally, to closing the deal. For all of these search process elements, the most effective organizations are also the most creative, open-minded, flexible, and partnership-oriented as they recruit.

In order for an organization to make recruiting a genuine and effective part of overall talent management, there needs to be active participation, and commitment, on the part of the executives who will be the new person's boss, peers, and direct reports. The absence of this participation, and overly bureaucratic approaches by staff managing external search, often leads to unsuccessful searches, or at least to long and drawn-out processes where the actual perspectives of the hiring executive are brought into the process late, incompletely, in a "second-hand" manner, or, sometimes, they are not at all involved.

Recruitment as Strategy—Some Key Dos and Don'ts

Our discussion here assumes that a company already has a strategy for talent management and executes a program of strong performance accountability and assessment for its executives. Assumed too is a company system of professional development, mentoring, career-broadening assignments and outside educational opportunities, and focused annual succession planning. That succession planning is crucial, in that it should in turn drive individual decisions on all the other talent management tools and actions noted here.

Assuming that these key elements are in place and effective, we can then characterize a number of dos and don'ts for external recruitment as it plays its integral role in talent management:

Do plan ahead, and build your "bench" in each key functional and market area. Create a corporate culture where cross-training and diversity of all sorts, including experience, functionally and geographically, are fostered and valued.

Don't automatically assume that your top internal succession candidate is the best you can have, or even that the person is competitive with the outside market's alternatives. The more you look externally in executive searches, the more sophisticated and current your understanding will be of what the total market's "best" look like.

Do stay current on your options regarding outside executive search firms and key partners in those firms able to lead search assignments for you. Update your knowledge of which firms deliver regular and frequent successes for the positions you need, at the level you operate, and in your relevant markets.

Don't assume that an outside search resource who is expert and did, for example, an excellent job for you on a finance role is necessarily the best, or even competitive, to do the same level of search a year later in a different function. In our executive search profession, the days of the highly successful "generalist" are behind us, given the sophistication of executive roles and competencies across each organization chart.

Do develop ongoing and regularly updated descriptions of the key responsibilities, executive competencies, and style aspects needed for success for each executive role. Use these both in your internal benchmarking and succession planning, and in getting an external executive search off to a focused and prompt start. If you can simply and accurately characterize your company culture and the way people at the top interact, you are much better positioned for successful searches.

Don't use peers or direct reports to the position being recruited as substitutes for the supervisor/boss of that role in selection interviews of external candidates. While it can be useful at a later point in a candidate's assessment to meet these other internal players, they can and do sometimes disrupt or even derail executive searches.

Do use your partnership with outside executive search firms to obtain or update your knowledge of talent in competitors' organizations and the broader market, compensation trends and levels, and other factors influencing the current search market.

Don't assume that your highly capable in-house recruiting team, who regularly fills large and demanding needs for lower-level sales, technical, manufacturing, and other skills can successfully do the same for senior executives. The trends outlined in the next section of this chapter underline the extreme difficulty faced by in-house recruiters, and some outside firms, in recruiting senior executives today.

Do create a culture where the CEO and the other top leaders in the company are actively engaged in the most senior searches. This is in our view absolutely correlated to search and corporate success.

Don't assume that your decision to conduct an external search in turn warrants leaving out search process consideration and assessment of your top internal candidates. As part of the search engagement, executive recruiters can and will assess your internal succession candidates, providing both those executives and top management a professional appraisal of how each stacks up on key leadership, know-how, strategic thinking, and other key competencies. For example, a current CEO of a major technology organization—a person now nationally recognized as outstanding in his marketplace— was politely dismissed several years ago as an internal candidate by the board of directors during the search as being "a wonderful guy, but not really ready to lead this complex operation." The executive recruiter, having interviewed and assessed that same person, was able to help the board see that the internal candidate was indeed stronger than the best outside candidates available.

Do recognize the value of diversity in people, in backgrounds, and in career roles as you go outside to recruit executive talent. Use your external recruiting strategy to emphasize bringing in new breadth, different perspectives, and a more diverse executive team. This is an especially important talent management strategy in the twenty-first century, in that your ability to recruit and retain diverse new hires is greatly influenced by those new young men and women being able to see people like themselves already in management roles. If you do not have a sufficiently diverse middle and senior leadership team, you risk that both your entry-level recruiting and your retention of earlier diverse hires during their fourth to sixth years will suffer as a result.

Don't wait too long to fill vacuums in your annual succession plan. Consider a proactive strategy to bring in one or more new executives who could move up in a relatively short time to a top role.

Current Trends That Make Executive Recruiting Even Tougher Going Forward

If all the elements described here are not challenging enough, there are in the marketplace at least three mega-trends that are complicating successful executive team building and search, and that will likely increase the degree of difficulty even more in the years ahead. A successful talent management strategy can and should recognize and strive to account for these factors, even as they complicate executive recruiting.

Post-Baby Boomer Demographics

It is well documented that talent management faces the highest annual retirement rate of senior executives now compared to any prior decade. Driven by the the giant Baby Boomer generation born in the two decades following the end of World War II, this reality affects organizations well beyond the executive ranks. In many companies, years of succession planning were complicated by the "age bunching" of key succession candidates for most top roles. As Baby Boomers retire, these companies see holes appear not only in the top boxes of the succession planning chart but in the "ready to step up to the lead role" boxes as well.

Today there is a total population of qualified individuals for executive succession that is profoundly smaller than its predecessor. Beyond the simple numbers, there are also factors of educational choice, early career selection, and perceptions regarding life in corporate or other large institutional settings that make qualified and interested pools much smaller. While executive recruiters have not necessarily been able to quantify the exact magnitude of this reduction, anecdotal evidence regarding length of time to complete searches, number of fully qualified candidates able to be attracted to an opportunity, and greater degrees of difficulty in closing the deal all support this premise.

The Increasingly Sophisticated and Technical Nature of Corporate and Other Large-Scale Organizations

For most Baby Boomers, in their early careers, there were no computers, cell phones, Internet sales, MRP systems, ERP systems, global supply chain operations, or just-in-time manufacturing. A generation of successful executives came into the marketplace, developed, and grew in their chosen functional area and market, and ascended to senior management often without any technical or business training in their academic past. Currently all businesses involve much more sophisticated management tools, products, services, and market environments, all demanding a higher entry-level baseline of both technical and business savvy and competence.

To the extent that many Generation X members chose, in the unique cultural setting of the 70s and 80s, to study things not well-aligned with this new business environment, the pool today of fully qualified individuals for next-generation executive recruitment is reduced even further. While the number of students trained in science and engineering at both the undergraduate and graduate levels has slowly risen for the past 30 years, that growth rate has not come close to keeping pace with the entry-level, middle management, and executive needs for these skills. Technical competency is a baseline talent management requirement for every organization today. Gone are the days where executive recruiters could simply "use their network" to bring forward strong lists of qualified candidates.

When Technical Competence and Performance Count: U.S. Brain Drain

A broad range of organizational leadership requires significant technical skill. For the three decades since the Baby Boomers finished college and the Generation X and Y members made their higher-education choices, we have seen science and engineering students/graduates at both the undergraduate and graduate levels characterized by an ever-increasing percentage of non-U.S. citizens. For years, this trend benefited U.S. industry, even as other nations complained vociferously about their "brain drain."

In the 80s, 90s, and first decade of this century, leading technology markets were able to benefit from this strong pool of non-U.S. citizens graduates in building their technical, management, and executive teams. More recently, the U.S. Census Bureau has documented a much higher rate of these foreign citizens returning to their home countries. As economies improve globally, as countries help develop their own businesses and other institutions that have technical skill requirements, and as other nations' political stability and standards of living improve, more people decide to return home after short working stints in the United States.

Hiring in the Dual-Income Family: Relocation and Other Issues

Over three-fourths (77 percent, per the U.S. Census Bureau) of the top income families in America are dual-income households. Because these families depend on the two incomes, or at least place high value on the standard of living afforded by that circumstance, the two people are much harder to recruit if and when the new position requires relocation. So significant has this challenge become in some situations that high-performing companies actually have developed strong capability to conduct their own "parallel search" to help place the spouse in an acceptable new position—either in their organization or elsewhere in the community—as part of the recruiting process. Ironically, success by these firms in this dual-recruiting strategy creates issues on the other end. The company that faces the potential loss of a key player may be faced with trying to counter not just their executive's offer and lure to leave but the corresponding new attractive situation offered to the spouse.

Conclusion

With the discussed constraints, roadblocks, and trends making executive recruiting increasingly more challenging and crucial, we hope the guidelines and suggestions set forth enlighten your understanding of the value and need for talent management strategies that include truly "best practices."

Chapter 48

Making Outplacement Part of Your Talent Strategy

Tony Santora, Executive Vice President, Global Solutions
Melvin Scales, Senior Vice President, Global Solutions
Right Management

THIS CHAPTER OUTLINES HOW THE INDUSTRY HAS EVOLVED, DETAILS THE EMERGING NEEDS and expectations of both organizations and individuals, and highlights the new standards of service required from outplacement providers. We also share some best practices for transitioning employees, supported by success stories to illustrate how outplacement is an important part of an organization's overall talent plan and, when well executed, how it fosters a culture of success.

Outplacement's Role in Business

Companies are operating in unpredictable times. The fast-changing and demanding global market is placing increased pressure on companies to compete more effectively. The subsequent result may be frequent restructuring, downsizing, and cutbacks, as organizations seek to align their talent strategies with their evolving business objectives. When those initiatives are implemented, departing employees need to be supported with outplacement services to aid in a successful career transition.

Outplacement is an established management practice that helps both the organization undergoing change and the employees affected. Since it was formally introduced as a business practice in 1969, the industry has matured to provide a range of management and employee services to help plan, manage, and execute organizational restructuring.

Your organization's workforce is a dynamic asset, requiring constant adjustments in response to changing marketing conditions and emerging business opportunities. As an integral part of your talent management strategy, outplacement strategically mobilizes and sizes your workforce to meet the changing needs of your business. The benefits include minimizing turnover, maintaining productivity of retained employees, demonstrating respect and commitment to your workforce and the community, and enhancing your overall employer brand.

Why Companies Use Outplacement

Never before has there been such a demand for quality outplacement services. Talent management is cited as the top issue for leaders to address.[1] Today some 73 percent of companies worldwide offer outplacement, although many are not legally required to do so. Companies in the Americas typically offer outplacement where it is not legally required (83 percent), significantly more often than companies in Europe (67 percent) or Asia Pacific (61 percent). Similarly, countries in developed markets more frequently (76 percent) provide outplacement than in emerging markets (58 percent).

Why do companies offer outplacement? Seventy-one percent of employers do so because "it's the right thing to do," followed closely by 69 percent believing "it sends positive signals to remaining employees" and 67 percent feeling "it ensures that former employees receive the skills and training to transition to a new career quickly and successfully." Forty-nine percent of employers also believe that outplacement "makes good business sense."[2]

Outplacement Needs Change Over Time

Outplacement is evolving, with breakthrough solutions to meet the progressive demands of both organizations undergoing change and their employees affected by career transition. Technological revolutions have impacted how people manage their networks and identify new employment opportunities. The growing presence of professional online networking sites facilitates faster connections to prospective employers and helps expand networking contacts.

Following are some of the most significant changes noted over time:

- **Greater focus on outcomes and meaningful results**
  - *Then*   The norm used to be process-driven outplacement solutions, conducted in a physical location, with content that was delivered based on a one-size-fits-all delivery approach and limited options for individual career choice and exploration. Once the program time allotted was over, so was all related support for the individual, irrespective of whether he or she had landed a new career opportunity.
  - *Now*   Our research has found that candidates and companies want a commitment from the outplacement provider to deliver meaningful outcomes and share in the responsibility to achieve success. There is greater emphasis on

results, and demand has created the need to provide ongoing support for individuals until they land meaningful outcomes for themselves, regardless of program length. Greater value is provided through more robust services, giving candidates program choices about how services are accessed and delivered, enabling personalized approaches to the transition goals of both the organization and its former employees.

- **Increasing opportunities to exercise individual choice**

  Then   Candidates, historically, could only access their outplacement services by going to a physical office location and either meeting with a consultant or participating in a group event. Focus groups and topic forums were generalized and broadly applicable to job search techniques.

  Now   Our research identified that individuals are demanding more choice and flexibility to access services when and where they need them most. Up to 30 percent of our candidates[3] access their services virtually from a location of their choosing. The balance continues to utilize the service through physical office locations or even a combination of both. Not all outplacement providers offer this option, but there is a growing trend that candidates want to have the choice of how they receive their services. Candidates can participate in Web-based group events, or even consult one-on-one with a specialized career coach who is not limited by time zones or geography. Candidates tell us that the one-on-one coaching is still the most important and valued component of the services they receive. Individuals have greater choice and flexibility to determine when, where, and how to access their service. They also have access to relevant and current learning modules that account for where they are in their career, generational differences, functional and industry expertise, and special-interest areas such as active retirement or entrepreneurship.

- **Rising client sophistication**

  Then   Organizations used to focus more on just making sure departing individuals were offered outplacement, with the hope of minimizing their exposure to litigation. Once the transition programs were implemented, many did not track the outcomes or experience of those who were displaced.

  Now   Through our research, clients have told us they expect rigorous reporting and proof of value. They are demonstrating increasing sophistication about talent management. Their operating and purchasing behavior is more global, with increasing complexity of relationships and specificity of demands. Companies should conduct regular research to ensure high levels of quality service, assessment of the value / relevance of tools, continuation of investing in new tools to meet changing needs, and staying on the cutting edge to uncover new needs as required.

Best Practice for Making Outplacement Part of Your Talent Plan

Releasing valued associates requires sensitivity, tact, preparation, practice, and a formal process. The most influential factor in the decision to seek legal or other redress against an ex-employer can almost always be traced back to the way the separation process was handled.

The following best practices are recommended to successfully make outplacement part of your talent plan and foster a culture of success:

1. Create the transition plan.
2. Consider redeployment.
3. Notify and support affected employees.
4. Manage change for remaining employees.

1. Create the Transition Plan

Creating a transition plan enables you to assess and outline the big picture for the whole organizational restructure, before you get into the detail of specific employee separations. Consideration should be given to the legal requirements in your country, the time frame for the restructure, and, most importantly, the objectives. Perhaps there is an opportunity to redeploy some of your workers instead of separating them from the organization. Perhaps you could offer voluntary separations before enforcing involuntary separations, as a tool to manage employee morale while also meeting your business objectives. This is the time to engage with an outplacement specialist. By working with a trusted partner to create your transition plan, you will be able to objectively define the positions to be eliminated.

2. Consider Redeployment

Redeployment can be an alternative to separation or conducted simultaneously with employee separations. It is a way of leveraging the skills and talents of existing employees and reassigning them to new roles within the organization. Redeployment provides an opportunity to retain valued talent, reduce the cost of turnover, and leverage knowledge transfers within the company. While this can be a complex process, the benefits also include increased employee engagement and morale during a difficult or tumultuous organizational change.

Our research has found that less than one-in-two companies offer redeployment before outplacement,[4] but as many as 18 percent of candidates are rehired by their previous employer.[5] Offering a redeployment solution can play a valuable role in your strategy to effectively manage your workforce. Tools and resources in a redeployment solution assist individuals to effectively manage their own careers and identifying new roles that align their competencies with organizational needs. This commitment to your employees' continued success will help them to effectively navigate change, ensure high levels of engagement, and position the organization to achieve strategic goals, while creating a powerful brand image—all important elements for creating a culture of success.

Case Study

How can redeployment be part of your outplacement strategy?

Objective:

- In an attempt to remain competitive, an organization was forced to both let people go from one part of the organization and seek to hire in other areas, often involving people with the same skill sets.

Solution:

- We identified an opportunity for the client to recognize cost savings through a new, more targeted redeployment process.
- A flexible, multifaceted process was designed to connect internal candidates to the hiring opportunities with greater speed and accuracy for more successful connections.

Result:

- In the first year, the process saved an estimated US$2.4 million in direct costs that would have been spent on severance and hiring from outside the organization.
- In one particular initiative, more than 400 interviews were scheduled in just three days, resulting in 59 offers extended and 51 offers accepted by internal candidates.

---

3. Notify and Support Affected Employees

The task of transitioning employees is fraught with challenges. Not only is there a moral responsibility to treat people with dignity and respect, helping them to land new positions as quickly as possible, there is also a social responsibility to do the right thing—these people live in your community. To maintain morale and engagement with the retained staff, care and support for separated employees need to be demonstrated and, at the same time that you are fulfilling business objectives, an effective plan needs to be implemented to contain various costs associated with transitioning staff, as well as minimize the organization's exposure to litigation.

If a restructure calls for employee separations, then it must be ensured that managers are prepared to conduct the notifications. The manager's role is paramount. A well-handled separation meeting means that the manager achieves the following objectives: Communicates a decision, provides facts clearly and sensitively, presents the decision as irrevocable, offers support and compassion, and encourages the employee to take positive actions.

Conducting the separation can be an anxiety-filled experience, both for the person being let go and for the manager responsible for delivering the news. The following five-step process for separating employees is recommended:

1. *Prepare the materials.*

   Assemble all supporting written documentation. This includes the notification letter, severance package, benefits, provision of outplacement/career transition services, and other pertinent information. It could also include performance reviews and warning notices, if the separation is involuntary and performance-related.

2. *Prepare the message.*
Script out in writing what needs to be said during the meeting. If the separation is due to a restructuring or downsizing, be prepared to explain the rationale, list factual reasons behind the change, be brief and concise, and develop a formal statement. Follow your country's legal requirements and recommendations for what to include, or not include, in your message to departing employees.

3. *Arrange all "next steps."*
Schedule in advance who should join you at the separation meeting and also the meetings that will need to take place immediately after the news has been communicated, such as meeting with an outplacement consultant, a financial advisor, and a human resources representative. The manager should be able to direct the departing employee to specific next steps, such as the date of departure, the procedures that need to be completed to finalize the separation (like returning keys or computers, what should be done with personal belongings, goodbyes to colleagues, transition of work responsibilities, etc.) and outlining the severance package on offer.

4. *Anticipate employee reactions.*
While no two people react to the loss of a job in the same manner, most employees experience denial, shock or even anger when the news is conveyed. Acknowledge these reactions and learn to recognize them so that you are prepared to handle it in a professional and supportive way.

5. *Conduct the meeting.*
Define the separation clearly and succinctly. Present the decision as definite and final in a statement that may be repeated as necessary and includes reasons for the decision so that the statement can be clearly understood and absorbed. Keep the meeting to less than 15 minutes. Listen and support, but return attention to the next steps in the separation process. Outline the separation package benefits, and connect the person with a representative from human resources and an outplacement consultant to review the career transition assistance to be provided.

4. Manage Change for Remaining Employees.

Managing change for those who remain is an essential component for a successful restructure. We work with clients to design and implement large-scale change interventions, ensuring that these strategic shifts lead to improved business performance. This is a real sticking point for many organizations. Senior leadership and HR drives home the restructure and often want to "get back to business" after the layoffs are made. But it doesn't work like that. The remaining employees need to be reengaged in the mission, vision, and business strategy. Productivity needs to be rebuilt. If you factor in all of the changes that impact us, managing change after a downsizing or reorganization has significant importance if the company wants to achieve the results expected from making the changes in the first place. The focus needs to be on ensuring that these strategic shifts lead to improved business performance.

While a traditional view of change management attempts to guide an organization from point "A" to point "B," we focus on taking organizations from point "A" to "Agility." Organizational agility is having the attitudes, processes, and energy to execute new business strategies quickly and effectively. An agile organization can accomplish its intended strategic objectives more quickly, confidently, and productively, leading to better business results sooner. Personal agility is the ability to stay focused and productive during times of change, and to be flexible enough to adapt strategies and plans to new events and conditions. It also involves being proactive and facilitative by assisting colleagues who are struggling with change. These competencies allow people to move through the change process faster each time it occurs.

Case Study

How do you secure employee engagement during periods of organizational change?

Objective:
- To increase worldwide growth initiatives while maintaining sales and profitability levels an organization wanted to maintain a nimble, fully engaged workforce necessary for embracing the changes to come, including new streamlined manufacturing, technology, and personnel processes, and the elimination of operational silos.

Solution:
- We implemented a comprehensive change program for managers and employees to address the emotional journey and career implications of the organizational changes.
- Services included change readiness assessment, 1:1 coaching, and transition or redeployment services to enable employees to successfully navigate change.
- Managers developed skills to manage career decision conversations.

Result:

Before
After
Variance

- Managers Ready to Lead Change
  Before: 35 percent
  After: 94 percent
  Variance: +59 percent
- Employee Confidence Level in Ability to Adapt to Change
  Before: 14 percent
  After: 94 percent
  Variance: +80 percent
- Employee Confidence Level in Ability to Determine Short- and Long-term Career Plans
  Before: 53 percent
  After: 90 percent
  Variance: +37 percent

Conclusion

Workforce reductions are a strategic imperative employed to realign talent needs with business strategy. In order to keep pace with changing business demands, organizations may need to realign their workforce, eliminating roles and functions in areas that are no longer viable while growing other areas of the business. How an organization approaches this strategic initiative has a powerful impact on those who are transitioning out of the company and those who remain. Successfully navigating such changes can mean the difference between an engaged, committed, and productive workforce and a company unable to meet the business goals intended as a result of the change in business strategy.

Navigating a workforce restructuring is a complex responsibility. Outplacement today is not an isolated event. It needs to be an integral part of your talent plan. When changes necessitate a reduction in the workforce, they need to be handled with dignity and respect. Remaining employees need to be engaged and productive. Outplacement helps to achieve this. Its benefits foster the creation of an engaged organizational culture, while also protecting your organization from litigation, damaged morale, and negative brand image.

Note

1. Right Management conducted an online poll of 461 senior executives via LinkedIn. The survey was conducted between September 17 and October 20, 2009, in the United States, Canada, and Latin America.
2. Per Right Management's global study on "Severance Practices around the World," conducted in 2008 and including responses of more than 1,500 human resource and line leaders representing 19 industries in 28 countries.
3. Based on Right Management's 2009 Candidate Satisfaction and Usage research of more than 35,000 candidates globally.
4. Based on a Right Management survey of 268 senior business and HR leaders conducted in 2009.
5. Right Management surveyed 17,413 outplacement candidates in North America between June 2008 and June 2009. Of that number, 3,179 were rehired by the employer that had previously laid them off.

Chapter 49

Developing Talent Management Information Systems

Craig M. Berger, Director of Education
Society for Environmental and Graphic Design

T ALENT MANAGEMENT IS BY ITS NATURE A DATA- AND METRIC-DRIVEN DISCIPLINE. IT IS also a discipline that relies on data from a variety of sources and an understanding of how corporate hierarchies process and utilize employee information. Developing an information strategy comes from an understanding of not only what results are desired but also the required corporate culture to support the system successfully.

Factors for Developing Talent Management Information Systems

A number of factors must be taken into account when developing a talent management information system. These organization and outcome factors should be closely measured when articulating a strategy. They include the following:

Accessibility. How many people will be using the system? How readily will information be required? For example: Will the system be used by only senior management or by all employees?

Complexity. For how many different purposes and how many times will the data be manipulated?

System time management. How much time will be needed to manage the system? For example: Will it need to be updated and monitored on a daily basis, or is the information needed only a few times per year? System time management is generally split into two areas: management of the data input process and management of the reporting process.

Integration into overall corporate data. How closely will the data used for talent management be integrated with the overall human resources management system? The integration decision affects software purchasing and customization decisions as well as the management of the system.

Security level. How secure does the system need to be? Is the data extremely sensitive, or can it be viewed by a large pool of people? Many systems need levels of security for both input and reporting.

These metrics are applied to the components of the talent information systems, as defined in the text that follows, using a scale of high, medium, and low.

Talent Information Systems

Talent information systems come in a number of different formats and are integrated in numerous ways, but there are five major system approaches.

1. Employee Assessment

Assessing employees is the central building block of talent management systems and serves as the underlying data system for compensation, training, recruitment, and succession. As a database that can be used to manage individual employees and corporate direction, most companies look to this information system to be basic and yet robust with multiple possible directions. When large database companies like PeopleSoft and SAP began developing HR software, employee assessment metrics served as the base data source. Companies developing talent management software also tied into the assessment building block. Accessibility and security are often the trickiest issue with assessment software, since the data will be used in many formats.

Employee Metrics	
Accessibility	Medium
Complexity	Medium
System time management	Medium
Integration into overall corporate data	Medium
Security level	High

2. Internal and External Selection

Large international companies in industries as disparate as oil, retail, and computer software have extensive information systems designed around recruiting new employees and moving employees to new positions in the organization. Generally, the most successful of these systems are highly accessible to recruits interested in a position, employees looking to change positions, and employers trying to gauge recruits. Ten years ago this manifested itself in kiosk recruitment stations in companies like Wal-Mart and McDonalds. Today most of these systems are Web-based, sacrificing high-level security for accessibility among a wide group. While recruitment systems generally need to respond to employee strategy and succession planning needs, there is little need to integrate recruitment information into other talent data in an organization. This allows the use of cheaper Web database tools in system development but requires rigorous daily management of the system.

Selection Metrics	
Accessibility	High
Complexity	Medium
System time management	High
Integration into overall corporate data	Low
Security level	High

3. Executive-Level Succession Planning

Organizations have grown increasingly more conscious of the need to closely align succession planning with high-level assessment data of their employees. The systems created to manage succession planning generally require input from a broad swath of employee information. However, the evaluative and analytical data generated by this information is restricted to a small constituency of senior executives. Internet-based software has been most effective for this combination of talent management components, but it requires a higher level of security. Some organizations have resorted to putting a firewall between data input evaluation and analysis.

Executive-Level Succession Planning	
Accessibility	Low
Complexity	Medium
System time management	Medium
Integration into overall corporate data	High
Security level	High

4. Training

A central component of talent management is the assessment, development, training, and promotion of employees. Training information should be used by line managers, but it must be closely linked to employee assessment data. Training systems can be simple, but to be effective, they must be updated continuously with new information and tools.

Training Metrics	
Accessibility	High
Complexity	Low
System time management	High
Integration into overall corporate data	Medium
Security level	Low

5. Compensation

Analyzing compensation including base salary, bonuses, and incentives requires a combination of position planning and employee assessment. Decision making is also spread out, with line managers making narrow decisions on raises and bonuses and senior executives making broader decisions on incentive compensation. The information systems tend to be very secure but must be integrated into the overall information system database. A number of high-level security breaches in recent years have made companies tread carefully. Compensation systems are usually continually updated.

Compensation Metrics	
Accessibility	Low
Information system complexity	Medium
Management time	Low
Integration into overall corporate data	High
Level of security	High

Integrating Information Systems

Most organizations have talent management needs that combine two or more of these information system approaches. In order to successfully integrate multiple systems, it is important to build a management scenario to determine how the information system will meet organizational needs. Three factors to be considered when integrating an information system are organizational strategy, information system selection, and implementation.

The following case studies illustrate the use of these factors.

TalentReservoir© at KenCrest

KenCrest is a human services nonprofit that assists people with developmental disabilities. The organization relies heavily on career and succession management for its success. To maintain KenCrest's edge, it needed comprehensive and integrated systems to manage employee assessment, career training, and succession.

Information System Strategy

Accessibility	**High**

The system needs to be accessed by all employees and their managers.

Complexity	**High**

The system integrates assessment, succession planning, and training in one system, requiring complex manipulation of data and multiple reporting approaches.

System time management	**Medium**

There is a yearly large-scale assessment program, with minor updating the rest of the year.

Integration into overall organization data	**High**

Data needs to be integrated with basic employee data.

Security level	**High**

Multiple levels of the organization have access to the data.

Information System Selection

KenCrest installed a comprehensive talent management methodology based on a model developed by Lance A. Berger & Associates. This was based on a talent management information system that provided succession and career planning. Training and development programs for individual employees were also included based on the succession and career plan assessments. The initial software approach used Microsoft Access. Two levels of security were also developed: one for managers to review their employee reports and a roll-up for HR to provide reports to senior management. The initial program became unwieldy with the increased size and complexity of the organization and was replaced with a Web-based system that provided enhanced security and reporting ability.

Administration

The system is managed through the HR department. Yearly, line managers assess their employees and can continuously access their reports through the information system throughout the year. The HR department periodically updates the system—for example, training programs or adding and deleting employees.

Recruitment as a Strategic Tool: Valero Energy Corporation

Oil discovery and refining is among the most talent-intensive fields. Years of constant growth has created a continuous shortage of qualified employees. Valero is among the most aggressive oil companies at recruiting talent. At Valero, staffing is treated like a leading strategic business function, with clear goals to dominate the industry in the attraction and retention of talent. At Valero, the term "labor supply chain" is used for the recruiting process, and it is treated like a profit center inside the company.

Information System Strategy

Accessibility   **High**

The system needs to be accessible to all managers as well as the entire recruitment team.

Complexity   **Medium**

The system focuses on recruitment (job openings, sources of recruitment, recruitment strategy, and selection processes).

System time management   **High**

The labor-intensive system needs constant management attention to the mountain of application and recruitment data.

Integration into overall corporate data   **Medium**

The recruitment and selection systems component provide ongoing input to the central payroll and internal employee database.

Level of Security   **Low**

The information is intended to be viewed by many levels of the organization.

Information System Selection

Valero hired HRsmart to develop an integrated Web-based recruitment tracking system tied into the company's internal SAP HR software system. The information system is also linked to employee tracking and career management by software from Success Factors.

Administration

The system works effectively because the HR department at Valero ensures the database is up-to-date. The organization has a dedicated staff member to input data. Another important aspect is that the talent system is able to be accessed by managers at all times and managers make strategic decisions from the system. The company is also dedicated to making continual updates to the system, including adding new search features and metrics for linking employer job openings with available recruits.

Compensation Management: Exelon Corporation

Developing compensation guidelines for large organizations is a difficult task. It requires frequent benchmarking and strategic review. Exelon is a leading example of this complexity, with a compensation structure containing over 250 plans developed by Towers Perrin and utilizing various industry benchmarks. These plans consist of base compensation programs, merit increase metrics, and equity and bonus programs. This structure was previously fragmented among multiple individual spreadsheets that were difficult to access by managers.

The system is managed through the HR department. Once a year, line managers assess their employees and can access their reports throughout the year. The HR department updates training programs quarterly, as well as adds new employees to the system.

Information System Strategy

Accessibility   **Medium**

The system metrics need to be accessed by managers, but the report, benchmarks, and metrics must be secure from changes by most of the organization.

Complexity   **High**

The system requires complex calculations based on extensive data analysis.

System time management   **Low**

The system requires periodic updates and metric restructuring.

Integration into overall corporate data   **Low**

As a secure management tool, it can be separate from broader HR data.

Security level   **High**

Compensation information must be tightly controlled from system access to management. Exelon wanted to develop a tightly controlled compensation tool based on the plan metrics developed by their consulting team. They also wanted a software system that would stay robust and current, with frequent access from managers and demands for new metrics and tools.

Information System Selection

In order to get the most up-to-date software, Exelon decided to use a new and innovative software approach using a Software as a Service (SaaS) system created by Authoria. This meant the software would be hosted by the software company, making the company responsible for the constant reporting changes while minimizing HR management.

Administration

Human resources have limited administrative responsibilities, with the software company ensuring system quality and security. Managers can make incentive and compensation changes within the tight guidelines embedded in the system.

Developing Your Information System Strategy

There are dozens of companies and consulting firms with effective talent management software solutions. The major issue is aligning these tools with both everyday and long-term goals. All information strategy should begin with clearly articulating a management approach before defining a specific information system.

Chapter 50

Implementing an Automated Talent Management System

Guy Gauvin, Executive Vice President of Global Services
Taleo

T HE PURPOSE OF THE CHAPTER IS TO OUTLINE WELL-TESTED, BEST-PRACTICE STEPS AND considerations for putting an automated talent management system in your organization—a system that will be adopted and used company-wide, not relegated to a silo of good intentions. These steps include the following:

1. Isolate your biggest exposure . . . or opportunity
2. Build executive advocates and infrastructure
3. Assess risk and creating a pilot project
4. Choose a technology that works for your company
5. Apply implementation methodology
6. Communicate to drive long-term value

1. Getting Started: Isolate Your Biggest Exposure . . . or Opportunity

The best talent management technology holistically supports all the levers for optimizing the workforce, including:

Hiring. Supports best practices in sourcing, assessment, background checking, and alignment with your organization's culture and success criteria.

Performance management. Captures goal setting, development, performance reviews, leadership and career development, and succession planning.

Compensation. Ideally links all of these factors to ensure performance-based compensation, incentivizing the key players in your organization to deliver on goals aligned directly to your business priorities.

Strategic organizations render impressive returns that can do all of the above and get a centralized view of their talent. A study conducted in 2009 by analyst firm Bersin & Associates showed that companies that integrated talent management (bringing together strategies, processes, and supporting technologies across hiring, developing, engaging, and paying staff) have 26 percent more revenue per employee, 41 percent less turnover in high-performing staff, 17 percent less voluntary turnover, and 28 percent less probability to need a significant layoff.

Yet many organizations are not ready to implement total talent management and technology in a single project. Therefore, the best place to start is to focus on the biggest pain or the biggest opportunity. Review the most pivotal talent issues in your organization and determine what needs to be corrected. Following are examples of business performance issues that can drive a project for implementing an automated talent management solution:

- *Marketing organization.* Minimizing burnout in a corporate call center
- *Insurance firm.* Creating and maintaining a talent pool of actuaries
- *Hospital.* Bolstering quality of care by ensuring a shared focus from surgeons to administrative personnel

For challenges or pain points, first identify the root cause. Then objectively and quantifiably look at solution options. With strategy and process in place, apply technology to help add scale and cadence to your approach.

Similarly, in the case of business expansion or growth, an organization should start by building a business case that includes defining success metrics and exploring the hurdles or risks endemic to its potential strategies. From there, apply technology to support the plan and help measure value realization.

2. Build Executive Advocates and Infrastructure

Though it is tempting to think that technology is a quick fix to scaling talent management, without the right foundation, you are susceptible to the single biggest pitfall of talent management initiatives: the inability to show benefit or ROI.

After you have identified a problem area, there are three steps to setting the scalable foundation for solving the issue:

- Build the internal champions and your data infrastructure.
- Ensure a solid process for implementing.
- Add technology, measure results, and communicate.

The first step in any project should be ensuring approval and sponsorship from your executive-level management. Choose someone in a position to clear obstacles and make the necessary resources available. This alignment between HR and the executive team ensures your key stakeholders fully understand the value of the talent management solution. In addition, having a "project champion" in a different business unit or geography can help with senior management embracing the project. These types of employees are well-respected within the organization and provide an additional layer of confidence that the new project is the "right thing to do."

Finally, a project team including line of business, HR, information technology, and change management experts should round out the steering committee for a talent management project. It is not enough to simply assign resources. The resources have to be knowledgeable about the project and possess the level of experience required to quickly contribute. Also, establishing a talented project manager who has a good understanding of the entire business process that will be affected is critical to building a strong project A-team. Remember, help is available. The talent management vendor, or third-party consultants, should be able to provide a resource schema or matrix and, based on the results, make recommendations on internal team makeup. Next, create or update and document the jobs, priorities, career paths, and supporting models that support your corporate "DNA."

Most companies have organizational charts showing the executive team, key business units or departments, leaders, and teams. This is the "who" in your organization. But for businesses to get the full benefits of automating talent management practices, it is just as critical to ascertain "what" jobs those people fill and the skills needed to succeed in each, "how" the jobs map to the company's priorities, "when" individuals in each position might be ready to move to the next level or to another position of leadership, and "why" some positions are aligned to succession plans for executive management.

Therefore, the content infrastructure at the core of strategic, automated talent management should include the following:

Job models. Job families within a group outlining levels, career paths, and criteria. This in turn can be stratified across the organization to identify the skill and contribution levels expected of, for example, all directors in the company or division.

Skill and capability models. Another level of granularity that pinpoints specific certifications, languages, proficiencies, and leadership behaviors required.

Compensation models. Vary widely by company but can include salary and/or a plethora of differentiated compensation options from MBO-driven incentives to stock grants and educational support to work/life balance alternatives.

3. Assess Risk and Create a Pilot Project

"If you have a process that doesn't work when applied 'offline' or manually, if you add technology to that process, what you get is a broken process . . . on steroids,"—Joseph Cabral, senior vice president of human resources at North Shore-Long Island Jewish Health Systems

Smooth, successful projects begin with a thorough risk and impact analysis. This means evaluating all aspects of the project, including scope of deployment, span of control of the project lead, and percentage of the team assigned full-time to the project. This helps project leaders understand areas of strength and identify areas that need improvement and that if left unattended could negatively impact the overall outcome. Teams examine the results of the risk assessment and devise ways to mitigate any potential negative impacts.

With this foundation in place, follow the cardinal rule of project management: Keep it simple, make it measurable, and keep communication open.

Enforce a tight scope among stakeholders, and be prepared to provide adequate justification (too expensive, time intensive, lack of consensus, etc.) to prevent scope creep. One approach is to limit the deployment to a pilot group. From there, identify metrics that show if you are moving the needle with your initiatives.

Projects thrive on the free flow of information, so it is imperative to draft a communications plan as early as possible. The plan must not only include how and when to communicate goals and progress, it should also outline a plan to communicate what the new system will mean for the end users—that is, how they will use it and how their roles and their day-to-day work lives will be affected. Different audiences have different needs concerning project information.

4. Choose a Technology That Works for Your Company

Talent management technology needs to fit your culture and your operating budget, and align with your business goals. Further, your technology vendor's team needs to work well with your organization.

Culture Counts

Cultural fit might seem like an odd alignment with software, but for the ultimate leverage of talent management technology, the technology solution must provide a tool set everyone in your organization *wants* to use. The mass culture shift in the past decade to consumer-friendly technology used by toddlers, teens, and seniors alike is driving expectations for similarly easy—even fun—technology at work.

Talent management systems that have intuitive, easy-to-use interfaces draw on familiar Web 2.0 consumer-like functionality such as Amazon, Google, and eBay. These applications offer an unprecedented opportunity for acceptance and self-service among employees, line managers, and executives. Embedding optimized talent management processes throughout the talent life cycle—from recruitment through onboarding and development—requires solutions that are at their core usable by all stakeholders.

Many technology solutions for recruiting, performance management, and succession were largely built independently of each other, resulting in separate applications for each solution. That produced silos of applications and fragmented data sets and talent pools. The visibility those systems provide into data is largely backwards-looking. Reports account for what happened last month or last year, but poorly predict the future. The applications themselves are used inconsistently, typically two to three times per year. They are difficult to use and used only when absolutely necessary. Without access to the needed information, HR is very reactive.

Separate systems and incompatible platforms result in redundancy of data, with data not matching up across systems. However, new talent management systems have evolved to provide the opportunity to base practices on a unified talent management platform.

Cost Considerations

Cost is always a front-line issue in determining technology decisions. But as with the criticality of building the infrastructure and process, management must review carefully total cost of ownership (TCO) and the return on, and value from, the investment. Essentially, the choice is build the system yourself, buy new talent management technology (often available on demand as a subscription), or try to make the most of existing enterprise-wide installed software, such as in enterprise resource planning (ERP) system that most large organizations have in place for accounting, manufacturing, HR administration, and payroll.

Today, the most popular talent management applications are available via on-demand subscription, also called "Software as a Service" (SaaS). On-demand solutions require no software license purchase or costly maintenance. Secure, configurable, best-practice processes run on the Internet. Users access the system on a Web browser—anytime, anywhere.

Total cost of operation with SaaS, as opposed to total cost of ownership when you buy a traditional license, means no maintenance costs and low-cost or included support services. Innovative, regularly updated SaaS technologies can more quickly empower business-centric talent management.

Key concerns include the following:

- Cost of software
- Time and cost of implementation
- Organizational skills and knowledge needed to add to system
- Ease of use/extent of adoption
- Amount and cost of training needed
- Flexibility
- Scalability
- Repository of best practices
- Depth of talent management insights possible

Reporting and Analytics to Support Your Key Business Decisions

Concerning the last point above, depth of insights, it is important to understand what information you will ultimately want to analyze and report on to drive business decisions. For example, the level and type of information that comes with typical fixed-asset-focused ERP software that most large businesses have in place is very different from that captured in "talent profiles" from a talent-management-specific solution.

Fixed-asset software inventories some data about your people—primarily about their function, their cost, and the associated benefits allotted to them. For example, with fixed-asset software, you can find out the number of laptops designated for your workforce. But you *can't* tell which employee using a laptop will help design your company's next big breakthrough product. Talent management software is built to help provide context about your staff, their skills, their success, and their aspirations. This provides your business with insight to make personnel decisions that can bolster your innovation, drive better sales, or create the best global marketing campaign ideas.

The Right Technology Team

Beyond the technology, evaluate the team you would be partnering with from your technology vendor; this can make or break a technology project. It is important to be in complete alignment with vendor or consulting resources from a cultural/organizational perspective, as they will help provide long-term growth capabilities. A Talent Management Systems Customer Satisfaction 2010 report by Bersin & Associates found that the factor most highly correlated with a customer's total satisfaction was the vendor's consulting expertise. Perform due diligence up front by contacting a variety of past customers and gauging their experiences. This is the best way to discover the real story regarding the vendor's service level and overall capability.

5. Apply Implementation Methodology

A talent management solution is a function-rich software product. It is highly configurable, and its implementation can have a significant impact on the business processes and resources within an organization. To ensure successful technology implementation, your vendor must have a structured implementation approach and consistent methodology. Without a documented, repeatable process, it is impossible to compare performance to expected levels and, therefore, difficult to plan improvements.

First-rate implementation methodologies address all the cultural, technical, and business-related factors to be planned and managed by an implementation methodology. Understanding the proposed implementation methodology should be considered an important part in choosing the best talent management solution for your company. Change management procedures should be factored in.

Phases of Implementation

An implementation methodology should outline the major phases including discovery, design, development, and delivery of a talent management system. Further, it should plan for continuing optimization as your business evolves.

Discovery. Important tasks for the discovery phase are project definition, the selection of the implementation project team, and the documentation of the implementation project plan. This sets the tone and clarifies the goals for the remainder of the implementation project.

Design. Implementation, where the specific requirements of the project are mapped out in detail, is the most important step of the design phase. The design phase includes a detailed analysis of the company's business practices, to determine not only its current procedures and workflow but also how those procedures ought to be reengineered as they become incorporated into the new system.

Development. The development phase involves the configuration and prototyping of the system, including the importing of legacy data. Integration with HRIS systems is a technical task, as is thorough testing and optimization within the company's existing infrastructure.

Delivery. Employee training is a crucial aspect of the delivery phase. Behavioral issues that arise during training can influence the critical adoption of the new system. A thorough implementation methodology will anticipate change management issues. The strategy for dealing with change management should already have been detailed in the project plan.

MIE: Measure, Improve, Evolve. Implementation of the talent management system typically takes three to six months to "go live" within your organization. Once you go live, ensure that your team and your vendor plan to measure initial results, then refine and optimize the tool to get increasingly better return, and continue this measure/improve cycle to evolve the system in lockstep with the evolution of your business.

Ask your prospective vendors about their implementation methodology. It is imperative that the vendor has a clear vision of its implementation methodology and the requirements of each step. There is more to an implementation methodology than simply documenting a business process and then following the documentation. A vendor should be prepared to invest in the ongoing development and maintenance of its implementation methodology in an ever-evolving way.

Your company should expect—and receive—superior service from highly experienced professionals during all the phases for implementation of your new system.

Implementation Review: Dos and Don'ts

Do

- Create an implementation team: executive champion from relevant line of business(es); HR partner; IT liaison; company-wide supporters to ensure widest adoption.
- Keep it simple. Workflow is the number 1 culprit of "over-complexification."
- Stage a multiyear roadmap of bite-sized goals and implementation.
- Drive business, not process.
- Adopt a philosophy of active dialogue (don't relegate decision making to either e-mail or just the technology).
- Adhere to 40/20/40 priorities rule: 40 percent process; 20 percent technology; 40 percent change management.
- Work with services or profit-driving departments initially.

Don't

- "Abandon" HR without business input. Otherwise, you risk siloed ideas you can't easily leverage.

- Be afraid to experiment or pilot. If you fail small, it's relatively fast and cheap and provides good learning.
- Forget that talent-related business problems usually have multiple causes and effects. You might not solve churn, for example, with just better hiring; you will likely need to look at development and incentive programs as well.

6. Communicating to Drive Long-Term Value

When the implementation is complete, find out what is and is not working and provide action plans as soon as possible. This will mitigate any concerns from staff who may not understand the value of the new solution. Employ the communication plan and promote successes, no matter how small.

Stay in touch with end users through user groups, discussion forums, and structured learn sessions. Make sure to implement key benchmarks and metrics that demonstrate the benefits of usage and undergo consistent root-cause analysis to uncover usability issues and implement an action plan to address them.

It also pays to be an active participant in a software vendor's customer programs such as regional user groups, steering committees, and annual conferences, to stay on top of key learnings and best practices.

Understanding Change

By now it should be clear to users that change is coming. But staff also needs to understand what the change is, and why the organization is doing it. The more transparent your decisions and reasoning, the greater will be the organizational adoption. This is critical; if end users feel that they have been heard and recognize that their needs have been addressed in the end design, they will more readily adopt the new process/system.

Marketing tactics can also prove very beneficial in selling new ideas and align with end users so there is a common understanding of the new talent management model or methodologies. Consider branding the project, or engage in key message crafting to get all users on the same page. Sensitivity to a change in jobs/roles as a result of the process reengineering is paramount and should be dealt with honestly and effectively.

Conclusion

Implementing automated technology needs to go hand-in-glove with the overall talent management strategy and process. Define a strategy, outline a usable and scalable process and talent management system, and obtain strong buy-in throughout the organization from employees, line management, executive leadership, and the board. Decisive action on talent management technology initiatives today will positively impact and grow your business for years to come.

Part VI

Innovative Thinking that Can Shape Your Organization's Approach to Talent Management

Chapter 51

Rethinking Talent Management Using a People Equity Framework

William A. Schiemann, CEO
Metrus Institute

MOST LEADERS HAVE SIMILAR ACCESS TO CAPITAL, RAW MATERIALS, TECHNOLOGY, AND markets. The major differences among them lie in two areas: their strategy—how they have chosen to uniquely position their company in the marketplace—and their ability to execute that strategy. And, as Rosabeth Moss Kanter has observed, there are far more firms floundering because of poor execution than because of poor strategy.[1]

Arguably, people are the most crucial ingredient in strategy execution. Dealing with talent issues was the number one concern related to strategy execution among a group of 75 executives that were interviewed for *Reinventing Talent Management*.[2] "Talent," they said, "is what will make or break their success in the new marketplace."

Recent interviews and executive forums suggest that "traditional talent models are broken," as observed by Anna Tavis, a senior HR executive with AIG and leader of a Financial Services HR Roundtable group in New York City. Recognizing that talent is clearly important and traditional talent models seem inadequate, the Metrus Institute began examining talent in the context of the new marketplace. We sought to better understand what was deficient about traditional models of talent and what was needed to overcome these deficiencies. As part of this research, the Metrus Institute reviewed and conducted numerous research studies and examined successful versus unsuccessful firms, with the goal of better understanding how talent is or could be optimized in organizations.

We will discuss the results of this endeavor by first addressing *the context in which talent management is being shaped*. Second, we will examine *the role of talent in value creation*. Third, *a new model for thinking about talent optimization* will be described, along with ways to measure how effectively talent is being deployed. Finally, we will discuss *the implications for several parts of the talent life cycle*, such as performance management and leader development.

The Talent Context

As we began conducting interviews and research, we realized that there were important trends and changes taking place in the environment, which were influencing how talent is acquired, grown, and leveraged. Here are a few of the most significant changes:

- *More for less.* While this statement may sound trite, the global balance of supply and demand has changed dramatically, which has had profound implications on business. During the twentieth century, fewer suppliers existed, and customers had to accept the limited products and services that were available—for example, one telephone company that offered limited choices. Throughout the world, many suppliers are now competing for the same customers.
- *More with less.* Organizations need to become leaner, producing ever more value with scarcer resources. They must optimize productivity in every area—operations, services, ideas, and *talent*. Those who can produce better service enhancements, more innovations, and higher productivity than their competitors will have a value advantage.
- *Agility.* Change is the one constant. Technology and emerging global competitors are two major factors that are changing the game constantly for many organizations. Competitors are innovating each day, and customer needs and wants will continue to change at unprecedented levels. This also means that talent will obsolesce faster, presenting a clear challenge and threat to both individuals and organizations.
- *Good talent has choices.* Many senior leaders lament losing talent; individuals with specialized skills, such as nurses and engineers; and workers whose jobs required very specific, hard-to-come-by knowledge. These scarce, top-performing players are difficult to replace and demand a premium in good and bad economic conditions.
- *Just-in-time talent.* Dr. Peter Cappelli of The Wharton School and others have argued that traditional methods of labor and talent forecasting perform abysmally when it comes to actually predicting talent needs. To remain competitive, organizations are morphing rapidly, making it difficult to stick to the rigid planning models that worked in the past. Cappelli points out that, under normal circumstances, if recently developed people are not deployed in ways that utilize their new skills, they are likely to move on in as few as ten months.
- *Cornering the talent market.* If you think about cornering talent, the way Curtis Jadwin thought about cornering markets in *The Pit*,[3] you are unlikely to be gratified. While a few rare organizations, such as Google, have been able to skim the

cream from the top, most firms don't have that privilege. Furthermore, if you were able to select only the best and brightest, how would you continue to develop and reward those premier players so they weren't tempted to leave? Garry Ridge, the CEO of WD–40 Corporation, and Will Kutcha, a vice president of human resources for Paychex, have followed more realistic talent management models, in which they chose instead to make average players great.[4] Ridge's organization generates over $1.4 million in revenue per employee and has optimized talent without selecting and paying for only premier players. His philosophy of "helping each employee get an 'A'" is a hallmark of a servant-leader model that has proven successful in his company.

- *Many slots competing for the "right" talent.* China and India were already pounding out GDP numbers over 5 percent in 2009, while the United States and many other Western nations had negative GDPs. This will mean a "pull" on the labor market in many areas. But don't assume that this will be universal. Some jobs in some locales may be sidelined forever, such as rust-belt jobs in the United States or Europe. In contrast, there will be high demand for people with the right skills and the right attitude in professions such as health care, energy, high technology, and the right role such as management, which is already scarce in numerous economies.

These changes are fueling the need to find new models for managing the talent life cycle (depicted in Figure 51-1). Our research indicates that in many organizations the

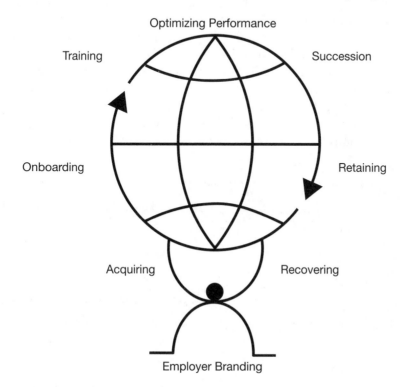

Figure 51-1 Managing the Talent Life Cycle

talent life cycle is still being managed within silos: with recruiters, for example, who are totally disconnected from those responsible for onboarding, training, or performance management. To optimize their investment in talent, organizations must stop handling each phase of the talent life cycle in isolation from the others. They must find effective ways to link their business strategy and their people strategy to the talent life cycle. Then they must design adaptable processes, capabilities, and messages to support the integrated model.

Given the growing importance of creating value, let us now turn to the process by which value is created and the role of talent in that process.

In Search of Value

Value represents the perceived benefits gained from anything—products, relationships, services—compared to the perceived costs—monetary, psychological, social—of obtaining that thing. There have been a number of models describing how organizations differentiate themselves in the marketplace through the value they create. Treacy and Wiersema[5] describe three alternative models for creating value for consumers: being an operational leader and, therefore, lowest-cost producer; being an innovation leader; and being a leader in customer intimacy. Everyone can think of familiar retail brands that follow these different models. Each has merits, and each can survive and thrive in the marketplace because a sufficient number of consumers find its benefits greater than its costs. For example, Nordstrom's follow the high customer intimacy model; it must find customers who value and are willing to pay for a much higher level of service. Apple is a leader in innovation; it attracts customers who value innovation and design and are willing to pay a premium for them. Each of the two companies follows a value creation model that effectively differentiates it in the marketplace.

Connecting this back to the importance of talent in strategy execution, what people or talent strategy will be most effective in each model? As Figure 51-2 depicts, employees of a company that embraces the operational leader model need different

Possible People Measures	Cost Leader	Innovation Leader	Customer Intimacy
What Values?	Efficiency	Autonomy	Empowerment
What Competencies?	Cost analysis	Idea generation	Customer knowledge
What Engages?	Task fulfillment	Creative fulfillment	Service fulfillment

Figure 51-2 Different Strategies, Different Measures

characteristics from those whose employer follows the innovation model, and those who work within a customer intimacy organization require still other characteristics. Performing your job successfully at Nordstrom's requires being focused on, trained in, and committed to service, while Wal-Mart workers are rewarded for efficiency. The most successful Apple employees may not be paragons of efficiency, but they can probably extol the latest and greatest features of new products. Table 51-1 provides a summary of some of the implications of our findings regarding the new talent marketplace and some key questions that every organization should be prepared to answer.

- "Perceived value" is making or breaking every organization, including internal functions—talent plays a critical role in the value equation.
- A clear people and talent strategy, which is aligned with the business strategy, is a must.
  - What makes you different from your competitors, and what talent strategy will best fit that model?
  - What are the "A" roles—the roles that are crucial to successfully executing your business strategy?
  - Are those roles populated by "A" talent?
  - Why do you deserve to get and keep the best talent, especially for "A" roles?
  - How will you optimize your talent, given limited resources?
  - How will you find the "right" talent? Talent that is aligned with your business model? Right skills? Committed to the organization?
- Great metrics are required to evaluate and guide strategy (including talent) execution.
  - How will you know if you are optimizing your talent?
  - How will you know if HR is effective?
- Does the organization have the Human Resource talent needed to support the business? Do they have the necessary industry and business acumen and a strong understanding of talent best practices?

Table 51-1 Implications and Key Questions for Managing Talent

Three Powerful Factors

Within the context of the identified changes and armed with an understanding of the critical role that value plays, we set out to determine whether or not there is a specific set of strategic talent factors that drive organizational success. If so, discovering these factors would enable organizations to strategically focus resources on initiatives, people processes, and behaviors that are most likely to optimize those factors. It would also reduce the scattered usage, and questionable value, of tactical metrics that are used without focus and purpose in organizations: head count, appraisals completed, time to hire, benefits processed, training cost per employee, exit interview data, suggestions submitted, and so on. We also sought to discover how such factors would influence talent decisions for organizations with different value propositions.

An additional goal of this long-term research was to help answer a key question: What is the connection between investments in human capital (people) and shareholder value or goal attainment in not-for-profit enterprises? Until now, there has been no integrated way for senior management to determine which of the investments they were making in their employees were paying off and which were a waste of resources. In short, there was no way for an organization to measure its "people equity."

In the late twentieth century, the concept of "customer equity" emerged as a way to capture the value of customers and connect it to shareholder value. But, on the people side, no such unifying concept had emerged[6] until we introduced the People Equity concept.[7]

From an extensive review of the literature and from interviews with individuals in many organizations, we were able to identify three powerful factors that drive organizational success: Alignment, Capabilities, and Engagement (the ACE model, described in Figure 51-3). People Equity is the sum total of the three powerful factors.

All three factors have been discussed in the research literature in isolated and varied ways. But as we discovered, all three factors play crucial and interrelated roles in success no matter what the organization's business strategy, industry, geography, or size. Each ACE factor contains some elements that are common across all organizations (e.g., clear goals, under Alignment). There are also elements that are unique to a particular organization and its strategy (e.g., goals that are aligned with a business strategy of being the most customer-intimate organization in the industry).

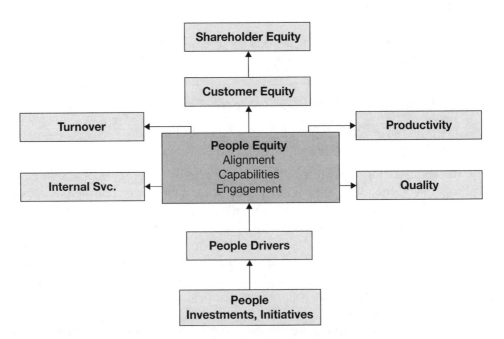

Figure 51-3 The ACE Model: Alignment, Capabilities, Engagement

Let's look more closely at each of the three factors:

- Alignment is the extent to which employees are connected to the organization's business strategy and goals and the extent to which work units are effectively aligned with one another to deliver high-value products or services to customers.
- Capabilities are the extent to which the organization effectively creates talent, information, and resources to grow customer value.
- Engagement is the extent to which employees are willing to go beyond the minimum requirements of their role to provide additional energy or to advocate for their organization as a great place to work, purchase from, or invest in.

Impact of ACE

Our findings demonstrate that the three ACE factors are drivers and predictors of quality, customer loyalty, talent retention, internal-function effectiveness, productivity, goal achievement, operating effectiveness, and, ultimately, financial performance. Figure 51-4 contains a few of the facts that a good CFO would want to know. Alignment is frequently the best predictor of operating and financial performance, for example, while Capabilities is most often the strongest predictor of customer outcomes, such as satisfaction or retention. Engagement is a strong predictor of employee retention and performance. Collectively, these three factors are a good predictor of overall organizational success.

Companies with high ACE

- Averaged half the turnover of low ACE companies

- Were **3x** more likely to be quality leaders in their industry

- Were **2x** more likely to be financial leaders in their industry

- Averaged **56 percentage points higher** on Internal Customer Service ratings

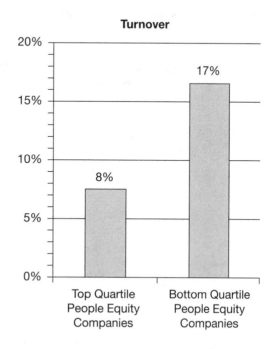

Figure 51-4 Impact of Ace

Source: Kostman & Schiemann, *People Equity: The Hidden Driver, Quality Progress, 2005; Seibert & Lingle, Internal Customer Service: Has it Improved?* Quality Progress 2007

We find that People Equity scores vary dramatically not only across but within organizations. For example, a recent study of over 70 hospitals within one hospital group found People Equity scores that ranged from over 90 (out of a maximum of 100) in one hospital to as low as 21 in another. Corroborating the importance of these findings was an acknowledgment by the CEO that the best People Equity hospitals were also the best performers and vice versa in terms of financial performance and patient satisfaction.

Which Profile Do You Manage?

The three factors of ACE can also display unique codes across an organization, function, or unit of any size. The eight profiles shown in Figure 51-5 capture the combinations of high and low ACE. Each profile carries implications for where value is lost and improvement can occur. For example, in "Strategic Disconnect" units, it often appears that people are working hard, but in reality many activities may not be adding the most value because they are not fully aligned with the organization's overall strategy, brand, or customers. Similarly, the "Under Equipped" profile indicates units that are Engaged and Aligned but perhaps don't have the talent, information, or resources to meet customer expectations.

What is interesting to note is that while the first four profiles all look high in Engagement, only one is optimal, demonstrating that Engagement alone is not enough. Total organizational performance is driven by all three factors.

The implications of these findings are important from a resource and credibility standpoint: Different profiles require different fixes, enabling an organization to target its resources in the areas where they will do the most good.

Alignment	Capabilities	Engagement	Profile
↑	↑	↑	Superior Performance
↓	↓	↑	Cheerleader
↑	↓	↑	Under Equipped
↓	↑	↑	Strategic Disconnect
↑	↑	↓	Under Achiever
↑	↓	↓	Indifferent
↓	↑	↓	Talent Waste
↓	↓	↓	Performance Laggard

Figure 51-5 People Equity Profiles

Measuring ACE

How can ACE be measured? After exploring many other approaches to measuring ACE, we realized that we could obtain most of the information we needed through surveys of employees specifically designed to probe A, C, and E. After all, who is in the best position to comment on ACE? Employees interface with internal and external customers, they are close to resources and information, they either do or do not understand the strategy, and they decide if they are going to expend above-average effort. Ideally, such ACE-focused employee surveys are complemented by customer and internal-stakeholder surveys—essentially organizational 360s—that effectively pinpoint important gaps.

We embarked on a process to capture the essential ACE information by using a calibrated employee survey that enabled us to compare the ACE dimensions on a common 100-point scale, allowing us the ability to compare the relative weakness or strength across the three factors. We also used these data to predict important business outcomes, such as those already shown in Figure 51-4.

The Drivers of ACE

While the full set of drivers and enablers are discussed in more detail in *Reinventing Talent Management*, the biggest causes of low scores in the three critical areas include the following:

Alignment

- Lack of clear direction
- Weak unit or personal goals
- Measures that fail to connect goals or establish stretch targets
- Gaps in performance management; most notably, poor feedback and coaching
- Lack of accountability—often connected to rewards

Capabilities

- Poor person-role fit
- Poorly defined customer expectations and measures
- A low degree of teamwork
- Insufficient resources or tools
- Missing the "right" information needed to create deliverables in an efficient and effective manner

Engagement

- Supervisory practices that stem from poor communication, lack of respect, or fairness issues
- Lack of a values fit (e.g., diversity, work-life balance, ethics)
- Few opportunities for growth/advancement
- Lack of recognition
- Leaders who are not respected or inspiring and who fail to model the behaviors they preach

The Implications of ACE

As part of our research, we have held numerous roundtables and discussions about the ACE factors with managers and executives from a wide variety of organizations. Out of these sessions have come the following observations and suggestions for improving an organization's ACE scores and, subsequently, its bottom line:

- The HR function, senior leadership, and direct managers are in a key position to influence ACE, given their roles and ability to influence the drivers of ACE.
- Supervisors are a very powerful weapon in managing ACE, given their day-to-day involvement with a number of the ACE drivers. However, the degree of freedom they have to manage ACE is shaped and limited by HR systems and senior leader behaviors, priorities, and policies. For example, supervisors cannot reward employees outside of organization-wide reward policies.
- Similar HR processes—recruiting, selection, onboarding, compensation—*do not guarantee* the same ACE scores
- Stop one-size-fits-all programs; they are a waste of resources, unless there is fact-based evidence that a particular gap exists across the organization. Instead, tailor solutions—that is, coaching, manager training, processes, reward—to fit unique gaps or opportunities revealed in the ACE profiles.
- You can't manage ACE if you don't measure it at every phase of the talent life cycle. For example, it doesn't help to only conduct exit interviews after talent has left; instead, use an ACE survey that is predictive of turnover, especially for "A" roles and "A" talent.
- To achieve maximum impact, it is usually best to first attack the area of ACE that has received the lowest score.

Implications for Talent Management

What are the implications for and applications of this new thinking about the talent context and the People Equity model? While this chapter cannot cover this subject in depth, we will share a few implications for various stages of the talent life cycle.[8]

In each of the management areas below are some "Fast Facts" that come from a review of research and from interviews with experts in each field. Following these are "Potential Actions" you can take to improve results in these areas.

Rethinking Performance Management

Fast Facts:

- Performance appraisals are only one component of performance management, but they are often the most damaging one because they create a fundamental conflict between Alignment and Engagement, while minimally improving Capabilities, and they are not helpful in development and performance improvement.[9]

Potential Actions:

- Make performance review discussions part of everyday life. Organizations like Intel expect their managers to have five- to ten-minute conversations with their employees weekly. These conversations afford opportunities to managers and employees alike to share successes, problems, and challenges. They make performance reviews a regular part of organizational life, enhancing Alignment and gaining manager understanding and support for Capabilities gaps, without driving Engagement down.
- Helping employees get an "A." Organizations like Smith Bucklin and WD–40 Corporation focus on making average employees great by building motivational and reward models that drive high ACE. They assume that all employees want to excel. They communicate clear values and performance norms that create peer pressure to perform. They establish leadership roles that call for managers to help employees maximize their potential.

Talent Acquisition

Fast Facts:

- Talent acquisition metrics are often weak and drive inappropriate behaviors.
- The hiring process for many organizations is expensive and far from effective; the average failure rate is about one in three with even good selection systems. With poor ones, it is no better than chance.[10]
- There continues to be an over-reliance on the interview, which, as used, often has poor validity.
- Organizations have been their best at hiring for the "C factor" (i.e., selecting for specific skills, abilities, or experiences).
- Organizations have been weakest at hiring for fit on Alignment and Engagement (i.e., hiring people who have the propensity to become Aligned and Engaged).

Potential Actions:

- Build more strategic talent acquisition metrics, reducing the importance of transactional metrics, such as time to hire or fill rates, and replace with more strategic ones, such as the percentage of hires that hit performance or retention targets. ACE is also a good success criterion. How many hires hit high ACE scores after 3, 6, or 12 months on the job?
- One improvement to the interview process is building in behavioral indicators that predict hires who will be high on Alignment and Engagement with their role, manager, and the organization.

Developing Leadership Talent

Fast Facts:

- Leaders are far better at hitting the "What" than the "How." That is, leaders and managers are held more accountable for "hitting the numbers" than they are for how they hit them—which is largely through strong talent.

- Most managers are far more proficient in technical skills than in people skills. A large percentage of hires are based on past performance and not on the potential to grow and leverage talent. This is a key reason why the failure rate is so high when organizations attempt to promote sales reps to managers.
- A recent review of the research on Leader Development commissioned by the SHRM Foundation shows that it is too much "art" and not enough based on fact and evidence.[11]

Potential Actions:

- There is a strong need for better people measures, which provide stronger evidence as to how well managers are optimizing talent. Without such measures, senior leaders must rely on hearsay and the intuition of a limited sample of managers—sometimes only the boss—about how well talent is being developed and managed. The ACE survey measures described earlier enable leaders to get an organizational view of their talent reservoir and how it is being developed and utilized.
- Teach ACE holistically. Because ACE represents the three key factors that optimize talent, managers must be educated on how they can manage each of the factors, how to detect gaps, and how to get to the root-cause fix. Engagement training alone will not do this. Talent management capabilities must be viewed and developed holistically.

We have just touched the surface of potential changes that can be made to the talent management framework and life cycle (see Figure 51-1).

Notes

1. Kanter, Rosabeth Moss. *When giants learn to dance*. New York: Simon & Schuster, Inc. (1989).
2. Schiemann, William. *Reinventing talent management: How to maximize performance in the new marketplace*. New York: John Wiley & Sons, Inc. (2009).
3. Norris, Frank. *The pit*. (Lenox, MA: Hard Press, 2006).
4. The 11th Annual SHRM Foundation Thought Leaders Retreat, "Positioning Your Organization for Recovery," October 5–6, 2009, Scottsdale, AZ.
5. Treacy, Michael, and Fred Wiersema. *The discipline of market leaders*. (Reading, Mass: Addison-Wesley Publishing Co., 1995.
6. Except perhaps the broad notion of Human Capital, but this was flawed because it either drove macro-economic treatment of people, missing important individual factors, or it was used as a catchall for anything dealing with people. Also, it was often used within the context of capital conservation, rather than value creation.
7. We labeled this concept "People Equity" to be consistent with the notion of value that can be grown or depleted over time, representing the aggregate value of people as it relates to customer equity and shareholder equity.
8. For a further treatment of these subjects, please see *Reinventing Talent Management* (Schiemann, 2009) or articles at www.metrus.com.

9. For example, Jerry Seibert, Global Director of Diagnostic Services for Metrus, reports that only 60 percent of employees say that their last performance review helped improve their performance.

10. Levin, Robert A., and Joseph G. Rosse. *Talent flow: A strategic approach to keeping good employees, helping them grow, and letting them go.* (San Francisco: Jossey-Bass, 2001).

11. McCauley, Cynthia. *Leader development: A review of research.* Center for Creative Leadership, Literature Review commissioned by the SHRM Foundation (2008).

Chapter 52

Marshalling Talent: A Collaborative Approach to Talent Management

Dave Ulrich, Ph.D., Professor
Ross School of Business, University of Michigan
Partner, *The RBL Group*
Michael Ulrich, Research Associate
The RBL Group

Introduction

We know *it* matters. Wars are fought over *it*. Professional sports teams draft *it*. Actors audition to demonstrate that they have *it*. Agents contract for *it*. Some are innately endowed with *it*, while others strive diligently to earn *it*. Organizations compete for *it*. All try to grow *it*. The *it* is Talent. *It* is evolving into a science for HR professionals and a critical determinant of success for general managers. A multitude of programs and investments have been developed to attract, retain, and upgrade talent. In 2008 companies in the United States spent over $130 billion dollars in training to raise the level of talent and improve performance (American Society of Training and Development 2009). Yet sometimes after stipulating that talent matters, it is easy to get lost in the myriad of promises, programs, and processes and lose sight of the basics.

This chapter synthesizes and simplifies what scholars and general managers should study and know to improve the science of talent and upgrade the quality of talent in organizations. We propose an emerging metaphor for talent and distill 11 insights from the talent research landscape that may guide talent theory and practice.

Metaphor for Talent

Perhaps the most dominant metaphor for talent in the last decade has been the "war for talent" (Michaels, Handfeld-Jones, and Axelrod 2001). This metaphor was based on work by the McKinsey consulting firm where they showed that companies compete not by products or services, but by access to talent. Their work highlighted how companies can secure scarce talent by outbidding or out-competing their competitors. Talent is seen as a win/lose game where a company gains more talent than another, leading to business success. Their work has recently shown that talent continues to be a significant issue for leaders and needs to be shared throughout the organization (Guthridge, Komm, and Lawson 2008).

One concern with a "war" metaphor is that it implies winners and losers. In an economy where talent is transient and where relationships with a company are transactional, there are short-term winners and losers. The "war" metaphor needs modernizing. This metaphor is similar to the way the Allies ended World War I. The Treaty of Versailles advocated "to the victor go the spoils." This victor's mind-set set in motion events leading to World War II. After WWII, the allies devised the Marshall Plan to collaborate with and rebuild those who lost. In his classic speech in 1947, George Marshall, the U.S. Secretary of State, suggested that collaborative reconstruction would help build sustainable European economies more than the winner-take-all mentality of WWI. He suggested that a long-term, collaborative approach to reconstruction would help build sustainable European economies more than a win/lose approach.

Likewise, the War for Talent metaphor is bettered by a Marshalling Talent analog. In both the War and Marshall Plan metaphors, talent is a critical and scarce resource. In the Marshall Plan, talent is intended as a long-term investment, not a short-term victory; as a collaboration where people work together in high-performing teams; as a way to look across boundaries between an organization and its external stakeholders; and as a way to retain and develop talent.

When we filter the myriad of studies and ideas on talent through the lens of Marshalling Talent, we distill 11 insights that define what Marshalling Talent might look like.

Eleven Talent Insights

We have reviewed the ideas, research, and best practices on talent to create a talent menu. This talent menu captures 11 insights and shapes the Marshalling Talent metaphor that general managers should adopt in order to make talent happen.

Insight 1: Talent matters inside a company ... and outside. Few would argue with the premise that organizations with better talent will be more successful. However, the specific ways that improved talent builds success may be delineated and expanded. Often, improved talent is measured through increased productivity, the ability to execute a strategy, the extent to which there are backups in place for key positions, and employee engagement scores. These internal mechanisms imply that talent helps what happens inside a company.

We agree with these measures, but in the spirit of working in a world without boundaries where value is defined not by who we are but by the value that our actions create for others, we posit that internal talent may also be linked to external stakeholder outcomes. If a company has better talent, then we are likely to see the following:

- *Increased customer value.* Customer value may be seen as attitudes of the customer toward the organization or the willingness of a customer to spend a higher portion of his or her money with the company. Each of these may be impacted by talent. A talent-customer value proposition exists where organizations with employees who have a more positive attitude will likely have customers who match that attitude. Positive customer attitudes will lead to discretionary spending where customers spend more on the targeted company (Schneider, Macey, Barbera, and Martin 2009).
- *Increased investor value.* Increasingly, there is a shared understanding that intangibles represent up to 50 percent of the market value of a public traded company. These intangibles represent the confidence that investors have in a firm's ability to predictably deliver future earnings (Ulrich and Smallwood 2003). Many of these intangibles come from how investors perceive quality of internal organization employees.
- *Increased community reputation.* Companies work hard to build a reputation within their communities to both enable them to attract better employees and help employees feel better about their work (Dowling 2002).

With technology making the world more accessible, talent becomes important for both internal and external organizational outcomes.

Insight 2: Talent requires individual ability . . . and teamwork. For the 2004 Olympics, the United States assembled one of the most talented groups of basketball players ever assembled. They had been all-stars, leading scorers, and leading rebounders in the NBA; they were the elite of their profession. They were expected to win because not since 1992 when NBA players were allowed to play in the Olympics had a United States team lost a game. They were routed by Puerto Rico (92–73), beat Greece (77–71), lost to Lithuania (94–90), beat Angola (89–53) and Spain (102–94), then lost to Argentina (89–81), and beat Lithuania (104–96), to take the bronze medal. Previous U.S. Olympic teams were a combined 109–2 prior to the 2004 U.S. Olympic team.

While there is a major focus in the talent field on individual talent, it is not enough. Just hiring people who have great personal abilities may not help deliver long-term organization success. No one would doubt that the above U.S. Olympic team had the most gifted athletes. Yet they lost, not only once but three times, and most of their victories were closer than their talent would suggest.

Talent without teamwork is insufficient, and while it may lead to individual records, it generally does not lead to long-term organization success. Following the basketball (or other team sport) metaphor, the top scorer in the league is seldom on the team that wins the championship. Consistent with a Marshalling Talent metaphor, teamwork matters because it makes ordinary people good and good people great.

The 2008 Olympics were a different story. Again, the team was composed of exceptional athletes, but this team committed not just to winning (as the other had pledged) but to playing together as a team. The 2008 team won the Olympic gold medal, and among the 12 teams, the United States were ranked first in 11of 19 team statistical categories, including scoring margin (+27.8), field goal percentage (.550), defensive field goal percentage (.403), and were ranked second in another four team areas. The stark contrast of these two assembled groups of talented players shows the importance not just of individual talent (war for talent), but of teamwork (Marshalling Talent).

Insight 3: Talent should align competencies with strategy inside . . . and stakeholders outside. Most talent work begins with competencies. Competencies represent the knowledge, skills, and abilities of employees. Competencies have been aligned with the strategy of a business (Byham and Moyer 1996). Competencies have more impact when they help a business deliver its goals. Going forward, we suggest that with a Marshall Plan mentality, competencies inside a company may be aligned with the expectations of customers, suppliers, communities, and investors outside the company. The "right" competencies are those that align external expectations and internal actions (Ulrich and Smallwood 2007). These customer-centric competencies then become standards for leaders and employees throughout the company. When competence models start with future customer expectations, they direct employee attention to what they should know and do. The simplest test of the competence standard is to ask target or key customers, "If our employees lived up to these standards, would they inspire confidence from you in our firm?" When customers answer yes, the competence model is appropriate; if they answer no, it needs more work.

Insight 4: Talent requires assessment both inside . . . and out. Based on defined competencies, standards may be established whereby employees may be assessed on how they perform. In recent years, most individual talent assessments have some form of a balanced scorecard (Kaplan and Norton 1996). For individuals, this logic has led to evaluating individuals on both results and behaviors (Welch and Welch 2005). Talented employees deliver results which may be related to financial, customer, and organization outcomes. In addition, talented employees behave the right way based on how well they demonstrate the defined competencies. These competencies may be assessed by the employee, subordinates, peers, and supervisors through 360 feedback. But to provide a holistic view, employees may also be evaluated by those outside the organization: suppliers, customers, investors, community leaders, and other external stakeholders. This shifts the 360 to a 720 (360 times 2 = 720). 720 feedback initiatives assess internal employee actions against external customer expectations.

Insight 5: Talent comes from thoughtful investment . . . that crosses boundaries and encourages collaboration. The billions of dollars spent on upgrading talent may be seen as investments in building future talent. We synthesize six types of investments that upgrade global talent with 6 B's. To Marshall talent, these six investments may be extended to create cooperation across boundaries. Some examples follow:

- *Buy.* Involve customers or suppliers to source, interview, and orient new talent.
- *Build.* Create executive exchanges where employees take assignments in customer or supplier organizations; involve customers or investors in design and delivery of development programs.
- *Borrow.* Source knowledge from contractors or others outside the organization; create Web-based social networks to find ways of doing work.
- *Bound.* Involve customers in defining criteria of future senior jobs; allow customers to participate in succession planning processes.
- *Bounce.* Use customer criteria as part of the downsizing process; outplace employees into supplier or customer networks.
- *Bind.* Be willing to rehire talented employees who have left; use employee referral programs of future employees as a way to retain the best employees.

As these collaborative approaches to talent emerge, employees inside and customers, suppliers, and investors outside may feel more connected to each other. Collaboration through talent programs across boundaries may connect social and interorganizational networks.

Insight 6: Talent has to be mindful of, and gain the benefits from, individual differences (diversity) . . . and build unity. Diversity thinking encourages organizations to vary in thinking and acting along a number of dimensions: race, age (generational shifts), gender, national culture, psychological orientation, career drivers, and global perspective. Managing diversity has social implications as societies assimilate people with different backgrounds, political ramifications as legislation attempts to serve multiple stakeholders, and economic consequences as organizations increase innovation and creativity by bringing people together with different backgrounds (Thomas 2005). Internal diversity matters more as organizations operate in increasingly complex social and economic settings.

While many organizations have implemented diversity or inclusion initiatives which foster respect for individual differences, we would also suggest that diversity without unity creates chaos. Simply respecting, responding to, or encouraging people who are different to come together will not result in organization performance if those people do not have a common goal and ability to work together. The premise of the Marshall Plan is that heretofore enemies can put aside differences and work together on shared interests. When they do so, societies, political systems, and organizations move forward. Organizations that maximize diversity without unity will devolve into disorder, with respect for differences being an excuse for disconnected actions. Organizations that foster true diversity also have explicit unity. Unity needs to be around working for common goals that generally begin with customer orientation.

Insight 7: Talent should focus on the A players and match them to A positions . . . but also pay attention to B players. Top performers produce a disproportionate amount of results (Smart 2005). More recently, top performers have been labeled as "A" players and leaders have been encouraged to match "A" players to "A" positions. "A" positions are those wealth-creating roles where top individuals can have maximum impact (Huselid, Beatty, and Becker 2005). Top performers in key roles will generally produce higher results. Scholars are finding that it is even more important to retain top players than to attract them (Fernandez-Araoz, Groysberg, and Nohria 2009). This is consistent with the metaphor of the Marshall Plan where an effort is made to upgrade and strengthen existing talent rather than seeking new talent.

In addition, following the collaboration logic of a Marshall Plan, we would suggest that "B" players are also important. "B" players are more likely to stay with the company (vs. A players, who are more mobile); there are more "B" players; "B" players are the heart and soul of a company and carry the institutional memory of the company (DeLong and Vijayaraghavan 2003). When leaders find ways to engage "B" players without having to make them into "A" players, the organization builds a more comprehensive commitment throughout the organization.

Insight 8: Talent requires not only competence and commitment . . . but also contribution. A simple formula for talent has been Competence * Commitment (Ulrich 1998). Competence means that individuals have the knowledge, skills, and values required for today's and tomorrow's jobs. One company clarified competence as *right skills, right place, right job.* Competence clearly matters because incompetence leads to poor decision making. But without commitment, competence is discounted. Highly competent employees who are not committed are smart but don't work very hard. Committed or engaged employees work hard, put in their time, and do what they are asked to do.

However, the next generation of employees may be competent (able to do the work) and committed (willing to do the work), but unless they are making a real contribution through the work (finding meaning and purpose in their work), their interest in what they are doing diminishes and their productivity wanes. Contribution occurs when employees feel that their personal needs are being met through their participation in their organization. Organizations are the universal setting where individuals find abundance in their lives through their work and they want this investment of their time to be meaningful. An emerging talent formula might be this: Competence * Commitment * Contribution.

A Marshall Plan for talent helps people find meaning and purpose in work, to answer the question, "Why am I working?" Based on theory and research from positive and developmental psychology, individual motivation, personal growth, and organization theory, we can identify what organizations and leaders can do to help employees find abundance at work (Ulrich and Ulrich 2010). Leaders may help employees answer seven questions so that employees feel abundance in their work.

- *Who am I?* How does the employee identity meld with the company reputation?
- *Where am I going and why?* How can the organization help the employee reach his or her goals?
- *Whom do I travel with?* How does the organization build a community of support so that an employee feels connected?
- *How well do I practice spiritual disciplines?* How well does the organization practice spiritual disciplines of humility, service, forgiveness, gratitude, and others?

- *What challenges do I enjoy?* How does the organization help an employee find challenges that are easy, enjoyable, and energizing?
- *How well can I access resources?* How does the organization help the employee manage health, space, and financial requirements?
- *What are my sources for delight?* How does the organization help the employee have fun?

When managers help employees find answers to these seven questions by participating in the organization, these employees may find abundance in their lives by feeling that they contribute.

Insight 9: Technology facilitates talent management processes . . . and connection among people. Technology has changed the way talent work is organized and delivered through information sharing, improved processes, redefinition of work, and social networks. Technology enables individuals to source and share information from people who are not personally accessible. In the talent arena, a simple example would be that potential employees could source information on organizations where they interviewed to have at least a cursory background on the company. In addition, people inside and outside an organization blog to share information about their organization experiences. More shared information increases decisions made about sourcing and using talent.

Technology also improves talent processes (Kavanagh and Thite 2008). Technology-enabled staffing includes employee databases like Monster.com and Web-based succession planning systems. Technology facilitates training and development by facilitating definition and assessment of competencies and by video and other Web-based training programs. In addition, technology-enhanced reward systems more efficiently administrate setting goals, holding people accountable for goals, and allocating rewards. In this way, technology handles the administrative requirements of talent management.

Technology also redefines work boundaries. Through technology, knowledge is an asset that does not have to be owned to be accessed. With technology, employees may work in a company without physical presence. With technology, organizations can now accomplish work by individuals who have no formal or long-term relationship with the organization. A number of firms in India perform services with organizations around the world by contracting for specific project-based assignments. For example, oDesk, founded in 2006, connects talented employees with companies needing specific projects. This service becomes a global job marketplace where employees freelance and work on company projects requiring specific skills. In December of 2009, oDesk reported over 420,000 providers having worked on projects with more than $130 million in value in the previous 90 days. This, and similar services, make talent more transparent, adaptable, and global.

Technology also creates social networks that enable people to connect with each other, not just to share information but to become part of a personal and professional community (Safko and Brake 2009). As technology evolves from wireless networks to satellite transmissions to cloud computing to artificial neural networks, people become connected across time and space. These swarms of talented individuals focus attention, make decisions, and sustain social support.

Imagine a present-day Marshall Plan where technology could streamline the processes of allocating resources, shape how people come together to get work done, and become a means of personal bonding across boundaries. Technology that changes the flow of information and money also will change the flow of talent within and across organizations.

Insight 10: Talent activities need to be measured . . . as do talent outcomes. Talent measures traditionally track activities related to talent: How many were hired, how they were hired, where they were hired from, what percent of leaders received 40 hours of training, how participants felt about training, or what percent were promoted based on succession plans (Fitz-enz 2009). These activity talent metrics help assess the processes related to talent, but they do not fully capture the outcomes of talent initiatives. The initiatives related to the Marshall Plan were important to measure (e.g., the amount of economic support given each country and how the money was invested). However, the outcomes of Marshall Plan had longer-term significance (the country-by-country economic development and viability).

In the talent arena, a number of outcomes could be articulated. These outcomes would be the response to the question: If we have better talent, what happens? Some of these outcomes could be related to individuals, for example, retention, productivity, preparation for promotion, or engagement. Some of the talent outcomes could be tracked with regard to organizational capabilities, for example, speed of response, innovation, or customer service (Ulrich 1997; Ulrich and Smallwood 2004).

Complete measures of talent should include (a) the processes of what is done (this would capture much of the legendary Kirkpatrick measures; Kirkpatrick and Kirkpatrick 2006), (b) the individual outcomes that occur because of talent investments, (c) the organizational capability outcomes as a result of talent investments, and (d) the customer, investor, and community implications of talent investments. We have proposed that the new ROI of human resources (or talent) is *return on intangibles*, where investor confidence in future business success is measured by intangible shareholder value (Ulrich and Smallwood 2006).

Insight 11: Talent efforts need to be owned by line managers . . . and architected by HR professionals. Four groups of stakeholders might be involved with building talent (Ulrich Allen, Brockbank, Younger, and Nyman 2009). Line managers own talent initiatives and ensure that they align to business goals. HR leaders architect talent initiatives. Consultants/advisors offer frameworks and insights from others and point out lessons learned. External customers and investors guide the relevance of talent work.

Line managers are ultimately accountable for ensuring that the organization has the right talent and right organization in place to deliver on expectations to customers, shareholders, and communities. The term "line manager" refers to leaders at all levels of the organization. Members of the board of directors should be informed about the rationale and outcomes of talent investments. Line managers in the C suite (governing or executive committee) should be informed advisors for talent initiatives. Line managers through the organization should also be aware of talent, how it will affect their ability to reach their goals, and their role in helping it move forward.

Talent depends on the quality of HR professionals and their relationships with line managers (Ulrich, Brockbank, Johnson, and Sandholtz 2008). If they cannot respond to the increased expectations raised by talent demands, they will quickly lose credibility and be relegated to second-tier status. Three targets are important among HR professionals: chief HR officer (CHRO), the HR leadership team, and HR professionals. The CHRO needs to be the talent sponsor by allocating money, and time to the talent effort. The CHRO should initiate, take lead in the design, and monitor the talent plan and ensure that robust measurements are in place to credibly and accurately monitor progress. The HR leadership team includes HR professionals in businesses or key geographic units, the heads of centers for expertise, and the shared services or transactional (or HR operations) HR leader. This team is critical for talent success and should not be overlooked or assumed. A talent transformation may be sponsored by the CHRO, but it must be enacted and lived by HR professionals throughout the organization. HR professionals who embrace talent initiatives recognize that their personal success is linked to the success of the HR transformation. HR professionals become architects who build frameworks and offer ideas to line managers.

Consultants or advisors bring insights and ideas into the talent arena. A colleague who has deep expertise in merger and acquisition integration recently shared that he had been retained to help a client manage a merger integration. But the client, in an effort to cut costs, opted to not use these services and worked to integrate the merger without outside council. Six months later, the client still had not realized the synergies it promised the investment community when the merger was made. Key employees had left, the combined company strategy was haphazard, and leaders were questioning if they had made the right choice to merge. No one can guarantee that our colleague could have averted these problems, but he had experience from dozens of companies who had faced and overcome these and other problems. Judicious and targeted use of outside consultants as partners may advance talent investments. Consultants may add value by bringing in experiences from other companies, by previewing and averting common challenges, by not being beholden to a political system that might limit creative problem solving, and by being independent contributors to the talent management process.

Conclusion

Traditionally talent is perceived as a finite resource, and if you fail to attract key talent, then your competitor will. The Marshall Plan for talent places greater emphasis on lifting your current talent to new levels. In this way, talent is no longer a scarce commodity but can be cultivated and grown much like a farmer's crop. We have distilled the ambitious and growing talent literature into 11 insights and shown how a Marshalling metaphor extends current thinking about talent. We have also shown that when organizations perform talent practices based on these insights, they will be more successful.

There are also many implications for practice. General managers and HR professionals who recognize the value of talent may begin to see talent as a win/win solution (Marshalling Talent metaphor). This implies that organizations invest in talent for the long term, that retention matters as much as recruitment, and that people need to feel connected to their organization. In addition, the preliminary research suggests that given limited resources, those charged with talent may want to invest in some areas more than others (e.g., building the business case for talent). Not all talent investments are equal, and those that create more value deserve more attention. This work explores what might be next as we order the talent domain into specific insights and as we show the relative impact of those insights on business performance.

References

American Society of Training and Development. 2009. *2009 State of the Industry Report.* www.ASTD.org.

Byham, William, and Reed Moyer. 1996. *Using competencies to build a successful organization.* Minneapolis: Development Dimensions Inc.

DeLong, Tom, and V. Vijayaraghavan. 2003. Let's hear it for B players. *Harvard Business Review.* June: 96–102.

Dowling, Graham. 2002. *Creating corporate reputations.* London: Oxford University Press.

Fernandez-Araoz, Claudio, Boris Groysberg, and Nitin Nohria. 2009. The definitive guide to recruiting in good times and bad. 2009. *Harvard Business Review* 87(5): 74–84.

Fitz-enz, Jac. 2009 *The ROI of human capital: Measuring the economic value of employee performance.* New York: AMACOM.

Guthridge, Matthew, Asmus Komm, and Emily Lawson. 2008. Making talent a strategic priority. *McKinsey Quarterly* 1, pp. 49–59

Kaplan, Robert, and David Norton. 1996. *The balanced scorecard: Translating strategy into action.* Boston: Harvard Business Press.

Kavanagh, Michael, and Mohan Thite. 2008. *Human resource information systems: Applications and future directions.* San Francisco: Sage.

Kirkpatrick, Donald, and James Kirkpatrick. 2006. *Evaluating training programs* (3rd edition). San Francisco: Berrett-Koehler Publishers.

Huselid, Mark, Richard Beatty, and Brian Becker. 2005. "A players" or "A positions"? The strategic logic of workforce management. *Harvard Business Review* 83(6).

Michaels, Ed, Helen Handfield-Jones, and Beth Axelrod. 2001. *The war for talent.* Boston: Harvard Business Press.

Safko, Lon, and David Brake. 2009. *The social media bible: Tactics, tools, and strategies for business success.* New York: Wiley.

Schneider, Benjamin, William Macey, Karen Barbera, and Nigel Martin. 2009. Driving customer satisfaction and financial success through employee engagement. *People and Strategy,* 32(2):24–27.

Smart, Bradford. 2005. *Topgrading: How leading companies win by hiring, coaching, and keeping the best people.* New York: Prentice Hall.

Thomas, Roosevelt. 2005. *Building on the promise of diversity: How we can move to the next level in our workplaces, our communities, and our society.* Washington, D.C.: AMACOM.

Ulrich, Dave. 1997. *Human resource champions: The next agenda for adding value and delivering results.* Boston: Harvard Business Press.

Ulrich, Dave. 1998. Intellectual capital = Competence * Commitment. *Sloan Management Review.* Winter: 15–26.

Ulrich, Dave, and Norm Smallwood. 2003. *Why the bottom line isn't: How to build value through people and organization.* Boston: Harvard Business Press.

———. 2004. Capitalizing on capabilities. *Harvard Business Review* 82(3).

———. 2006. HR's new ROI: Return on intangibles. *Human Resource Management* 44(2): 137–142.

———. 2007. *Leadership brand: Developing customer focused leaders to drive performance and build lasting value.* Boston: Harvard Business Press.

Ulrich, Dave, Wayne Brockbank, Dani Johnson, and Kurt Sandholtz. 2008. *HR competencies: Mastery at the intersection of people and business.* Washington D.C.: Society of Human Resource Management.

Ulrich, Dave, Justin Allen, Wayne Brockbank, Jon Younger, and Mark Nyman. 2009. *HR transformation: Building human resources from the outside/in.* New York: McGraw-Hill.

Ulrich, Dave, and Wendy Ulrich, 2010. *The why of work: How great leaders build abundant organizations to deliver value to employees, customers, investors, and communities.* New York: McGraw-Hill.

Welch, Jack, and Suzy Welch. 2005. *Winning.* New York: HarperBusiness.

Chapter 53

The Global State of Talent Management

David C. Forman, Chief Learning Officer
Human Capital Institute

"The key factor in the global economy is no longer goods, services or flows of capital, but the competition for people."

Richard Florida

"Work flows to the places where it will be done best—that is, the most efficiently and with the highest quality."

Sam Palmisano, IBM

"The jobs are going to go where the best educated workforce is with the most competitive infrastructure and environment for creativity and supportive government. It is inevitable. And by definition, those people will have the best standard of living. These may or may not be the countries who led the Industrial Revolution."

John Chambers, CEO, Cisco

A S SUCCESS ON THE INTERNATIONAL STAGE IS COVETED, TALENT MANAGEMENT BECOMES A critical ingredient to achieving this result. Organizations cannot be successful without their talented employees being aligned, engaged, and productive throughout all locations, markets, and initiatives. Effective talent practices lead to successful business results, and this finding is true for local, regional, and global enterprises. Global talent management does, however, pose different and more complex challenges than those for an organization that just competes locally.

The global state of talent management concerns organizations operating globally beyond their own country's boundaries that seek to be more globally integrated. These organizations are termed multinational enterprises (MNEs); this term has replaced "multinational corporations (MNCs)" because the definition of corporation varies across countries and regions. More specifically, this chapter focuses on the new global context, drivers for globalization, the impact of culture and regulations, the delicate global dilemma of balancing standardization and localization, and the current state of nine different talent management practices and processes.

The New Global Context

Global borders are no longer barriers to goods, companies, and talent. The world is flat, with a level playing field (Friedman 2006). Consider the following examples:

- Billions of people are new entrants into the world economy, and entire nations have skipped stages of economic growth to get there faster than could have been anticipated.
- IBM's revenues are more than 60 percent from outside the United States, and it employs people in 170 countries with almost as many people in India as in the United States.
- Recent examples of the world's leading "vanguard" companies include examples from all over the world such as Mexico's Cemex, Brazil's Banco Real, and India's ICICI Bank (Kanter 2010).
- 95 percent of Nestle's employees are outside of Switzerland.
- A Dell laptop ordered in San Diego is shipped from Malaysia with parts from 12 different countries.
- Russia has thousands of scientists working for Intel, Motorola, Cisco, and HP.
- Microsoft's R&D center in Beijing is among the best-performing software research units in the corporation. Google has research centers in South Korea, Japan, Switzerland, Norway, and Israel. Denmark is a hot innovation center for alternative energy.

Organizations used to proceed through a series of steps to become global: from local to domestic to regional to international to global. It often took decades to move a company with a few international satellite offices to a fully integrated MNE. But now, many companies are "born global." This includes small to medium-sized businesses that previously did not have the "scale" to consider global operations.

The Global Drivers

For thousands of years, international borders have been crossed and even trampled. First, the reasons were conquest and religious conversion; then it was furs, spices, and raw materials to fuel the industrial revolution. In the twenty-first century it is still about economic advantage, but of a different kind: talent to fuel innovation, creativity, agility, and greater global reach.

The drivers for this twenty-first-century globalization are technology infrastructure, markets, cost, and the demographics of talent supply. The Internet revolution has created untold opportunity for 3 billion new participants in the global economy. People worldwide now have access to the technology, tools, and information that was once available only through sophisticated computer centers. But, of course, none of this is viable if the electricity isn't working, the roads cannot bear traffic, digital information cannot be transferred, and communications are not in place.

The *market driver* for globalization is clear: Most organization's revenues and profits are now derived from international, as opposed to domestic, operations. The BRIC countries (Brazil, Russia, India, and China) are where the action is, and where Foreign Direct Investment (FDI) is also the highest. The *cost driver* is also very apparent, although this advantage is fleeting. As low-cost countries strive to not just build products but also design them, the low-cost advantage shifts to other countries. During recent years, for example, China has lost more manufacturing jobs than the United States. China is losing manufacturing jobs to countries such as Vietnam and Indonesia. Cost is a driver, but not as critical as the supply of talented employees.

The demographics of the supply of talent actually involve three different drivers. The first is simply the number of people that are available to participate in the new economy. For countries like Japan, Italy, and Russia, this is a major issue; they are in danger of losing 20 percent to even 40 percent of their population through declining birth rates. Russia has recently incented its citizens to solve this problem. The second is the quality of the output from the educational system so that people are skilled and talented. While the United States was once on solid footing in terms of educational quality, this is no longer the case. Our educational system is getting failing grades, especially as children progress from primary to secondary school. Our colleges and universities were once unrivaled throughout the world, but now that mantel is shared. The Indian Institutes of Technology may well be the finest technical school in the world. The third is the barrier for immigrating new talent. As Richard Florida suggests, a huge part of the Untied States competitive advantage is our international talent. Look who founded Intel, Google, eBay, Yahoo, and Sun. Roughly 10 percent of America's 500 leading CEOs were born outside the United States. Now, after 9/11 there are strict rules and regulations that limit the influx of people into the country. For the first time in recent memory, the number of foreign students has declined in the United States, and other countries are taking advantage of this rich talent source.

The drivers for globalization are powerful. The question is how to operate organizations within this new context so that strategies are executed, business goals are achieved, employees are engaged and rewarded, and global communities are strengthened.

Global Cultures, Policies, and Regulations

Before looking at the state of global talent practices, we must discuss two further topics because they have such a direct and immediate impact on employees and organizations. The first is culture, and the second is the different rules, regulations, and policies that affect behavior in different countries. Culture has been studied for centuries by social scientists, and while there are a myriad of definitions, Edward Schein has a practical one: "Culture is the way that people solve problems." It is clear from this definition that culture significantly impacts organizations and people.

Richard Gesteland, based on 30 years of international experience, offers a practical approach to the world of business on theoretical definitions of culture (Briscoe, Schuler, and Claus 2009).

All of these dimensions inform business decisions and how talent management is practiced. It is important to remember, however, that as valuable and descriptive as these categories are, they can also be restrictive if taken to the level of a blanket stereotype (Kanter 2009).

Cultural Patterns	Description
Deal Focus versus Relationship Focus	This is the "great divide" between low-context cultures such as the United States and United Kingdom, and higher-context cultures such as those in Asia and South America.
Informal versus Formal Cultures	This is the distinction between informal, egalitarian cultures and those that are more formal and hierarchical.
Rigid-time versus Fluid-time Cultures	The "let's get it done" versus the "later is fine" approach.
Expressive versus Reserved Cultures	Communication preferences and patterns are very different among cultures; this certainly impacts feedback and negotiations.

Global rules, policies, and regulations also impact individual and organizational behavior. In some countries, workers must get six months' notice before a personnel action occurs, and then the severance package can extend into years, not months. Unions, collective bargaining agreements, and works councils are very prominent in some parts of the world and not in others. Barriers to conducting business in different countries can also be extreme. It takes two days to go through the process of starting a business in Australia and over 200 days in many African countries. A simple commercial contract can be enforced in the Netherlands in 39 days, but it takes almost 1,500 days in Guatemala (Friedman 2006).

Cultural traditions, although they are not policies or legal statutes, can also have a powerful impact. In the Wynn Hotel in Las Vegas, for example, floors that begin with 4 don't exist. The number 4 signifies death in the Chinese, Japanese, and Korean cultures, and would be viewed as bad luck for gamblers from these countries.

Talent management is more complex and varied for global organizations than for local or domestic entities. Global talent management needs to address such mundane matters as time zones and virtual team meetings scheduled for 3:00 a.m., and subtle differences on how messages and meaning are conveyed. International legal and procedural issues need to be understood and properly addressed to avoid major operational malfunctions and financial disasters. And while all companies face issues of organizational silos and proprietary mind-sets, these are particularly difficult barriers for a unified global enterprise.

The Global Dilemma: Standardization versus Localization

The central issue faced by global organization is the extent to which strategy, operations, processes, and practices are standardized or localized across the globe. McDonald's, for example, allows wine to be served in their French locations, Wal-Mart stores in China have fish tanks where customers can make their selection, and Cemex has relaxed its whistle-blowing policies in Europe to respect local traditions.

In general, for organizations seeking more global integration, the "upstream-downstream" metaphor pertains to this standardization versus localization dilemma: Standardization for those functions close to the center of the organization, and localization for those closer to markets and customers. The standardized platform is often composed of strategy, business objectives, values, and key processes. While McDonald's continues to promote other local variations such as beer in Germany and lamb burgers in India, the core values of quality, cleanliness, speed, and branding are nonnegotiable (Briscoe, Schuler, and Claus 2009).

For talent management, the balance between standardization and localization can also be delicate depending on the maturity, strategy, and success of the organization. A guideline for MNEs seeking more global integration is that global talent practices should focus on "principles, not necessarily tactics." A principle, for example, is that *employees will be evaluated on their performance and contribution.* How this happens may differ across geographic boundaries and cultures. In some cases, a 360-degree survey may be used as an assessment tool, while in others, assessment will primarily be based on interviews with selected senior individuals. Global organizations need to select the principles that are vital for leveraging talent across the enterprise (the what) and then accept different ways to accomplish the task (the how).

The three most common organizational practices that are consistent across global entities, departments, and locations are budgeting, succession management, and performance management; two of the three are talent management practices. Succession management establishes the pipeline of global talent that will run the enterprise. Performance management aligns the organization to accomplish its strategy and business objectives, and budgeting provides a common language upon which organizational decisions are made. Each of these practices is vital to align and synchronize globally dispersed organizations.

Global Talent Practices

In their article "Winning the Race for Talent in Emerging Markets," Ready, Hill, and Conger (2008) state that talent strategies that work in the home country often have abysmal results internationally. They propose a framework based on research in the BRIC countries. Their new "talent compact" is based on *promises made and promises kept.*

An employment brand, for example, is a promise made to an employee. If that promise is not fulfilled, the employee will become disengaged or leave. Following are the components of this new compact:

Component	Specifics	What Matters
Brand	Known for excellence Leading global company Inspirational leadership	A reputation for excellence and a ticket to future success
Purpose	Guiding mission and values Global citizenship Committed to the region	Opportunity to be part of something big and transformative
Opportunity	Challenging work Accelerated career track Continual development Competitive pay	Accelerated development and career path from day one; unlimited prospects for individual growth
Culture	Authenticity Meritocracy Connection Talent-centricity	Meritocracy, transparency, and follow-through on promises

This "promises made and promises kept" compact is very useful, but it is also valuable to examine the current state of specific global talent management practices. Following are nine key talent management practices and processes that are experienced during the employee life cycle:

1. **Workforce Planning.** *Identifying the workforce that can implement the organization's strategy both now and in the future, and protecting the organization from unforeseen difficulties.* Workforce planning is the least developed talent management function and is therefore behind other practices and processes in implementation. The most important factors to consider for global workforce planning are as follows:
   - Internal talent supply data are often inconsistent across multiple locations, IT systems, and platforms.
   - It is difficult to acquire external talent supply data on labor markets in various countries; this is especially vital for decisions on expansion and use of expatriates. China, for example, lacks mid-level manager talent pools, so talent has to be imported to meet these gaps.
   - It is difficult to monitor external demand for a full spectrum of national economic, political, social and market needs, technology breakthroughs, and legal policies and compliance. This global landscape is infinitely more complex than that of a domestic organization, and balancing all these priorities is difficult to accomplish.

- Strategic workforce planning is difficult if not impossible without common talent management platforms such as performance and succession management.
- Multiyear expatriate assignments are very costly and should be replaced by shorter-term assignments (as required) and the development of local national talent.
- Staffing philosophies must move away from a "headquarters-centric" view of talent and also to a more inclusive workforce that includes females and other groups who previously were excluded.

2. **Talent Acquisition.** *Attracting, finding, and hiring the best talent for the job.* Unlike workforce planning, recruiting is one of the most mature talent management practices. But because it involves messaging and communicating directly with people, there are significant cultural variations that can impact recruiters. Following are the most important factors to consider for global talent acquisition:
   - The relevance of a brand across cultures must be analyzed.
   - The Web career center must be easy to use for people speaking different languages.
   - The use of the Internet and social media as recruiting tools can vary significantly across cultures and countries with a poor technology infrastructure.
   - The etiquette of an internal recruiter and what they are allowed to do vary in different parts of the world. In many countries, an internal recruiter should not contact someone in another firm because this is the province of the external recruiter only.
   - Logistical issues such as visas and work permits are critically important.
   - Selection assessments need to be scrutinized for cultural bias.
   - Negotiation with candidates is very different across cultures.

3. **Engaging Global Talent.** *Having employees who are committed to the organization's goals and values and are willing to expend their discretionary effort to make the organization successful.* There is a global engagement issue of significant proportions. In Japan, for example, only 3 percent of employees are highly engaged, as compared to 14 percent in the United Kingdom and 21 percent in the United States. The global average is 21 percent (Towers Perrin 2008). Following are the most important factors to consider for global engagement:
   - Global differences in engagement criteria must be understood. The wording of some engagement questions must be carefully examined in terms of translation and cultural meaning.
   - There is a difference among countries in why someone is attracted to an organization, is engaged with their work, and decides to stay. People want different things from their employers at different stages of their lifetime.
   - "Promises made and promises kept" is a very good engagement equation for each country.
   - People are more likely to stay with companies that they perceive to be talent friendly.
   - People place a huge premium on the ability to learn and grow in an organization.

4. **Developing Global Talent.** *Improving the knowledge, skill, and performance of employees.* Increasingly, development is understood to be much more than training. The 70/20/10 developmental model applies internationally as well as domestically: 70 percent of development is through workplace experiences; 20 percent through connecting with others, coaching, and mentoring; and 10 percent through formal training programs. Following are the most important factors to consider for global development:
   - Short-term international assignments and global virtual teams are very important, developmental assignments for global workforces.
   - Obtaining a "global mind-set" is a vital behavioral competency for organizations seeking to be more globally integrated.
   - The acceptability of different training approaches varies from culture to culture, usually based on the status awarded to the teacher and the likelihood of taking risks and trying new approaches. While in the United States, techniques that foster interactivity and problem solving are preferred, in other parts of the world, the lecture is the preferred teaching method and techniques such as "role plays" are not well accepted.
   - All global employees value an organization that provides strong and varied developmental opportunities.

5. **Deploying Global Talent**. *Having the right person with the right skills in the right job.* Global enterprises that seek greater integration must find ways to share talent, expertise, and knowledge so that the interests of the employees and the organization are balanced. Following are the most important factors to consider for global deployment:
   - Internal movement across the enterprise must be easy to accomplish and supported by the culture.
   - Enterprise technology systems can be used to connect different countries and groups so that new opportunities and vacancies are visible and there is an effort to match employees with targeted new opportunities.
   - Knowledge and expertise management systems can ensure that the right people and knowledge are applied to each project.
   - If employees feel stuck in a place or job and if they cannot take charge of their own career, then engagement and productivity suffers.

6. **Talent Retention**. *Keeping the best people and losing nonperformers.* Organizations struggle if there is too much or too little turnover, and if talented employees leave in greater proportion than the general employee population. Following are the most important factors to consider for global retention:
   - The employee's immediate manager is the most significant predictor of turnover. Managers must be developed to improve engagement and retention of key employees.
   - Retention issues vary from country to country, and can differ from attraction and engagement factors.
   - Data need to be gathered on turnover by talent level and then by location, department, and even manager to determine if patterns exist and need to be addressed.
   - The use of exit interviews varies by country and culture.

7. **Performance Management.** *Being able to evaluate employee performance on business results, and performance, and to align employees to the goals of the organization.* Performance management is one of the core talent management processes that need to be in place for enterprises that strive to be more globally integrated. Following are the most important factors to consider for global performance management:

- The balance between standardization and localization must be determined; in most organizations there is agreement on the principles and criteria of performance management, but how it gets implemented varies.
- According to Briscoe, Schuler, and Claus (2009), the three aspects of performance management most influenced by cultural attributes are specificity of performance objectives (broad versus narrowly defined tasks), method of appraisal (multiple assessors, formal, and systematic versus single assessor, informal, and top-down) and type of performance feedback (explicit and direct versus subtle, indirect, and nonconfrontational).
- Feedback on performance objectives needs to occur more frequently than just at the yearly, formal performance appraisal.

8. **Succession Planning and Leadership Development**. *Developing talent pipelines and preparing future leaders.* This is another foundational talent practice that is based on the assumption that key talent belongs to the enterprise and not a country, department, or location. Global talent pools are the keys to the future success of the organization. The most important factors to consider for global succession planning and leadership development are as follows:

- The building block for succession management is a global leadership competency model that truly reflects the complexity of managing in an international context and is not just recycled domestic competencies.
- The way in which future leaders are identified and potential is measured needs to be consistent across the enterprise. The criteria should be on job performance and not seniority or prestige of the university attended.
- The best future leaders may come from surprising sources. It is important, for example, to ignore a headquarters-biased or an English-language-fluency-only succession pool. There is recent research that suggests that the best future global leaders will come from countries like the Netherlands and Singapore, not the United States or Japan, because these leaders are used to dealing with different cultures and markets.
- Many organizations have a global talent pool of, for example, the top 300 to 500 future leaders, and this is supported by regional and domestic talent pools with slightly reduced criteria.
- It is also important to identify feeder positions and talent pools lower in the organization.
- The most important part of succession management is the leadership development programs; these should include deployment to international sites with stretch assignments in new areas of responsibility.

9. **Recognition and Reward Programs.** *Reinforcing behaviors that impact performance, contribution, and social responsibility.* These incentives continue to be important, but Pink (2009) suggests that a whole new set of rewards will be more effective in the future. The most important factors to consider for global recognition and reward programs are as follows:

- Compensation has both standard and local aspects that must be addressed.
- Global incentive and recognition programs must be vetted locally because there may be different ways to incent the same principle without unanticipated consequences.
- Pink (2009) makes the case that old-style incentives, rewards, and punishments are part of a past that believes that external "if-then" carrots and sticks are primary motivators. He believes that new organizations must respond to "our innate need to direct our own lives, to learn more, and create things, and to do better by ourselves and our world." Pink calls these three attributes autonomy, mastery, and purpose; and they would seem to correlate with criteria in some engagement and "Great Places to Work" surveys.

Conclusion

The global state of talent management is more important than ever before as more organizations seek to be globally integrated. As international organizations attempt to be more than the sum of their parts, common platforms such as technology, budgeting, and talent management are essential connectors. It is clear that global talent management is more complex and varied than its local or domestic counterpart. There is more cultural, policy, legal, economic, social, and political factors to weigh and balance. The standardization versus localization dilemma is always present, and that fulcrum will move over time. But the most critical factor that must be developed, supported, and enhanced in organizations is a global talent mind-set. If organizations think globally first, are inclusive, are not ethnocentric, and value performance, hard work, and education, then more global integration and stronger talent management practices will result.

References

Briscoe, D., R. Schuler, and L. Claus. 2009. *International human resource management.* New York: Routledge.

Florida, R. 2005. *The flight of the creative class.* New York: HarperBusiness.

Friedman, T. 2006. *The world is flat.* New York: Farrar, Straus, and Giroux.

Kanter, R. 2009. *Supercorp.* New York: Crown Business.

Pink, D. *Drive.* New York, NY: Riverhead Books, 2009.

Ready, D., L. Hill, and J. Conger. 2008. Winning the race for talent in emerging markets. *Harvard Business Review.* November.

SHRM. 2003. *SHRM global learning system.* Alexandria, VA: Society for Human Resource Management.

Towers Perrin. 2008. *Winning strategies for a global workforce.* Study.

Chapter 54

A Model for Talent Manager Excellence

Marc Effron, President
The Talent Strategy Group
Jim Shanley, Partner
The Shanley Group

I F CORPORATE PRIORITIES WERE SET BY UNANIMOUS AGREEMENT ABOUT THEIR IMPORTANCE, executives would be focused on little other than talent management (TM). With regularity, a survey emerges reporting that corporate executives view growing talent as their first priority. In those same surveys, the executives lament the actual state of talent in their organization and the survey authors lament the fractional amount of time the executives invest in building talent.

This increasingly predictable dialogue obscures the fact that the real work of talent building isn't getting done in most organizations. As TM professionals, we must try to understand the few capabilities that differentiate those companies who consistently produce great talent and great business results. As experienced practitioners and consultants in this field, we believe a critical and often-overlooked element is the capabilities of the TM staff. In this chapter, we describe the factors that differentiate great TM leaders.

Defining Talent Management

To provide both context and urgency for our model, we start by outlining the functional boundaries of TM and offer a brief overview of the state of the field. The functional boundaries are important, since as a field that emerged only in the last decade, there's understandable uncertainty about what work constitutes TM. We look to the research of the New Talent Management Network (NTMN), the world's largest organization of TM professionals, to help inform us in both areas.

The NTMN conducts an annual State of TM survey that assesses what TM does, the structure of TM departments, compensation levels, and so on. Their survey shows that the types of activities done by TM groups are becoming more universal and are different than the work done by other HR specialties. The data shows that groups that are officially called "TM" are typically focused on talent reviews and succession planning, high-potential identification, career development, and assessment and feedback. Groups identifying themselves as organization development or organization effectiveness engage in these activities much less frequently. This suggests a shift of these activities from those groups (or generalists) to this new specialty area. A notable exclusion from the areas of TM focus is talent acquisition or recruiting, which is done by only four in ten TM groups.

It makes sense that the activities listed above are the focus of TM, since these are the core processes that build talent in organizations. Together they compose the heart of the talent growth cycle—identify, develop, and deploy talent across the organization. In this article, when we refer to TM activities and the work done by TM practitioners, we are speaking about these activities.

The NTMN survey also asks respondents to assess how their executives would rate the effectiveness of their company's talent practices. You might expect that skewed self-perception or efforts at "impression management" would inflate the response to this question. Given the findings, we hope it didn't. Fewer than half of respondents rated core TM practices like high-potential identification, development planning, and assessing leaders as Always or Often Effective. Succession planning scraped by, with 51 percent rating this practice as effective.

Survey questions about the simplicity, transparency, and accountability of those practices fared even worse. As a few examples, barely 30 percent of respondents considered their development planning process Extremely or Mostly Easy to Use. In only one of the eight TM processes did a majority of companies say that managers were held accountable for follow-up. In the core process for TM leaders—the talent review and succession planning process—just over 40 percent rated managers as being Always Held Accountable. But it was transparency around talent practices that fared the worst of all. Just over 20 percent of companies said that practices like executive coaching or talent reviews were Totally or Mostly Transparent.

While there may be many reasons that these practices aren't working and that executives are unhappy with their company's talent, only one is under our control. As a TM community, we own our capabilities, and we need to collectively own improving them. The increased demand for great talent in our organizations makes this not only the ideal time to focus on this issue, but perhaps the last time we'll have an opportunity to. It's doubtful that corporate executives will tolerate much longer a department that is so clearly underperforming its potential.

The TM 4 + 2 Capability Model

TM's recent emergence as a field means that no clear success model has been developed yet. Based on our experience as TM consultants and practitioners, interviews with other well-regarded practitioners, and input over the years from executive search leaders, we believe we have identified the factors that differentiate successful TM leaders.

We propose that there are six characteristics that differentiate a high-performing TM leader. We consider four of these to be core—the proverbial "price of admission" required to operate at an acceptable level of effectiveness. Being great at these will bring a modicum of success, but they are only part of the equation. The other two are factors that separate the great from the merely very good. It is these two that elevate TM leaders to their highest level of effectiveness.

The Core Four

Business Junkie. *Knows and loves business.* Great talent leaders are permanently addicted to business. At a practical level, they are deep experts in their organization's business. They understand the company's strategy, how the products or services are produced, how the R&D process operates, and how the company goes to market. They can dissect their company's (or any other company's) income statement and balance sheet, and are able to trace human capital decisions back to the relevant line items. Their understanding comes from firsthand involvement in the business—sitting through marketing meetings, wandering the floor at the factory, going on sales calls.

In addition to knowing their business, they genuinely love business. They enjoy waking up each morning to participate in the capitalistic pursuit of making and selling things that produce a profit for their company, jobs for their employees, and returns for their shareholders. They advance a business-first agenda, in which they are responsible to get the best return from that corporation's talent investment.

According to Kevin Wilde, VP, Organization Effectiveness & Chief Learning Officer at General Mills, being a business junkie isn't "only knowing how to read a balance sheet. It's getting underneath." He suggests an easy way to make that happen. "Talent leaders should be sure to make friends in two departments—investor relations and business development. Have lunch with them. Bring them into leadership courses. They can share with you the items that the CEO and business unit leaders care most about, and provide insights that no one else can."

HR Disciple. *Has comprehensive, firsthand knowledge of human resource disciplines.* The HR Disciple has a broad understanding of the core TM areas along with compensation, recruiting, organization development, and engagement. He or she is an avid student of the human resource discipline and is able to effectively translate ideas from academic abstraction to practical reality. According to Julian Kaufman, who held the top TM jobs at Honeywell and Tyco, and now AIG, "Academic knowledge is great, but you must have a practitioner's mind-set—how do I apply this knowledge to actually solve problems? You have to put your skills *on trial* to see if they really work."

According to a number of top TM leaders, there's no substitute for broad-based experience to grow one's capabilities as an HR Disciple. Kaufman feels that executive recruiting experience is a great way to calibrate the gold standard for good talent. Exposure to other HR specialty areas (compensation, generalist, organization development, etc.) is equally important to ensure the TM leader has a holistic understanding of how these levers interact to drive performance. Another critical differentiator? Multicompany experience. There's just no better way to gain perspective and depth than by seeing how HR challenges are handled in operating environments and under different business cultures.

Those desiring success in this field should actively seek out assignments, projects, and other opportunities that broaden their experience in both different HR disciplines and operating environments. No matter how superior one's TM technical skills are, without this additional knowledge and experience, it will be difficult to develop the credibility and perspective needed to excel.

Production Manager. *Can build and consistently execute talent production processes.* Some in the TM field think of themselves as experienced craftspeople, building individual leaders in a labor of love. The best in the field know that they are actually the production line managers on the talent factory floor. Their job is to build and operate a process that turns out leaders who meet the specifications agreed to, in the time frame that was agreed upon. To them, the "talent factory" is reality, not just an analogy.

They approach their task with the same disciplined approach to process management as any other production leader. They understand the raw materials available to them, the tools that can most effectively cut, shape, and polish that material, and how to ensure that the finished product meets quality standards and is distributed appropriately. They know how to keep the production line moving to produce leaders when needed. Excelling in this role means keeping those production processes simple. As Roger Cude, VP Talent Management for Wal-Mart, says, "Your processes must be elegant but simple. As a craft, we tend to overcomplicate things."

Production manager skills can be gained through practice with classic project management tools like PERT (Performance Evaluation and Review Technique) and Gantt charts, through exposure to Six Sigma methodology, and most powerfully, through firsthand experience in operations or supply chain roles. More important, and more challenging to develop, is the belief that talent *should be* produced with this mind-set.

Talent Authority. *Understands the backgrounds, strengths, weaknesses, and development needs of top talent.* Great talent leaders know their talent. When the CEO asks for a slate of candidates, they can immediately list five names along with the strengths and weaknesses of each. The most expensive TM technology is no substitute for a talent leader's nuanced knowledge about his or her charges. Talent profiles are at best a two-dimensional recitation of facts. The talent leader brings those facts to life through a deeper understanding of the stories and influences behind them.

A successful talent authority also has a great "eye for talent." As subjective as that might sound, certain individuals have a talent for selecting talent. They understand what it takes to succeed in a given role and have the ability to quickly summarize how well a candidate fits with those needs. This likely stems from matching an understanding of the business, its culture, and the patterns of past success with an ability to ascertain how well someone would fit with the intellectual, cultural, political, and relationship-based factor of the job.

Becoming a talent authority only happens when the talent leader has a deep, personal knowledge of the organization's talent. This means having one-on-one meetings with key talent where the talent leader builds trust as he or she gathers information about leaders' careers, their ambitions, and their management style. The talent leader must then integrate that information with all the other data about that leader—derailer factors, business performance, engagement performance—into a comprehensive three-dimensional leadership profile. That effort requires a large investment of time but yields very high returns through more accurate and timely talent decisions.

The Differentiating Two

While TM leaders must have the above described attributes, achieving full potential requires even more. A TM leader must also be a Trusted Executive Advisor and Courageous Advocate.

Trusted Executive Advisor. Uses credibility and relationships with executives to influence key decisions. As a trusted advisor, the TM leader uses his or her knowledge, experience, and insights to guide key people decisions. But even with a strong level of technical expertise, a talent leader can only become a trusted advisor by flexing a different set of muscles. Being a trusted advisor transcends a professional relationship. The TM leader provides wise counsel on talent issues in a way that considers the client's ego, personal hopes, and fears, and reflects a deeper understanding of the organization's financial, operational, and political realities. This requires that the TM leader

Is professionally credible. Professional credibility doesn't come from impressive educational credentials or long tenure in the role. Demonstrating the Core Four provides the necessary ingredients for becoming professionally credible. The credible TM leader can integrate those ingredients in a way that allows the leader to continually make the "right" talent decisions for the organization This includes being able to persuasively present and argue for a position using the right balance of facts and emotion. Without that capability, the individual is destined to remain a technical specialist.

Forms strong executive relationships. The quality of a TM leader's personal relationships with senior executives will determine whether he or she becomes a trusted advisor on talent issues in that organization. That strong relationship can only happen after the senior leader trusts that the TM leader has the senior leader's best interest at heart. To get there, the TM leader will need to demonstrate an understanding of the executive's personal and professional agendas and the executive's ego needs. The TM leader will increase the relationship's strength after each interaction where the executive sees that the leader genuinely represents his or her best interests.

Courageous Advocate. Has a theory in the case and is appropriately aggressive in advancing a point of view on talent, independent of its popularity. The Courageous Advocate has a theory of the case about why specific talent choices should be made, and he or she is appropriately aggressive in voicing that opinion. Those who effectively balance these two factors ensure that the right talent decisions get made. We'll look at each factor in turn:

- **Has a Theory of the Case.** *A fact-based, brief, logical, and credible argument about why a talent decision should or shouldn't be taken.* It is the concise expression of a deeply held viewpoint on why talent succeeds, the best way to develop talent, why talent fails, and the aggregated learning from many other talent interactions. A theory of the case might be that Mary can succeed as a new general manager even though she's never led teams before because
  - Point 1: She is highly motivated to succeed in that role and she's breached similarly large gaps in her career development driven by that motivation
  - Point 2: Her personality characteristics are consistent with those who have successfully led teams through challenging times
  - Point 3: We have strong development and support mechanisms for general managers in our company
  - Point 4: She has a strong functional team around her who will provide support as she learns.

A well-developed point of view is at the core of being persuasive.

- **Is Appropriately Aggressive.** This phrase, provided by Kevin Wilde, captures a variety of nuanced behaviors that differentiate great TM leaders. To us, "appropriate" means knowing how to select which battles are worth fighting, knowing in which situations pushing back will be most productive, and knowing the politically productive way to bring a potentially incendiary issue to the table. "Aggressiveness" means not being afraid to voice your opinions, to fight for what you believe is right, and to not be afraid of pushing back just one more time. A difficult capability to master, many TM leaders fail on their path to greatness because they over or under use it.

The combination of a theory of the case and the appropriate amount of aggressiveness creates a TM leader who drives the right talent decisions in the right way.

Conclusion

We believe that 4 + 2 Talent Management model highlights the most differentiating capabilities for talent management leaders. Given that this field is still in its infancy, it's possible that our view on these critical capabilities will change over time. We are confident that the closer that TM leaders fit with the 4 + 2 profile, the better odds we have for this profession realizing its true potential.

Chapter 55

Talent Management Leadership in Government

Allen Zeman, Ph.D., President
Anne Kelly, Principal
Allan Schweyer, Principal
Center for Human Capital Innovation (CHCI)

"Two decades of empirical evidence show that organizations perform to the highest levels when they invest heavily in their employees. These organizations do better in terms of financial returns, innovation, and job creation. In particular, companies that embrace this philosophy have survived and prospered through many economic cycles and have consistently outperformed their peers."

—*Linda Bilmes and Scott Gould,* The People Factor

Introduction

The United States is faced with a crisis in government. Problems are increasing in complexity just as the most experienced civil servants are set to retire in droves. It is well known that about half the nation's federal civil servants will become eligible for retirement by 2014, including 6,100 of the 7,000 leaders in the Senior Executive Service, the very top of the public service workforce. The federal government will lose an enormous knowledge and leadership asset this decade just as the country's challenges in defense, the economy, the environment, security, financial regulation, and a host of other areas become more complex and more critical.

To make matters worse, unprecedented debt and deficits give the President, Congress, and their state and local equivalents little flexibility when it comes to making investments in the government workforce. Indeed, it is more likely that budgets for government will be cut in the coming decade than expanded, at the same time, demands on government—with the aging population, global instability, climate change, and a host of other problems—will be much greater.

The challenges the country faces as it enters the second decade of the twenty-first century put at stake the quality of life of future generations of Americans. Government infrastructure, and especially the workforce that constitutes the federal government, is a pillar upon which the strength of the nation rests. That pillar, while not yet crumbling, is severely strained.

HR leaders in government must do their part to reverse the trend toward weaker and less effective government, but they must do so in an environment that will be wary where budgets are concerned. This has already happened in the private sector. There, HR and talent management executives are increasingly called upon to articulate the business reasons for their budget requests and to frame their proposals in the context of the organization's overall business objectives or mission. This higher standard of scrutiny and demand for metrics-based budget requests is at least as important in government today as it is in the private sector.

It is understandable and right that government leaders who are accountable for financial management should ask why their agency or department must invest in a particular training course or purchase a workforce management technology. Government HR leaders have failed to quantify the real costs of underperforming supervisors, or of poor hiring, turnover, and employee disengagement. This failure has eroded their credibility.

In the past, government HR leaders were largely excused from the common business practice of justifying expenditures with ROI-based business cases. As a result, the field has often attracted practitioners and executives without financial skills and acumen—"people persons" who are not only incapable of speaking the language of business but often disdain it. Over time, this has led to HR's marginalization and its failure to gain "a seat at the table," despite overwhelming agreement among government executives that talent is the most important part of a modern agency or department.

HR and talent management executives certainly lead the most important part of government today. Indeed, in government, the depth and quality of talent can make the difference between reasonable value for taxes and outrageous waste, and even between life and death for citizens. Governments, like companies, should strive to recruit, develop, and retain the best talent possible. Governments increasingly compete for tax payers, who more than ever are prepared to vote with their feet when government in one jurisdiction is superior to government in another—nations included.

Integrated and Aligned Talent Management

The interdependent talent life cycle model of human capital management (Figure 55-1) considers the impact that actions or initiatives taken within one aspect will have on the other aspects. Whether referred to as "integrated" talent management or "holistic" talent management, leading organizations are increasingly breaking down the internal silos that have traditionally prevented a more effective approach to workforce management. Equipped with this understanding, action plans can be prioritized and leveraged in order to maximize results around the talent life cycle.

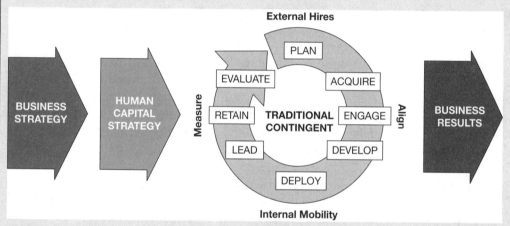

Figure 55-1 Holistic and Integrated Workforce Management

Integrated talent management, as important as it is, is not valuable if it is not also aligned with the organization's greater strategic plans and objectives. Holistic talent management requires careful alignment with the organization's established goals, objectives, and current and strategic business plans. Shown conceptually in the figure, this ensures that integrated talent management initiatives are aligned with both organizational and human capital strategies and objectives to achieve desired results.

Talent Management Leadership in Government

The challenges of deep economic recession, debt, two wars, health-care reform, global climate change, and national security seem easy to prioritize over human capital reform in government. Yet each of these challenges depends on a strong civil service for resolution. Worse, ignoring civil service reform and the need for better talent management in government is almost certain to generate new challenges on the magnitude of those above or, at the very least, create conditions in which current and new challenges cannot be confronted in any practical way.

Under any plausible scenario, the federal government will soon have fewer resources than it has today. That doesn't mean government can't improve. There is room for greater efficiency. Some of it will come from better and more integrated talent management practices whose foundation is based on measureable business outcomes. Indeed, leadership and cost control, particularly with regard to the management of people in the federal government workforce, is critical; labor, after all, is by far the greatest single expense item for government.

The government must curb its robust appetite for ever larger budgets, but measurable and meaningful improvements must still be made. Convinced of the reality of this dilemma, the Center for Human Capital Innovation (CHCI) has spent the past two years exploring investments in talent management that will yield the largest payoff for government, both in money saved and performance increased. One key area is in front-line leadership—managers and supervisors.

Throughout most of 2009, we examined the business case for investing in leadership development in government.[1] Through data gathered from more than 22,000 federal government workers, a case study analysis, and a literature review, we attempted to answer the questions: Are organizations that invest in leadership development more successful? Is leadership development the cause of organizational improvements? Could the federal government benefit similarly from a leadership development program?

Overwhelmingly, evidence suggests the answers to these questions are positive. The organizations in our case studies reported higher levels of employee inspiration, lower turnover, and more productive workforces. If agencies and departments of the federal government increased their investment in leadership development, our research and the case studies suggest they would experience enormous financial benefits. By using real data from recent research involving thousands of federal government employees, we are confident that the information in this report can be used by any federal government department or agency as a basis for building their own business case.

As shown in Table 55-1 (based on a large government organization), the federal government currently spends less on leadership development as a percentage of their employee payroll than private-sector averages. Indeed, in their 2009 book, *The People Factor*, Scott Gould (currently the Deputy Secretary of the Department of Veterans Affairs) and Linda Bilmes (currently a professor at Harvard's JFK School of Government) state the following:

> Professionals, including doctors, lawyers, architects and accountants, are all required to undergo periodic training in order to maintain their credentials. By contrast, the federal government trusts important government workers with similar levels of responsibility for America's safety, security and health but fails to train them. The United States spends on its civilian government employees less than one-third per capita what private firms and the military spend, and training is one of the first line items to be cut when money gets tight.

	Expenditure as % of Payroll	Total Investment
Federal Organization Studies	0.23%	$47.3M
National Average	0.46%	$94.7M (equiv.)
Best Practice	0.57%	$116.2M (equiv.)
Highest ROI	0.84%	$172.2M (equiv.)

Table 55.1 Leader Development Training in One Federal Government Organization
From American Society for Training and Development (ASTD) 2008 State of the Industry Report

To the extent that our samples can be used as a proxy for agencies and departments across government, current (and historic levels) of leadership development investment are low. Thus, the federal government has an opportunity to realize high payoffs from more effective leadership development programs. In the case illustrated in Table 55-1 involving just one federal government organization, an additional investment of $47 million would be required to meet the national average expenditure on leadership development. An additional $125 million would meet the level of firms that achieve the highest ROI on their leadership development investments.

By establishing such benchmarks against industry standards, the federal government can better understand how its leadership development investment compares to what other organizations typically spend on their supervisors, managers, and senior executives. The calculation of the same government organization's current investment includes leadership development centrally funded by headquarters and those resourced independently by other parts of the organization.

The leadership costs of programs were gathered through a data call requesting total training and development budgets of each subagency. CHCI then conducted a line-by-line review of entries to isolate only those programs which truly represented leadership development. To ensure that our cost analysis was comparable to private industry assessments, CHCI followed the American Society for Training and Development's (ASTD) cost definition defined in their 2008 "State of the Industry Report."[2]

Overall, it is estimated that the organization in our example spent roughly $47.3 million in leadership development in 2008, or 0.23 percent of a $20.5 billion annual payroll expenditure. This is significantly lower than private-sector norms. According to *Training* magazine and the ASTD's most recent annual reports, private companies allocated between 0.46 percent to 0.57 percent of direct payroll expenditures to leadership development, or 21 percent of their total training budgets.[3]

To make matters worse, our research determined that not only are most front-line supervisors and manager underinvested in, they are poorly chosen, rarely if ever trained in the management of people, too busy to coach and provide feedback, and largely not skilled or credible to conduct meaningful performance reviews. As front-line leaders, the impact this group has on the workforce is almost inestimable.

From our survey results, we were able to approximate engagement/morale levels across some parts of government and, by extrapolation, the potential yields for improving employee engagement through better frontline leadership across the entire federal government. Through our analysis (available at www.tmgov.org), we estimated that modest efforts to elevate the engagement levels of the current federal government workforce through improved leadership alone (there are other factors that impact employee engagement) would result in a net financial gain of approximately $9.6 billion to the organization overall. As the action cycle is repeated annually, greater gains could be expected as more disengaged employees become engaged and highly motivated.

Realizing a financial gain of this magnitude is possible because the quality of supervision, the biggest lever for raising engagement levels, has much room for improvement, according to our research results. Equipping managers with the interpersonal and managerial skills to inspire and motivate others to high performance can be accomplished through quality leadership development programs. The development of supervisors and frontline managers, who can inspire employees and make sound decisions regarding their development, is a high-benefit action that the federal government must take to both cut costs and improve the quality of government across the board.

Better frontline leadership not only impacts engagement and performance, it keeps talented people in the government service. The direct and indirect costs of turnover are substantial in government, just as they are elsewhere. Government recruiting efforts and expenditures are being wasted through much higher than necessary (or desired) turnover. According to Staffing.org, Saratoga Institute, and others, the cost of recruiting a single individual is between 25 to 30 percent of their salary. Thus, reducing turnover (now about 9.6 percent) by an aggressive one-third (3.2 percent) or 63,333 people across the federal government, would likely result in a recruiting cost savings of about $1.2 billion per year (0.25 × $71,260 × 66,333). Of course, this calculation doesn't factor the post-hire costs of onboarding and training, which usually exceed the cost of hiring.

If the federal government invests in effective, high-quality leadership development for its civilian workforce, it can conservatively expect measurable performance and cost reductions to total between $12.3 and $40 billion over a five-year period (even assuming that no savings accrue until at least year 3). The cost for such a leadership development investment is estimated between $500 million to $800 million, depending on the standard adopted for the program (industry norms, best practice, or highest ROI; See Table 55-1).

The above is just one example of how government might improve in an era of almost inconceivable challenges and (soon-to-be) strict budget restraints. This is a critical time for talent management in the federal workforce. Human capital leaders need to be aware of the greater challenge that they face. To begin the process of developing a workforce capable of meeting the challenges of this decade, leaders need to take aggressive action now. This includes conducting similar ROI analyses to exploit other opportunities, such as those in HCM technology adoption, streamlining hiring processes, making other investments in talent development, and so on. The federal government workforce can simultaneously improve and cut costs, but only through wise investments and measured outcomes.

Conclusions

The results of our research indicate that the federal government has a tremendous opportunity to increase its leadership capacity and employee productivity by investing a reasonable amount of resources to establish a comprehensive and robust leadership development program. By investing in frontline leaders, the government not only saves billions of dollars and realizes greater productivity, it sets in motion the foundation for even greater results around the talent life cycle. Leaders who are skilled talent managers will make better hiring decisions; they will onboard new recruits more effectively; they will recognize, coach, and reward their reports, help them navigate their careers, and plan their development. Better frontline leaders will inspire the workforce to greater heights, better deploy their teams, and more effectively identify future leaders.

The challenges faced by the nation are immense, but with a strong government, they are not insurmountable. Like most other sectors of the economy, government is only as good as its people. It's time to make targeted, strategic investments in that talent that will generate far greater returns for the country and its citizens.

Notes

1. "Leadership Development in Government: A Business Case Analysis," *Center for Human Capital Innovation*, February 2010.
2. Paradise, Andrew, "State of the Industry Report 2008," American Society for Training and Development, 2008, http://www.astd.org/content/research/stateOfIndustry.htm. To facilitate comparison with private-industry averages, we applied the ASTDs definition of "direct expenditures" or "direct learning investments" in evaluating the Army's leadership development costs. The ASTD's cost definition includes learning and performance staff salaries, travel costs for learning and performance staff, administrative costs, non-salary delivery costs (including classroom facilities), and outsourced activities.
3. "Training 2007 Industry Report," *Training*, November/December 2007, vol. 44, no. 10, p. 8. Leadership development training as a percent of total training expenditures is reported by *Training* magazine's "Industry Report," an annual survey of annual training trends in the United States. Our definition of "leadership development" included both "management/supervisory training" and "executive development" costs. The 2007 survey included responses from private companies across various sectors. Twenty-eight percent of responses were from "small" companies employing 100 to 999 employees, 39 percent of respondents were "mid-sized" organizations with 1,000 to 9,999 employees, and "large" organizations 10,000 or more employees composed the remaining 33 percent.

   The annual ASTD report records training expenditures of 316 organizations, including 25 large Fortune 500 companies averaging 64,000 employees. Employee averages for all organizations reporting data in the ASTD Industry report in 2007 was 18,000. The upper bound of leadership development expenditures as a percentage of payroll were calculated using data reported by BMF organizations and BEST Award Winners for 2007.

Index